# THE "JEWISH QUESTION" IN GERMAN-SPEAKING COUNTRIES 1848–1914

GARLAND REFERENCE LIBRARY
OF THE HUMANITIES
(Vol. 1571)

*A special publication of*

# THE FELIX POSEN BIBLIOGRAPHIC PROJECT ON ANTISEMITISM

MANAGING EDITOR: *Sara Grosvald*
PRODUCTION EDITOR: *Rosalind N. Arzt*
EDITORIAL ADVISOR: *Susan S. Cohen*

The Vidal Sassoon International Center
for the Study of Antisemitism
The Hebrew University of Jerusalem

# THE "JEWISH QUESTION" IN GERMAN-SPEAKING COUNTRIES, 1848–1914
## A Bibliography

*Edited by*
Rena R. Auerbach

GARLAND PUBLISHING, INC. • NEW YORK & LONDON
1994

## Library of Congress Cataloging-in-Publication Data

The "Jewish question" in German-speaking countries, 1848–
1914 : a bibliography / edited by Rena R. Auerbach.
    p.    cm. — (Garland reference library of the human-
ties ; vol. 1571)
    Works cited chiefly in German with additional entries in
English, French, Hebrew, and other European languages.
    At head of title: The Vidal Sassoon International Center
for the Study of Antisemitism, the Hebrew University of
Jerusalem.
    A special publication of the Felix Posen Bibliographic
Project on Antisemitism.
    Continues the Bibliographie zur Geschichte der Judenfrage
by Volkmar Eichstädt.
    Includes indexes.
    ISBN 0–8153–0812–4
    1. Jews—Europe, German-speaking—History—19th cen-
tury—Bibliography.  2. Jews—Europe, German-speaking—
History—20th century—Bibliography. 3. Antisemitism—
Europe, German-speaking—History—19th century—Biblio-
graphy.    4. Antisemitism—Europe, German-speaking—His-
tory—20th century—Bibliography.    5. Europe, German-
speaking—Ethnic relations—Bibliography.   6. Europe,
German-speaking—Imprints.    I. Auerbach, Rena R.
II. Eichstädt, Volkmar. Bibliographie zur Geschichte der
Judenfrage.    III. Vidal Sassoon International Center for the
Study of Antisemitism (Universiṭah ha-'Ivrit bi-Yerushala-
yim    IV. Felix Posen Bibliographic Project on Antisemitism.    V. Series.
Z6373.E86J48   1994
[DS135.E83]
940'.04924—dc20                                94–18554
                                                                CIP

Printed on acid-free, 250-year-life paper
Manufactured in the United States of America

# CONTENTS

# PREFACE

*The Vidal Sassoon International Center for the Study of Antisemitism of the Hebrew University of Jerusalem was established in 1982 as an interdisciplinary research center dedicated to an independent, non-political approach to the accumulation and dissemination of knowledge necessary for understanding the phenomenon of antisemitism. The Center engages in research on antisemitism throughout the ages, focusing on relations between Jews and non-Jews, particularly in situations of tension and crisis.*

*The Felix Posen Bibliographic Project of the Center comprises an on-line data base accessible through the Israeli University Libraries Network, and a printed bibliography.*

*The "Jewish Question" in German-Speaking Countries, 1848-1914*, lists works documenting Jewish life, thought, and development during the period of emancipation and thereafter, and the relations of the host countries — Germany, Austria-Hungary and Switzerland — with the Jews living in their midst.

It continues the *Bibliographie zur Geschichte der Judenfrage*, by Volkmar Eichstädt, published in 1938 and reprinted in 1969. Eichstädt's work contains material published in German during the period 1750–1848. The subjects treated are: tolerance, improvement of civil rights, equality, emancipation, and the "Jewish Question," selected material on missionary work, Judaism in literature, and the internal Jewish debate about religious reform of Judaism.

The bibliography lists both the literature *of* and *about* the period. The subjects treated reflect changes in the attitude and approach to the "Jewish Question" in German-speaking countries after 1848. Among the subjects which have been added are: army, demography and statistics, economics and finance, ideologies, law and justice, racism, and the 'solution of the Jewish

viii                                                           *Preface*

Question.' The arrangement is according to subject, whereas Eichstädt's bibliography is arranged, in the main part, chronologically.

Most of the items listed have been published — books, articles in periodicals and collections, periodicals and newspapers, and pamphlets — except for a few items of archival materials. Pamphlets of this period are numerous — particularly attacks against the Jews and Jewish apologetics.

The location of each item is given at the end of each entry. Material which was found only in bibliographies is designated 'Unseen.'

The format of each entry follows the rules of the *Chicago Manual of Style*, with slight modifications. Most titles are self-explanatory. In some cases, a brief annotation is given. In a number of entries, the exact pagination was not obtainable.

Most entries are in German, with additional entries in English, French, Hebrew, and several other European languages. Modern spelling has been used for German entries of the nineteenth century.

Before I left for Germany in 1985, Dr. Henry Wassermann of the Open University in Israel suggested that I take advantage of my stay there to work on a bibliography about the "Jewish Question" in German-speaking countries from 1848 to 1914. To test his suggestion, I began to collect material in various libraries. After a year in Germany, I called on Prof. Herbert A. Strauss at the Zentrum für Antisemitismusforschung in Berlin asking for support of my project. Prof. Strauss consented to the plan and applied for a grant to the Deutsche Forschungsgemeinschaft, which I then received for a period of two years. My thanks go to Dr. Wassermann for his suggestion and to Prof. H.A. Strauss for accepting it and getting the grant for this project. As happens ever so often, the completion of my task took longer than anticipated.

I wish to express deep-felt thanks to my colleagues in all the libraries, but in particular to my former colleagues in the Jewish National and University Library in Jerusalem, and my gratitude and appreciation to the Vidal Sassoon International Center for the Study of Antisemitism of the Hebrew University in Jerusalem for accepting the project and preparing it for publication in the framework of its various bibliographical projects.

*Rena R. Auerbach*
*Jerusalem, March 1994 — Adar 5754*

# INTRODUCTION

The term "Jewish Question" appears for the first time during the great "Jew Bill" controversy on the naturalization of the Jews in England in 1753-54.[1] But it was not until a century later, within the broad and heated public discussion regarding Jewish emancipation — particularly in the German-speaking countries — that the term emerged as a key token in discourse, expanding to encompass virtually all aspects of Jewish existence in modern society.[2] The theological world view based on religious antagonism, that had fixed and circumscribed the place and status of the Jew in Christian society throughout the course of previous centuries, had by that time lost its claim to exclusive validity. Increasingly, the continued existence of the Jews as a separate community came to be viewed as a secular question demanding a secular solution.

Alongside the conservative Christian position, openly opposed to any change in the time-honored traditional legal and social status of the Jews, new perspectives had entered the arena of discourse, proposing a "solution to the Jewish Question" by means of assimilation and emancipation. However, this development was accompanied by a mounting wave of opposition to the civil emancipation and social integration of the Jews — based now on secular rather than religious motives. Within the matrix of this melange of anti-Jewish attitudes, fueled and shaped by social, national or racist sentiments, the old traditional antagonism reared its head in a new guise: the form of modern antisemitism.[3] Even the most extreme manifestation of modern antisemitism, the genocidal Nazi enterprise aimed at the physical annihilation of European Jewry, made use of the term "final solution to the Jewish Question."

Parallel with the widespread use of the expression "the Jewish Question" in polemical writings on Jewish emancipation and antisemitism, this signifier has, since the end of the nineteenth century, also served to characterize modern Jewish political and social thought, occupying a central discursive function in their own discussions about the identity, place and role of the Jews in the modern world.[4] Thus, Theodor Herzl subtitled *The Jewish State*, published in 1896: "An Attempt at a Modern Solution of the Jewish Question." In a similar vein, Leo Pinsker's pre-Zionist 1882 pamphlet *Auto-Emancipation* begins with the sentence: "The eternal problem presented by the Jewish Question stirs men today as it did ages ago. It remains unsolved like the squaring of the circle, but unlike it, it is still a burning question."[5] Eight decades later, Kurt Blumenfeld, the last chairman of the German Zionist Federation before the Nazi takeover, chose to call his autobiography, written from the perspective of the second half of our century, *Erlebte Judenfrage* (Living the Jewish Question).[6] Moses Hess, the mentor of Karl Marx and precursor of the modern conception of Jewish nationalism, had significantly subtitled his *Rome and Jerusalem*: "The Last Question of Nationalities."[7]

Thus, it should be evident that throughout the stormy history of the Jewish people in recent centuries, hardly any domain has been left untouched, directly or indirectly, by the crucial concept of the "Jewish Question." The standard bibliography by Volkmar Eichstädt on the history of the *Judenfrage* is also based on such a broad perception of the term. Although the book appeared in 1938 in Nazi Germany, Eichstädt's comprehensive approach justified its reprinting in England in 1969.[8] His bibliography covers the years 1750–1848, focusing on Jewish emancipation and its opponents.

The aim of the present work by Rena Auerbach, one of the most experienced and able bibliographers at the Jewish National and University Library in Jerusalem, is to continue the bibliography begun by Eichstädt down to 1914, supplementing and extending it in certain areas. The principal thematic foci during this period were the process of struggle for achievement of full emancipation, the rise of modern antisemitism, and the beginnings of the Jewish national movement. In conceptual terms, Auerbach's work complements the other bibliographies in the overall framework of the Felix Posen Bibliographical Project of the Vidal Sassoon International Center for the Study of Antisemitism at the Hebrew University of Jerusalem,[9] and it was thus that the Center elected to take on and support the present project, including this long-needed bibliography in the Center's expanding series of monographs and standard studies on antisemitism.

*Otto D. Kulka*
*The Hebrew University of Jerusalem, March 1994*

## Notes

1. Cf. Jacob Toury, "'The Jewish Question'. A Semantic Approach," *Leo Baeck Institute Year Book XI* (1966), 85–89.

2. The first publication of this kind in German-speaking Europe appeared in 1838 in the periodical *Deutsche Vierteljahrsschrift* entitled "Beiträge zur Lösung der jüdischen Frage" (Contributions toward a Solution of the Jewish Question). The best-known polemical pamphlets from the period are Bruno Bauer's "Die Judenfrage" in 1842/43 and the 1844 response by Karl Marx "Zur Judenfrage," see Toury, 'The Jewish Question,' p. 93, fn. 42e and p. 99, fn. 65.

3. See the broadly conceived studies on this topic by Reinhard Rürup, *Emanzipation und Antisemitismus. Studien zur "Judenfrage" der bürgerlichen Gesellschaft* (Göttingen, 1975) and Alexander Bein, *Die Judenfrage. Biographie eines Weltproblems* (Stuttgart, 1982). On clarification of semantic aspects, cf. Alexander Bein, "Der moderne Antisemitismus und seine Bedeutung für die Judenfrage," *Vierteljahrshefte für Zeitgeschichte* 6 (1958), 340–60. A characteristic example of the use of the term "Jewish question" in antisemitic literature is Eugen Dühring, *Die Judenfrage als Racen-, Sitten- und Culturfrage* (Karlsruhe, 1881).

4. See Toury, 'The Jewish Question,' 102–106.

5. Leo Pinsker, *Autoemanzipation. Mahnung an seine Stammesgenossen von einem russischen Juden* (Berlin, 1882). In English translation: "Auto-Emancipation," in his *Road to Freedom: Writings and Addresses* (New York, 1944).

6. Kurt Blumenfeld, *Erlebte Judenfrage. Ein Vierteljahrhundert deutscher Zionismus* (Stuttgart, 1962).

7. *Rom und Jerusalem. Die letzte Nationalitätenfrage* (Leipzig, 1862). In English translation: *Rome and Jerusalem* (New York, 1918).

8. Volkmar Eichstädt, *Bibliographie zur Geschichte der Judenfrage, Band 1, 1750–1848* (Hamburg, 1938), repr. Farnborough Hants, 1969.

9. *Antisemitism, An Annotated Bibliography*, ed. Susan S. Cohen (New York and London, 1987 ff.) [on publications from 1984 on]; *Retrospective Bibliography of Antisemitism* [prior to 1984], eds. Sylviane Stampfer, Jane Singer (in preparation).

# ABBREVIATIONS

## Location of Publications

| | |
|---|---|
| *LB* | Zentrum für Antisemitismusforschung, Berlin |
| *LC* | Germania Judaica, Cologne |
| *LF* | Stadt- und Universitätsbibliothek, Frankfurt a.M. |
| *LJ* | Jewish National and University Library, Jerusalem |
| *LM* | Bayerische Staatsbibliothek, Munich |
| *LTA* | Wiener Library, Tel Aviv |
| *LV* | Oesterreichische Nationalbibliothek, Vienna |

## Geographical Abbreviations

| | |
|---|---|
| Bruck a.d.M. | Bruck an der Mur (Styria) |
| E. | Elsaß (Alsace) |
| Frankfurt a.M. | Frankfurt am Main |
| Freiburg i.Br. | Freiburg im Breisgau |
| Halle a.d. S. | Halle an der Saale |
| M. | Mecklenburg |
| Münster i.W. | Münster in Westfalen |
| Nossen i.S. | Nossen im Saarland |
| O.S. | Oberschlesien (Upper Silesia) |
| Rostock i.M. | Rostock in Mecklenburg |
| Thür. | Thüringen (Thuringia) |
| Ts. | Taunus |
| Westf. | Westfalen (Westphalia) |
| Westpr. | Westpreußen (Westprussia) |
| Zell i.W. | Zell im Wiesental |

## General Abbreviations

| | | | |
|---|---|---|---|
| a.o. | and others | Lfg. | Lieferung |
| Abt. | Abteilung | luth. | lutherisch |
| akad. | akademische | ms., mss. | manuscript(s) |
| Aufl. | Auflage | n. Chr. | nach Christi Geburt |
| Ausg. | Ausgabe | n.d. | no date |
| ausgearb. | ausgearbeitet | N.F. | Neue Folge |
| Bd(e). | Band, Bände | N.S. | Neue Serie |
| bearb. | bearbeitet | n.s. | new series |
| betr. | betreffs, betreffend | n.p. | no place |
| Bro., Bros. | Brother, Brothers | Nachf. | Nachfolger |
| Buchdr. | Buchdruckerei | no(s). | number(s) |
| Buchhdlg. | Buchhandlung | Nr. | Nummer |
| Bull. | Bulletin | öst. | österreichisch(e, er, es) |
| bzw. | beziehungsweise | | |
| cf. | confer | p.t. | pleno titulo |
| col. | column | per. | period |
| Diss. | Dissertation | pp. | pages |
| Dr. | Doktor | Prof. | Professor |
| E.H. | Euer Hochwürden | pseud. | pseudonym |
| e.V. | eingetragener Verein | pt(s). | part(s) |
| ed. | edited, editor | ptie. | partie |
| erg. | ergänzt | rev. | revidiert, revised, revue |
| erw. | erweiterte | | |
| etc. | et cetera | sen. | senior |
| ev. | evangelisch | spez. | speziell |
| ff. | following | suppl. | supplement |
| fol. | folio | t. | tome |
| Gebr. | Gebrüder | T., Tle. | Teil, Teile |
| Geh. | Geheimer | tr. | translator, translated |
| H.H. | Herren | typ. | typography |
| Hl. | Heiliger, Heilige | u.a. | und andere(s) |
| hrsg. | herausgegeben | überarb. | überarbeitet |
| Hrsg. | Herausgeber | übers. | übersetzt |
| i. | in | unveränd. | unveränderte |
| i.e. | id est | ungar. | ungarisch (Hungarian) |
| illus. | illustration(s) | usw. | und so weiter |
| in Komm. | in Kommission | V. | Vers |
| Jhrg. | Jahrgang | veränd. | veränderte |
| jr. | junior | verb. | verbesserte |
| Jun. | Junior | Verlagshdlg. | Verlagshandlung |
| Jzn | Jezuieten | verm. | vermehrte |
| k.k. | Kaiserlich-königlich | vol(s). | volume(s) |
| koenigl. | königlich(er, e, es) | Wwe. | Witwe |
| l. | leaf, leaves | | |

## Newspapers and Periodicals

| | |
|---|---|
| AZJ | Allgemeine Zeitung des Judentums |
| Freimann, A. Dt. anon. Schriften . . . | Freimann, Aron: Deutsche anonyme Schriften über Juden und judentum. In: Zeitschrift für Hebräische Bibliographie, 1915. Vol. 18, pp. 73-101 |
| Hist. Jud. | Historia Judaica |
| I.Dt. R. | Im Deutschen Reich |
| J.Q.R. | Jewish Quarterly Review |
| J.S.St. | Jewish Social Studies |
| J.C.E.A. | Journal of Central European Affairs |
| J.J.St. | Journal of Jewish Studies |
| LBI Bull. | Leo-Baeck-Institute Bulletin |
| LBIYB | Leo-Baeck-Institute Yearbook |
| MGWJ | Monatsschrift für Geschichte und Wissenschaft des Judentums |
| N.Z. | Neue Zeit |
| Pol.Anthrop.Rev. | Politisch-Anthropologische Revue |
| Pr. Jhrb. | Preußische Jahrbücher |
| SaH | Saat auf Hoffnung |
| TAJfDG | Tel-Aviver Jahrbuch für Deutsche Geschichte |
| Wien.Lib.Bull. | Wiener Library Bulletin |
| ZfDSJ | Zeitschrift für Demographie und Statistik der Juden |
| ZfGJ | Zeitschrift für die Geschichte der Juden |
| ZfGJD | Zeitschrift für die Geschichte der Juden in Deutschland |

# LIST OF PERIODICALS AND COLLECTIONS

900 Jahre Geschichte der Juden in Hessen. Wiesbaden, Kommission für die Geschichte der Juden in Hessen, 1983 (no. 1381)

Allgemeine Konservative Monatsschrift für das Christliche Deutschland. Leipzig, 1843– (no. 1381)

Allgemeine Zeitung des Judentums. Berlin: Mosse, 1837–1922

Allgemeines Handbuch der Freimaurerei. 3rd, rev. ed., Leipzig: M. Hesse, 1900–1901 (no. 1053)

American Economic Review. Stanford, Cal.: American Economic Association, 1911–

The American Hebrew. New York, 1879–

American Historical Review. New York, 1895/96–

The American Journal of Sociology. Chicago, 1895–

Antisemitisches Jahrbuch. Berlin, 1897–

Antisemitism through the Ages; A Collection of Essays, ed. Shmuel Almog. Jerusalem: The Zalman Shazar Center for the Study of Jewish History, 1980 (no. 1140)

Antisemitism through the Ages, ed. Shmuel Almog. Oxford: Pergamon Press, 1988 (no. 2289)

Antisemitismus und jüdische Geschichte. Berlin: Wissenschaftlicher Autoren-Verlag, 1987 (nos. 392, 1108, 1885)

Antisemitismus; von der Judenfeindschaft zum Holocaust, eds. Herbert Strauss, Norbert Kampe. Frankfurt a.M.: Campus Verlag, 1985 (nos. 1041, 1799)

Antisemitismus; zur Pathologie der bürgerlichen Gesellschaft, eds. Hermann Huss, Andrea Schröder. Frankfurt a.M.: Europäische Verlagsanstalt, 1965 (no. 660)

Archiv für Kriminalanthropologie und Kriminalistik. Leipzig: F.C.W. Vogel, 1898–1916

Archiv für Rassen- und Gesellschaftsbiologie. Berlin, 1904–
Archiv für Sozialgeschichte. Hannover, 1961–
Aristocracy and the Middle Classes in Germany. Social Types in German
    Literature, 1830–1900. Rev. ed. With a foreword by G.P. Gooch.
    Chicago: University of Chicago Press, 1964 (no. 2335)
Das Ausland. Stuttgart, 1828–1893
Austriaca; Betrachtungen und Streiflichter. Leipzig: Dunker & Humblot, 1882
    (no. 3553)
Bayreuther Blätter. Leipzig, 1878–
Der Bayreuther Kreis von seiner Entstehung bis zum Ausgang der
    Wilhelminischen Aera. Münster: Verlag Aschendorff, 1971 (no. 1889)
Beiträge zur Geschichte der deutschen Arbeiterbewegung. Berlin: Dietz 1959–
Berliner Straßeneckenliteratur 1848–1849. Stuttgart: Ph. Reclam Jun., 1977
    (nos. 951, 1429)
Bernstein und der demokratische Sozialismus, eds. Horst Heimann, Thomas
    Meyer. Berlin, 1978 (no. 2234)
Berühmte Kriminalprozesse der Gegenwart. Wien: Alois Reichmann [n.d.]
    (nos. 1526, 1667)
Between East and West; Essays Dedicated to the Memory of Bela Horowitz,
    ed. A. Altmann. London: East & West Library, 1958 (no. 201)
Das Bild des Juden in der Volks- und Jugendliteratur vom 18. Jahrhundert bis
    1945, ed. Heinrich Pleticha. Würzburg: Königshausen und Neumann,
    1985 (nos. 641, 2410)
Die bürgerlichen Parteien in Deutschland. Handbuch der Geschichte der
    bürgerlichen Parteien. Vol. 1. Berlin: Das Europäische Buch, 1968
    (no. 721).
Cahiers de l'Institut de Science Economique Appliquée. Paris: I.S.E.A. 1960–
Central European History. Atlanta, GA: Emory University, 1968–
Christen und Juden, ed. Wolf-Dieter Marsch. Göttingen: Vandenhoeck &
    Ruprecht, 1961 (no. 993)
Christen und Juden, eds. Wolf-Dieter Marsch, Karl Thieme. Mainz: Matthias-
    Grünewald-Verlag, 1961 (no. 154)
Colloquium; A Journal of Historical and Social Thought. New York: J. Wiley
    & Sons, 1964–1968
Commentary. New York, 1945–
Conservative Judaism. New York, 1945–
Contemporary Review. London, 1886–
Deutsch-Soziale Blätter. Leipzig, 1885–
Deutsche Jugend, ed. Will Vesper. Berlin, 1934 (no. 1494)

Das Deutsche Kaiserreich, 1871–1918. Göttingen: Vandenhoeck & Ruprecht, 1973 (no. 2167)
Deutsche Revue. Berlin, 1877–
Deutsche Rundschau. Berlin, 1874–
Deutsche Vierteljahrsschrift. Stuttgart, 1923–
Deutsche Worte. Leipzig, 1881–
Deutsche Worte. Wien: Verlag Deutsche Worte, 1904 (no. 98)
Deutscher Staat und deutsche Parteien. Beiträge zur deutschen Partei- und Ideengeschichte, ed. Paul Wentzke. München, 1922 (no. 1087)
Deutsches Judentum — Aufstieg und Krise. Stuttgart: Deutsche Verlagsanstalt, 1963 (no. 1252)
Dionysian Art and Populist Politics in Austria. New Haven: Yale University Press, 1974 (no. 1413)
Dispersion and Unity; Journal on Zionism and the Jewish World. Jerusalem: World Zionist Organization, 1960–
The Economic Journal. London–New York, 1891–
Elite and Leading Groups in the History of Israel and the Nations. Jerusalem, 1966 (no. 17)
Emuna; Horizonte zur Diskussion über Israel und Judentum. Frankfurt a.M., 1966–1975
Encyclopaedia Judaica. Berlin: Verlag Eschkol, 1928–1934 (nos. 99, 258)
Encyclopaedia Judaica. Jerusalem: Encyclopaedia Judaica, 1971–1972 (no. 95)
Die Erben Bismarcks; Parteien und Verbände in der Spätphase des Wilhelminischen Deutschlands-Sammlungspolitik 1897–1918. Köln: Kiepenheuer & Witsch, 1970 (no. 1969)
Es werde Licht. Leipzig, 1869–
European Judaism. Amsterdam: World Union for Progressive Judaism, 1966–
European Studies Review. London, 1971–
Evidences. Paris: American Jewish Committee, 1961–
Familiengeschichtliche Blätter — Deutscher Herold; Monatsschrift für wissenschaftliche Genealogie. Leipzig, 1903–1939
Festschrift für Jacob Rosenheim. Frankfurt a.M.: J. Kauffmann, 1931 (no. 1500)
Forschung am Judentum. Festschrift zum 60. Geburtstag von Rabbiner Dr. Dr.H.C. Lothar Rothschild. Dargereicht von der Vereinigung für Religiös-Liberales Judentum in der Schweiz. Bern, 1970. (no. 588)
Forschungen zur Judenfrage. Hamburg: Hanseatische Verlagsanstalt, 1936–
Frankfurter Hefte; Zeitschrift für Kultur und Politik. Frankfurt a.M., 1945–

Das freie Wort. Frankfurter Halbmonatsschrift für Fortschritt auf den Gebieten des geistigen Lebens. Frankfurt a.m.: Neuer Frankfurter Verlag, 1902–

Gedenkschrift Martin Gähring; Studien zur europäischen Geschichte. Mit einem Geleitwort von Jacques Droz, ed. Ernst Schulin. Wiesbaden: F. Steiner, 1968. (no. 1801)

Gegen die Antisemiten; eine Streitschrift zusammengestellt von J. S. Bloch. Wien: D. Löwy, 1882 (no. 867)

Gegenwart im Rückblick. Festgabe für die jüdische Gemeinde zu Berlin, 25 Jahre nach dem Neubeginn, eds. Herbert A. Strauss, Kurt R. Grossmann. Heidelberg, 1970 (no. 897)

Die Gegenwart; Wochenschrift für Literatur, Kunst und öffentliches Leben. Berlin: Stilke, 1872–1908

Germania Judaica. Köln: Germania Judaica, 1962 (no. 1422)

Germania; Zentralorgan der deutschen Katholiken. Berlin, 1871–1938

Germans, Poles and Jews; the Nationality Conflict in the Prussian East 1772–1914. Chicago: University of Chicago Press, 1980 (no. 890)

Geschichte der Juden, ed. Franz Bautz. München: C.H. Beck, 1983 (no. 834)

Geschichte in der Gegenwart. Festschrift für Kurt Kloxen. Paderborn, 1972 (no. 936)

Geschichte in Wissenschaft und Unterricht. Stuttgart, 1950–

Geschichte und Gesellschaft. Göttingen, 1975–

Geschichte und Kultur der Juden in Bayern, eds. Manfred Treml, Wolf Weigand. München, 1988 (no. 758)

Die Gesellschaft; internationale Revue für Sozialismus und Politik. Berlin: Y.H.W. Dietz Nachf., 1924–1933

Die Gesellschaft; Münchner Halbmonatsshrift für Kunst und Kultur. München: G. Franz, 1885–1902

Gesellschaft, Recht und Politik. Neuwied: Luchterhand, 1968 (no. 1879)

Die Grenzboten. Leipzig, 1841–1944

Das größere Deutschland, ed. Eugen Stamm. Breslau: W. Korn, 1935 (no. 2589)

Gutzkow-Funde. Beiträge zur Literatur- und Kulturgeschichte des 19. Jahrhunderts. Berlin: A.L. Wolff, 1901 (no. 3397)

Hammer; Blätter für deutschen Sinn. Leipzig, 1902–

Der Hammer; Zeitschrift des nationalen Arbeiterbundes in Wien. Wien, 1895–

Hebrew Union College Annual. Cincinnati, 1924–

Heimkehr; Essays jüdischer Denker, ed. Jüdischer Nationaler Akademischer Verein "Emunah". Czernowitz: L. Lamm, 1912 (no. 1781)

Herzl Yearbook. New York: Theodor Herzl Foundation, 1958–
Historia Judaica; Journal of Studies in Jewish History. New York, 1938–1961
The Historical Journal. London, 1958–
Historisch-Politische Blätter für das Katholische Deutschland. München, 1838–1923
Historische Zeitschrift. München, 1859–
Historisches Jahrbuch der Görres-Gesellschaft. München, 1880–
The History of the Jewish People, ed. H.H. Ben-Sasson. Cambridge, Mass.: Harvard University Press, 1969 (no. 631)
Hochland; Monatsschrift. Kempten: J. Kösel, 1903–1907
Hungarian-Jewish Studies. New York: World Federation of Hungarian Jews 1966–1973
Idea; Jahrbuch der Hamburger Kunsthalle. München: Prestel, 1982–
Im Deutschen Reich. Berlin: Expedition, 1895–1922
In zwei Welten. Tel-Aviv, 1962 (no. 366)
Interessante Kriminal-Prozesse. Vols. 3–5. Berlin: H. Barsdorf, 1911–1912 (nos. 730, 734–736)
Interessante Kriminalprozesse von kulturhistorischer Bedeutung. Berlin: Berliner Buchversand, 1920-1921 (nos. 731, 737)
International Council for Philosophy and Humanistic Studies; The Third Reich. London: Weidenfeld & Nicolson, 1955 (no. 1703)
International Review of Social History. Amsterdam: International Institute of Social History, 1956–
Der Israelit. Frankfurt a.M., 1860–1938
Israelitische Monatsschrift; Suppl. to Jüdische Presse. Berlin: H. Itzkowski, 1870–1923
Israelitische Wochenschrift für die religiösen und sozialen Interessen des Judentums. Magdeburg, 1870–1914
Israelitisches Familienblatt. Hamburg, 1898–1938
Jahrbuch der jüdischen literarischen Gesellschaft. Frankfurt a.M., 1903–1932
Jahrbuch der sächsischen Missionskonferenz. Leipzig: Buchhdlg. des Vereinshauses, 1888–
Jahrbuch für Berlin-Brandenburgische Kirchengeschichte. Berlin, 1904–
Jahrbuch für die Geschichte der Juden und des Judentums. Leipzig, 1860–1869
Jahrbuch für Gesetzgebung, Verwaltung und Volkswirtschaft im Deutschen Reich. Berlin, 1871–1912
Jahrbücher für Nationalökonomie und Statistik. Jena, 1863–
Jewish Affairs. Johannesburg, 1941–
Jewish Chronicle. London, 1841–

The Jewish Encyclopedia. New York: Funk & Wagnalls Co., 1901 (no. 96)

Jewish Quarterly Review. Philadelphia, 1888–

The Jewish Response to German Culture; from the Enlightenment to the Second World War, ed. Jehuda Reinharz, Walter Schatzberg. Hanover, NH: University Press of New England, 1985 (nos. 1136, 1487, 2118, 2297)

The Jewish Review. London, 1910–1914, 1932–1934

Jewish Social Studies. New York, 1939–

Jews in a Gentile World, eds. Isaque Graeber, Stewart Henderson Britt. New York: Macmillan Co., 1942 (no. 185)

The Jews of Austria; Essays on Their Life, History and Destruction, ed. Josef Fraenkel. London: Vallentine, Mitchell, 1967 (no. 1680)

The Jews of Czechoslovakia. Vol. 1. Philadelphia: Jewish Publication Society, 1968 (no. 1162)

Journal of Jewish Studies. London, 1948–

Journal of Central European Affairs. Boulder, CO 1941–1964

Journal of Contemporary History. London, 1966–

Journal of Modern History. Chicago, 1929–

Journal of the History of Ideas. New York, 1940–

Judaean Addresses. New York, 1917 (no. 1917)

Judaica; Beiträge zum Verständnis des jüdischen Schicksals in Vergangenheit und Gegenwart. Zürich: Zwingli-Verlag, 1945–

Judaica. Buenos Aires, 1933–

Judaism. New York, 1952–

Der Jude. Berlin, 1916–1928

Juden als Darmstädter Bürger. Darmstadt: Eduard Röther Verlag, 1984 (nos. 703, 2152)

Die Juden als Minderheit in der Geschichte, eds. Bernd Martin, Ernst Schulin. München: Deutscher Taschenbuch-Verlag, 1981 (nos. 922, 923, 2295)

Juden im wilhelminischen Deutschland, 1890–1914, ed. Werner E. Mosse. Tübingen: J.C.B. Mohr, 1976 (nos. 408, 849, 1049)

Die Juden in den böhmischen Ländern. Vorträge der Tagung des Collegium Carolinum in Bad Wiessee vom 27.–29. November 1981. München: R. Oldenbourg, 1983 (no. 1567)

Juden in der Schweiz; Glaube, Geschichte, Gegenwart. Zürich: Edition Kürz, 1982 (no. 2181)

Judenfeindschaft in Altertum, Mittelalter und Neuzeit, ed. Anneliese Mannzmann. Königstein, Ts.: Scriptor 1981 (no. 1291)

Das Judentum in der deutschen Umwelt, 1800–1850, ed. Hans Liebeschütz, Arnold Pauker. Tübingen: J.C.B. Mohr, 1977 (no. 1601)

Judentum, Schicksal, Wesen und Gegenwart, eds. F. Böhm, W. Dirks. Wiesbaden: Steiner, 1975 (no. 688)

Judentum und Antisemitismus von der Antike bis zur Gegenwart, eds. Thomas Klein a.o. Düsseldorf: Droste, 1984 (nos. 336, 1365, 1384)

Jüdische Statistik. Berlin, 1903 (nos. 290, 1474)

Jüdische Zeitung für Ostdeutschland. Breslau, 1896–1937

Jüdischer Almanach. Köln: Jüdischer Verlag, 1910 (no. 1582)

Jüdisches Lexikon. Berlin: Jüdischer Verlag, 1927–1930

Jüdisches Literatur-Blatt. Berlin, 1872–1913

Le juif antisémite. Paris: Vita, 1935 (nos. 227, 228)

Kampf; sozialdemokratische Monatsschrift. Wien, 1907–

Kirche und Synagoge; Handbuch zur Geschichte von Christen un Juden. Darstellung mit Quellen. Stuttgart: E.Klett, 1968–1970 (no. 1337)

Köln und das Rheinische Judentum, ed. Jutta Bohnke-Kollwitz a.o. Köln: J.P. Bachem, 1984 (no. 2027)

Kommunisten zur Judenfrage; zur Geschichte von Theorie und Praxis des Kommunismus. Pt. 1–2. Opladen: Westdeutscher Verlag, 1983 (nos. 1926, 1930)

Konferenzblätter; Monatschrift für das gesamte Unterrichts- und Erziehungswesen. Quedlinburg: Voges, 1893–1898

Konservatives Wochenblatt. Berlin, 1890–1893

Der Kulturkämpfer. Berlin: F. Luckhardt, 1880–1888

Der Kunstwart. München, 1887–1926

Lebenslauf und Gesellschaft, ed. Wilhelm Heinz Schröder. Stuttgart: Klett-Cotta, 1985 (no. 1492)

Leo Baeck Institute Bulletin. Tel-Aviv: Bitaon, 1957–

Leo Baeck Institute Yearbook. London, 1956–

Liberalismus; die deutschliberale Bewegung in der Habsburgischen Monarchie. München: Callwey, 1955 (no. 704)

Literarische Rundschau für das Katholische Deutschland. Freiburg i.Br.: Herder, 1875–1914

März; Halbmonatsschrift für deutsche Kultur. München: A. Langen, 1907–

Masaryk und das Judentum, ed. Ernst Rychnowsky. Prag, 1931 (no. 1810)

Medizinhistorisches Journal. Mainz, 1966–

Men and Events; Historical Essays. New York: Harper & Bros., 1958 (no. 2081)

Menorah Journal. New York, 1915–1942

Mitteilungen des Oberhessischen Geschichtsvereins. Giessen, 1889–

Mitteilungen des Vereins zur Abwehr des Antisemitismus. Berlin, 1891–1933

Monatsschrift der Österreichisch-Israelitischen Union. Wien, 1889–1919

Monatsschrift für Geschichte und Wissenschaft des Judentums. Dresden, 1851–1939

Monatsschrift für Kriminalpsychologie und Strafrechtsreform. Köln, 1904–

Monatsschrift für Kriminologie und Strafrechtsreform see Monatsschrift für Kriminalpsychologie und Strafrechtsreform.

Monumenta Judaica, Handbuch. Köln: J. Melzer, 1963 (no. 1181)

Der Morgen; Monatsschrift der Juden in Deutschland. Berlin, 1925–1938

Nathanael; Zeitschrift der Berliner Gesellschaft zur Beförderung des Christentums unter den Juden. Berlin, 1885–1918

The Nation. New York, 1865–

Die Nation; Wochenschrift für Politik, Volkswirtschaft und Literatur. Berlin, 1883–1907

National Life and Thought of the Various Nations throughout the World. A Series of Addresses. London: T.E. Unwin, 1891 (no. 3650)

Die Nationalitätenfrage und die Sozialdemokratie in Wien. 2nd ed. Wien: Wiener Volksbuchhdlg., 1924 (no. 178)

Neohelicon. Budapest, 1973–

Neue Demokratie — Richtlinien fuer bürgerliche Politik. Berlin: Walther, 1909 (no. 2282)

Neue Deutsche Rundschau see Die Neue Rundschau

Neue Evangelische Kirchenzeitung. Leipzig, 1859-1886

Neue Jüdische Monatshefte. Berlin, 1916–1920

Die Neue Rundschau. Frankfurt a.M.: S. Fischer, 1890–

Die Neue Zeit; Wochenschrift der deutschen Sozialdemokratie. Stuttgart: Dietz, 1883–1923

Neue Zeitschrift für Musik. Mainz, 1834–

New York Times. New York, 1851–

Österreichische Akademie der Wissenschaften. Phil. Hist. Klasse. Anzeiger. Wien, 1864–

Das Oesterreichische Judentum. Wien: Jugend und Volk, 1974 (no. 888)

Oesterreichische Monatsschrift für Tierheilkunde. [n.p], [n.d] (no. 1334)

Oesterreichische Parteiprogramme. PT. 1: Parteiprogramme von 1868–1918. München: R. Oldenbourg, 1967 (no. 209)

Oesterreichische Rundschau. Wien, 1904–

Olam (World Union of Jewish Students). London, 1976–

Ost und West; Monatsschrift für modernes Judentum. Berlin, 1901–1923

Die Peitsche; kritische Halbmonatschrift. Düsseldorf, 1924–1925

Politisch Anthropologische Revue. Eisenach, 1902–

Politische Studien; Monatshefte der Hochschule für politische Studien. München, 1950–

Populärwissenschaftliche Monatsblätter zur Belehrung über das Judentum. Frankfurt a.M., 1881–

Preußische Jahrbücher. Berlin: Stilke, 1858–1938

Propheten des Nationalismus, ed. Karl Schwedhelm. München: List-Verlag, 1969 (nos. 1006, 1103, 1104, 1430, 1674, 1675)

Protestantismus und Politik. Werk und Wirkung Adolf Stöckers, ed. Günther Brakelmann a.o. Hamburg: Christians, 1982 (no. 1039)

Realenzyklopädie für Bibel und Talmud, ed. Jakob Hamburger. Strelitz: Selbstverlag, 1870–1883 (no. 900)

Rehearsal for Destruction, by Paul W. Massing. New York: Harper & Brothers, 1949 (no. 3097)

Die Republik, Berlin, 1918–

Revue des Deux Mondes. Paris, 1831–

Revue des Études Juives. Paris: Durlacher, 1880–

Revue des Revues. Paris, 1890–1900

Revue Juive de Génève. Génève, 1932–

Saat auf Hoffnung; Zeitschrift für die Mission der Kirche an Israel. Erlangen, 1863–

Saeculum; Jahrbuch für Universalgeschichte. Freiburg, 1950–

Schlesische Presse. [n.p.], [n.d] (no. 840)

Schlesische Zeitung. Breslau, 1848–1945

Schmollers Jahrbuch für Gesetzgebung, Verwaltung und Volkswirtschaft im Deutschen Reich. Berlin, 1877–

Schmollers Jahrbuch für Wirtschafts- und Sozialwissenschaften see Schmollers Jahrbuch für Gesetzgebung, Verwaltung und Volkswirtschaft im Deutschen Reich.

Soviet Jewish Affairs. London, 1971–

Soziale Revue. Böhmisch-Kamnitz, 1892–1893

Sozialgeschichte heute. Festschrift für Hans Rosenberg zum 70. Geburtstag, ed. Hans Ulrich Wehler. Göttingen: Vandenhoeck & Ruprecht, 1974 (nos. 1802, 2123, 2197)

Sozialistische Monatshefte; internationale Revue des Sozialismus. Berlin, 1895–1923

Staats-Lexikon. 3rd ed, eds. C. Rotteck, C. Welcker. Leipzig: Brockhaus, 1863–66 (no. 1998)

Staats- und Gesellschaftslexikon. Berlin: F. Heinicke, 1859–1867 (no. 169)

Staatsbürgerzeitung, 2. Beilage (no. 1863)

Stadtbibliothek Frankfurt am Main. Katalog der Judaica und Hebraica. Vol.1: Judaica, ed. Aron Freimann. Frankfurt a.m., 1932 (no. 711)

Die Standarte, ed. M. Handl. Berlin: Verlag der Standarte, 1906-1909

Statistische Monatsschrift. Wien: Hölder, 1875-1921

Student und Hochschule im 19. Jahrhundert; Studien und Materialien. Göttingen: Vandenhoek & Ruprecht, 1975 (no. 854)

Studi Storici. Roma: Istituto Gramsci, 1954-

Studia Judaica Austriaca. Wien, 1974-

Studien zur deutschen Geschichte des 19. und 20. Jahrhunderts. Göttingen: Vandenhoeck & Ruprecht, 1961 (no. 1086)

Studies in Contemporary Jewry. Hebrew University, Jerusalem; Institute of Contemporary Jewry. Bloomingdale, Ind., 1984-

Studies in Nineteenth Century Jewish Intellectual History, ed. Alexander Altmann. Cambridge, Mass.: Harvard University Press, 1964 (no. 1329)

Studies of the Leo Baeck Institute. New York: Ungar Pub. Co., 1967 (no. 1137)

Ein Stück von uns; deutsche Juden in deutschen Armeen, 1813-1976. Eine Dokumentation. Mainz: v. Hase & Köhler Verlag, 1977 (no. 2114)

Tel-Aviver Jahrbuch für Deutsche Geschichte. Tel-Aviv, 1972-

Texts and Responses, eds. Michael A. Fishbane, Paul R. Flohr. Leiden: E.J. Brill, 1975 (no. 1713)

Theologie und Glaube. Paderborn: Verlag F. Schöningh, 1908-

Tribüne; Zeitschrift zum Verständnis des Judentums. Frankfurt a.M., 1962-

The Universal Jewish Encyclopedia. New York: The Universal Jewish Encyclopedia, 1939 (no. 97)

Das Verbrechen und seine Bekämpfung. 2nd ed. Heidelberg: C. Winter, 1906 (no. 116)

Victor Adlers Aufsätze; Reden und Briefe. Vienna: Verlag der Wiener Volksbuchhandlung, 1922 (no. 614)

Vierteljahrshefte für Zeitgeschichte. Stuttgart: Institut für Zeitgeschichte, 1953-

Vierteljahrsschrift für gerichtliche Medizin und öffentliches Sanitätswesen. Berlin: A. Hirschwald, 1852-

Von Juden in München. München: Ner-Tamid Verlag, 1958 (no. 1870)

Weckstimmen für das Katholische Volk. Wien, 1870-

Die Welt; Zentralorgan der zionistischen Bewegung. Wien, 1897-1914

Weltkampf; Monatsschrift für Weltpolitik, völkische Kultur und die Judenfrage aller Länder. München, 1924-1941

Weltwirtschaftliches Archiv. Tübingen: Institut für Weltwirtschaft, 1913-

Werkshagen; der Protestantismus am Ende des XIX. Jahrhunderts. Vol. 1. Berlin, 1902 (no. 2163)

Who's Afraid of Richard Wagner. Jerusalem: Keter, 1984 (nos. 7, 22)

Wien 1879–1930; Traum und Wirklichkeit, ed. Robert Waissenberger. Salzburg: Residenz-Verlag, 1984 (no. 1471)

Wiener Library Bulletin. London: Wiener Library, 1946–1981

Wirtschaft, Gesellschaft, Geschichte. Stuttgart: Metzler, 1974 (no. 1588)

Yad va-Shem Studies on the European Jewish Catastrophe and Resistance. Jerusalem: Yad va-Shem, 1974 (nos. 200, 2186)

Yalkut Moreshet. Tel-Aviv, 1963– (Hebrew)

YIVO Annual of Jewish Social Science. New York: Yidisher visnshaftlikher Institut, 1946–

Zeitschrift des Vereins für Hamburgische Geschichte. Hamburg, 1848–

Zeitschrift für Demographie und Statistik der Juden. Berlin: Bureau für Statistik der Juden, 1905–1931

Zeitschrift für die Geschichte der Juden. Tel-Aviv, 1964–1974

Zeitschrift für die Geschichte der Juden in Deutschland, ed. Ismar Elbogen. Berlin, 1929–1938

Zeitschrift für die Geschichte der Juden in Deutschland, ed. Ludwig Geiger. Braunschweig, 1887–1892

Zeitschrift für die Geschichte des Oberrheins. Heidelberg: Landesarchiv zu Karlsruhe, 1850–

Zeitschrift für Geschichtswissenschaft. Berlin, 1953–

Zeitschrift für Hebräische Bibliographie, eds. H. Brody, A. Freimann. Berlin, 1896–1921

Zeitschrift für Ostforschung. Marburg, 1952–

Zeitschrift für Politik. Berlin: C. Heymann, 1908–

Zeitschrift für Religions- und Geistesgeschichte. Köln, 1948–

Zeitschrift für Sozialwissenschaft. Leipzig, 1897–1921

Zeitschrift für Unternehmergeschichte. Wiesbaden, F. Steiner, 1955–

Zeitungswissenschaft; Mitteilungsblatt des Deutschen Zeitungswissenschaftlichen Verbandes. [n.p.], [n.d.] (no. 2821)

Zion. Jerusalem, 1936– (Hebrew)

Die Zukunft. Berlin, 1892-1922

Die Zukunft des deutschen Volkstums. München: J.F. Lehmann, 1907 (no. 922)

Zur Geschichte der Juden in Deutschland. Jerusalem: Academic Press, 1971 (no. 1482)

# WORKS ON THE JEWISH QUESTION

0001

אבינרי, שלמה: לבירור עמדתו של הגל לשאלת האמנציפציה. ציון 25 (1960)
‎134-137.

[Avineri, Shlomo: The Hegelian Position in the Emancipation of the Jews. *Zion* 25 (1960) 134-137.] *LJ*

English summary.

0002

אילוני, יהודה: בעיות אידיולוגיות, ארגוניות ומבניות בציונות הגרמנית
מראשיתה עד מלחמת העולם הראשונה. תל-אביב, 1981. 759 ע'. דיס.
אוניברסיטת תל-אביב.

[Eloni, Yehuda: *Ideological, Organizational and Structural Problems in the German Zionist Movement from its Beginning to World War I.* Tel-Aviv: 1981. 759 pp.] *LJ*

Diss. Tel-Aviv University. English summary.

0003

אליאב, מרדכי: החנוך היהודי בימי ההשכלה והאמנציפציה. ירושלים:
הסוכנות היהודית, 1960. יד', 370, 8 ע'.

[Eliav, Mordechai: *Jewish Education in Germany in the Period of Enlightenment and Emancipation.* Jerusalem: The Jewish Agency, 1960. 14, 370, 8 pp.] *LJ*

0004

אלכסנדר, גבריאל: ד"ר קארל לואגר; התנועה הנוצרית הסוציאליסטית
והיהודים בוינה בשלהי הקיסרות ההבסבורגית. ירושלים, תשמ"ד, 126 ע'.
עבודת גמר MA האוניברסיטה העברית.

[Alexander, Gabriel: *Dr. Karl Lueger, the Christian Social Party and the Jews of Vienna at the End of the Habsburg Empire*. Jerusalem: 1984. 126 pp.] *LJ*

M.A. thesis, Hebrew University.

0005

בורנשטיין, אהרון: מקבצנים לדורשי עבודה; יהודים נודדים בגרמניה, 1869–1914. תל-אביב, 1987, 428 ע'. דיס. אונ. ת"א.

[Bornstein, Ahron: *From Beggars to Seekers of Work*. Tel-Aviv: 1987. 428 pp.] *LJ*

Diss. Tel-Aviv University. English summary.

0006

בכרך, צבי: גזענות בשרות הפוליטיקה; מן המוניזם אל הנאציזם. ירושלים: הוצאת מאגנס, 1985, 182 ע'.

[Bachrach, Walter Zwi: *Racism — the Tool of Politics; From Monism Toward Nazism*. Jerusalem: Magnes Press, 1985. 182 pp.] *LJ*

0007

בכרך, צבי: ריכרד ואגנר — ההומניסט האנטי הומני. מי מפחד מריכרד ואגנר. ירושלים: הוצאת כתר, 1984, 219–229 ע'.

[Bachrach, Walter Zwi: Richard Wagner — the Anti-Humane Humanist. *Who's Afraid of Richard Wagner*. Jerusalem: Keter, 1984. Pp. 229–219.] *LJ*

0008

בן-אבנר, יהודה: המעמד האזרחי של יהודי הקיסרות האוסטרית בעשור הראשון לשלטון הקיסר פרנץ יוסף I (1849–1859). רמת גן, תשל"ח, 160, II ע'. דיס. אוניברסיטת בר-אילן.

[Ben-Avner, Yehuda: *The Civil State of Jews in the Austrian Empire in the First Decade of the Reign of Emperor Francis Joseph I*. Ramat Gan: 1978. II, 160 pp.] *LJ*

Diss. Bar-Ilan University.

0009

דורון, יהויקים: הציונות המרכז-אירופית מול אידיאולוגיות גרמניות בין השנים 1885–1914, הקבלות והשפעות. תל-אביב, תשל"ז, XXII, 133, 436 ד'. דיס' אוניברסיטת תל-אביב.

[Doron, Yehoyakim: *The Impact of German Ideologies on Central European Zionism, 1885–1914*. Tel-Aviv: 1977. XXII, 133, 436 l.] *LJ*

Diss. Tel-Aviv University. English summary.

0010

וסרמן, הנרי: יהודים, בורגנות "וחברה בורגנית" בעידן ליברלי בגרמניה
(1840–1880). ירושלים, 1979, 343 ע'. דיס. אונ. עברית.

[Wassermann, Henry: *Jews, Bürgertum and "bürgerliche Gesellschaft" in a Liberal Era (1840–1880)*. Jerusalem: 1979. 343 pp.] *LJ*

Diss. Hebrew University. English summary.

0011

זילברנר, אדמונד (1910–): הסוציאליזם המערבי ושאלת היהודים; מחקר
בתולדות המחשבה הסוציאליסטית במאה התשע עשרה. ירושלים: מוסד
ביאליק, תשט"ו, 484 ע'.

[Silberner, Edmund (1910-): *Western Socialism and the Jewish Problem 1800–1918*. Jerusalem: Mossad Bialik, 1955. 484 pp.] *LJ*

Extensive bibliography.

0012

טורי, יעקב: האורינטציות הפוליטיות של היהודים בגרמניה במאה הי"ט (עד
לאיחוד גרמניה). ירושלים: 1960, VI, 326 ע'. דיס. האונ. העברית.

[Toury, Jakob: *Jewish Political Orientations in XIXth Century Germany*. Jerusalem: 1960. VI, 326 pp.] *LJ*

Diss. Heb. Univ. English summary.

0013

טורי, יעקב: נסיונות לניהול מדיניות יהודית עצמאית בגרמניה, 1893–1918.
ציון כ"ח , ג'–ד' (תשכ"ג) 166–205.

[Toury, Jakob: Plans for a Jewish Political Organization in Germany, 1893–1918. *Zion* 28, 3-4 (1963) 166–205.] *LJ*

English summary.

0014

טל, אוריאל: האנטישמיות ברייך הגרמני השני, 1870–1914. ירושלים,
תשכ"ג. 4, IX, 309, IX, 6, 19 ד'. דיס. ירושלים, תשכ"ג.

[Tal, Uriel: *Antisemitism in the Second German Reich, 1870–1914*. Jerusalem: 1963. 4, IX, 309, IX, 6, 19 l.] *LJ*

Diss. Jerusalem, 1963. English summary.

0015

טל, אוריאל: יהדות ונוצרות ברייך השני 1870–1914; תהליכים היסטוריים
בדרך לטוטליטריות. ירושלים: הוצאת מאגנס, תשמ"ה, 315 ע'.

[Tal, Uriel: *Judaism and Christianity in the Second Reich; Historical Development on the Way to Totalitarianism.* Jerusalem: Magnes Press, 1985. 315 pp.] *LJ*

0016

טל, אוריאל: "מלחמת התרבות" ומעמד היהודים בגרמניה. ציון 29 (1964)
208–242.

[Tal, Uriel: The "Kulturkampf" and the Position of the Jews in Germany. *Zion* 29 (1964) 208–242.] *LJ*

English summary.

0017

טל, אוריאל: העילית האינטלקטואלית בגרמניה ועמדתה כלפי היהודים
בתקופת ביסמארק. קבוצות עילית ושכבות מנהיגות בתולדות העמים.
ירושלים: החברה ההסטורית הישראלית תשכ"ז, 1966, 98–130 ע'.

[Tal, Uriel: The Intellectual Elite in Germany and its Position to the Jews During the Bismarck Period. *Elite and Leading Groups in the History of Israel and the Nations.* Jerusalem: Israel Historical Society, 1966. Pp. 98–130.] *LJ*

0018

טל, אוריאל: הפרוטסטנטיות השמרנית ומעמד היהודים ברייך הגרמני השני
1870–1914. ציון 27 (1962) 27–111.

[Tal, Uriel: Conservative Protestantism and the Jewish Status in the German Second Reich 1870–1914. *Zion* 27 (1962) 27–111.] *LJ*

English summary.

0019

נדב, דניאל ש.: מדיניות של "היגיינה סוציאלית" בגרמניה; יוליוס מוזס
(1868–1942) ואסכולת ההיגיינה הסוציאלית בתקופת הקיסרות ובריפובליקת
ויימר. תל-אביב, 1981. 2 כרכים. דיס. אוניב. ת"א.

[Nadav, Daniel S.: *Politics of Social Hygiene in Germany.* Tel-Aviv: 1981. 2 vols.] *LJ*

Diss. Tel-Aviv University. English summary.

0020

סוקולוב, נחום (1859–1936): שנאת עולם לעם עולם. תולדות השנאה
לישראל . . . ווארשא: דפוס גאלדמאן, תרמ"ב, IX, 212 ע'.

[Sokolow, Nahum (1859–1936): *The Ancient Hatred Against the Jewish People,
its Origin and Development of the Jew Hatred from the Historical and
Psychological Point of View.* Warsaw: Typ. Goldmann, 1882. IX, 212 pp.] *LJ*

0021

צימרמן, משה: המאבק על האמנציפציה ואינטגרציה של היהודים
בקונטקסט העימות בין פרטיקולריזם ואחדות לאומית בהמבורג 1830–1865.
ירושלים, 1976. 396, XXII, 3 ע'. דיס. אונ. עברית.

[Zimmermann, Moshe: *The Struggle for Jewish Emancipation and Integration
in the Framework of the Confrontation between Particularism and the Trend
Towards German Unity in Hamburg.* Jerusalem: 1976. 396, XXII, 3 pp.] *LJ*

Diss. Hebrew University. English summary.

0022

קולקה, אוטו דב: ריכרד ואגנר — מרדיקליזם דימוקרטי לאנטישמיות
גזענית. מי מפחד מריכרד ואגנר. ירושלים: הוצאת כתר, 1984. ע' 230–246.

[Kulka, Otto Dov: Richard Wagner: From Democratic Radicalism to Racial
Antisemitism. *Who's Afraid of Richard Wagner.* Jerusalem: Keter, 1984. Pp.
230–246.] *LJ*

0023

קטצבורג, נתנאל: האנטישמיות הפוליטית בהונגריה בשנות 1867–1914. תל
אביב: דביר, 1969. X, 294 ע'. (אוניברסיטת בר-אילן: סדרת מחקרים ע"ש פ.
חורגין, 6).

[Katzburg, Nathanael: *Political Antisemitism in Hungary 1867–1914.* Tel-Aviv:
Dvir, 1969. X, 294 pp.] *LJ*

0024

קירשנבוים, שמשון ליב: ההגירה היהודית מרוסיה ופולין לגרמניה, צרפת
ואנגליה ברבע האחרון של המאה הי"ט והתערותה בארצות אלה. ירושלים,
תש"ט. 26, 365 ד'. דיס. אוניברסיטה עברית בירושלים.

[Kirschenbaum, Shimshon: *The Immigration of Jews from Russia and Poland
into Germany, France and England in the Last Quarter of the 19th Century.*
1950. 26, 365 l.] *LJ*

Diss. Hebrew University, Jerusalem. English summary.

0025

רודקינזון, מיכאל לוי: מצת מצוה ועלילת הדם. פרעסבורג: דפוס לאווי
ואלקאלאי, 1883, VIII, 32 ע'.

[Rodkinssohn, Michael Levi (1845–1904): *Matza (unleavened bread) and the Accusation of Using Blood at the Passover Festival*. Pressburg: Typ. Alkalai, 1883. VIII, 32 pp.] *LJ*

0026

שטרן, אליהו: קורותיהם של יהודי דאנציג מאז האמנציפציה ועד הגירוש
בימי השלטון הנאצי. ירושלים: אונ. עברית, תשל"ח. יג, 664 ע'. דיס. אונ.
עברית, 1978.

[Stern, Eliyahu: *The History of the Jews of Danzig from the Emancipation until their Deportation in the Nazi Era*. Jerusalem: 1978. 664 pp.] *LJ*

Diss. Hebrew University. English summary.

0027  Aargau (Switzerland) Großer Rat: *Die Judenfrage vor dem Hohen Großen Rate des Kantons Aargau in zweiter Beratung am 15. Mai 1862*. Aargau: Albrecht, 1862. 48 pp. *LJ*

0028  *ABC für Konservative Wähler. Hrsg. unter Mitwirkung namhafter Konservativer*. Berlin: M. Schulze, 1881. 56 pp. *LV*

0029  Aberbach, Alan David: *The Ideas of Richard Wagner; an Examination and Analysis of his Major Aesthetic, Political, Economic, Social and Religious Thoughts*. Lanham, MD.: University Press of America, 1984. x, 385 pp. *LJ*

Chapter 7 deals with Wagner's *Judemtum in der Musik*.

0030  *Die abergläubischen und sehr beschwerlichen Religionsgebräuche der talmudischen Juden von Rabbinen vorgeschrieben, aber nur hie und da durchwegs noch beobachtet. Das hierin meistens unwissenden Christen, gläubigen wie ungläubigen zur Belehrung*. Aus älteren und neueren Schriften. Bern: R. Jenni, 1874. 88 pp. *LJ*

0031  Achterberg, Erich: *Berliner Hochfinanz; Kaiser, Fürsten, Millionäre um 1900*. Frankfurt a.M.: F. Knapp, 1965. 240 pp. *LJ*

0032  Ackermann, Aron: *Vogelfrei! Ein Blick auf das erste Jahr des 20. Jahrhunderts*. Brandenburg an der Havel: Evenius, 1901. 20 pp. *LJ*

0033  Adler, Bruno (1889–): *Kampf um Polna; ein Tatsachenroman*. Prag: Kacha-Verlag, 1934. 276 pp. *LJ*

0034  Adler, Marcus: *Chronik der Gesellschaft zur Verbreitung der Handwerke und des Ackerbaues unter den Juden im Preußischen Staate*. Berlin: Typ. R. Boll, 1899. 60 pp. *LJ*

Founded in 1812.

0035 Adler-Rudel, Schalom (1894–): *Ostjuden in Deutschland 1880–1940; zugleich eine Geschichte der Organisationen, die sie betreuten.* Mit einem Vorwort von S. Moses. Tübingen: Mohr, 1959. XII, 169 pp. (Schriftenreihe wissenschaftlicher Abhandlungen des LBI, 1) *LJ*

0036 Adler, Salo: *Für und wider die jüdische Volksschule in Preußen. Mit einem 2. Teil: Die jüdische Volksschule in Süddeutschland, von S. Dingfelder.* Hrsg. von dem Verband der Jüdischen Lehrervereine im Deutschen Reiche. Frankfurt a.M.: Kauffmann, 1913. 34 pp. *LJ*

0037 Adler, Salo: *Das Schulunterhaltungsgesetz und die preußischen Bürger jüdischen Glaubens.* 3. durch einen Anhang: "Der neue Schulgesetzentwurf und die jüdische Schule" verm. Aufl. Frankfurt a.M.: J. Kauffmann, 1906. 44 pp. *LJ*

0038 Adler, Sigismund: *Assimilation oder Nationaljudentum.* Berlin: Apolant, 1894. 15 pp. *LJ*

0039 *Adolf Stoecker; der Herold für Volk und Kirche. Es arbeiteten mit: Karl Veidt u.a.* Berlin: Hochweg-Verlag, 1935. 79 pp. *Unseen*

0040 *Adolf Stoecker und die Angriffe seiner Gegner im Lichte der Wahrheit, von einem Nichtpolitiker.* Berlin: M. Warneck, 1901. 63 pp. *LJ*

0041 *Adolf von Stoecker.* München: 1913. 297–316 pp. *LJ*

Offprint from: *Historisch-Politische Blätter für das Katholische Deutschland,* vol. 152, no. 4, 1913.

0042 *Die Aechtung Bismarcks durch den neuesten Kurs und das Echo des nationalen Gewissens.* Berlin: P. Heichen, 1892. 56 pp. *LV*

0043 Agnes, Duchess of Sachsen-Altenburg (Princess of Anhalt): *Ein Wort an Israel.* Mit einem Vorwort von Friedrich Ahlfeld. Leipzig: W. Faber, 1893. 74 pp. (Schriften des Institutum Judaicum in Leipzig, 37–38) *LJ*

0044 Ahlwardt, Hermann (1846–1914): *Des deutschen Volkes Rettung aus jüdischer Knechtschaft. Worte an alle deutschen Handwerker und Gewerbetreibende. Vortrag gehalten im "Deutschen Bunde zur Hebung des Mittelstandes."* Berlin: G.A. Dewald, 1892. 16 pp. *Unseen*

0045 Ahlwardt, Hermann (1846–1914): *Judenflinten.* Dresden: Druckerei Glöss, 1892. 62 pp. *LTA*

0046  Ahlwardt, Hermann (1846–1914): *Die Judenfrage. Ein Vortrag gehalten zu New York im Januar 1896. 2. Aufl.* Hoboken, N.Y.: Amerikanische Antisemitische Association, 1896. 30 pp. *Unseen*

0047  Ahlwardt, Hermann (1846–1914): *Die Judenfrage. Vortrag gehalten zu Leipzig am 5. Juli 1892.* Stenographischer Bericht von Armin Graf. Leipzig: Verlag der Neuen Deutschen Zeitung, 1892. 26 pp. *LJ*

0048  Ahlwardt, Hermann (1846–1914): *Der Kampf des Germanentums mit dem Judentum. Vortrag nach kurzschriftlichen Aufzeichnungen in der Versammlung vom 23. Mai 1894 auf dem Johannisberg in Elberfeld.* Elberfeld: Deutsch-Sozialer Antisemitischer Verein, 1894. 23 pp. *LJ*

0049  Ahlwardt, Hermann (1846–1914): *Mehr Licht! Der Orden Jesu in seiner wahren Gestalt und in seinem Verhältnis zum Freimaurer- und Judentum.* Dresden: Freideutscher Verlag, 1910. 92 pp. *LJ*

0050  Ahlwardt, Hermann (1846–1914): *Meine Verhaftung. Rede gehalten in Dresden, 8. Juli 1892.* Dresden: Verlag der Druckerei Glöss, 1892. 46 pp. *LJ*

0051  Ahlwardt, Hermann (1846–1914): *Mephistos Kinder bei der Arbeit.* Rixdorf: M. Ahlwardt, 1906. 112 pp. *LJ*

0052  Ahlwardt, Hermann (1846–1914): *Neue Enthüllungen; "Judenflinten."* Dresden: Verlag der Druckerei Glöss, 1892. 37 pp. *LJ*

Attack on the weapons manufacturer Ludwig Löwe.

0053  Ahlwardt, Hermann (1846–1914): *Oeffentlicher Vortrag über die Judenfrage gehalten im Tivoli zu Dresden am 28. April 1892.* Stenographische Aufnahme von Max Trömel. Dresden: Hertwig, 1892. 32 pp. *LV*

0054  Ahlwardt, Hermann (1846–1914): *Otterngezücht.* Dresden: Typ. Glöss, 1892. 56 pp. *LJ*

0055  Ahlwardt, Hermann (1846–1914): *Prozeß Ahlwardt; "Judenflinten," 29. November bis 9. Dezember 1892.* Berlin: 1892. 308 pp. *LJ*

0056  Ahlwardt, Hermann (1846–1914): *Die Prozeße Manché und Bleichröder.* Berlin: G.A. Dewald, 1891. 16 pp. *LJ*

0057  Ahlwardt, Hermann (1846–1914): *Rede über "Judenflinten," gehalten Montag, den 16. Mai 1892. Stenographischer Bericht.* Berlin: G. A. Dewald, 1892. 24 pp. *Unseen*

0058 Ahlwardt, Hermann (1846–1914): *Schwerin und Bleichröder, Edelmann und Jude*. Dresden: Glöss, 1893. VII, 95 pp. *LJ*
Rudolf Plack-Podgorski has been also named as author.

0059 Ahlwardt, Hermann (1846–1914): *Ueber die Judenfrage; öffentlicher Vortrag . . . gehalten im Tivoli zu Dresden am 28. April 1892*. 2. Aufl. Dresden: H. Hertwig, 1892. 31 pp. *LJ*

0060 Ahlwardt, Hermann (1846–1914): *Der Verzweiflungskampf der arischen Völker mit dem Judentum*. Berlin: F. Grobhäuser, 1890. 250 pp. *LJ*
*Der Eid eines Juden* and *Jüdische Taktik* are included as pt. II and pt. III respectively in this publication.

0061 Ahlwardt, Hermann (1846–1914): *Vor seinen Wählern; Rede gehalten in Waldenberg am 14. Mai 1893*. Dresden: Typ. Glöss, 1893. 23 pp. *LTA*

0062 Ahlwardt, Hermann (1846–1914): *Wach' auf deutscher Michel! Sensationelle Enthüllungen. Vortrag gehalten am 1. November 1891 in Mühlheim a.d. Ruhr*. Nossen i.S.: P. Westphal, 1892. 32 pp. *LJ*

0063 Ahlwardt, Hermann (1846–1914): *Wahrer und falscher Patriotismus; Vortrag gehalten im Deutsch-Sozialen Verein zu Zwickau am 28. Mai 1892*. Zwickau: F. Badstübner, 1892. 48 pp. *Unseen*

0064 Ahlwardt, Hermann (1846–1914): *Wie es der Jude treibt. Vortrag gehalten nach seiner Verurteilung zu 4 Monaten Gefängnis am 24. Februar 1892*. Berlin: G.A. Dewald, 1892. 16 pp. *LJ*

0065 *Ahlwardt und seine "Judenflinten"; Ansichten eines deutschen Waffenoffiziers*. Berlin: Schreiter, 1892. 16 PP. *LJ*

0066 *Ahlwardtflinten; Kritik und sachliche Widerlegung der "Judenflinten," von einem deutschen Offizier*. Leipzig: M. Spohr, 1892. 18 pp. *LJ*

0067 *Akten und Gutachten in dem Prozeße Rohling kontra Bloch*. Wien: M. Breitenstein, 1890. 395 pp. *LJ*

0068 Albert, Johann: *Heinrich Heine und der Antisemitismus*. Nossen i. S.: P. Westphal, 1892. 45 pp. *LJ*

0069 Alexander, Kurt: Die soziale Unruhe der modernen Juden; ein soziologischer Versuch. *Pr. Jhrb.* 127 (1907) 35–57. *LJ*

0070 Alldeutsche Schüler der Ostmark: *Georg Schönerer und die Entwicklung des Alldeutschtums in der Ostmark*. Wien: Detjens, [n.d.]. 97 pp. *LB*

0071  Alldeutscher Verband: *Handbuch.* München: J. F. Lehmann, 1906. 105 pp.
      *LTA*

0072  Alldeutscher Verband: *Kundgebungen, Beschlüße und Forderungen des Alldeutschen Verbandes, zusammengestellt in der Geschäftsstelle des Alldeutschen Verbandes.* München: J.F. Lehmann, 1902. 131 pp. (Flugschriften des Alldeutschen Verbandes, 14) *LJ*

0073  Allgemeine Vereinigung zur Bekämpfung des Judentums: *Die Ziele des Antisemitismus. Ein Resumé in Gestalt des stenographischen Berichtes über den 2. Antijüdischen Kongreß zu Chemnitz.* Leipzig: Th. Fritsch, 1883. 68 pp. *LJ*
      First published in: *Schmeitzners Internationale Monatsschrift*, vol. 1883, no. 5, pp. 255-322.

0074  Allmeyer-Beck, Johann Christoph: *Vogelsang; vom Feudalismus zur Volksbewegung.* Wien: Herold, 1952. 172 pp. (Beiträge zur neueren Geschichte des christlichen Oesterreichs) *LB*

0075  Alsberg, Moritz: *Rassenmischung im Judentum.* Hamburg: J. F. Richter, 1891. 40 pp. (Sammlung gemeinverständlicher wissenschaftlicher Vorträge. N.S., Ser. 5, no. 116) *LJ*

0076  *Am Sterbebett des entschiedenen Liberalismus.* Leipzig: Th. Fritsch, 1887. 8 pp. (Brennende Fragen, 27) *LJ*

0077  Ammann,J.:*Die Irreführung des Antisemitismus. Vortrag.*Berlin:Selbstverlag, 1883. 15 pp. *LJ*

0078  Anacker, Friedrich Heinrich: *Das rechte Verhalten der Christenheit gegen Israel. Ein Mahnwort . . .* Leipzig: W. Faber, 1887. 40 pp. (Schriften des Institutum Judaicum in Leipzig, 17) *LJ*

0079  Andree, Richard: *Zur Volkskunde der Juden. Mit einer Karte über die Verbreitung der Juden in Mitteleuropa.* Bielefeld: Velhagen & Klasing, 1881. VIII, 296 pp. *LTA*

0080  Angerer, Johann: *Die Judenfrage im österreichischen Parlament.* Wien: Deutsche Worte, 1888. 11 pp. *LJ*
      Offprint from: *Deutsche Worte*, May 5, 1888.

0081  Angress, Werner T.: The Impact of the "Judenwahlen" of 1912 and the Jewish Question; a Synthesis. *LBIYB* 28 (1983) 367-410. *LJ*

0082 Angress, Werner T.: Prussia's Army and the Jewish Reserve Officer. Controversy before World War I. *LBIYB* 17 (1972) 19–42. *LJ*

0083 *Der Anteil der Juden am Verbrechen. Auf Grund der amtlichen Statistik über die Tätigkeit der Schwurgerichte in vergleichender Darstellung mit den christlichen Konfessionen.* 3. Aufl. Berlin: Hentze-Verlag, 1881. 19 pp. *LF*

0084 Anticlodius, pseud.: *Zum ewigen Gedächtnis.* Zürich: Schröter & Meyer, 1889. 2 vols. *LTA*

  Vol. 1: *Aktenstücke aus dem Prozeße Schönerer — Tagblatt von 1884.* Vol. 2: *Einige Fragen an die unverfälschte deutsche Studentenschaft.*

0085 *Die Antisemiten im Reichstag.* 2. Aufl. Berlin: C. Kundel, 1903. 48 pp. *LJ*

0086 *Antisemiten-Kalender, 1896.* Hrsg. vom Deutsch-Sozialen Reform-Verein in Berlin. Berlin: Verlag des Deutsch-Sozialen Reform-Vereins, 1896. 48 pp. *LJ* No more published.

0087 Antisemiten-Liga, Berlin: *Aufruf.* Berlin: Bureau der Antisemiten-Liga, 1879. 2 pp. (Flugblatt der Antisemiten-Liga, 1) *LJ*

0088 Antisemiten-Liga, Berlin: *Statuten des Vereins "Antisemiten-Liga."* Berlin: O. Hentze, 1879. 7 pp. *LJ*

0089 *Antisemitische Harfenklänge. Illustriertes humoristisches Taschenliederbuch nebst ernster und vaterländischer Gedichte.* Berlin: M. Schulze, 1883. 96 pp. *LJ*

0090 *Der antisemitische Parteitag zu Erfurt am 6. Juli 1890. Reden von Böckel, Pickenbach, Werner und Zimmermann.* 1.–5. Aufl. Berlin: Dewald, 1890. 22 pp. *Unseen*

0091 Antisemitische Vereinigung für Norddeutschland: *Gemeinplätze wie sie von Jüdisch-Freisinnigen und Sozialdemokraten gegen den Antisemitismus gebraucht werden und deren Widerlegung.* Berlin: Antisemitische Vereinigung für Norddeutschland, 1894. 32 pp. *LJ*

0092 *Antisemitischer Volkskalender für das Jahr 1888 und 1889.* Leipzig: Fritsch, 1888–1889. 2 vols. *LJ*

0093 *Antisemitisches Adressbuch für Berlin.* Berlin: W. Giese, 1897–1899. 3 vols. *LC*

0094 Antisemitisches Volksblatt: *Judentum und Revolution; drei Plaudereien.* Kassel: L. Werner, 1888. 8 pp. *LJ*

*Abdruck aus dem Reichsgeldmonopol, Postkatalog Nr. 4840*. I. Die vertrauten
Brüder Salomo's; oder Die Fortschrittspartei; II. Die tiefste Ursache der
Judenherrschaft; III. Liberalismus, Judenherrschaft und Anarchismus.

0095  Antisemitism. *Encyclopaedia Judaica. Vol. 3*. Jerusalem: Encyclopaedia
      Judaica, 1971. Col. 111–135. *LJ*

0096  Antisemitism. *The Jewish Encyclopedia. Vol. 1*. New York: Funk and Wagnalls
      Co., 1901. Pp. 641–649. *LJ*

0097  Antisemitism. *The Universal Jewish Encyclopedia. Vol. 1*. New York: The
      Universal Jewish Encyclopedia, 1939. Pp. 341–409. *LJ*

0098  Antisemitismus. *Deutsche Worte*. Wien: Verlag Deutsche Worte, 1904. Pp.
      337–366. *LF*

0099  Antisemitismus. *Encyclopaedia Judaica, Bd. 2*. Berlin: Verlag Eschkol, 1928.
      Col. 956–1104. *LJ*

0100  Antisemitismus. *Jüdisches Lexikon. Bd. 1*. Berlin: Jüdischer Verlag, 1927. Col.
      331–371. *LJ*

0101  *Der Antisemitismus; Berechtigung und Notwendigkeit so wie die Zwecke und
      Ziele desselben. Die preußische Judengesetzgebung mit besonderer Berück-
      sichtigung der Landtags-Verhandlungen von 1847 über die Emanzipation der
      Juden*. Dortmund: E. Otten, 1889. 107 pp. *LJ*

0102  *Der Antisemitismus in seinen Ursachen und Wirkungen. Unter besonderer
      Berücksichtigung des Prozeßes Buschhoff. Kulturhistorische Skizze von einem
      Laien*. München: K. Mehrlich, 1892. 15 pp. *Unseen*

0103  *Der Antisemitismus: sein Entstehen und Vergehen. Briefe eines Arieres an einen
      Semiten*. See entry no. 0114.

0104  *Antisemitismus und Sozialdemokratie*. Leipzig: Th. Fritsch, 1887. 8 pp.
      (Brennende Fragen, 13) *LJ*

0105  *Aphorismen zur Judenfrage*. Leipzig: Th. Fritsch, 1888. 8 pp. (Brennende
      Fragen, 35) *LJ*

0106  Appelbaum (lawyer): *Zum Meineidsprozeß gegen Moritz Lewy in Konitz,
      Westpr.; Verteidigungsrede des Rechtsanwalts Appelbaum in Konitz*. Berlin:
      H.S. Hermann, 1901. 16 pp. *LJ*

0107 Arendt, Hannah (1906–1975): *Elemente und Ursprünge totaler Herrschaft.* Frankfurt a.m.: Europäische Verlagsanstalt, 1958. Pp. 5–189. *LJ*

Original title: *The Origins of Totalitarianism.*

0108 Arendt, Hannah (1906–1975): *The Origins of Totalitarianism.* Cleveland: World Pub. Co., 1958. Pp. 3–88, 222–243. *LJ*

0109 Arianus, Friedrich: *Ist die Judenfrage eine Glaubens- oder Magenfrage?* Leipzig: Kommissions-Verlag des "Deutschen Müller," 1890. 11 pp. *LJ*

0110 *Arier und Semiten.* Leipzig: Th. Fritsch, 1888. 8 pp. (Brennende Fragen, 31) *LJ*

0111 Ark, B.: *Historische Enthüllungen über die Juden-Moral und das Blutgeheimnis.* Rom: G. Zappa, 1894. 42 pp. *LJ*

0112 Arkel, Dirk van: *Antisemitism in Austria.* Leiden: Sociologisch Instituut der Rijksuniversiteit, 1966. XIX, 210 l. *LJ*

Diss. Leiden.

0113 Arndt, Hans: *Herunter mit der Maske! Die Führer der deutschen Antisemiten im Lichte der Wahrheit.* Zürich: C. Schmidt, 1898. 122 pp. *LJ*

0114 Aryan, pseud.: *Der Antisemitismus: sein Entstehen und Vergehen. Briefe eines Arieres an einen Semiten.* Leipzig: E. Thiele, 1886. 45 pp. *LV*

See also D. Almogen: *Worte der Abwehr.*

0115 Asch, Adolf: *Self-Defence at the Turn of the Century: the Emergence of the K.C. LBIYB* 3 (1958) 122–138. *LJ*

0116 Aschaffenburg, Gustav (1861–1944): Rasse und Religion. *Das Verbrechen und seine Bekämpfung.* 2. Aufl. Heidelberg: C. Winter, 1906. Pp. 45–50. *LJ*

0117 Ascher, Arnold: *Die Juden im statistischen Jahrbuche der Stadt Wien für das Jahr 1909.* Wien: Typ. L. Beck & Sohn, 1911. 20 pp. *LJ*

Offprint from: *Oesterreichische Wochenschrift.*

0118 Ascher, Arnold: *Die Juden im statistischen Jahrbuche der Stadt Wien für das Jahr 1910.* Wien: Typ. L. Beck & Sohn, 1912. 25 pp. *LJ*

Offprint from: *Oesterreischische Wochenschrift.*

0119 Aschheim, Steven Edward: *Brothers and Strangers, the East European Jews in Germany and German Jewish Consciousness, 1800–1923.* Madison: University of Wisconsin, 1982. Pp. 3–138. *LJ*

Chapters 1–6 deal with the period 1800–1914.

0120 Aschheim, Steven Edward: The East European Jew and German Jewish Identity. *Studies in Contemporary Jewry* 1 (1984) 3–25. *LJ*

0121 Aschkewitz, Max (1901–): Der Anteil der Juden am wirtschaftlichen Leben Westpreußens um die Mitte des 19. Jahrhunderts. *Zeitschrift für Ostforschung* 11 (1962) 482–491. *LJ*

0122 Astfalck, Caesar: *Ein Beitrag zur Lösung der Judenfrage.* Köln: Selbstverlag, 1892. 46 pp. *LJ*

0123 Astfalck, Caesar: *Der kategorische Imperativ für den Mittelstand; 3. Beitrag zur Lösung der sozialen Frage.* Köln: Selbstverlag, 1893. 44 pp. *LC*

0124 Astfalck, Caesar: *Ruhende Kampfmittel des Nationalliberalismus und Antisemitismus und die äußerste Notwendigkeit ihrer Verwendung. 2. Beitrag zur Lösung der sozialen Frage.* Köln: Selbstverlag, 1892. 88 pp. *LTA*

0125 Auerbach, Berthold (1812–1882): *Briefe an seinen Freund Jacob Auerbach; ein biographisches Denkmal.* Mit Vorbemerkungen von Friedrich Spielhagen. Frankfurt a.M.: Rütten and Löning, 1884. 2 vols. *LJ*

0126 Auerbach, Elias (1882–1971): Die jüdische Rassenfrage. *Archiv für Rassen- und Gesellschaftsbiologie* 4 (1907) 333–361. *LJ*

0127 *Die Aufhebung der Judenemanzipation und ihre rechtliche Begründung.* Leipzig: H. Beyer, 1895. 116 pp. *LJ*

Contents: Der Talmudstreit vor den deutschen Richtern. Was hat Herr Strack bewiesen "zur Blutopfer-Frage." Die Unhaltbarkeit der staatsrechtlichen Stellung der Juden.

0128 *Aufruf an wahrhaft aufgeklärte Israeliten zur zeitgemäßen Besserung des religiösen Zustandes ihres Volkes, mit Rücksicht auf die Reformvereine Frankfurt a.M., Breslau, Königsberg i. Pr., Offenbach und alle Reformfreunde in Deutschland.* Frankfurt a.M.: Stritt, 1849. 72 pp. *Unseen*

0129 Austerlitz, Friedrich: Karl Lueger. *N.Z.* 2 (1900–1901) 36–45. *LJ*

0130 Avé-Lallemant, Friedrich Christian Benedict: *Das deutsche Gaunertum in seiner sozial-politischen, literarischen und linguistischen Ausbildung in seinem heutigen Bestande.* T. 1-4. Leipzig: Brockhaus, 1856-1862. 4 vols. in 3. *LJ*

0131 Avé-Lallemant, Friedrich Christian Benedict: *Dolmetsch der Geheimsprache.* Bearb. nach dem Avé-Lallemant für Beamte, Gerichtspersonen und besonders Kaufleute. 2. Ausg. des Buches "Sem und Japhet." Leipzig: A. Glockner, 1889. 63 pp. *LJ*

0132 Avé-Lallemant, Friedrich Christian Benedict: *Die Mechulle-Leut; ein Polizeiroman.* 2. Aufl. Leipzig: Brockhaus, 1870. 2 vols. *LV*

0133 Avineri, Shlomo (1933–): Marx and Jewish Emancipation. *Journal of the History of Ideas* 25 (1964) 445-450. *LJ*

0134 Axenfeld, Karl: *Rückblick auf 25 Jahre der Wirksamkeit des Rheinisch-Westfälischen Vereins für Israel.* Köln: Römke in Komm., 1868. 56 pp. *LC*

0135 Ayerst, William: *Glauben in Israel, erläutert durch das von Gliedern des Hauses Israel abgelegte Zeugnis für die Kraft des Evangeliums.* Nach dem Englischen hrsg. von H.P. Frankfurt a.M.: Typ. C. Naumann, 1852. 40 pp. *LJ*

0136 Bach, Albert: Die Lösung der Judenfrage und die Aufgaben des C.V. Neustadt: 1913. 13 pp. *LJ*

First published November 1912 in the Journal *Nord und Süd.*

0137 Bachem, Julius (1845-1921): *Erinnerungen eines alten Publizisten und Politikers.* Köln: J.P. Bachem, 1913. 195 pp. *LF*

0138 Bachem, Julius (1845-1921): *Der unlautere Wettbewerb im Handel und Gewerbe und dessen Bekämpfung.* Köln: Bachem, 1892. 42 pp. *Unseen*

0139 Bacher, Albert: *Die Stuttgarter Oberbürgermeisterwahl vom November 1892 als Beitrag zur Auslegung des Reichsgesetzes betreffend die Gleichberechtigung der Konfessionen und damit insbesondere zur Feststellung des in der "Judenfrage" geltenden Rechts.* Stuttgart: Metzler, 1892. 16 pp. *Unseen*

0140 Bachrach, Walter Zwi: Bemerkungen zu Richard Wagners Kunsttheorie, Deutschtum und Judentum. *TAJfDG* 9 (1980) 375-388. *LJ*

0141 Bachrach, Walter Zwi: Die Ideologie des deutschen Rassenantisemitismus und seine praktischen Folgerungen. *TAJfDG* 4 (1975) 369-386. *LJ*

0142   Bachrach, Walter Zwi: Jews in Confrontation with Racist Antisemitism, 1879–1933. *LBIYB* 25 (1980) 197–219. *LJ*

0143   Back, Wilhelm: *Schächten oder Betäuben? Eine Bedürfnisfrage; ein Beitrag zum Erlaß eines Reichsschlachtgesetzes.* Straßburg: E.D. Olière und Rasch, 1911. 28 pp. *LF*

0144   Backhaus, Simon: *Die Germanen; ein semitischer Volksstamm. Geschichtlicher und sprachlicher Nachweis.* Berlin: M. Driesner, 1879. 57 pp. *Unseen*

0145   Baentsch, Bruno: *H.St. Chamberlains Vorstellungen über die Religion der Semiten, spez. der Israeliten.* Langensalza: Beyer, 1905. 83 pp. (Pädagogisches Magazin, 246) *LB*

0146   Bahr, Hermann (1863–1934): *Der Antisemitismus; ein internationales Interview.* Berlin: S. Fischer, 1894. 215 pp. *LJ*

0147   Balder, Benno, pseud.: *Die Wahrheit über Bismarck; ein offenes Wort an die deutsche Nation.* Leipzig: C. Minde, 1892. 164 pp. *LF*

0148   Bamberger, Ludwig (1823–1899): *Deutschtum und Judentum.* Leipzig: F.A. Brockhaus, 1880. VI, 38 pp. *LJ*

       Offprint from: *Unsere Zeit,* 1880.

0149   Bamberger, Seligmann Beer (1807–1878): *Einige Worte des Aufschlußes im Betreffe der Emanzipation der Juden.* Fürth: J. Sommer, 1850. 2, 16 pp. *LJ*

0150   Barasch, Iuliu: *Offenes Sendschreiben an Herrn Israel Pick von einem Bukarester Juden.* Leipzig: in Komm. bei C.L. Fritzsche, 1854. 44 pp. *LJ*

       Reply to his pamphlet *Israel hat eine Idee zu tragen* . . .

0151   Barkai, Abraham: *Jüdische Minderheit und Industrialisierung Demographie, Berufe und Einkommen der Juden in Deutschland, 1850–1914.* Unter Mitarbeit von Schoschanna Barkai-Lasker. Tübingen: J.C.B. Mohr, 1988. XIV, 177 pp. (Wissenschaftliche Abhandlungen des LBI, 46) *LJ*

0152   Barkai, Abraham: Sozialgeschichtliche Aspekte der deutschen Judenheit in der Zeit der Industrialisierung. *TAJfDG* 11 (1982) 237–260. *LJ*

0153   Barkai, Abraham: Die sozio-ökonomische Entwicklung der Juden in Rheinland-Westfalen in der Industrialisierung 1850–1910. *LBI Bull.* 66 (1983) 53–81. *LJ*

0154   Barkenings, Hans-Joachim: Die Stimme der Anderen; der "heilgeschichtliche Beruf Israels" in der Sicht evangelischer Theologen des 19. Jahrhunderts.

*Christen und Juden.* Eds. Wolf-Dieter Marsch, Karl Thieme. Mainz: Matthias-Grünewald-Verlag, 1961. Pp. 201–231. *LJ*

0155 Baron, Salo Wittmayer (1895–1989): Aspects of the Jewish Communal Crisis in 1848. *J.S.St.* 14 (1952) 99–144. *LJ*

0156 Baron, Salo Wittmayer (1895–1989): The Impact of the Revolution of 1848 on Jewish Emancipation. *J.S.St.* 11 (1949) 195–248. *LJ*

0157 Baron, Salo Wittmayer (1895–1989): The Jewish Question in the 19th Century. *Journal of Modern History* 10 (1938) 51–65. *LJ*

0158 Bartels, Adolf (1862–1945): *Der deutsche Verfall; Vortrag gehalten am 21. Januar 1913 zu Berlin.* Leipzig: Armanen-Verlag, 1913. 47 pp. *LB*

0159 Bartels, Adolf (1862–1945): *Heine-Genossen. Zur Charakteristik der deutschen Presse und der deutschen Parteien.* Dresden: C.A. Koch, 1907. 130 pp. *LJ*

0160 Bartels, Adolf (1862–1945): *Heinrich Heine. Auch ein Denkmal.* Dresden: C.A. Koch, 1906. XV, 375 pp. *LJ*

0161 Bartels, Adolf (1862–1945): Heinrich Heine. Berthold Auerbach. Paul Heyse. *Geschichte der deutschen Literatur. Bd. 2.* Leipzig: E. Avenarius, 1905. Pp. 139–157, 313–319, 571–583. *LJ*

0162 Bartels, Adolf (1862–1945): *Rasse. 16 Aufsätze zur nationalen Weltanschauung.* Hamburg: Hanseatische Druck- und Verlagsanstalt, 1909. 199 pp. *LJ*

0163 Bartels, Adolf (1862–1945): Rassenzucht. *Pol.Anthrop.Rev.* 8 (1909) 629–642. *LJ*

0164 Bartels, Adolf (1862–1945): *Ein ruhiges Wort in der Heine-Denkmal Angelegenheit.* Weimar: Roltsch, 1909. 4 pp. *Unseen*

0165 Barth, Theodor: Ludwig Bamberger. *Politische Portraits.* Berlin: G. Reimer, 1904. Pp. 16–28. *LTA*

0166 Bartys, Julian: Grand Duchy of Poznan under Prussian Rule; Changes in the Economic Position of the Jewish Population. *LBIYB* 17 (1972) 191–204. *LJ*

0167 Bary, József: *A tiszaeszlári bűnper. Bary József vizsgálobiro emlékiratai.* Budapest: Kir. Magy Egyetemi Nyomda, 1933. 612 pp. *LJ*

Posthumous memoir on the trial of Salomon Schwarcz and others on the charge of having murdered Eszter Solymosi.

0168 Baudisch, Ursula: *Der Antisemitismus der Christlichsozialen im Spiegel der parteinahen Presse, 1890–April 1897.* Wien: 1967. IV, 282 pp. *LJ*
Diss.

0169 Bauer, Bruno (1809–1882): Das Judentum in der Fremde. *Staats- und Gesellschaftslexikon* 10 (1862) 614–692. *LF*

0170 Bauer, Erwin (1857–1901): *Caveat populus. (Deutsches Volk sei auf deiner Hut.) Wider den neuen Kurs.* Leipzig: Werther, 1892. 124 pp. *LF*

0171 Bauer, Erwin (1857–1901): *Der Fall Bleichröder. Vortrag gehalten am 17. September 1891 im Konzerthaus "Battenberg" zu Leipzig. Mit dem Programm der Deutsch-Sozialen Partei und mehreren Anlagen.* Leipzig: Germanicus-Verlag, 1891. 24 pp. *LJ*

0172 Bauer, Erwin (1857–1901): *Die Israeliten als "Träger der Kultur." Streiflichter auf unsern modernen Bücherhandel und Skizzen etwelcher Jünger desselben. Offener Brief an den Journalisten Dr. Isidor Feilchenfeld, von Sally Simon Tilles, pseud.* Berlin: Paul Heichen's Verlag, 1892. 29 pp. *LJ*

0173 Bauer, Erwin (1857–1901): *Der Jude im Zitat und im Sprichwort. Ein Bädeker für Anti- und Philo-Semiten.* Zusammengestellt von Sally Simon Tilles, pseud. Berlin: P. Heichen, 1892. 64 pp. *LJ*

0174 Bauer, Erwin (1857–1901): *Die Mischpoke im Berliner Buchhandel. Offener Brief an den Journalisten Dr. Isidor Feilchenfeld, von Sally Simon Tilles, pseud.* Berlin: Hans Lüstenöder, 1891. 24 pp. *LJ*
Offprint from: *20. Jahrhundert.*

0175 Bauer, Erwin (1857–1901): *Moment-Photographien aus den Kreisen unserer israelitischen Herren Kollegen.* 2. Aufl. Berlin: K.F. Köhler, 1892. 36 pp. *Unseen*

0176 Bauer, Erwin (1857–1901): *Der Sensationsfall Carl Paasch; Vortrag.* Leipzig: W. Wauer, 1891. 23 pp. *LJ*
Offprint from: *Leipziger Tages-Anzeiger.*

0177 Bauer, Erwin (1857–1901): *Der Untergang der antisemitischen Parteien. Ein Mahnwort an die nationale Bewegung im Deutschen Reiche von einem alten Antisemiten.* Leipzig: G.A. Müller, 1895. 62 pp. *LJ*

0178 Bauer, Otto (1881–1938): Nationale Autonomie der Juden? *Die Nationalitätenfrage und die Sozialdemokratie in Wien.* 2. Aufl. Wien: Wiener Volksbuchhdlg., 1924. Pp. 366–381. *LJ*

First published in 1907 in *Marx Studien* 2.

0179 Bauer, Otto (1881–1938): Sozialismus und Antisemitismus. *Kampf* 4 (1910–11) 94–95. *LJ*

0180 Baumgarten, Emanuel Mendel (1828–1908): *Die Blutbeschuldigung gegen die Juden. Stimmen christlicher Theologen, Orientalisten und Historiker. Die Bullen der Päpste. Simon von Trient.* Wien: Dr. Bloch's Oesterreichische Wochenschrift, 1900. 2 vols. (Dokumente zur Aufklärung, 1–2) *LJ*

An abbreviated ed. is titled: *Die Blutbeschuldigung gegen die Juden von christlicher Seite beurteilt.*

0181 Baumgarten, Emanuel Mendel (1828–1908): *Die Blutbeschuldigung gegen die Juden von christlicher Seite beurteilt.* Wien: Steyrermühl, 1883. 70 pp. *LJ*

0182 Baumgarten, Michael (1812–1889): *Stoecker's gefälschtes Christentum. Rede gehalten am 15. Oktober 1881 in Berlin.* Berlin: Stuhr, 1881. 33 pp. *LJ*

0183 Baumgarten, Michael (1812–1889): *Wider Herrn Hofprediger Stoecker; eine christliche Stimme über die Judenfrage.* 3., mit einem Anhang, verm. Aufl. Berlin: Stuhr, 1881. 33 pp. *LJ*

0184 Bauwerker, Carl: *Das rituelle Schächten der Israeliten im Lichte der Wissenschaft. Ein Vortrag . . .* Kaiserslautern: A. Gotthold, 1882. 46 pp. *LJ*

0185 Beard, Miriam (1901–): Antisemitism; Product of Economic Myths. *Jews in a Gentile World.* Eds. Isaque Graeber, Stewart Henderson Britt. New York: Macmillan Co., 1942. Pp. 362–401. *LJ*

0186 Bech, Hugo: *Die große Frage.* Teutoburg: Aachen-Verlag, 1912. 55 pp. *LC*

0187 Becker, Hartmut: *Antisemitismus in der Deutschen Turnerschaft.* Sankt Augustin: H. Richarz, 1980. 155 pp. (Schriften der Deutschen Sporthochschule Köln, 3) *LJ*

0188 Becker, Wilhelm (1853–): *Antisemit oder Philosemit? Wer hat recht? Bündig beantwortet.* Gotha: F.A. Perthes, 1891. 34 pp. (Zimmers Handbibliothek der praktischen Theologie, 11–14, pt. 35a) *LJ*

0189 Becker, Wilhelm (1853–): *Ferdinand Wilhelm Becker; eine Heldengestalt in der Judenmission des 19. Jahrhunderts.* Berlin: Evangelische Vereinsbuchhdlg, 1893. 72 pp. (Schriften des Institutum Judaicum in Berlin, 16) *LC*

0190   Becker, Wilhelm (1853–): *Immanuel Tremellius; ein Proselytenleben im Zeitalter der Reformation.* 2. veränd. Aufl. Leipzig: J.C. Hinrichs, 1890. 60 pp. (Schriften des Institutum Judaicum in Berlin, 8) *LJ*

0191   Becker, Wilhelm (1853–): *Ist die Judenmission wirklich eine Christenpflicht?* Stuttgart: Belser, 1894. 43 pp. (Zeitfragen des christlichen Volkslebens, 19, 2) *Unseen*

0192   Becker, Wilhelm (1853–): *Das Menschenopfer bei den Israeliten. Der Synagoge und der Kirche gewidmet.* Berlin: Gossnersche Buchhdlg, 1898. 16 pp. *LJ*

0193   *Die Bedeutung der Kandidatur des Fürsten Alois Liechtenstein für den Antisemitismus und die christlich soziale Reform in Oesterreich.* Wien: Verlag Austria, 1891. 16 pp. *LJ*

0194   Beer, Max (1864–1949): Literarische Rundschau; Leopold Caro, die Judenfrage, eine ethische Frage. *N.Z.* 11, 2 (1892–3) 118–119. *LJ*

0195   Beer, Max (1864–1949): Der Talmud. *N.Z.* 12, 2 (1893–94) 379–384, 408–416, 603. *LJ*

0196   Behr, Alexander: The Judaism of Ferdinand Lassalle. *The Jewish Review* 3 (1912) 259–270. *LJ*

0197   Behrendt, Bernd: *Zwischen Paradox und Paralogismus; weltanschauliche Grundzüge einer Kulturkritik in den neunziger Jahren des 19. Jahrhunderts am Beispiel August Julius Langbehn.* Frankfurt a.M.: Lang, 1984. 549 pp. (Europäische Hochschulschriften. Reihe 1: Deutsche Sprache und Literatur, 804) *LC*

0198   Bein, Alex (1903–): The Jewish Parasite. *LBIYB* 9 (1964) 3–40. *LJ*

0199   Bein, Alex (1903–): *Die Judenfrage; Biographie eines Weltproblems.* Stuttgart: Deutsche Verlags-Anstalt, 1980. 2 vols. *LJ*

0200   Bein, Alex (1903–): Modern Antisemitism and its Effect on the Jewish Question. *Yad Vashem Studies on the European Jewish Catastrophe and Resistance* 2 (1958) 7–15. *LJ*

0201   Bein, Alex (1903–): Modern Antisemitism and its Place in the History of the Jewish Question. *Between East and West; Essays Dedicated to the Memory of Bela Horowitz.* Ed. A. Altmann. London: East & West Library, 1958. Pp. 164–193. *LJ*

0202 Bein, Alex (1903–): Der moderne Antisemitismus und seine Bedeutung für die Judenfrage. *Vierteljahrshefte für Zeitgeschichte* 6 (1958) 340–360. *LJ*

0203 Beiträge zur Beurteilung der Judenfrage; die polnischen Juden. *Die Grenzboten* 39 (1880) 55–67, 155–167, 177–194. *LC*

0204 *Der bekehrte Judenknabe; eine Geschichte.* Berlin: Deutsche Evangelische Buch- und Traktatgesellschaft, 1894. 12 pp. *Unseen*

0205 Belke, Ingrid: Liberal Voices on Antisemitism in the 1880s; Letters to Moritz Lazarus, 1880–1883. *LBIYB* 23 (1978) 61–87. *LJ*

0206 Below, Georg von (1858–1927): Literaturbericht — "Die Juden und das Wirtschaftsleben," von Werner Sombart. *Historische Zeitschrift* 108 (1912) 614–624. *LJ*

0207 Ben Akiba der Jüngere, pseud.: *Deutschnational, der im Deutschtum, nicht im Christentum aufgeht.* Mit einer Kundgebung eines geheimen Regierungsrats und Universitäts-Professors in Berlin. Leipzig: P. Schimmelwitz, 1899. 22 pp. *LJ*

0208 Bendokat, Bruno: *Adolf Stoeckers Stellung zur Judenfrage; ein Beitrag zur Geschichte der Gegenwart.* Witten: Westdeutscher Lutherverlag, 1937. 72 pp. *LJ*

0209 Berchtold, Klaus, ed.: Das christlich-konservative Lager; das deutsch-nationale Lager. *Oesterreichische Parteiprogramme. PT. 1: Parteiprogramme von 1868–1918.* München: R. Oldenbourg, 1967. Pp. 165–229. *LJ*

0210 Berend, A.L.& Co.: *Der jüdische Spaßvogel; oder, Jocosus hebricosus. Ahne Versammling von allerhand lustige Jüdengeschichtcher . . .* 2. Aufl. München: Braun & Schneider, 1877. VIII, 352 pp. *LJ*

0211 Berg, Alexander: *Juden-Bordelle; Enthüllungen aus dunklen Häusern.* Berlin: P. Heichen, 1892. 42 pp. *LJ*

0212 Berg, Alexander: *Judenhyänen vor dem Strafgericht in Lemberg: ein bestätigter Nachtrag zu seiner Schrift "Judenbordelle."* Berlin: G.A. Dewald, 1893. 31 pp. *LTA*

0213 Berg, Alexander: *Judentum und Sozialdemokratie. Ein Beitrag zur Beförderung der Einsicht in die sozialistisch-jüdische Koalitionserscheinung unserer Zeit.* Berlin: Dewald, 1891. IV, 61 pp. *LJ*

0214  Berg, Alexander: *Die Straflosigkeit des Verbrechens vor Gericht; ein Produkt der Verjudung unseres Anwaltsstandes.* Randbemerkungen zum Saling'schen Meineidsprozeß. Berlin: G.A. Dewald, 1893. 32 pp. *Unseen*

0215  Bergel, Siegmund: *Die Entwicklung des Ordens und seine Aufgaben.* Berlin: 1910. 35 pp. *Unseen*

0216  Berglar Peter: Harden und Rathenau; zur Problematik ihrer Freundschaft. *Historische Zeitschrift* 209 (1969) 75-94. *LJ*

0217  Bergmann, Eugen von: *Zur Geschichte der Entwickelung deutscher, polnischer und jüdischer Bevölkerung in der Provinz Posen seit 1824.* Tübingen: Laupp, 1883. VIII, 368 pp. (Beiträge zur Geschichte der Bevölkerung in Deutschland, 1) *LTA*

0218  Bergner, Rudolf (1860-1899): *Die Judenherrschaft in den Karpatenländern. Sensationelle Enthüllungen.* Marburg: Reichs-Herold, 1889. 61 pp. *LJ*

0219  Bering, Dietz: *Der Name als Stigma; Antisemitismus im deutschen Alltag, 1812-1933.* Stuttgart: Klett-Cotta, 1987. 567 pp. *LJ*

0220  Berlin, Isaiah (1909-): *The Life and Opinions of Moses Hess.* Cambridge: Heffer, 1959. 49 pp. (The Lucien Wolf Memorial Lecture, London, 1957) *LJ*

0221  Berliner, Abraham (1833-1915): *Professor Paul de Lagarde nach seiner Natur gezeichnet.* Berlin: J. Benzian, 1887. 32 pp. *LJ*

0222  Berliner, Cora: Wandervogel. *I.Dt.R.* 19 (1913) 547-555. *LJ*

0223  Berliner, Hanania: *Der Erlöser und Erretter; Leben, Taten und Lehren des Messias Jeschua. In jüdisch-deutscher Sprache und hebräischer Schrift.* Leipzig: J.C. Hinrichs Verlag, 1898. III, 123 pp. (Schriften des Institutum Judaicum in Berlin, 23) *LF*

0224  Berliner, Hanania, ed: *Die Juden und das Evangelium. Aeußerungen hervorragender evangelischer Christen der Gegenwart veranlasst und zum Erwägen für Christen und Juden.* Hrsg. von G.M. Löwen, pseud. Leipzig: J.C. Hinrichs, 1913. 47 pp. (Schriften des Institutum Judaicum in Berlin, 42) *LJ*

0225  Die Berliner Stadtverordneten über die Anstellung jüdischer Lehrerinnen. *Israelitische Wochenschrift* (1899) 697-700. *LJ*

0226  *Berliner Straßeneckenliteratur; humoristisch-satirische Flugschriften aus der Revolutionszeit.* Zusammengestellt und kommentiert von Gesine Abert u.a. Stuttgart: P. Reclam jun., 1977. 342 pp. (Universal-Bibliothek, 9856) *LJ*

0227 Berneri, Camillo: Karl Marx antisémite. *Le juif antisémite*. Paris: Vita, 1935. Pp. 62–78. *LJ*

0228 Berneri, Camillo: Otto Weininger. *Le juif antisémite*. Paris: Vita, 1935. Pp. 45–47. *LJ*

0229 Bernfeld, Simon (1860–1940): *Juden und Judentum im neunzehnten Jahrhundert*. Berlin: S. Cronbach, 1898. 167 pp. (Am Ende des Jahrhunderts; Rückschau auf 100 Jahre geistiger Entwicklung, 3) *LJ*

0230 Bernfeld, Simon (1860–1940): *Der Talmud*. Frankfurt a.M.: J. Kauffmann, 1914. 55 pp. (Volksschriften über die jüdische Religion, vol. 2, 4) *LJ*

0231 Bernfeld, Simon (1860–1940): *Der Talmud; sein Wesen, seine Bedeutung und seine Geschichte*. Berlin: S. Calvary, 1900. IV, 120 pp. *LJ*

0232 Bernsdorf, E.: K. Freigedank und das Judentum in der Musik. *Neue Zeitschrift für Musik* 32–33 (1850) 165–168. *LJ*

0233 Bernstein, Aaron David (1812–1884): *Herrn Stoeckers Rede im Lichte der Wahrheit, 22.11.1810*. Berlin: G. Schade, 1880. 33 pp. *LC*

0234 Bernstein, Aaron David (1812–1884): *Herrn Stoeckers Treiben und Lehren*. Berlin: Verlag der Volkszeitung, 1880. 27 pp. *LJ*

Offprint from: *Volkszeitung*.

0235 Bernstein, Eduard (1850–1932): Literarische Rundschau; C. Lombroso. Der Antisemitismus und die Juden im Lichte der modernen Wissenschaft. *N.Z.* 12, 2 (1893–94) 405–407. *LJ*

0236 Bernstein, George: *Antisemitism in Imperial Germany, 1871–1914; Selected Documents*. Ann Arbor: Mich. University Microfilms, 1980. 433 l. *LJ*

Columbia University, diss. 1973.

0237 Bernstein, Richard: Die Sozialdemokratie und die Lösung der Judenfrage durch planmäßige Ansiedlung des jüdischen Volkes. *Deutsche Worte* 24 (1904) 307–312. *LF*

0238 Berthold, Hans: *Die Judengefahr*. Klagenfurt, Carinthia: Buchdruckerei und Buchhdlg. des St. Josefs Vereines, 1912. 31 pp. (Volksaufklärung, 159) *Unseen*

0239 Berthold, Ludwig: *Cassel! Predige deinen Juden und dir selbst. Ein Mahnwort an Herrn Judenmissionar Prof. Dr. P. Cassel und dessen Stammesgenossen*. Berlin: F. Luckhardt, 1881. 34 pp. *LJ*

0240  Bertold: *Wiener Judenalbum für das Jahr 1852: den p.t. Herren Juden Deutschlands, Oesterreichs, Ungarns, Galiziens — vielleicht auch ganz Europas — mit besonderer Zärtlichkeit gewidmet.* Augsburg: Anton Herzog, 1852. VI, 103 pp. *LB*

0241  Die beruflichen und sozialen Verhältnisse der Juden in Deutschland. *Ost und West* 12 (1912) col. 513–524. *LJ*

       Review of Jakob Segall's book: *Die beruflichen und sozialen Verhältnisse der Juden in Deutschland . . . 1912.*

0242  Beskiba, Marianne: *Aus meinen Erinnerungen an Dr. Karl Lueger.* Wien: Selbstverlag, 1911. VIII, 144 pp. *LJ*

0243  Besser, Max: *Die Juden in der modernen Rassentheorie.* Köln: Jüdischer Verlag, 1911. 29 pp. *LJ*

0244  Bettziech, Ottomar (1845–1913): *Darwin, Deutschland und die Juden; oder, Der Juda Jesuitismus. 33 Thesen nebst einer Nachschrift über den vergessenen Faktor der Volkswirtschaft.* Leipzig: Selbstverlag, 1876. 46 pp. *LJ*

0245  Bettziech, Ottomar (1845–1913): *Der Geist Bleichröders und der Geist Friedrichs des Großen; ein Nachklang vom Sedantage.* Berlin: P. Westphal, 1893. 8 pp. *Unseen*

0246  Bettziech, Ottomar (1845–1913): *Warum? Warum liegen wir Deutsche in den Ketten der Schuldknechtschaft. Nach einem Vortrag über Real- und Personal-Credit.* Hrsg. vom Deutsch-Sozialen Antisemitischen Verein für Berlin und Umgegend. Berlin: S. Schneider, 1892. 48 pp. *LJ*

0247  *Beurteilung der Verhältnisse der Israeliten zu Frankfurt und der Stellung der letzteren zu der christlichen Bürgerschaft vom Standpunkte des Rechtes und der Selbsterhaltung.* Frankfurt a.M.: Krebs-Schmitt, 1851. 28 pp. *LJ*

0248  Bewer, Max (1861–1921): *Bismarck im Reichstage.* Dresden: Glöss, 1891. 64 pp. *LB*

0249  Bewer, Max (1861–1921): *Bismarck und Rothschild.* Dresden: Typ. Glöss, 1891. 43 pp. *LJ*

0250  Bewer, Max (1861–1921): *Der deutsche Christus. War Christus Jude? War Christus Sozialdemokrat? Wie wird Deutschland glaubenseinig?* Dresden: Goethe-Verlag, 1907. 238 pp. *LJ*

0251  Bewer, Max (1861–1921): *Gedanken, Ritualmorde und Isopathie.* Dresden: Glöss, 1892. 238 pp. *Unseen*

0252 Bewer, Max (1861–1921): *Ein Goethepreis.* Dresden: Glöss, 1900. 80 pp. *LF*

0253 Bewer, Max (1861–1921): Hebräer als deutsche Offiziere. *Der Hammer* 3 (1904) 296–298. *LB*

0254 Bewer, Max (1861–1921): Ritual-Morde? *Deutsch-Soziale Blätter* 8 (1893) 206–207. *LB*

0255 Bewer, Max (1861–1921): Zum Mord in Xanten. *Deutsch-Soziale Blätter* 8 (1893) 240–241. *LB*

0256 Biberfeld, Eduard: *Halsschnitt nicht Hirnzertrümmerung! Eine Antwort auf die Backsche Streitschrift "Schächten oder Betäuben?"* Berlin: L. Lamm, 1911. 39 pp. *LJ*

0257 Bibl, Viktor: *Georg von Schönerer; ein Vorkämpfer des Großdeutschen Reiches.* Leipzig: Fr. Brandstetter, 1942. 23 pp. *Unseen*

0258 Bibliographie. *Encyclopaedia Judaica.* Berlin: Verlag Eschkol, 1929. Col. 765–769. *LJ*

0259 Biddiss, Michael Denis: *Father of Racist Ideology; the Social and Political Thought of Count Gobineau.* London: Weidenfeld & Nicolson, 1970. X, 314 pp. *LJ*

0260 Bieling, Richard: *Friedrich Händess, 1797–1838; ein Zeuge des Herrn unter Israel. Zumeist nach seinen Tagebüchern und Briefen geschildert.* 2. Aufl. Berlin: Verlag der Gesellschaft zur Beförderung des Christentums unter den Juden, 1911. 63 pp. (Schriften des Institutum Judaicum in Berlin, 20) *LC*

0261 Bieling, Richard: *Die Juden vornehmlich; ein geschichtlicher Ueberblick über die Arbeit der Gesellschaft zur Beförderung des Christentums unter den Juden zu Berlin.* Berlin: Selbstverlag der Gesellschaft, 1898. 87 pp. *LJ*

0262 Bihl, Wolfdieter: *Bibliographie der Dissertationen über Judentum und jüdische Persönlichkeiten, die 1872–1962 an österreichischen Hochschulen approbiert wurden.* Wien: Verlag Notring der Wissenschaftlichen Verbände Oesterreichs, 1965. 51 pp. *LJ*

0263 Bihl, Wolfdieter: Die Juden in der Habsburger Monarchie 1848–1918. *Studia Judaica Austriaca* 8 (1980) 5–73. *LJ*

0264 Bihl, Wolfdieter: Das Judentum in Ungarn 1780–1914. *Studia Judaica Austriaca* 3 (1976) 17–31. *LJ*

0265  Billerbeck, Paul: Vereinsorganisationen innerhalb der Judenschaft Deutschlands, *Nathanael* 20 (1904) 33–61, 65–92; 21 (1905) 1–31 *LJ*

0266  Billroth, Theodor (1829–1894): *Ueber das Lehren und Lernen der medizinischen Wissenschaften an den Universitäten der deutschen Nation.* Nebst allgemeinen Bemerkungen über Universitäten; eine kulturhistorische Studie. Wien: Gerold, 1876. X, 508 pp. *LF*

0267  Birnbaum, Nathan (1864–1937): Einige Gedanken über den Antisemitismus, von Mathias Acher, pseud. *Ost und West* 2 (1902) col. 517–526. *LJ*

0268  Birnbaum, Nathan (1864–1937): *Die jüdische Moderne, Vortrag gehalten im akademischen Vereine "Kadimah" in Wien.* Leipzig: A. Schulze, 1896. 38 pp. *LJ*

0269  Birnbaum, Nathan (1864–1937): *Die nationale Wiedergeburt des jüdischen Volkes in seinem Lande, als Mittel zur Lösung der Judenfrage; ein Appell an die Guten und Edlen aller Nationen.* Wien: Selbstverlag, 1893. 44 pp. *LJ*

0270  Birnbaum, Nathan (1864–1937): *Das Stiefkind der Sozialdemokratie.* Wien: C. W. Stern, 1905. 31 pp. *LJ*

0271  Birnbaum, Nathan (1864–1937): *Zwei Vorträge über Zionismus. 1. Die kulturelle Bedeutung des Zionismus; 2. Wissenschaft und Zionismus.* Berlin: H. Schildberger, 1898. 30 pp. *LJ*

0272  Bischoff, Erich (1865–1936): *Jesus und die Rabbinen; Jesu Bergpredigt und "Himmelreich" in ihrer Unabhängigkeit vom Rabbinismus dargestellt.* Leipzig: J.C. Hinrichs, 1905. VI, 114 pp. (Schriften des Institutum Judaicum in Berlin, 33) *LJ*

0273  Bischoff, Erich (1865–1936): *Die Juden und das Christenblut. Beiträge zur Erklärung der Hypothese eines jüdischen "Blutrituals."* Berlin: G.A. Dewald, 1891. 16 pp. *LJ*

0274  Bischoff, Erich (1865–1936): *Jüdisch-deutscher Dolmetscher; ein praktisches Jargon-Wörterbuch . . .* 3. völlig neubearb. Aufl. Leipzig: T. Grieben, 1901. 96 pp. *LJ*

0275  Bischoff, Erich (1865–1936): *Kritische Geschichte der Talmud-Uebersetzungen aller Zeiten und Zungen.* Frankfurt a.M.: J. Kauffmann, 1899. 111 pp. *Unseen*

0276  Bischoff, Erich (1865–1936): *Talmud-Katechismus.* Leipzig: T. Grieben, 1904. XII, 112 pp. (Morgenländische Bücherei, 3) *LJ*

0277 Blach, Friedrich: *Die Juden in Deutschland, von einem jüdischen Deutschen.* Berlin: K. Curtius, 1911. 77 pp. *LJ*

0278 Blau, Bruno (1881–1954): *Die Kriminalität der deutschen Juden.* Berlin: L. Lamm, 1906. 15 pp. *LJ*

0279 Blau, Bruno (1881–1954): Sociology and Statistics of the Jews. *Hist. Jud.* 11 (1949) 145–162. *LJ*

0280 Blavier, V., ed: *Adressbuch der Juden Berlins; praktisches Handbuch für das kaufende Publikum zusammengestellt auf Grund authentischer Listen und enthaltend 10,000 selbständige Juden.* Zusammengestellt von V. Blavier. Berlin: V. Blavier, 1888. iv, 277 pp. *Unseen*

0281 Blechmann, Bernhard: *Ein Beitrag zur Anthropologie der Juden.* Dorpat: Typ. W. Just, 1882. 64 pp. *LJ*

Diss.

0282 Bleibtreu, Karl (1859–1928): *Der große Dreyfus-Schwindel. Ein Beitrag zur Psychologie des Pansemitismus.* Berlin: C.A. Schwetschke, 1899. 136 pp. *LJ*

0283 Bloch, Joseph Samuel (1850–1923): *Des k.k. Prof. Rohling neueste Fälschungen.* Wien: Wiener Allgemeine Zeitung, 1883. 31 pp. *LJ*

Offprint from: *Wiener Allgemeine Zeitung.*

0284 Bloch, Joseph Samuel (1850–1923): *Israel und die Völker nach jüdischer Lehre. Mit Berücksichtigung sämtlicher antisemitischer Textfälschungen in Talmud, Schulchan Aruch, Sohar und anderen rabbinischen und kabbalistischen Schriften, auf Grund der dem Wiener Landesgericht aus Anlaß des Prozeßes Rohling kontra Bloch 1885 erstatteten schriftlichen Gutachten, der in Eid genommenen Sachverständigen Professor Dr. Theodor Nöldecke und Dr. August Wünsche.* Berlin: B. Harz, 1922. LII, 830 pp. *LJ*

Trial of Rohling against Bloch.

0285 Bloch, Joseph Samuel (1850–1923): Der Justizfrevel an Leopold Hilsner, Thomas G. Masaryk. *Erinnerungen aus meinem Leben. Bd. 3.* Wien: Appel, 1933. Pp. 1–19. *LJ*

0286 Bloch, Joseph Samuel (1850–1923): *Prof. Rohling und das Wiener Rabbinat; oder, Die arge Schelmerei.* Wien: Selbstverlag des Verfassers, 1882. 29 pp. *LJ*

Offprint from: *Wiener Allgemeine Zeitung.*

0287   Bloch, Joseph Samuel (1850–1923): *Schwurgerichtsprozeß kontra Pfarrer Dr. Joseph Deckert und Paulus Meyer.* Wien: R. Löwit, 1922. 235 pp. *LJ*

In: Bloch, J.S.: *Erinnerungen aus meinem Leben, vol. 2.* The trial took place in Vienna, 1893.

0288   Bloch, Philipp (1841–1923): *Prof. Rohlings Falschmünzerei auf talmudischem Gebiet.* Posen: L. Merzbach, 1876. 31 pp. *LJ*

0289   Bloom, Solomon Frank (1903–1962): Karl Marx and the Jews. *J.S.St.* 4 (1942) 3–16. *LJ*

0290   Blum Alfons: Enquête über die wirtschaftliche Lage der jüdischen Landbevölkerung in Baden; Ergebnisse einer Erhebung vom Jahre 1900. *Jüdische Statistik.* Berlin, 1903. Pp. 191–201. *LJ*

0291   Blum Alfons: *Die wirtschaftliche Lage der jüdischen Landbevölkerung im Großherzogtum Baden; eine sozial-politische Studie.* Mannheim: Mannheimer Vereins-Druckerei, 1901. 47 pp. *LJ*

0292   Blumenberg, Werner: Ein unbekanntes Kapitel aus Marx' Leben; Briefe an die holländischen Verwandten. *International Review of Social History* 1 (1956) 55–111. *LJ*

0293   Blumenthal, Adolf: *Offener Brief an Herrn Prof. Franz Delitzsch, Geheimer Oberkirchenrat zu Leipzig.* Frankfurt a.M.: A.J. Hofmann, 1889. 28 pp. *LJ*

0294   *Blut-Aberglaube.* 3. Aufl. Wien: "Oesterreichische Wochenschrift," 1891. 70 pp. *LJ*

Offprint from: *Oesterreichische Wochenschrift.*

0295   *Der Blut-Prozeß von Tísza-Eslár in Ungarn.* New York: Schnitzer Bros., 1883. X, 206 pp. *LJ*

Prehistory of the accusation and the complete account about the trial proceedings in the law court of Nyiregyhaza, based on the official stenographic protocols and tr. from Hungarian.

0296   *Blutbeschuldigung.* Danzig: Kafemann, 1900. 51 pp. *LTA*

Reprinted from: *Antisemitenspiegel,* 1900.

0297   *Die Blutbeschuldigung gegen die Juden. Von christlicher Seite beurteilt.* Wien: Hölder, 1883. VII, 62 pp. *LJ*

0298 *Die Blutbeschuldigung gegen die Juden. Die Bullen der Päpste, Simon von Trient. Stimmen christlicher Theologen, Orientalisten und Historiker.* Zagreb: Typ. V. Eisenstädter, 1910. XII, 200 pp. (Dokumente zur Aufklärung, 2) *LJ*

0299 *Der Blutmord in Konitz mit Streiflichtern auf die staatsrechtliche Stellung der Juden im Deutschen Reiche. Nach authentischen Quellen dargestellt von einem besorgten Vaterlandsfreunde.* Vorwort von Max Liebermann von Sonnenberg. 11. verm. und verb. Aufl. Berlin: Deutsch-Nationale Buchhdlg. und Verlagsanstalt, 1901. VII, 79 pp. *LJ*

0300 Bode, Wilhelm Arnold von (1845–1929): Rembrandt als Erzieher; von einem Deutschen. Besprochen von . . . *Pr. Jhrb.* 65 (1890) 301–314. *LF*

0301 Bodemeyer, Hildebrand: *Die Juden; ein Beitrag zur Hannoverschen Rechtsgeschichte.* Göttingen: Verlag der Dieterichschen Buchhdlg, 1855. IV, 108 pp. *LJ*

0302 Bodenheimer, Max Isidor (1865–1946): *Zionismus und Judentag. Rede gehalten . . . bei Gelegenheit des Delegiertentages in Berlin . . .* Köln: Verlag der Zionistischen Vereinigung für Deutschland, 1901. 23 pp. *LJ*

0303 Böckel, Otto (1859–1923): *Güterschlächterei in Hessen; ein Mahnruf an das deutsche Volk.* 5. Aufl. Leipzig: Th. Fritsch, 1890. 8 pp. (Brennende Fragen, 21) *Unseen*

0304 Böckel, Otto (1859–1923): *Die Juden — Die Könige unserer Zeit. Rede gehalten in der öffentlichen Versammlung des Deutschen Antisemiten-Bundes auf der Bockbrauerei zu Berlin am 4. Oktober 1886.* 13. Aufl. Berlin: A. Rusch, 1887. 15 pp. *LJ*

0305 Böckel, Otto (1859–1923): *Die Judenfrage als nationale Existenzfrage. Rede gehalten im großen Saal der Tonhalle zu Saarbrücken, Samstag, den 24. Juli 1886.* St. Johann a.d. Saar: A. Allenspach, 1886. 14 pp. *LJ*

0306 Böckel, Otto (1859–1923): *Nochmals: "Die Juden — die Könige unserer Zeit"! Eine neue Ansprache an das deutsche Volk.* Berlin: Deutsche Hochwacht, 1901. 40 pp. (Flugschrift des Deutschen Volksbundes, 1) *Unseen*

0307 Böckel, Otto (1859–1923): *Die Quintessenz der Judenfrage. Ansprache an seine Wähler und alle deutsch-nationalen Männer im Vaterlande.* 9. verm. Aufl. Berlin: G.A. Dewald, 1888. 24 pp. *LJ*

0308 Böhm, Franz (1895–): Antisemitismus im 19. Jahrhundert. *LBI Bull.* 4 (1961) 268–276. *LJ*

0309  Bönigk, Otto von (1867–): *Grundzüge zur Judenfrage; soziologisch-ökonomische Studie.* Leipzig: W. Friedrich, 1894. III, 154 pp. *LJ*

0310  Böning, Holger: Bürgerliche Revolution und Judenemanzipation in der Schweiz. *TAJfDG* 14 (1985) 157–189. *LJ*

0311  Börne, Ludwig (1786–1837): *Ludwig Börne über die Juden; ein Beitrag zur Emanzipationsfrage für die Reichstage.* Wien: C. Rosenthal, 1848. 15 pp. *Unseen*

0312  *Börsen-Kirmess.* Dresden: Glöss, 1892. 1 l. (Politischer Bilderbogen, 5) *LJ*

0313  Böttger, Ernst: Offene Antwort an den Zentralverein Deutscher Staatsbürger Jüdischen Glaubens. *Der Hammer* 11 (1912) 126–127. *LB*

0314  Bötticher, Wilhelm: *Die Herrschaft der Juden; ein Wort zur Belehrung zum Trost und zur Warnung für Juden und Christen, Jesaias, 55, V. 3–9.* Berlin: Typ. C. Striefe, 1848. 8 pp. *LJ*

0315  Bötticher, Wilhelm: *Die Zukunft Israels und der Christenheit; oder, Die Erfüllung der biblischen Weissagungen über Israels Bekehrung und die darausfolgende Verpflichtung aller evangelischen Christen, vornehmlich der deutschen . . . jetzt schon dazu mitzuwirken Ein Buch für Fürst und Volk.* Berlin: Thome in Komm., 1848. XIV, 466 pp. *LF*

0316  Boh, Felix: *Der Konservatismus und die Judenfrage.* Dresden: Konservativer Verein, 1892. 20 pp. *LJ*

0317  Bolle, Henri Jean: Frédéric Nietzsche et l'antisémitisme. *Revue Juive de Génève* 2 (1933) 75–80. *LJ*

0318  *Die Bombe; Enthüllungen über den Bau und die Verwaltung der serbischen Staatsbahnen.* Aus dem Serbischen übers. von W. Rudow. Mit einem Vorwort von Karl Paasch. 2. Aufl. Leipzig: Germanicus-Verlag, 1893. 100 pp. *LF*

0319  Bondi, Dr.: Die wirtschaftliche Tätigkeit der Juden. *Jahrbuch der jüdischen literarischen Gesellschaft. Frankfurt a.M.* 8 (1910) 378–431. *LJ*

0320  Bonger, W.A.: Rezension zu Dr. Rudolf Wassermann's "Beruf, Konfession und Verbrechen; eine Studie über die Kriminalität der Juden in Vergangenheit und Gegenwart." *N.Z.* 26, 1 (1907–1908) 47. *LJ*

0321  Bonhard, Otto: *Geschichte des "Alldeutschen Verbandes."* Leipzig: Th. Weicher, 1920. 291 pp. *LJ*

0322 Bonnet, J.: *Die Stellung der Judenmission in der Reihe der christlichen Reichsarbeiten. Vortrag. 2. verb. Aufl.* Norden: D. Soltan, 1877. 29 pp. *LJ*

0323 Bonus, Arthur (1864–1941): Shylock; zur Judenfrage. Acht Briefe an eine Jüdin. *Pr. Jhrb.* 83 (1896) 414–437. *LJ*

0324 Bonus, Arthur (1864–1941): *Von Stoecker zu Naumann; ein Wort zur Germanisierung des Christentums.* Heilbronn: Eugen Salzer, 1896. 84 pp. *LM*

0325 Boom, Willem ten: *Die Entstehung des modernen Rassen-Antisemitismus, besonders in Deutschland.* Leipzig: Typ. R. König, 1928. 50 pp. (Schriften des Institutum Judaicum Delitzschianum zu Leipzig, 5) *LJ*

0326 Borries, Hans Joachim von: *Deutschtum und Judentum; Studien zum Selbstverständnis des deutschen Judentums 1879–1880.* Hamburg: Typ. R. Himmelheber, 1971. 162 pp. *LJ*

Diss. Zürich.

0327 Borus, Salomon: *Sollen und dürfen die Juden zum Christentum übertreten? Ein Beitrag zur Lösung der Judenfrage.* Straßburg i. E.: Wolfstein & Teilhaber, 1906. 13 pp. *LJ*

0328 Bosse, Friedrich: *Die Verbreitung der Juden im Deutschen Reiche, auf Grundlage der Volkzählung vom 1. Dezember 1880. Nach amtlichen Materialien zusammengestellt.* Berlin: Puttkammer & Mühlbrecht, 1885. VIII, 136 pp. *LJ*

0329 Boudin: Der Kosmopolitismus der jüdischen Rasse. *MGWJ* 9 (1860) 401–406. *LJ*

Offprint from: *La vérité Israélite,* vol. 1, no. 44, published in Paris.

0330 Bournand, François (1853–): *Juifs et antisémites en Europe.* Paris: Tolra, 1891. VIII, 388 pp. *LJ*

Les Juifs et l'antisémitisme en Allemagne: Pp. 171–247. En Autriche-Hongrie: Pp. 289–324.

0331 Bournand, François (1853–): *Les juifs et nos contemporains: l'antisémitisme et la question juive.* Introduction par Edmond Picard. Paris: A. Pierret, 1899. 316 pp. *LB*

0332 Boyer, John W.: *Political Radicalism in Late Imperial Vienna; Origins of the Christian Social Movement, 1848–1897.* Chicago: University of Chicago Press, 1981. XVI, 577 pp. *LJ*

Discusses Karl Lueger's central role in the Christian Social movement.

0333 Braatz, Werner: Antisemitismus, Antimodernismus und Antiliberalismus im ausgehenden 19. Jahrhundert. *Politische Studien* 10 (1971) 20–33. *Unseen*

0334 Brake, Georg: *Zur deutschen Judenfrage. Ein Wort zum Frieden.* Gotha: F.A. Perthes, 1880. 100 pp. *LJ*

0335 Brammer, Annegret H.: *Judenpolitik und Judengesetzgebung in Preußen 1812-1847; mit einem Ausblick auf das Gleichberechtigungsgesetz des Norddeutschen Bundes von 1869.* Berlin: Schelzky und Jeipp, 1987. 569 pp. *LJ*

0336 Brandt, Hartwig: Stufen der Judenemanzipation im 18. und 19. Jahrhundert. *Judentum und Antisemitismus von der Antike bis zur Gegenwart.* Eds. Thomas Klein a.o. Düsseldorf: Droste, 1984. Pp. 103–112. *LJ*

0337 Brann, Henry Walter: *Schopenhauer und das Judentum.* Bonn: Bouvier Verlag, 1975. 114 pp. (Abhandlungen zur Philosophie, Psychologie und Pädagogik, 97) *LJ*

0338 Braumann, A.: *Die Anteilnahme der deutschen Frau an dem Kampfe wider das Judentum: Vortrag.* Berlin: Dewald, 1892. 16 pp. (Deutsche Weckschriften, 1) *Unseen*

0339 Braumann, A.: *Die Juden als Hauptfeinde deutscher Sprache und Schrift; Vortrag.* Berlin: Dewald, 1892. 16 pp. (Deutsche Weckschriften, 2) *Unseen*

0340 Braun, Adolf (1862–1929): *Die Parteien des Deutschen Reichstages, ihre Programme, Entwicklung und Stärke; ein unentbehrliches Handbüchlein für jeden Reichstagswähler.* Stuttgart: J.H.W. Dietz, 1893. 36 pp. *Unseen*

0341 Braun, Max: *Adolf Stoecker.* Berlin: Verlag der Vaterländischen Verlags- und Kunstanstalt, 1913. 286 pp. *LJ*

0342 Braune, Ernst: *Die Juden. Von einem Christen.* Berlin: E. Großer, 1877. 61 pp. *LJ*

0343 Brendel, Franz (1811–1868): Das Judentum in der Musik. *Neue Zeitschrift für Musik* 34 (1851) 4–6. *LJ*

0344 Brenner, Harry L.: *Judentum und Christentum.* Hamburg: Zions-Freund, 1910. 24 pp. *LM*

0345 Brentano, Lujo (1844–1931): Judentum und Kapitalismus. *Die Anfänge des modernen Kapitalismus.* München: Verlag der Akademie der Wissenschaften, 1916. Pp. 158–198. *LJ*

"Festrede gehalten in der öffentlichen Sitzung der K. Akademie der Wissenschaften am 15. Maerz 1913."

0346  Breslauer, Bernhard (1851-1928): *Die Abwanderung der Juden aus der Provinz Posen; Denkschrift im Auftrage des Verbandes der Deutschen Juden.* Berlin: Typ. B. Levy, 1909. 19 pp. *LJ*

0347  Breslauer, Bernhard (1851-1928): Die gesellschaftliche Stellung der Juden in Deutschland. *I.Dt.R.* 12 (1906) 279-298. *LJ*

0348  Breslauer, Bernhard (1851-1928): *Die Zurücksetzung der Juden an den Universitäten Deutschlands.* Denkschrift im Auftrage des Verbandes der Deutschen Juden. Berlin: B. Levy, 1911. 22 pp. *LJ*

0349  Breslauer, Bernhard (1851-1928): *Die Zurücksetzung der Juden im Justizdienst. Denkschrift im Auftrage des Verbandes der Deutschen Juden.* Berlin: B. Levy, 1907. 9 pp. *LJ*

0350  Breslauer, Emil: *Herr Richard Wagner und seine neueste Schrift "Das Judentum in der Musik."* Breslau: B. Heidenfeld, 1869. 13 pp. *Unseen*

0351  Breslauer, Walter: Jews in the City of Posen. *LBIYB* 8 (1963) 229-237. *LJ*

About the relationship among Germans, Jews and Poles in Poznan.

0352  Breslauer, Walter: Der Verband der Deutschen Juden, 1904-1922. *LBI Bull.* 4 (1964) 345-379. *LJ*

0353  Breslauer, Walter: Die "Vereinigung für das Liberale Judentum" und die Richtlinien zu einem Progamm für das liberale Judentum; Erinnerungen aus den Jahren 1908-1914. *LBI Bull.* 9 (1966) 302-329. *LJ*

0354  Breuer, Isaak (1883-1946): Sombart und die Juden. *Der Israelit* 52, 36 (1911) 1-3; 52, 37 (1911) 1-2; 52, 38 (1911) 5-6; 52, 40 (1911) 5-6 *LJ*

A review.

0355  Breuer, Raphael (1881-1932): *Aus dem Tagebuch einer jüdischen Studentin.* Frankfurt a.M.: Knaur, 1907. 16 pp. *LF*

0356  Briegleb, Otto: *Rassennot — Rassenschutz.* Hamburg: Deutsch-Nationale Buchhdlg. und Verlagsanstalt, 1913. 30 pp. *LF*

0357  Briemann, August: *Judenspiegel; oder, 100 neuenthüllte, heutzutage noch geltende, den Verkehr der Juden mit den Christen betreffende Gesetze der Juden, nach der wissenschaftlichen Untersuchung des Herrn Dr. Jakob Ecker.* 5. rev. Aufl. Paderborn: Bonifacius Druckerei, 1892. 112 pp. *LJ*

0358 Briemann, August: *"Talmudische Weisheit."* 400 *höchst interessante märchen-hafte Aussprüche der Rabbinen, direkt aus der Quelle geschöpft und dem christlichen Volke vorgetragen.* Paderborn: Bonifacius Druckerei, 1884. IV, 67 pp. *LJ*

0359 Brilling, Bernhard (1906–): Breslauer Judentaufen im 19. Jahrhundert. *Jüdische Zeitung für Ostdeutschland,* Breslau 6 (1929) Suppl. 17. *LJ*

0360 Bröker, Walburga (Kröger): *Der Rassengedanke in der deutschen Presse des 19. Jahrhunderts.* Leipzig: 1944. 136 l. *Unseen*

Diss. 1944 (ms).

0361 Bronder, Dietrich: *Bevor Hitler kam; eine historische Studie.* Hannover: H. Pfeiffer, 1964. Pp. 316–392. *LJ*

0362 Broszat, Martin: *Die antisemitische Bewegung im Wilhelminischen Deutschland.* Köln: 1953. 156 pp. *LC*

Diss. 1953.

0363 Brüggen, Ernst von der: Das Deutsche Judentum in seiner Heimat. Der Talmud. *Russland und die Juden; kulturgeschichtliche Skizzen. Ausland und die Juden; kulturgeschichtliche Skizzen.* Leipzig: Veit & Co., 1882. Pp. 20–100. *LJ*

0364 Brüggen, Ernst von der: Das deutsche Judentum in seiner Heimat. *Die Grenzboten* 39 (1880) 181–191, 212–226, 258–266, 296–311. *LC*

0365 Brüll, Adolf (1846–1908): *Presse und Judentum; Vortrag gehalten am 7. Dezember 1882 im Mendelssohn Verein zu Frankfurt a.M.* Frankfurt a.M.: [n.pub.], 1883. 7 pp. *LJ*

Offprint from: *Populär-Wissenschaftliche Monatsblätter.*

0366 Brunner, Frederick H.: Juden als Bankiers und ihre völkerverbindende Tätigkeit. *In zwei Welten.* Tel-Aviv, 1962. Pp. 509–535. *LJ*

0367 Brunner, Sebastian (1814–1893): *Die jüdischen Federhelden; oder, Das politisch-literarische Schabesgärtle in Wien, von Max Veitel Stern, pseud.* Wien: Lesk, [n.d.]. 12 pp. *Unseen*

Edited, with an appendix, by Richard Maria Werner.

0368 Brunner, Sebastian (1814–1893): *Lessingiasis und Nathanologie. Eine Religionsstörung im Lessing- und Nathan-Kultus.* Paderborn: F. Schöningh, 1890. VIII, 370 pp. *LJ*

0369  Brunner, Sebastian (1814–1893): *Zwei Buschmänner, Börne und Heine. Aktenmäßig geschildert.* Paderborn: F. Schöningh, 1891. XII, 407 pp. *LJ*

0370  Bruno, Max: *Gemauschel. Illustriert von Fritz Bindewald.* Marburg: Selbstverlag des Verfassers, 1892. 55 pp. *Unseen*

0371  Brunstäd, Friedrich: *Adolf Stoecker; Wille und Schicksal.* Berlin: Wichern-Verlag, 1935. 167 pp. *LJ*

0372  Buber, Martin (1878–1965): *Die jüdische Bewegung; gesammelte Aufsätze und Ansprachen, 1900–1915.* Berlin: Jüdischer Verlag, 1916. 251 pp. *LJ*

0373  Buber, Martin (1878–1965): Moses Hess. *J.S.St.* 7 (1945) 137–148. *LJ*

0374  Buchheim, Karl (1889–): *Geschichte der christlichen Parteien in Deutschland.* München: Kösel-Verlag, 1953. 466 pp. *LF*

0375  Buchow, Wilhelm (1883–): *Fünfzig Jahre antisemitische Bewegung. Beitrag zu ihrer Geschichte.* Berlin: Deutscher Volksverlag, 1937. 101 pp. *LJ*

0376  Bückeburg. Synagogen-Gemeinde: *Gesuch an das Fürstlich Schaumburg-Lippische Ministerium.* Berlin: 1907. 51 pp. *LJ*

0377  *Die bürgerliche und staatsrechtliche Stellung der Juden in Preußen; eine Sammlung der wichtigsten, über die Verhältnisse der jüdischen Staatsbürger geltenden, gesetzlichen Bestimmungen.* Danzig: Kafemann, 1867. 55 pp. *Unseen*

0378  Die bürgerlichen Verhältnisse der Juden in Deutschland. *Gegenwart* 1 (1848) 353–407. *LJ*

0379  Bulova, Josef Adolf: *Das Polnaer Verbrechen; ein Sittenbild aus Oesterreichs jüngster Vergangenheit aufgenommen. Rekapitulation und 2. Teil zu der Broschüre "Zum Polnaer Ritualmordprozeße."* Als Manuskript gedruckt. Berlin: Gorber and Co., 1901. 38 pp. *Unseen*

0380  Bulova, Josef Adolf: *Zum Polnaer Ritualmordprozeß im Stadium vor dem 2. Urteile; ein Brief an die Herren Professoren der gerichtlichen Medizin, Juristen und an alle ehrlichen Menschen überhaupt.* Berlin: G.E. Kitzler, 1900. 32, LXXVI pp. *LJ*

0381  Bunke, Ernst: *Adolf Stoecker, ein deutscher Prophet.* Giessen: Brunnen-Verlag, 1938. 86 pp. (Menschen, die den Ruf vernommen, 22) *Unseen*

0382  Bunke, Ernst: *Adolf Stoecker und die Angriffe seiner Gegner im Lichte der Wahrheit. Von einem Nichtpolitker.* Berlin: M. Warneck, 1901. 63 pp. *LJ*

0383  Bunke, Ernst, ed.: *Erinnerungsblätter.* Berlin: Vaterländischer Verlag und Kunstanstalt, 1909. 218 pp. *LB*

0384  Bureau für Statistik der Juden, Berlin: *Die Juden in Oesterreich.* Im Auftrag des Verbandes der Israelitischen Humanitätsvereine Bnai Brith für Oesterreich, von Jakob Thon. Berlin: L. Lamm, 1908. 160 pp. (Veröffentlichungen des Bureaus für Statistik der Juden, 4) *LJ*

0385  Bureau für Statistik der Juden, Berlin: *Die jüdischen Gemeinden und Vereine in Deutschland.* Berlin: Verlag des Bureau für Statistik der Juden, 1906. 85 pp. (Its Veröffentlichungen, 3) *LJ*

0386  Bureau für Statistik der Juden, Berlin: *Statistik der Juden; eine Sammelschrift.* Berlin: Kommissions-Verlag Jüdischer Verlag, 1917. 171 pp. *LJ*

       This collection of articles should have been published on October 1, 1914. The outbreak of the First World War delayed publication till 1917.

0387  Burg, Meno (1787–1853): *Geschichte meines Dienstlebens.* 2. Aufl. Mit einem Geleitwort von Ludwig Geiger. Leipzig: M.W. Kaufmann, 1916. XVI, 172 pp. *LJ*

       First published in 1854.

0388  Burger, Alexander: *Die Parteien der wirtschaftlichen Vereinigung; Christlich-Soziale Partei, Antisemiten, Bund der Landwirte. T. 4 der Geschichte der Parteien des Deutschen Reichstages.* Gautzsch bei Leipzig: F. Dietrich, 1910. 14 pp. (Kultur und Fortschritt, 314) *Unseen*

0389  Burkhardt, Carl August: Aus der Zeitschriften-Literatur zur Geschichte der Juden in Deutschland; Verzeichnis von Abhandlungen und Notizen. *ZfGJD* [Ed. Ludwig Geiger] 2 (1888) 1–46, 109–149. *LJ*

0390  Busch, Helmut: *Die Stoecker-Bewegung im Siegerland; ein Beitrag zur Geschichte der Christlich-Sozialen Partei.* Marburg: 1964. XVI, 263 pp. *LC*

       Diss.

0391  Busch, Moritz (1821–1899): *Israel und die Gojim; Beiträge zur Beurteilung der Judenfrage.* Leipzig: F.W. Grunow, 1880. III, 316 pp. *LJ*

0392  Busch, Ralf: Die jüdischen Reformschulen in Wolfenbüttel und Seesen und ihre
      Bibliotheken. *Antisemitismus und jüdische Geschichte.* Berlin: Wissen-
      schaftlicher Autoren-Verlag, 1987. 173–183. *LJ*

0393  *Buschhof Prozeß: Der Xantener Knabenmord vor dem Schwurgericht zu Cleve
      vom 4.–14. Juli 1892.* Mit Situationsplänen und nach stenographischen
      Aufzeichnungen. Hagen i. Westfalen: L. Wrietzner, 1892. 112 pp. *LJ*

0394  Cahn, Michael: *Das Plaidoyer des Herrn Justizrat Makower für den Verband
      der Deutschen Juden; eine Replik.* Frankfurt a.M.: Verlag des "Israelit," 1913.
      58 pp. *LJ*

      Offprint from *Israelit.*

0395  Cahnman, Werner J. (1902–): Adolf Fischhof and his Jewish Followers. *LBIYB*
      4 (1959) 111–139. *LJ*

0396  Calthrop, Gordon: *Die jüdische Kolonisationsfrage. Ansprache . . .* Aus dem
      Englischen übers. von C. Wagner. Berlin: Deutsche Evangelische Buch- und
      Traktat-Gesellschaft, 1892. 14 pp. *LJ*

0397  Calvary, Moses: *Die Aufgabe des deutschen Zionismus.* Berlin: Typ. W.R.
      Saling & Co., 1911. 20 pp. *LJ*

      Offprint from: *Jüdische Studenten,* 1911, vol. 9, no. 6.

0398  Calwer, Richard (1868–1927): *Das Kommunisitische Manifest und die heutige
      Sozialdemokratie.* Braunschweig: A. Günther, 1894. 52 pp. *LJ*

      Antisemitic publication by a social democrat.

0399  Carlebach, Julius: *Karl Marx and the radical critique of Judaism.* London:
      Routledge & Kegan Paul, 1978. XI, 466 pp. (The Littman Library of Jewish
      Civilization) *LJ*

      "The antisemitism of Marx and the use of Marx in antisemitism": Pp.
      344–358.

0400  Caro, Jecheskel (1844–1916): *Den Judenfeinden Treitschke, Marr und Stoecker.*
      Erfurt: Typ. F. Bartholomäus, 1879. 8 pp. *LJ*

0401  Caro, Jecheskel (1844–1916): *Die Frankisten und der Archivarius der Stadt
      Lemberg; eine Antwort auf dessen Abhandlung über Ritualmord.* Lemberg:
      Verlag des Verfassers, 1899. 8 pp. *LJ*

0402  Caro, Joseph ben Ephraim (1488–1575): *Zitatenschatz aus dem Schulchan Aruch
      nach der Uebersetzung von Johannes A.F.E.L. von Pavly.* Zur Information für
      jedermann. Dortmund: Otten, 1888. 16 pp. (Flugschriften-Sammlung, 1) *LJ*

Excerpts chosen in order to deprecate the book.

0403 Caro, Leopold (1864–1939): *Der Wucher; eine sozialpolitische Studie.* Leipzig: Duncker & Humblot, 1893. XV, 311 pp. *LJ*

0404 Cassel, Paulus Stephanus (1821–1892): *Der Judengott und Richard Wagner; eine Antwort an die Bayreuther Blätter zum 28. Mai 1881.* Berlin: Wohlgemuth's Verlag, 1881. 44 pp. *LTA*

0405 Cassel, Paulus Stephanus (1821–1892): *Wie ich über Judenmission denke: ein kurzes Sendschreiben an englische Freunde.* Berlin: K. Siegismund, 1886. 35 pp. *Unseen*

0406 Cecil, Lamar: *Albert Ballin; Business and Politics in Imperial Germany 1888–1918.* Princeton, NJ: Princeton University Press, 1967. XXI, 338 pp. *LJ*

0407 Cecil, Lamar: Jew and Junker in Imperial Berlin. *LBIYB* 20 (1975) 47–58. *LJ*

0408 Cecil, Lamar: Wilhelm II und die Juden. *Juden im wilhelminischen Deutschland, 1890–1914.* Ed. Werner E. Mosse. Tübingen: J.C.B. Mohr, 1976. Pp. 313– 348. (Schriftenreiche wissenschaftlicher Abhandlungen des LBI, 33) *LJ*

0409 Centralverein Deutscher Staatsbürger Jüdischen Glaubens: *Generalversammlung des Centralvereins . . .* Berlin: 1893. 4 pp. *LJ*

0410 Centralverein Deutscher Staatsbürger Jüdischen Glaubens: *Die Gutachten der Sachverständigen über den Konitzer Mord.* Nach den amtlichen Akten veröffentlicht. Berlin: Selbstverlag, 1903. 87 pp. *LJ*

0411 Centralverein Deutscher Staatsbürger Jüdischen Glaubens: *Satzungen des Centralvereins . . .* Berlin: 189-. 3 pp. *LJ*

0412 Centralverein Deutscher Staatsbürger Jüdischen Glaubens: *Zur Frage des Ritualmordes.* Berlin: R. Moffe, 189-. 1 l. *Unseen*

0413 Červinka, František: The Hilsner Affair. *LBIYB* 13 (1968) 142–157. *LJ*

0414 Chamberlain, Houston Stewart (1855–1927): *Arische Weltanschauung.* Berlin: Bard, Marquard und Co., 1905. VI, 86 pp. (Kultur; Sammlung illustrierter Einzeldarstellungen, 1) *LJ*

0415 Chamberlain, Houston Stewart (1855–1927): *Dilettantismus, Rasse, Monotheismus, Rom.* Vorwort zur 4. Aufl. der Grundlagen des XIX Jahrhunderts. München: F. Bruckmann, 1903. 80 pp. *LJ*

0416 Chamberlain, Houston Stewart (1855–1927): *Foundations of the 19th Century.* A translation from the German by John Lees, with an introduction by Lord Redesdale. München: F. Bruckmann, 1910. 2 vols. *LJ*

Original title: *Die Grundlagen des 19. Jahrhunderts.*

0417 Chamberlain, Houston Stewart (1855–1927): *Die Grundlagen des 19. Jahrhunderts.* 4. Aufl. München: F. Bruckmann, 1903. 2 vols. *LJ*

0418 Chamberlain, Houston Stewart (1855–1927): *Richard Wagner.* München: Verlag für Kunst und Wissenschaft, 1896. 368 pp. *LJ*

On antisemitism and racism, in particular in the 2nd chapter.

0419 Chamberlain, Houston Stewart (1855–1927): *Wehr und Gegenwehr.* Vorworte zur 3. und 4. Aufl. der Grundlagen des 19. Jahrhunderts. München: F. Bruckmann, 1912. 108 pp. *LJ*

0420 Charmatz, Richard: *Dr. Karl Lueger.* Berlin: 1904. 64–81 pp. *LJ*

Offprint from: Berliner Monatsschrift *Deutschland.*

0421 Cherbuliez, Victor: L'affaire de Tísza–Eslár. *Revue des Deux Mondes* 53, 3. per. (1883) 681–692. *LJ*

0422 Cherbuliez, Victor: La question des juifs en Allemagne. *Revue des Deux Mondes* 50, 3. per. (1880) 203–245. *LJ*

0423 Chevalier, pseud.: *Börsen-Silhouetten.* Berlin: W.H. Kühl, 1880. 52 pp. *Unseen*

Offprint from: *Börsen-Wochenblatt.*

0424 Chiarloni, Anna Pegoraro: Antisemitismo in Germania, 1848–1870. *Studi Storici* 11 (1970) 97–112. *LJ*

0425 Chickering, Roger: *We Men Who Feel Most German; a Cultural Study of the Pan-German League, 1886–1914.* Boston: G. Allen and Unwin, 1984. XIV, 365 pp. *LJ*

0426 *Die Cholera und die Juden; ein zeitgemäßes Gespräch mit dramatischem Abschluß.* Berlin: Th. Heinrich, 1892. 40 pp. *LF*

0427 Cholewa von Pawlikowski, Konstantin: *Eine Christenantwort auf die Judenfrage.* 3 Tle. Wien: Mayer und Comp., 1859. 79 pp. *LJ*

0428 Cholewa von Pawlikowski, Konstantin: *Hundert Bogen aus mehr als fünfhundert alten und neuen Büchern über die Juden neben den Christen.* T. 1. Freiburg: Herder, 1859. LIX, 926 pp. *LTA*

No more published.

0429 Cholewa von Pawlikowski, Konstantin: *Lelewel; Kämpfer für Recht und Wahrheit und die Judenfeinde.* Wien: 1880. 24 pp. *Unseen*

0430 Cholewa von Pawlikowski, Konstantin: *Der Talmud in der Theorie und in der Praxis; eine literarhistorische Zusammenstellung.* Regensburg: Manz, 1866. VIII, 340 pp. *LJ*

0431 Cholewa von Pawlikowski, Konstantin: *Die unschuldig verfolgten, wehrlosen Juden und Rabbiner Mayer Mintz, der Kämpfer für Recht und Wahrheit.* Wien: Mayer und Comp., 1860. 24 pp. *LV*

0432 *Christenschutz oder Judenschutz? Erwägungen über Ursprung, Umfang und Berechtigung der Judenfrage vom katholisch-konservativen Standpunkt.* Linz: Redaktion des Linzer Volksblatt, 1893. 82 pp. *LC*

0433 *Christliche Zeugnisse gegen die Blutbeschuldigung der Juden.* Berlin: Walther & Apolant, 1882. VI, 58 pp. *LJ*

0434 Chvolson, Daniil Abramovič (1819-1911): *Die Blutanklage und sonstige mittelalterliche Beschuldigungen der Juden; eine historische Untersuchung nach den Quellen.* Nach der 2. vielfach verb. Ausg. von 1880 aus dem Russischen übers. und mit vielen Verbesserungen und Zusätzen vom Autor versehen. Frankfurt a.M.: J. Kauffmann, 1901. XV, 362 pp. *LJ*

0435 Class, Heinrich (1868-): *Die Bilanz des neuen Kurses; Vortrag von Rechtsanwalt Heinrich Class in Mainz gehalten auf dem Alldeutschen Verbandstag 1903.* Berlin: Alldeutscher Verband, 1903. 42 pp. (Flugschriften des Alldeutschen Verbandes, 16) *LV*

0436 Class, Heinrich (1868-): *Deutsche Geschichte, von Einhart, pseud.* 5. vollkommen neu bearb. und erw. Aufl. Leipzig: Dietrich, 1914. XII, 511 pp. *LJ*

0437 Class, Heinrich (1868-): *Wenn ich der Kaiser wär' — politische Wahrheiten und Notwendigkeiten.* 2. Aufl. Leipzig: Dieterichsche Verlags-Buchhdlg., 1912. XI, 235 pp. *LJ*

0438 Class, Heinrich (1868-): *Wider den Strom; vom Werden und Wachsen der nationalen Opposition im Alten Reich.* Leipzig: K.F. Köhler, 1932. 421 pp. *LTA*

0439 Cobet, Christoph: *Der Wortschatz des Antisemitismus in der Bismarckzeit.* München: Fink, 1973. 269 pp. (Münchener germanistische Beiträge, 11) *LJ*

0440 Cohen, Arthur (1864–1940): Die Münchener Judenschaft 1750–1861; eine bevölkerungs- und wirtschaftsgeschichtliche Studie. *ZfDSJ* 2 (1930) 262–283. *LJ*

0441 Cohen, Carl: The Road to Conversion. *LBIYB* 6 (1961) 259–279. *LJ*

0442 Cohen, Gustav G.: *Drei Stadien, 1885.* [n.p.]: 1906? 48 pp. *LJ*
Printed as ms. "Nachwort" dated 1906.

0443 Cohen, Hermann (1842–1918): Emanzipation. *Jüdische Schriften. Bd. 2.* Berlin: C.A. Schwetschke, 1924. Pp. 220–228. *LJ*
First published in *Israelitisches Familienblatt* March 7, 1912, pp. 1–3.

0444 Cohen, Hermann (1842–1918): Heinrich Heine und das Judentum. *Jüdische Schriften. Bd. 2.* Berlin: C.A. Schwetschke, 1924. Pp. 2–44. *LJ*
First published under the pseudonym Ben-Jechiel in the Berlin weekly *Die Gegenwart*; Berliner Wochenschrift für jüdische Angelegenheiten, 1867.

0445 Cohen, Hermann (1842–1918): *Die Nächstenliebe im Talmud.* Ein Gutachten dem Königlichen Landgerichte zu Marburg erstattet. Marburg: Elwert, 1888. 35 pp. *LJ*

0446 Cohen, Hermann (1842–1918): Der Religionswechsel in der neuen Aera des Antisemitismus. *Jüdische Schriften. Bd. 2.* Berlin: C.A. Schwetschke, 1924. Pp. 342–345. *LJ*
First published in *AZJ*, 1890, pp. 489–490.

0447 Cohen, Hermann (1842–1918): Virchow und die Juden. *Jüdische Schriften. Bd. 2.* Berlin: C.A. Schwetschke, 1924. Pp. 457–462. *LJ*
First published in *Die Zukunft*, August 14, 1868.

0448 Cohen, Israel (1879–): *Antisemitism in Germany.* London: Offices of the "Jewish Chronicle" and the Jewish World, 1918. 20 pp. *LJ*

0449 Cohn, Emil (1881–1948): Probleme im modernen Judentum. *Pr. Jhrb.* 129 (1907) 302–324. *LJ*

0450 Cohn, Emil (1881–1948): Die religiöse Judenfrage. *Pr. Jhrb.* 143 (1911) 432–440. *LF*

0451 Cohn, Gustav (1840–1918): *Robert von Mohl wider die Gleichstellung der Juden. Zur Kritik der neuesten Angriffe, von einem getauften Juden.* Berlin: W. Adolf, 1869. 21 pp. *LJ*

Deals with an article in *Staatsrecht, Völkerrecht und Politik*. Vol. 3, II. Politik, Monographien von Robert von Mohl.

0452 Cohn, Heinrich Meyer: *Houston Stewart Chamberlain — Die Grundlagen des neunzehnten Jahrhunderts.* Dresden: E. Pierson, 1901. 44 pp. *LJ*

0453 Cohn, Heinrich Meyer: *Wie Treitschke zitiert und Geschichte schreibt, von H.C.* Berlin: R. Mosse, 1902. 15 pp. *LJ*

Offprint from: *AZJ*.

0454 Cohn Tobias: Eduard Lasker; biographische Skizze. *Jahrbuch für die Geschichte der Juden und des Judentums* 4 (1869) 1–141. *LJ*

0455 Collet, Peter Franz: *Warum bin ich Antisemit: 1. Weil ich Deutscher bin! 2. Weil ich Christ bin. Allen Denkenden zur Beherzigung empfohlen.* Leipzig: O. Gottwald, 1894. 24 pp. *LV*

0456 Comite zur Abwehr antisemitischer Angriffe in Berlin: *Die Juden als Soldaten.* Berlin: S. Cronbach, 1896. X, 167 pp. (Die Juden in Deutschland, II) *LJ*

0457 Conti, Berthold W.: *Ahlwardt's Bubenstreiche und die hierfür applizierten Ohrfeigen erteilt, von dem Rasse-Juden Berthold W. Conti.* [n.p.]: 189–. 2 pp. *LJ*

0458 Corti, Egon Caesar von: *Das Haus Rothschild in der Zeit seiner Blüte, 1830–1871. Mit einem Ausblick in die neuste Zeit.* Leipzig: Insel-Verlag, 1928. 511 pp. *LJ*

Sequel to *Aufstieg des Hauses Rotschild, 1770–1830*, 1927.

0459 Coudenhove-Kalergi, Heinrich von (1859–1906): *Anti-Semitism throughout the Ages.* Edited and brought up-to-date by Count Richard Coudenhove-Kalergi. Authorized English translation by Dr. Angelo S. Rappaport. London: Hutchinson, 1935. 288 pp. *LJ*

First published in German in 1901 under the title: *Das Wesen des Antisemitismus* . . .

0460 Coudenhove-Kalergi, Heinrich von (1859–1906): *Das Wesen des Antisemitismus.* Berlin: S. Calvary, 1901. 526 pp. *LJ*

0461 Coudenhove-Kalergi, Heinrich von (1859–1906): *Das Wesen des Antisemitismus.* Hrsg. von Richard Nikolaus Coudenhove-Kalergi. 2. Aufl. Wien: Gesellschaft für Graphische Industrie, 1923. 206 pp. *LJ*

First published in 1901.

0462 Coudenhove-Kalergi, Heinrich von (1859–1906): *Das Wesen des Antisemitismus. Eingeleitet durch "Antisemitismus nach dem Weltkrieg," von Richard Nikolaus Coudenhove.* Wien: Paneuropa-Verlag, 1929. 284 pp. *LJ*

0463 Cramer, Franz Josef: *Das antisemitische Theater.* Leipzig: O. Mutze, 1900. 36 pp. *LJ*
About the aryan Raimund-Theater, Vienna.

0464 Cremer, Christoph Joseph: *Die angeblichen 10.000 Mark des Herrn von Bleichröder.* Berlin: F. Luckhardt, 1889. 48 pp. *LJ*

0465 Croner, Else: *Die moderne Jüdin.* Berlin: A. Juncker, 1913. 148 pp. *LB*

0466 Croner, Johannes: *Die Geschichte der agrarischen Bewegung in Deutschland.* Berlin: G. Reimer, 1909. VII, 269 pp. *LV*

0467 Crzellitzer A: Besprechungen — Ignaz Zollschan's "Das Rassenproblem unter besonderer Berücksichtigung der theoretischen Grundlagen der jüdischen Rassenfrage." *MGWJ* 54 (1910) 114–118. *LJ*

0468 Cunow, Heinrich (1862–1936): Literarische Rundschau; Otto Freiherr von Bönigk's Grundzüge zur Judenfrage. *N.Z.* 13, 1 (1894–1895) 823–824. *LJ*

0469 Cunow, L.: *Die Gemeingefährlichkeit des jüdischen Einflußes. Vortrag gehalten am 19. Mai 1882 zu Berlin.* Berlin: O. Lorentz, 1882. 8 pp. *LJ*

0470 Curtius, Lorenz: *Der politische Antisemitismus von 1907–1911.* München: Kommissions-Verlag des National-Vereins für das Liberale Deutschland, 1911. 120 pp. *LJ*

0471 Czaczkes-Tissenboim, Schmeril: *Der Anteil der Juden an der Wiener Revolution im Jahre 1848.* Wien: 1926. 216 l. *LJ*
Diss. Photo-copy of the typescript, 1980.

0472 Daab, H.: *Der Talmud in Vorträgen.* Leipzig: G. Böhme, 1883. 204 pp. *LJ*

0473 *Dämonen der Unzucht! Notschrei einer deutschen Frau.* Leipzig: Uhl, 1894. 80 pp. *Unseen*

0474 Daim, Wilfried: *Der Mann, der Hitler die Ideen gab; von den religiösen Verirrungen eines Sektierers zum Rassenwahn des Diktators.* München: Isar Verlag, 1958. 286 pp. *LJ*

0475  Dalman, Gustaf Hermann (1855–): *Die Allgemeine Konferenz der Judenmission in Leipzig vom 6.–8. Juni 1895. Die Ansprachen der Referenten und Bericht über den Verlauf der Konferenz.* Leipzig: W. Faber, 1896. 130 pp. *LJ*

0476  Dalman, Gustaf Hermann (1855–): *Jesaja 53, das Prophetenwort vom Sühneleiden des Heilsmittlers mit besonderer Berücksichtigung der synagogalen Literatur erörtert.* 2. umgearb. Aufl. Leipzig: J.C. Hinrichs, 1914. IV, 59 pp. (Schriften des Institutum Judaicum in Berlin, 13) *LJ*

0477  Dalman, Gustaf Hermann (1855–): *Jüdisches Fremdenrecht, antisemitische Polemik und jüdische Apologetik. Kritische Blätter für Antisemiten und Juden.* Erw. Sonderabdruck aus "Nathanael," Jhrg. 1. Berlin: H. Reuther's Verlag, 1886. III, 80 pp. (Schriften des Institutum Judaicum in Berlin, 1) *LJ*

0478  Dalman, Gustaf Hermann (1855–): *Kurzgefaßtes Handbuch der Mission unter Israel.* Mit Beiträgen von P.E. Gottheil und R. Bieling. Berlin: Reuther & Reichard, 1893. 144 pp. (Schriften des Institutum Judaicum in Berlin, 18) *LJ*

0479  Dalman, Gustaf Hermann (1855–): *Der leidende und der sterbende Messias der Synagoge im ersten nachchristlichen Jahrhundert.* Berlin: H. Reuther's Verlag, 1888. IV, 100 pp. (Schriften des Institutum Judaicum in Berlin, 4) *LJ*

0480  Dalman, Gustaf Hermann (1855–): Statistik der Judenmission. *SaH, Rundschau* (1888) 1–67. *LJ*

0481  Dalman, Gustaf Hermann (1855–): *Die Tötung Ungläubiger nach talmudisch-rabbinischem Recht. Quellenmäßig dargestellt.* Leipzig: Dörffling & Franke, 1885. 48 pp. (Schriften des Institutum Judaicum in Leipzig, 6) *LJ*

0482  Dalman, Gustaf Hermann (1855–): *Was sagt der Talmud über Jesum? Beantwortet durch Mitteilung des unzensierten Grundtextes der talmudischen Angaben.* Berlin: Reuther und Reichard, 1891. 19 pp. (Schriften des Institutum Judaicum in Berlin, 11) *LJ*

0483  Dalman, Gustaf Hermann (1855–): *Zinzendorf und Lieberkühn; Studien zur Geschichte der Judenmission.* Leipzig: J.C. Hinrichs' Verlag, 1903. 102 pp. (Schriften des Institutum Judaicum in Berlin, 32) *LJ*

0484  Damaschke, Adolf (1865–): *Manchestertum, Antisemitismus oder Bodenbesitzreform.* Berlin: Deutscher Bund für Bodenbesitzreform, 1891. 32 pp. *LJ*

0485  Dammann, Karl (1839–1914): *Gutachten über das jüdische Schlachtverfahren.* Hannover: L. Ey, 1886. 13 pp. *LJ*

0486 Danzer, Dionys: *Das Judentum im Hopfenhandel.* Leipzig: H. Beyer, 1888. 40 pp. *Unseen*

Offprint from: *Unverfälschte Worte.*

0487 Dasbach, Georg Friedrich: *Der Wucher im trierischen Lande.* Trier: Verlag der Paulinus-Druckerei, 1887. 32 pp. *LJ*

Offprint from: *Schriften des Vereins für Sozialpolitik,* vol. 35: Wucher auf dem Lande.

0488 Davis, Gustav (1856-1951): *An die sehr gescheidten Herren Juden in Oesterreich.* Wien: Typ. G. David & A. Keiss, 1901. 32 pp. (Blitzblaue Briefe, 2) *LJ*

0489 Deckert, Joseph (1843-1901): *Die ältesten und gefährlichsten Feinde des Christentums und christlichen Volkes.* Konferenzreden. Mit einem Anhang: Zivilehe und Judenehe. Wien: Verlag des "Sendbote des hl. Joseph," 1895. VIII, 103 pp. *LJ*

0490 Deckert, Joseph (1843-1901): *Arbeit, Lohn und Wucher; 3 Konferenzreden gehalten am 7., 8. und 9. September 1894 in der St. Joseph-Votiv-Kirche zu Weinhaus, Wien.* Wien: H. Kirsch, 1895. 40 pp. *LC*

0491 Deckert, Joseph (1843-1901): *Briefe eines Erleuchteten; oder, Ehrenrettung des Exrabbi Itzig Schmul Bloch.* Aus dem Hebräischen übers. und hrsg. von Jainkef Frischmaul, pseud. Wien: Selbstverlag, 1894. 1 vol. (without paging). *LJ*

0492 Deckert, Joseph (1843-1901): *Der ewige Jude "Ahasver." Zur Abwehr eines philosemitischen Mahnrufes in der Judenfrage.* Wien: Selbstverlag, 1894. 31 pp. *LJ*

Offprint from: *Sendbote des hl. Joseph.*

0493 Deckert, Joseph (1843-1901): *Inquisition und Hexenprozeße; Greuel der Katholischen Kirche.* Wien: "Sendbote des hl. Joseph" in Komm. bei H. Kirsch, 1896. 34 pp. *LTA*

Offprint from: *Sendbote des hl. Joseph.*

0494 Deckert, Joseph (1843-1901): *Juden raus; 8 Konferenzreden gehalten in der St. Joseph-Votivkirche zu Wien-Weinhaus vom 26.4. bis 3.5.1896.* Wien: 1896. 62 pp. *LC*

0495 Deckert, Joseph (1843-1901): *Jüdische Richter, Judeneid, Kol-nidre! Zeitgemäße Gedanken.* Wien: Verlag der "Reichspost," 1898. 24 pp. *LJ*

0496  Deckert, Joseph (1843–1901): *Kann ein Katholik Antisemit sein.* Dresden: Typ. Glöss, 1893. 40 pp. *LJ*

0497  Deckert, Joseph (1843–1901): *Ein Ritualmord.* Aktenmäßig nachgewiesen. Dresden: Typ. Glöss, 1893. 39 pp. *LJ*

0498  Delitzsch, Elisabeth: *Franz Delitzsch als Freund Israels; ein Gedenkblatt.* Leipzig: Evangelisch-LutherischerZentralverein für Mission unter Israel, 1910. 31 pp. (Kleine Schriften zur Judenmission, 5) *LJ*

0499  Delitzsch, Franz Julius (1813–1890): *Die Bibel und der Wein; ein Thirza-Vortrag.* Leipzig: Dörffling & Franke, 1885. 18 pp. (Schriften des Institutum Judaicum in Leipzig, 7) *LJ*

0500  Delitzsch, Franz Julius (1813–1890): *Ein Briefwechsel zwischen Franz Delitzsch in Leipzig und Dr. Hermann Riess, praktischer Arzt in Auspitz.* Hrsg. von Dr. Riess. Wien: Typ. von M. Knöpflmacher, 1888. 38 pp. *LJ*

0501  Delitzsch, Franz Julius (1813–1890): *Dokumente der nationaljüdischen christgläubigen Bewegung in Südrussland.* In deutscher Uebersetzung. 2. rev. Aufl. Erlangen: A. Deichert, 1885. VIII, 44 pp. *LJ*

0502  Delitzsch, Franz Julius (1813–1890): *Ernste Fragen an die Gebildeten jüdischer Religion.* 2. Aufl. Leipzig: W. Faber, 1890. 68 pp. (Schriften des Institutum Judaicum, 18–19) *LJ*

0503  Delitzsch, Franz Julius (1813–1890): *Fortgesetzte Dokumente der national-jüdischen christgläubigen Bewegung in Südrussland. Nebst Aufruf zur Herstellung eines Bethauses für die christgläubigen aus Israel in Kischinew.* Erlangen: W. Faber, 1885. 40 pp. (Schriften des Institutum Judaicum in Leipzig, 5) *LF*

0504  Delitzsch, Franz Julius (1813–1890): *Jesus und Hillel. Mit Rücksicht auf Renan und Geiger verglichen.* 2. rev. Aufl. Erlangen: A. Deichert, 1867. 42 pp. (Schriften für Israel, 1) *LJ*

0505  Delitzsch, Franz Julius (1813–1890): *Der Katechismus des XIX.Jahrhunderts für Juden und Protestanten, den auch Katholiken lesen dürfen.* Mainz: Franz Kirchheim, 1877. VIII, 272 pp. *Unseen*

0506  Delitzsch, Franz Julius (1813–1890): *Messianische Weissagungen in geschichtlicher Folge.* Leipzig: W. Faber, 1890. VII, 160 pp. *LJ*

0507  Delitzsch, Franz Julius (1813–1890): *Der Messias als Versöhner; ein begründetes Zeugnis an die Gebildeten im jüdischen Volke.* Hrsg. von der

Londoner Gesellschaft zur Verbreitung des Christentums unter den Juden. Straßburg: Typ. Berger-Levrault, 1867. 24 pp. *LJ*

0508 Delitzsch, Franz Julius (1813–1890): *Missionsvorträge. Gesammelt aus "Saat auf Hoffnung."* Leipzig: W. Faber, 1892. 32 pp. (Schriften des Institutum Judaicum in Leipzig, 32) *Unseen*

0509 Delitzsch, Franz Julius (1813–1890): *Die Polemik des Rabbinismus; eine wissenschaftliche Antwort ohne Polemik für die Rabbiner und ihre Genossen.* Paderborn: 1883. 108 pp. *Unseen*

0510 Delitzsch, Franz Julius (1813–1890): *Eine Uebersetzungsarbeit von 52 Jahren. Aueßerungen des weiland Professor Franz Delitzsch über sein hebräisches Neues Testament für die Förderer seiner Verbreitung zusammengestellt.* Leipzig: W. Faber, 1891. 40 pp. (Schriften des Institutum Judaicum in Leipzig, 27) *LJ*

0511 Delitzsch, Franz Julius (1813–1890): *Welche Anforderungen stellt die Gegenwart an die Missions-Arbeit unter den Juden? Vortrag gehalten zu Berlin, am 28. April 1870 in der Konferenz der in Deutschland an der Verbreitung des Christentum unter den Juden arbeitenden Gesellschaften.* Erlangen: A. Deichert, 1870. 14 pp. *LJ*

0512 Dellin, Martin-Gregor: Erlösung dem Erlöser; eine Betrachtung zu Richard Wagner. *Neohelicon* 11, 2 (1984) 8–26. *LJ*

0513 Dembo, Isaak Aleksandrovich (1846–1906): *Das Schächten im Vergleich mit anderen Schlachtmethoden. Vom Standpunkte der Humanität und Hygiene beleuchtet.* Leipzig: H. Roskoschny, 1894. VIII, 116 pp. *LJ*

0514 Denkler, Horst: Flugblätter in "jüdisch-deutschem" Dialekt aus dem revolutionären Berlin, 1848–49. *TAJfDG* 6 (1977) 215–257. *LJ*

0515 *Denkschrift die gesetzliche Regelung des jüdischen Gemeindewesens betreffend.* Trier: 1874. 7 pp. *LC*

0516 *Denkschrift über die Judenfrage in dem Gesetz betreffend den Austritt aus der Kirche.* Berlin: Typ. M. Driesner, 1873. 14 pp. *LJ*

0517 *Denkschrift über die Stellung der Juden in Oesterreich.* Wien: C. Gerold's Sohn, 1859. 45 pp. *LC*

0518 *Der Juden Anteil am Verbrechen. Auf Grund der amtlichen Statistik über die Tätigkeit der Schwurgerichte in vergleichender Darstellung mit den christlichen Konfessionen.* Berlin: O. Hentze's Verlag, 1881. 19 pp. *LJ*

0519  *Der Wahrheit die Ehre.* Leipzig: A. Lorentz, 1893. 60 pp. *LTA*

0520  Deschner, Günther: *Gobineau und Deutschland; der Einfluß J.A. de Gobineaus "Essai sur l'inégalité des races humaines" auf die deutsche Geistesgeschichte, 1853-1917.* Erlangen: 1968. 194, XIX pp. *LC*
       Diss.

0521  Deutsch, Gotthard (1859-1921): *Antisemitism in Austria.* Chicago: 190-. 22 pp. *LJ*
       Offprint from: *The Reform Advocate.*

0522  Deutsch, Ignaz: *Beitrag zur Geschichte jüdischer Tartuffe. Eingaben an das ehemalige K.K. Kultusministerium in Wien über die religiösen Zustände der Juden in Oesterreich.* Hrsg. von Israel Levi Kohn. Leipzig: C.G. Naumann, 1864. 47 pp. *LJ*

0523  Deutsch-Israelitischer Gemeindebund, Leipzig: *Grundsätze der jüdischen Sittenlehre.* Berlin: Typ. H. Friedländer, 188-. 8 pp. *LJ*

0524  Deutsch-Israelitischer Gemeindebund, Leipzig: *Hat das Judentum dem Wucherunwesen Vorschub geleistet.* Leipzig: Typ. W. Schuwardt, 1879. 17 pp. *LJ*

0525  Deutsch-Israelitischer Gemeindebund, Leipzig: *Neue Satzungen des Deutsch-Israelitischen Gemeindebund bestätigt durch den allerhöchsten Erlaß vom 13. Februar 1899.* Berlin: Typ. R. Boll, 1899. 10 pp. *LJ*

0526  Deutsch-Israelitischer Gemeindebund, Leipzig: *Die preußisch-jüdische Gemeinde-Verfassungsfrage; Denkschrift zur Verteidigung des einheitlichen Rechtsverbandes der jüdischen Gemeinden in Deutschland.* Leipzig: 1873. 27 pp. *LJ*

0527  Deutsch-Israelitischer Gemeindebund, Leipzig: *Stenographisches Protokoll des Deutsch-Israelitischen Verbandstages, Sonntag, den 22. Juni 1913 . . .* Berlin: Typ. R. Boll, 1913. 46 pp. *LJ*

0528  Deutsch-Israelitischer Gemeindebund, Leipzig: *Verhandlungen der vom Deutsch-Israelitischen Gemeindebunde einberufenen Konferenz über die Frage der Wanderbettelei am Sonntag den 5. Dezember 1909 zu Berlin.* Berlin: Typ. R. Boll, 1909. 28 pp. *LJ*

0529  Deutsch-Israelitischer Gemeindebund, Leipzig: *Was ist, will und leistet der Deutsch-Israelitische Gemeindebund.* Berlin: Typ. R. Boll, 1904. 20 pp. *LJ*

0530 Deutsch-Konservative Partei: *Konservatives Handbuch; hrsg. unter Mitwirkung der parlamentarischen Vertretung der konservativen Parteien.* 2. umgearb. Aufl. Berlin: H. Walther, 1894. VIII, 444 pp. *LF*

0531 Deutsch-Konservative Partei: *Stenographischer Bericht über den Allgemeinen Konservativen Parteitag abgehalten am 8. Dezember 1892 zu Berlin.* Hrsg. vom Wahlverein der Deutschen Konservativen. Berlin: W. Issleib, 1893. 48 pp. *Unseen*

0532 Deutsch-Konservative Partei: *Unkorrigierter stenographischer Bericht über die Verhandlungen des Allgemeinen Konservativen Parteitages in Dresden am 2. Februar 1898.* Hrsg. vom Wahlverein der Deutschen Konservativen. Berlin: W. Müller, 1898. 98 pp. *Unseen*

0533 Deutsch-Konservative Partei: *Vademecum zur Reichstagswahl 1893; Wahlbüchlein zur Aufklärung für die deutschen Wähler in Stadt und Land.* Hrsg. von dem Wahlverein der Deutschen Konservativen. Berlin: W. Issleib, 1893. 72 pp. *Unseen*

0534 *Deutsche Antisemiten-Chronik 1888–1894. Eine Sammlung von Tatsachen zur Unterhaltung und Belehrung für jedermann.* Zürich: Schabelitz, 1894. 205 pp. *LJ*

0535 *Deutsche Parteichronik 1866–1890: mit besonderer Berücksichtigung der Nationalliberalen Partei.* Leipzig: Renger, 1892. III, 112 pp. *Unseen*

0536 Deutscher Antisemiten-Bund: *Der Talmud.* Berlin: M. Schulze, 188– . 8 pp. (Flugschrift no. 2 des Deutschen Antisemiten Bundes, D.A.B.) *LJ*

0537 Deutscher Antisemiten-Bund: *Verhandlungsbericht des ersten Norddeutschen Antisemitentages abgehalten in den Germania-Sälen zu Berlin am 26.6.1892.* Berlin: Deutscher Antisemitenbund, 1892. 23 pp. *Unseen*

0538 Deutscher Reformverein, Kassel: *Programm und Statut.* Kassel: Typ. Richarts, [n.d.]. 8 pp. *LJ*

0539 Deutscher Reichstag: *Aus den Verhandlungen des Deutschen Reichstags über das Schächten, 18. Mai, 1887; 25. April 1899 und 9. Mai 1899.* Berlin: 1909. 37 pp. *LJ*

0540 Deutscher Reichstag: *Die Tätigkeit der Antisemiten in der abgelaufenen Sitzungsperiode des Reichstages.* Leipzig: Th. Fritsch, 1890. 4 pp. *Unseen*

0541  *Deutscher Schulverein.* Wien: Schönerer, 1886. 14 pp. *LJ*
Offprint from: *Unverfälschte Deutsche Worte.*

0542  Deutscher Schulverein: *Auflösung der Wiener akademischen Ortsgruppe.* Wien: J.Ursin, 1886. 13 pp. *LJ*

0543  Deutscher Studententag: *Beschlüße des ersten deutschen Studententages, 8. und 9. Eismond, 1897.* Wien: Statzer, 1897. 48 pp. *Unseen*

0544  Diebold, Bernhard (1886–): *Der Fall Wagner; eine Revision.* Frankfurt a.M.: Frankfurter Societäts-Druckerei, 1928. 46 pp. *LJ*
Deals chiefly with Nietzsche's views on Wagner.

0545  Diethart, Otto: *Rassennot — Rassenschutz.* Hamburg: Deutschnationale Buchhdlg. und Verlags-Gesellschaft, 1913. 30 pp. *LJ*

0546  *Ein Disput über die Judenfrage.* Leipzig: Th. Fritsch, 1887. 8 pp. (Brennende Fragen, 15) *LJ*

0547  Dithmar (minister): Protestantismus und Antisemitismus. *Die Zukunft* 4 (1893) 613–616. *LJ*

0548  Dittmar, Peter: "Der zwölfjaehrige Christus im Tempel von Adolph Menzel"; ein Beispiel für den Antijudaismus im 19. Jahrhundert. *Idea; Jahrbuch der Hamburger Kunsthalle* 6 (1987) 81–96. *LB*

0549  Dix, Arthur (1875–): *Der Bund der Landwirte: Entstehung, Wesen und politische Tätigkeit.* Berlin: Buchhdlg. der Nationalliberalen Partei, 1909. 68 pp. *Unseen*

0550  Dönges, Emil: *Die Judenfrage.* 5. Aufl. Dillenburg: Dönges, 1912. 24 pp. *LJ*

0551  Donath, Endre: *Solymosi, Eszter legujabb társadalami regény két kőtetben.* I. kőtet 11. füzet. Klausenburg: 1883. 32 pp. *Unseen*

0552  Dorée, Nadage: *Jesu wahres Christentum; von einer Jüdin.* 2. Aufl. Berlin: S. Calvary, 1904. 135 pp. *LJ*

0553  Doron, Joachim: Rassenbewußtsein und naturwissenschaftliches Denken im deutschen Zionismus während der Wilhelminischen Aera. *TAJfDG* 9 (1980) 389–427. *LJ*

0554  *Dr. M. Luther und die Juden; den deutschen Studenten gewidmet, von einem Kommilitonen.* Leipzig: Frohberg, 1881. 32 pp. *Unseen*

0555  *Dr. Martin Luther und die Judenfrage.* Elberfeld: E. Seitz, 189-. 8 pp. *LJ*

0556  Dreifus, Markus G.: *Ehrerbietige Vorstellung der israelitischen Gemeinden Endingen und Lengnau an den Hohen Vorort in Bern zu Händen der Hohen Bundesrevisions-Kommission und der Hohen Tagsatzung.* Zum Drucke befördert durch die beiden Gemeinden zur Erlangung der bürgerlichen Gleichstellung aufgestellte Kommission. Baden: J. Zehnder, 1848. 19 pp. *Unseen*

0557  Dreifuss, Emil: *Juden in Bern; ein Gang durch die Jahrhunderte.* Bern: Verlag der Verbandsdruckerei Betadruck, 1983. 64 pp. *LJ*

0558  Dreydorff, Johann Georg: *Warum und wie? Ein Beitrag zur Lösung der Judenfrage.* Berlin: P. Mödebeck, 1895. 27 pp. *LJ*

0559  Dreyfus, Robert (1873–1939): *La vie et les prophéties du comte de Gobineau.* Paris: Calmann-Lévy, 1905. 344 pp. *LJ*

0560  Dubnow, Semen Markovich (1860–1941): *History of the Jews.* Tr. from the Russian. 4th definitive rev. Ed. Moshe Spiegel. South Brunswick: T. Yoseloff, 1967–1973. 10 vols. in 5. *LJ*

0561  Dubnow, Semen Markovich (1860–1941): *Die neueste Geschichte des jüdischen Volkes.* Autorisierte Uebersetzung aus dem Russischen von A. Steinberg. Berlin: Jüdischer Verlag, 1925–29. 10 vols. *LJ*

Partial contents — Vol. 9: *Das Zeitalter der zweiten Emanzipation, 1848–1881*, pp. 319–394. Vol. 10: *Die antisemitische Bewegung und die große Wanderung, 1880–1900*, pp. 11–118, 406–427. See also English translation, item no. 0560

0562  Dubnow, Semen Markovich (1860–1941): *Die neueste Geschichte des jüdischen Volkes, 1789–1914.* Deutsch von Alexander Eliasberg. Berlin: Jüdischer Verlag, 1920–1923. 3 vols. *LJ*

Partial contents — Vol. 2, pt. 3: *Das Zeitalter der zweiten Emanzipation 1848–1881*, pp. 309–383, 476–481. Vol. 3, pt. 4: *Die Epoche der zweiten Reaktion 1881–1914*, pp. 3–105, 269–270, 327–372, 458–482, 496–519.

0563  Düding, Dieter: *Der Nationalsoziale Verein 1896–1903; Versuch einer parteipolitischen Synthese von Nationalismus, Sozialismus und Liberalismus.* München: Oldenbourg, 1972. 211 pp. (Studien zur Geschichte des 19ten Jahrhunderts, 6) *LF*

0564  Dühring, Eugen Karl (1833–1921): *Soziale Rettung durch wirkliches Recht statt Raubpolitik und Knechtsjuristerei.* Leipzig: O.R. Reisland, 1907. VIII, 315 pp. *LTA*

0565  Dühring, Eugen Karl (1833–1921): *Die Ueberschätzung Lessing's und dessen Anwaltschaft für die Juden.* Karlsruhe: H. Reuther, 1881. VI, 93 pp. *LJ*

0566  Duggan, Paul R.: German-Jewish Relations in the Wilhelminian Period.; Comments on the Papers of Marjorie Lamberti and Werner T. Angress. *LBIYB* 17 (1972) 43–54. *LJ*

0567  Dukmeyer, Friedrich: *Kritik der reinen und praktischen Unvernuft in der gemeinen Verjudung.* 7. unveränd. Aufl. Berlin: E. Rentzel, 1892. 48 pp. *LJ*

0568  Duschak, Moritz (1815–1890): *Mittel gegen die falschen Blutbeschuldigungen, nebst einem Anhang zur Sage und Geschichte Polens.* Krakau: Typ. Fischer und Deutscher, 1883. II, 66 pp. *LJ*

0569  Duschak, Moritz (1815–1890): *Die Moral der Evangelien und des Talmud; eine vergleichende Studie im Geiste unserer Zeit.* Breslau: W. Jacobsohn, 1885. 58 pp. *LJ*

   An answer to August Rohling's *Der Talmudjude.*

0570  Eberle, Josef: *Großmacht Presse: Enthüllungen für Zeitungsgläubige, Forderungen für Männer.* München: K. Ohlinger, 1912. VII, 262 pp. *LJ*

0571  Eberstein, Alfred von: *1892 (achtzehnhundert . . .).* Wiesbaden: Selbstverlag des Verfassers, 1893. 70 pp. *LJ*

0572  Eberstein, Alfred von: *Hervortreten des Judentums seit Anfang dieses Jahrhunderts.* Wiesbaden: Typ. G. Weiser, 1893. 15 pp. *LJ*

0573  Eberswalde. Synagogengemeinde: *Replik der Synagogen-Gemeinde auf die Eingabe des Tierschutzvereins, betreffend Verbot des jüdisch-rituellen Schlachtverfahrens "Schächtens."* Eberswalde: 1906. 39 l. *LJ*

0574  *Der echte "Talmud-Auszug (Schulchan-Aruch)"; enthaltend die wichtigsten bisher übersetzten, noch heute gültigen Gesetze der jüdischen Religion.* Berlin: Dewald, 1892. 4 pp. *Unseen*

0575  Ecker, Jakob (1851–1912): *Der "Judenspiegel" im Lichte der Wahrheit; eine wissenschaftliche Untersuchung.* Paderborn: Verlag der Bonifacius-Druckerei, 1884. XVII, 74 pp. *LJ*

0576  Eckert, Willehard Paul: Ludwig Philippson und seine "Allgemeine Zeitung des Judentums" [AZJ] in den Jahren 1848/49 — Die Revolution im Spiegel der Zeitung. *Studia Judaica Austriaca* 1 (1974) 112–125. *LJ*

0577 Eckstein, Adolf (1857–1935): *Die bayerischen Parlamentarier jüdischen Glaubens*. Bamberg: Verlag der Handels-Druckerei, 1902. 47 pp. *LJ*

0578 Eckstein, Adolf (1857–1935): Die Emanzipationsbestrebungen in Bayern. *MGWJ* 54 (1910) 257–267, 474–480. *LJ*

0579 Eckstein, Adolf (1857–1935): *Der Kampf der Juden um ihre Emanzipation in Bayern*. Auf Grund handschriftlichen Quellenmaterials. Fürth: G. Rosenberg, 1905. VIII, 127 pp. *LJ*

0580 Eckstein, Gustav: "Das Rassenproblem unter besonderer Berücksichtigung der theoretischen Grundlagen der jüdischen Rassenfrage," von Ignaz Zollschan. *N.Z.* 29, 1 (1910–1911) 60–63. *LJ*

0581 Edinger, Dora: Bertha Pappenheim; a German-Jewish Feminist. *J.S.St.* 20 (1958) 180–186. *LJ*

0582 Eduard, Daniel: *Dem Friedensfürsten, sein unveräußerlicher Vorzug bewahrt; offenes Sendschreiben an den Herrn Oberrabbiner Dr. Frankel mit Beziehung auf seinen jüngst gehaltenen Festvortrag*. Breslau: A. Goschorsky, 1855. 29 pp. *LJ*

0583 *Eduard von Hartmann und seine Judenfreundschaft*. Magdeburg: Israelitische Wochenschrift, 1885. 31 pp. *LJ*

0584 Effertz, Otto: *Einige Worte zur Judenfrage*. 2. verm. Aufl. Berlin: G.A. Dewald, 1892. VII, 107 pp. *LJ*

0585 Eger, Heinrich: *Formulierte Vorschläge zur Gesetzgebung gegen den Wucher auf dem Lande*. Marburg: N.G. Elwert, 1893. 51 pp. *LTA*

0586 Eheberg, Karl Theodor von (1855–): Die neueste Wuchergesetzgebung und die bäuerliche Kreditnot. *Schmollers Jahrbuch für Gesetzgebung, Verwaltung und Volkswirtschaft im Deutschen Reich* 19 (1895) 442–463. *LJ*

0587 Ehrke, Thomas: *Antisemitismus in der Medizin im Spiegel der "Mitteilungen aus dem Verein zur Abwehr des Antisemitismus" 1891–1931*. Giessen: Gahmig, 1978. 118 pp. *LJ*

0588 Ehrlich, Ernst Ludwig: Das Jahr 1912 in der Geschichte der Juden in Deutschland. *Forschung am Judentum. Festschrift zum 60. Geburtstag von Rabbiner Dr. H.C. Lothar Rothschild. Dargereicht von der Vereinigung für Religiös-Liberales Judentum in der Schweiz*. Bern, 1970. Pp. 127–141. *LJ*

0589   Ehrmann, Herz: *Tier-Schutz und Menschen-Trutz. Sämtliche für und gegen das Schächten geltend gemachten Momente.* Kritisch beleuchtet nebst einer Sammlung aller älteren und neueren Gutachten hervorragender Fachgelehrten . . . Frankfurt a.M.: I. Kauffmann, 1885. 167 pp. *LJ*

0590   Einig, Peter: *Offene Antwort an Herrn Abgeordneten Adolf Stoecker, Hof- und Domprediger a.D. in Berlin.* Trier: Paulinus Druckerei, 1895. 32 pp. *LJ*
       Offprint from: Zeitschrift *Pastor Bonus.*

0591   *Einige Worte des Aufschlußes über die beabsichtigte sogenannte Israelitische Synode zu Augsburg. Von einem Freunde der Wahrheit.* Mainz: Le Roux'sche Hofbuchhdlg., 1871. 12 pp. *LJ*

0592   Eisen, Arnold M: Nietzsche and the Jews Reconsidered. *J.S.St.* 48 (1986) 1–14. *LJ*

0593   Eisenmenger, Johann Andreas (1654–1704): *Entdecktes Judentum. Das ist; wortgetreue Verdeutschung der wichtigsten Stellen des Talmuds. Zeitgemäß überarbeitet und hrsg. von Franz Xaver Schiefer.* Dresden: Brandner, 1893. 591 pp. *LJ*

0594   Eisenmenger, Johann Andreas (1654–1704): *Die Sittenlehre der Juden; Zusammenstellung rabbinischer Lehren und jüdischer Sittengesetze, dem Talmud und Schulchan Aruch entnommen.* Veröffentlicht auf Grund des eidlichen Gutachtens des gerichtlichen Sachverständigen Prof. Dr. Jakob Ecker in Trier. Stuttgart: Deutsch-Völkischer Schutz- und Trutzbund, 1885. 16 pp. *LJ*

0595   Elbogen Friedrich: *Ein Mahnruf an das arbeitende Volk. (Die Arbeiter und der Antisemitismus).* Wien: Selbstverlag, 1885. 16 pp. (Economic pamphlets, 137) *Unseen*

0596   Elbogen, Ismar (1874–1973): *Die Geschichte der Juden in Deutschland.* Frankfurt a.M.: Europäische Verlagsanstalt, 1966. Pp. 172–283. (Bibliotheca Judaica) *LJ*

0597   Elbogen, Ismar (1874–1973): *Ein Jahrhundert jüdischen Lebens; die Geschichte des neuzeitlichen Judentums.* Hrsg. von Ellen Littman. Frankfurt a.M.: Europäische Verlagsanstalt, 1967. Pp. 35–58, 61–62, 102–120, 151–201, 264–287, 379–394. (Bibliotheca Judaica) *LJ*

0598   Eliav, Mordechai: Philippsons Allgemeine Zeitung des Judentums [AZJ] und Erez Israel. *LBI Bull.* 12 (1969) 155–182. *LJ*

0599   Eliav, Mordechai: Zur Vorgeschichte der jüdischen Nationalbewegung in Deutschland. *LBI Bull.* 12 (1969) 282–314. *LJ*

0600 Ellenbogen, Wilhelm (1863–1951): Die Gemeinderatswahlen in Wien. *N.Z.* 14, 1 (1895–96) 21–25. *LJ*

About the election victory of Karl Lueger and his party, the clericals.

0601 Elmayer-Vestenbrugg, Rudolf von (1881–): *Georg Ritter von Schönerer; der Vater des politischen Antisemitismus, von einem, der ihn selbst erlebt hat.* München: F. Eher, Nachf, 1936. 140 pp. *LJ*

0602 Emanuel, B.: Ueber den Zionismus. *N.Z.* 13 (1894–1895) 599–603. *LJ*

0603 Die Emanzipation der Juden in Holstein. *MGWJ* 12 (1863) 347–355. *LJ*

0604 Emmerich, Wolfgang: *Zur Kritik der Volkstumsideologie.* Frankfurt a.M.: Suhrkamp, 1971. Pp. 7–94. *LC*

0605 Endlich, Johann Quirin: *Eine Stimme gegen die Judenemanzipation.* Wien: Mayer und Comp., 1859. 41 pp. *Unseen*

0606 *Das Endziel des Judentums. Entweder — oder: Atheismus oder Christentum.* Breslau: Dülfers Verlag, 1887. 38 pp. *Unseen*

0607 Engel de Janosi, Joseph (1851–): *Das Antisemitentum in der Musik.* Zürich: Almathea-Verlag, 1933. 284 pp. *LB*

Deals mainly with Richard Wagner's anti-Jewish views.

0608 Engel, Joseph: *Richard Wagner's "Das Judentum in der Musik." Eine Abwehr.* Leipzig: O. Leiner, 1869. 32 pp. *LJ*

0609 Engelbert, Hermann: *Ist das Schlachten der Tiere nach jüdischem Ritus wirklich Tierquälerei? Ein Wort der Verwahrung und der Abwehr.* St. Gallen: Zollikofer, 1867. 16 pp. *LJ*

Offprint from: *Tagblatt der Stadt St. Gallen, 27th February, 1867.*

0610 Engelbert, Hermann: *Das Schächten und die Bouterole; Denkschrift für den Hohen Großen Rat des Kantons St. Gallen zur Beleuchtung des diesbezüglichen regierungsrätlichen Antrags und mit Zugrundlegung der neuesten mitab- gedruckten Gutachten von Adam Bagge u.a.* St. Gallen: Zollikofersche Buchdruckerei, 1876. 47 pp. *LJ*

0611 Engelbert, Hermann: *Statistik des Judentums im Deutschen Reich ausschließlich Preußens und in der Schweiz.* Frankfurt a.M.: Kauffmann, 1875. XII, 100 pp. *LJ*

0612  Engelmann, Hans: *Die Entwicklung des Antisemitismus im 19. Jahrhundert und Adolf Stoeckers "Antijüdische Bewegung."* Erlangen: 1953. 146 pp. *LC* Diss. 1953.

0613  Engelmann, Hans: *Kirche am Abgrund; Stoecker und seine antijüdische Bewegung.* Berlin: Institut Kirche und Judentum, 1984. 185 pp. (Studien zu jüdischem Volk und christlicher Gemeinde, 5) *LJ*

0614  Engels, Friedrich (1820–1895): Ein privater Brief Friedrich Engels', veröffentlicht in der Sozial-Demokratischen Arbeiter Zeitung Wiens, am 9. Mai 1890. *Victor Adlers Aufsätze: Reden und Briefe.* Wien: Verlag der Wiener Volksbuchhandlung, 1922. Pp. 6–8. *LF*

0615  Engländer, Martin: *Die auffallend häufigen Krankheitserscheinungen der jüdischen Rasse.* Wien: J.L. Pollak, 1902. 46 pp. *LJ*

0616  Epstein, M.: Review on Werner Sombarts "Die Juden und das Wirtschaftsleben." *The Economic Journal* 21 (1911) 445–447. *Unseen*

0617  Erasmus, Siegfried: *Die Juden in der ersten deutschen Nationalversammlung.* Weimar: Fink, 1941. 104 pp. (Thüringer Untersuchungen zur Judenfrage, 5) *LB*

0618  Erb, Reiner: *Die Nachtseite der Judenemanzipation; der Widerstand gegen die Integration der Juden in Deutschland, 1780–1860.* Berlin: Metropol, 1989. 303 pp. *LJ*

0619  Erbsreich, Kunibert: *Brauchen die Juden Christenblut? Entgegnung auf den von Prof. Strack in der "Evangelischen Kirchenzeitung" veröffentlichten Aufsatz "Tísza-Eszlár — oder brauchen die Juden Christenblut." Eine kulturhistorische Studie.* Berlin: M. Schulze, 1882. 23 pp. *Unseen*

0620  Erdmannsdörffer, Hans Gustav: *Dem Abgrunde zu! Die deutschsoziale Reformpartei in kritischer Betrachtung.* Hannover: R. Werther, 1898. 46 pp. *Unseen*

0621  Erdmannsdörffer, Hans Gustav: *Die Juden und die Cholera; eine intolerante Schrift.* Leipzig: R. Werther, 1892. 32 pp. *LC*

0622  *Erklärung! Im Vertrauen auf den Beistand Gottes erklären wir, die unterzeichneten Rabbiner der jüdischen Gemeinden Deutschlands zur Steuer der Wahrheit gegenüber falschen Vorstellungen, die über das Schrifttum und die Sittenlehre des Judentums verbreitet werden, was folgt . . .* Berlin: Itzkowski, 1893. 2 l. *LC*

0623 *Ernest Renans Vortrag über das Judentum vom Gesichtspunkt der Rasse und der Religion 1883 im Vergleich zu seinem früheren Aueßerungen über das Judentum in den Werken: Histoire des origines du Christianisme u.a., 1873-1879.* Berlin: F. Luckhardt, 1884. 22 pp. *LJ*

0624 Ernst, Ludwig: *Kalte und warme Herzen; ein Nachtrag zur Broschüre "Kein Judenstaat, sondern Gewissensfreiheit."* 2. verm. Aufl. Leipzig: Literarische Anstalt, 1896. 12, IV pp. *LJ*

0625 Ernst, Ludwig: *Kein Judenstaat, sondern Gewissensfreiheit! Eine Entgegnung auf Theodor Herzl's "Der Judenstaat."* 2. Aufl. Leipzig: Literarische Anstalt, 1896. 23 pp. *LJ*

0626 Ernst, W. von: *Noch etwas vom besiegten Germanentum. Offener Brief an die Herren Marr u.a. über sein Buch: Der Sieg des Judentums über das Germanentum.* Dresden: Grumbkow, 1879. 23 pp. *LJ*

0627 Eschelbacher, Josef (1848-1916): *Das Judentum im Urteile der modernen protestantischen Theologie.* Leipzig: G. Fock, 1907. 64 pp. (Schriften hrsg. von der Gesellschaft zur Förderung der Wissenschaft des Judentums) *LJ*

0628 Eschelbacher, Max (1880-1964): Das jüngste Bild vom Judentum. *Ost und West* 11 (1911) col. 1042-1052; 12 (1912) col. 114-123 *LJ*

0629 Escherich, A.: Die Judenemanzipationsfrage vom naturhistorischen Standpunkt. *Deutsche Vierteljahrsschrift* 1, 4 (1848) 97-118. *LJ*

0630 Escherich, A.: Der Judenstamm in naturhistorischer Beziehung. *Das Ausland* (1880) 453-456, 474-476, 483-488, 509-513, 536-539. *LF*

0631 Ettinger, Samuel (1919-1988): The Modern Period. Pt. 6. *The History of the Jewish People.* Ed. H.H. Ben-Sasson. Cambridge, Mass.: Harvard University Press, 1969. Pp. 727-1075. *LJ*

0632 Ettinger, Samuel (1919-1988): The Origins of Modern Antisemitism. *Dispersion and Unity; Journal on Zionism and the Jewish World* 9 (1969) 17-37. *LJ*

0633 Ettinger, Samuel (1919-1988): *Vom 17. Jahrhundert bis zur Gegenwart. Die Neuzeit.* München: C.H. Beck, 1980. Pp. 81-236. (Geschichte des jüdischen Volkes, ed. H.H. Ben-Sasson, 3) *LJ*

0634  *Étudiants socialistes révolutionnaires internationalistes de Paris: Antisémitisme et sionisme; rapport présenté au Congrès ouvrier révolutionnaire international.* Paris: Édition du "Libertaire," 1900. Pp. 332–339. (L'Humanité Nouvelle, 7) *Unseen*

0635  Eulenberg, Herbert (1876–1949): Die Judenfrage. *Die Zukunft* 67 (1909) 213–215. *LJ*

0636  Evangelisch-Lutherischer Zentralverein für die Mission unter Israel: *Bericht über den Evangelisch-Lutherischen Zentralverein für die Mission an Israel.* Leipzig: Typ. Ackermann, 1891. 15 pp. *LJ*

0637  Evangelisch-Lutherischer Zentralverein für Judenmission: Bericht über die 25-jährige Tätigkeit des Evangelisch-LutherischenZentralvereins für Judenmission. *SaH* 33 (1896) 177–192. *LJ*

0638  Ewald, Ferdinand Christian (1802–1874): *Aboda Sara; oder, Der Götzendienst. Ein Traktat aus dem Talmud vollständig übers. mit Einleitung und Anmerkungen.* Nürnberg: J.P. Raw, 1856. XXV, 546 pp. *LJ*

0639  F.O.: *Der Wucher und der deutsche Michel.* Berlin: E. Rentzel, 1895. 36 pp. (Die Knute, 1) *LTA*

0640  Faber, Wilhelm: *Der Kampf des Lichtes mit der Finsternis unter den Juden Osteuropas; Beobachtungen und Erlebnisse.* Leipzig: Akademische Buchhdlg, 1891. 31 pp. (Schriften des Institutum Judaicum in Leipzig, 28) *LJ*

0641  Fährmann, Willi: Die Buschoff Affäre in Xanten. *Das Bild des Juden in der Volks- und Jugendliteratur vom 18. Jahrhundert bis 1945.* Ed. Heinrich Pleticha. Würzburg: Königshausen und Neumann, 1985. Pp. 127–139. *LJ*

0642  *Der Fahrkartenschwindel auf norddeutschen Bahnen.* Leipzig: H. Beyer, 1894. 40 pp. *LF*

0643  Falk, Kurt: *Antisemitismus und Sozialdemokratie.* Hrsg. vom Rheinischen Agitationskomitee. 2. Aufl. Elberfeld: Typ. Grimpe, 1892. 34 pp. *Unseen*

0644  *Der Fall Buschhoff; aktenmäßige Darstellung des Xantener Knabenmord-Prozeßes.* Frankfurt a.M.: C. Könitzer, 1892. 56 pp. (Interessante Kriminalfälle, 2) *Unseen*

0645  *Der Fall Buschoff; die Untersuchung über den Xantener Knabenmord, von einem Eingeweihten.* Berlin: Vaterländische Verlagsanstalt, 1892. 42 pp. *LJ*

0646 *Der Fall Buschoff; die Untersuchung über den Xantener Knabenmord, von einem Eingeweihten.* 2. stark verm. Aufl. Berlin: Vaterländische Verlagsanstalt, 1892. 56 pp. *Unseen*

0647 Fall, Gustav Heinrich: *Die rechtliche Stellung der Juden in Oesterreich.* Wien: Verlag des Vereins zur Abwehr des Antisemitismus, 1892. 14 pp. *LJ*

0648 *Der Fall Hilsner; ein europäisches Justizverbrechen.* Berlin: A.W. Hayn, 1911. 24 pp. *LJ*

0649 *Der falsche und der wahre Stoecker. Von einem Mitgliede des Deutschen Reichstages.* 2. Aufl. Leipzig: Böhme, 1885. 31 pp. *Unseen*

0650 Farbstein, David (1868–1953): *Der Zionismus und die Judenfrage, ökonomisch und ethisch.* Bern: Steiger, 1898. 29 pp. *LJ*

0651 Fassbender, Martin: *Das Vorkommen des Wuchers auf dem Lande im Bereiche der Provinz Westfalen. Bericht im Auftrage des Westfälischen Bauernvereins erstattet.* [n.p.]: 188–. 227–244 pp. *LJ*

0652 Fauerholdt, Irenius Vilhelm Ravn (1877–): Aufgaben der Judenmission. *Jahrbuch der sächsischen Missionskonferenz für 1913* (1914) 121–131. *Unseen*

0653 Fauerholdt, Irenius Vilhelm Ravn (1877–): *Joseph Rabinowitsch; eine prophetische Gestalt aus dem neueren Judentum.* Leipzig: Evangelisch-Lutherischer Zentralverein für Mission unter Israel, 1914. 35 pp. (Kleine Schriften zur Judenmission, 8) *LJ*

0654 Fauerholdt, Irenius Vilhelm Ravn (1877–): *Warum Mission unter den Juden; ein Friedenswort zur Verständigung mit aufrichtig und gebildeten Juden.* Leipzig: Ev.-Luth. Zentralverein für Mission unter Israel, 1912. 30 pp. (Kleine Schriften zur Judenmission, 7) *Unseen*

0655 Fay, Theodor Sedgwick: *Denkschrift der Vereinigten Staaten von Nordamerika gerichtet an Schweizerischen Bundesrat betreffend die Zulassung der nordamerikanischen Israeliten zur Niederlassung in der Schweiz vom 26. Mai 1859.* Biel: Typ. E. Schüler, 1863. 45 pp. *LJ*

0656 Feder, Ernst (1881–1964): Paul Nathan, the Man and His Work. *LBIYB* 3 (1958). 60–80. *LJ*

0657 Feist, Siegmund (1865–): Zur Geschichte des Rassenantisemitismus in Deutschland. *ZfGJD* [Ed. Ismar Elbogen] 2 (1930) 40–67. *LJ*

0658  Felden, Klemens (1936-): *Die Uebernahme des antisemitischen Stereotyps als soziale Norm durch die bürgerliche Gesellschaft Deutschlands, 1875-1900.* Heidelberg: 1965. 175 l. *LJ*

Diss. Heidelberg 1965.

0659  Fern, Athanasius: *Die jüdische Moral und das Blutmysterium.* Leipzig: H. Beyer, 1893. 47 pp. *LJ*

0660  Fetscher, Iring: Zur Entstehung des politischen Antisemitismus in Deutschland. *Antisemitismus: zur Pathologie der bürgerlichen Gesellschaft.* Eds. Hermann Huss, Andreas Schröder. Frankfurt a.M.: Europäische Verlagsanstalt, 1965. Pp. 9-33. (Sammlung "res novae," 36) *LJ*

0661  Fetscher, Iring, ed.: *Marxisten gegen Antisemitismus.* Hamburg: Hoffmann und Campe, 1974. Pp. 54-119. (Standpunkte) *LJ*

0662  Feuchtwanger, Ludwig: Besprechung von Felix Theilhaber's "Der Untergang der deutschen Juden" München 1911 und Werner Sombart's "Die Zukunft der Juden," Leipzig 1912. *Schmollers Jahrbuch für Wirtschafts- und Sozialwissenschaften* 36 (1912) 954-957. *LJ*

0663  Feuchtwanger, Ludwig: Die Juden und das Wirtschaftsleben. *Schmollers Jahrbuch für Wirtschafts- und Sozialwissenschaften* 35 (1911) 1433-1466. *LJ*

About Werner Sombart's book: *Die Juden und das Wirtschaftsleben.*

0664  Feuchtwanger, Ludwig: Die Juden und die Entstehung des Kapitalismus. *März* 6 (1912) 92-99. *LJ*

0665  Feuerstein, Otto: *Der Ritualmord in Konitz an dem Gymnasiasten Ernst Winter.* Lorch: K. Rohm, 1925. 24 pp. *LC*

0666  Fey, Carl: *Bausteine zur Geschichte des Antisemitismus, von F. Carley, pseud.* Zell i. W.: Fr. Bauer, 1895. 15 pp. *LF*

0667  Field, Geoffrey G.: Antisemitism and Weltpolitik. *LBIYB* 18 (1973) 65-91. *LJ*

0668  Field, Geoffrey G.: *Evangelist of Race; The Germanic Vision of Houston Stewart Chamberlain.* New York: Columbia University Press, 1981. X, 565 pp. *LJ*

0669  Findel, Joseph Gabriel: *Der freimaurerische Kampf für die Juden und die Settegast'sche Großloge.* Leipzig: Verlag von J. G. Findel, 1894. 24 pp. *LJ*

0670  Findel, Joseph Gabriel: *Die Juden als Freimaurer; zur Beleuchtung der gegenwärtigen Krisis innerhalb des deutschen Maurertums.* Leipzig: J.G. Findel, 1893. 39 pp. *LJ*

0671  Finot, Jean (1858–1922): *The Death-Agony of the "Science of Race."* Tr. from the French. London: Stead, 1911. 164 pp. *LTA*

0672  Fischer, Bernard (1821–1906): *Talmud und Schulchan Aruch; ein Vortrag für den Leipziger Antisemiten Verein.* Leipzig: Teutonia-Verlag, 1902. 110 pp. *LJ*

0673  Fischer, Karl (1755–1844): *Gutmeinung über den Talmud der Hebräer; verfasst von Karl Fischer, k.k. Zensor, Revisor und Translator im hebräischen Fache zu Prag.* Nach einem Manuskript von 1802. Wien: A. Hölder, 1883. VI, 112 pp. *LJ*

Preface by E. Baumgarten.

0674  Fischer, Karl (1840–): *Heinrich von Treitschke und sein Wort über unser Judentum; ein Wort zur Verständigung.* München-Gladbach: Schellmann's Verlag, 1880. 40 pp. *LJ*

0675  Fischer, Rolf: *Entwicklungsstufen des Antisemitismus in Ungarn, 1869–1939; die Zerstörung der magyarisch-jüdischen Symbiose.* München: R. Oldenbourg, 1988. 206 pp. (Südosteuropäische Arbeiten. Süd-Ost Institut, München, 85) *LJ*

0676  Fishberg, Maurice (1872–1934): *The Jews; a Study of Race and Environment.* London: Walter Scott Publ. Co., 1911. XIX, 578 pp. *LJ*

0677  Fishberg, Maurice (1872–1934): *Die Rassenmerkmale der Juden; eine Einführung in ihre Anthropologie.* München: E. Reinhardt, 1913. XI, 272 pp. *LJ*

0678  Fishberg, Maurice (1872–1934): *Zur Frage der Herkunft des blonden Elements im Judentum.* Berlin: 1907. 11 pp. *LJ*

Offprint from: *ZfDSJ* 3 (1907).

0679  Förster, Bernhard (1843–): *Das Verhältnis des modernen Judentums zur deutschen Kunst.* Vortrag gehalten im Berliner Zweigverein des Bayreuther Patronats-Vereins. Berlin: M. Schulze, 1881. IV, 59 pp. *LJ*

0680  Förster, Paul (1844–): *Deutsch-Sozial. Gedenke, daß Du ein Deutscher bist; einer für alle! Alle für einen!* Leipzig: H. Beyer, [n.d.]. 7 pp. *LJ*

0681  Förster, Paul (1844–): *Deutsche Bildung, deutscher Glaube, deutsche Erziehung; eine Streitschrift.* Leipzig: E. Wunderlich, 1906. V, 147 pp. *Unseen*

0682    Förster, Paul (1844–): *Der Fall Ahlwardt in der öffentlichen Meinung und im Lichte der Wahrheit. Eine Streitschrift.* 3. veränd. und um ein Nachwort über den Prozeß "Judenflinten" verm. Aufl. Berlin: G.A. Dewald, 1893. 56 pp. *LJ*

0683    Förster, Paul (1844–): *Der Jude und die deutsche Frau; Vortrag.* Leipzig: Deutscher Verlag, 1892. 22 pp. *Unseen*

0684    Förster, Paul (1844–): *Der Kampf des deutschen Volkes um sein Dasein; Vortrag.* Leipzig: Th. Fritsch, 1889. 20 pp. *LTA*

0685    Förster, Paul (1844–): *Talmud und Schulchan-Aruch; ein Vortrag gehalten am 11. April 1892 zu Breslau.* Berlin: G.A. Dewald, 1892. IV, 54 pp. *LJ*
         Appendix: Programm der Deutsch-Sozialen (antisemitischen) Partei. 4 pp.

0686    Förster, Paul (1844–): *Unsere deutsch-sozialen Grundsätze und Forderungen; Vortrag gehalten auf dem Deutsch-Sozialen Parteitage in Breslau.* Mit dem Programm der Deutsch-Sozialen (antisemitischen) Partei. Leipzig: H. Beyer, 1892. 26 pp. (Sammlung deutsch-sozialer Flugschriften, 4) *Unseen*

0687    Förster, Paul (1844–): *Wie stehen wir — wie siegen wir? Rede gehalten zur Begründung der "Antisemitischen Vereinigung für Norddeutschland auf dem 2. Norddeutschen Antisemitentage am 17. September 1893.* Berlin: Geschäftsstelle der "Antisemitischen Vereinigung für Norddeutschland," 1893. 16 pp. *LJ*

0688    Fränkel, Ernst: Der Beitrag der deutschen Juden auf wirtschaftlichem Gebiet. *Judentum, Schicksal, Wesen und Gegenwart. Bd. 2.* Eds. F. Böhm, W. Dirks. Wiesbaden: Steiner, 1975. Pp. 552–600. *LJ*

0689    Fränkel, Michael: Heinrich Graetz und Theodor Mommsen. *Der Morgen* 11 (1935–1936) 365–366. *LJ*

0690    Frank, Arnold: *Die Hamburger Judenmission in Wort und Bild.* Hamburg: Verlag des "Zionsfreund," 1912. 40 pp. *LJ*

0691    Frank, Arnold, ed.: *Zeugen aus Israel.* Hamburg: "Zionsfreund," 19––. 80 pp. *LJ*

0692    Frank, Friedrich (1832–1904): *Nachträge zu "Der Ritualmord vor den Gerichtshöfen der Wahrheit und Gerechtigkeit." I. Die letzten Schlupfwinkel des Ritualmord-Aberglaubens. II. Der Ritualmord-Aberglaube in den letzten Zügen. III. Das Leichenbegängnis des Ritualmord-Aberglaubens.* Regensburg: Verlagsanstalt vormals J.G. Manz, 1902. 100 pp. *LJ*

0693  Frank, Friedrich (1832–1904): *Der Ritualmord vor den Gerichtshöfen der Wahrheit und der Gerechtigkeit*. 2. Aufl. Regensburg: Verlagsanstalt vormals J.G. Manz, 1901. VIII, 327 pp. *LJ*

0694  Frank, Friedrich (1832–1904): *Die Schächtfrage vor der Bayerischen Volksvertretung*. 7. Aufl. Würzburg: L. Woerl, 1894. 48 pp. *LJ*

0695  Frank, Walter (1905–1945): "Apostata" Maximilian Harden und das Wilhelminische Deutschland. *Forschungen zur Judenfrage* 3 (1937) 9–60. *LJ*

0696  Frank, Walter (1905–1945): *Hofprediger Stoecker und die christlichsoziale Bewegung*. Berlin: Reimar Hobbing, 1928. 450 pp. *LJ*

0697  Frankel, Zacharias (1801–1875): *Der Judeneid vor den Preußichen Kammern*. Breslau: Schletter, 1861. 10 pp. *LJ*

0698  Frankfurter, S.: *Erste Generalversammlung des Vereins für die jüdischen Interessen des Rheinlands am Mittwoch den 19. Marcheschwan 5663 in Köln im Englischen Saale der "Philharmonie."* Mainz: Wirth, 1902. 40 pp. *LJ*

0699  Frankl-Grün, Adolf (1847–1916): *Houston Stewart Chamberlain's Beurteilung des Judentums*. Wien: M. Waizner, 1901. 18 pp. *LJ*

Offprint from: *Neuzeit*, 1901.

0700  Frantz, Gustav Adolph Constantin (1817–1891): Eugen Stamm, Ahasverus; oder, Ueber die Judenfrage. *Schriften und Leben*. Pt. 1: *1817–1856*. Heidelberg: C. Winter, 1907. Pp. 59–65. (Heidelberger Abhandlungen, 19) *LJ*

No more published.

0701  Frantz, Gustav Adolph Constantin (1817–1891): *Die Weltpolitik unter besonderer Bezugnahme auf Deutschland*. Chemnitz: E. Schmeitzner, 1882–83. 3 vols. *Unseen*

0702  Franz, A.: *Das Judentum und sein Verhältnis zu anderen Religionen. Nach christlichen und jüdischen Quellen*. 2. Aufl. Stuttgart: A. Pfautsch, 1890. 136 pp. *LC*

0703  Franz, Eckhart G.: Fabrikanten, Kaufleute, Bankiers; die wirtschaftliche Bedeutung der Darmstädter Juden im beginnenden Industriezeitalter. *Juden als Darmstädter Bürger*. Darmstadt: E. Röther, 1984. Pp. 93–106. *LJ*

0704  Franz, Georg: Judentum. *Liberalismus; die deutschliberale Bewegung in der Habsburgischen Monarchie*. München: Callwey, 1955. Pp. 186–214. *LJ*

0705  Franzos, Karl Emil (1848–1904): Aus Briefen Berthold Auerbach's. *ZfGJD* [Ed. Ludwig Geiger] 4 (1890) 385–391. *LJ*

About antisemitism and the antisemitic movement in the second half of the 19th century.

0706  Frei, Philipp: Pathologie der jüdischen Volksseele. *Die Zukunft* 26 (1899) 339–344. *LJ*

0707  Freie Vereinigung für die Interessen des Orthodoxen Judentums: *Auszüge aus dem Gutachten der hervorragendsten Physiologen und Veterinärärzte über das Schächten*. 2. durch neueingegangeneGutachten verm. Aufl. Frankfurt a.M.: Typ. L. Golde, 1887. 66 pp. *LJ*

0708  Freie Vereinigung für die Interessen des Orthodoxen Judentums: *Gutachten betreffend das jüdischrituelle Schlachtverfahren, das Schächten, auf Grund experimenteller Untersuchungen, erstattet vom Geheimen Regierungsrat Dr. Tereg*. Berlin: Typ. Braunbeck — Gutenberg, 1911–1913. 16, 9 pp. *LJ*

0709  Freie Vereinigung für die Interessen des Orthodoxen Judentums: *Gutachten der hervorragendsten Physiologen und Veterinärärzte über das Schächten*. 3. durch neu eingegangene Gutachten verm. Aufl. Frankfurt a.M.: Typ. L. Golde, 1894. 186 pp. *LJ*

0710  Freimann, Aron (1871–1948): Deutsche anonyme Schriften über Juden und Judentum. *Zeitschrift für Hebräische Bibliographie* 18 (1915) 73–101. *LJ*

0711  Freimann, Aron (1871–1948), ed.: Judenmission, Taufe, Proselyten. *Stadtbibliothek Frankfurt am Main. Katalog der Judaica und Hebraica. Bd. 1. Judaica* Frankfurt a.M., 1932. Pp. 416–427. *LJ*

Reprinted: Graz, 1968.

0712  Freimut, Bernardin: *Altjüdische Religionsgeheimnisse und neujüdische Praktiken im Lichte christlicher Wahrheit; eine Kritik des Talmud*. 2. verm. und verb. Aufl. von "Jüdische Religionsgeheimnisse nach dem Talmud." Münster: A. Russell, 1893. 144 pp. *LJ*

0713  Freimut, Bernardin: *Jüdische Religionsgeheimnisse nach dem Talmud; eine Lehre und Mahnung für das christliche Volk*. München-Gladbach: Josef Schlesiger, 1893. 83 pp. *LJ*

0714  Freimut, Bernardin: *Die jüdischen Blutmorde von ihrem ersten Erscheinen in der Geschichte bis auf unsere Zeit*. Münster: A. Russell, 1895. 187 pp. *LJ*

0715 Freund, Ismar (1876–1956): *Die Rechtsstellung der Juden im preußischen Volksschulrecht, nebst den bezüglichen Gesetzen, Verordnungen und Entscheidungen.* Im Auftrage des Verbandes der Deutschen Juden systematisch dargestellt. Berlin: J. Guttentag, 1908. XIII, 401 pp. *LJ*

0716 Freund, Ismar (1876–1956): *Staat, Kirche und Judentum in Preußen.* Berlin: M. Poppelauer, 1911. 109–138 pp. *LJ*
Offprint from: *Jahrbuch für Jüdische Geschichte und Literatur.*

0717 Freund, Leonhard: *Hinaus! Ein Kulturbild aus dem Zentrum des modernen deutschen Antisemitismus. Skizziert von O. Lenhard, pseud.* Leipzig: A. Thiele, 1889. VII, 56 pp. *LJ*

0718 Freund, Wilhelm (1806–1894): *Die Anstellung israelitischer Lehrer an preußischen Gymnasien und Realschulen; ein Wort zur Aufhellung der Sachlage, von einem praktischen Schulmann.* Berlin: Springer, 1860. 43 pp. *LJ*

0719 Freytag, Gustav (1816–1895): Der Streit über das Judentum in der Musik. *Die Grenzboten* 28 (1869) 336. *LJ*
Against Wagner's critique. The author's opinion: Music composed by Jews should be accepted as music and not as Jewish music.

0720 Fricke, Dieter: Antisemitische Parteien, 1879–1894. *Die bürgerlichen Parteien in Deutschland; Handbuch der Geschichte der bürgerlichen Parteien. Bd. 1.* Berlin: Das Europäische Buch, 1968. Pp. 36–40. *LJ*

0721 Fricke, Dieter: Bund der Landwirte. *Die bürgerlichen Parteien in Deutschland. Handbuch der Geschichte der bürgerlichen Parteien. Bd. 1.* Berlin: Das Europäische Buch, 1968. Pp. 129–149. *LJ*

0722 Friedegg, Ernst: *Millionen und Millionäre; wie die Riesenvermögen entstehen.* Berlin: Vita Deutsches Verlagshaus, 1914. 383 pp. *LTA*

0723 Friedemann, Adolf: *Was will der Zionismus.* Hrsg. von der Zionistischen Vereinigung für Deutschland. Berlin: Jüdische Rundschau, 1903. 39 pp. *LJ*

0724 Friedemann, Edmund (1847–): *Das Judentum und Richard Wagner.* Berlin: W. Adolf & Comp., 1869. 15 pp. *LJ*

0725 Friedenheim, Constantin Ignatz Anton: *Des bekehrten Juden Caspar Josef Buch über die Torheiten und Geheimnisse des Judentums, nachgewiesen aus der Vernunft der Hl. Schrift, besonders dem Talmud und andern rabbinischen Schriften.* Neue Aufl. Würzburg: Halm, 1853. VIII, 114 pp. *Unseen*

0726  Friedenheim, Constantin Ignatz Anton: *Die Irrtümer und Geheimnisse des Judentums, nachgewiesen aus der Vernunft der Hl. Schrift, besonders aus dem Talmud und andern rabbinischen Schriften, von dem jüdischen Konvertiten K.J.A. Fr.* Neu hrsg. von Anton Christianus. Würzburg: Bucher, 1892. XI, 165 pp. *Unseen*

0727  Friedländer, Ernst (1841–1903): *Das Handlungshaus Joachim Moses Friedländer et Söhne zu Königsberg in Preußen für die Familie hrsg.* Hamburg: Petermann, 1913. 58 pp. *LC*

0728  Friedländer, Fritz: *Das Leben Gabriel Riessers; ein Beitrag zur inneren Geschichte Deutschlands im neunzehnten Jahrhundert.* Berlin: Philo-Verlag, 1926. 185 pp. *LJ*

0729  Friedländer, Hugo: *Der Brand der Synagoge in Neustettin; Verhandlung vor dem Schwurgericht in Cöslin vom 18. bis 22. Oktober 1883.* Redigiert nach den vom demselben prima vista niedergeschriebenen Zeitungsberichten. Cöslin: C.G. Henden, 1883. 51 pp. *LJ*

0730  Friedländer, Hugo: Die Ermordung des Gymnasiasten Ernst Winter. *Interessante Kriminal-Prozeße* Berlin: H. Barsdorf, 1911. Vol. 3, Pp. 75–136. *LJ*

0731  Friedländer, Hugo: Der Judenflinten Prozeß. *Interessante Kriminalprozeße von kulturhistorischer Bedeutung.* Berlin: Berliner Buchversand, 1921. Pp. 137–149. *LJ*

0732  Friedländer, Hugo: *Der Knabenmord in Xanten. Interessante Kriminalprozeße von kulturhistorischer Bedeutung.* Berlin: Verlag Berliner Buchversand, 1921. Pp. 67–88. *LJ*

0733  Friedländer, Hugo: *Der Knabenmord in Xanten vor dem Schwurgericht zu Cleve.* Cleve: W. Startz, 1892. 151 pp. *LJ*

0734  Friedländer, Hugo: Der Königliche Hof- und Domprediger Adolf Stoecker in dem Beleidigungsprozeß wider den Redakteur Heinrich Bäcker als Zeuge. *Interessante Kriminal-Prozeße. Bd. 4.* Berlin: H. Barsdorf, 1912. Pp. 104–175. *LJ*

0735  Friedländer, Hugo: Ein Nachspiel zu der Ermordung des Gymnasiasten Ernst Winter in Konitz. *Interessante Kriminal-Prozeße. Bd. 5.* Berlin: H. Barsdorf, 1912. Pp. 238–246. *LJ*

0736 Friedländer, Hugo: Ein "Ritualmord" Prozeß; eine Verhandlung vor dem Schwurgericht zu Danzig, April 1885. *Interessante Kriminal-Prozeße. Bd. 4.* Berlin: H. Barsdorf, 1912. Pp. 65–123. *LJ*

0737 Friedländer, Hugo: Der Synagogenbrand von Neustettin. *Interessante Kriminal-Prozeße.* Berlin: Berliner Buchversand, 1920. Pp. 13–134. *LJ*

0738 Friedländer, Markus Hirsch: *Zur Geschichte der Blutbeschuldigungen gegen die Juden im Mittelalter und in der Neuzeit, 1171–1883.* Nach den Quellen dargestellt. 3. Aufl. Brünn: B. Epstein, 1883. 32 pp. *LJ*

0739 Friedman, Elisha Michael: *Antisemitism; an Essay in Social Science.* [n.p.]: 1922. 8 pp. *LJ*

Offprint from: *Menorah Journal*, February 1922.

0740 Friedman, Isaiah: The Austro-Hungarian Government and Zionism. *J.S.St.* 27 (1965) 147–167, 236–249. *LJ*

0741 Friedman, Philip (1901–1960): *Die galizischen Juden im Kampfe um ihre Gleichberechtigung, 1848–1868.* Frankfurt: J. Kauffmann, 1929. VIII, 216 pp. (Veröffentlichungen des Dr. S.A. Bettelheim Memorial Foundation, 3) *LJ*

0742 Friedman, Philip (1901–1960): Die Judenfrage im galizischen Landtag, 1861–1868. *MGWJ* 72 (1928) 379–390, 457–477. *LJ*

0743 Friedrich, Johannes (1836–1917): *Die moderne Judenfrage nach ihrer geschichtlichen Entstehung und einzig möglichen Lösung. Ein Warn- und Mahnruf an das deutsche Volk.* Berlin: K. G. Wiegandt, 1894. 23 pp. *LJ*

0744 Fritsch, Theodor (1852–1933): *Beweismaterial gegen Jahwe.* 2. Aufl. Leipzig: Hammer-Verlag, 1911. 232 pp. *LJ*

This publication includes also the author's essay "Der falsche Gott."

0745 Fritsch, Theodor (1852–1933): *Halb-Antisemiten; ein Wort zur Klärung.* Leipzig: H. Beyer, 1893. 8 pp. *Unseen*

0746 Fritsch, Theodor (1852–1933): Zur Auseinandersetzung mit Driesmans. *Der Hammer* 11 (1912) 659–664. *LJ*

0747 *Fritz Reuter und die Juden.* Dresden: Glöss, 1895. 31 pp. *LJ*

0748 Frölich, Ernst: *Das Schächten — ein mosaischer Ritualgebrauch? Beitrag zur Lösung der Schächtfrage.* Potsdam: Selbstverlag, 1899. 31 pp. *LJ*

0749  Fromer, Jakob (1865–): Die Juden in der Wirtschaft. *Die Zukunft* 77 (1911) 103–115. *LJ*

A comment on Sombart's *Die Juden und das Wirtschaftsleben.*

0750  Fromer, Jakob (1865–): *Das Wesen des Judentums.* Berlin: Hüpeden & Merzyn, 1905. VII, 183 pp. (Kulturprobleme der Gegenwart, 2nd. ser., 1) *LJ*

0751  Frühling, Moritz: *Biographisches Handbuch der in der k. und k. Oesterr. Ungar. Armee und Kriegsmarine aktiv gedienten Offiziere, Aerzte, Truppenrechnungsführer und sonstigen Militärbeamten jüdischen Stammes.* Wien: Oester. Ungarn Juden im Heer und Marine, 1911. 224 pp. *LJ*

0752  Fuchs, Eugen (1856–1923): *"Die Zukunft der Juden." Ein Referat über Werner Sombarts Schrift.* Berlin: Central-Verein Deutscher Staatsbürger Jüdischen Glaubens, 1912. 20 pp. *LJ*

0753  Fuchs, Max: *Noch ein Wort über Richard Wagners Judentum in der Musik.* München: im Selbstverlage des Verfassers, 1869. 32 pp. *LF*

0754  Fürst, Arthur: *Christen und Juden; Licht- und Schattenbilder aus Kirche und Synagoge.* Straßburg: Straßburger Druckerei & Verlagsanstalt, 1892. IV, 316 pp. *LJ*

0755  Fürst, Arthur: Die jüdischen Realschulen in Deutschland. *MGWJ* 58 (1914) 430–453, 513–541. *LJ*

0756  *Fürst Bismarcks Verhältnis zum Glauben, insbesondere zum Judentum.* 2. Aufl. Leipzig: R. Friese, 1879. 16 pp. *LJ*

0757  Fürstenberg, Karl (1850–1933): *Die Lebensgeschichte eines Bankiers, 1870–1914.* Hrsg. von Hans Fürstenberg. Berlin: Ullstein, 1931. X, 577 pp. *LJ*

0758  Füssl, Wilhelm: Friedrich Julius Stahl; vom bayerischen Juden zum preußischen Konvertiten. *Geschichte und Kultur der Juden in Bayern.* Eds. Manfed Treml, Wolf Weigand. München, 1988. Pp. 121–128. *LJ*

0759  Ganzer, Karl Richard: Richard Wagner und das Judentum. *Forschungen zur Judenfrage* 3 (1937) 105–120. *LJ*

0760  Gaulke, Johannes (1869–): Judenfrage als Wirtschafts- und Rassenproblem. *Gegenwart* 31 (1902) 161–163. *LF*

0761  Gay, Peter: Die Begegnung mit der Moderne; die deutschen Juden in der Wilhelminischen Kultur. *Freud, Juden und andere Deutsche. Aus dem*

*Amerikanischen von Karl Berisch.* Hamburg: Hoffmann und Campe, 1986. Pp. 115–188. *LJ*

0762  Gay, Peter: Encounter with Modernism; German Jews in Wilhelminian Culture. *Freud, Jews and other Germans; Martyrs and Victims in Modernist Culture.* Oxford: Oxford University Press, 1978. Pp. 93–168. *LJ*

0763  Gay, Peter: Hermann Levi; a Study in Service and Self-Hatred. *Freud, Jews and other Germans; Masters and Victims in Modernist Culture.* Oxford: Oxford Univeristy Press, 1978. Pp. 207–237. *LJ*

German translation: Herman Levi; eine Studie über Unterwerfung und Selbsthaß. Published in *Freud, Juden und andere Deutsche*, 1986.

0764  Gedalius, Ed. E.: *Die jüdische Missionsfrage; im Sinne der Heiligen Schrift beleuchtet.* Berlin: Selbstverlag, 1891. 14 pp. *LJ*

0765  Gedalius, Ed. E.: *Wie begegnen wir dem Antisemitismus; ein Wort an meine jüdischen Volksgenossen.* Leipzig: W. Faber, 1893. 39 pp. *LJ*

0766  *Gedanken eines Juden.* Berlin: Walther und Apolant, 1885. 24 pp. *LJ*

0767  *Die geheime Geschäftssprache der Israeliten, Ein Hand- und Hilfsbuch für alle, welche mit Israeliten in Geschäftsverbindung stehen und der hebräischen Sprache, der sogenannenten Marktsprache unkundig sind.* 7. verm. Aufl. Neustadt an der Aisch: Engelhardt, 1886. 46 pp. *LJ*

0768  *Die geheime Geschäftssprache der Juden; ein Hand- und Hilfsbuch für alle, welche mit Juden in Geschäftsverbindung stehen und der hebräischen Sprache, der sogenannten Marktsprache unkundig sind.* Neue verm. Aufl. Neustadt an der Aisch: Engelhardt, 1900. 53 pp. *LJ*

0769  Geiger, Abraham (1810–1874): Ueber den Austritt aus dem Judentum. Ein aufgefundener Briefwechsel. *Nachgelassene Schriften. Bd. 1.* Berlin: L. Gerschel, 1875. Pp. 230–246. *LJ*

0770  Geiger, Abraham (1810–1874): *Ueber den Austritt aus dem Judentume; offenes Sendschreiben an Herrn M. Maass.* Breslau: J. U. Kern, 1858. 32 pp. *LJ*

0771  Geiger, Ludwig (1848–1919): *Geschichte der Juden in Berlin. Als Festschrift* . . . Berlin: J. v. Guttentag, 1871. IX, 358 pp. *LJ*

0772  Geiss, Imanuel: Die jüdische Frage auf dem Berliner Kongreß, 1878. *TAJfDG* 10 (1981) 413–422. *LJ*

0773  Gelber, Nathan Michael (1891–): The Berlin Congress. *LBIYB* 5 (1960) 221–247. *LJ*

0774  Gelber, Nathan Michael (1891–): The Intervention of German Jews at the Berliner Congress, 1878. *LBIYB* 5 (1960) 221–247. *LJ*

0775  Gellately, Robert: *The Politics of Economic Despair; Shopkeepers and German Politics 1890–1914.* London: Sage Publications, 1974. XVI, 317 pp. (Sage Studies in 20th Century History, 1) *LJ*

0776  Geller, Leo: *Gesetz betreffend die äußeren Rechtsverhältnisse der israelitischen Religionsgesellschaften. Mit Erläuterung aus den Materialien.* Wien: M. Perles, 1890. 32 pp. *Unseen*

0777  Geller, Leo, ed.: *Vorschriften betreffend die Verfassung der israelitischen Religionsgemeinschaft; Namenwesen und Matrikeln der Israeliten.* Mit Erläuterungen an den Materialien der Rechtssprechung. 2. erheblich verm. Aufl. Wien: M. Perles, 1896. 104 pp. *LC*

0778  George, Gustav: *Enthüllungen zur Konitzer Mordaffaire. Auf Grund eigener Ermittlungen und Beobachtungen.* Berlin: G. König, 1903. 78 pp. *LJ*

0779  Gerhard, C.J. Paul: *Lessing und Christus; ein Friedenswort an Israel.* Breslau: Max und Co., 1881. 31 pp. *Unseen*

0780  Gerhardt, Dagobert von (1831–1910): *Eine moderne Abendgesellschaft.* Berlin: Issleib, 1881. 64 pp. *LJ*

Pro and contra; dialogue about the Jewish question.

0781  Gerlach (Director of the Royal Veterinary School in Hannover): Ueber das Schächten vom physiologischen Standpunkte. *MGWJ* 16 (1867) 93–100. *LJ*

0782  Gerlach, Hans Christian: *Agitation und parlamentarische Wirksamkeit der deutschen Antisemitenparteien, 1873–1895.* Kiel: 1956. X, 247 l. *LC*

Diss. Kiel (ms), 1956.

0783  Gerlach, Hellmut von (1866–1935): *Erinnerungen eines Junkers.* Berlin: Die Welt am Montag, 1924. 158 pp. *LF*

0784  Gerlach, Hellmut von (1866–1935): *Von rechts nach links.* Zürich: Europa-Verlag, 1937. 275 pp. *LJ*

0785  Germanus, Michael, ed.: *Die Geheimnisse der Hölle; oder, Miss Diana Vaughan, ihre Bekehrung und ihre Enthüllungen über die Freimaurerei, den*

*Kultus und die Erscheinungen des Teufels in den palladistischen Triangeln.*
Feldkirch: Verlag des Pelikans, 1896. 101 pp. *LTA*

0786 Gersdorff, Julius: *Das internationale Judentum und die schwarze Magie; ein Beitrag zur Unduldsamkeit der jüdischen Nation.* Usingen: Selbstverlag, 1899. 16 pp. *Unseen*

0787 Gerson, Christian (1569–1627): *Der jüdische Talmud; Auslegung und Widerlegung.* Neu bearb. von Joseph Deckert. Wien: H. Kirsch, 1895. 250 pp. *LJ*

0788 Gerstenhauer, Max Robert: *Rassenlehre und Rassenpflege.* Leipzig: Armanen-Verlag R. Burger, 1913. 56 pp. *LJ*

"Verzeichnis der Rassenliteratur": Pp. 53–56.

0789 *Geschichte der Handelskammer zu Frankfurt a.M., 1707–1908; Beitrag zur Frankfurter Handelsgeschichte.* Frankfurt: J. Bär, 1908. XV, 1371 pp. *LF*

Ed. by the Handelskammer Frankfort o.M.

0790 *Geschriebene Photographien aus der Ersten Israelitischen Synode in Leipzig am 29. Juni 1869.* Berlin: L. Gerschel, 1869. IV, 38 pp. *LJ*

0791 Gesellschaft zur Beförderung des Christentums unter den Juden zu Berlin: *Bericht, 1823–1905.* Berlin: 1824–1905. *LJ*

0792 Gesellschaft zur Beförderung des Christentums unter den Juden zu Berlin: *Friedrich Albert Augusti, ein Bekehrter aus dem Judentum, der . . . als Prediger zu Eschenberge . . . sein Amt als ein wahrhaftiger Diener Jesu verwaltet und in einem Alter von beinahe 91 Jahren in's Land der Ruhe eingegangen ist.* 5. Aufl. Berlin: Selbstverlag, 1863. 36 pp. *LJ*

0793 Gesellschaft zur Beförderung des Christentums unter den Juden zu Berlin: *Fünfzig Jahre der Judenmission; eine Denkschrift zur fünfzigjährigen Jubelfeier der Berliner Gesellschaft zur Beförderung des Christentums unter den Juden und im Auftrage derselben verfasst, von W. Ziethe.* Berlin: Selbstverlag der Gesellschaft, 1872. 66 pp. *LJ*

0794 Gesellschaft zur Beförderung des Christentums unter den Juden zu Berlin: *Kurze Uebersicht der Geschichte der Gesellschaft . . . seit der Stiftung im Jahre 1822 bis zum Jahre 1853.* Berlin: Typ. Trowitzsch, 1854. 22 pp. *LJ*

0795 Gesellschaft zur Verbreitung der Handwerke und des Ackerbaus unter den Juden im Preußischen Staate: *Jahres-Bericht.* Berlin: 1896–1913. *LJ*

                                        

0796  Gesellschaft zur Verbreitung der Handwerke und des Ackerbaus unter den Juden im Preußischen Staate: *Revidiertes Statut*. Berlin: Typ. Boll, 1894. 13 pp. *LJ*

0797  Gesellschaft zur Verbreitung der Handwerke und des Ackerbaus unter den Juden im Preußischen Staate: *Satzung der Gesellschaft . . . Gegründet im Jahre 1812*. Berlin: Typ. L. Borchardt, 1902. 11 pp. *Unseen*

0798  *Gesetz betreffend die Verhältnisse der hiesigen Israelitischen Gemeinden. Auf Befehl E.H. Senats der Freien und Hansestadt Hamburg publiziert den 7. November, 1864*. Hamburg: Typ. Th. G. Meissner, 1864. 8 pp. *LTA*

0799  *Gibt es einen jüdischen Ritualmord? Verhandlungen über die Judenfrage im Hause der Oesterreichischen Abgeordneten am 10. und 16. November 1899*. Lorch: Rohm, 1922. 32 pp. *LF*

      Excerpts from *Staatsbürgerzeitung*, Berlin, 580, 12, December 1899.

0800  Giese, Wilhelm: *Die Herren Raab und von Liebermann der Deutsch-Sozialen Reformpartei*. Berlin: W. Giese, 1900. VIII, 110 pp. *Unseen*

0801  Giese, Wilhelm: *Die Juden und die deutsche Kriminalstatistik*. Leipzig: F.W. Grunow, 1893. 107 pp. *LJ*

0802  Gilbert, Felix (1905-), ed.: *Bankiers, Künstler und Gelehrte; unveröffentlichte Briefe der Familie Mendelssohn aus dem 19. Jahrhundert*. Tübingen: J.C.B. Mohr, 1975. LII, 328 pp. (Schriften wissenschaftlicher Abhandlungen des LBI, 31) *LJ*

0803  Gilbert, Felix (1905-): *Bismarckian Society's Image of the Jew*. New York: LBI, 1978. 31 pp. (Leo Baeck Memorial Lecture, 22) *LJ*

0804  Gildemeister, Johann (1812-1890): *Gutachten über den Schulchan Aruch*. Neu hrsg. von Adolf Tesdorpf. Neue Ausg. Lorch, Württemberg: Karl Rohm, 1921. 16 pp. *LJ*

      First published in 1892.

0805  Gildemeister, Johann (1812-1890): *Der Schulchan Aruch und was daran hängt; ein gerichtlich erfordertes Gutachten*. Bonn: Neusser, 1884. 16 pp. *LJ*

0806  Gilman, Sander L: Hofprediger Stoecker and the Wandering Jew. *J.S.St.* 19 (1968) 63-69. *LJ*

0807  Gladius, Dr.: *A tisza-eszlári ügy ismeretlen hullája. Orvosi szakvelemeny a közzétett bonczlelet alapjan*. Budapest: Z. Samuel, 1882. 38 pp. *LJ*

0808  Glagau, Otto (1834–1892): *Hofprediger Stoecker und sein Prozeß.* Berlin: Kulturkämpfer, 1885. 37 pp. (Der Kulturkämpfer, vol. 5, 120) *LJ*

0809  Glanz, Rudolf: *Geschichte des niederen jüdischen Volks in Deutschland; eine Studie des historischen Gaunertum, Bettelwesen und Vagantentum.* New York: Waldon Pr., 1968. 395 pp. *LB*

0810  Glatter, Eduard: *Ueber die Lebenschancen der Israeliten gegenüber den christlichen Konfessionen; biostatistische Studie.* Wetzlar: Rathgeber u. Cobet, 1856. 44 pp. *LJ*

0811  Glatzer, Nahum Norbert (1903–): Leopold Zunz and the Revolution of 1848. With the Publication of 4 Letters by Zunz. *LBIYB* 5 (1960) 122–139. *LJ*

0812  Gliksman, Arthur: *Der ärztliche Standesverein der Königsstadt, 1871–1921.* Berlin: 1922. 23 pp. *LTA*

0813  Gobineau, Joseph Arthur, Comte de (1816–1882): *Essai sur l'inegalité des races humaines.* Paris: Librairie de Firmin Didot, 1853–1855. 4 vols. *LJ*

0814  Gobineau, Joseph Arthur, Comte de (1816–1882): *Versuch über die Ungleichheit der Menschenrassen.* Deutsch von Ludwig Schemann. Stuttgart: F. Frommanns Verlag, 1898–1901. 4 vols. *LJ*

0815  *Götzendienst; Satiren.* Frankfurt a.M.: Verlag von W. Hartenfels, 1909. 62 pp. *LC*

0816  *Gold-Währung oder Doppel-Währung?* Leipzig: Th. Fritsch, 1887. 8 pp. (Brennende Fragen, 12) *LJ*

0817  Goldenberg, Berisch (1825–1898): *Die Assimilation der Juden.* Tarnopol: Selbstverlag, 1883. 36 pp. *LF*

0818  Goldenweiser, Emanuel Aleksandrovich (1883–1953): "Die Zukunft der Juden," by Werner Sombart; Review. *American Economic Review* 2 (1912) 678–679. *LJ*

0819  Goldhammer, Leo (1884–1949): Jewish Emigration from Austria-Hungary in 1848–1849. *YIVO Annual of Jewish Social Science* 9 (1954) 332–362. *LJ*

0820  Goldmann, Felix (1882–): *Taufjudentum und Antisemitismus.* Frankfurt a.M.: J. Kauffmann, 1914. 95 pp. *LJ*

0821  Goldmann, Felix (1882–): *Zionismus oder Liberalismus; Atheismus oder Religion.* Frankfurt a.M.: Voigt und Gluber, 1911. 79 pp. *LJ*

0822   Goldschmidt, Levin (1829–1897): An Prof. Heinrich von Treitschke, Berlin den
       4. Mai, 1881. *Ein Lebensbild in Briefen.* Berlin: Verlag Emil Goldschmidt,
       1898. Pp. 432–436. *LJ*

0823   Goldschmidt, Levin (1829–1897): *Zur Reichstagswahl vom 21. Februar und 2.*
       *März 1887.* Berlin: Puttkammer und Mühlbrecht, 1887. 61 pp. *LJ*

0824   Goldschneider, Anton: Die Entwicklung der jüdischen Bevölkerung in Preußen
       im 19. Jahrhundert, 1816–1875. *ZfDSJ* 3 (1907) 70–75. *LJ*

0825   Goldstein, Julius (1873–1929): *Moderne Rassentheorien; Vortrag gehalten in*
       *der Generalversammlung des Vereins zur Abwehr des Antisemitismus in Berlin*
       *am 9. Mai 1910.* Berlin: Braunsbeck und Gutenberg, 1910. 12 pp. *LTA*

0826   Goldstein, Julius (1873–1929): *Moritz Goldsteins "Deutsch-Jüdischer Parnass";*
       *kritische Bemerkungen.* [n.p.]: 191–. 16 pp. *LJ*

0827   Goldstein, Moritz: Die Juden und Europa. *Die Grenzboten* 72 (1913) 543–554.
       *LJ*

0828   Goldstücker, Eduard (1913–): Jews Between Czechs and Germans around 1848.
       *LBIYB* 17 (1972) 61–71. *LJ*

0829   Gompertz, G., comte de Gueldhonoren: *Sem-Min-Thora; Vorläufer des*
       *projektierten Weltkongreßes (Cosmoreligiös) behufs endgiltiger Lösung der*
       *"Judenfrage," von einem Semminthoranar.* Dresden: Albanus, 1891. 70 pp. *LJ*

0830   Gorel, Ludwig: *Das Blutmärchen, seine Entstehung und Folgen bis zu den*
       *jüngsten Vorgängen auf Korfu. An Hand der Geschichte dargestellt.* Berlin:
       Gnadenfeld & Co., 1891. 46 pp. *LJ*

0831   Goslar, Hans (1888–1945): *Jüdische Weltherrschaft! Phantasiegebilde oder*
       *Wirklichkeit?* Berlin: Philo-Verlag, 1910. 32 pp. *LJ*

0832   Goslar, Hans (1888–1945): *Die Krisis der jüdischen Jugend in Deutschland; ein*
       *Beitrag zur Geschichte der jüdischen Jugendbewegung.* Berlin: L. Lamm,
       1911. 32 pp. *LTA*

0833   Gotthelf, Jakob: *Die Rechtsverhältnisse der Juden in Bayern auf Grundlage der*
       *neuesten bayerischen Gesetze.* München: G. Franz, 1852. 196, VIII pp. *LJ*

0834   Grab, Walter: Der preußisch-deutsche Weg der Judenemanzipation. *Geschichte*
       *der Juden.* Ed. Franz Bautz. München: C.H. Beck, 1983. Pp. 140–164. *LJ*

0835 Grab, Walter , ed.: *Juden im Vormärz und in der Revolution von 1848.* Stuttgart: Burg Verlag, 1983. 400 pp. (Studien zur Geistesgeschichte, 3) *LJ*

0836 Graetz, Heinrich Hirsch (1817–1891): *Briefe an Moses Hess, 1861–1872.* Hrsg. von Edmund Silberner. Milano: Feltrinelli Editore, 1961. Pp. 326–400. *LJ*

Dedicated to the 100th anniversary of Moses Hess' book *Rom und Jerusalem.*

0837 Graetz, Heinrich Hirsch (1817–1891): *Briefwechsel einer englischen Dame über Judentum und Semitismus.* Stuttgart: Levy & Müller, 1883. 78 pp. *LJ*

0838 Graetz, Heinrich Hirsch (1817–1891): Erwiderung an Herrn von Treitschke. *Israelitische Wochenschrift* 10 (1879) 433–435. *LJ*

0839 Graetz, Heinrich Hirsch (1817–1891): *Gedanken einer Jüdin über das Judentum in Vergangenheit und Zukunft.* Stuttgart: Levy & Müller, 1885. 78 pp. *LJ*

0840 Graetz, Heinrich Hirsch (1817–1891): Mein letztes Wort an Professor von Treitschke. *Schlesische Presse* December 28 (1879) *Unseen*

Cited in Böhlich's *Berliner Antisemiten-Streit*, published 1965.

0841 Graetz, Heinrich Hirsch (1817–1891): Offener Brief an Herrn Prof. H.v. Treitschke. *Schlesische Zeitung.* December (1879) *Unseen*

0842 Graf, Armin: *Herrenhaus redivivus; der Fall Paasch im Preußischen Herrenhaus am 1. April 1892. Ein einstimmiges Verdikt dieses Hohen Hauses über die gemeingefährlichen Bestrebungen des internationalen Judentums . . . nebst einem Anhang über die Verjudung unserer Aristokratie.* Berlin: Kommissionsverlag G.A. Dewald, 1892. 32 pp. *LJ*

0843 Graf, Curt: *Das Recht der Israelitischen Religionsgemeinschaft im Königreich Sachsen.* Frankfurt a.M.: Kauffmann, 1914. 48 pp. *LJ*

0844 Grau, Wilhelm: *Heinrich von Treitschke und die Judenfrage.* München: C.H. Beck, 1934. Pp. 81–90. *LJ*

From: *Zeitwende*, November 1934.

0845 Grauenhorst, C: *Der Hofprediger Stoecker; seine Feinde und sein Prozeß.* Berlin: Selbstverlag, 1885. 27 pp. *LTA*

0846 Green, Max: *Die Judenfrage und der Schlüssel zu ihrer Lösung.* Aus dem Englischen übers. von Elisabeth Delitzsch. Leipzig: J.C. Hinrichs, 1911. VI, 119 pp. (Schriften des Institutum Delitzschianum, 3) *LJ*

0847  Gregor-Dellin, Martin: Erlösung dem Erlöser; eine Betrachtung zu Richard Wagner. *Neohelicon* 11 (1984) 9–26. *LJ*

0848  Greive, Hermann: *Geschichte des modernen Antisemitismus.* Darmstadt: Wissenschaftliche Buchgesellschaft, 1983. Pp. 1–103. *LJ*

0849  Greive, Hermann: Die gesellschaftliche Bedeutung der christlich-jüdischen Differenz. *Juden im wilhelminischen Deutschland, 1890–1914.* Tübingen: J.C.B. Mohr, 1976. Pp. 349–388. *LJ*

0850  Greive, Hermann: Der "umgekehrte Talmud" des völkischen Nationalismus. *Judaica; Beitraege zum Verständnis des jüdischen Schicksals in Vergangenheit und Gegenwart* 23 (1967) 1–27. *LJ*

0851  Greive, Hermann: Zu den Ursachen des Antisemitismus im deutschen Kaiserreich von 1870–71. *Judaica* 27 (1971) 184–192. *LJ*

0852  Grell, Hugo: *Der Alldeutsche Verband; seine Geschichte, seine Bestrebungen und Erfolge.* München: J.F. Lehmann, 1898. 25 pp. (Flugschriften des Alldeutschen Verbandes, 8) *Unseen*

0853  Griebel, Karl: *Das Judentum in der Naturheilkunde; nebst einem Vorschlag zur Reinhaltung der letzteren und einer Kritik der Kuhne- und Kneipkur.* Lichtenthal bei Baden-Baden: Selbstverlag, 1892. 39 pp. *LB*

0854  Grieswelle, Detlef: Antisemitismus in deutschen Studentenverbindungen des 19. Jahrhunderts. *Student und Hochschule im 19. Jahrhundert; Studien und Materialien.* Göttingen: Vandenhoek & Ruprecht, 1975. Pp. 366–379. (Studien zum Wandel von Gesellschaft und Bildung im 19ten Jahrhundert, 12) *LJ*

0855  Grimpen, Albert: *Die Eisenacher Einigung und die Magdeburger Spaltung der deutschen Antisemiten; zur Klärung der Parteiverhältnisse dargestellt.* Hamburg: A. Grimpen, 1904. 42 pp. *LC*

0856  Gröbler, F.: *Das Blutopfer der talmudischen Juden; eine Untersuchung der Frage, ob dieselben Christenblut zu geheimen Zwecken gebrauchen und ob der Talmud den Christenmord gestattet oder sogar zur Pflicht macht. Auf Grund sorgfältigen Quellenstudiums beleuchtet.* München: Gentner, 1883. 15 pp. *LJ*

0857  Grotewold, Christian (1873–): *Die Parteien des Deutschen Reichstages.* Leipzig: G.H. Wigand, 1908. 338 pp. (Die Politik des Deutschen Reiches in Einzeldarstellungen, 1) *Unseen*

0858  Grüneberg, Emil: *Grünebergs Enthüllungen über die Christlich-Soziale Partei der Herren Stoecker und Wagner.* Berlin: Volks-Zeitung, 1878. 8 pp. *LJ*

Offprint from: *Demokratische Blätter*, nos. 14, 15, 16.

0859   Gruenspan, Karl: *De rituele moord in de geschiedenis der volken.* Amsterdam: "De Ploeger," [n.d.]. 88 pp. *LTA*

0860   *"Die Grundlagen des 19. Jahrhunderts" von Houston Stewart Chamberlain; kritische Urteile.* München: F. Bruckmann, 1901. VIII, 108 pp. *LJ*

0861   Grunsfeld, M: *Aus dem Leben; oder, Jesus ist Sieger; eine Bekehrungsgeschichte, von ihm selbst erzählt.* 2. Aufl. Berlin: Selbstverlag, 1911. 38 pp. *LM*

0862   Grunwald, Kurt (1901-): Europe's Railways and Jewish Enterprise; German Jews as Pioneers of Railway Promotion. *LBIYB* 12 (1967) 163-209. *LJ*

0863   Grunwald, Max (1871-1953): *Geschichte der Wiener Juden bis 1914.* Wien: Selbstverlag der Israelitischen Kultusgemeinde, 1926. 80 pp. *LJ*

0864   Grunwald, Max (1871-1953): *Juden als Reeder und Seefahrer.* Berlin: Poppelauer, 1902. 13 pp. *LC*

0865   Grunwald, Max (1871-1953): *Zur Psychologie und Geschichte des Blutritualwahnes; der Prozeß Simon von Trient und Leopold Hilsner. Vortrag.* Berlin: S. Calvary & Co., 1906. 24 pp. *LJ*

0866   Güdemann, Moritz (1835-1918): "Die Juden und das Wirtschaftsleben." *MGWJ* 55 (1911) 257-275. *LJ*

0867   Güdemann, Moritz (1835-1918): Kinderschlächter. *Gegen die Antisemiten; eine Streitschrift, zusammengestellt von J.S. Bloch.* Wien: D. Löwy, 1882. Pp. 13-19. *Unseen*

0868   Günter, Michael: *Die Juden in Lippe von 1648 bis zur Emanzipation 1858.* Detmold: Naturwissenschaftlicher und Historischer Verein für das Land Lippe, 1973. 214 pp. (Sonderveröffentlichung des Naturwissenschaftlichen Vereins, 20) *LC*

0869   Guggenheim, Paul: *Zur Geschichte der Schweizer Juden.* Zürich: Typ. Kopp-Tanner, 1934. 16 pp. *LJ*

Offprint from: *Jüdische Presszentrale Zürich*, 1933, vol. 16.

0870   *Gutachten Ganganelli's — Clemens XIV — in Angelegenheit der Blutbeschuldigung der Juden. Aus dem Italienischen übersetzt von A. Berliner.* Berlin: Deutsch, 1888. 48 pp. *LJ*

0871 *Gutachten über das jüdisch-rituelle Schlachten, erstattet von den Herren: Adam Bagge, Berdez u.a.* [n.p.]: 18--. 29 pp. *Unseen*

0872 *Gutachten über das jüdisch-rituelle Schlachtverfahren, "Schächten."* Auszug aus dem Gutachten . . . Marburg: N.G. Elwert, 1897. 30 pp. *LJ*

0873 *Gutachten über das rituelle Schlachtverfahren, "Schächten."* Berlin: E. Apolant, 1894. XVI, 122 pp. *LJ*

Preface signed: Das Komite zur Abwehr Antisemitischer Angriffe.

0874 *Gutachten über das rituelle Schlachtverfahren, Schächten. Nachtrag zu der Gutachten-Sammlung über das jüdisch-rituelle Schlachtverfahren, "Schächten."* Berlin: Typ. H.S. Hermann, 1899. 11 pp. *LJ*

0875 *Gutachten über das rituelle Schlachtverfahren, "Schächten." Nachtrag zu der Gutachten-Sammlung . . .* Berlin: Typ. H.S. Hermann, 1902. 44 pp. *LJ*

0876 *Gutachten über das rituelle Schlachtverfahren, "Schächten": Neues Gutachten über das jüdisch-rituelle Schlachtverfahren, "Schächten."* Gesammelt von *Hirsch Hildesheimer.* Hrsg. vom Verband der Deutschen Juden. Berlin: G. Braunbeck & Gutenberg-Druckerei, 1908. 70 pp. *LJ*

Preface, February 1909. Initiated by the "Kommission zur Abwehr gegen das Schächten gerichtete Angriffe."

0877 Gutman, Robert William: *Richard Wagner; the Man, his Mind and his Music.* London: Secker & Warburg, 1968. XX, 490 pp. *LJ*

0878 Gutmann, Moses: *Richard Wagner, der Judenfresser; Entgegnung auf Wagners Schrift "Das Judentum in der Musik."* Dresden: Conrad Weiske, 1869. 17 pp. *LB*

0879 Gutteridge, Richard Joseph Cooke: *Open the Mouth for the Dumb! The German Evangelical Church and the Jews, 1879-1950.* Oxford: B. Blackwell, 1976. Pp. 1–34, 326–344. *LJ*

Partial contents: The Roots of Christian Antisemitism, 1879-1918 (1–34). Judenmission (326–344).

0880 Guttmann, Jakob (1845–1919): Die moderne Kultur und das Judentum. *MGWJ* 19 ( 1870) 364–375. *LJ*

Review of Wilhelm Herzberg's book *Jüdische Familienpapiere.*

0881 Guttmann, Julius (1880–1950): *Die Juden und das Wirtschaftsleben.* Tübingen: J.C.B. Mohr, 1913. 149–212. *LJ*

Offprint from: *Archiv für Sozialwissenschaft und Sozialpolitik*, vol. 36, no. 1.

0882 Haas, Theodor: *Die Juden in Mähren; Darstellung der Rechtsgeschichte und Statistik unter besonderer Berücksichtigung des 19. Jahrhunderts*. Brünn: Jüdischer Buch- und Kunstverlag, 1908. 73 pp. *LJ*

0883 Haase, Amine: *Katholische Presse und die Judenfrage; Inhaltsanalyse katholischer Periodika am Ende des 19. Jahrhunderts*. Pullach bei München: Verlag Dokumentation, 1975. 262 pp. (Dortmunder Beiträge zur Zeitungsforschung, 20) *LJ*

0884 Habel, Werner: *Deutsch-Jüdische Geschichte am Ausgang des 19. Jahrhunderts; Untersuchungen zur Geschichte der innerjüdischen Sammelbewegung, 1880-1900 als Beitrag zu einem wissenschafts-propädeutischen Geschichtsunterricht*. Kastellaun: Aloys-Heim-Verlag, 1977. 321 pp. *LJ*

0885 Häusler, Wolfgang: Assimilation und Emanzipation des ungarischen Judentums um die Mitte des 19. Jahrhunderts. *Studia Judaica Austriaca* 3 (1976) 33-79. *LJ*

0886 Häusler, Wolfgang: Demokratie und Emanzipation, 1848. *Studia Judaica Austriaca* 1 (1974) 92-111. *LJ*

0887 Häusler, Wolfgang: Konfessionelle Probleme in der Wiener Revolution von 1848. *Studia Judaica Austriaca* 1 (1974) 64-77. *LJ*

0888 Häusler, Wolfgang: Toleranz, Emanzipation und Antisemitismus; das österreichische Judentum des bürgerlichen Zeitalters, 1782-1918. *Das Oesterreichische Judentum*. Wien: Jugend und Volk, 1974. Pp. 83-140. *LJ*

0889 Hagedűs, Sándor: *A tiszaeszlán vervád*. Budapest: Kossuth Kőnyvkiado, 1966. 205 pp. *LJ*

0890 Hagen, William W.: The German Liberal Movement, the Jews, and Zionism. *Germans, Poles and Jews; the Nationality Conflict in the Prussian East 1772-1914*. Chicago: University of Chicago Press, 1980. Pp. 288-319. *LJ*

0891 Hahn, Adele: *Historische Grundlage des jüdischen Ritualmordes*. Königsberg i. Pr.: Ostpreußische Druckerei und Verlagsanstalt, 1906. 64 pp. *LC*

0892 Haid, F.S.: *Emanzipation; eine Untersuchung über die staatsrechtlichen Prinzipien des Mosaismus im Verhältnis zu den Prinzipien der Gegenwart*. Ellwangen: Brantegger, 1848. VI, 210 pp. *LJ*

0893 Haller, Ernst: *Die rechtliche Stellung der Juden im Kanton Aargau.* Aarau: H.R. Sauerländer, 1901. XII, 310. *LJ*

0894 Hamburger, Edwin: *Der Antisemitismus und die deutsche Studentenschaft; Entgegnung auf Kurt Müller's "Das Judentum in der deutschen Studentenschaft."* Leipzig: O. Gottwald, 1891. 16 pp. (Cyclus akademischer Broschüren, 1) *Unseen*

0895 Hamburger, Ernest (1890-): Jews in Public Service under the German Monarchy. *LBIYB* 9 (1964) 206-238. *LJ*

0896 Hamburger, Ernest (1890-): *Juden im öffentlichen Leben Deutschlands; Regierungsmitglieder, Beamte und Parlamentarier in der monarchischen Zeit, 1848-1918.* Tübingen: J.C.B. Mohr, 1968. XXII, 595 pp. (Schriftenreihe wissenschaftlicher Abhandlungen des Leo Baeck Instituts, 19) *LJ*

0897 Hamburger, Ernest (1890-): Jüdische Parlamentarier in 1848-1933. *Gegenwart im Rückblick. Festgabe für die jüdische Gemeinde zu Berlin, 25 Jahre nach dem Neubeginn.* Eds. Herbert A. Strauss, Kurt R. Grossmann. Heidelberg, 1970. Pp. 56-85. *LJ*

0898 Hamburger, Hermann: *Der Konitzer Mord; ein Beitrag zur Klärung.* Breslau: Preuß & Jünger, 1900. 48 pp. *LJ*

0899 Hamburger, Jakob (1826-1911): *Die Nichtjuden und die Sekten im talmudischen Schrifttum; Vortrag.* 2. Aufl. Neustrelitz: G. Barnewitz, 1880. 16 pp. *LJ*

0900 Hamburger, Jakob (1826-1911): Zurückweisung der Blutbeschuldigung. *Realenzyklopädie für Bibel und Talmud. Bd. 2.* 1883. Pp. 1315-1321. *LJ*

0901 Hamburger, Leopold: *Herr Otto Hartmann in Köln und sein Kampf gegen die Schlachtweise der Israeliten.* Den verehrlichen Mitgliedern der Tierschutzvereine gewidmet, von einem Kollegen. Frankfurt a.M.: Typ. M. Slobotzky, 1889. 20 pp. *LJ*

0902 Hamel, Iris: *Völkischer Verband und nationale Gewerkschaft; der Deutsch-nationale Handlungsgehilfen-Verband, 1893-1933.* Frankfurt a.M.: Europäische Verlagsanstalt, 1967. 289 pp. (Veröffentlichungen der Forschungsstelle für die Geschichte des Nationalsozialismus in Hamburg, 6) *LJ* Diss. Hamburg.

0903 Hammer, Käthe: *Die Judenfrage in den westlichen Kronländern Oesterreichs im Jahre 1848.* Wien: 1948. 195 l. *Unseen* Diss.

0904 *Handbuch der Jüdischen Gemeindeverwaltung und Wohlfahrtspflege; statistisches Jahrbuch.* Hrsg. von dem Deutsch-Israelitischen Gemeindebund und von der Zentralwohlfahrtsstelle der deutschen Juden. Bearb. von dem Bureau der Statistik der Juden. Berlin: Deutsch-Israelitischer Gemeindebund, 1886–1914. 22 vols. *LJ*

0905 Handler, Andrew: *Blood Libel at Tíszaeszlár.* Boulder: East European Monographs, 1980. 273 pp. (East European Monographs, 68) *LJ*

0906 Handler, Andrew: *An Early Blueprint for Zionism; Győző Istoczy's Political Antisemitism.* Boulder, Colo.: East European Monographs, 1989. 206 pp. (East European monographs, 261) *LJ*

0907 Hanslick, Eduard (1825–1904): Richard Wagner's "Judentum in der Musik," 1869. *Eduard Hanslicks Wagner Kritiken.* Wien: Europa-Verlag, 1947. *Unseen*

0908 Harden, Maximilian (1861–1927): Fürst Bismarck und der Antisemitismus. *Die Zukunft* 3 (1893) 193–201. *LJ*

0909 Harden, Maximilian (1861–1927): Stoecker. *Köpfe. Bd. 1, 40.–41. Aufl.* Berlin: Reis, 1916. Pp. 175–194. *LJ*

0910 Harling, Otto von (1864–): *"Du Tochter Zion freue Dich." Die Heilige Nacht. Weihnachtsspiel. Die Macht der göttlichen Liebe. Weihnachtsgedicht, von C. Hermann.* Leipzig: Ev.-Luth. Zentralverein für Mission unter Israel, 1912. 14 pp. (Kleine Schriften zur Judenmission, 6) *Unseen*

0911 Harling, Otto von (1864–): *Hundert Jahre Judenmission; Vortrag gehalten auf der XII. allgemeinen evangelischen lutherischen Konferenz zu Hannover.* Leipzig: Ev.-Luth. Zentralverein für Mission unter Israel, 1909. 15 pp. (Kleine Schriften zur Judenmission, 4) *Unseen*

0912 Harmelin, Wilhelm: Jews in the Leipzig Fur Industry. *LBIYB* 9 (1964) 239–266. *LJ*

0913 Harpf, Adolf: *Die Zeit des ewigen Friedens; eine Apologie des Krieges als Kultur- und Rassenauffrischer.* Rodaun bei Wien: Verlag der Ostara, 1908. 39 pp. (Ostara, 19–20) *LB*

0914 Harpf, Adolf: *Zur Lösung der brennendsten Rassenfrage der heutigen europäischen Menschheit; eine soziologische Studie mit einem Anhange zur Begründung der Sozialethik.* Wien: M. Breitenstein, 1898. 73 pp. *LJ*

0915 Harrassowitz, Otto: *Bibliotheca Judaica-Hebraica-Rabbinica Pinczower-Porges.* Mit einer Einleitung von Felix Daniel Pinczower. Wiesbaden: M. Sändig, 1971. XXX, 759 pp. *LJ*

"Erstausg. 1931-1932."

0916 Harris, James F.: Eduard Lasker, the Jew as National German Politician. *LBIYB* 20 (1975) 151-177. *LJ*

0917 Hartleben, A., ed.: *Der Prozeß von Tísza-Eslár, verhandelt in Nyiregyhaza im Jahre 1883. Eine genaue Darstellung der Anklage der Zeugenverhöre, der Verteidigung und des Urteils nach authentischen Berichten bearb.* 4. Aufl. Wien: A. Hartleben, 1883. 96 pp. (A. Hartleben's Chronik der Zeit, 7) *LJ*

0918 Hartmann, Eduard von (1842-1906): *Das Judentum in Gegenwart und Zukunft; sozialpolitische Abhandlungen.* Leipzig: W. Friedrich, 1885. 194 pp. *LJ*

0919 Hartmann, Moritz (1821-1872): *Revolutionäre Erinnerungen.* Hrsg. von H.H. Houben. Leipzig: W. Klinkhardt, 19--. 96 pp. *LC*

0920 Hartwig, Edgar: *Zur Politik und Entwicklung des Alldeutschen Verbandes von seiner Gründung bis zum Beginn des Weltkrieges, 1891-1914.* Jena: 1966. 327 l. *Unseen*

Diss. 1966, typescript.

0921 Hartwig, Otto (1830-1903): *Ludwig Bamberger; eine biographische Skizze.* Marburg: C.L. Pfeil, 1900. VIII, 85 pp. *Unseen*

0922 Hasse, Ernst (1846-1908): *Rasse. Die Zukunft des deutschen Volkstums.* München: J.F. Lehmann, 1907. Pp. 46-68. (Deutsche Politik. Vol. 1: Heimatpolitik, 1) *LJ*

0923 Haumann, Heiko (1945-): Das jüdische Prag, 1850-1914. *Die Juden als Minderheit in der Geschichte.* Eds. Bernd Martin, Ernst Schulin. München: Deutscher Taschenbuch-Verlag, 1981. Pp. 209-230. *LJ*

0924 Hausmeister, Jakob August: *Die evangelische Mission unter Israel; Winke und Mitteilungen.* Mit dem Lebenslauf des Verewigten. Hrsg. von Ernst Fink. Basel: F. Schneider, 1861. VI, 97 pp. *LJ*

0925 Hausmeister, Jakob August: *Der Unterricht und die Pflege jüdischer Proselyten; ein Beitrag zum Religionsunterricht und zur Seelenpflege überhaupt.* Heidelberg: K. Winter, 1852. VI, 124 pp. *LJ*

0926 Hawlik, Johannes: *Der Bürgerkaiser; Karl Lueger und seine Zeit.* Wien: Herold Verlag, 1985. 224 pp. *LJ*

0927 Hayn, Hugo (1843-1923): *Uebersicht der meist in Deutschland erschienenen Literatur über die angeblich von Juden verübten Ritualmorde und Hostienfrevel.* Jena: H.W. Schmidt, 1906. 30 pp. *LJ*

0928 Hecht, Alexander: *Der Bund B'nai B'rith und seine Bedeutung für das österreichische Judentum.* Hrsg. vom Israelitischen Humanitätsverein "Eintracht" B'nai B'rith. Wien: Typ. H. Liebermann, 1914. 36 pp. *LJ*

0929 Hecht, Georg: *Der neue Jude.* Leipzig: G. Engel, 1911. 169 pp. *LJ*

0930 Heckel, Johannes (1889-1963): Der Einbruch des jüdischen Geistes in das deutsche Staats- und Kirchenrecht durch Friedrich Julius Stahl. *Forschungen zur Judenfrage* 1 (1937) 110-135. *LJ*

Also published in *Historische Zeitschift 1937*, vol. 155. Pp. 506-541.

0931 Heckscher, M: *Die Börsensteuer; eine gemeinfaßliche Darstellung.* Minden, Westf.: J.C.C. Brun, 1885. 18 pp. (Soziale Zeitfragen, 9) *Unseen*

0932 Heger, Adolf: *Adolf Stoecker als Vorkämpfer der Kirche und als Vorkämpfer völkischen Erwachens. Zur 100. Wiederkehr seines Geburtstages.* Oldenburg i.O.: Verlag des Oldenburger Sonntagsblattes, 1935. 24 pp. *LTA*

0933 Heilbrunn, Rudolf M.: Bismarcks blinder Hofjude. *TAJfDG* 10 (1981) 283-317. *LJ*

0934 Heimberger, Joseph: *Die staatskirchenrechtliche Stellung der Israeliten in Bayern; ein Beitrag zur Lehre von den Privatkirchengesellschaften.* Freiburg i.Br.: J.C.B. Mohr, 1893. VII, 207 pp. *LJ*

0935 Hein, Oskar: *Ein offenes Wort an die Gewerbetreibenden Oesterreichs.* Wien: Schwarzinger, 1890. 8 pp. *LTA*

"Anti-Schneider."

0936 Heinen, Ernst: Antisemitische Strömungen im politischen Katholizismus während des Kulturkampfes. *Geschichte in der Gegenwart; Festschrift für Kurt Kloxen.* Paderborn, 1972. Pp. 259-299. *LJ*

0937  Hellwig, Albert Ernst Karl Max (1880–): Jüdischer Meineidsaberglaube. *Archiv für Kriminalanthropologie und Kriminalistik* 41 (1911) 126–141. *LJ*

0938  Hellwig, Albert Ernst Karl Max (1880–): Ritualmord und Blutaberglaube. *Die Grenzboten* 72 (1913) 149–160. *LJ*

0939  Hellwig, Albert Ernst Karl Max (1880–): *Ritualmord und Blutaberglaube.* Minden: J.C.C. Bruns, 1914. 174 pp. *LJ*

0940  Hellwing, Isak A.: *Der konfessionelle Antisemitismus im 19. Jahrhundert in Oesterreich.* Wien: Herder, 1972. 311 pp. (Veröffentlichungen des Instituts für Kirchliche Zeitgeschichte am Internationalen Forschungszentrum für Grundlagen der Wissenschaften, Salzburg, Ser. 2, Studien 2) *LJ*

0941  Heman, Karl Friedrich (1839–1919): *Das Erwachen der jüdischen Nation; der Weg zur endgültigen Lösung der Judenfrage.* Basel: P. Kober, 1897. 114 pp. *LC*

0942  Heman, Karl Friedrich (1839–1919): *Die historische und religiöse Weltstellung der Juden und die moderne Judenfrage.* 2. unveränd. Abdruck. Leipzig: J.C. Hinrichs'sche Buchhdlg., 1882. 76 pp. *LJ*

0943  Heman, Karl Friedrich (1839–1919): *Die religiöse Weltstellung des jüdischen Volkes.* Leipzig: Hinrichs'sche Buchhdlg., 1882. X, 130 pp. *LJ*

0944  Henrici, Ernst (1854–1915): An Wilhelm Marr, 14.3.1881. *Staatsarchiv Hamburg.* Nachlaß Wilhelm Marr-StA Hbg. NL Marr A99. *Unseen*

0945  Hentsch, Gerhard: *Gewerbeordnung und Emanzipation der Juden im Kurfürstentum Heßen.* Wiesbaden: Kommission für die Geschichte der Juden in Hessen, 1979. VIII, 204 pp. (Schriften der Kommission . . . 4) *LJ*

0946  Hentschel, Willibald: *Varuna: das Gesetz des ansteigenden Lebens und sinkenden Lebens in der Geschichte.* 2. Aufl. Leipzig: Th. Fritsch, 1907. 128 pp. *LB*

0947  Heppner, Ernst: *Juden als Erfinder und Entdecker; Biographien jüdischer Erfinder und Entdecker.* Einführung von N. Birnbaum. Berlin: Welt-Verlag, 1913. 125 pp. (Veröffentlichung der Henriette-Becker-Stiftung) *LC*

0948  Hermann, C.: *Die Macht der göttlichen Liebe; Weihnachtsgedicht.* Leipzig: Evangelisch-Lutherischer Zentralverein für Mission unter Israel, 1912. (Kleine Schriften zur Judenmission, 6) *Unseen*

0949 *Herr Liebermann von Sonnenberg als Parteiführer und Gesinnungsgenosse. Aufschlüße über die Vorgänge in der deutsch-sozialen Bewegung Leipzigs, von einigen Deutsch-Sozialen.* Leipzig: Kommissinsverlag H. Träger, 1893. 139 pp. *LJ*

0950 Hersch, Isaac Moses: *Schreibebrief an den graussen Keiser Napauljon ibber de heintje pollitsche Looge in Ejropa.* Leipzig: H. Matthes, 1867. 56 pp. *LJ*

"Vun maane mool ssu hinterlassende Peppiere Nommero aans."

0951 Hersch, Jekef Mosche: Offener Brief des Rebb Jekef Mosche Hersch an den König von Preußen. *Berliner Straßeneckenliteratur 1848-1849.* Stuttgart: Ph. Reclam Jun., 1977. Pp. 103-106. *LJ*

0952 Hertl, Paul: *Der jüdisch-freimaurerische Weltbund.* Warnsdorf: A. Opitz, 1907. 5 vols. (Volksaufklärung, 102-107) *LJ*

0953 Hertz, Friedrich Otto (1878-): *Moderne Rassentheorien; kritische Essays.* Wien: C.W. Stern, 1904. 354 pp. *LJ*

0954 Herz, Hugo: *Die Kriminalität der Juden in Oesterreich.* Berlin: 1907. 36 pp. *LJ*

0955 Herz, Sophony (1905-): *Treitschkes kritische Haltung gegenüber Berthold Auerbach, Rahel Varnhagen und Fanny Lewald. TAJfDG* 1 (1972) 119-144. *LJ*

0956 Herzfeld, Michael: *Das Scheker bilbul von Tísza-Eszlár; Eszter und Haman. Interessante Hirtenbriefe.* Wien: M. Herzfeld, 1883. 15 pp. *LJ*

0957 Herzig, Arno: *Judentum und Emanzipation in Westfalen.* Münster: Aschendorffsche Verlagsbuchhdlg., 1973. XV, 162 pp. (Veröffentlichungen des Provinzialinstituts für Westfälische Landes- und Volkskunde, ser. 1, 17) *LJ*

0958 Herzl, Hechler, the Grand Duke of Baden and the German Emperor, 1896-1904. Documents found by Hermann and Bessi Ellern. Tr. by Harry Zohn. *Herzl Yearbook* 4 (1961-62) 207-270. *LJ*

0959 Herzl, Theodor (1860-1904): Die Jagd in Böhmen. *Gesammelte Zionistische Werke. Bd. 1.* Tel Aviv: Hoza'ah Ivrith, 1934. Pp. 216-222. *LJ*

First published in 1904.

0960 Herzl, Theodor (1860-1904): *Der Judenstaat; Versuch einer modernen Lösung der Judenfrage.* Leipzig: Breitenstein, 1896. 86 pp. *LJ*

0961 Herzl, Theodor (1860-1904): A Solution to the Jewish Question. *Jewish Chronicle* 17.1.1896, no. 1, 398, n.s. Pp. 12-13. *LJ*

0962   Herzstein, Robert Edwin: Richard Wagner at the Crossroads of German Antisemitism, 1848–1933. *ZfGJ* 4 (1967) 119–140. *LJ*

0963   Hess, Moses (1812–1875): *Rom und Jerusalem; die letzte Nationalitätsfrage, Briefe und Noten.* Leipzig: E. Wengler, 1862. XVI, 239 pp. *LJ*

0964   Heuch, F.C.: *Reform-jüdische Polemik gegen das Christentum im Gewande moderner Aesthetik.* Uebers. aus dem Norwegischen. Flensburg: A. Westphalen, 1879. 52 pp. *LJ*

0965   Heynemann, Sigismund Sussmann: *Zwei Briefe eines jüdischen Getauften.* 2. Aufl. Leipzig: Dörffling & Franke, 1909. 48 pp. (Schriften des Institutum Judaicum in Leipzig, 10) *LJ*

0966   Hieber, Otto: *Zur Abwehr; eine Beleuchtung der Schrift des Prof. Dr. Settegast "Die deutsche Freimaurerei, ihr Wesen, ihre Ziele und Zukunft im Hinblick auf den freimaurerischen Notstand in Preußen."* Berlin: Mittler, 1892. 34 pp. *LTA*

0967   Hildesheimer, Hirsch: *Erklärung des Dr. H. Hildesheimer auf die Privatklagesache des Schriftstellers Ludwig Schwennhagen wider Dr. H. Hildesheimer.* Berlin: H.S. Hermann, 189–. 22 pp. *LJ*

0968   Hildesheimer, Hirsch: *Erklärung des Hirsch Hildesheimer in der Privatklagesache des Schriftstellers Oberwinder wider H. Hildesheimer.* Berlin: Typ. H.S. Hermann, 1893. 73 pp. *LJ*

"Anlage zur Klagebeantwortung des Rechtanwalts Dr. Stranz."

0969   Hildesheimer, Hirsch: *Ich nehme den Schutz des Paragraph 193 für mich in Anspruch.* Berlin: Typ. H.S. Hermann, 1893. 22 pp. *LJ*

About the Oberwinder-Hildesheimer law suit in the Buschhoff blood libel case.

0970   Hildesheimer, Hirsch: *Replik des Dr. Hirsch Hildesheimer auf das Druckwerk welches der Buchdruckerei-Besitzer F.W. Glöss seiner Klage entgegengestellt hat.* [n.p.], 1895. 125 pp. *LJ*

0971   Hildesheimer, Hirsch: *Das Schächten; eine vorläufige Auseinandersetzung.* Berlin: Typ. Haasenstein & Vogler, 1905. 23 pp. *LJ*

Commissioned by "Centralverein Deutscher Staatsbürger Jüdischen Glaubens." Enlarged offprint from the June issue of *Blätter für höheres Schulwesen.*

0972   Hildesheimer, Hirsch: *Widerklage.* Berlin: 1893. 7 pp. *LJ*

Hildesheimer's defence in the Oberwinder-Hildesheimer trial of the Buschhoff case.

0973 Hilfsverein der Deutschen Juden: *Bericht über die Hilfsaktion für die durch die Ausschreitungen geschädigte jüdische Bevölkerung in Kischinew.* Erstattet vom eingesetzten Komitee am 7. (20.) Juni 1903. [n.p.]: [n.d.]. 14 pp. *LTA*

0974 Hirsch, Felix (1902–): Eduard von Simson; das Problem der deutsch-jüdischen Symbiose im Schatten Goethes und Bismarcks. *Geschichte in Wissenschaft und Unterricht* 16, 5 ( 1965) 261–277. *LJ*

0975 Hirsch, Helmut (1907–): Karl Marx und die Bittschriften für die Gleichberechtigung der Juden. *Archiv für Sozialgeschichte* 8 (1968) 229–245. LJ

0976 Hirsch, Helmut (1907–): *Marxiana Judaica. Cahiers de l'Institut de Science Economique Appliquée* Suppl. 140 (1963) 5–52. (Etudes de Marxologie, 7) *Unseen*

0977 Hirsch, Isaak: *Verträgt sich die Talmud-Moral mit dem deutschen Staatsbürgerrecht.* Hannover: Manz & Lange, 1893. 16 pp. *LJ*

0978 Hirsch, Max (1832–1905): *Was bezwecken die Gewerkvereine; ein Merk- und Mahnwort für alle deutschen Handwerker und Arbeiter.* 5. Aufl. Berlin: Verband deutscher Gewerkvereine, 1883. 15 pp. *Unseen*

0979 Hirsch, Samson Raphael (1808–1888): *Ueber die Beziehung des Talmuds zum Judentum und zu der sozialen Stellung seiner Bekenner.* Frankfurt a.M.: Kauffmann, 1884. 38 pp. *LJ*

0980 *Hoch Schönerer; ein Justizmord in Oesterreich.* Wien: 1888. 16 pp. *Unseen*

0981 Hönighaus, R., ed.: *Das neue preußische Gesetz betreffend den Austritt aus den jüdischen Synagogengemeinden; nebst den älteren und noch giltigen, die Verhältnisse der Juden betreffenden Gesetzen. Mit den amtlichen Motiven und den bedeutendsten Reden der Landtags-Mitglieder in authentischem Wortlaut.* Berlin: G. Hempel, 1876. 55 pp. *LJ*

0982 Hoffmann, [?]: *Der Blutmord zu Konitz. Wortlaut der Eingabe die der des Mordes verdächtigte Fleischermeister H. am 6.VI.1900 dem Amtsgerichte zu Konitz einreichte.* 4. Aufl. Berlin: Deutschnationale Buchhdlg. und Verlagsanstalt, 1900. 4 pp. *Unseen*

0983 Hoffmann, Christhard (1952–): *Juden und Judentum im Werk deutscher Althistoriker des 19. und 20. Jahrhunderts.* Leiden: E.J. Brill, 1988. IX, 302 pp. (Studies in Judaism in modern times, vol. 9) *LJ*

0984 Hoffmann, (Dr.): *Der Katechismus der Juden; oder, Die Vorschriften des Schulchan Aruch verglichen mit denen des Talmud. Nebst einem Referat über den vor dem Königlichen Landgericht zu Münster verhandelten Strafprozeß in Sachen des Schulchan Aruchs. Wohlfeile Volksausg.* Berlin: Schulze, 1884. 48 pp. *LTA*

0985  Hoffmann, Moses: *Judentum und Kapitalismus; eine kritische Würdigung von Werner Sombarts "Die Juden und das Wirtschaftsleben."* Berlin: Itzkowski, 1912. 192 pp. *LJ*

0986  Hofmann, Eduard von (1837-1897): *Gutachten über die am 18. Juni 1882 bei Tísza-Dada aus der Theisz gezogene, am 19. Juni gerichtlich obduzirte und am 7. Dezember 1882 behufs neuerlicher Untersuchung exhumirte weibliche Leiche.* Budapest: Pester Buchdruckerei-Aktien Gesellschaft, 1883. 39 pp. *LJ*

0987  Hofmann, Johann Christian Konrad von: *Die Mission in der Heidenwelt und unter Israel; ein Vortrag.* Nürnberg: Raw, 1856. 16 pp. *Unseen*

0988  Hofmann von Wellenhof, Paul: *Das Heinrich-Heine-Denkmal; oder, Der Skandal auf dem Parnasse. Ein dramatisches Capricio, von Christophorus Treumund, pseud.* 2. Aufl. Wien: Vetter, 1888. 40 pp. *Unseen*

Offprint from: *Oesterreichischer Reformer*, no. 83.

0989  *Hofprediger Stoecker und der Hof.* Berlin: R. Eckstein, Nachf., 1889. 56 pp. *LJ*

0990  Holdheim, Samuel (1806-1860): *Gemischte Ehen zwischen Juden und Christen, die Gutachten der Berliner Rabbinatsverwaltung und des Königsberger Konsistoriums, beleuchtet von . . .* Berlin: L. Lassar, 1850. VIII, 88 pp. *LJ*

0991  Holdheim, Samuel (1806-1860): *Stahl's christliche Toleranz.* 2. unveränd. Abdruck. Berlin: J. Abelsdorff, 1856. 46 pp. *LJ*

0992  Holeczek, Heinz: Die Judenemanzipation in Preußen. *Die Juden als Minderheit in der Geschichte.* 3. Aufl. Eds. Bernd Martin, Ernst Schulin. München: DTV, 1985. Pp. 131-160. *LJ*

0993  Holsten, Walter: Adolf Stoecker als Symptom seiner Zeit; Antisemitismus in der evangelischen Kirche des 19. Jahrhunderts. *Christen und Juden.* Ed. Wolf-Dieter Marsch. Göttingen: Vandenhoeck & Ruprecht, 1961. Pp. 182-200. *LJ*

0994  Holzer, Heribert: *Dr. Josef Deckert, Pfarrer von Weinhaus, 1843-1901; sein Leben und Wirken.* Wien: 1959. 98 l. *Unseen*

Diss., typescript.

0995 Hoppe, Hugo: *Hervorragende Nichtjuden über den Zionismus; eine Sammlung von Urteilen hervorragender Persönlichkeiten aller Länder.* Königsberg i. Pr.: Ostdeutsche Buchhdlg., 1904. X, 198 pp. *LJ*

0996 Hoppe, Hugo: *Krankheiten und Sterblichkeit bei Juden und Nichtjuden, unter besonderer Brücksichtigung der Alkoholfrage.* Berlin: S. Calvary, 1903. 64 pp. *LJ*

0997 Horn, Ede: *Die Revolution und die Juden in Ungarn. Nebst einem Rückblick auf die Geschichte der letzteren, von J. Einhorn, pseud.* Leipzig: Carl Geibel, 1851. VI, 137 pp. *LJ*

0998 Horovicz, Jonathan Benjamin: *Der erste allgemeine Rabbinerkongreß zu Krakau 9.-13. August 1903.* Also-Kubin: D. Fried, 1903. 47 pp. *LJ*

0999 Horovicz, Jonathan Benjamin: *Gegen die Blutbeschuldigung; der Schwur des in Krakau am 9.-13. August 1903 abgehaltenen Rabbiner Kongreßes.* Wien: J. Schlesinger, 1904. 56 pp. *LJ*

1000 Horovitz, Markus (1844-1910): *Korfu; Vortrag, gehalten am 28. Mai 1891.* Frankfurt a.M.: J. Kauffmann, 1891. 15 pp. *LJ*

1001 Hortzitz, Nicoline: *"Früh-Antisemitismus" in Deutschland, 1789-1871/72; strukturelle Untersuchungen zu Wortschatz, Text und Argumentation.* Tübingen: M. Niemeyer, 1988. XI, 347 pp. (Reihe Germanistische Linguistik, 83) *LJ*

1002 Hrabal, Bohŭmil: Die Moritat von der Ermordung Anežka Hruzovás. *Moritaten und Legenden. Aus dem Tschechischen von Franz Peter Künzel.* Frankfurt a.M.: Suhrkamp, 1973. Pp. 129-146. (Bibliothek Suhrkamp, 360) *LF*

1003 Hrabal, Bohŭmil: *Tanzstunden für Erwachsene und Fortgeschrittene. Aus dem Tschechischen von Franz Peter Künzel.* Frankfurt a.M.: Suhrkamp, 1965. 93 pp. (Edition Suhrkamp, 126) *LF*

1004 Hron, Karl: *Wiens antisemitische Bewegung.* Wien: Selbstverlag, 1890. 146 pp. *LJ*

1005 Hübner, Paul Gerhard: *Adolf Stoeckers sozial-ethische Anschauungen; ein Beitrag zur christlich-sozialen Zielsetzung.* Leipzig: A. Deichert, 1930. 95 pp. *LJ*

1006 Hülsen Hans von: Neid als Gesinnung — der manische Antisemitismus des Adolf Bartels. *Propheten des Nationalismus.* Ed. Karl Schwedhelm. München: List-Verlag, 1969. Pp. 176-188. *LC*

1007  Huret, Jules (1864–1915): *L'antisémitisme en Allemagne*. Paris: Bibliothèque Charpentier, 1909. Pp. 341–391. *LJ*

1008  Ilschner, Liselotte: *Rembrandt als Erzieher und seine Bedeutung; Studie über die kulturelle Struktur der neunziger Jahre*. Danzig: Kafemann, 1928. 94 pp. *Unseen*

1009  *Interessante Enthüllungen aus der geheimen Werkstätte der Freimaurerei, mit besonderer Berücksichtigung auf Oesterreich-Ungarn*. Würzburg: Wörl, 1888. 26 pp. *Unseen*

1010  Irwahn, Hans: *Bilder aus der Urgeschichte des DHV (Deutschnationaler Handlungsgehilfenverband)*. Hamburg: Hanseatische Verlagsanstalt, 1920. 94 pp. *Unseen*

1011  *Israel Goldstern; Bild aus der neuesten Juden-Mission*. Hrsg. vom Rheinisch-Westfälischen Verein für Israel in Köln am Rhein. 2. Aufl. Köln: in Komm. bei C. Römke, 1885. 77 pp. *LJ*

1012  *Israel in Alarm über den Mahnruf der Zeit und den deutschen Bescheid der Stimme aus dem Judenspiegel*. Beleuchtet von A-Z. Hamburg: Selbstverlag des Verfassers, 1862. 16 pp. *LJ*

About Wilhelm Marr's *Judenspiegel*.

1013  Israelitische Synode 1 and 2: *Die Beschlüße der ersten und zweiten Israelitischen Synode*. Mainz: J. Gottesleben, 1871. 16 pp. *LJ*

1014  Israelitische Synode 1 and 2: *Referate über die der Israelitischen Synode zu Leipzig überreichten Anträge*. Berlin: L. Gerschel, 1871. 246 pp. *LJ*

1015  Israelitische Synode 1 and 2: *Verhandlungen der ersten Israelitischen Synode zu Leipzig vom 29. Juni bis 4. Juli 1869*. Berlin: L. Gerschel, 1869. VI, 260 pp. *LJ*

1016  Israelitische Synode 1 and 2: *Verhandlungen der Zweiten Israelitischen Synode zu Augsburg von 11.–17. Juli 1871*. Nach stenographischen Aufzeichnungen. Berlin: L. Gerschel, 1873. VI, 262 pp. *LJ*

1017  Istoczy, Győző (1842–1915): *Statuten-Entwurf des Zentral-Vereins des Nichtjuden-Bundes von Ungarn*. Ausgearb. vom ungarischen Reichstags-Abgeordneten Istoczy. Berlin: O. Hentze, 1880. 12 pp. *Unseen*

1018  Jab, pseud.: *Le sang chrétien dans les rites de la synagogue moderne*. Paris: Gautier, 1888. 404 pp. *LTA*

1019 Jacobs, Joseph (1854–1916): Excursus on Sombart. *Jewish Contributions to Civilization; An Estimate.* Philadelphia: The Conat Press, 1920. Pp. 247–267. *LJ*

1020 Jacobs, Joseph (1854–1916): *The Jewish Question, 1875–1884; Bibliographical Handlist.* London: Trubner, 1885. XI, 96 pp. *LJ*

1021 Jacobs, Joseph (1854–1916): The Jews and Commerce; How History Ought and Ought Not to Be Written. *The American Hebrew* 88 (1911) 767–768. *LJ*

1022 Jacobsohn, Bernhard: *Der Deutsch-Israelitische Gemeindebund nach Ablauf des ersten Decenniums seit seiner Begründung von 1869 bis 1879; eine Erinnerungsschrift.* Leipzig: Typ. W. Schuwardt, 1879. VI, 70 pp. *LJ*

1023 Jacoby, Johann (1805–1877): *Gesammelte Schriften und Reden.* T. 1–2. Hamburg: O. Meissner, 1877. 2 vols. *LJ*

1024 Jacoby, P: *Beiträge zur Lösung der Judenfrage in Preußen. I. Die rechtliche Stellung der Juden vor der Emanation der Verfassungsurkunde.* Leipzig: O. Wigand, 1858. 60 pp. *Unseen*

1025 Jäger, Hans: *Unternehmer in der deutschen Politik, 1890–1918.* Bonn: Röhrscheid, 1967. Pp, 354–369 (Bonner Historische Forschungen, 30) *LTA*

1026 Jäger, Johannes (1862–): *Steht im Talmud etwas über Fleisch- und Fettbesudeln? Beantwortet von J. Jäger.* Mit einem Anhang: I. Gutachten des Herrn Strack, II. Rabbiner-Erklärung. Gerolzhofen: Kommissions-Verlag von Fr. Büchner's Buchdruckerei, 1900. XIII, 48 pp. *LJ*

1027 Jaffe, Max: *Die nationale Wiedergeburt der Juden; eine volkswirtschaftliche Studie.* Berlin: H. Steinitz, 1897. 56 pp. *LJ*

1028 *Jahrbuch der evangelischen Judenmission.* Im Auftrage des Ausschußes der Internationalen Konferenz für Judenmission, hrsg. von Hermann L. Strack. Bd. 1–2. Leipzig: J.C. Hinrichs, 1906–1913. 2 vols. *LJ*

1029 Jakobowski, Ludwig (1868–1900): *Der Juden Anteil am Verbrechen. Nach amtlichen Quellen dargestellt.* Berlin: M. Hoffschläger, 1892. 40 pp. *LJ*

1030 Janasz, Adolf: *Die Zukunft des Volkes Israel.* Berlin: Otto Bouillon, 1882. 15 pp. *LJ*

1031 Jansen, Theodor: *Das jüdische Blutmysterium; Vortrag gehalten in einer Versammlung des Vereins "Christenschutz" zu Aachen am 3. September 1895.* 2. Aufl. Leipzig: H. Beyer, 1895. 30 pp. *LJ*

1032  Jaques, Heinrich (1831–1894): *Denkschrift über die Stellung der Juden in Oesterreich.* 4. verm. Aufl. nebst einer antikritisch-juristischen Einleitung. Wien: Carl Gerold, 1859. 119, 51 pp. *LJ*

1033  Jellinek, Adolf (1821–1893): *Der Talmudjude. Reden: 1. Womit beginnt und womit schließt der Talmud? 2. Die Lebensfülle des Talmud! 3. Wozu und von wem wurde der Talmud studiert? 4. Die Rede- und Vortragsweise der Talmudlehrer zunächst Adam betreffend.* Wien: Löwy, 1882. 4 vols. in 1. *LJ*

1034  Jenks, William Alexander: The Jews in the Habsburg Empire, 1879–1918. *LBIYB* 16 (1971) 155–162. *LJ*

1035  Jenks, William Alexander: *Vienna and the young Hitler.* New York: Columbia University, 1960. VIII, 252 pp. *LJ*

1036  *Jews, Antisemitism and Culture in Vienna.* Ed. Ivar Uxaal, Michael Pollak and Gerhard Botz. London: Routledge & Kegan Paul, 1987. XIV, 300 pp. *LJ*

1037  The Jews in Economic Life; The Judaeans Discuss Prof. Sombart's Work and Incidentally Japan and the American Passport in Russia. *The American Hebrew* 90 (1912) 523. *LJ*

1038  Jochmann, Werner (1921–): *Gesellschaftskrise und Judenfeindschaft in Deutschland, 1870–1945.* Hamburg: Christians, 1988. 443 pp. (Hamburger Beiträge zur Sozial- und Zeitgeschichte, 23) *LJ*

1039  Jochmann, Werner (1921–): Stoecker als nationalkonservativer Politiker und antisemitischer Agitator. *Protestantismus und Politik. Werk und Wirkung Adolf Stoeckers.* Ed. Günther Brakelmann a.o. Hamburg: Christians, 1982. Pp. 123–196. *LJ*

1040  Jochmann, Werner (1921–): Struktur und Funktion des deutschen Antisemitismus. *Juden im Wilhelminischen Deutschland, 1890–1914.* Ed. Werner E. Mosse. Tübingen, 1976. Pp. 389–477. *LJ*

1041  Jochmann, Werner (1921–): Struktur und Funktion des deutschen Antisemitismus, 1878–1914. *Antisemitismus: Von der Judenfeindschaftt zum Holocaust.* Eds. Herbert Strauss, Norbert Kampe. Frankfurt a.M.: Campus Verlag, 1985. Pp. 99–142. *LJ*

1042  Jöhlinger, Otto (1883–1924): *Bismarck und die Juden.* Berlin: D. Reimer, 1921. VIII, 206 pp. *LJ*

1043 Joel, Manuel (1826–1890): *Lasker's Resolution den Austritt aus der Synagogen-gemeinde betreffend und ihre etwaigen Folgen für das bevorstehende Judengesetz beleuchtet.* Breslau: Commissions-Verlag Priebatsch, 1875. 11 pp. *LJ*

1044 Joel, Manuel (1826–1890): Leistung des Advokaten Dr. Kopp im Prozeße Rohling-Bloch. *MGWJ* 35 (1886) 145–155 pp. *LJ*

1045 Joel, Manuel (1826–1890): *Meine in Veranlassung eines Prozeßes abgegebenen Gutachten über den Talmud in erw. Form hrsg.* Breslau: Schletter'sche Buchhdlg., 1877. 33 pp. *LJ*

1046 Jonge, Moritz de: *Ein Akt moderner Tortur. I. Die Wahnbriefe.* Berlin: Verlag der Vaterländischen Verlagsanstalt, 1890. 116 pp. *LJ*

1047 Jonge, Moritz de: *Höret Rathenau und Genossen; Kritik des Dogma's von der assimilatio gojica.* Berlin: H. Schildberger, 1903. 56 pp. (Jüdische Schriften, ser. 1, I) *LJ*

1048 Jonge, Moritz de: *Messias, der kommende jüdische Mann; Sturz der kirchlichen Stabilierung der jüdischen Messias-Lehre.* Berlin: H. Schildberger, 1904. 200 pp. (Jüdische Schriften, 3–4) *LJ*

1049 Josaphet, Don, pseud.: *Bibel und Judentum; ein Blick auf Israels Vergangenheit, Gegenwart und Zukunft.* Passau: Coppenrath, 1893. VIII, 155 pp. *LC*

1050 *Der Jude als Deutschkatholik; oder, Der neue Johannes Ronge am alten Fleischmarkt. Noch ein halbes Dutzend "Bremsen" für den "Freimütigen."* Wien: Mayer, 1848. 23 pp. *Unseen*

1051 *Ein Jude deutscher Kultur; unsere Judenfrage.* Berlin: Louis Lamm, 1906. 35 pp. *Unseen*

1052 *Der Jude Salomon Kaufmann von Viernheim; einer der größten jüdischen Wucherer und Betrüger, dessen Prozeß vor der Strafkammer des Landgerichts Mannheim vom 11. bis 13. September 1881 stattfand.* 3. verb. Aufl. Mannheim: Zahn, 1882. 20 pp. *LJ*

1053 Juden. *Allgemeines Handbuch der Freimaurerei. 3. vollständig rev. Aufl. Bd. 1.* Leipzig: M. Hesse, 1900–1901. Pp. 513–516. *LJ*

1054 Die Juden der Schweiz. *MGWJ* 8 (1859) 413–419. *LJ*

1055 *Die Juden des Altertums.* Leipzig: Th. Fritsch, 1886. 8 pp. (Brennende Fragen, 34) *LJ*

1056  *Die Juden im Jahrzehnt der deutschen Revolution 1848 und ihr Einfluß auf die
      Arbeiterbewegung; ein Grundriß.* Berlin: Arbeitswissenschaftliches Institut der
      Deutschen Arbeitsfront, 1942. 34 pp. *Unseen*

      Typescript.

1057  *Die Juden in Böhmen und ihre Stellung in der Gegenwart.* Prag: Silber und
      Schenk, 1863. IV, 90 pp. *LJ*

1058  *Die Juden in Ungarn und ihre bevorstehende Emanzipation, von J. G.W.* Pest:
      Gebr. Lauffer, 1866. 15 pp. *Unseen*

1059  *Die Juden-Mission; eine evangelische Christenpflicht und der Gewinn, den sie
      uns Christen bringt.* Köln: Typ. W. Hassel, 1864. 33 pp. *LJ*

      Lectures given at the general meeting of the Rheinisch–Westfälischer Verein
      für Israel on May 18, 1864.

1060  *Die Juden und das Christenblut; geschichtliche Beiträge zur Frage des jüdischen
      Blutrituals.* Leipzig: Germanicus–Verlag, 1892. XV, 46 pp. (Sammlung
      deutsch-sozialer Flugschriften, 5–6) *LJ*

1061  Juden und jüdische Aspekte in der deutschen Arbeiterbewegung, 1848–1918.
      Internationales Symposium Dezember 1976. Leitung: Shlomo Na'aman. Hrsg.:
      Walter Grab. *TAJfDG* Beiheft 2 (1977) 260 pp. *LJ*

1062  *Die Juden verlangen Emanzipation. Soll man die Juden emanzipieren?* Pest:
      Emich, 1848. 15 pp. *Unseen*

1063  *Das Judenchristentum in der religiösen Volkserziehung des deutschen
      Protestantismus, von einem christlichen Theologen.* Leipzig: F.W. Grunow,
      1893. VII, 182 pp. *LJ*

1064  *Der Judeneid betrachtet vom mosaisch-religiösen und humanitären Standpunkte.*
      Semlin: Soppron, 1864. 16 pp. *LV*

      Signed: S . . . n, Belgrad.

1065  *Der "Judenflinten" Prozeß.* Sonderabdruck der stenografischen Berichte der
      "Neuen Deutschen Zeitung" über die Verhandlungen des Königlichen
      Landgerichtes zu Berlin in der Beleidigungssache Ludwig Isidor Löwe und
      Kühne wider den Rektor Hermann Ahlwardt, Mitglied des Deutschen
      Reichstags. Leipzig: Verlag der "Neuen Deutschen Zeitung," 1892. 154 pp.
      *LJ*

1066  *Die Judenfrage; "Denkschrift" über die Ursachen eines erfolgten Uebertritts zur
      christlichen Kirche und die sich — aus demselben, wie auf Grundlage*

*vorherrschend spezifisch christlichen Weltanschauung — ergebende Veranlassung für die gebildeten deutschen insbesondere ungläubigen Juden zur Ueberantwortung der künftigen Generation an die christliche Kirche.* Von einem Offizier a.D. München: G. Franz Buchdruckerei, 1881. XII, 98 pp. *LJ*
The author's name: von Henle.

1067 *Die Judenfrage; ein offenes Sendschreiben an das deutsche Parlament in Frankfurt a.M.* Clausthal: Schweigersche Buchhdlg, 1848. 38 pp. *LTA*

1068 Die Judenfrage noch einmal vor beiden Häusern des Landtags. *Pr. Jhrb.* 7 (1861) 11–50. *LF*

1069 *Die Judenfrage vor Gericht; Klage des Deutsch-Israelitischen Gemeindebundes in Leipzig gegen Autor und Verleger der "Egon Waldegg'schen Judenfrage."* Nach den Prozeßakten veröffentlicht. Dresden: R. von Grumbkow, 1883. 33 pp. *LJ*

1070 *Judenhaß und Antisemitismus im 19. Jahrhundert.* Hrsg. Karlheinz Schneider, Nikolaus Simon. 2. durchges. Aufl. Frankfurt a.M.: Haag & Herchen, 1991. 119 pp. *LJ*

1071 *Das Judentum im Staate.* Berlin: Verlag der Redaktion des "Reichsbote," 1884. 46 pp. *LJ*
Offprint from: *Der Reichsbote.*

1072 Das Judentum in den deutschen Freimaurerlogen. *Der Hammer* 11 (1912) 123–125. *LB*

1073 *Das Judentum und das einige wahre Christentum.* Bremen: Valett und Comp., 1892. 28 pp. *LJ*
Offprint from: *Einiges wahres Christentum.*

1074 *Das Judentum und seine Aufgabe im neuen Deutschen Reich; Sendschreiben an die deutschen Juden von einem Glaubensgenossen.* Leipzig: Leiner, 1871. 24 pp. *LJ*

1075 Judt, Ignacy Maurycy: *Die Juden als Rasse; eine Analyse aus dem Gebiete der Anthropologie.* Berlin: Jüdischer Verlag, 1903. 243 pp. *LJ*

1076 Jüdische Bibliographie. *Jüdisches Lexikon. Bd. 1.* Berlin: Jüdischer Verlag, 1927. Col. 1022–1026. *LJ*
Entered in vol. 1 under: Bibliographie, Jüdische.

1077  *Der Jüdische Einjährig-Freiwillige im deutschen Heere.* Berlin: Walther & Apolant, 1888. 22 pp. *LJ*

1078  *Jüdische Integration und Identität in Deutschland und Oesterreich, 1848–1918; internationales Symposium, April 1983.* Leitung Walter Grab. Tel Aviv: Universität, Institut für deutsche Geschichte, 1984. 368 pp. (TAJfDG, Beiheft 6) *LJ*

1079  *Der jüdische Soldat im deutschen Heere.* Hamburg: A. Goldschmidt, 1890. 24 pp. *LJ*

1080  *Die jüdische und die christliche Moral von Pfr. K. in Dr. bei M.* Leipzig: Faber, 1895. 16 pp. *LJ*

1081  *Die jüdischen Gemeinden und Vereine in Deutschland.* Berlin: Verlag des Bureaus für Statistik der Juden, 1906. 85 pp. (Veröffentlichungen des Bureaus für Statistik der Juden, 3) *LJ*

1082  *Jüdisches Litteraturblatt.* See Appendix: Newspapers and Periodicals, Jewish

1083  Jung, Dr.: Die Vorschriften über Eidesleistung der Juden. *Pr. Jhrb.* 5 (1859) *Unseen*

1084  Jungmann, Max: Ist das Jüdische Volk degeneriert? *Die Welt* 6 (1902) 3–4. *LJ*

1085  Kadisch, Hermann: *Jungjuden und Jungösterreich.* Wien: Im Verlag der "Jüdischen Vereinigung," 1905. 36 pp. *LJ*

       Offprint from: *Jüdisches Volksblatt!*

1086  Kähler, Siegfried August: Adolf Stoecker, 1835–1909. *Studien zur deutschen Geschichte des 19. und 20. Jahrhunderts.* Göttingen: Vandenhoeck & Ruprecht, 1961. Pp. 184–203. *LJ*

1087  Kähler, Siegfried August: Stoeckers Versuch eine Christliche-Soziale Arbeiter-Partei in Berlin zu begründen (1878). *Deutscher Staat und deutsche Parteien. Beiträge zur deutschen Partei- und Ideengeschichte.* Ed. Paul Wentzke. München, 1922. Pp. 227–265. *LJ*

1088  Kaelble, Hartmut: *Berliner Unternehmer während der frühen Industrialisierung; Herkunft sozialer Status und politischer Einfluß.* Mit einem Vorwort von Otto Büsch. Berlin: W. de Gruyter, 1972. X, 302 pp. (Veröffentlichungen der Historischen Kommission zu Berlin, 40) *LJ*

1089 Kahn, Arnold: *Die berufliche, soziale und wirtschaftliche Entwicklung der Juden in Frankfurt a.M. während der Emanzipationszeit, 1806-1866.* Frankfurt: 1923. IV, 108, XXVI pp. *LF*

Diss. 1923 (ms)

1090 Kahn, Lehman: *Assimilation, par L.K. Amitai (pseud.).* Bruxelles: M. van Dantzig, 1900. 227 pp. *LJ*

1091 Kahn, Lehman: *Offener Brief an die Adresse des Herrn Stoecker, Hofprediger in Berlin, Vater des Antisemitismus unserer Zeit in Deutschland. Von einem Freunde der Wahrheit . . .* Brüssel: Tr. Rein, 1888. 20 pp. *LJ*

1092 Kahn, Lothar: Moritz Gottlieb Saphir. *LBIYB* 20 (1975) 247-257. *LJ*

1093 Kahn, Siegbert: *Antisemitismus und Rassenhetze: eine Uebersicht über ihre Entwicklung in Deutschland.* Berlin: Dietz, 1948. 94 pp. *LC*

1094 Kahn, Siegbert: Dokumente des Kampfes der revolutionären Arbeiterbewegung gegen Antisemitismus und Judenverfolgung. *Beiträge zur Geschichte der deutschen Arbeiterbewegung* 2 (1960) 552-564. *LF*

1095 Kaim, Isidor: *Ein Jahrhundert der Judenemanzipation und deren christliche Verteidiger. Rückblick auf Literatur und Geschichte.* Leipzig: A. Fritsch, 1869. VIII, 90 pp. *LJ*

1096 Kalisch, Moritz: *Die Judenfrage in ihrer wahren Bedeutung für Preußen.* Leipzig: Veit & Comp., 1860. XIV, 410 pp. *LJ*

1097 Kalischer, Alfred Christlieb: *Was uns in der Religion Not tut; ein Weckruf an die Bekenner Jesu und an die Bekenner Mose.* Berlin: C. Chun, 1879. 51 pp. *LJ*

1098 Kalischer, Arnold: *Offener Brief eines deutschen Israeliten an den Königlichen Geheimen Regierungsrat Heinrich von Treitschke, ordentlichen Professor an der Universität Berlin.* 3. Aufl. Berlin: Walther & Apolant, 1888. 15 pp. *LJ*

1099 Kalkar, Chr. K.: *Israel und die Kirche; geschichtlicher Ueberblick der Bekehrungen der Juden zum Christentum in allen Jahrhunderten.* Uebers. von A. Michelsen. Hamburg: Agentur des Rauten-Hauses, 1869. 194 pp. *LJ*

1100 Kallner, Josef: *Einiges zur jüdischen Fleischhygiene; Vortrag gehalten auf der Internationalen Hygiene Ausstellung zu Dresden.* Berlin: Verlag des Central-Vereins Deutscher Staatsbürger Jüdischen Glaubens, 1912. 19 pp. *LJ*

1101  Kallner, Rudolf: *Herzl und Rathenau; Wege jüdischer Existenz an der Wende des 20. Jahrhunderts.* Stuttgart: Klett, 1976. 446 pp. *LJ*

1102  Kaltenbrunner, Gerd-Klaus: Houston Stewart Chamberlain, the Most Germanic of Germans. *Wien.Lib.Bull.* 22 (1967-1968) 6-12. *LJ*

1103  Kaltenbrunner, Gerd-Klaus: Vom Konkurrenten des Karl Marx zum Vorläufer Hitlers; Eugen Dühring. *Propheten des Nationalismus.* Ed. Karl Schwedhelm. München: List-Verlag, 1969. Pp. 36-55. *LC*

1104  Kaltenbrunner, Gerd-Klaus: Wahnfried und die "Grundlagen"; Houston Stewart Chamberlain. *Propheten des Nationalismus.* Ed. Karl Schwedhelm. München: List-Verlag, 1969. Pp. 105-123. *LC*

1105  Kameras, N.: Für Juden und für Antisemiten; Vortrag gehalten am 9. Jänner 1890 in einer christlichen Versammlung. Hrsg. und bevorwortet von J. Priluker. Wien: Selbstverlag des Herausgebers, 1890. 14 pp. *LJ*

1106  Kamis-Mueller, Aaron (1946-): *Antisemitismus in der Schweiz, 1900-1930.* Zürich: Chronos, 1990. 547 pp. *LJ*

      Summaries in English, French and Hebrew.

1107  Kampe, Norbert (1948-): Jews and Antisemites at Universities in Imperial Germany. I. Jewish Students — Social History and Social Conflict. *LBIYB* 30 (1985) 357-394. *LJ*

1108  Kampe, Norbert (1948-): Jüdische Professoren im Deutschen Kaiserreich; zu einer vergessenen Enquête Bernhard Breslauers. *Antisemitismus und jüdische Geschichte.* Berlin: Wissenschaftlicher Autoren-Verlag, 1987. Pp. 185-211. *LJ*

1109  Kampe, Norbert (1948-): *Studenten und "Judenfrage" im Deutschen Kaiserreich; die Entstehung einer akademischen Trägerschicht des Antisemitismus.* Göttingen: Vandenhoeck and Ruprecht, 1988. 327 pp. (Kritische Studien zur Geschichtswissenschaft, 761) *LJ*

1110  *Der Kampf gegen das Judentum; eine Würdigung des gleichnamigen Werkes von Dr. med. Gustav Stille. Mit dem Programm der Deutschsozialen <antisemitischen> Partei und drei Anlagen.* Leipzig: Germanicus, 189-. 16 pp. *LJ*

      Offprint from: *Deutsch-Soziale Blätter.*

1111  Kamphausen, Adolf Hermann Heinrich (1829-1909): *Das Verhältnis des Menschenopfers zur israelitischen Religion.* Bonn: Röhrscheid & Ebbecke, 1896. 75 pp. *LJ*

Offprint from: *Programm zur Geburtstagfeier des Stifters der Rheinischen Friedrich-Wilhelm Universität.*

1112 Kampmann, Wanda: Adolf Stoecker und die Berliner-Bewegung; ein Beitrag zur Geschichte des Antisemitismus. *Geschichte in Wissenschaft und Unterricht* 113 (1962) 558–579. *LJ*

1113 Kampmann, Wanda: *Deutsche und Juden; die Geschichte der Juden in Deutschland vom Mittelalter bis zum Beginn des Ersten Weltkrieges.* Frankfurt a.M.: Fischer Taschenbuch-Verlag, 1979. Pp. 206–450. *LJ*

1114 Kann, Robert Adolf: Assimilation and Antisemitism in the German-French Orbit in the Nineteenth and Early Twentieth Century. *LBIYB* 14 (1969) 92–115. *LJ*

1115 Kann, Robert Adolf: Friedrich Julius Stahl. *LBIYB* 12 (1967) 55–74. *LJ*

1116 Kann, Robert Adolf: German Speaking Jewry During Austria-Hungary's Constitutional Era, 1867–1918. *J.S.St.* 10 (1948) 239–256. *LJ*

1117 Kann, Robert Adolf: Hungarian Jewry during Austria-Hungary's Constitutional Period, 1867–1918. *J.S.St.* 7 (1945) 357–386. *LJ*

1118 Kann, Robert Adolf: *The Multinational Empire; Nationalism and National Reform in the Habsburg Monarchy 1848–1918.* New York: Columbia University Press, 1950. 2 vols. *LJ*

Vol. 1: *Empire and Nationalities.* Vol. 2: *Empire Reform.*

1119 Kaplan, Marion A.: German-Jewish Feminism in the Twentieth Century. *J.S.St.* 38 (1976) 39–53. *LJ*

1120 Karbach, Oscar: Die politischen Grundlagen des deutsch-österreichischen Antisemitismus. *ZfGJ* 1 (1964) 1–8, 103–116, 169–178. *LJ*

1121 Kartell-Convent: *Protokoll über die Verhandlungen des XII ordentlichen K.C. Tages in München vom 20. und 21. Juli 1907.* München: 1907. 46 pp. *LJ*

1122 Kartell Jüdischer Verbindungen: *Der zionistische Student; Flugschrift des KZV.* Berlin: in Komm. beim Jüdischen Verlag, 1912. 64 pp. *LJ*

1123 Kaskel, Joachim Felix: Vom Hoffaktor zur Dresdner Bank; die Unternehmerfamilie Kaskel im 18. und 19. Jahrhundert. *Zeitschrift für Unternehmergeschichte* 28, 4, 3 (1983) 159–187. *LC*

1124 Kastan, Isidor (1840–1931): *Herr Robert von Mohl und die Judenemanzipation; eine Erwiderung.* Berlin: J.M. Späth, 1869. 30 pp. *LJ*

1125  Kaszony, Daniel von: *Esther Solymosi, das Blutopfer von Tísza-Eslár; Sozial-Roman aus der Gegenwart.* Budapest: G.P. Grimm, 1883. VI, 257 pp. *Unseen*

1126  Katary, Karl: *Die Rasse im Denken der zweiten Hälfte des 19. Jahrhunderts, unter besonderer Berücksichtigung Julius Langbehns.* Wien: 1936. 172 l. *Unseen*

Diss. 1936.

1127  *Der Katechismus der Juden; oder, Die Vorschriften des Schulchan Aruch verglichen mit denen des Talmud. Nebst einem ausführlichen Referat über den vor dem kgl. Landgericht zu Münster verhandelten. Strafprozeß in Sachen des Schulchan Aruch. Wohlfeile Volksausg.* Berlin: M. Schulze, 1884. 48 pp. *LJ*

1128  Katz, Albert (1858–1923): *Der wahre Talmudjude; die wichtigsten Grundsätze des talmudischen Schrifttums über das sittliche Leben des Menschen.* Uebers. und in 70 Kapiteln systematisch geordnet. 2. Aufl. Berlin: Apolant, 1893. 165 pp. *LJ*

1129  Katz, Jakob (1904–): Die Anfänge der Judenemanzipation. *LBI Bull.* 13 (1974) 12–31. *LJ*

1130  Katz, Jakob (1904–): *The Darker Side of Genius; Richard Wagner's Antisemitism.* Hannover: University Press of New England, 1986. 158 pp. *LJ*

Orginal title: *Richard Wagner; Vorbote des Antisemitismus.*

1131  Katz, Jakob (1904–): "Die Juden sind unser Unglück"; Reflexionen über ein antisemitisches Schlagwort. *Tribüne* 92 (1984) 58–66. *LJ*

1132  Katz, Jakob (1904–): *Emancipation and Assimilation; Studies in Modern Jewish History.* Westmead: Farnborough, Gregg International, 1972. XII, 293 pp. *LJ*

1133  Katz, Jakob (1904–): *Die Entstehung der Judenassimilation in Deutschland und deren Ideologie.* Frankfurt a.M.: 1935. 83 pp. *LJ*

Diss. 1935.

1134  Katz, Jakob (1904–): *From Prejudice to Destruction; Antisemitism, 1700–1933.* Cambridge, Mass.: Harvard University Press, 1980. VIII, 392 pp. *LJ*

1135  Katz, Jakob (1904–): German Culture and the Jews. *Commentary* 77 (1984) 54–59. *LJ*

1136  Katz, Jakob (1904–): German Culture and the Jews. *The Jewish Response to German Culture; from the Enlightenment to the Second World War.* Eds. Jehuda Reinharz, Walter Schatzberg. Hannover, N.H., 1985. Pp. 85–99. *LJ*

1137 Katz, Jakob (1904–): The German-Jewish Utopia of Social Emancipation. *Studies of the Leo Baeck Institute*. New York: Ungar Pub. Co., 1967. Pp. 61–80. *LJ*

1138 Katz, Jakob (1904–): *Jews and Freemasons in Europe 1723–1939*. Cambridge: Harvard University Press, 1970. VIII, 293 pp. *LJ*

Tr. from the Hebrew by Leonard Oschry.

1139 Katz, Jakob (1904–): *Out of the Ghetto; the Social Background of Jewish Emancipation 1770 till 1870*. Cambridge, Mass.: Harvard University Press, 1973. 271 pp. *LJ*

1140 Katz, Jakob (1904–): The Preparatory Stage of the Modern Antisemitic Movement (1873–1879). *Antisemitism through the Ages; a Collection of Essays*. Ed. Shmuel Almog. Jerusalem: The Zalman Shazar Center for the Study of Jewish History, 1980. Pp. 279–299. *LJ*

1141 Katz, Jakob (1904–): *Richard Wagner; Vorbote des Antisemitismus*. Königstein, Ts.: Jüdischer Verlag Athenäum, 1985. 216 pp. *LJ*

"Eine Veröffentlichung des Leo Baecks Instituts."

1142 Katz, Jakob (1904–): *A State within a State*. Jerusalem: Israel Academy of Sciences, 1969. 30 pp. (Proceedings, vol. 4, 3) *LJ*

1143 Katz, Jakob (1904–): *Zur Assimilation und Emanzipation der Juden; ausgewählte Schriften*. Darmstadt: Wissenschaftliche Buchgesellschaft, 1982. VIII, 209 pp. *LJ*

1144 Katz, Leopold (1878–): *Die rechtliche Stellung der Israeliten nach dem Staatskirchenrecht des Großherzogtums Hessen*. Giessen: Töpelmann, 1906. VIII, 95 pp. *LJ*

1145 Katzburg, Nathanael: The Jewish Congress in Hungary. *Hungarian-Jewish Studies* 2 (1969) 1–33. *LJ*

1146 Kaufmann, David (1852–1899): *Franz Delitzsch; ein Palmblatt aus Juda auf sein frisches Grab*. Berlin: Verlag der Jüdischen Presse, 1890. 22 pp. *LJ*

1147 Kaufmann, David (1852–1899): *Paul de Lagarde's jüdische Gelehrsamkeit; eine Erwiederung*. Leipzig: O. Schulze, 1887. 53 pp. *LJ*

1148 Kautsky, Karl (1854–1938): Kritik des Buches "Das Judentum und Sozialdemokratie." Ein Beitrag zur Beförderung der Einsicht in die sozialistisch-jüdische Koalitionserscheinung unserer Zeit, von Alexander Berg. *N.Z.* 10 (1891–1892) 757. *LJ*

1149 Kautsky, Karl (1854–1938): Das Massaker von Kischineff und die Judenfrage. *N.Z.* 21, 2 (1903) 303–309. *LJ*

1150 Kautsky, Karl (1854–1938): *Rasse und Judentum.* Stuttgart: Dietz, 1914. 94 pp. *LJ*
Offprint from: *Die Neue Zeit, Ergänzungs-Heft 20,* 1883.

1151 Kayser, Rudolf (1889–1964): Bettina von Arnim and the Jews. *Hist. Jud.* 20 (1958) 47–60. *LJ*

1152 Kayserling, Meier (1829–1905): *Die Blutbeschuldigung von Tísza-Eslár.* Budapest: Selbstverlag, 1882. 16 pp. *LJ*

1153 Kayserling, Meier (1829–1905): *Das Moralgesetz des Judentums in Beziehung auf Familie, Staat und Gesellschaft.* Wien: M. Waizner, 1882. 75, 27 pp. *LJ*

1154 Kayserling, Meier (1829–1905): *Die rituale Schlachtfrage; oder, Ist Schächten Tierquälerei?* Auf Grund der eingeholten und mit abgedruckten Gutachten von Adam Bagge, u.a. beantwortet und beleuchtet. Aarau: H.R. Sauerländer, 1867. 95 pp. *LJ*

1155 Kayserling, Meier (1829–1905): Zur Geschichte der Juden in der Schweiz. *MGWJ* 12 (1863) 405–417, 444–454. *LJ*

1156 Keim, Anton Maria: *Die Judenfrage im Landtag des Großherzogtums Hessen, 1820–1849; ein Beitrag zur Geschichte der Juden im Vormärz.* Darmstadt: Selbstverlag der Hessischen Historischen Kommission Darmstadt und der Historischen Kommission für Hessen, 1983. 258 pp. (Quellen und Forschungen zur Hessischen Geschichte, 46) *LJ*

1157 Keller, Augustin (1805–1883): *Die Emanzipation der Juden im Kanton Aargau; Rede gehalten vor dem großen Rat des Kanton Aargau am 15. Mai 1862.* Baden: Jäger, 1889. 16 pp. *Unseen*

1158 Keller, Augustin (1805–1883): *Das Schächten der Israeliten; Referat gehalten in einer Versammlung von Tierschutzfreunden am 2. April 1890.* Aarau: Typ. P. Wirz-Christen, 1890. 26 pp. *LJ*

1159 Kenyeres, Balàzs: Falsche Auslegungen der Sachverständigen bei Anklagen wegen Ritualmord. *Vierteljahrsschrift für gerichtliche Medizin und öffentliches Sanitätswesen* Suppl. 57–62 (1908) *LF*

1160 Kessler, Adolf: *Die Juden in Oesterreich unter Kaiser Franz Josef I.* Wien: 1932. VII, 216 l. *Unseen*
Diss.

1161 Kessler, Gerhard (1883–): Judentaufen und judenchristliche Familien in Ostpreußen. *Familiengeschichtliche Blätter — Deutscher Herold; Monatschrift für wissenschaftliche Genealogie* 36 (1938) col. 201–232, 261–272, 297–306. *LJ*

1162 Kestenberg-Gladstein, Ruth: The Jews between Czechs and Germans in the Historic Lands, 1848–1918. *The Jews of Czechoslovakia. Vol. 1.* Philadelphia: Jewish Publication Society, 1968. Pp. 21–71. *LJ*

1163 Kettner, Friedrich: *Ueber Constantin Brunners Werk "Der Judenhaß und die Juden."* Wien: Löwit, 1922. 53 pp. *LJ*

1164 Kindt, Werner, ed.: *Die Wandervogelzeit; Quellenschriften zur deutschen Jugendbewegung, 1896–1919.* Düsseldorf: E. Diederichs, 1968. 1097 pp. (Dokumentation der Jugendbewegung, 2) *LJ*

1165 Kirchholtes Hans-Dieter: *Jüdische Privatbanken in Frankfurt am Main.* Frankfurt a.M.: Kramer, 1969. 79 pp. *LJ*

1166 Kisch, Guido (1889–): Book Review: The Jews and Modern Capitalism, by Werner Sombart. With an Introduction to the American ed. by Bert F. Hoselitz. *Hist. Jud.* 13 (1951) 157–159. *LJ*

1167 Kisch, Guido (1889–): Die deutsch-jüdische Bibliographie seit dem 19. Jahrhundert. *Zeitschrift für Religions- und Geistesgeschichte* 22 (1970) 143–152. *LJ*

1168 Kisch, Guido (1889–): *Judaistische Bibliographie; ein Verzeichnis der in Deutschland und der Schweiz von 1956–1970 erschienenen Dissertationen und Habilitationsschriften.* Basel: Helbing & Lichtenhahn, 1972. 104 pp. *LJ*

1169 Kisch, Guido (1889–): *Judentaufen; eine historisch-biographisch, psychologisch-soziologische Studie, besonders für Berlin und Königsberg.* Berlin: Colloquium Verlag, 1973. VIII, 134 pp. (Einzelveröffentlichungen der Historischen Kommission zu Berlin, 14) *LJ*

1170 Kittseer, Jakob, Jun.: *Inhalt des Talmuds und seine Autorität aus den ersten Quellen geschöpft und unparteiisch behandelt.* Preßburg: Verlag des Verfassers, 1857. 201 pp. *LC*

1171 Klein, Charlotte: Damaskus to Kiev; Civiltà Cattolica on Ritual Murder. *Wien.Lib.Bull.* 27, n.s. 32 (1974) 18–25. *LJ*

1172 Klein, K.: *Aus öffentlichen und privaten Schlachthäusern Deutschlands.* München: M. Kupferschmid, 1912. X, 141 pp. *Unseen*

1173  Klein, K.: *Ein Gutachten des Geheimen Regierungsrates Prof. Dr. Tereg über das jüdisch-rituelle Schlachtverfahren.* Leipzig: 1914. 12 pp. (Leipziger Flugschriften-Sammlung zur Betäubungsfrage der Schlachttiere, 36) *LF*
Offprint from: *Deutsche Schlacht- und Viehhof-Zeitung,* 1913.

1174  Klein, Paula: *Der Antisemitismus in der Wiener Presse von 1848-1873.* Wien: 1938. 128 l. *LC*
Diss. 1938, typescript.

1175  Klein, Salomon (1814-1867): *Das Judentum; oder, Die Wahrheit über den Talmud.* Uebers. von S. Mannheimer. Basel: Chr. Krüsi, 1860. 151 pp. *LB*

1176  Kleinecke, Paul: *Gobineaus Rassenphilosophie; Essai sur l'inégalité des races humaines.* Berlin: Hermann Walther, 1902. 84 pp. *LJ*

1177  Kleinpaul, Rudolf Alexander Reinhold (1845-1918): *Menschenopfer und Ritualmorde.* Leipzig: H. Schmidt & C. Günther, 1892. 80 pp. *LJ*

1178  Kleinpaul, Rudolf Alexander Reinhold (1845-1918): *Der Mord von Konitz und der Blutaberglaube des Mittelalters.* Leipzig: H. Schmidt &. C. Günther, 1900. 32 pp. *LJ*

1179  Klemperer, Wilhelm: *Voltaire und die Juden; Vortrag.* Berlin: Bibliographisches Bureau, 1894. 35 pp. *LJ*

1180  Klesse, Max: Neuzeit der Juden. *Vom alten zum neuen Israel; ein Beitrag zur Genese der Judenfrage und des Antisemitismus. Bd. 3.* Frankfurt a.M.: Ner-Tamid-Verlag, 1965. Pp. 149-231. *LJ*

1181  Klinkenberg, Hans Martin: Zwischen Liberalismus und Nationalismus im Zweiten Kaiserreich, 1870-1918. *Monumenta Judaica, Handbuch.* Köln: J. Melzer, 1963. Pp. 309-384. *LJ*

1182  *Der Knabenmord in Xanten vor dem Schwurgericht in Kleve.* Zweibrücken: H. Reiselt, 1892. 36 pp. *LJ*

1183  Knauss, Erwin: Der politische Antisemitismus im Kaiserreich, 1871-1900. *Mitteilungen des Oberhessischen Geschichtsvereins* 53-54 (1969) 43-68. *LF*

1184  Kober, Adolf (1879-1958): Emancipation's Impact on the Education and Vocational Training of German Jewry. *J.S.St.* 16 (1954) 3-32, 151-176. *LJ*

1185  Kober, Adolf (1879-1958): Jews in the Revolution of 1848 in Germany. *J.S.St.* 10 (1948) 135-164. *LJ*

1186  Koch, Paul: *Der Ritualmord; eine Forderung des Alten Testamentes.* Berlin: Selbstverlag, 1902. 39 pp. *LJ*

1187  König, Adolf: *Heinrich Heine, der Schmutzfink im deutschen Dichterwald.* Düsseldorf: Komm. Verlag Schaber, 1888. 32 pp. *LJ*

1188  *Können den Israeliten die Staatsämter gegeben werden? Von einem Freunde Israels. Aus den Papieren eines Verstorbenen.* Berlin: Nicolai, 1861. 78 pp. *LJ*

1189  Koeri: *Die wahre Erlösung vom Antisemitismus. Von einem getauften Juden.* Leipzig: O. Wigand, 1883. 61 pp. *LJ*

1190  Kohler, Max James (1871-1934): Review of the German Edition of Werner Sombart's "Die Juden und das Wirtschaftsleben." *American Economic Review* 2 (1912) 81. *LJ*

1191  Kohn, Hans (1891-): Germany; Treitschke. *Prophets and Peoples; Studies in 19th Century Nationalism.* New York: Macmillan, 1946. Pp. 105-130. *LJ*

1192  Kohn, Jakob: *Assimilation, Antisemitismus und Nationaljudentum.* Wien: L. Rosner, 1894. 25 pp. *LJ*

1193  Kohut, Adolph (1848-1917): *Alexander Humboldt und das Judentum; ein Beitrag zur Kulturgeschichte des 19. Jahrhunderts.* 2. Aufl. Leipzig: F.W. Pardubitz, 1871. XV, 198 pp. *LJ*

1194  Kohut, Adolph (1848-1917): *Ferdinand Lassalle; sein Leben und Wirken.* Leipzig: O. Wigand, 1889. IX, 210 pp. *LJ*

1195  Kohut, Adolph (1848-1917): *Ritualmordprozeße; bedeutsame Fälle aus der Vergangenheit.* Berlin: Basch & Co., 1913. 64 pp. (Fragen des Tages, 1) *LJ*

Discussion of cases in Fulda, Skurz, Konitz, Polna, and Xanten.

1196  Kollenscher, Max (1875-): *Jüdische Gemeindepolitik.* Berlin: Verlag Zionistisches Zentralbureau, 1909. 32 pp. *LJ*

1197  Kollenscher, Max (1875-): *Zionismus oder liberales Judentum.* Berlin: Zionistische Vereinigung, 1912. 25 pp. *LJ*

1198  Kollenscher, Max (1875-): *Zionismus und Staatsbürgertum.* Berlin: Verlag Zionistisches Zentralbureau, 1910. 15 pp. *LJ*

1199  Kollenscher, Max (1875-), ed.: *Rechtsverhältnisse der Juden in Preußen.* Textausg. mit Einleitung, Anmerkungen und Sachregister. Berlin: J. Guttentag, 1910. VIII, 199 pp. (Guttentag'sche Sammlung preußischer Gesetze, 45) *LJ*

1200  *Der Konitzer Blutmord vor dem Berliner Gericht.* Berlin: G.A. Dewald, 1902.
      58 pp. *Unseen*

1201  *Der Konitzer Mord; ein Beitrag zur Klärung.* Breslau: Preuß & Jünger, 1900.
      48 pp. *LJ*

1202  Kopelovitz, Jakob: *Bibel und Talmud; oder, Ist der rituelle Mord möglich?*
      Wien: Selbstverlag des Verfassers, 1883. 40 pp. *LJ*

1203  Kopp, Josef (1827–1907): *Zur Judenfrage nach den Akten des Prozeßes
      Rohling-Bloch.* 3. Aufl. Leipzig: J. Klinkhardt, 1886. V, 196 pp. *LJ*

1204  Kornfeld, Hermann: *Zionismus und Kirchenstaat, von H.K. (Samuelo).* Berlin:
      J. Singer, 1905. 23 pp. *LJ*
      The author favors territorialism.

1205  *Der Kornwucher an der Börse, I und II.* Leipzig: Th. Fritsch, 1888. 2 vols.
      (Brennende Fragen, 36–37) *LJ*

1206  Kosmopolitus, Etfra, pseud.: *Die Lösung der Judenfrage in humanitärster
      Weise.* Leipzig: A. Schulze, 1892. 82 pp. *LJ*

1207  Kralik, Richard: *Dr. Karl Lueger und der christliche Sozialismus. Bd. 1: Vom
      Beginn bis 1900.* Wien: Hilfsbund für Heimat und Volk, 1923. 280 pp. *LB*

1208  Kraus, Karl (1874–1936): *Eine Krone für Zion.* Wien: Frisch, 1898. 31 pp. *LJ*

1209  Krause, Fritz: *Der Wucher und seine Geldleute.* 8. Aufl. Berlin: G. A. Dewald,
      1894. 27 pp. *LJ*

1210  Krause, H. von: *Zum Austritt Stoeckers aus der Konservativen Partei.* Hrsg.
      von Oberst von Krause. Berlin: M. Pasch, 1896. 48 pp. *LJ*

1211  Kretzer, Eugen: *Joseph Arthur, Graf von Gobineau; sein Leben und sein Werk.*
      Leipzig: H. Seemann Nachf., 1902. 264 pp. (Männer der Zeit, 11) *LC*

1212  Kretzer, W.: *Die Fraktion der Antisemiten im Reichstage.* Berlin: G. Höppner,
      1890. 59 pp. *LJ*

1213  Kristeller, Samuel (1820–1900): *Liebe deinen Nächsten wie dich selbst.* Berlin:
      Typ. S. Preuß, 1891. 48 pp. *LTA*

1214  Krohn, Helga: *Die Juden in Hamburg; die politische, soziale und kulturelle
      Entwicklung einer jüdischen Großstadtgemeinde nach der Emanzipation,*

*1848-1918.* Hamburg: Christians, 1974. 247 pp. (Hamburger Beiträge zur Geschichte der Deutschen Juden, 4) *LJ*

Diss. Hamburg.

1215 Krohn, Helga: *Die Juden in Hamburg, 1800-1850; ihre soziale, kulturelle und politische Entwicklung während der Emanzipationszeit.* Frankfurt a.m.: Europäische Verlagsanstalt, 1967. 110 pp. (Hamburger Studien zur neueren Geschichte, 9) *LJ*

1216 Krollmann, C.: *Warum gab es im Jahre 1819 eine "Judenhetze"? Ein Beitrag zur Geschichte des Antisemitismus.* Berlin: W. Giese, 1899. 24 pp. *LJ*

Offprint from: *Antisemitisches Jahrbuch für 1899.*

1217 Kroner, Theodor (1845-1923): Gegen den Wucher. *Israelitische Wochenschrift* 10 (1879) 53-54, 63, 71, 78, 106-107, 115-116. *LJ*

A series of articles against usury among the Jews and the fight of the Jewish communities against it.

1218 Kruck, Alfred: Kampf gegen das Judentum. *Geschichte des Alldeutschen Verbandes 1890-1893.* Wiesbaden: F. Steiner, 1954. Pp. 130-134. (Veröffentlichungen des Instituts für Europäische Geschichte, Mainz, 3) *LJ*

1219 Krudy, Gyula: *A tiszaeszlári Solymosi Eszter.* Budapest: Magveto Kőnyvkiado, 1975. 548 pp. (Tények és tanúk) *LJ*

1220 Kruk, Josef: *Die Rolle der auswärtigen Staaten für die Emanzipation der Juden in der Schweiz.* Zürich: Typ. v. Ostheim, 1913. 61 pp. *LJ*

1221 Kubinszky, Judit: *Politikai antiszemitizmus Magyarorszagon 1875-1890.* Budapest: Kossuth Konyvkiado, 1976. 272 pp. *LJ*

1222 Kühleborn, pseud.: Der Konitzer Mord; eine Kriminalstudie. *Antisemitisches Jahrbuch* (1901) 162-198. *LJ*

1223 Külling, Friedrich T.: *Antisemitismus bei uns wie überall; Judenfeindschaft in der Schweiz, 1866-1900.* Zürich: Juris-Verlag, 1978. XXV, 412 pp. *LJ*

1224 Küpfer (minister): *Was hältst Du von Israels Rettung? Ein Vortrag.* Straßburg: Typ. Berger-Levrault, 1862. 32 pp. *LJ*

1225 Kuhlenbeck, Ludwig (1857-1920): *Das Evangelium der Rasse; Briefe über das Rassenproblem.* Prenzlau: A. Mieck, 1905. 72 pp. (Deutsches Wollen, 2) *LJ*

1226 Kulka, Otto Dov (1933–): Richard Wagner und die Anfänge des modernen
Antisemitismus. *LBI Bull.* 4 (1961) 281–300. *LJ*

1227 Kunert, Karl (1870–): *Die Anfänge des Talmuds und die Entstehung des
Christentums; eine Beleuchtung zu dem gleichlautenden Vortrag von H.
Vogelstein.* 2. erw. Aufl. Leipzig: Dörffling & Franke, 1914. 19 pp. *LJ*

1228 Kunert, Karl (1870–): *Die Geschichte der Judenmission; Vortrag gehalten am
1.12.1903.* Königsberg: Evangelische Buchhdlg. des Ostpreußischen
Provinzial-Vereins für Innere Mission, 1904. 16 pp. *Unseen*

1229 Kunert, Karl (1870–): *Jom Kippur, der große Versöhnungstag der Juden.*
Königsberg i. Pr.: Emil Rautenberg, 1902. 16 pp. *LJ*

1230 Kunert, Karl (1870–): *Kann ein Jude aus Ueberzeugung Christ werden?*
Königsberg: Evangelische Buchhdlg. des Ostpreußischen Provinzial-Vereins
für Innere Mission, 1911. 24 pp. *Unseen*

1231 Kunert, Karl (1870–): *Lieder für Judenmissionsfeste; zusammengestellt von Karl
Kunert.* Königsberg: E. Rautenberg, 1904. 4 l. *Unseen*

1232 Kunert, Karl (1870–): *Müssen wir Judenmission treiben?* Königsberg i. Pr.:
Selbstverlag, 1911. 43 pp. *LF*

1233 Kunert, Karl (1870–): *Offener Brief an Herrn Rabbiner Dr. F. Perles in
Königsberg.* Königsberg i. Pr.: Evangelische Buchhdlg. des Ostpreußischen
Provinzial-Vereins für Innere Mission, 1902. 8 pp. *Unseen*

1234 Kunert, Karl (1870–): *Rabbiner Dr. H. Vogelstein's Vortrag; die Anfänge des
Talmuds und die Entstehung des Christentums.* Missionspredigt in Königsberg.
Königsberg i. Pr.: Evangelische Buchhdlg. des Ostpreußischen
Provinzialvereins für Innere Mission, 1902. 20 pp. *LJ*

1235 Kunert, Karl (1870–): *Was lernen Juden und Christen von Dr. Perles; ein
bescheidener Beitrag zur Harnack Literatur.* Königsberg i. Pr.: Evangelische
Buchhdlg. des Ostpreußischen Provinzial-Vereins für Innere Mission, 1902. 16
pp. *LJ*

1236 Kunert, Karl (1870–): *Was treibt uns zur Judenmission? Vortrag gehalten am
20.10.1903.* Königsberg i. Pr.: Evangelische Buchhdlg. des Ostpreußischen
Provinzial-Vereins für Innere Mission, 1904. 16 pp. *Unseen*

1237 Kunert, Karl (1870–): *Ein Wort zu seiner Zeit; für Juden und Christen
mitgeteilt.* Königsberg i. Pr.: Evangelische Buchhdlg, 1912. 16 pp. *LJ*
Offprint from: *Saat auf Hoffnung*, 1903.

1238 Kupisch, Karl: *Adolf Stoecker, Hofprediger und Volkstribun; ein historisches Porträt.* Berlin: Haude & Spener, 1970. 94 pp. *LJ*

1239 Kupisch, Karl: *Judenfeindschaft im 19. Jahrhundert; Ursachen, Formen und Folgen.* Berlin: Institut Kirche und Judentum, 1977. 55 pp. (Veröffentlichungen aus dem Institut Kirche und Judentum bei der Kirchlichen Hochschule, Berlin, 4) *LJ*

1240 Kuppe, Rudolf: *Dr. Karl Lueger; Persönlichkeit und Wirken.* Wien: Brüder Hollinek, 1947. 195 pp. (Oesterreichische Heimat, 12) *Unseen*

1241 Kuppe, Rudolf: *Karl Lueger und seine Zeit.* Wien: Oesterreichische Volksschriften, 1933. 583 pp. *LB*

1242 Kurrein, Adolf (1846–1919): *Brauchen die Juden Christenblut?* Prag: J. Brandeis, 1900. 49 pp. *LJ*

1243 Kynades, Ludwig: *Herkules am Scheidewege; oder, Stoecker und die Konservative Fraktion.* Leipzig: Werther, 1896. 15 pp. *Unseen*

1244 Lademacher, Horst: *Moses Hess in seiner Zeit.* Bonn: L. Röhrscheid, 1977. 194 pp. (Veröffentlichungen des Stadtarchivs Bonn, 17) *LJ*

1245 Laible, Heinrich: *Jesus Christus im Talmud. Mit einem Anhang: Die talmudischen Texte mitgeteilt von Gustaf Dalman.* Berlin: Reuther und Reinhard, 1891. VI, 96, 19 pp. (Schriften des Institutum Judaicum in Berlin, 10) *LJ*

1246 Lamberti, Marjorie (1937–): The Attempt to Form a Jewish Bloc; Jewish Notables and Politics in Wilhelminian Germany. *Central European History, Atlanta, GA* 3 (1970) 73–93. *LJ*

1247 Lamberti, Marjorie (1937–): From Coexistence to Conflict; Zionism and the Jewish Community in Germany, 1897–1914. *LBIYB* 27 (1982) 53–86. *LJ*

1248 Lamberti, Marjorie (1937–): The Jewish Struggle for the Legal Equality of the Religions in Imperial Germany. *LBIYB* 23 (1978) 101–116. *LJ*

1249 Lamberti, Marjorie (1937–): Liberals, Socialists and the Defence Against Antisemitism in the Wilhelminian Period. *LBIYB* 25 (1980) 147–162. *LJ*

1250 Lamm, Hans: *Karl Marx und das Judentum.* München: M. Hüber, 1969. 78 pp. (Hüber, 7195) *LJ*

1251  Landau, Fab: Die erwerbstätigen Israeliten in Deutschland. *Israelitisches Familienblatt, Hamburg* 15, 32 (1913) 3. *LJ*

1252  Landes, David Saul (1924–): Das Bankhaus Bleichröder, Gerson von Bleichröder, 1822–1893. *Deutsches Judentum — Aufstieg und Krise.* Stuttgart: Deutsche Verlagsanstalt, 1963. Pp. 187–215. *LJ*

1253  Landes, David Saul (1924–): The Bleichröder Bank; an Interim Report. *LBIYB* 5 (1960) 201–220. *LJ*

1254  Landes, David Saul (1924–): The Jewish Merchant; Typology and Stereotypology in Germany. *LBIYB* 19 (1974) 11–23. *LJ*

1255  Landsberg, Wilhelm: *Das rituelle Schächten der Israeliten im Lichte der Wahrheit.* Kaiserslauten: E. Grusius, 1882. 15 pp. *LJ*

1256  Lang, Julius (Munich): *Zur Versöhnung des Judentums mit Richard Wagner; mit Benutzung zweier noch nicht veröffentlichter auf diese Angelegenheit bezug habenden Briefe Richard Wagners. Ein unparteiisches Votum.* Berlin: Stilke und van Muyden, 1869. 47 pp. *LJ*

1257  Langbehn, August Julius (1851–1907): *Rembrandt als Erzieher, von einem Deutschen.* Leipzig: C.L. Hirschfeld, 1890. V, 356 pp. *LJ*

1258  Langen, Friedrich Ernst, von (1860–1935): *Talmudische Täuschungen; das jüdische Geheimgesetz und die deutschen Landesvertretungen. Ein Handbüchlein für Politiker.* Leipzig: H. Beyer, 1895. VI, 113 pp. *LJ*

1259  Lanz-Liebenfels, Jörg (1874–1954): *Revolution oder Evolution? Eine freikonservative Osterpredigt für das Herrentum europäischer Rasse.* Wien: "Ostara," 1906. 14 pp. ("Ostara," österreichisches Flugschriftenmagazin freikonservativer Richtung, 3) *LV*

1260  Lanz-Liebenfels, Jörg (1874–1954): *Der Taxil-Schwindel; ein welthistorischer Ulk nach den Quellen bearb.* Frankfurt a.M.: Neuer Frankfurter Verlag, 1906. 151 pp. (Bibliothek der Aufklärung) *Unseen*

1261  Laqueur, Walter Zeev (1921–): The German Youth Movement and the Jewish Question; a Preliminary Survey. *LBIYB* 6 (1961) 193–205. *LJ*

1262  Laqueur, Walter Zeev (1921–): Die Judenfrage. *Die deutsche Jugendbewegung.* Köln: Verlag Wissenschaft und Politik, 1962. Pp. 89–99. *LJ*

1263 Laser, W.: *Ein dunkler Punkt im Leben des Geh. Kommerzienrats von Bleichröder zu Berlin; zugleich ein Gegensatz zur Anklage gegen Prof. Gräf.* Zürich: Verlags–Magazin, 1886. 48 pp. *Unseen*

1264 Lassalle, Ferdinand (1825–1864): *Ferdinand Lassalle; der Mensch und Politiker in Selbstzeugnissen.* Hrsg. Konrad Hänisch. Leipzig: A. Kröner, 1925. 214 pp. *LJ*

1265 Lazare, Bernard (1865–1903): *L'Antisémitisme, son histoire et ses causes.* Paris: L. Chailley, 1894. VII, 420 pp. *LJ*

1266 Lazarus, Moritz (1824–1903), ed.: *Christliche Zeugnisse gegen die Blutbeschuldigung der Juden.* Berlin: Walther und Apolant, 1882. 58 pp. *LJ*

1267 Lazarus, Moritz (1824–1903): *Reden zur Eröffenung und zum Schluß der Zweiten Israelitischen Synode in Augsburg am 11. und 17. Juli 1871.* Augsburg: G.A. Reichel, 1871. 40 pp. *LJ*

1268 Le Rider, Jaques: Ein antisemitischer Jude. *Der Fall Otto Weininger.* Wien: Löcker–Verlag, 1985. Pp. 189–219. *LJ*

1269 Le Seur, Paul (1877–): *Adolf Stoecker; ein Gedenken und ein Ruf.* Berlin: Hochweg–Verlag, 1928. 55 pp. *LB*

1270 *Leben, Schicksale und Bekehrung Friedrich Albrecht Augusti's vormaligen jüdischen Rabbi's und nachherigen Verkündiger des göttlichen Wortes zu Eschenberge im Herzogtum Sachsen-Gotha.* Berlin: Beck, 1859. 36 pp. *LC*

1271 Lehmann, Emil (1829–1898): *Der Deutsche jüdischen Bekenntnisses; Vortrag gehalten im Centralverein Deutscher Staatsbürger Jüdischen Glaubens zu Berlin.* Berlin: P. Mödebeck, 1894. 15 pp. *LJ*

1272 Lehmann, Emil (1829–1898): *Höre Israel! Aufruf an die deutschen Glaubensgenossen.* Dresden: L. Wolf, 1869. IV, 89 pp. *LJ*

1273 Lehmann, Emil (1829–1898): *Die Rechtsverhältnisse der Juden in Sachsen; Petition an den Landtag des Königreichs Sachsen um Aufhebung der mit Paragraph 33 der Verfassungsurkunde im Widerspruch stehenden Bestimmungen.* Dresden: H. Henkler, 1869. 18 pp. *LJ*

1274 Lehmann, Johannes Georg (1851–1925): *Die Mündigerklärung der Israeliten im teutschen Völkerbunde und die Einsetzung derselben in alle bürgerlichen und staatlichen Rechte.* Eine Denkschrift an die Mitglieder der hohen teutschen Reichsversammlung in Frankfurt a.M. Landau: in Komm E. Kaussler, 1849. VII, 84 pp. *LJ*

1275   Lehr, Stefan: *Antisemitismus — religiöse Motive im sozialen Vorurteil; aus der Frühgeschichte des Antisemitismus in Deutschland, 1870–1914.* München: Kaiser, 1974. VIII, 291 pp. (Abhandlungen zum christlich–jüdischen Dialog, 5) *LJ*

1276   Leib, Mausche Mochuls, pseud.: *Ein Wort an die deutschen Juden.* Zürich: Schmidt, 1881. 18 pp. *LJ*

1277   Leitner, Rudolf: *Die Judenpolitik der österreichischen Regierung in den Jahren 1848–1859.* Wien: 1924. 122 l. *LC*
       Diss.

1278   Leo Baeck Institute, New York: *Bibliothek und Archiv. Katalog.* Bd. 1. Hrsg. von Max Kreutzberger. Tübingen: Mohr, 1970. XLI, 623 pp. (Schriftenreihe wissenschaftlicher Abhandlungen des LBI, 22) *LJ*

1279   Leon, S.: *Unser heutiges Judentum; eine Selbstkritik.* Berlin: Walther und Apolant, 1890. 40 pp. *LJ*

1280   Leroy–Beaulieu, Anatole (1842–1912): *L'antisémitisme.* Paris: C. Lévy, 1897. III, 78 pp. *LJ*

1281   Leroy–Beaulieu, Anatole (1842–1912): *L'antisémitisme et les amis de la paix.* [n.p.]: 1899. 36–41 pp. *Unseen*
       Detached from: *Almanach de la paix, 1899.*

1282   Leroy–Beaulieu, Anatole (1842–1912): *Les doctrines de haine; l'antisémitisme, l'antiprotestantisime, l'anticléricalisme.* Paris: C. Lévy, 1902. III, 309 pp. *LJ*

1283   Leroy–Beaulieu, Anatole (1842–1912): *Israel Among the Nations; a Study of the Jews and Antisemitism.* Tr. by Frances Hellman. New York: G.P. Putnam's Sons, 1895. XXIII, 385 pp. *LJ*

1284   Leroy–Beaulieu, Anatole (1842–1912): *The Jew and Antisemitism.* Tr. from the Revue des Deux Mondes by A. Blum. Cincinnati: 189-. 83 pp. *Unseen*

1285   Leroy–Beaulieu, Anatole (1842–1912): *Les juifs et l'antisémitisme; Israël chez les nations.* Paris: C. Lévy, 1893. XI, 441 pp. *LJ*

1286   Leroy–Beaulieu, Anatole (1842–1912): *Les juifs et l'antisémitisme; les griefs contre les juifs.* Paris: 1891. 771–813 pp. *LF*
       Detached from: *Revue des Deux Mondes.*

1287 Lestschinsky, Jakob: Jüdische Wanderungen und Staatsräume im Lichte der Vergangenheit. *MGWJ* 75 (1931) 429-443. *LJ*

1288 Lestschinsky, Jakob: Die Umsiedlung und Umschichtung des jüdischen Volkes im Laufe des letzten Jahrhunderts. *Weltwirtschaftliches Archiv* 30 (1929) 123-156; 32 (1930) 563-599 *LJ*

1289 Leszczynski, Hermann: *Unser Bruder bist Du! Achenu Attah! Ueber eine volle staatsbürgerliche, gesellschaftliche und militärische Gleichstellung der modernen, gebildeten Israeliten. Auf Grund eines überzeugungsvollen Anschlußes an M.v. Egidy's "Einiges Christentum" und einer innigen Rassenverschmelzung mit dem deutschen Wirtsvolke.* Leipzig: C.F. Müller, 1893. 96 pp. *LJ*

1290 Leuschen-Seppel, Rosemarie: *Sozialdemokratie und Antisemitismus im Kaiserreich, 1871-1914.* Bonn: Neue Gesellschaft, 1978. 347 pp. (Politik und Gesellschaftsgeschichte) *LJ*

1291 Leuschen-Seppel, Rosemarie: Sozialdemokratie und Antisemitismus im Kaiserreich, 1871-1914. *Judenfeindschaft in Altertum, Mittelalter und Neuzeit.* Ed. Anneliese Mannzmann. Königstein, Ts.: Scriptor 1981. Pp. 65-79. *LJ*

1292 Leuss, Hans (1861-1920): *Wilhelm Freiherr von Hammerstein, 1881-1895, Chefredakteur der Kreuzzeitung.* Auf Grund hinterlassener Briefe und Aufzeichnungen. Berlin: Herm. Walther, 1905. 158 pp. *LV*

1293 Leuthner, Karl (1869-1944): Junker und Juden. *Sozialistische Monatshefte* 2 (1908) 912-922. *LJ*

1294 Leven, Narcisse (1833-1915): *Cinquante ans d'histoire; l'Alliance Isráelite Universelle, 1860-1910.* Paris: Alcan, 1911-1920. 2 vols. *LJ*

1295 Levin, A.: *Der Kriegszug gegen das Schächten.* Sagan: R. Schönborn'sche Buchhdlg., 1889. 12 pp. *LJ*

1296 Levin, A.M.: *Ganz untertänigste Petition an ein Hohes Herrenhaus des Rabbiners A.M. Levin in Landsberg in Ober-Schlesien namens der altgläubigen Juden und in Vollmacht ihrer angesehensten Rabbiner, sowohl des In- und Auslandes betreffend die Revision und demnächstige Aufhebung des "Juden-Gesetzes" vom 23. Juli 1847.* Berlin: Typ. Heinticke, 1858. 96 pp. *LJ*

1297 Levinstein, Gustav (1842-1910): *Jüdische Kindertaufen; Vortrag gehalten am 9. Februar 1910.* Berlin: F. Weber, 1910. 12 pp. *LJ*

1298 Levinstein, Gustav (1842–1910): *Professor Ladenburg und der Unsterblichkeitsgedanke im Judentum.* Berlin: F. Weber, 1904. 32 pp. *LJ*

1299 Levinstein, Gustav (1842–1910): *Die Taufe.* Berlin: F. Weber, 1899. 30 pp. *LJ*

1300 Levinstein, Gustav (1842–1910): *Ueber die Erlösung des Judentums.* Berlin: 1900. 23 pp. *LJ*

A refutation of Benedictus Levita's article "Erlösung des Judentums."

1301 Levinstein, Gustav (1842–1910): *Warum die Juden nicht Christen werden können. Antwort auf den offenen Brief des Herrn Pastor Gebhardt.* Berlin: F. Weber, 1899. 24 pp. *LJ*

1302 Levita, Benedictus, pseud.: Aemterbesetzungsrecht und die Juden. *Das freie Wort* 3 (1903) 427–434. *LJ*

1303 Levita, Benedictus, pseud.: Antwort zu H. Vogelstein's Die Erlösung des Judentums. Bemerkungen zu dem . . . Aufsatze. *Pr. Jhrb.* 102 (1900) 515–516. *LJ*

1304 Levita, Benedictus, pseud.: Die Erlösung des Judentums. *Pr. Jhrb.* 102 (1900) 131–140. *LJ*

1305 Levy, Alphonse (1838–1917): *Die Erziehung der jüdischen Jugend zu Handwerk und Bodenkultur.* Berlin: E. Billig, 1895. 14 pp. *LJ*

1306 Lévy, George Raphael: Le rôle des juifs dans la vie économique. *Revue des études juives* 62 (1911) 161–189. *LJ*

Review of: Werner Sombart's *Die Juden und das Wirtschaftsleben.*

1307 Levy, J.H.: Werner Sombart's: "Die Juden und das Wirtschaftsleben." *The Jewish Chronicle* June 23 (1911) 19. *LJ*

Book review.

1308 Levy, Meyer (1833–1896): *Der Staat und die Juden im Norddeutschen Bund; ein Mahnruf an das norddeutsche Parlament.* Lissa: T. Scheibel, 1867. 40 pp. *LJ*

1309 Levy, Richard Simon: *The Downfall of the Antisemitic Political Parties in Imperial Germany.* New Haven: Yale University Press, 1975. VII, 335 pp. (Yale Historical Publications, Miscellany ser., 106) *LJ*

1310  Levy, Salomon: Ueber den Kampf ums Dasein in Bezug auf die Juden nach Prof. Dodel. *Populärwissenschaftliche Monatsblätter zur Belehrung über das Judentum* (1896) 63–64. *LJ*

1311  Lewin, Adolf (1843–1910): *Geschichte der badischen Juden seit der Regierung Karl Friedrichs, 1738–1909.* Karlsruhe: Braun, 1909. VI, 508 pp. *LJ*

1312  Lewin, Adolf (1843–1910): *Der Judenspiegel des Dr. Justus ins Licht der Wahrheit gerückt.* Magdeburg: Typ. D.L. Wolff, 1884. 89 pp. *LJ*

1313  Lewinnek, Artur: *Die Freunde des Kronprinzen; auch eine Schrift zum 25-jährigen Regierungsjubiläum unsers Kaisers.* Königsberg: Hartung, 1913. 40 pp. *LJ*

1314  Lewinsohn, Isaac Bär: *Die Blutlüge, Efess damim.* Aus dem Hebräischen übers., mit einem Vorwort und Anmerkungen versehen von Albert Katz. Berlin: Schildberger, 1892. 102 pp. *LJ*

1315  Lewinsohn, Isaac Bär: *Das Damokles-Schwert.* Aus dem Russischen von M. Friedländer. Petersburg: Düntz, 1884. 132 pp. *LJ*

1316  Lewkowitz, Albert (1883–1954): *Das Judentum und die geistigen Strömungen des 19. Jahrhunderts.* Breslau: Marcus, 1935. XII, 570 pp. (Grundriß der Gesamtwissenschaft des Judentums) *LJ*

1317  Lewy, Moritz: *Der Prozeß gegen Moritz Lewy, Konitz, 13–16 Februar 1901. nach stenographischer Aufnahme.* Berlin: H.S. Hermann, 1901. 434 pp. *LJ*

1318  *Liberalismus, Freiheit und Reaktion.* Leipzig: Th. Fritsch, 1887. 8 pp. (Brennende Fragen, 7) *LJ*

1319  Lichtenstein, Isaak: *Begegnungspunkte zwischen Juden und Christen; Gesetz und Evangelium.* 2. Ausg. London: Hebrew Christian Testimony to Israel, 1902. 20 pp. *LJ*

1320  Lichtenstein, Isaak: *Eine Bitte an die geehrten Leser.* Wien: L. Schönberger, 189–. 24 pp. *LJ*

1321  Lichtenstein, Isaak: *Eine Bitte an mein Volk.* Budapest: 189–. 24 pp. *LJ*

1322  Lichtenstein, Isaak: *Ein Geheimnis aus dem Talmud.* Wien: L. Schönberger, 189–. 41 pp. *LJ*

1323  Lichtenstein, Isaak: *Judenspiegel.* Wien: L. Schönberger, 1896. 35 pp. *LJ*

1324  Lichtenstein, Isaak: *Judentum und Christentum*. Hamburg: A. Scheibenhuber, [n.d.]. 97 pp. *LJ*

1325  Lichtenstein, Isaak: *Die Liebe und die Bekehrung; ein sehr ernstes Wort zu sehr ernster Zeit.* Budapest: Typ. V. Hornyavszky, 1887. 39 pp. *LJ*

1326  Lichtenstein, Isaak: *Der Talmud auf der Anklagebank durch einen begeisterten Verehrer des Judentums.* Budapest: 1886. 21, 14, 37 pp. *Unseen*

1327  Lichtenstein, Isaak: *Zwei Briefe; oder, Was ich eigentlich wirklich will.* Leipzig: W. Faber, 1893. 38 pp. *LJ*

1328  Liebermann, Arthur: *Der Schulchan Aruch.* 2. erw. Aufl. Berlin: M. Poppelauer, 1912. 40 pp. *LC*

1329  Liebeschütz, Hans (1893–): German Radicalism and the Formation of Jewish Political Attitudes during the Earlier Part of the Nineteenth Century. *Studies in Nineteenth Century Jewish Intellectual History.* Ed. Alexander Altmann. Cambridge, Mass.: Harvard University Press, 1964. Pp. 141–170. *LJ*

1330  Liebeschütz, Hans (1893–): *Das Judentum im deutschen Geschichtsbild von Hegel bis Max Weber.* Tübingen: Mohr, 1967. X, 360 pp. (Schriftenreihe wissenschaftlicher Abhandlungen des LBI, 17) *LJ*

1331  Liebeschütz, Hans (1893–), ed.: *Das Judentum in der deutschen Umwelt, 1800–1850.* Tübingen: J.C.B. Mohr, 1977. XII, 445 pp. (Schriftenreihe wissenschaftlicher Abhandlungen des LBI, 35) *LJ*

1332  Liebeschütz, Hans (1893–): Problems of Diaspora History in 19th Century Germany. *J.J.St.* 8 (1957) 103–111. *LJ*

1333  Liebeschütz, Hans (1893–): Treitschke and Mommsen on Jewry and Judaism. *LBIYB* 7 (1962) 153–182. *LJ*

1334  Liebling, U.: Die rituelle Fleischbeschau der Juden. *Oesterreichische Monatsschrift für Tierheilkunde* (1901) 241–250. *Unseen*

1335  Liese, Wilhelm: Werner Sombart's "Die Juden und das Wirtschaftsleben." *Theologie und Glaube* 4 (1912) 402–404. *Unseen*
      Review.

1336  Lilienhain, A. von: *Dunkle Morde; Xanten, Konitz, Gumbinnen.* Leipzig: K. Minde, 1902. 49 pp. *LJ*

1337 Lill, Rudolf: Katholizismus nach 1848. A: Der Heilige Stuhl und die Juden. B: Die deutschen Katholiken und die Juden in der Zeit von 1850 bis zur Machtübernahme Hitlers. *Kirche und Synagoge, Handbuch zur Geschichte von Christen und Juden. Darstellung mit Quellen. Bd. 2.* Eds. Karl Heinrich Rengstorf, Siegfried von Kortzfleisch, Stuttgart: E. Klett, 1970. Pp. 358-393. *LJ*

1338 Lill, Rudolf: Zu den Anfängen des Antisemitismus im Bismarck-Reich. *Saeculum* 26 (1975) 214-231. *LF*

1339 Linvald, Axel Steffensen (1886-): *Die dänische Regierung und die Juden in Dänemark und den Herzogtümern um den Anfang des 19. Jahrhunderts. Beiträge zur Emanzipationsgeschichte der Juden.* Kiel: Vollbehr & Riepen, 1927. 292-364 pp. *Unseen*

From: *Zeitschrift der Gesellschaft für Schleswig-Holsteinische Geschichte*, vol. 57.

1340 Lippe, Chaim David: *Bibliographisches Lexikon der gesamten jüdischen Literatur der Gegenwart . . .* Bd. 1-2. Wien: D. Löwy, 1879-1881. 2 vols. *LJ*

1341 Lippe, Chaim David: *Bibliographisches Lexikon der gesamten jüdischen Literatur der Gegenwart.* N.S., Bd. 1. Wien: Ch. D. Lippe's Buchhdlg., 1899. XXXII, 496 pp. *LJ*

1342 Lipschütz, Leopold, ed.: *Zeugnisse gegen die Blutbeschuldigung der Juden.* Berlin: Walther & Apolant, 1882. VI, 58 pp. *Unseen*

1343 Lipshytz, Christlieb T.: *Der Ebionitismus in der Judenmission; oder, Christentum und national-jüdisches Bewußtsein; Vortrag.* Leipzig: J.C. Hinrichs, 1912. 15 pp. (Schriften des Institutum Judaicum in Berlin, 41) *LJ*

1344 Liszt, Franz von (1851-1919): Die Kriminalität der Juden in Deutschland; Vortrag. *Mitteilungen des Vereins zur Abwehr des Antisemitismus* 16 (1906) 74-78. *LJ*

1345 Liszt, Franz von (1851-1919): *Das Problem der Kriminalität bei den Juden.* Giessen: A. Töpelmann, 1907. 11 pp. *LC*

Excerpt from: Festschrift der juristischen Fakultät der Universität Giessen zur dritten Jahrhundertfeier der Alma Mater Ludoviciana.

1346 Literarische Rundschau; Das Talmudjudentum von W. Rubens, pseud. *N.Z.* 12, 1 (1893-1894) 724-725. *LJ*

1347  Litten, Julius: *Die Juden und die politischen Parteien; eine Antwort an den Verfasser der Schrift "Schutzjuden oder Staatsbürger?"* Berlin: A. Wilhelm, 1893. 19 pp. *LJ*

1348  Lochner, Rudolf: *Georg von Schönerer, ein Erzieher zu Großdeutschland.* Bonn: Gebr. Scheur, 1942. 19 pp. (Kriegsvorträge der Rheinischen Friedrich–Wilhelms–Universität, Bonn a.Rh., 99) *LJ*

1349  Löb, Abraham: *Die Rechtsverhältnisse der Juden im ehemaligen Königreiche und der jetzigen Provinz Hannover.* Frankfurt a.M.: J. Kauffmann, 1908. VIII, 140 pp. *LC*

1350  Löb, Moritz: *Berliner Konfektion.* 5. Aufl. Berlin: H. Seemann, Nachf., 1906. 91 pp. (Großstadt-Dokumente, 15) *LC*

1351  Löb, Moritz: *Seine Majestät, der Reisende; Glossen aus dem Geschäftsleben.* Mit Illustrationen von Richard Guttschmidt. Stuttgart: Franckh'sche Verlagsbuchhdlg., 190–. 100 pp. *LC*

1352  Löbenstein, Mathias Emanuel: *Juden laßt Euch taufen.* 2. Aufl. Wien: Typ. C. Gerold, 1848. 15 pp. *LJ*

1353  Löffler, Lorenz: *W. Marr's "Sieg des Judentums über das Germanentum"; vom positiv christlichen Standpunkte aus betrachtet.* Stockach: Selbstverlag, 1879. 16 pp. *LC*

1354  Löwe, Heinrich (1869–1951): *Antisemitismus und Zionismus; eine zeitgemäße Betrachtung. Von Heinrich Sachse, pseud.* 2. Aufl. Berlin: H. Schildberger, 1903. 22 pp. (Jüdische Aufklärungsschrift, 1) *LJ*

1355  Löwe, Heinrich (1869–1951): *Die Juden in Deutschland; bibliographische Notizen.* ZfGJD *(ed. Ismar Elbogen)* 1 (1929) 75–87, 337–360; 2 (1930) 310–332; 3 (1931) 151–170, 282–306; 4 (1932) 157–172 *LJ*

1356  Löwenfeld, Samuel (1854–): *Die Wahrheit über der Juden Anteil am Verbrechen.* Auf Grund amtlicher Statistik. Berlin: Stuhr, 1881. 16 pp. *LJ*

1357  Löwenstein, Lipmann Hirsch: *An die Hohe Verfassungsgebende Versammlung der Freien Stadt Frankfurt a.M.* Rödelheim: 1848. 8 pp. *LF*

1358  Löwenthal, Max J.: *Das jüdische Bekenntnis als Hinderungsgrund bei der Beförderung zum preußischen Reserveoffizier.* Im Auftrage des Verbandes der Deutschen Juden. Berlin: H.S. Hermann, 1911. 134 pp. *LJ*

1359 Löwenthal, Max J., ed.: *Jüdische Reserveoffiziere. Im Auftrage des Verbandes der Deutschen Juden von seinem Generalsekretär.* Berlin: Typ. R. Boll, 1914. 152 pp. *LJ*

1360 Lombroso, Cesare (1836–1909): *Der Antisemitismus und die Juden im Lichte der modernen Wissenschaft.* Autorisierte deutsche Ausg. von H. Kurella. Leipzig: G.H. Wigand, 1894. VIII, 114 pp. *LJ*
Orginal title: *L'Antisemitismo e le scienze moderne, 1894.*

1361 Lomer, Georg: Der Massenaufstieg der Juden. *Die Zukunft* 69 (1909). 380–384. *LJ*

1362 Lorens, Carl: *Jüdisch Lozelach; oder, Koschere Witze.* Wien: Hagenauer, [n.d.]. 1 vol. *Unseen*

1363 Lorenz, Otto: Karl Marx. *Forschungen zur Judenfrage* 2 (1937) 143–153. *LJ*

1364 Lorenzen, Friedrich: *Die Antisemiten.* Berlin: Verlag "Die Hilfe," 1912. 56 pp. *LJ*

1365 Losemann, Volker: Rassenideologien und antisemitische Publizistik in Deutschland im 19. und 20. Jahrhundert. *Judentum und Antisemitismus.* Eds. Thomas Klein a.o. Düsseldorf, 1984. Pp. 137–159. *LJ*

1366 Lougee, Robert Wayne: *Paul de Lagarde, 1827–1891; a Study of Radical Conservatism in Germany.* Cambridge, Mass.: Harvard University Press, 1962. VIII, 357 pp. *LJ*

1367 Low, Alfred D.: *Jews in the Eyes of the Germans; from the Enlightenment to Imperial Germany.* Philadelphia: Institute for the Study of Human Issues, 1979. X, 509 pp. *LJ*

1368 Lowenstein, Steven M.: The Pace of Modernisation of German Jewry in the 19th Century. *LBIYB* 21 (1976) 41–56. *LJ*

1369 Luba, F.: *Enthüllungen über die internationale russisch-jüdische Gaunerbande des "Rigaer Goldklub und seine Mitglieder"; soziales Sittenbild aus der Gegenwart.* Berlin: G.A. Dewald, 1892. VI, 53 pp. *Unseen*

1370 Lublinski, Samuel (1868–1910): Der Antisemitismus. *Neue Deutsche Rundschau* 3-4 (1896) 1145–1162. *LJ*

1371 Lütgenau, Franz (1857–): *Die Judenfrage, ökonomisch und ethisch.* Berlin: F. Dümmler, 1893. 22 pp. *LJ*

1372  Lüth, Erich: *Isaac Wolffson, 1817-1895; ein hamburgischer Wegbereiter des Rechts und der deutschen Emanzipation.* Hamburg: Freie Akademie der Künste, 1963. 46 pp. *LJ*

1373  Lüttwitz, Arthur Maria von: *Wir sind die Juden; eine biblische Studie.* Trier: Jubiläumsdruckerei, 1894. 29 pp. *LF*

1374  M.: *Das Judentum und die Emanzipation der Juden; oder, Gleichstellung derselben in allen staatsbürgerlichen Rechten mit den Christen in jeder Beziehung . . . Mit einer kurzen Beleuchtung der von 27 Juden des Kreises von Unterfranken und Aschaffenburg um Emanzipation bei der Hohen Stände-Versammlung des Königreichs Bayern eingereichten Vorstellung.* Würzburg: 1849. 63 pp. *LJ*

1375  Maass, Martin (1820-): *G.E. Lessing's Erziehung des Menschengeschlechtes; oder, Der Entwicklungsgang der religiösen Idee vom Judentume zum Christentume, den modernen Apologeten des Judentums gegenüber nachgewiesen.* Berlin: G. Reimer, 1862. VI, 67 pp. *LJ*

1376  Maass, Martin (1820-): *Die Mischehe, das einzig wirksame Mittel einer dauernden Vereinigung zwischen der jüdischen und christlichen Bevölkerung Deutschlands.* Aus Anlaß der jüngst in der sogenannten Judenfrage geführten Debatten. Mit kritischen Nachträgen. Löbau, Westpr.: Skrzeczek, 1881. 50 pp. *LJ*

1377  Maass, Martin (1820-): *Die Religion des Judentums und die politisch-sozialen Prinzipien unseres Jahrhunderts. Zur Kritik der Philippsonschen Resolution auf der 1. Israelitischen Synode zu Leipzig, 29. Juni-4. Juli 1869.* Leipzig: J.G. Findel, 1870. VIII, 184 pp. *LJ*

1378  Maass, Martin (1820-): *Die soziale Stellung der Juden in Deutschland und das Zivil-Ehegesetz . . .* Mit Bezug auf die Schrift des Herrn Dr. J. Kolkmann: "Die gesellschaftliche Stellung der Juden." Löbau, Westpr.: Skrzeczek, 1876. 85 pp. *LJ*

1379  Maass, Martin (1820-): *Zwei Gespräche über den Austritt aus dem Judentume.* Veranlasst durch den über diese Frage, hrsg. Briefwechsel des Dr. A. Geiger. Leipzig: O. Wigand, 1858. 48 pp. *LJ*

1380  Macaulay, Thomas Babington, 1st baron (1800-1859): *Dokumente zur Emanzipation der Juden; 4 Reden von Th. Macaulay, Gabriel Riesser, Suter und Freiherrn Georg von Vincke.* Halle: Hendel, 1912. 122 pp. *LJ*

1381 Mack, Rüdiger: Otto Böckel und die antisemitische Bauernbewegung in Hessen, 1887–1894. *900 Jahre Geschichte der Juden in Hessen.* Wiesbaden, 1983. Pp. 377–410. *LJ*

1382 Mahler, Arthur (1871–1916): *Rede gehalten in der Universitätsdebatte zum Dringlichkeitsantrag Prof. Masaryks im Oesterreichischen Abgeordnetenhaus am 3. Dezember 1907.* Hrsg. von der jüdischen akademischen Verbindung "Unitas" Wien. Wien: Unitas, 1908. 20 pp. *LJ*

About equal rights for Jewish students.

1383 Mahler, Karl: *Die Programme der politischen Parteien in Deutschland.* 3. Aufl. Leipzig: Gradlauer, 1911. 82 pp. *LV*

1384 Mai, Gunther: Sozialgeschichtliche Bedingungen von Judentum und Antisemitismus im Kaiserreich. *Judentum und Antisemitismus von der Antike bis zur Gegenwart.* Eds. Thomas Klein a.o. Düsseldorf, 1984. Pp. 113–136. *LJ*

1385 Maier, Joseph von: *Ueber den Judeneid.* Stuttgart: Zu Guttenberg, 1852. 22 p. *LJ*

1386 Makower, Hermann: *Ueber die Gemeindeverhältnisse der Juden in Preußen.* Berlin: J. Guttentag, 1873. 115 pp. *LJ*

1387 Malbeck, Gerhard (1909–): *Der Einfluß des Judentums auf die Berliner Presse von 1800–1879; ein Nachweis der Berechtigung des Auftretens Adolf Stoeckers gegen die Verjudung der Berliner Presse.* Dresden: M. Dittert, 1935. 87 pp. *LC*

Diss. 1935.

1388 Mandel, Jules: *Ueber Tötung der Schlachttiere nach israelitischem Ritus und über Aenderungen, welche diesfalls passend einzuführen wären.* Wien: Hölder, 1883. 20 pp. *LV*

1389 Mandl, Leopold: *Zum Verständnis der Blutlüge; eine Studie.* Wien: Moriz Waizner, 1900. 12 pp. *LJ*

1390 Mann, Thomas (1875–1955): Die Lösung der Judenfrage. *Gesammelte Werke in Dreizehn Bänden. Bd. 13.* Frankfurt a.M.: S. Fischer Verlag, 1974. Pp. 459–462. *LJ*

First published in *Münchener Neueste Nachrichten*, no. 430. Reprinted in: *Die Lösung der Judenfrage; eine Rundfrage by Julius Moses.* München, Modernes Verlagsbureau, 1907, pp. 242–246.

1391 Marczianyi, Georg von: *Esther Solymosi; oder, Der jüdische rituelle Jungfrauenmord in Tísza-Eslár*. Autorisierte deutsche Uebersetzung aus dem Ungarischen. Berlin: M. Schulze, 1882. 52 pp. *LJ*

1392 Maretzki, Louis: *Geschichte des Ordens Bnei Briss in Deutschland, 1882-1907*. Berlin: M. Cohn, 1907. XVI, 283 pp. *LJ*

1393 Marschalko, Lajos: *Tísza-eszlár, a magyar fajvédelem hőskora*. Debrecen: Typ. Magyar nemzeti Kőnyv-és lapkíadovállalat, 1943. 246 pp. *LJ*

1394 Martin, Rudolf: *Jahrbuch des Vermögens und Einkommens der Millionäre in Berlin*. Berlin: R. Martin, 1913. X, 228 pp. *LC*

1395 Martin, Rudolf: *Jahrbuch des Vermögens und Einkommens der Millionäre in der Provinz Brandenburg, einschließlich Charlottenburg, Wilmersdorf und alle anderen Vororte Berlins*. Berlin: Rudolf Martin, 1913. VIII, 168 pp. *LJ*

1396 Martin, Rudolf: *Unter dem Scheinwerfer*. Berlin: Schuster & Löffler, 1910. 378 pp. *LC*

1397 Marx, Karl (1818-1883): Ein unbekanntes Kapitel aus Marx' Leben; Briefe an die holländischen Verwandten. *International Review of Social History* 1 (1956) 55-111. *LJ*

1398 Masaidek, Franz Friedrich: *Georg von Schönerer: eine Schutz- und Trutzschrift, von einem Deutschnationalen*. Wien: Kubasta & Voigt, 1887. 19 pp. *LV*

1399 Masaidek, Franz Friedrich: *Georg von Schönerer und die deutschnationale Bewegung*. Wien: F. Schalk, 1898. 39 pp. *LV*

1400 Masaryk, Tomáš Garrigue (1850-1937): *Die Bedeutung des Polnaer Verbrechens für den Ritualglauben*. Berlin: H.S. Hermann, 1900. 94 pp. *LJ*

1401 Masaryk, Tomáš Garrigue (1850-1937): *Die Notwendigkeit der Revision des Polanaer Prozeßes. (Interpellation Kronawetter im Abgeordnetenhause am 9.11.1899)*. Wien: Administration "Die Zeit," 1899. 31 pp. *LV*
Offprint from: *Die Zeit*.

1402 Massiczek, Albert: *Der menschliche Mensch, Karl Marx's jüdischer Humanismus*. Wien: Europa-Verlag, 1968. 654 pp. *LJ*

1403 Massing, Paul W.: *Rehearsal for Destruction; a Study of Political Antisemitism in Imperial Germany*. New York: Harper, 1949. XVIII, 341 pp. (Studies in Prejudice. The American Jewish Committee. Social Studies Ser. Publ., 2) *LJ*

1404  Massing, Paul W.: *Vorgeschichte des politischen Antisemitismus.* Aus dem Amerikanischem übersetzt und für die deutsche Ausg. bearb. von Felix J. Weil. Frankfurt a.M.: Europäische Verlagsanstalt, 1959. VIII, 258 pp. (Frankfurter Beiträge zur Soziologie. Institut für Sozialforschung, 8) *LJ*
Original title: *Rehearsal for Destruction.*

1405  Masur, Gerhard (1901–): *Imperial Berlin.* London: Routledge & Kegan Paul, 1971. 353 pp. *LJ*

1406  Maurer, W.: *Kirche und Synagoge; Motive und Formen der Auseinandersetzung der Kirche mit dem Judentum.* Stuttgart: Kohlhammer, 1953. 135 pp. *LJ*

1407  Mayer, Gustav (1871–): Der Jude in Karl Marx. *Neue Jüdische Monatshefte* 2 (1918) 327–331. *LJ*

1408  Mayer, Gustav (1871–): Lassalle und das Judentum. *Der Jude* 8 (1924) 727–736. *LJ*

1409  Mayer-Löwenschwerdt, Erwin: *Schönerer der Vorkämpfer; eine politische Biographie.* Wien: W. Graumüller, 1938. VII, 390 pp. *LJ*

1410  Mayer, Sigmund (1831–1920?): *Die Aufhebung der Gewerbefreiheit; Streit- und Fehdeschrift gegen die Wiederherstellung der Zunft in Oesterreich.* 2. Aufl. Wien: Bermann & Altmann, 1883. 106 pp. *LJ*

1411  Mayer, Sigmund (1831–1920?): *Ein jüdischer Kaufmann, 1831–1911; Lebenserinnerungen. Anhang: Die Juden als Handelsvolk in der Geschichte.* Leipzig: Duncker & Humblot, 1911. VII, 401 pp. *LJ*

1412  Mayer, Sigmund (1831–1920?): Die Wiener Juden von der Revolution 1848 bis zur Gegenwart. *Die Wiener Juden; Kommerz, Kultur, Politik, 1700–1900. Buch 3.* Wien: R. Löwit, 1917. Pp. 309–521. *LJ*

1413  McGrath, William James: The Linz Program. *Dionysian Art and Populist Politics in Austria.* New Haven: Yale University Press, 1974. Pp. 165–181. *LJ*

1414  McGrath, William James: *Wagnerism in Austria; the Regeneration of Culture Through the Spirit of Music.* Berkeley: 1965. 308 l. *LV*

Diss.

1415  Mehring, Franz (1846–1919): Anti- und Philosemitisches. *N.Z.* 9, II (1891) 585–588. *LJ*

Attack on the two "isms" and German policy seen as from the socialist standpoint.

1416  Mehring, Franz (1846–1919): Bleichröder's Kommis'. *N.Z.* 16, 1 (1897–8) 706–708. *LJ*

1417  Mehring, Franz (1846–1919): Das Ende eines Demagogen. *N.Z.* 11, 2 (1892–1893) 545–548. *LJ*
Contra Stoecker as viewed from the socialist viewpoint.

1418  Mehring, Franz (1846–1919): *Herr Hardens Fabeln.* Berlin: H. Walther, 1899. 45 pp. *LF*

1419  Mehring, Franz (1846–1919): *Herr Hofprediger Stoecker der Sozialpolitiker.* Bremen: C. Schünemann, 1882. X, 104 pp. (Broschüren zur antisemitischen Bewegung, 3) *LJ*

1420  Mehring, Franz (1846–1919): *Kapital und Presse; ein Nachspiel zum Falle Lindau.* Berlin: K. Brachvogel, 1891. 138 pp. *LJ*

1421  Mehring, Franz (1846–1919): Mönch und Rabbi. *N.Z.* 11, II (1892–1893) 841–844. *LJ*

1422  Meier-Cronemeyer, Hermann: Jüdische Jugendbewegung. T. 1. *Germania Judaica* 8, N.F. 27–28 (1969) 1–34. *LJ*

1423  Meinecke, Friedrich (1862–1954): Walter Frank, Hofprediger Stoecker und die christlich-soziale Bewegung. *Historische Zeitschrift* 140 (1929) 151–154. *LJ*
A book review.

1424  *Der Meineidsprozeß in Konitz; eine kritische Untersuchung.* Berlin: Hermann Walther, 1901. 19 pp. *LJ*

1425  Meinhold, Eberhard: *Deutsche Rassenpolitik und die Erziehung zu nationalem Ehrgefühl.* München: Lehmann, 1908. 28 pp. *LV*

1426  Meissner, W.: *Galizien und seine Juden.* Aus einem Berichte unseres Missionars Schmeisser. Leipzig: Evangelisch-Lutherischer Zentralverein für Mission unter Israel, 1901. 32 pp. (Kleine Schriften zur Judenmission, 1) *Unseen*

1427  Memminger, Anton (1846–1923):*Die Hinrichtung des "Judenheiligen" Gotthold Ephraim Lessing durch Dr. Eugen Dühring in Berlin; ein Echo aus dem Bregenzer Schriftstellerwinkel . . .* Bregenz am Bodensee: Wagner'sche Buch- und Kunsthdlg., 1881. 15 pp. *Unseen*

1428 Memminger, Anton (1846–1923): *Der Talmud.* 2. Aufl. Würzburg: Memminger's Verlagsanstalt, 1897. 103 pp. *LJ*

1429 Menasche, Falek Esre: Die erste Stootsparade der Nazional-Bergerwehr von Berlin vor unsern allergenedigsten König, beschrieben von den baumwollenen Handelsmann Falek Esre Menasche. Zur Unterhaltung vor die Berliner und Frankforther Parlamenter. *Berliner Straßenecken-literatur 1848–1849.* Stuttgart: Ph. Reclam, Jun. 1977. Pp. 71–72. *LJ*

1430 Menck, Klara: Die falsch gestellte Weltenuhr; der Rembrandtdeutsche Julius Langbehn. *Propheten des Nationalismus.* Ed. Karl Schwedhelm. München: List-Verlag, 1969. Pp. 88–104. *LC*

1431 Mendes-Flohr, Paul R. (1941–): Werner Sombart's The Jews and Modern Capitalism; an Analysis of Its Ideological Premises. *LBIYB* 21 (1976) 87–107. *LJ*

1432 Menes, Abraham (1897–1969): The Conversion Movement in Prussia During the First Half of the 19th Century. *YIVO Annual of Jewish Social Science* 6 (1951) 187–205. *LJ*

First published in *YIVO Historishe Shriftn,* 1929.

1433 Menes, Abraham (1897–1969): Zur Statistik des jüdischen Schulwesens in Preußen um die Mitte des vorigen Jahrhunderts. *ZfGJD (Ed. Ismar Elbogen)* 3 (1931) 203–206. *LJ*

1434 Menscher, Isak: *Der Beilis-Prozeß und seine Vorläufer in der Geschichte.* Czernowitz: M. Landau, 1914. 30 pp. *LJ*

1435 *Die menschlichen Rassen und die ältesten Völker.* Leipzig: Th. Fritsch, 1886. 8 pp. (Brennende Fragen, 24) *LJ*

1436 Menzinger, Johannes: *Friede der Judenfrage. Mit einem Anhang: Zur Geschichte des Antisemitismus.* Berlin: Schuster & Löffler, 1896. 247 pp. *LJ*

1437 Metz, Rudolph: *Das Gesetz, die bürgerlichen Rechte der israelitischen Glaubensgenossen betreffend vom 29. Juni 1851.* Erlangen: Palm & Enke, 1855. 40 pp. *Unseen*

1438 Metzger, Heinz Klaus, ed.: *Richard Wagner — Wie antisemitisch darf ein Künstler sein.* Hrsg. von Heinz Klaus Metzger und Rainer Riehn. München: Ed. Text und Kritik, 1978. 112 pp. (Musik-Konzepte, 5) *LJ*

1439  Mewes, Rudolf (1858–): *Dr. Eugen Dühring als wissenschaftlicher Gladiator und Plagiator; nach Tatsachenmaterial.* Berlin: R. Mewes, 1904. 46 pp. *Unseen*

1440  Meyer, Louis: Juden und Judenmission; eine Uebersicht für den Weltmissionskongreß in Edinburg, Juni 1910. Aus dem Englischen übers. von H.L. Strack. *Nathanael* 27 (1911) 1–9. *LJ*

1441  Meyer, Michael A.: Great Debate on Antisemitism; Jewish Reaction to New Hostility in Germany, 1879–1881. *LBIYB* 11 (1966) 136–170. *LJ*

1442  Meyer, Michael A.: Jewish Religious Reform and "Wissenschaft des Judentums"; the Position of Zunz, Geiger and Frankel. *LBIYB* 16 (1971) 19–41. *LJ*

1443  Meyer, Michael A.: Review on Ismar Schorsch's Jewish Reactions to German Antisemitism. *Conservative Judaism* 27 (1973) 84–87. *LJ*

1444  Meyer, Paul: *Erinnerungen an Theodor Fontane, 1819–1898. Aus dem Nachlaß seines Freundes und Testamentsvollstreckers Justizrat Paul Meyer.* Berlin: Privatdruck, 1936. 62 pp. *LTA*

1445  Meyer, Seligmann (1853–1925): *Der Austritt aus der Synagogengemeinde; das Gesetz und dessen Beratung im Hause der Abgeordneten in erster, zweiter und dritter Lesung.* Nach den stenografischen Berichten zusammengestellt und mit einem Vorwort versehen. Berlin: Jüdische Presse, 1876. 88 pp. *LJ*

1446  Meyer, Seligmann (1853–1925): *Contra Delitzsch; die Babel-Hypothesen widerlegt. Mit einem Briefe des Herrn Professor Friedrich Delitzsch an den Verfasser.* 2. Aufl. Frankfurt a.M.: J. Kauffmann, 1903. 2 vols. *LJ*

1447  Meyer, Seligmann (1853–1925): *Ein Wort an Herrn von Treitschke.* Berlin: Jüdische Presse, 1880. 37 pp. *LJ*

1448  Michael, Emil (1852–1917): *Ignaz von Döllinger; eine Charakteristik.* 2. Aufl. Innsbruck: F. Rauch, 1892. XIII, 600 pp. *Unseen*

1449  Michael, Reuwen: Graetz and Hess. *LBIYB* 9 (1964) 91–121. *LJ*

1450  Michael, Reuwen: Graetz contra Treitschke. *LBI Bull.* 4 (1961) 301–322. *LJ*

1451  Michaelis, Alfred, ed.: *Die Rechtsverhältnisse der Juden in Preußen seit dem Beginn des 19. Jahrhunderts; Gesetze, Erlaße, Verordnungen, Entscheidungen.* Berlin: Louis Lamm, 1910. XIV, 744 pp. *LJ*

1452 Mintz, Meir: *Ein Wort zur Zeit; Gutachten über die Verhältnisse und Uebelstände der galizischen Juden in einer löblich k.k. kreisamtlichen Aufforderung von M. . .r M. . .tz.* Lemberg: 1848. VI,43 pp. *LF*

1453 Misrahi, Robert: *Marx et la question juive.* Paris: Gallimard, 1972. 252 pp. (Collection Idées, 259) *LJ*

1454 Mittermaier, K.: *Das Schächten geschildert und erläutert auf Grund zahlreicher neuerer Gutachten.* Im Auftrage des Heidelberger Tierschutzvereins dargelegt. Heidelberg: C. Winter, 1902. 82 pp. *LJ*

1455 Modlinger, Samuel: *Lessing's Verdienste um das Judentum; eine Studie.* Frankfurt: Selbstverlag, 1869. 52 pp. *LJ*

1456 Mogge, Brigitte: *Rhetorik des Hasses; Eugen Dühring und die Genese seines antisemitischen Wortschatzes.* Neuss: Gesellschaft für Buchdruckerei, 1977. 243 pp. (Aus Zeit und Geschichte, 1) *LJ*

1457 Mohl, Robert von (1799–1875): Die Judenemanzipation. *Staatsrecht, Völkerrecht und Politik.* Vol. 3. Tübingen: H. Laupp, 1869. Pp. 673–680. *LJ*

1458 Moldenhauer, R.: Jewish Petitions to the German National Assembly in Frankfurt, 1848–49. *LBIYB* 16 (1971) 185–223. *LJ*

1459 Molisch, Paul: *Geschichte der deutschnationalen Bewegung in Oesterreich von ihren Anfängen bis zum Verfall der Monarchie.* Jena: G. Fischer, 1926. X, 277 pp. *LJ*

1460 Molisch, Paul: Die Judenfrage. *Politische Geschichte der deutschen Hochschulen in Oesterreich von 1848–1918.* 2. erw. Aufl. Wien: S. Braumüller, 1939. Pp. 118–137. *LC*

   2nd enl. ed. of the publication: *Die deutschen Hochschulen in Oesterreich und die politisch-nationale Entwicklung im Jahre 1848.*

1461 Mombert, Alfred (1872–): Werner Sombarts "Die Juden und das Wirtschaftsleben." *Literarische Rundschau für das Katholische Deutschland* 93 (1913) col. 227–228. *Unseen*

   A review.

1462 Mommert, Carl (1840–): *Menschenopfer bei den alten Hebräern.* Leipzig: E. Haberland, 1905. 88 pp. *LJ*

1463 Mommert, Carl (1840–): *Der Ritualmord bei den Talmud-Juden.* Leipzig: E. Haberland, 1905. 127 pp. *LJ*

1464  Mommert, Carl (1840–): *Widerlegung der Widersprüche frommer Juden und Christen gegen die Blutbeschuldigung der Juden.* Leipzig: E. Haberland, 1906. 144 pp. *LJ*

1465  Mommsen, Wilhelm (1892–1966): *Paul de Lagarde als Politiker; zu seinem 100. Geburtstag am 2.XI.1927.* Göttingen: Vandenhoeck & Ruprecht, 1927. 30 pp. *LV*
      Offprint from : *Göttinger Beiträge zur deutschen Kulturgeschichte.*

1466  Mommsen, Wilhelm (1892–1966): Vom Vormärz bis zum Ausgang des Ersten Weltkrieges. *Deutsche Parteiprogramme. 2. Aufl.* München: Isar-Verlag, 1960. Pp. 1–421. (Deutsches Handbuch der Politik, 1) *LJ*

1467  *Der Mord zu Damaskus; oder, Wie ein christlicher Priester von Juden geschächtet wurde.* Nach den Akten zu Nutz und Frommen dem Volk erzählt. Marburg: Verlag des "Reichsherold," 1888. 24 pp. *LJ*

1468  *Der Mord zu Lutscha; Darstellung des in Galizien von Judenhand begangenen Mordes an Franziska Mnich, sowie der darüber gepflogenen Gerichtsverhandlungen, nebst einer Schlußbetrachtung.* 3. Aufl. Marburg: Verlag des "Reichsherold," 1890. 14 pp. *LJ*

1469  Morel, L.: *Les Juifs et La Hongrie devant l'Europe; Affaire de Tísza-Eszlár.* Paris: en vente chez les auteurs, 1883. 63 pp. *LJ*

1470  Mork, Gordon R.: German Nationalism and Jewish Assimilation, the Bismarck Period. *LBIYB* 22 (1977). 81–90. *LJ*

1471  Moser, Jonny: Antisemitismus zwischen Doppeladler und Krukenkreuz. *Wien 1879–1930; Traum und Wirklichkeit.* Ed. Robert Waissenberger. Salzburg: Residenz-Verlag, 1984. Pp. 64–70. *LJ*

1472  Moser, Jonny: *Von der Emanzipation zur antisemitischen Bewegung; die Stellung Georg Ritter von Schönerers und Heinrich Friedjungs in der Entwicklungsgeschichte des Antisemitismus in Oesterreich, 1848–1896.* Wien: 1962. 156 l. *LV*
      Diss. 1965.

1473  Moses, Julius (1868–1944): *Die Lösung der Judenfrage; eine Rundfrage.* Berlin: K. Wigand, 1907. 309 pp. *LJ*

1474  Moses, Julius (1868–1944): Statistische Erhebungen über die Berufswahl der jüdischen Jugend in Landgemeinden Badens. *Jüdische Statistik.* Berlin, 1903. Pp. 202–208. *LJ*

1475 Mosse, George Lachman (1918–): *The Crisis of German Ideology; Intellectual Origins of the Third Reich.* New York: Grosset and Dunlap, 1964. VI, 373 pp. (The Universal Library, UL 173) *LJ*

1476 Mosse, George Lachman (1918–): Culture, Civilisation and German Antisemitism. *Judaism* 7 (1958) 256–266. *LJ*

1477 Mosse, George Lachman (1918–): *Die Nationalisierung der Massen; politische Symbolik und Massenbewegungen in Deutschland von den Napoleonischen Kriegen bis zum 3. Reich.* Aus dem Englischen von Otto Weith. Frankfurt a.M.: Ullstein, 1976. 283 pp. *LJ*

Original title: *The Nationalisation of the Masses.*

1478 Mosse, George Lachman (1918–): *The Nationalization of the Masses; Political Symbolism and Mass Movements in Germany from the Napoleonic Wars through the Third Reich.* New York: H. Fertig, 1975. XVI, 252 pp. *LJ*

1479 Mosse, George Lachman (1918–): *Rassismus; ein Krankheitssymptom in der europäischen Geschichte des 19. und 20. Jahrhunderts.* Aus dem Englischen von Elfriede Burau. Königstein i. Taunus: Athenäum, 1978. Pp. 91–139. *LJ*

Original title: *Toward the Final Solution.*

1480 Mosse, George Lachman (1918–): *Toward the Final Solution, a History of European Racism.* New York: H. Fertig, 1978. Pp. 1–168. *LJ*

1481 Mosse, George Lachman (1918–): *Ein Volk, ein Reich, ein Führer; die völkischen Ursprünge des Nationalsozialismus.* Uebertragung der amerikanischen Vorlage Renate Becker. Königstein i. Taunus: Athenäum, 1979. VII, 368 pp. *LJ*

Original title: *The Crisis of German Ideology,* pts. I–II. Covers the period until 1918.

1482 Mosse, Werner Eugen: Bamberger und Sonnemann; zwei deutsch-jüdische Politiker in dem Konflikt zwischen Liberalismus und Nationalismus. *Zur Geschichte der Juden in Deutschland.* Jerusalem: Academic Press, 1971. Pp. 76–80. *LJ*

1483 Mosse, Werner Eugen: The Conflict of Liberalism and Nationalism and Its Effect on German Jewry. *LBIYB* 15 (1970) 125–139. *LJ*

1484 Mosse, Werner Eugen: Judaism, Jews and Capitalism; Weber, Sombart and Beyond. *LBIYB* 24 (1979) 3–15. *LJ*

1485  Mosse, Werner Eugen: Rudolf Mosse and the House of Mosse, 1867-1920. *LBIYB* 4 (1959) 237-259. *LJ*

1486  Mosse, Werner Eugen: Terms of Successfull Integration; the Tietz Family, 1858-1923. *LBIYB* 34 (1989) 131-161. *LJ*

1487  Mosse, Werner Eugen: Wilhelm II and the "Kaiserjuden"; a Problematic Encounter. *The Jewish Response to German Culture; from the Enlightenment to the Second World War.* Eds. Jehuda Reinharz, Walter Schatzberg. Hanover, NH: University Press of New England, 1985. Pp. 164-194. *LJ*

1488  Mosse, Werner Eugen, ed.: *Juden im Wilhelminischen Deutschland 1890-1914; ein Sammelband.* Tübingen: Mohr, 1976. XIV, 786 pp. (Schriften wissenschaftlicher Abhandlungen des LBI, 33) *LJ*

1489  Mosse, Werner Eugen, ed.: *Revolution and Evolution in German Jewish History.* Tübingen: J.C.B. Mohr, 1981. XII, 431 pp. (Schriftenreihe wissenschaftlicher Abhandlungen des LBI, 39) *LJ*

1490  Müller, A.: *Jesus, ein Arier; ein Beitrag zur völkischen Erziehung.* Leipzig: M. Sängewald, 1904. 74 pp. *Unseen*

1491  Müller, Alois (1835-1901): *Brauchen die Juden Christenblut? Ein offenes Wort an denkende Christen.* Wien: O. Frank, 1884. 16 pp. *LJ*

1492  Müller, Alwin: Minderheit und sozialer Aufstieg; Juden in Köln zwischen 1808 und 1850. *Lebenslauf und Gesellschaft.* Ed. Wilhelm Heinz Schröder. Stuttgart: Klett-Cotta, 1985. Pp. 48-75. *LC*

1493  Müller, Franz Heinrich: *Stoecker's angeblich ethisch-soziale Judenfrage; eine allseitige Beleuchtung derselben vom politischen und sittlichen Standpunkte aus mit besonderer Berücksichtigung der Mischehe.* 2. verb. Aufl. Würzburg: Typ. "Würzburger Telegraph," 1880. 77 pp. *LC*

1494  Müller, Georg: Rings um den "Hohen Meissner." *Deutsche Jugend.* Ed. Will Vesper. Berlin, 1934. Pp. 58-59. *LJ*

1495  Müller-Guttenbrunn, Adam (1852-1923): *Die Kreuzzeitungs-Politik und die Aera Hammerstein-Stoecker; regieren und intrigieren. Adolf Stoecker, der Unvorsichtige. 2 Artikel aus der Wochenschrift "Die Nation."* Berlin: Rosenbaum & Hart, 1895. 36 pp. *LTA*

1496  Müller, Johannes (1864-): *Die Aufgabe der evangelischen-lutherischen Christenheit gegenüber den Juden der Heimat; Vortrag gehalten auf der VI.*

*Allgemeinen Lutherischen Konferenz in Hannover.* Leipzig: W. Faber, 1891. 15 pp. *LJ*

Offprint from: *Saat auf Hoffnung*, 1891, vol. 1.

1497 Müller, Johannes (1864–): *Proselytenpflege.* Leipzig: Typ. Ackermann & Glaser, 1892. Pp. 75–115. *LJ*

Offprint from: *Saat auf Hoffnung*, 1892, no. 2.

1498 Münz, Wilhelm (1856–): *Die Judenmetzeleien in Russland; ein offener Brief an die regierenden Fürsten und Staatsoberhäupter der Kulturwelt.* Breslau: Köbner, 1906. 10 pp. *LJ*

1499 Münz, Wilhelm (1856–): *Ritualmord und Eid; ein offener Brief an den Reichstagabgeordenten Herrn Liebermann von Sonnenberg in Groß-Lichterfelde.* Gleiwitz: Neumanns Staatsbuchdruckerei, 1902. 12 pp. *LJ*

1500 Munk, Esra (1867–1940): Die Entwicklung der Verhältnisse der preußischen Synagogengemeinde. (Im Geltungsbereich des Gesetzes vom 23. Juli 1874 über die Verhältnisse der Juden). *Festschrift für Jacob Rosenhein.* Frankfurt a.M.: J. Kauffmann, 1931. Pp. 172–195. *LJ*

1501 Muscat, Perez Paul: *Die Taten der Kaiser und Könige in Bezug auf Emanzipation Mendelssohns und Victor Hugos Zeiten. Dieses sind die 3 ersten Abschnitte des Werkes "Das Leben und die Krone Israels."* Mainz: 1886. 65 pp. *LF*

1502 Muth, Karl (1867–1944): Ueber Antisemitismus. *Hochland* 9, 1 (1911–12) 119; 11, 2 (1913–14) 545 *Unseen*

1503 Myers, Alfred Moritz: *Der Jude.* Nach der 5. Aufl. des englischen Originals. Allen Freunden des Reiches Gottes dargeboten. Frankfurt a.M.: M. Brönner, 1856. VI, 270 pp. *Unseen*

1504 Myers, Alfred Moritz: *Moses & Samuel; ein Gespräch.* 3. Aufl. Frankfurt a.M.: Typ. Brönner, 1864. 78 pp. *LJ*

From his publication *Der Jude*, Frankfurt a.M., 1856.

1505 Myers, Asher Isaac (1848–1902): *The "Blood Accusation," Its Origin and Occurrence in the Middle Ages; an Historical Commentary on the Tísza–Eszlár Trial.* London: Jewish Chronicle, 1883. 12 pp. *Unseen*

1506 N. . .r, Josef: *Hat Istoczy der Judenfresser recht oder unrecht.* Budapest: Typ. E. Bartalitz, 1878. 16 pp. *LJ*

1507 Naaman, Shlomo (1912–): *Ferdinand Lassalle, Deutscher und Jude; eine sozial-geschichtliche Studie.* Hannover: Niedersächsische Landeszentrale für politische Bildung, 1968. 151 pp. *LJ*

1508 Naaman, Shlomo (1912–): Heine und Lassalle; ihre Beziehungen im Zeichen der Dämonie des Geldes. *Archiv für Sozialgeschichte* 4 (1964) 45–86. *LJ*

1509 Naaman, Shlomo (1912–): Jüdische Aspekte des Deutschen Nationalvereins, 1859–1867. *TAJfDG* 15 (1986) 285–307. *LJ*

1510 Naaman, Shlomo (1912–): Rom und Jerusalem als nationaljüdische Verjüngung und Heilige Geschichte. *Emanzipation und Messianismus; Leben und Werk des Moses Hess.* Frankfurt a.M.: Campus Verlag, 1982. Pp. 299–333. *LJ*

1511 Naaman, Shlomo (1912–): Die Selbstdeutung von "Rom und Jerusalem" durch Moses Hess; seine Artikelserie in der Niederrheinischen Volkszeitung. *TAJfDG* 11 (1982) 173–201. *LJ*

1512 Nagel, G.: *Heilige Rätsel und ihre Lösung; oder, Das jüdische Volk und die christliche Gemeinde in ihren gegenseitigen Beziehungen und ihren Zielen. Ein biblisch-historisches Zeugnis.* Witten a.d.R.: Buchhdlg. der Stadtmission, 1899. VIII, 235 pp. *LJ*

1513 Nathan, Paul (1857–1927): *Der jüdische Blutmord und der Freiherr von Wackerbarth-Linderode, Mitglied des preußischen Abgeordneten-Hauses. Ein antisemitisches-parlamentarisches Kulturbild.* Berlin: F. Fontane & Co., 1892. 37 pp. *LJ*

   Offprint of the preface to: *Der Prozeß von Tísza-Eszlár.*

1514 Nathan, Paul (1857–1927): *Die Kriminalität der Juden in Deutschland.* Hrsg. von dem Comite zur Abwehr antisemitischer Angriffe in Berlin. Berlin: Cronbach, 1896. 56 pp. (Die Juden in Deutschland, 1) *LJ*

1515 Nathan, Paul (1857–1927): *Der Prozeß von Tísza-Eszlár; ein antisemitisches Kulturbild.* Berlin: F. Fontane & Co., 1892. XL, 416 pp. *LJ*

1516 Nathan, Paul (1857–1927): *Xanten-Cleve; Betrachtungen zum Prozeße Buschhof.* Berlin: H.S. Hermann, 1892. 16 pp. *LJ*

   Offprint from: *"Nation," Wochenschrift für Politik, Volkswirtschaft und Literatur.*

1517 Nathan, Sally: *Motivia; die Tragödie von Konitz.* Berlin: W. Schröder, 1901. 65 pp. *LJ*

1518 Nationalliberale Partei: *Politisches Handbuch der Nationalliberalen Partei.* Berlin: Verlag der Buchhdlg. der Nationalliberalen Partei, 1907. 1229, VII pp. *LJ*

About political parties, antisemitism, Jews, etc. Very informative.

1519 Nauen, Franz (1938–): Hermann Cohen's Concept of the State and the Problem of Antisemitism, 1867–1907. *TAJfDG* 8 (1979) 257–282. *LJ*

1520 Naumann, Friedrich (1860–1919): *Die politischen Parteien. 4 Vorträge gehalten im Januar–Februar 1910 in der Philharmonie zu Berlin.* Berlin: Buchverlag der "Hilfe," 1910. 111 pp. *LJ*

1521 Néher, André (1913–): Une carte antisémite de la Suisse au XIX siècle. *Evidences* 4 (1952) 40–44. *LJ*

1522 Nendtvich, Karoly Miksa: *Die Judenfrage in Oesterreich-Ungarn; eine kultur-historische Studie.* Budapest: Bartalits, 1884. VI, 138 pp. *LJ*

1523 *Neu-Judäa; Entwurf zum Wiederaufbau eines selbständigen jüdischen Reiches, von C.L.K. Als Beitrag zur Vorgeschichte des Zionismus.* Hrsg. von Heinrich Löwe. 2. Aufl. Berlin: Jüdische Rundschau, 1903. 23 pp. *LJ*

Colonization in North-America in order to gather the Jewish people and unite them into an independent nation.

1524 Neubach, Helmut: *Die Ausweisungen von Polen und Juden aus Preußen 1885–1886; ein Beitrag zu Bismarcks Polenpolitik und zur Geschichte des deutsch-polnischen Verhältnisses.* Wiesbaden: O. Harrassowitz, 1967. XI, 293 pp. *LJ*

1525 Neufville, Wilhelm Karl de: *Lebensdauer und Todesursachen 22 verschiedener Stände und Gewerbe, nebst vergleichender Statistik der christlichen und israelitischen Bevölkerung Frankfurts.* Nach zuverläßigen Quellen bearb. Frankfurt a.M.: Sauerländer's Verlag, 1855. IV, 116 pp. *Unseen*

1526 Neumann, Fred: Der Skurczer Mord vor dem Schwurgerichte zu Danzig vom 22. April bis einschließlich 27. April 1881; aktenmäßige Darstellung. *Berühmte Kriminalprozeße der Gegenwart.* Wien: Alois Reichmann, [n.d.]. Pp. 516–526. *LTA*

1527 Neumann, Friedrich Julius (1835–1910): Die Sterblichkeit ehelicher und unehelicher Kinder, insbesondere innerhalb der jüdischen Bevölkerung in Baden. *Jahrbuch für Gesetzgebung, Verwaltung und Volkswirtschaft im Deutschen Reich* 1 (1877) 411–424. *LF*

1528 Neumann, Friedrich Julius (1835–1910): *Volk und Nation; eine Studie.* Tübingen: H. Laupp, 1888. XVI, 164 pp. *LF*

1529 Neumann, Hermann: *Die Judenjagd und die deutsche Meute. Ein Nachtrag zu den Judenflinten. Mit einer Einleitung von Hermann Ahlwardt.* Berlin: G.A. Dewald, 1892. 33 pp. *LJ*

1530 Neumann, Salomon (1819–1908): *Die Fabel von der jüdischen Masseneinwanderung; ein Kapitel aus der preußischen Statistik.* Berlin: L. Simion, 1880. 46 pp. *LJ*

1531 Neumann, Salomon (1819–1908): *Die Fabel von der jüdischen Masseneinwanderung; ein Kapitel aus der preußischen Statistik. 3. Aufl.* Berlin: L. Simion, 1881. 46, 22 pp. *LJ*

The 3rd edition is supplemented by: "Mit einer Nachschrift, enthaltend I. Antwort an Herrn Adolf Wagner. II. Herr Heinrich von Treitschke und seine jüdische Masseneinwanderung. III. Die Antwort des Königlich–Preußischen Statistischen Bureaus."

1532 Neumann, Salomon (1819–1908): *Die neueste Lüge über die israelitische Allianz; ein Probestück aus der antisemitischen Moral.* Berlin: Druck und Verlag der Volks-Zeitung, 1883. 21 pp. *LJ*

Offprint from: *Volks-Zeitung.*

1533 Neumann, Salomon (1819–1908): *Zur Statistik der Juden in Preußen von 1816–1880.* 2. Beitrag aus den amtlichen Veröffentlichungen. Berlin: Louis Gerschel, 1884. 50 pp. *LJ*

1534 Neuschäfer, Fritz Albrecht: *Georg Ritter von Schönerer.* Hamburg: 1935. 83 pp. *LJ*
Diss.

1535 *Der Neustettiner Synagogenbrand; Prozeß vor den Geschworenen zu Cöslin und Konitz.* Eine genaue Darstellung der Anklage, der Zeugenverhöre, der Verteidigung und des Urteils. Stuttgart: Levy & Müller, 1884. 46 pp. *LJ*

1536 The new "Cultur" War in Germany. *The Nation* 30 (1880) 74–75. *LJ*

1537 *Nicht das falsche, sondern nur das wahre Israel hat je und je die Welt überwunden, und wird sie überwinden.* Von Pfarrer K. in Dr. bei M. Leipzig: Typ. Ackermann and Glaser, 1897. 39 pp. *LJ*

1538 Nielsen, Frederik Kristian: *Das moderne Judentum; seiner Emanzipation und Reform entgegen geführt durch die Verdienste Lessings, Moses Mendelssohns und Abraham Geigers.* Eine historische Charakteristik. Aus dem Dänischen übers. von C. Schumacher. Flensburg: Westphalen, 1880. 46 pp. *LJ*

1539 Nietzsche, Friedrich Wilhelm (1844–1900): Der Fall Wagner. *Werke in 2 Bänden. Bd. 2.* Leipzig: Alfred Kröner Verlag, 1930. Pp. 299–305. *LJ*

Written about 1890.

1540 Nobel, Josef (1840–1917): *Kritisches Richtschwert für Rohling's "Talmudjude"; eine quellengemäße, streng kritische Beurteilung des obengennanten Buches, etc.* Totis: Meyer, 1881. III, 86 pp. *LJ*

1541 Nöltingk, G.C.: *Die Christlich-Soziale Partei in Deutschland; eine Zeitbetrachtung.* Bernburg: Baumeister, 1882. 30 pp. *LTA*

1542 Nordau, Max Simon (1849–1923): *Das Judentum im 19. und 20. Jahrhundert; Vortrag.* 2. Aufl. Köln: Jüdischer Verlag, 1911. 22 pp. *LJ*

1543 Nordau, Max Simon (1849–1923): *Zionism and Antisemitism.* New York: Fox, Duffield, 1905. 76 pp. *LJ*

Contents: Zionism, by Max Nordau. Antisemitism in Europe, by Gustav Gottheil.

1544 Norel, Okke, Jzn.: *Adolf Stoecker en zijn sociaal-ethisch streven.* Utrecht: Kemink, 1914. 219 pp. *LF*

"Proefschrift"-Utrecht.

1545 Nossig, Alfred (1864–1943): Die Auserwähltheit der Juden im Lichte der Biologie. *ZfDSJ* 1 (1905) 1–5. *LJ*

1546 Nossig, Alfred (1864–1943): *Deutschland und die Schweiz, Oesterreich; Materialien zur Statistik des jüdischen Stammes.* Wien: Bei C. Konegen, 1887. 38–69. *LJ*

1547 Novgoratz, Hans: *Sebastian Brunner und der frühe Antisemitismus.* Wien: 1978. IX, 319 l. *LJ*

Diss. Vienna.

1548 Nussbaum, Arthur (1877–1964): *Der Polnaer Ritualmordprozeß; eine kriminalpsychologische Untersuchung auf aktenmäßiger Grundlage.* Mit einem Vorwort von Franz von Liszt. Berlin: A. W. Hayn's Erben, 1906. VIII, 259 pp. *LJ*

1549 Nussbaum, Arthur (1877–1964): The Ritual Murder Trial of Polna. *Hist. Jud.* 9 (1947) 57–79. *LJ*

1550 Obergruber, Rudolf: *Die Zeitschriften für jüdische Kulturinteressen im 19. Jahrhundert in Wien.* Wien: 1941. 97 l. *LJ*

Diss. Includes also periodicals of political interest and internal Jewish matters.

1551  Oberlandesgerichtspräsident Hagens in Frankfurt a.m. und der Antisemitismus. *I.Dt.R.* 7 (1901) 443–449. *LJ*

1552  Oberwinder, Heinrich (1845–1914): Das Stoeckerblatt. *Die Zukunft* 16 (1896) 160–174. *LJ*

1553  Oelsner, Toni (1907–): The Place of the Jews in Economic History as Viewed by German Scholars; a Critical Comparative Analysis. *LBIYB* 7 (1962) 183–212. *LJ*

1554  Oelsner, Toni (1907–): Three Jewish Families in Modern Germany; a Study of the Process of Emancipation. *J.S.St.* 4 (1942) 241–268, 349–398. *LJ*

1555  Oertzen, Dietrich von (1849–): *Adolf Stoecker; Lebensbild und Zeitgeschichte.* Berlin: Vaterländische Verlags- und Kunstanstalt, 1910. 2 vols. *LJ*

1556  Oesterreichische Polizei-Direktion, Wien. Zentral-Evidenz Bureau: *Wörterbuch der Diebes- Gauner- oder Kochemersprache, enthaltend alle ihre Abartungen und Dialekte als . . . die jüdische.* Wien: 1853. 82 pp. *LJ*

1557  *Oesterreichisches statistisches Handbuch für die im Reichsrate vertretenen Königreiche und Länder.* Wien: K.K. Statistische Zentral-Kommission, 1886. 1 vol. *LV*

1558  Oncken, Hermann (1869–): *Lassalle.* 2. durchgearb. Aufl. Stuttgart: F. Frommann, 1912. VI, 526 pp. (Politiker und Nationalökonomen, 2) *LJ*

1559  Onody, Géza von (1848–?): *Tísza-Eszlár in der Vergangenheit und Gegenwart.* Autorisierte Uebersetzung aus dem Ungarischen von Georg von Marczianyi. Budapest: 1883. 215 pp. *LJ*

1560  Oort, Henricus (1836–1927): *Der Ursprung der Blutbeschuldigung gegen die Juden; Vortrag beim sechsten Orientalisten-Kongreß.* Leipzig: Otto Harrassowitz, 1883. 31 pp. *LJ*

1561  *Die Opfer der Börse; eine beherzigenswerte Mahnung an alle Kapitalisten, von xxx.* Berlin: G. Schuhr, 1891. 32 pp. *LTA*

1562  Oppenheimer, Franz (1864–1943): Werner Sombart; "Die Juden und das Wirtschaftsleben." *Die Welt* 15 (1911) 535–537. *LJ*

Book review.

1563 Orandt, J.: *Der Hofprediger Stoecker; seine Feinde und sein Prozeß*. Berlin: Selbstverlag des Verfassers, 1888. 31 pp. *Unseen*

1564 Orel, Anton (1881–1959): *Gibt es jüdische Ritualmorde? Eine Sichtung und Erklärung des geschichtlichen Materials; die Prozeße von Trient, Damaskus, Tísza-Eszlár und Polna*. 2. stark erw. Aufl. Wien: Vogelsang-Verlag, 1928. 32 pp. (Der Rufer in der Wüste, vol. 4, 1) *LJ*

1565 Osiander, Andreas (1498–1552): *Schrift über die Blutbeschuldigung*. Wiederaufgefunden und im Neudruck hrsg. von M. Stern. Berlin: Verlag Hausfreund, 1893. XX, 44 pp. *LJ*

1566 Ostwald, Hans (1873–): *Die Assimilation der Juden*. Berlin: Verlag der Diskussion, 1913. 54 pp. (Diskussion; eine Monatsschrift für aktuelle Kulturfragen, 1913, 4) *LJ*

1567 Otruba, Gustav: Der Anteil der Juden am Wirtschaftsleben der böhmischen Länder seit dem Beginn der Industrialisierung. *Die Juden in den böhmischen Ländern; Vorträge der Tagung des Collegium Carolinum in Bad Wiessee vom 27.–29. November 1981*. München: R. Oldenbourg, 1983. Pp. 209–268. *LJ*

1568 Ottel, Michael: *Versuch einer Beantwortung der Frage: Kann den Juden im österreichischen Kaiserstaate eine volle politische Emanzipation gestattet werden*. Parteilos und offenherzig besprochen. Wien: F. Ullrich, 185–. 15 pp. *LJ*

1569 O'Wickedone, P.R.: *Emporgepeitscht! Einschmelzen oder totschlagen? Germania Gouvernante bei Israels. Zur arischjüdischen Pantomime*. Zürich: J. Schabelitz, 1898. 91 pp. *LJ*

1570 Paasch, Karl (1848–1916): *"Der Minister sagts ja auch!" Freiherr von Manteuffel, Herr von der Gröben-Arenstein, Freiherr Dr. jur F.E. von Langen; Ehrengerichtliches und Politisches*. Zürich: J. Schabelitz, 1898. 42 pp. *Unseen*

1571 Paasch, Karl (1848–1916): *Dr. jur. Freiherr F.E. von Langen, Mitglied des Deutschen Reichstages und der Fall Paasch*. Berlin: G.A. Dewald, 1896. 72 pp. *Unseen*

 Contents: 1. Eine Petition an die deutschen Landesvertretungen. 2. Ein Justiz- und politischer Mordversuch am Ende des XIX. Jahrhunderts 3. Der Reichstagsabgeordnete Dr. jur. Freiherr F.E. von Langen.

1572 Paasch, Karl (1848–1916): *Eine Protest-Eingabe an Seine Excellenz den Herrn Reichskanzler von Caprivi*. Leipzig: C. Paasch, 1892. 12 pp. *LJ*

1573  Pacher, Alexander: *Die Judenfrage der 80er Jahre des 19. Jahrhunderts, ihre wissenschaftliche Bearbeitung und deren Widerhall in der Wiener liberalen Presse.* Wien: 1941. III, 146 l. Unseen
      Diss.

1574  Pacher, Paul: *Der klägliche Versuch, Eugen Dühring totzuschweigen.* Salzburg: Selbstverlag, 1904. 127 pp. *LV*

1575  Pacher, Paul: *Verbreitung der Schrift "Der klägliche Versuch Eugen Dühring totzuschweigen."* Salzburg: P. Pacher, 1904. 34 pp. *LV*

1576  Pappenheim, Bertha (1859–1936): *Zur Lage der jüdischen Bevölkerung in Galizien, Reiseeindrücke und Vorschläge zur Besserung der Verhältnisse.* Frankfurt a.M.: Neuer Frankfurter Verlag, 1904. 98 pp. *LJ*

1577  Paranaitis, Justin Bonaventura (–1917): *Das Christentum im Talmud der Juden; oder, die Geheimnisse der rabbinischen Lehre über die Christen. Uebers. und erw. von Joseph Deckert.* Wien: Verlag des Sendboten des hl. Joseph, 1894. 173 pp. *LV*

1578  Paranaitis, Justin Bonaventura (–1917): *Christianus in Talmude Iudäorum; sive Rabbinicae doctrinae de Christianis secreta quae patere, fecit I.B. Paranaitis.* Petropoli: Officina typographia Academiae Caesareae Scientiarum, 1892. 130 pp. *LV*
      With Hebrew translation.

1579  Parkes, James William (1896–): *Antisemitism.* London: Vallentine, Mitchell, 1963. Pp. 20–44. *LJ*

1580  Parkes, James William (1896–): *Antisemitism before 1914. The Emergence of the Jewish Problem, 1878–1939.* London: Oxford University Press, 1946. Pp. 195–208. *LJ*
      Issued under the auspices of the Royal Institute of International Affairs.

1581  Parkes, James William (1896–): *Die Juden als politische Prügelknaben, 1879–1914. Antisemitismus.* München: Rütten & Löning, 1964. Pp. 38–57. *LJ*
      Tr. from the English by Arno Dohm.

1582  Pasmanik, Daniel (1869–1930): *Die Judenassimilation seit Mendelssohn; ein geschichtlicher Ueberblick. Jüdischer Almanach.* Köln: Jüdischer Verlag, 1910. Pp. 50–65. *LJ*

1583  Paul-Schiff, Maximilian: *Der Prozeß Hilsner; Aktenauszug.* Wien: L. Rosner, 1908. 155 pp. *LJ*

1584 Paul-Schiff, Maximilian: Zur Statistik der Kriminalität. *ZfDSJ* 5 (1909) 70–75. *LJ*

1585 Pazi, Margarita: Die Juden in der ersten deutschen Nationalversammlung, 1848–49. *TAJfDG* 5 (1976) 177–209. *LJ*

1586 Peal, David: Jewish Responses to German Antisemitism; the Case of the Böckel Movement, 1887–1894. *J.S.St.* 48 (1986) 269–282. *LJ*

1587 Pellens, Eugen, of Leipzig: An Wilhelm Marr, 19.10.1879. *Staatsarchiv Hamburg.* Nachlaß Marr STA-Hbg NL Marr A 173. *Unseen*

1588 Penzkofer, Peter: Wirtschaftliche und gesellschaftliche Einflüße auf die Entstehung und Entwicklung der privaten Geschäftsbanken Ende des 19. und im 20. Jahrhundert. *Wirtschaft, Gesellschaft, Geschichte.* Stuttgart: Metzler, 1974. Pp. 43–201. *LJ*

1589 Perles, Felix (1874–1933): *Der Krieg und die polnischen Juden in ihrem Verhältnis zu Deutschland.* Königsberg i. Pr.: Gräfe & Unzer, 1914. 16 pp. *LJ*

1590 Perles, Felix (1874–1933): *Was nach dem Herrn Missionsprediger Juden und Christen von mir lernen können.* Königsberg: Ostdeutsche Buchhdlg., 1902. 8 pp. *LJ*

1591 Perles, Felix (1874–1933): What Jews May Learn from Harnack. *J.Q.R.* 14 (1902) 517–542. *LJ*

1592 Perles, Rosalie (1839–1932): *Ein moderner Erlöser des Judentums; Benedictus Levita. Vortrag gehalten im Verein für jüdische Geschichte und Literatur zu Königsberg Pr.* Königsberg, Pr.: Ostdeutsche Buchhdlg., 1901. 16 pp. *LJ*

1593 Perls, Arnold (1856–1907): *Herr Stoecker und sein Prozeß. Zeitbetrachtungen.* 2. Aufl. Leipzig: A. Unflad, 1885. 40 pp. *LJ*

1594 Pestalozzi, Johannes: Herr Hofprediger Stoecker und die Christlich-Soziale Arbeiterpartei; ein Beitrag zur Wegleitung des öffentlichen Urteils. Halle: E. Strien, 1885. V, 35 pp. *LJ*

1595 Petermann, Reinhard E.: *Wien im Zeitalter Franz Josephs I.* Wien: R. Lechner, 1908. IV, 412 pp. *LV*

1596 Die Petition der Antisemiten und die Judenhetze. *AZJ* (1880) 552–553, 741–743, 757–762, 769–776, 822–825. *LJ*

About the deliberations in the Prussian Abgeordnetenhaus and reactions by American Jews.

1597  Petting, Otto: *Wiens antisemitische Presse*. Wien: Selbstverlag, 1896. 24 pp. *LV*

1598  Phelps, Reginald H.: Theodor Fritsch und der Antisemitismus. *Deutsche Rundschau* 87 (1961) 442-449. *LJ*

1599  Philipp, Alfred (1904-): *Die Juden und das Wirtschaftsleben; eine antikritisch-bibliographische Studie zu W. Sombart's "Die Juden und das Wirtschaftsleben."* Straßburg: Heitz, 1920. VI, 120 pp. (Die Volkswirtschaft, 2) *LJ*

1600  Philippson, Johanna: Constantin Frantz. *LBIYB* 13 (1968) 102-119. *LJ*

1601  Philippson, Johanna: Ludwig Philippson und die Allgemeine Zeitung des Judentums [AZJ]. *Das Judentum in der deutschen Umwelt, 1800-1850.* Eds. Hans Liebeschütz, Arnold Pauker. Tübingen: J.C.B. Mohr, 1977. Pp. 243-291. (Schriftenreihe wissenschaftlicher Abhandlungen des LBI, 35) *LJ*

1602  Philippson, Ludwig (1811-1889): *An ein Hohes Abgeordnetenhaus; Petition in Angelegenheit der jüdischen Gemeindeverfassung.* Bonn: 1874. 3 pp. *LTA*

1603  Philippson, Ludwig (1811-1889): *Der Kampf der Preußischen Juden für die Sache der Gewissensfreiheit.* Magdeburg: Bänsch, 1856. XLIV, 218 pp. *LJ*

1604  Philippson, Ludwig (1811-1889): *Zur Charakteristik der Ersten Jüdischen Synode; die erste Resolution der Synode beantragt und motiviert.* Berlin: L. Gerschel, 1869. 19 pp. *LJ*

1605  Philippson, Martin (1846-1916): *Neueste Geschichte des jüdischen Volkes.* Bd. 1-2. 2. verm. Aufl. Frankfurt a.M.: Kauffmann, 1922-1930. Vol. 1, pp. 298-398; vol. 2, pp. 1-101, 130-326. *LJ*

1606  Picard, Jacob (1883-1967): The Childhood in the Village. *LBIYB* 4 (1959) 273-293. *LJ*

1607  Pichl, Eduard (1872-): *Georg Ritter von Schönerer.* Volksausg. Wien: Deutscher Verlag für Jugend und Volk, 1940. 337 pp. *LJ*

1608  Pichl, Eduard (1872-): *Georg Schönerer und die Entwicklung des Alldeutschtums in der Ostmark; ein Lebensbild, von Herwig, pseud.* Wien: Selbstverlag des Verfassers, 1913-1923. 4 vols. *LV*

1609  Pichl, Eduard (1872-): *Georg Schönerer und die Entwicklung des Alldeutschtums in der Ostmark; die Alldeutschen Hochschüler der Ostmark.* Wien: F. Schalk, 1909. VII,V, 97 pp. *Unseen*

1610 Pichler, Hiltrud: *Die Brüder Pereire und die Oesterreichisch-Ungarische Monarchie; Unternehmensprojekte als Beitrag zur österreichischen Wirtschaftsentwicklung, 1850–1880.* Wien: 1974. VI, 233 l. *LC*
Diss. Typescript.

1611 Pick, Israel: *Bekenntnisse aus der Tiefe eines jüdischen Herzens; mit Erläuterungen von Franz Delitzsch.* Leipzig: Selbstverlag des Instituts, 1883. 31 pp. (Schriften des Institutum Judaicum in Leipzig, 2) *LJ*

1612 Pick, Israel: *Briefe an meine Stammgenossen.* Hamburg: in. Komm. bei Berendsohn, 1854. 62 pp. *LJ*

1613 Pick, Israel: *Der Gott der Synagoge und der Gott der Judenchristen; Antwort auf das offene Sendschreiben des "Bukarester Juden," i.e. Iuliu Barasch.* Breslau: in Komm. bei K. Dülfer, 1854. 32 pp. *LJ*

1614 Pick, Israel: *"Israel hat eine Idee zu tragen"; die letzte Lüge einer sterbenden Synagoge. Ein Wort an mein Volk . . . gesprochen in der Hofkirche zu Breslau am 1. Januar 1854.* Breslau: K. Dülfer, 1854. 31 pp. *LJ*

1615 Pick, Israel: *Ist kein Arzt da? oder, Israel und dessen Propheten. Von Ithiel (pseud.).* Hamburg: Nolte & Köhler, 1859. 184 pp. *LJ*

1616 Pick, Israel: *Die Lösung der Judenfrage; Briefe an meine Stammesgenossen.* 2. Aufl. Leipzig: W. Faber, 1894. 59 pp. *LJ*

1617 Pick, Israel: *Die sterbende Jüdin im Gitschiner Spitale; aus meinem Leben.* 3. Aufl. Leipzig: W. Faber, 1895. 47 pp. (Schriften des Institutum Judaicum in Leipzig, 42) *Unseen*

1618 Piloty, Robert: *Zur Revision des bayerischen Judenedikts; Vortrag gehalten am 12. Februar 1914 . . . zu Würzburg.* Frankfurt a.M.: Verlag des Israelit, 1914. 43 pp. *LJ*

1619 Pinkus, Lazar Felix (1881–): Jüdische Wirtschaftsgeschichte. *Ost und West* 3 (1903) col. 527–534. *LJ*

1620 Pinkus, Lazar Felix (1881–): *Die moderne Judenfrage; von den Grundlagen der jüdischen Wirtschaftsgeschichte und des Zionismus.* Breslau: W. Köbner, 1903. 48 pp. *LJ*

1621 Pinkus, Lazar Felix (1881–): *Studien zur Wirtschaftstellung der Juden von der Völkerwanderung bis zur Neuzeit; ein Beitrag zur jüdischen Wirtschaftsgeschichte.* Berlin: Louis Lamm, 1905. 56 pp. *LJ*

1622  Pinner, Efraim Moses: *Offenes Sendschreiben an den Hohen Reichstag des*
*NorddeutschenBundes; die Eheschliessung, EhescheidungundEidesleistung der*
*Juden nach ihren Ritualgesetzen im Vergleich mit den darauf bezüglichen.*
*Gesetzen in den Staaten des Norddeutschen Bundes und der Notwendigkeit*
*gleichmäßiger Gesetze. Ein Beitrag zur Geschichte Deutschlands und der*
*Juden.* Berlin: Selbstverlag des Verfassers, 1870. LXXIV, 82 pp. *LJ*

1623  Pinsker, Lev Semenovich (1821-1891): *Autoemanzipation! Mahnruf an seine*
*Stammesgenossen, von einem russischen Juden.* Berlin: W. Issleib in Komm.,
1882. III, 36 pp. *LJ*

1624  Plath, Karl Heinrich Christian: *Shakespeare's Kaufmann von Venedig. Ein*
*Beitrag zum Verständnisse der Judenfrage.* Greifswald: J. Abel, 1882. 36 pp.
*LJ*

1625  Plath, Karl Heinrich Christian: *Was machen wir Christen mit unsern Juden?*
Nördlingen: C.H. Beck, 1881. IV, 187 pp. *LJ*

1626  Plath, Karl Heinrich Christian: *Welche Stellung haben die Glieder der*
*christlichen Kirche dem modernen Judentum gegenüber einzunehmen?* Berlin:
Buchhdlg. der Gossner'schen Mission, 1881. 38 pp. *LJ*

1627  Platter, Julius: *Der Wucher in der Bukowina.* Jena: Fischer, 1878. 54 pp.
(Soziale Studien in der Bukowina, I) *LJ*

1628  Pleyer, Karl: *Johann Emanuel Veith (Veit, Jonas) und sein Kreis.* Wien: 1934.
153 l. *Unseen*

      Diss.

1629  Pois, Robert A.: Walter Rathenau's Jewish Quandary. *LBIYB* 13 (1968)
120-131. *LJ*

1630  Polakowsky, Helmut: *Was soll mit den Juden geschehen; eine Anleitung zur*
*gesetzlichen Lösung der Judenfrage.* Berlin: M. Schulze, 1881. 60 pp. *LJ*

1631  Poliakov, Leon (1910-): Die deutschen Länder. *Geschichte des Antisemitismus.*
*Bd. 1: Zwischen Assimilation und Weltverschwörung.* Frankfurt a.M.:
Athenäum, 1988. Pp. 13-43. *LJ*

      Orginal Title: *Histoire de l'antisémitisme — L'Europe suicidaire.* 1. ptie.
1870-1914.

1632  Poliakov, Leon (1910-): Deutschland. *Geschichte des Antisemitismus. Bd. 6:*
*Emanzipation und Rassenwahn.* Worms: Verlag Georg Heintz, 1987. Pp.
184-265. *LJ*

Orginal title: *Histoire de l'antisémitisme*.

1633 Poliakov, Leon (1910–): From Voltaire to Wagner. *The History of Antisemitism, vol. 3*. London: Routledge & K. Paul, 1975. Pp. 380–457. (The Littman Library of Jewish Civilization) *LJ*

1634 Poliakov, Leon (1910–): Gobineau and His Contemporaries and the Aryan Epoch. *The Aryan Myth; A History of Racist and Nationalist Ideas in Europe*. London: Chatto & Windus, 1974. Pp. 215–330. (The Columbus Centre Series) *LJ*

Original title: *Le mythe aryen*.

1635 Poll, Bernhard: *Jüdische Presse im 19. Jahrhundert*. Aus dem Internationalen Zeitungsmuseum der Stadt Aachen . . . Aachen: Internationales Zeitungsmuseum, 1967. 147 pp. *LC*

1636 Pollack, Heinrich (1835–1908): *30 (Dreißig) Jahre aus dem Leben eines Journalisten*. Wien: A. Hölder, 1894–1898. 3 vols. *LV*

1637 Pollak, Johann: Der politische Zionismus. *N.Z.* 16, I (1897–1898) 596–600. *LJ*

Attack on Zionism from the socialist point of view.

1638 Pollak, Michael: *Vienne 1900; une identité blessée*. Paris: Edition Gallimard-Julliard, 1984. 220 pp. (Collection: Archives) *LJ*

About antisemitism in Vienna at the end of the 19th century, pp. 75–107.

1639 *Der Polnaer Ritualmordprozeß; sein Stand vor der Revision*. Wien: Kraus, 1900. 16 pp. *LJ*

1640 Popper-Lynkeus, Josef (1838–1921): *Fürst Bismarck und der Antisemitismus*. Wien: Hugo Engel, 1886. 150 pp. *LJ*

1641 Porsch, J. K.: *Kleiner Juden-Spiegel, darinnen man klar und deutlich sehen kann, wie beim Viehhandel der Bauer von den Juden schändlich betrogen wird*. Schleusingen: Conrad Glaser, 1880. 47 pp. *LJ*

Reprint of the 1848 edition.

1642 Preissler, Dietmar: *Frühantisemitismus in der Freien Stadt Frankfurt und im Großherzogtum Hessen (1810 bis 1860)*. Heidelberg: C. Winter, Universitätsverlag, 1989. XII, 409 pp. (Heidelberger Abhandlungen zur mittleren und neueren Geschichte, N.S., 3) *LJ*

1643 Pressel, Wilhelm (1818–): *Israel, seine gegenwärtige Lage und welthistorische Bedeutung. Referat bei der 5. General-Versammlung der evangelischen Allianz, dem 19. August 1867 erstattet.* Tübingen: Osiander'sche Buchhdl., 1868. 16 pp. *LJ*

1644 Pressel, Wilhelm (1818–): *Die Juden-Mission, eine evangelische Christenpflicht und der Gewinn, den sie uns Christen bringt; beleuchtet in zweien am 18. Mai 1864 gehaltenen Vorträgen.* Köln: Typ. W. Hassel, 1864. 33 pp. *LJ*

1645 Pressel, Wilhelm (1818–): *Der Talmud vor dem Schwurgericht am Ende des XIX. Jahrhunderts; ein Zeugnis für die Wahrheit.* Leipzig: Dörffling & Franke, 1893. 68 pp. *LJ*

1646 Pressel, Wilhelm (1818–): *Die Zerstreuung des Volkes Israel.* Nr. 1–5. Heilbronn: Henninger, 1887. 5 vols. in 1. *LJ*

1647 Preston, David L.: The German Jews in Secular Education; University, Teaching and Science. A Preliminary Inquiry. *J.S.St.* 38 (1976) 99–116. *LJ*

1648 Preuß, Hugo (1860–1925): Konfessionelle Kandidaturen. *Die Nation* 16 (1898) 17–19. *LJ*

1649 Preuß, Hugo (1860–1925): *Die Maßregelung jüdischer Lehrerinnen in den Berliner Gemeindeschulen; Rede gehalten in der Sitzung der Stadtverordneten am 1.XII.1898.* Stenographischer Bericht nebst einer orientierenden Vorbemerkung. Berlin: S. Cronbach, 1898. 36 pp. *LJ*

1650 Preußisches Abgeordnetenhaus: *Die bürgerliche Gleichstellung der Juden in Preußen; Verhandlungen des Hauses der Abgeordneten vom 24.–27. April 1860 und vom 10. Mai 1860.* Berlin: W. Adolf & Comp., 1860. 127 pp. *LJ*

Debate and voting about the report of the Petitions Commission.

1651 Preußisches Abgeordnetenhaus: *Der Fall Kantorowicz und die Judenfrage vor dem Preußischen Abgeordnetenhause am 20. und 22. November 1880.* Abdruck der an die Interpellation geknüpften Reden nach dem amtlichen . . . Berlin: Werkenthin, 1881. 199 pp. *LJ*

1652 Preußisches Abgeordnetenhaus: *Die Judenfrage im preußischen Volkshause.* Abdruck der Verhandlungen des Hauses der Abgeordneten über die Petition der Rabbiner Sutro zu Münster. Aus dem stenographischen Berichte der 25. Sitzung am Mittwoch, den 23. März 1859. Hrsg. und mit einigen kritischen Anmerkungen versehen von Spinoza, dem Jüngeren. Berlin: Behrendt, 1859. 67 pp. *Unseen*

1653 Preußisches Abgeordnetenhaus:*Die Judenfrage; Verhandlungen des Preußischen Abgeordnetenhauses über die Interpellation des Abgeordneten Dr. Hänel am 20. und 22. November 1880. 2 Aufl.* Berlin: Möser, 1880. 211 pp. *LJ*

Offprint from: *Stenographische Berichte des Hauses der Abgeordneten*.

1654   Preußisches Abgeordnetenhaus: *Stenographischer Bericht. 20. Sitzung am 25. Februar 1882*. Berlin: Preußische Verlagsanstalt, Pp. 483-515. *LJ*

The speakers: Stoecker, Virchow, von Puttkammer, Strosser, E. Richter, Cremer and Schröder.

1655   Preußisches Abgeordnetenhaus: *Stenographischer Bericht der Sitzung des Preußischen Abgeordnetenhauses vom 9. Februar 1892*. Berlin: 1892. 1 vol. *Unseen*

Debate on the murder of a boy in Xanten.

1656   Preußisches Herrenhaus: *Die bürgerlichen Rechte der Juden und Dissidenten vor dem Forum der Ersten Kammer*. Nach den Druckschriften der Kammer und dem stenographischen Bericht. Berlin: W. Adolf, 1852. 61 pp. *LJ*

1657   Preußisches Herrenhaus: *Einige Erklärungen über die Judenfrage aus früheren Sitzungen des Preußischen Herrenhauses. Abdruck aus den stenographischen Berichten*. Berlin: Heinicke, 1880. 40 pp. *LJ*

1658   Prinz, Arthur: *Juden im deutschen Wirtschaftsleben; soziale und wirtschaftliche Struktur im Wandel, 1850-1914*. Tübingen: Mohr, 1984. IX, 202 pp. (Schriftenreihe wissenschaftlicher Abhandlungen des LBI, 43) *LJ*

A section about the political antisemitism is included in chapter 3: Industrialisierung und Gründerkrise, 1871-1874. Ed. Abraham Barkai.

1659   Prinz, Arthur: New Perspectives on Marx as a Jew. *LBIYB* 15 (1970) 107–124. *LJ*

1660   *Prof. Dr. August Rohling in Prag vor dem Gerichtshof deutscher Gelehrter; zum Presssprozeß wider den Bezirksrabbiner und Reichsratsabgeordneten Dr. J.S. Bloch*. Wien: D. Löwy, 1883. 20 pp. *LJ*

1661   *Protestantismus und Politik; Werk und Wirkung Adolf Stoeckers, von Günther Brakelmann, Martin Greschat, Werner Jochmann*. Hamburg: Christians, 1982. 252 pp. (Hamburger Beiträge zur Sozial- und Zeitgeschichte, 17) *LJ*

1662   *Protokolle der in Köln am Rhein vom 6. bis zum 9.10. 1900 abgehaltenen Missionskonferenz für die Arbeit der evangelischen Kirche an Israel*. Leipzig: J.C. Hinrichs' Verlag, 1901. 99 pp. (Schriften des Institutum Judaicum in Berlin, 29) *LJ*

1663   *Der Prozeß Ahlwardt; ein Zeichen der Zeit und eine lehrreiche Studie. Von einem Deutsch-Nationalen*. Berlin: P. Heichen, 1892. 56 pp. *LJ*

1664  *Der Prozeß Ahlwardt; stenographischer Bericht über die Verhandlungen vor der 2. Strafkammer . . . am 11. April und 5. Mai 1891.* Berlin: G. Höppner, 1891. 32 pp. *LJ*

1665  *Prozeß Fritsch; Anklage wegen Beleidigung der sogenannten "Jüdischen Religionsgemeinde"; verhandelt Leipzig den 19.5.1911.* Stenographischer Bericht. 3. Aufl. Leipzig: Hammer-Verlag, 1911. 16 pp. (Hammer-Schriften, 4) *LC*

1666  *Prozeß gegen den jüdischen Wucherer Markus Löb von Mainz und Hirsch Süsser von Würzburg; geführt gegen Löb vor der Strafkammer zu Mainz am 14., 15., und 16. Februar 1883 und gegen Süsser vor der Strafkammer zu Würzburg am 15., 16. und 17. Februar.* Mannheim: Diesbach, 1883. 16 pp. *LJ*

1667  Prozeß gegen den Reichsratsabgeordneten Georg Ritter von Schönerer und den Stenographen Eduard Gerstgrasser. *Berühmte Kriminalprozeße der Gegenwart.* Wien: Reichmann, [n.d.]. Pp. 49–94, 205–213. *Unseen*

1668  *Der Prozeß gegen den Reichsratsabgeordneten Georg Ritter von Schönerer und den Stenographen Eduard Gerstgrasser; verhandelt vor dem Erkenntnissenate des Wiener Landgerichtes am 4. und 5. Mai 1888.* Wien: 1888. 49–96 pp. *LJ*

   From: A. Hartleben's *Gerichtsbibliothek*, vol. 1, no. 2.

1669  *Der Prozeß gegen Masloff und Genossen, Konitz, 25. Oktober–10. November 1900, nach stenographischer Aufnahme.* Berlin: H.S. Hermann, 1900. 1074 pp. *LJ*

   About the blood libel affair in Konitz.

1670  *Prozeß Oberwinder; eine Beleuchtung des Falles Buschoff.* Berlin: Vaterländische Verlagsanstalt, 1892. 96 pp. *Unseen*

1671  *Der Prozeß Rohling kontra Bloch.* Berlin: M.Hoffschläger, 1892. 22 pp. *LJ*

   Offprint from: *Mitteilungen aus dem Verein zur Abwehr des Antisemitismus.*

1672  *Prozeß: Schönerer — Neues Wiener Tagblatt. (Beschuldigte: G. Ritter von Schönerer, F. Gerstgrasser). Unverkürzte stenographische Aufnahme.* Wien: Verlag A. Amonesta, 1888. 176 pp. *LB*

1673  Der Prozeß von Tísza-Eszlár und die antisemitische Bewegung. *Der Kulturkämpfer* 4 (1883) 41–50. *LJ*

1674  Prugel, Alfred: Ein großer Verführer; Heinrich von Treitschke. *Propheten des Nationalismus.* Ed. Karl Schwedhelm. München: List-Verlag, 1969. Pp. 72–87. *LC*

1675 Prugel, Alfred: Träumereien am großen deutschen Kamin: Paul de Lagarde. *Propheten des Nationalismus.* Ed. Karl Schwedhelm. München: List-Verlag, 1969. Pp. 36–55. *LC*

1676 Pucher, Solomon: *Mitgefühl mit den Tieren; eine heilige Pflicht der jüdischen Religion, ein Wort an meine Glaubensgenossen.* Mitau: Typ. J.F. Steffenhagen, 1876. 19 pp. *LJ*

Commissioned by Kurlandischer Tierschutz-Verein.

1677 Pudor, Heinrich (1865–): Das Schächten und der Fall Fritsch. *Der Hammer* 10 (1911) 166. *LJ*

1678 Puhle, Hans Jürgen: Der militante Antisemitismus der Agrarier. *Agrarische Interessenpolitik und Preußischer Konservatismus im Wilhelminischen Reich, 1893-1914.* 2. erw. Aufl. Bonn-Bad Godesberg: Verlag Neue Gesellschaft, 1975. Pp. 111–140. (Schriftenreihe des Forschungsinstitut der Friedrich-Ebert-Stiftung, 51) *LJ*

1679 Pulzer, Peter George Julius: The Austrian Liberals and the Jewish Question, 1867-1914. *Journal of Central European Affairs* 23 (1963) 131–142. *LJ*

1680 Pulzer, Peter George Julius: The Development of Political Antisemitism in Austria. *The Jews of Austria; Essays on Their Life, History and Destruction.* Ed. Josef Fraenkel. London: Vallentine, Mitchell, 1967. Pp. 429–443. *LJ*

1681 Pulzer, Peter George Julius: *Die Entstehung des politischen Antisemitismus in Deutschland und Oesterreich, 1867-1914.* Gütersloh: S. Mohn, 1966. 312 pp. *LJ*

Original title: *The Rise of Political Antisemitism in Germany and Austria.*

1682 Pulzer, Peter George Julius: *The Rise of Political Antisemitism in Germany and Austria.* New York: Wiley, 1964. XIV, 364 pp. (New Dimensions in History; Essays in Comparative History) *LJ*

1683 Pulzer, Peter George Julius: The Roots of Political Antisemitism in Germany and Austria. *Colloquium* (1964) 12–17. *LTA*

1684 Pulzer, Peter George Julius: Why was there a Jewish Question in Imperial Germany? *LBIYB* 25 (1980) 133–146. *LJ*

1685 *La question juive en Allemagne.* Extrait du Correspondant. Paris: Jules Gervais, 1881. 49 pp. *Unseen*

Offprint from: *Correspondant.*

1686  R-g: *Was ist Wucher? Zwei Briefe in dieser Frage.* Wien: Stein, 1880. 1 vol.
       *LV*

1687  Raabe-Johnsdorf, B.A., ed.: *Neunzehn Jahrhunderte Christen- und Judentum.*
       Wien: Typ. H. Liebermann, 1894. 45 pp. *LJ*

1688  Rabben, Ernst: *Die Gaunersprache. (Chochum loschen).* Gesammelt und
       zusammengestellt aus der Praxis für die Praxis. Hamm i. Westf.: Breer &
       Thiemann, 1906. 196 pp. *LV*

1689  Rabinowitz, Joseph (1837–1899): *Neue Dokumente der südrussischen
       Christentumsbewegung; Selbstbiographie und Predigten.* Hrsg. von Franz
       Delitzsch. Leipzig: Dörffling & Franke, 1887. X, 54 pp. (Schriften des
       Institutum Judaicum in Leipzig, 16) *LJ*

1690  Rabinowitz, Joseph (1837–1899): *Zwei Predigten in dem Gotteshause Bethlehem
       in Kischniew gehalten.* Leipzig: Dörffling & Franke, 1885. 32 pp. (Schriften
       des Institutum Judaicum in Leipzig, 9) *LJ*

1691  Rachfahl, Felix (1867–1925): Das Judentum und die Genesis des modernen
       Kapitalismus. *Pr. Jhrb.* 147 (1912) 13–86. *LJ*

1692  *Die rätselhafte Ermordung des Gymnasiasten Ernst Winter in Konitz am 11. 3.
       1900.* Chemnitz: C.A. Hager, 1900. 16 pp. *Unseen*

1693  Ragins, Sanford: *Jewish Responses to Antisemitism in Germany, 1870 to 1914.*
       Ann Arbor: Mich. University Microfilm, 1972. VI, 280, 76, 18 pp. *LJ*
       Brandeis University, Ph.D., 1972.

1694  Ramer, Christa: *Heinrich von Treitschke, Theodor Mommsen und Rudolf
       Virchow in ihrem Verhältnis zum Problem des Antisemitismus.* Bamberg: 1965.
       71, 18 pp. *LTA*
       Typescript.

1695  Raphael, Jacob: Gustav Heine in Wien. *ZfGJ* 5 (1968) 110–117. *LJ*

1696  Raphael, Jacob: Die Hamburger Familie Gumpel und der Dichter Heinrich
       Heine. *ZfGJ* 6 (1969) 33–38. *LJ*

1697  Raphael, Paul: *La France, l'Allemagne et les Juifs (1789–1915). Antisémitisme
       et Pangermanisme.* Paris: F. Alcan, 1916. 89 pp. *LJ*

1698  Rathenau, Walther (1867–1922): "Höre Israel." *Die Zukunft* 18 (1897)
       454–462. *LJ*

1699 Ratzinger, Georg (1844–1899): *Die Volkswirtschaft in ihren sittlichen Grundlagen.* Freiburg i. Br.: Herder, 1881. XIV, 532 pp. *LV*

1700 Rauchberg, Heinrich: *Die Bevölkerung Oesterreichs auf Grund der Ergebnisse der Volkszählungen vom 31. Dezember 1890.* Wien: A. Hölder, 1895. X, 530 pp. *LV*

1701 Rauchberg, Heinrich: Die Hauptergebnisse der österreichischen Berufsstatistik. *Statistische Monatsschrift* 1 (1894) 128–; 2 (1894) 379–. *LV*

1702 Ravesteijn, Willem van: Kapitalismus und Judentum. *N.Z.* 2 (1911/12) 708–716. *LJ*

1703 Réal, Jean: The Religious Conception of Race; Houston Stewart Chamberlain and Germanic Christianity. *International Council for Philosophy and Humanistic Studies; the Third Reich.* London: Weidenfeld & Nicolson, 1955. Pp. 243–286. *LJ*

1704 *Die Rechtsirrtümer des Judeneides. Notizen zur neuen Prüfung einer alten Frage.* Speyer: G.L. Lang, 185–. 56 pp. *LJ*

1705 *Redet mit Jerusalem freundlich! Nachrichten über das Seminar des Institutum Judaicum zu Leipzig.* Gegengabe des Dankes an die Freunde und Förderer der Anstalt. Leipzig: W. Faber, 1887. 54 pp. (Schriften des Institutum Judaicum in Leipzig, 11) *Unseen*

1706 Reich, Nathan: Capitalism and the Jews; a Critical Examination of Sombart's Thesis. *Menorah Journal* 18 (1930) 5–19. *LJ*

1707 Reichardt, Johann Christian: *Der alte und der neue Bund; oder, Mosaismus und Christentum.* Frankfurt a.M.: 1856. 1 vol. *Unseen*

1708 Reichardt, Johann Christian: *Die Bestimmung des Volkes Israel; ein Wort über und für Israel.* Frankfurt a.M.: Typ. C. Naumann, 1856. 16 pp. *LJ*

1709 Reichmann, Eva Gabriele (Jungmann): *Die Flucht in den Haß; die Ursachen der deutschen Judenkatastrophe.* Frankfurt a.M.: Europäische Verlagsanstalt, 1956. Pp. 7–178. *LJ*

Original title: *Hostages of Civilisation.*

1710 Reichmann, Eva Gabriele (Jungmann): *Hostages of Civilisation.* London: V. Gollancz, 1950. Pp. 5–171. *LJ*

1711 Reichstagsverhandlungen über die Zurücksetzung der jüdischen Einjährigen-Freiwilligen. *I.Dt.R.* 14 (1908) 266–276. *LJ*

1712 Reinach, Salomon (1858–1932): *L'origine des aryens; histoire d'une controverse.* Paris: Leroux, 1892. II, 124 pp. *LV*

1713 Reinharz, Jehuda: Consensus and Conflict between Zionists and Liberals in Germany before World War I. *Texts and Responses. Studies presented to Nahum N. Glatzer.* Eds. Michael A. Fishbane, Paul R. Flohr. Leiden: E.J. Brill, 1975. Pp. 226–238. *LJ*

1714 Reinharz, Jehuda: Deutschtum and Judentum in the Ideology of the Centralverein Deutscher Staatsbürger Jüdischen Glaubens. *J.S.St.* 36 (1974) 19–39. *LJ*

1715 Reinharz, Jehuda: East European Jews in the Weltanschauung of German Zionists, 1882–1914. *Studies in Contemporary Jewry* 1 (1984) 55–95. *LJ*

1716 Reinharz, Jehuda: *Fatherland; or, Promised Land; the Dilemma of the German Jew, 1893–1914.* Ann Arbor, Mich.: University of Michigan, 1975. 320 pp. *LJ*

About the C.V. and ZVfD and their influence on German Jewry.

1717 Reinharz, Jehuda: Review of Ismar Schorsch's "Jewish Reactions to German Antisemitism, 1870–1914." *J.S.St.* 35 (1973) 297–299. *LJ*

1718 Reinharz, Jehuda: Zionisten und Liberale in deutschsprachigen Ländern (Deutschland, Oesterreich, Ungarn und Böhmen). *LBI Bull.* 82 (1989) 49–63. *LJ*

1719 *Religiöse Schwärmereien; ein kulturhistorischer Beitrag zur Legende der Blutopfer, von einem Katholiken.* Leipzig: Levien, 1891. 36 pp. *Unseen*

A new edition of *Die Teufelskralle.* First published in 1884.

1720 *Der Rembrandtdeutsche, von einem Wahrheitsfreund.* Dresden: Glöss, 1892. VIII, 194 pp. *LV*

1721 Renan, Ernest (1823–1892): *Das Judentum vom Gesichtspunkte der Rasse und der Religion; Vortrag.* Basel: Bernheim, 1883. 32 pp. *LJ*

Orginal title: *Le judaisme comme race et comme rèligion.* Paris, 1883.

1722 Rengstorf, K.H., ed.: *Kirche und Synagoge. Handbuch zur Geschichte von Christen und Juden.* Bd. 2. Stuttgart: E. Klett, 1970. Pp. 280–321, 358–393, 483–547, 587–593, 668–691. *LJ*

1723 Reuss, Rodolphe: *L'affaire de Tísza-Eszlár; une épisode de l'histoire de l'antisémitisme au dix-neuvième siècle.* Straßburg: Treuttel & Würtz, 1883. 53 pp. *LJ*

1724 Richarz, Monika: Jewish Social Mobility in Germany during the Time of Emancipation, 1790-1871. *LBIYB* 20 (1975) 69-77 pp. *LJ*

1725 Richarz, Monika, ed.: *Jüdisches Leben in Deutschland.* Stuttgart: Deutsche Verlagsanstalt, 1976-1979. 2 vols. (Veröffentlichungen des L.B.I.) *LJ*

Vol. 1: *Selbstzeugnisse zur Sozialgeschichte, 1780-1871;* Vol. 2: *Selbstzeugnisse zur Sozialgeschichte im Kaiserreich.*

1726 Richthofen, Gotthard von: *Der Antisemitismus im Lichte der Bibel; ein Brief.* Breslau: J. Mar, 1892. 34 pp. *LJ*

1727 Rieger, Paul (1870-1939): *Zur Jahrhundertfeier des Juden-Edikts vom 11. März 1812; im Rückblick auf den Kampf der preußischen Juden um die Gleichberechtigung.* Berlin: Typ. Rosenthal, 1912. 46 pp. *LJ*

1728 Riesser, Gabriel (1806-1863): *Eine Auswahl aus seinen Schriften und Briefen.* Frankfurt a.M.: J. Kauffmann, 1913. 124 pp. (Denkmäler jüdischen Geistes, 2) *LJ*

1729 Riesser, Gabriel (1806-1863): *Gesammelte Schriften.* Hrsg. im Auftrag des Comité der Riesser-Stiftung von M. Isler, Bd. 1-4. Frankfurt a.M.: Verlag der Riesser-Stiftung, 1867-1868. 4 vols. *LJ*

1730 Riesser, Gabriel (1806-1863): Die Rechte der Juden in Preußen. *Pr. Jhrb.* 5 (1860) 105-142. *Unseen*

1731 Riff, Michael E.: The Anti-Jewish Aspect of the Revolutionary Unrest of 1848 in Baden and Its Impact on Emancipation. *LBIYB* 21 (1976) 27-40. *LJ*

1732 Riff, Michael E.: Czech Antisemitism and the Jewish Response Before 1914. *Wien.Lib.Bull.* 39-40 (1976) 8-20. *LJ*

1733 Ring, Max (1817-1901): *David Kalisch; der Vater des "Kladderadatsch" und Begründer der "Berliner Posse."* Berlin: Staude, 1873. 40 pp. *LV*

1734 Rinott, Mosche: Gabriel Riesser, Fighter for Jewish Emancipation. *LBIYB* 7 (1962) 11-38. *LJ*

1735 Riquarts, Kurt Gerhard: *Der Antisemitismus als politische Partei in Schleswig-Holstein und Hamburg, 1871-1914.* Kiel: 1975. 442 pp. *LJ*

Diss. Kiel.

1736  Ritter Gerhard Albert, ed.: *Deutsche Parteien vor 1918.* Köln: Kiepenheuer &
      Witsch, 1973. 406 pp. (Neue wissenschaftliche Bibliothek, 61) *LJ*

1737  Ritter, Immanuel Heinrich: Die letzten zwölf Jahre; ein Beitrag zur Geschichte
      der Juden in Preußen. *Jahrbuch für die Geschichte der Juden und des
      Judentums* 1 (1860) 103-126. *LTA*

1738  Der Ritualmord bei den Talmud-Juden. *I.Dt.R.* 11 (1905) 574-579. *LJ*

1739  *Ritualmord. Blutbeschuldigung.* Danzig: A.W. Kafemann, 1900. 51 pp. *LJ*
      Offprint from: *Antisemitenspiegel.*

1740  Ritualmordmärchen. *I.Dt.R.* 18 (1912) 218-225. *LJ*
      Signed A.L.

1741  Rocholl, Heinrich Wilhelm (1845-): *Zur Weltstellung des israelitischen Volkes;
      ein Vortrag.* Leipzig: Akad. Buchhdlg., 1890. 15 pp. (Schriften des Institutum
      Judaicum in Leipzig, 26) *LJ*

1742  Röder, Adam: *Der Austritt Stoeckers aus der Konservativen Partei.* Karlsruhe:
      Müller & Gräff, 1896. 44 pp. *LJ*

1743  Röhl, J.: Higher Civil Servants in Germany, 1890-1900. *Journal of
      Contemporary History* 2 (1967) 101-102. *LJ*

1744  Rösel Georg: *Luther und die Juden; ein Beitrag zu der Frage "Hat die
      Reformation gegen Juda Toleranz geübt?"* Münster i.W.: Adolph Russell,
      1893. 40 pp. *LJ*

1745  Rohan, Karel J.: *Eine Ansicht über die Ursachen der Judenfrage und über die
      Mittel zur Lösung derselben.* Leipzig: O. Wigand, 1882. 27 pp. *LJ*

1746  Rohling, August (1839-1931): *Le juif selon le Talmud.* Ed. francaise
      considérablement augm. par A. Pontigny. Pref. Edouard Drumont. Paris: A.
      Savine, 1889. XVII, 285 pp. (Bibliothèque antisémitique) *LJ*

1747  Rohling, August (1839-1931): *Der Katechismus des 19. Jahrhunderts für Juden
      und Protestanten, den auch Katholiken lesen dürfen.* Mainz: F. Kirchheim,
      1877. VIII, 272 pp. *LJ*

1748  Rohling, August (1839-1931): *Meine Antworten an die Rabbiner; oder, Fünf
      Briefe über den Talmudismus und das Blut-Ritual der Juden.* Prag: Cyrillo-
      Method'sche Buchhdlg., 1883. 106 pp. *LJ*

1749 Rohling, August (1839–1931): *Die Polemik und das Menschenopfer des Rabbinismus; eine wissenschaftliche Antwort ohne Polemik für die Rabbiner und ihre Genossen.* Paderborn: Bonifatius-Druckerei, 1883. 108 pp. *LJ*

1750 Rohracher, Fr.: *Ursula von Lienz; ein von Juden gemartertes Christenkind. Ein spätes Gedenkblümelein.* Brixen: Pressereins–Buchhdlg., 1905. 24 pp. *LV*

1751 Roi, Johann Friedrich Alexander de la: Auf Missionsreisen unter den Juden in Mitteleuropa. *Nathanael* 29 (1913) 80–92, 97–109. *LJ*

1752 Roi, Johann Friedrich Alexander de la: Aus meinen Missionsjahren. *Nathanael* 28 (1912) 73–81. *LJ*

1753 Roi, Johann Friedrich Alexander de la: *Die evangelische Christenheit und die Juden unter dem Gesichtspunkte der Mission geschichtlich betrachtet.* Berlin: Reuther und Reinhard, 1892. 2 vols. (Schriften des Institutum Judaicum in Berlin, 9) *LTA*

1754 Roi, Johann Friedrich Alexander de la: *Ferdinand Christian Ewald; ein Lebensbild aus der neueren Judenmission.* Gütersloh: C. Bertelsmann, 1896. 160 pp. *LJ*

1755 Roi, Johann Friedrich Alexander de la: *Geschichte der evangelischen Judenmission seit Entstehung des neueren Judentums.* Leipzig: J.C. Hinrichs' Verlag, 1899. 354, 454 pp. (Schriften des Institutum Judaicum in Berlin, 9) *LJ*

1756 Roi, Johann Friedrich Alexander de la: Die heutige evangelische Judenmission. *Nathanael* 23 (1907) 1–19. *LJ*

1757 Roi, Johann Friedrich Alexander de la: *Isaak da Costa, der holländische Christ und Dichter aus Israel.* Leipzig: J.C. Hinrichs' Verlag, 1899. 42 pp. (Schriften des Institutum Judaicum in Berlin, 26) *LJ*
Offprint from: *Nathanael.*

1758 Roi, Johann Friedrich Alexander de la: Judenmission 1895 und 1896. *Nathanael* 13 (1897) 12–30, 33–49. *LJ*

1759 Roi, Johann Friedrich Alexander de la: Die Judenmission an der Wende des Jahrhunderts. *Nathanael* 16 (1900) 3–29. *LJ*

1760 Roi, Johann Friedrich Alexander de la: *Judentaufen im 19. Jahrhundert; ein statistischer Versuch.* Leipzig: J.C. Hinrichs' Verlag, 1899. 156 pp. (Schriften des Institutum Judaicum in Berlin, 27) *LJ*
Offprint from: *Nathanael.*

1761  Roi, Johann Friedrich Alexander de la: *Michael Solomon Alexander, der erste evangelische Bischof in Jerusalem; ein Beitrag zur orientalischen Frage.* Gütersloh: C. Bertelsmann, 1897. VII, 230 pp. (Schriften des Institutum Judaicum in Berlin, 22) *Unseen*

1762  Roi, Johann Friedrich Alexander de la: *Neujüdische Stimmen über Jesum Christum gesammelt.* Mit Benutzung eines gleichbetitelten Aufsatzes in H. Strack's Nathanael. Berlin: Institutum Judaicum, 1910. 54 pp. (Schriften des Institutum Judaicum in Berlin, 39) *Unseen*

1763  Roi, Johann Friedrich Alexander de la: *Rudolf Hermann Gurland.* Leipzig: J.C. Hinrichs' Verlag, 1906. 70 pp. (Schriften des Institutum Judaicum in Berlin, 35) *LJ*

      Offprint from: *Nathanael.*

1764  Roi, Johann Friedrich Alexander de la: *Stephan Schultz; ein Beitrag zum Verständnis der Juden und ihrer Bedeutung für das Leben der Völker.* 2. Aufl. Gotha: F.A. Perthes, 1878. 279 pp. *LJ*

1765  Ronge, Johannes (1813–1887): *Offenes Sendschreiben an die Herren Konsistorialräte Ebrand in Erlangen, von Otto in Eisenberg, an Hofprediger Stoecker, Superintendent Hechzermaier in Bielefeld, Pfarrvikar Stromberger in Biebesheim (Hessen) und an die andern fünf geistlichen Mitglieder des Antisemiten-Comités.* 2. Aufl. Darmstadt: 1881. 1 vol. Unseen

1766  Ronge, Johannes (1813–1887): *Sendschreiben an Herrn Dr. Förster und die andern Mitglieder des Antisemiten-Komitees.* 2. Aufl. Darmstadt: 1881, 1 vol. *Unseen*

1767  Roos, J.R.B. de: *Ueber die Kriminalität der Juden. Monatsschrift für Kriminalpsychologie und Strafrechtsreform* 6 (1909–1910) 193–205. *LJ*

1768  Rose, Paul Lawrence: The Noble Antisemitism of Richard Wagner. *The Historical Journal* 25, 3 (1982) 751–763. *LJ*

1769  Rose, Paul Lawrence: *Revolutionary Antisemitism in Germany from Kant to Wagner.* Princeton, N.J.: Princeton University Press, 1990. XVIII, 389 pp. *LJ*

1770  Rosenbacher, Arnold: *Vortrag des Herrn Arnold Rosenbacher über das Dr. Kopp'sche Werk "Stritt Rohling-Bloch."* Prag: Centralverein zur Pflege jüdischer Angelegenheiten, 1886. 28 pp. (Bericht des Centralvereins . . . 3) *LJ*

1771  Rosenbaum, Eduard: Albert Ballin; a Note on the Style of his Economic and Political Activities. *LBIYB* 3 (1958) 257–299. *LJ*

1772 Rosenbaum, Eduard: Ferdinand Lassalle; a Historiographical Meditation. *LBIYB* 9 (1964) 122–130. *LJ*

1773 Rosenbaum, Eduard: M.M. Warburg & Co.; Merchant Bankers of Hamburg. A Survey of the First 140 Years, 1798–1938. *LBIYB* 7 (1962) 121–149. *LJ*

1774 Rosenbaum, Eduard: Rathenau; a Supplementary Note. *LBIYB* 13 (1968) 132–134. *LJ*

1775 Rosenbaum, Eduard: Reflections on Walter Rathenau. *LBIYB* 4 (1959) 260–264. *LJ*

1776 Rosenbaum, Eduard: Some Reflections on the Jewish Participation in German Economic Life. *LBIYB* 1 (1956) 307–314. *LJ*

1777 Rosenberg, Alfred (1893–1946): *Houston Stewart Chamberlain als Verkünder und Begründer einer deutschen Zukunft.* München: Hugo Bruckmann, 1927. 128 pp. *LTA*

1778 Rosenberg, Aron: *Das Judentum und die Nationalitätsideen; eine völkerpsychologische Studie.* Wien: Kaposvar, 1882. 31 pp. *Unseen*

1779 Rosenberg, Arthur (1889–1943): Treitschke und die Juden; zur Soziologie der deutschen akademischen Reaktion. *Die Gesellschaft* 7 (1930) 78–83. *Unseen*

1780 Rosenberg, Hans (1904–): *Große Depression und Bismarckzeit; Wirtschaftsablauf, Gesellschaft und Politik in Mitteleuropa.* Berlin: W. De Gruyter, 1967. XII, 301 pp. (Veröffentlichungen der Historischen Kommission zu Berlin . . ., 24) *LJ*

1781 Rosenfeld, Max: Nationale Autonomie der Juden in Oesterreich. *Heimkehr; Essays jüdischer Denker.* Ed. Jüdischer Nationaler Akademischer Verein "Emunah." Czernowitz: L. Lamm, 1912. Pp. 30–96. *LJ*

1782 Rosensaft, Menachem Z.: Jews and Antisemites in Austria at the End of the 19th Century. *LBIYB* 21 (1976) 57–86. *LJ*

1783 Rosenzweig, Leon: *Wir Juden; Betrachtungen und Vorschläge eines Bukowiner Juden, pseud.* Zürich: C. Schmidt, 1883. 30 pp. *LJ*

1784 Rosin, B.: Die zionistisch-sozialistische Utopie. *N.Z.* 27 (1908–1909) 29–34 pp. *LJ*

Contra Zionism from the socialist point of view.

1785   Rosin, Heinrich (1855–1927): *Entwurf eines Gesetzes über die Organisation der israelitischen Religionsgemeinschaft in Preußen, nebst Einleitung, Begründung und Schluß. Im Auftrage des Ausschußes des Deutsch-Israelitischen Gemeindebundes verfasst.* Berlin: Boll, 1906. 60 pp. *LJ*

1786   Rost, Hans (1877–): Jüdische Statistik. *Historisch-Politische Blätter für das Katholische Deutschland* 133–134 (1904) 667–676. *LJ*

1787   Rost, Hans (1877–): Untergang der deutschen Juden. *Historisch-Politische Blätter für das Katholische Deutschland* 148 (1911) 751–758. *LJ*

1788   Rotenstreich, Nathan (1914–): Moses Hess and Karl Ludwig Michelet; on the ocassion of the Centenary of "Rome and Jerusalem." *LBIYB* 7 (1962) 283–286. *LJ*

1789   Rotholz, Julius: Die Berufe der preußischen Juden bis zum Jahre 1853. *MGWJ* 75 (1931) 394–396. *LJ*

       Refers to Heinrich Silbergleit's book *Die Bevölkerungs- und Berufsverhältnisse der Juden im Deutschen Reich . . . 1930.*

1790   Rothschild, Max M: *Jewish Social Studies; Cumulative Index, 1939–1964.* New York: Conference on Jewish Social Studies, 1967. 148 pp. *LJ*

1791   Rozenblit, Marsha Lea: *The Jews of Vienna, 1867–1914; Assimilation and Identity.* Albany: State University of New York Press, 1983. XVII, 284 pp. (SUNY Series in Modern Jewish History) *LJ*

1792   *Ruben und Lea; oder, Die Rückkehr zur Bundeslade.* Ein Vorspiel zu vielen Tragödien der Gegenwart, von xxx. Berlin: H. Lüstenöder, 1892. 35 pp. *LJ*

1793   Rudnitzky, Naphtali: *Die Blutbeschuldingungen gegen die Juden, der sogenannte Ritualmordprozeß; ein Wort zur Klärung.* Schmalkalden: A. Löhnert, 191–. 26 pp. *LJ*

1794   Rülf, Gutmann: *Einiges aus der ersten Zeit und über den Stifter der Jacobson-Schule in Seesen.* Braunschweig: B. Görlitz, 1890. 41 pp. *LTA*

1795   Rülf, Isaak (1831–1902): *Aruchas Bas Ammi; Israels Heilung. Ein ernstes Wort an Glaubens- und Nichtglaubensgenossen.* Frankfurt a.M.: J. Kauffmann, 1883. 94 pp. *LJ*

1796   Rülf, Isaak (1831–1902): *Jankel Widutzky, der den Händen der Judenbekehrungsmission entzogene Knabe. Keine Mortara — aber doch auch eine charakteristische Geschichte.* Memel: Schnee, 1867. 24 pp. *Unseen*

1797 Rürup, Reinhard: Emancipation and Crisis; the "Jewish Question" in Germany 1850–1890. *LBIYB* 20 (1975) 13–25. *LJ*

1798 Rürup, Reinhard: *Emanzipation und Antisemitismus. Studien zur "Judenfrage" der bürgerlichen Gesellschaft.* Göttingen: Vandenhoeck & Ruprecht, 1975. 208 pp. (Kritische Studien zur Geschichtswissenschaft, 15) *LJ*

1799 Rürup, Reinhard: Emanzipation und Antisemitismus; Verbindungslinien. *Antisemitismus* Eds. Herbert Strauss, Norbert Kampe. Frankfurt: Campus Verlag, 1985. Pp. 88–98. *LJ*

1800 Rürup, Reinhard: German Liberalism and the Emancipation of the Jews. *LBIYB* 20 (1975) 59–68. *LJ*

1801 Rürup, Reinhard: Die Judenemanzipation in Baden. *Zeitschrift für die Geschichte des Oberrheins* 114 (1966) 241–300. *LJ*

1802 Rürup, Reinhard: Judenemanzipation und bürgerliche Gesellschaft. *Gedenkschrift Martin Gähring; Studien zur europäischen Geschichte. Mit einem Geleitwort von Jacques Droz.* Ed. Ernst Schulin. Wiesbaden: F. Steiner, 1968. Pp. 174–199. (Europäische Geschichte, Mainz, 50) *LC*

1803 Rürup, Reinhard: Kontinuität und Diskontinuität der "Judenfrage" im 19. Jahrhundert; zur Entstehung des modernen Antisemitismus. *Sozialgeschichte heute. Festschrift für Hans Rosenberg zum 70. Geburtstag.* Ed. Hans Ulrich Wehler. Göttingen: Vandenhoeck & Ruprecht, 1974. Pp. 388–415. *LJ*

1804 Rürup, Reinhard: Sozialismus und Antisemitismus in Deutschland vor 1914. *TAJfDG* Beiheft 2 (1977) 203–227. *LJ*

1805 Rürup, Reinhard, ed.: *Antisemitismus und Judentum.* Göttingen: Vandenhoeck und Ruprecht, 1979. Pp. 440–581. (Geschichte und Gesellschaft, 5) *LJ*

1806 Rüsten, Rudolf: *Was tut not; ein Führer durch die gesamte Literatur der Deutschbewegung.* Leipzig: G. Hedeler, 1914. 112 pp. *LV*

1807 Ruppin, Arthur (1876–1943): *Die Juden der Gegenwart; eine sozialwissenschaftliche Studie.* Berlin: S. Calvary, 1904. VI, 296 pp. (Bureau für Statistik der Juden) *LJ*

1808 Ruppin, Arthur (1876–1943): *Die Juden im Großherzogtum Hessen. Im Auftrag der Großloge für Deutschland U.O. B'nei Briss bearb. vom Bureau für Statistik der Juden.* Berlin: L. Lamm, 1909. 137 pp. (Veröffentlichungen des Bureau für Statistik der Juden, 6) *LJ*

1809 Ruppin, Arthur (1876–1943): Die sozialen Verhältnisse der Juden in Preußen und Deutschland; statistisch dargestellt. *Jahrbücher für Nationalökonomie und Statistik* 23, 3 (1902) 374–386, 760–785. *LJ*

1810 Rychnowsky, Ernst: Im Kampf gegen den Ritualmord-Aberglauben. *Masaryk und das Judentum.* Ed. Ernst Rychnowsky. Prag, 1931. Pp. 166–273. *LJ*

1811 Rys-(Rozśevaé), Jan: *Hilsneriada a TGM.* Březen: Wiesner, 1939. 239 pp. *LTA* About the trial of Leopold Hilsner and Thomas G. Masaryk's actions on behalf of Leopold Hilsner, published on the 40th anniversary of the murder in Polna.

1812 Säusheim [?]: *Geschichte des großen Aufstandes der Pius-Vereine für religiöse Freiheit, gegen die Juden-Emanzipation des Jahres 1861.* [n.p.]: [n.d.], 1 l. *Unseen* Leaflet.

1813 Salis, Ludwig Rudolf von (1863–): *Die Entwicklung der Kultusfreiheit in der Schweiz. Festschrift des schweizerischen Juristenverein bei seiner Versammlung in Basel im Jahre 1894.* Ueberreicht von der juristischen Fakultät der Universität Basel. Basel: R. Reich, 1894. 100 pp. *Unseen*

1814 Salis, Ludwig Rudolf von (1863–): *Gegenmemorial für die sämtlichen israelitischen Kulturvereine in der Schweiz betreffend den Rekurs der Regierungen von Bern und Aargau gegen den Entscheid des Bundesrats vom 17. März 1890 in der Schächtfrage.* Bern: 1891. 1 vol. *Unseen*

1815 Salomon, Felix (1866–1928): *Die deutschen Parteiprogramme.* Bd. 2. Leipzig: B.G. Teubner, 1912. 49–178. (Quellensammlung zur deutschen Geschichte) *LJ*

1816 *Sammel-Gutachten über die Ritual- und Blutmordfrage. Von gebildeten deutschen Männern aller Stände.* Küstrin: H. Brandt, 1901. 66 pp. *LJ*

1817 Samter, Nathan: *Judentaufen im neunzehnten Jahrhundert. Mit besonderer Berücksichtigung Preußens dargestellt.* Berlin: M. Poppelauer, 1906. VII, 157 pp. *LJ*

1818 Samter, Nathan: Judentum und Proselytismus; Vortrag . . . Breslau: W. Jacobsohn, 1897. 40 pp. *LJ*

1819 Samter, Nathan: *Was tun? Ein Epilog zu den Judentaufen im 19. Jahrhundert.* Breslau: Th. Schatzky, 1900. 45 pp. *LC*

1820 Sandler, Aron: *Anthropologie und Zionismus; ein populär-wissenschaftlicher Vortrag.* Brünn: Jüdischer Buch- und Kunstverlag, 1904. 51 pp. *LJ*

1821  Sándor, Iván: *A viszgálat iratai; tudósitás a tísza-eszlárc per kőrűmenyeiről.* Budapest: Kozmosz, 1976. 202 pp. (Kozmosz kőnyvek) *LJ*

1822  Sandvoss, Franz: *Was dünket Euch um Heine; ein Bekenntnis, von Xantippus, pseud.* Leipzig: Grunow, 1888. VII, 104 pp. *Unseen*

1823  Saner, Marcel: *Freiherr Karl von Vogelsangs Gesellschafts- und Wirtschaftslehre.* Fribourg: 1939. XV, 170 pp. *Unseen*
      Diss. Fribourg.

1824  Saphir, Adolph (1831–1891): *Christus und die Schrift.* Aus dem Englischen von I. v. Lancizolle. Bevorwortet von Ober-Konsistorialrat D. Kögel und Prof. F. Delitzsch. 4. Aufl. Berlin: 1894. VIII, 138 pp. (Schriften des Institutum Judaicum in Berlin, 19) *LM*

1825  Saphir, Adolph (1831–1891): *"Ganz Israel wird selig werden," ein Geheimnis.* Nach dem Englischen des D.A. Saphir von W. Hochbaum. Bevorwortet von F. Delitzsch. Leipzig: Buchhdlg. des Vereinshauses, 1884. 27 pp. (Schriften des Institutum Judaicum in Leipzig, 3) *LJ*

1826  Saphir, Adolph (1831–1891): *Wer ist der Apostat? Eine Pesachgeschichte.* Autorisierte Ausg. Leipzig: 1889. 40 pp. (Schriften des Institutum Judaicum in Leipzig, 23) *LJ*

1827  Saphir, Adolph (1831–1891): *Wer ist ein Jude? Gespräch zwischen einem Namens- und einem wahren Juden.* Frankfurt a.M.: Typ. C. Naumann, 1865. 23 pp. *LJ*

1828  Schach, Fabius (1868–1930): Die Fremdenfrage. *Ost und West* 14 (1914) col. 10–20. *LJ*

1829  Schach, Fabius (1868–1930): *Ueber die Zukunft Israels; eine kritische Betrachtung.* Berlin: M. Poppelauer, 1904. 24 pp. *LJ*

1830  Schacht, Hjalmar Horace Greeley (1877–1970): Notizen und Besprechungen über jüdische Statistik. Hrsg. vom Verein für Jüdische Statistik. *Pr. Jhrb.* 113 (1903) 567–569. *LJ*

1831  Schadäus, Elias (fl.1591): *Judenmissions-Traktate des M. Elias Schadäus, Pfarrer an Alt-St. Peter, Prof. der Theologie und Münsterprediger in Straßburg, 1593.* Leipzig: Akad. Buchhdlg., 1892. IV, 65 pp. (Schriften des Institutum Judaicum in Leipzig, 33) *LJ*

1832  Schächter, Hersch: *Die Judenfrage in der Publizistik vor dem Jahre und während des Jahres 1848 in Oesterreich-Ungarn.* Wien: 1932. 154 l. *LC*

Diss.

1833  *Die Schächtfrage; Widerlegung, des von Herrn Vice-Direktor Preyer, in der Ausschuß-Sitzung des Wiener Tierschutz-Vereines vom 9. Dezember 1899 erstatteten und angenomenen Referates.* Wien: Verlag der Israelitischen Kultusgemeinde, 1900. 36 pp. *LC*

1834  Schäffer, Ernst: Die Juden als Soldaten. *Nathanael* 13 (1897) 97–105. *LJ*

1835  Schaffer, Schepsel: *Das Recht und seine Stellung zur Moral nach talmudischer Sitten- und Rechtslehre.* Frankfurt a.M.: Kauffmann, 1889. 131 pp. *LJ*

1836  Scharff von Scharffenstein, Herman von: *Das geheime Treiben, der Einfluß und die Macht des Judentums in Frankreich seit 100 Jahren, 1771–1871.* 2. Aufl. Wiesbaden: Killinger, 1872. IV, 160 pp. *LJ*
      Deals also with German and Austrian conditions.

1837  Scharlowski, Werner (1933–): *Die zivilrechtliche Stellung der Juden in Deutschland während der Neuzeit.* Tübingen: 1964. 79 pp. *Unseen*
      Diss. 1964.

1838  Schechter, Solomon (1850–1915): Dr. Solomon Schechter Dissects Some of the Views of Professor Werner Sombart as Expressed in "The Jews in Economic Life"; Novelty of Directions by the Author Excites Criticism and Comment. *New York Times* Sunday, March 3 (1912) 10. *LJ*

1839  Schedukat, Klaus: *Adolf Bartels und die völkische Bewegung; eine Analyse seines politischen Denkens und Wirkens.* Hamburg: 1969. 1 vol. *Unseen*
      State examination paper.

1840  Scheftelowitz, Isidor (1876–1934): *Das stellvertretende Huhnopfer. Mit besonderer Berücksichtigung des jüdischen Volksglaubens.* Giessen: A. Töpelmann, 1914. 66 pp. (Religionsgeschichtliche Versuche und Vorarbeiten, 14) *LJ*

1841  Scheicher, Josef: *Sebastian Brunner; ein Lebensbild, zugleich ein Stück Kirchengeschichte.* Würzburg: Wörl, 1888. 348 pp. *LM*

1842  Scheidemann, Philipp (1865–1939): Wandlungen des Antisemitismus. *N.Z.* 24, 2 (1906) 632–636. *LJ*

1843  Schemann, Ludwig (1852–1938): *Gobineau; eine Biographie.* Straßburg: K.J. Trübner, 1913–16. 2 vols. *LV*

1844 Schemann, Ludwig (1852–1938): *Gobineaus Rassenwerk; Aktenstücke und Betrachtungen zur Geschichte und Kritik des "Essai sur l'inégalité des races humaines."* Stuttgart: F. Frommanns Verlag, 1910. XLI, 544 pp. *LB*

1845 Schilling, Konrad: *Beiträge zu einer Geschichte des radikalen Nationalismus in der Wilhelminischen Aera 1890–1909.* Köln: 1968. 707 pp. *Unseen*

Diss. 1968.

1846 Schimmer, Gustav Adolf: *Die Juden in Oesterreich nach der Zählung vom 31. Dezember 1880.* Wien: A. Hölder, 1881. 17 pp. *LJ*

1847 Schimmer, Gustav Adolf: *Statistik des Judentums in den im Reichsrate vertretenen Königreichen und Ländern.* Hrsg. von der Statistischen Zentralkommission. Wien: K.u.K. Hof- und Staatsdruckerei, 1873. 71 pp. *LJ*

1848 Schippel, Max (1859–1928): Die Konservativen und der Antisemitismus. *N.Z.* 11, 2 (1892/93) 298–302. *LJ*

1849 Schläpfer, Rudolf: *Die Ausländerfrage in der Schweiz vor dem Ersten Weltkrieg.* Zürich: Juris-Verlag, 1969. II, 293 pp. *Unseen*

Diss. Zürich.

1850 Schleier, Hans: Zur Entwicklung und Rolle des Antisemitismus in Deutschland von 1871–1914. *Zeitschrift für Geschichtswissenschaft* 9 (1961) 1592–1597. *LJ*

1851 Schlotzhauer, Inge: *Ideologie und Organisation des politischen Antisemitismus in Frankfurt a.M., 1880–1914.* Frankfurt a.M.: W. Kramer, 1989. 327 pp. (Studien zur Frankfurter Geschichte, Frankfurter Verein für Geschichte und Landeskunde in Verbindung mit der Frankfurter Historischen Kommission, 28) *LJ*

1852 Schmeisser, E.: *Israel.* Leipzig: Ev.-Luth. Centralverein für Mission unter Israel, 1902. 26 pp. (Kleine Schriften zur Judenmission, 2) *LC*

1853 Schmidl, Erwin A.: Jews in the Austro-Hungarian Armed Forces, 1867–1918. *Studies in Contemporary Jewry* 3 (1987) 127–146. *LJ*

1854 Schmidt-Clausing, Fritz (1902–): *Judengegnerische Strömungen im deutschen Katholizismus des 19. Jahrhunderts; eine religionspolitische Untersuchung.* Jena: 1942. III, 169 l. *Unseen*

Diss. 1942. Manuscript.

1855 Schmidt, Ferdinand Jakob (1860–): Notizen und Besprechungen. Philosophie: Arische Weltanschaung, von Houston Stewart Chamberlain. *Pr. Jhrb.* 122 (1905) 514–518. *LJ*

1856 Schmidt, Gerhard Karl (1908–): Nietzsches Schau vom Judentum. *Weltkampf* 4 (1944) 78–88. *LB*

1857 Schmidt, K.: *Das heilige Blut von Sternberg.* Halle a. S.: Niemeyer, 1892. (Schriften für das deutsche Volk, 18) *Unseen*

1858 Schmidtbauer, Peter: Zur sozialen Situation der Wiener Juden im Jahre 1857. *Studia Judaica Austriaca* 1 (1974) 57–89. *LJ*

1859 Schnee, Heinrich (1871–1949): *Georg Ritter von Schönerer; ein Kämpfer für Alldeutschland.* 2. erg. Aufl. Reichenberg: F. Kraus, 1941. IX, 263 pp. *LJ*

1860 Schnee, Heinrich (1895–): *Bürgermeister Karl Lueger; Leben und Wirken eines großen Deutschen.* Heidelberg: Quelle & Meyer, 1936. 54 pp. *LB*

1861 Schnee, Heinrich (1895–): *Karl Lueger; Leben und Wirken eines großen Sozial- und Kommunalpolitikers.* Berlin: Duncker & Humblot, 1960. 123 pp. *LB*

1862 Schnee, Heinrich (1895–): Die politische Entwicklung des Wiener Bürgermeisters Dr. Karl Lueger; vom liberalen Politiker zum christlich-sozialen Führer. *Historisches Jahrbuch der Görres-Gesellschaft* 76 (1957) 64–78. *LJ*

1863 Schneider, Ernst: Gibt es einen jüdischen Ritualmord. *Staatsbürgerzeitung. 2. Beilage,* 12 December 1899. *Unseen*

Speech by Ernst Schneider, a member of the Austrian parliament.

1864 Schneider, J.: *Samuel Thalhofer; oder, Wie können die Landwirte von den Wucherern befreit werden.* Straßburg i. Elsaß: Vomhoff, 188–. 31 pp. *LJ*

1865 Schneidewin, Max Paul Ernst (1843–): *Die jüdische Frage im Deutschen Reich. Versuch eines unparteiischen und auf die salus publica zielenden Schiedsspruches zwischen Antisemitismus und Philosemitismus.* Hameln: T. Fündeling, 1894. X, 162 pp. *LJ*

1866 Schochow, Werner: *Deutsch-jüdische Geschichtswissenschaft; eine Geschichte ihrer Organisationsformen unter besonderer Berücksichtigung der Fachbibliographie.* Berlin: Colloquium Verlag, 1969. 327 pp. (Einzelveröffentlichungen der Historischen Kommission in Berlin, 3) *LJ*

1867 Schön, Theodor: *Geadelte jüdische Familien.* Salzburg: Kyffhäuser, 1891. 112 pp. *LJ*

1868 Schönerer, Georg von (1842–1921): *Die Ziele und Aufgaben der Deutschnationalen in der Ostmark: Vortrag gehalten in Halle a. d. Saale am 3. Dezember 1891.* Leipzig: Deutscher Verlag, 1892. 35 pp. *Unseen*

1869 Schönwald, Alfred (1835–1894): *Das Drama von Tísza-eszlár; Erinnerungsblätter an den Nyiregyhazaer Prozeß.* Wien: A. Schönwald, 1883. 100 pp. *Unseen*

1870 Schöps, Hans Joachim (1909–): Friedrich Julius Stahl und das Judentum. *Von Juden in München.* München: Ner-Tamid Verlag, 1958. Pp. 99–103. *LJ*

1871 Scholl, Karl (1820–1907): *Das Judentum und die Religion der Humanität; Vortrag zum 23. Stiftungsfest der freireligiösen Gemeinde in Mannheim am 17. August 1879.* Leipzig: R. Friese, 1879. 24 pp. *LJ*

1872 Scholl, Karl (1820–1907): Zur Ehrenrettung des Talmuds. *Es werde Licht* 13 (1882) 129–144. *LM*

1873 Schopenhauer, Arthur (1788–1860): Zur Rechtslehre und Politik. *Sämtliche Werke in 5 Bänden. Bd. 5: Parerga und Paralipomena.* Leipzig: Insel-Verlag, 192–. Pp. 283–286. *LJ*

First published in 1851.

1874 Schoppe, Wilhelm: *Die neuesten Ahlwardtschen Judenflinten betreffend.* Dresden: Dresdener-Verlags-Magazin, 1892. 15 pp. *LJ*

Contra Ahlwardt.

1875 Schorsch, Ismar (1935–): "Identity or Integration — Which?" Review of Uriel Tal's Book Christians and Jews in the "Second Reich," 1870–1914. *Judaism* 19 (1970) 373–377. *LJ*

1876 Schorske, Carl E.: Politics in a New Key; an Austrian Trio. *Fin de Siècle Vienna; Politics and Culture.* New York: Vintage Books, 1981. Pp. 116–180. *LJ*

1877 Schorske, Carl E.: Politics in a New Key; an Austrian Triptych. *Journal of Modern History* 39 (1967) 343–386. *LJ*

1878 Schottländer, Rudolf (1900–): Vom Judenhaß dreier Großer (Luther, Marx, Wagner). *Frankfurter Hefte* 12 (1983) 37–46. *LJ*

1879  Schramm, Gottfried: Die Ostjuden als soziales Problem des 19. Jahrhunderts. *Gesellschaft, Recht und Politik.* Neuwied: Luchterhand, 1968. Pp. 353–380. *LM*
      "Wolfgang Abendroth zum 60. Geburtstag."

1880  Schramm, Helmut: Der Doppelritualmord von Polna. *Der Weltkampf* 16 (1939) 339–349. *LJ*

1881  Schramm, Helmut: *Der jüdische Ritualmord; eine historische Untersuchung.* Berlin: Th. Fritsch, 1943. XXVII, 475 pp. *LB*

1882  Schreiber, Emanuel (1852–1932): *Graetz's Geschichtsbauerei; beleuchtet von . . .* Berlin: W. Issleib, 1881. IV, 108 pp. *LJ*

1883  Schreiber, Emanuel (1852–1932): *Der Talmud vom Standpunkte des modernen Judentums.* Berlin: W. Issleib, 1881. 52 pp. *LJ*

1884  Schreiner, Helmuth: *Macht und Dienst; Adolf Stoeckers Kampf um die Freiheit der Kirche.* Gütersloh: C. Bertelsmann, 1951. 92 pp. *LJ*

1885  Schroubek, Georg R.: Der Ritualmord von Polna; traditioneller und moderner Wahnglaube. *Antisemitismus und jüdische Geschichte.* Berlin: Wissenschaftlicher Autoren-Verlag, 1987. Pp. 149–171. *LJ*

1886  Schüler, Alexander: *Der Rassenadel der Juden; der Schlüssel zur Judenfrage.* Berlin: Jüdischer Verlag, 1912. 58 pp. (Die jüdische Gemeinschaft) *LJ*

1887  Schüler, Gottlieb August: *Die Judenfrage; eine Frage an das deutsche Volk und die deutschen Juden.* Marburg: N.G. Elwertsche Verlagsbuchhdlg., 1880. 87 pp. *LJ*

1888  Schüler, Gottlieb August: *Die Wurzeln der Judenfrage; Christen und Juden, zunächst den Studenten Deutschlands dargestellt.* Berlin: Deutsche Evangelische Buch- und Traktat-Gesellschaft, 1881. IV, 60 pp. *LJ*

1889  Schüler, Winfried: Völkisch-kultureller Nationalismus im Zeichen von Antisemitismus und Rassismus; von Wagners "Judentum in der Musik" zu Chamberlains "Grundlagen." *Der Bayreuther Kreis von seiner Entstehung bis zum Ausgang der Wilhelminischen Aera.* Münster: Verlag Aschendorff, 1971. Pp. 231–278. *LJ*

1890  Schultheiss, Franz Guntram: *Deutschnationales Vereinswesen; ein Beitrag zur Geschichte des deutschen Nationalgefühls.* München: J.F. Lehmann, 1897. VI, 82 pp. (Der Kampf um das Deutschtum, 2) *LB*

1891 Schulze, Ludwig: *August Neander; ein Gedenkblatt für Israel und die Kirche.* Leipzig: Akademische Buchhdlg., 1890. III, 64 pp. (Schriften des Institutum Judaicum in Leipzig, 24) *LJ*

1892 Schuon, Hermann: *Der Deutschnationale Handlungsgehilfen-Verband zu Hamburg, sein Werdegang und seine Arbeit.* Jena: G. Fischer, 1914. VIII, 249 pp. (Abhandlungen der Staatswissenschaftlichen Seminars zu Jena, vol. 13, 3) *LM*

1893 Schwabacher, Simeon Leon von (1819–1888): *Drei Gespenster; ritueller Mord — "Kabal" — Exploitation.* Stuttgart: Levy & Müller, 1883. 55 pp. *LJ*

1894 Schwabacher, Simeon Leon von (1819–1888): *Von Heliopolis nach Berlin.* Odessa: Typ. A. Schultze, 1885. 104 pp. *LJ*

About the antisemitism in Germany.

1895 Schwalb, Moritz (1833–1916): *Christus und das Judentum; Vortrag gehalten im protestantischen Reformverein zu Berlin am 27. Februar 1883.* Berlin: Walther & Apolant, 1883. 15 pp. *LJ*

1896 Schwartz, Dr. von: *Das betäubungslose Schächten der Israeliten. Vom Standpunkt des 20. Jahrhunderts auf Grund von Schächt-Tatsachen geschildert und erläutert.* Konstanz am Bodensee: E. Ackermann, 1905. 259 pp. *LJ*

1897 Schwartz, Jürgen: Deutsche Studenten und Politik im 19. Jahrbundert. *Geschichte in Wissenschaft und Unterricht* 20 (1969) 72–94. *LJ*

1898 Schwarz, F.W.S.: *Eines Kindes Gebet; eine Geschichte aus dem jüdischen Leben.* Mit einem Vorwort von Franz Delitzsch. Berlin: Wiegandt & Grieben, 1878. 176 pp. *Unseen*

1899 Schwarz, F.W.S.: *Saronsrosen; Geschichten aus Israel.* Berlin: Hauptverein für christliche Erbauungschriften, 1887. 2 vols. *LM*

1900 Schwarz, Walter: A Jewish Banker in the Nineteenth Century. *LBIYB* 3 (1958) 300–310. *LJ*

1901 Schwarzschild, Emanuel: *Herr Rabbiner Dr. Joel und die Lasker'sche Resolution, beleuchtet von Schwarzschild.* Frankfurt a.M.: Typ. Textor, 1875. 14 pp. *LJ*

1902 Schweizer Bundesrat: *Bundesratsbeschluß über den Rekurs der israelitischen Ortsbürgergemeinden Neu-Endingen und Neu-Lengnau vom 17. März 1890.* Bern: 1890. 25 pp. *Unseen*

1903   Schwer, Hanns Arnold: *Die Wahrheit über die Morde in Polna.* Wien: Selbstverlag, 1900. 220 pp. *LJ*

1904   Schwerin, Kurt: *Historia Judaica Index [for vols. 1-20].* New York: Historia Judaica, 1961. Vol. 23, pp. 23-166. *LJ*
       This index is part of vol. 23.

1905   Schweriner, Artur: *Die Reichstagswahlen vor der Tür. In die Front.* Liebenwerda: E. Helle, 1911. 28 pp. *LJ*
       Contents: Herr Raab als Schänder der Juden. Aeußerungen einiger Reichstagsabgeordneten. Wirkung der "Rede" im Reichstag.

1906   *Sechs Aktenstücke zum Prozeße von Tísza-Eslár.* Berlin: Simion, 1882. 120 pp. *LJ*

1907   Segall, Jakob (1883-): Der Anteil der Juden in Deutschland an den Beamtenstellen und den freien Berufen. *ZfDSJ* 8 (1912) 49-60. *LJ*

1908   Segall, Jakob (1883-): Die ausländischen Juden in München. *ZfDSJ* 5 (1909) 17-23, 33-38. *LJ*

1909   Segall, Jakob (1883-): *Die beruflichen und sozialen Verhältnisse der Juden in Deutschland.* Berlin: M. Schildberger, 1912. 86 pp. (Veröffentlichungen des Bureaus für Statistik der Juden, 9) *LJ*

1910   Segall, Jakob (1883-): *Die Entwicklung der jüdischen Bevölkerung in München 1875-1905; ein Beitrag zur Kommunalstatistik.* Hrsg. vom Verein für die Statistik der Juden. Berlin: Max Schildberger, 1910. VI, 108 pp. (Veröffentlichungen des Bureaus für Statistik der Juden, 7) *LJ*

1911   Segall, Jakob (1883-): Taufen und Austritte aus dem Judentum. *I.Dt.R.* 19 (1913) 338-343. *LJ*

1912   Segall, Jakob (1883-): Die wirtschaftliche und soziale Lage der Juden in Deutschland. *ZfDSJ* 7 (1911) 49-58, 76-80, 81-88, 97-112. *LJ*

1913   Selig, Dr. med.: *Reflexionen zu Walther Rathenaus "Höre Israel"; eine Erwiderung.* Worms: H. Krauter, 1902. 24 pp. *LJ*

1914   *Sem und Japheth. Die hebräischen Worte der jüdisch-deutschen Umgangsprache.* Zusammengestellt und erklärt nebst einer Vorrede, von J.H.M. Leipzig: Glökner, 1882. 56 pp. *LV*

1915  Semler, Johann Salomo (1725–1791): *Historisch-theologische Abhandlungen. 2. Sammlung, 2. Stück über die Blutbeschuldigung. Halle, 1762.* Neue Ausg. Wien: M. Waizner, 1897. 51 pp. *LJ*

1916  Shulman, Samuel: "Chamberlain's Foundations of the Nineteenth Century" and "the Claims of Judaism." *J.Q.R. (N.S.)* 5 (1914–15) 163–200. *LJ*

1917  Shulman, Samuel: The Jews and the Economic Life; a Review of Werner Sombart's Book. *Judaean Addresses* 2 (1917) 77–90. *Unseen*

1918  Shulman, Samuel: Review of Werner Sombart's "Die Juden und das Wirtschaftsleben." *The American Hebrew* 90 (1912) 695–697, 713. *LJ*

1919  Shunami, Shlomo: *Bibliography of Jewish Bibliographies.* 2nd ed. enl. Jerusalem: Magnes Press, 1965. XXIII, 997, XXIV pp. *LJ*

1920  Shunami, Shlomo: *Bibliography of Jewish Bibliographies.* Supplement to 2nd enl. ed., 1965. Jerusalem: Magnes Press, 1975. XVII, 464, XVI pp. *LJ*

1921  Silberner, Edmund (1910–): *The Antisemitic Tradition in Modern Socialism.* Jerusalem: 1953. 19 pp. *Unseen*

   Inaugural Lecture Delivered at the Hebrew University on January 4, 1953.

1922  Silberner, Edmund (1910–): Austrian Social Democracy and the Jewish Problem. *Hist. Jud.* 13 (1951) 121–140. *LJ*

1923  Silberner, Edmund (1910–): Deutsche und österreichische Sozialisten. *Sozialisten zur Judenfrage; ein Beitrag zur Geschichte des Sozialismus vom Anfang des 19. Jahrhunderts bis 1914. T. 2.* Berlin: Colloquium Verlag, 1962. Pp. 107–245. *LJ*

   Tr. from the English by Arthur Mandel.

1924  Silberner, Edmund (1910–): Ferdinand Lassalle. *Hebrew Union College Annual, Cincinnati* 24 (1952–53) 151–186. *LJ*

1925  Silberner, Edmund (1910–): German Social Democracy and the Jewish Problem Prior to World War I. *Hist. Jud.* 15 (1953) 3–48. *LJ*

1926  Silberner, Edmund (1910–): Ideologen und Parteiführer. *Kommunisten zur Judenfrage; zur Geschichte von Theorie und Praxis des Kommunismus. Pt. 2.* Opladen: Westdeutscher Verlag, 1983. Pp. 58–71. *LJ*

1927  Silberner, Edmund (1910–): *Johann Jacoby; Politiker und Mensch.* Bonn — Bad Godesberg: Verlag Neue Gesellschaft, 1976. 648 pp. (Veröffentlichungen des Instituts für Sozialgeschichte, Braunschweig) *LJ*

1928   Silberner, Edmund (1910–): Moses Hess. *Hist. Jud.* 13 (1954) 3–28. *LJ*

1929   Silberner, Edmund (1910–): *Moses Hess; Geschichte seines Lebens.* Leiden:
       E.J. Brill, 1966. XVIII, 691 pp. *LM*

1930   Silberner, Edmund (1910–): Wegbereiter. *Kommunisten zur Judenfrage; zur
       Geschichte von Theorie und Praxis des Kommunismus. Pt. 1.* Opladen:
       Westdeutscher Verlag, 1983. Pp. 16–56. *LJ*

1931   Simon, Alexander Moritz: *Soziales zur Judenfrage; ein Beitrag zu ihrer Lösung.*
       Frankfurt a.M.: Kauffmann, 1900. 20 pp. *LJ*

1932   Simon, Heinrich (1880–1941): *Leopold Sonnemann; seine Jugendgeschichte bis
       zur Entstehung der Frankfurter Zeitung.* Frankfurt a.M.: Frankfurter Societäts-
       Druckerei, 1931. 153 pp. *LJ*

1933   Simon, Heinrich: *Die rituelle Schlachtmethode der Juden vom Standpunkt der
       Kritik und der Geschichte.* Frankfurt a.M.: J. Kauffmann, 1893. 41 pp. *LJ*

1934   Sincerus, pseud.: *Ein geistiger Krach im Parlament; politische Erörterungen aus
       Anlaß der Stoecker'schen Rede in der Sitzung des Preußischen Landtags am 26.
       Februar. Ein Mahnruf an Hofprediger Stoecker und das Deutsche Volk.*
       Heidelberg: G. Weiss, 1883. 30 pp. *LJ*

1935   Singer, Isidore (1859–1939): *Presse und Judentum.* Mit einem Briefe Mr.
       Laurence Oliphant's an den Verfasser. Wien: D. Löwy, 1882. 163 pp. *LJ*

1936   Singer, Isidore (1859–1939): *Sollen die Juden Christen werden? Ein offenes
       Wort an Freund und Feind. Mit einem Facsimile Schreiben Ernest Renan's an
       den Verfasser.* 2. verm. und verb. Aufl. Wien: O. Frank, 1884. XV, 143 pp.
       *LJ*

1937   Sittenfeld, Konrad (1862–1918): Judentum und Antisemitismus, von Conrad
       Alberti, pseud. *Die Gesellschaft* 12 (1889) 1718–1733. *Unseen*

1938   *Sittenlehre des Talmuds und der zerstörende Einfluß des Judentums im
       Deutschen Reich.* Berlin: M.A. Niendorf, 1875. 138 pp. *LJ*

1939   Skalnik, Kurt: *Dr. Karl Lueger; der Mann zwischen den Zeiten.* Wien: Herold,
       1954. 182 pp. (Beiträge zur neueren Geschichte des christlichen Oesterreich)
       *LJ*

1940   Smotricz, Israel: Die österreichische Presse in der Revolution von 1848 und ihr
       Verhältnis zu den Juden. *ZfGJ* 1 (1964) 147–152. *LJ*

1941  Snyder, Louis Leo (1907–): *German Nationalism; the Tragedy of a People. Extremism contra Liberalism in Modern German History.* New York: Kennikat, 1969. 321 pp. *LJ*

1942  Snyder, Louis Leo (1907–): *The Idea of Racialism; Its Meaning and History.* Princeton: Van Nostraud Co., 1962. 192 pp. (Van Nostraud Anvil Books, 66) *LJ*

1943  Sofer, Leo: Zur Biologie und Pathologie der jüdischen Rasse. *ZfDSJ* 2 (1906) 85–92. *LJ*

1944  Solano, Arwed: *Der Geheimbund der Börse.* 2. Aufl. Leipzig: H. Beyer, 1893. 48 pp. *LM*

1945  Solov'ev, Vladimir Sergeevich (1853–1900): *Judentum und Christentum.* Uebers. und mit erläuterndem Vorwort von Ernst Keuchel. Dresden: P. Tietz, 1911. XLI, 103 pp. *LJ*

1946  Solov'ev, Vladimir Sergeevich (1853–1900): *Das Judentum und die christliche Frage, 1884.* Uebers. von Johannes Harder. Wuppertal: Jugenddienst Verlag, 1961. 32 pp. *LJ*

First published 1884, in Russian.

1947  Solov'ev, Vladimir Sergeevich (1853–1900): Der Talmud und die neueste polemische Literatur über ihn in Oesterreich und Deutschland. *Deutsche Gesamtausg. Bd. 4.* München: E. Wewel, 1972 Pp. 511–549. *LJ*

First published 1886 in Russian. Tr. into German by Fairy von Lilienfeld.

1948  Sombart, Werner (1863–1941): Anteil der Juden am Aufbau der modernen Volkswirtschaft. *Die Neue Rundschau* (1910) 145–173. *LJ*

1949  Sombart, Werner (1863–1941): Bedeutung des Einschlagens jüdischer Elemente für Deutschlands Wirtschaftsleben. *Ost und West* 4 (1904) col. 23–31. *LJ*

1950  Sombart, Werner (1863–1941): *The Jews and Modern Capitalism.* Tr. by M. Epstein. With an introduction to the American edition by Bert F. Hoselitz. London: T.E. Unwin, 1913. XLII, 402 pp. *LJ*

Translation of *Die Juden und das Wirtschaftsleben.*

1951  Sombart, Werner (1863–1941): *Die Juden und das Wirtschaftsleben.* Leipzig: Duncker & Humblot, 1911. XXVI, 476 pp. *LJ*

1952  Sombart, Werner (1863–1941): *Judentaufen.* 9. Aufl. München: Georg Müller, 1912. 146 pp. *LJ*

1953  Sombart, Werner (1863–1941): Jüdischer Geist im modernen Wirtschaftsleben. *Die Neue Rundschau* (1910) 585–615. *LJ*

1954  Somerville, Alexander N.: *Judentum und Christentum; ein Vortrag.* In rev. deutschem Texte. Hrsg. von Franz Delitzsch. Erlangen: A. Deichert, 1882. 25 pp. *LJ*

1955  Sonnenfeld, Hugo: *Zum Meineidsprozeß gegen Moritz Lewy in Konitz, Westpr.; Verteidigungsrede des Rechtsanwalts Hugo Sonnenfeld.* Mit einem Vorwort des Justizrats Dr. Erich Sello. Berlin: H.S. Hermann, 1901. 48 pp. *LJ*

1956  Soziale Verhältnisse der Juden in Preußen und Deutschland. *Soziale Revue* 2 (1902) 580–. *Unseen*

1957  Spät, Franz: *Die Gutachten der Sachverständigen über den Konitzer Mord.* München: J.F.Lehmann, 1903. 12 pp. *LJ*

Offprint from: *Münchener Medizinische Wochenschrift*, no. 51, 1903.

1958  Spanier, Moritz (1853–): *Ueber den Anteil der Juden, vorzugsweise der Magdeburger an den Vaterlandskriegen.* Magdeburg: Typ. Oskar Bendix, 1893. 19 pp. *LJ*

Offprint from: *Verwaltungsbericht des Vorstandes der Synagogengemeinde zu Magdeburg.*

1959  Specht, Fritz: *Die Reichstagswahlen von 1867 bis 1897; eine Statistik der Reichstagswahlen, nebst den Programmen der Parteien und dem Verzeichnis der gewählten Kandidaten.* Berlin: C. Heymann, 1898–1903. 2 vols. *LM*

Vol. 2 revised by Fritz Specht and Paul Schwabe.

1960  Spitzer, Rudolf (1920–): *Der Bürgermeister Lueger, Lumpen und Steuerträger.* Wien: Oesterreichischer Bundesverlag, 1988. 224 pp. *LJ*

1961  Spitzer, Samuel: *Das Blutgespenst auf seine wahre Quelle zurückgeführt.* Essek: J. Pfeiffer, 1883. 20 pp. *LJ*

1962  Die staatsbürgerliche Gleichstellung der Israeliten in Holstein. *MGWJ* 8 (1854) 135–137. *LJ*

1963  Stadtbibliothek Frankfurt a.M.: *Katalog der Judaica und Hebraica.* Bd. 1: Judaica. Frankfurt a.M.: Typ. M. Lehrberger, 1932. XII, 646 pp. *LJ*

1964  Stahlberg, Wolfgang, ed.: *Beiträge zur Geschichte des Kyffhäuser Verbandes der Vereine deutscher Studenten.* Berlin: Bernard & Gräfe, 1931. 218 pp. *LM*

1965 Stammler Jakob: *Die Ermordung des Knaben Rudolf von Bern durch die Juden, 1288?* Luzern: 1888? 49 pp. *LTA*

1966 Starke, Theodor: *Israel, so Du verdirbst, ist's Deine eigene Schuld. Ein Christenwort an die Juden.* 2. Aufl. Kaiserslauten: A. Gotthold, 1888. 42 pp. *LJ*

1967 *Statistisches zur modernen Judenfrage, von K.H.* Warnsdorf: A. Opitz, 1904. 70 pp. *LB*

1968 Stauracz, Franz (1855–1918): *Dr. Karl Lueger, zehn Jahre Bürgermeister im Lichte der Tatsachen und nach dem Urteile seiner Zeitgenossen.* Wien: W. Braumüller, 1907. VIII, 283 pp. *LJ*

1969 Stegmann, Dirk: Class' "Kaiserbuch"; nur eine "Alldeutsche" Programmschrift? *Die Erben Bismarcks; Parteien und Verbände in der Spätphase des Wilhelminischen Deutschlands. Sammlungspolitik, 1897–1918.* Köln: Kiepenheuer & Witsch, 1970. Pp. 293–304. *LJ*

1970 Stein, Adolf (1870–), ed.: *Der gefälschte Brief; stenographischer Bericht über den Witte — Stoecker Prozeß vom 29. und 30. Januar 1897 mit geschichtlicher Einleitung und Anmerkungen.* Berlin: Vaterländische Verlags-Anstalt, 1897. XVI, 278 pp. *LJ*

1971 Stein, Franz: *Linzer Programm und Arbeiterschaft.* Wien: Der Hammer, 1899. 1 vol. *Unseen*

1972 Stein, Franz: *Der Rufer der Ostmark; Georg Schönerers Leben und Kampf.* Krems: Faber, 1941. 94 pp. *LB*

1973 Stein, L.: Der Mörder von Konitz. *Die Peitsche; kritische Halbmonatschrift* 1 (1902) 33–44. *LJ*

1974 Stein, Leon: *The Racial Thinking of Richard Wagner.* New York: Philosophical Library, 1950. XIV, 252 pp. *LJ*

1975 Stein, Maximilian: *Judentum und Christentum; Vortrag gehalten in der Montefiore-Loge U.O.B.B.* Berlin: 1906. 22 pp. *LJ*

1976 Steiner, Karl: Das Ritual-Mord Märchen. *Konferenzblätter; Monatsschrift für das gesamte Unterrichts- und Erziehungswesen* 8 (1897) 205–215. *LJ*

1977 Steiner, Otto (1905–): *Ritualmord? Vier große Ritualmordprozeße.* Hamburg: Kriminalistik Verlag für Kriminalistische Fachliteratur, 1959. 111 pp. *LJ*

1978   Stempf, L., ed.: *Das Gesetz über die bürgerliche Gleichstellung der Israeliten
       im Großherzogtum Baden unter Beifügung der Motive.* Kommissionsberichte
       und landständliche Verhandlungen. Donaueschingen: Schmidt, 1862. 77 pp. *LJ*

1979   Sterling, Eleonore: *Er ist wie Du; aus der Frühgeschichte des Antisemitismus
       in Deutschland, 1815–1850.* Vorwort von Carlo Schmid. München: Ch. Kaiser,
       1956. 235 pp. *LJ*

1980   Sterling, Eleonore: *Judenhaß; die Anfänge des politischen Antisemitismus in
       Deutschland, 1815–1850.* Vorwort von Carlo Schmid. Frankfurt a.M.:
       Europäische Verlagsanstalt, 1969. 237 pp. *LB*

       Title of previous ed.: *Er ist wie du.*

1981   Stern, Edith: Gerichtsmedizinische Bezüge zu dem Ritualmordprozeß von
       Tíszaészlár, Ungarn 1882–83. *Monatsschrift für Kriminologie und
       Strafrechtsreform* 67 (1984) 38–47. *LJ*

1982   Stern, Fritz Richard (1926–): *Gold and Iron; Bismarck, Bleichröder and the
       Building of the German Empire.* New York: Knopf, 1977. xxiv, 620 pp. *LJ*

       German translation: *Gold und Eisen; Bismarck und sein Bankier Bleichröder.*
       Frankfurt a.M., 1978.

1983   Stern, Fritz Richard (1926–): Gold and Iron; the Collaboration and Friendship
       of Gerson Bleichröder and Otto von Bismarck. *Failure of Illiberalism.* New
       York: Alfred A. Knopf, 1972. Pp. 58–73. *LC*

1984   Stern, Fritz Richard (1926–): Gold and Iron; the Collaboration and Friendship
       of Gerson Bleichröder and Otto von Bismarck. *American Historical Review* 75
       (1969) 37–46. *LJ*

1985   Stern, Fritz Richard (1926–): *Kulturpessimismus als politische Gefahr; eine
       Analyse nationaler Ideologie in Deutschland.* Uebersetzung aus dem
       Amerikanischen von Alfred P. Zeller. Bern: Scherz, 1963. 420 pp. *LJ*

       Original title: *The Politics of Cultural Despair.*

1986   Stern, Fritz Richard (1926–): Money, Morals and the Pillars of Society. *Failure
       of Illiberalism.* New York: Alfred A. Knopf, 1972. Pp. 26–57. *LC*

1987   Stern, Fritz Richard (1926–): *The Politics of Cultural Despair; a Study in the
       Rise of the Germanic Ideology.* Berkeley: University of California Press, 1963.
       XXX, 367 pp. *LJ*

       Revision of the author's diss.: *Cultural Despair and the Politics of Discontent.*

1988  Stern, Jakob (1843–1911): *Jesus, ein Reformator des Judentums, von Dr. E. Molchow, pseud.* Zürich: Verlags-Magazin, 1880. 63 pp. *Unseen*

1989  Stern, Jakob (1843–1911): *Die Mischehe zwischen Juden und Christen. Mit einem Anhang: Der ächte Ring. Von Leo Rauchmann, pseud.* Zürich: Verlags-Magazin, 1880. 47 pp. *LJ*

1990  Stern, Jakob (1843–1911): Rezension zu: Theodor Herzl, Der Judenstaat. *N.Z.* 15, 1 (1896/97) 186. *LJ*

1991  Stern, Jakob (1843–1911): *Das Schächten; Streitschrift gegen den jüdischen Schlachtritus.* Leipzig: Kössling, 1883. VI, 23 pp. (Zeitbewegende Fragen, I) *LJ*

1992  Stern, Jakob (1843–1911): *Das Schächten; Streitschrift gegen den jüdischen Schlachtritus. Ein Mahnwort an die deutschen Tierschutzvereine, von einem Juden (J. St.).* 2. Aufl. Leipzig: G. Levien, 1891. VI, 23 pp. *LJ*

1993  Stern, Jakob (1843–1911): Der Talmud. *N.Z.* 12, 2 (1893/ 94) 536–539. *LJ*

1994  Stern, Jakob (1843–1911): *Das Talmudjudentum; nebst einem Anhang über den Talmud, von William Rubens, pseud.* Zürich: J. Schabelitz, 1893. IV, 96 pp. *LJ*

2nd ed. of *Der alte und der neue Glaube im Judentum.*

1995  Stern, Josef: Hermann Levi und seine jüdische Welt. *ZfGJ* 7 (1970) 17–25. *LJ*

1996  Stern, Moritz (1864–1939), ed.: *Die päpstlichen Bullen über die Blutbeschuldigung.* Berlin: S. Cronbach, 1893. 151 pp. *LJ*

1997  Stern, Moritz (1864–1939): *Quellenkunde zur Geschichte der deutschen Juden.* Bd. 1: Zeitschriftenliteratur. Kiel: H. Fienke, 1892. 104 pp. *LJ*

No more published.

1998  Stern, S. (1812–1867): *Juden und Judenemanzipation. Staats-Lexikon. 3. Aufl. Vol. 8.* Eds. C. Rotteck, C. Welcker. Leipzig: Brockhaus, 1863–66. Pp. 647–675. *LJ*

1999  Stern, Salomon: *Die politischen und kulturellen Kämpfe der Juden in Ungarn vom Jahre 1848-1871.* Wien: 1932. 192, XX 1. *LJ*

Diss.

2000  Steub, Ludwig: *Altbayerische Kulturbilder.* Leipzig: E. Keil, 1869. 229 pp. *LJ*

"Der Judenmord zu Deggendorf": Pp. 21–150.

2001 Stillschweig, Kurt: Jewish Assimilation as an Object of Legislation. *Hist. Jud.* 8 (1946) 1–12. *LJ*

2002 Stoecker, Adolf (1835–1909): *Sozialdemokratisch, sozialistisch und christlichsozial; Vortrag gehalten in Braunschweig am 30. März 1880.* 2 Aufl. Braunschweig: Grüneberg's Buchhdlg., 1880. 24 pp. *LB*

2003 *Stoecker in Leipzig; Bericht über die große Versammlung in der Albert-Halle (Krystall-Palast) am 19. Februar 1889.* Leipzig: H. Beyer, 1889. 7 pp. *Unseen*

2004 *Stoecker kontra "Freie Zeitung"; Bericht über den Prozeß.* Berlin: W. Issleib, 1885. 36 pp. *LJ*

2005 Stolle, Friedrich: *Die Bekehrung zweier Rabbinen, Selig Benjamin und Aron Mendel.* 4. Aufl. erg. und verb. von C. Wagner. Köln: Westdeutscher Verein für Israel, 1891. 32 pp. *LM*

2006 Stolle, Friedrich: *Ein halbes Jahrhundert, 1843–1893, in der Arbeit der Evangelischen Kirche an Israel.* Jubiläumschrift zur Gedächtnisfeier des Rheinischen Westfälischen-Westdeutschen Vereins für Israel in dessen Auftrage verfasst. Köln a. Rhein: Selbstverlag des Vereins für Israel, 1893. 58 pp. (Kölner Schriften für Christen und Israeliten, 1) *LJ*

2007 Stolz, Karl: *Die Männer um das "Linzer Programm" mit besonderer Berücksichtigung des Historikers Dr. Heinrich Friedjung.* Wien: 1941. 133 l. *Unseen*

Diss.

2008 Stourzh, Gerald: Galten die Juden als Nationalität Altösterreichs? *Studia Judaica Austriaca* 10 (1984) 73–117. *LJ*

2009 Strack, Hermann Leberecht (1848–1922): Geschichte und Wesen des Antisemitismus. *Nathanael* 25 (1909) 99–120. *LJ*

2010 Strack, Hermann Leberecht (1848–1922): *Das Institutum Judaicum Berolinense in den ersten 30 Jahren seines Bestehens.* Leipzig: J.C. Hinrichs, 1914. 16 pp. (Schriften des Institutum Judaicum in Berlin, 43) *LJ*

2011 Strack, Hermann Leberecht (1848–1922): *The Jew and Human Sacrifice; Human Blood and Jewish Ritual. An Historical and Sociological Inquiry.* The English translation by Henry Blanshamp. London: Cope & Fenwick, 1909. 289 pp. *LJ*

2012 Strack, Hermann Leberecht (1848–1922): Jubiläum der Londoner Gesellschaft zur Beförderung des Christentums unter den Juden. *Nathanael* 25 (1909) 3–12. *LJ*

2013 Strack, Hermann Leberecht (1848–1922): "Jüdische Presse" und Judenmission. *Nathanael* 13 (1897) 115–122. *LJ*

2014 Strack, Hermann Leberecht (1848–1922): Noch einmal die Juden als Soldaten. *Nathanael* 13 (1897) 145–148. *LJ*

2015 Strack, Hermann Leberecht (1848–1922): *Ritualmord; 2 Artikel in Münchner Neueste Nachrichten, Nr. 546–547 vom 26. und 27. November 1899.* München: 1899, Unpaged. *Unseen*

2016 Strack, Hermann Leberecht (1848–1922): *Das Wesen des Judentums; Vortrag gehalten auf der Internationalen Konferenz für Judenmission zu Amsterdam.* Leipzig: J.C. Hinrich's Verlag, 1906. 23 pp. (Schriften des Institutum Judaicum in Berlin, 36) *LJ*

2017 Strack, Hermann Leberecht (1848–1922): Wie gewinnen wir unsere Geistlichen für die Arbeit an Israel oder Erweiterung des Institutum Judaicum in Berlin. *Nathanael* 13 (1897) 50–55. *LJ*

2018 Straten, Arved: *Blutmord, Blutzauber, Aberglauben; eine Untersuchung über ihre Verbreitung und ihr gleichartiges Auftreten bei allen Völkern, mit besonderer Berücksichtigung des jüdischen Volkes. Zur Aufklärung der Blutmorde dargestellt.* Siegen: Westdeutsche Verlagsanstalt, 1901. 107 pp. *LJ*

2019 Stratz, Karl Heinrich: *Was sind Juden? Eine ethnographisch-anthropologische Studie.* Wien: F. Temsky, 1903. 30 pp. *LJ*

2020 Straus, Raphael: The Jews in the Economic Evolution of Central Europe. *J.S.St.* 3 (1941) 15–40. *LJ*

2021 Ströter, Ernst Ferdinand: *Israel, das Wundervolk; ein Wort an Juden und Christen.* 5. Aufl. Düsseldorf: E. Schaffnit, 1903. 35 pp. *LJ*

2022 Strousberg, Bethel Henry (1823–1884): *Dr. Strousberg und sein Wirken, von ihm selbst geschildert.* Berlin: J. Guttentag, 1876. 486 pp. *LJ*

2023 Stuckelberg, Roderick: Houston S. Chamberlain; from Monarchism to National Socialism. *Wien.Lib.Bull. (n.s.)* (1978) 118–125. *LJ*

2024  Sturm, Julius (1816-1896): *Israels Weg zur Herrlichkeit; Lieder der Liebe in Israels Herz gesungen.* Bevorwortet von F. Delitzsch. Erlangen: Bläsing, 1858. 100 pp. *Unseen*

2025  Sturm, Julius (1816-1896): *Neue Harfenklänge für Israel; jüdische Poesien.* Leipzig: W. Faber, 1891. 79 pp. (Schriften des Instítitum Judaicum in Leipzig, 28) *LJ*

2026  Suchsland, Emil: *Die Klippen des sozialen Friedens; ernste Gedanken über Konsumvereine und Warenhäuser.* 13. Aufl. Halle a.S.: Buchhdl. des Waisenhauses, 1907. 31 pp. *LM*

2027  Suchy, Barbara: Antisemitismus in den Jahren vor dem Ersten Weltkrieg. *Köln und das Rheinische Judentum.* Ed. Jutta Bohnke-Kollwitz a.o. Köln: J.P. Bachem, 1984. Pp. 252-286. *Unseen*

2028  Suchy, Barbara: Der Verein zur Abwehr des Antisemitismus. I. From Its Beginning to the First World War. *LBIYB* 28 (1983) 205-239. *LJ*

2029  Sutor, Gustav: *Der Konitzer Mord und seine Folgen.* Berlin: H. Schildberger, 1900. 32 pp. *LJ*

2030  Sutor, Gustav: *Die Konitzer Prozeße; ein weiteres Wort zur Aufklärung.* Konitz: C. Schulz, 1901. 101 pp. *LJ*

2031  Syrkin, Nachman (1868-1924): Die Judenfrage. *Deutsche Worte* 18 (1898) 289-313. *LF*

2032  Syrkin, Nachman (1868-1924): *Die Judenfrage und der sozialistische Judenstaat, von Ben Elieser, pseud.* Bern: Steiger, 1898. 67 pp. *LJ*

2033  Szajkowski, Zosa (1911-): Sufferings of Jewish Emigrants to America in Transit through Germany. *J.S.St.* 39 (1977) 105-116. *LJ*

2034  Tänzer, Arnold Aron (1871-): *Die Geschichte der Juden in Hohenems. Vorworte Fritz Tänzer und Otto Amann. Nachruf Rabbiner Dr. Auerbach. Anhang: Karl Heinz Burmeister: Die Juden in Vorarlberg im Mittelalter. Norbert Peter: Die Hohenemser Judengemeinde im. Spiegel antisemitischer Beschuldigungen.* Bregenz: H. Lingenhöle, 1982. IV, IV, 839 pp. *LJ*

Reprint of the Meran ed., 1905.

2035  Taglicht, Israel (1862-1943): *Juden und Judentum in der Darstellung Werner Sombarts.* Wien: M. Waizner & Sohn, 1911. 16 pp. *LJ*

2036 Tal, Uriel: *Christians and Jews in Germany; Religion, Politics and Ideology in the Second Reich, 1870–1914.* Tr. from the Hebrew by Noah Jonathan Jacobs. Ithaca: Cornell University Press, 1975. 359 pp. *LJ*

First published 1969 in Hebrew.

2037 Tal, Uriel: Liberal Protestantism and the Jews in the Second Reich 1870–1914. *J.S.St.* 26 (1964) 23–41. *LJ*

2038 *Der Talmud: In deutscher Uebersetzung.* Hrsg. von A. Szentesy. Wien: T. Mattern, 1912. 230 pp. *LJ*

A selection of passages from the Talmud intended to discredit this work.

2039 Tannenwald, Bruno: *Die rechtlichen Verhältnisse der Juden in Hamburg.* Hamburg: Boysen, 1911. 112 pp. *LJ*

2040 *Tatsachen der Gegenwart, insbesondere Judenverfolgungen und Exzesse gegen Guts- und Fabrikherren erklärt durch Tatsachen der Vergangenheit, nebst einigen Vorschlägen zur Heilung sozialer Uebel für die Zukunft, von einem "Kopfarbeiter."* Berlin: Aschendorff'sche Buchhdlg., 1848. 36 pp. *LJ*

2041 Taussig, Frank William (1859–): The Jew Question in Germany. *Nation, New York* 30 (1880) 468–469. *LJ*

2042 Taxil, Leo Gabriel (1854–1907), pseud. (1854–1907): Die Drei-Punkte-Brüder. . . *Vollständige Enthüllungen über die Freimaurerei.* Bd. 1. Freiburg (Switzerland): Buchdruckerei des Werkes vom Hl. Paulus, 1886–1887. 2 vols. *LB*

2043 Teifen, Theodor: *Das soziale Elend und die besitzenden Klassen in Oesterreich.* Wien: Wiener Volksbuchhdlg., 1894. IV, 180 pp. *LM*

2044 Teja, Heinz: *Die Maske herunter; ein Beitrag zur Judenfrage in Deutschland.* Berlin: E. Hahn, 1904. 60 pp. *LJ*

2045 Teller ?: *Die Juden in Böhmen und ihre Stellung in der Gegenwart.* Prag: Silber und Schenk, 1863. 2, 91 pp. *LJ*

Ascribed to Teller — cf. *Zeitschrift für hebräische Bibliographie, 1915,* vol. 18, pp. 87.

2046 Tellering [?]: *Freiheit und Juden; zur Beherzigung für alle Volksfreunde.* Wien: A. Dorfmeister, 1848. 26 pp. *LJ*

2047 Telushkin, Joseph: *Why the Jews? The Reason for Antisemitism.* New York: Simon & Schuster, 1983. 238 pp. *LJ*

2048  *Die Teufelkralle; eine düstere Erzählung von einst für jetzt. Zur Geschichte der Blutopfer.* Leipzig: G. Wolf, 1884. 36 pp. *LJ*

2049  Theilhaber, Felix Aaron (1884–1956): Beiträge zur jüdischen Rassenfrage. *ZfDSJ* 6 (1910) 40–44. *LJ*

2050  Theilhaber, Felix Aaron (1884–1956): *Die Schädigung der Rasse durch soziales und wirtschaftliches Aufsteigen bewiesen an den Berliner Juden.* Berlin: L. Lamm, 1914. 67–92. *LJ*
      Offprint from: *Archiv für Rassen- und Gesellschaftsbiologie, 1913,* 1–2.

2051  Theilhaber, Felix Aaron (1884–1956): *Der Untergang der deutschen Juden; eine volkswirtschaftliche Studie.* München: E. Reinhardt, 1911. VIII, 170 pp. *LJ*

2052  Theimer, Camilla: *Antisemitismus und Nationaljudentum: Ein arischer Beitrag zur Lösung der Judenfrage.* Wien: C.W. Stern, 1907. 52 pp. *LJ*

2053  *Die Theorien des Herrn Hofprediger Stoecker in der Pastoral-Konferenz und die Frauen. Von einem Gläubigen im Evangelium des Friedens.* Berlin: W. Issleib, 1882. 68 pp. *LJ*

2054  Thimme, Ludwig: *Antisemitismus und Christentum; eine religiöse Studie Vorurteilslosen unter Juden und Christen.* Wandsbeck: Verlagsbuchhdlg. "Bethel," 19––. 62 pp. *LJ*

2055  Thon, Jakob (1880–1950): Der Anteil der Juden am Hochschulstudium seit 1851. *ZfDSJ* 3 (1907) 33–38. *LJ*

2056  Thon, Jakob (1880–1950): *Der Anteil der Juden am Unterrichtswesen in Preußen.* Berlin: Verlag des Bureaus für Statistik der Juden, 1905. 50 pp. (Veröffentlichungen, 1) *LJ*

2057  Thon, Jakob (1880–1950): *Die jüdischen Gemeinden und Vereine in Deutschland.* Berlin: Verlag des Bureaus für Statistik der Juden, 1906. 85 pp. (Veröffentlichungen, 3) *LJ*

2058  Thon, Jakob (1880–1950): Kriminalität der Christen und Juden in Oesterreich. *ZfDSJ* 2 (1906) 6–10. *LJ*

2059  Thon, Jakob (1880–1950): Taufbewegung der Juden in Oesterreich. *ZfDSJ* 4 (1908) 6–12. *LJ*

2060  Tietz, Georg (1889–1953): *Hermann Tietz; Geschichte einer Familie und ihrer Warenhäuser.* Bearb. von Edith J. Hirsch und Edith Tietz unter Benutzung der

Anmerkungen von Prof. Julius Hirsch. Stuttgart: Deutsche Verlagsgesellschaft, 1965. 212 pp. (Veröffentlichung des LBI) *LJ*

2061 Tietze, Hans (1886–1954): Die Aera des Liberalismus. *Die Juden Wiens; Geschichte, Wirtschaft, Kultur.* Leipzig: E.P. Tal, 1933. Pp. 179–291. *LJ*

2062 Tiltack, Curt: Lagarde und die Judenfrage. *Weltkampf* (1944) 35–39. *LJ*

2063 Timann, Richard: *Die Judenfrage und die evangelische Kirche; ein Wort des Bekenntnisses und der Mahnung.* Halle: Strien, 1881. 39 pp. *LJ*

2064 Times of London, 1880: *About Jew-bating in Germany, Discussions in the Prussian Abgeordnetenhaus and Antisemitic Agitation — Antisemitenliga, etc.* London: Nov. 15, 6a; Nov. 18, 8a, 9d; Nov. 19, 5b, 5d, 6b; Nov. 20, 5c; Nov. 22, 5b, 9d; Nov. 23, 5b, 6b; Nov. 24, 5b; Nov. 25, 5b, 5d; Nov. 30, 5d. Dec. 2, 5f; Dec. 3, 5c; Dec. 13, 5c; Dec. 21, 5d; Dec. 22, 5f. *LJ*

2065 Tims, Richard Wonser (1912–): *Germanizing Russian Poland; the H.K.T. Society and the Struggle for the Eastern Marshes in the German Empire, 1894–1919.* New York: AMS Press, 1966. 312 pp. (Studies in History, Economics and Public Law, 487) *LTA*

2066 Tirrell, Sarah Rebecca: *German Agrarian Politics After Bismarck's Fall; the Formation of the Farmer's League.* New York: Columbia University Press, 1951. 354 pp. (Columbia University Studies in History, Economics and Public Law) *Unseen*

2067 Tolstoi, Lev Nikolaevich, Count (1828–1910): *Graf Leo Tolstoi über die Juden.* Vorwort von O. Pergament. Deutsch von S. Brunner. Berlin: E. Murawkin, 1908. 48 pp. *LJ*

2068 Toury, Jakob: Jüdische Buchhändler und Verleger in Deutschland vor 1860. *LBI Bull.* 3 (1960) 58–69. *LJ*

2069 Toury, Jakob: Jüdische Parteigänger des Antisemitismus. *LBI Bull.* 4 (1961) 323–335. *LJ*

2070 Toury, Jakob: *Die jüdische Presse im Oesterreichischen Kaiserreich; ein Beitrag zur Problematik der Akkulturation, 1802–1918.* Tübingen: J.C.B. Mohr, 1983. VIII, 171 pp. (Schriftenreihe wissenschaftlicher Abhandlungen des LBI, 41) *LJ*

2071 Toury, Jakob: Die jüdischen Schneider in Hamburg, 1848–1854. *TAJfDG* 1 (1972) 101–118. *LJ*

2072  Toury, Jakob: Neue hebräische Veröffentlichungen zur Geschichte der Juden im deutschen Lebenskreise. *LBI Bull.* 4 (1961) 55–73. *LJ*

2073  Toury, Jakob: Ostjüdische Handarbeiter in Deutschland vor 1914. *LBI Bull.* 6 (1963) 81–91. *LJ*

2074  Toury, Jakob: *Die politischen Orientierungen der Juden in Deutschland, von Jena bis Weimar.* Tübingen: Mohr (Siebeck), 1966. X, 387 pp. (Schriftenreihe wissenschaftlicher Abhandlungen des LBI, 15) *LJ*

2075  Toury, Jakob: Probleme jüdischer Gleichberechtigung auf lokalbürgerlicher Ebene; dargestellt am Beispiel einer thüringischen Gemeinde. *TAJfDG* 2 (1973) 267–286. *LJ*

2076  Toury, Jakob: *Soziale und politische Geschichte der Juden in Deutschland, 1847–1871; zwischen Revolution, Reaktion und Emanzipation.* Düsseldorf: Droste Verlag, 1977. 411 pp. (Veröffentlichungen des Diaspora Research Instituts, 20) (Schriftenreihe des Instituts für Deutsche Geschichte, Universität Tel-Aviv, 2) *LJ*

2077  Tramer, Hans: Die Hamburger Kaiserjuden. *LBI Bull.* 3 (1960) 177–189. *LJ*

2078  Treitschke, Heinrich Gotthard von (1834–1896): Zur inneren Lage am Jahresschluße. *Pr. Jhrb.* 46 (1880) 639–645. *LJ*

A justification of the antisemitic movement.

2079  Treter, Miecislaus von Lubomir: *Studien über die Judenfrage von einem Geächteten.* Lemberg: Sayfarth & Czajkowski, 1880. 3 vols.in one. *LJ*

2080  Treue, Wolfgang (1916–): *Deutsche Parteiprogramme, 1861–1956.* 2. erw. Aufl. Göttingen: Musterschmidt-Verlag, 1956. 371 pp. (Quellensammlung zur Kulturgeschichte, 3) *LJ*

2081  Trevor-Roper, Hugh Redwald: The Jews and Modern Capitalism. *Men and Events; Historical Essays.* New York: Harper & Bros. 1958. pp. 156–160. *LJ*

2082  Trocase, François: *L'Autriche juive. L'Autriche contemporaine, telle qu'elle est; politique, économique, militaire et sociale.* Paris: P. Dupont, 1900. 402 pp. *LJ*

2083  Truhart, Arthur von: *Offener Brief an Herrn Richard Wagner, den Verfasser der Broschüre "Das Judentum in der Musik."* St. Petersburg: Wilcken, 1869. 15 pp. *Unseen*

2084  Tugendhold, Jakob (1794–1871): *Der alte Wahn vom Blutgebrauch der Israeliten beim Osterfeste.* Berlin: Veit, 1858. IV, 90 pp. *LJ*

2085 Ulmer, Wilhelm: *Joreh Deah, der, für Lehrer der christlichen Erkenntnis, jüdischen Irrtümern entgegengesetzt.* 3. Aufl. nach der Callenberg Ausg. vom Jahre 1744, neu bearb. Leipzig: W. Faber, 1894. 48 pp. (Schriften des Institutum Judaicum in Leipzig, 41) *LJ*

2086 Ungern-Sternberg, Alexander von (1806-1868): *Der falsche und der wahre Stoecker, von einem Mitglied des Reichstags.* 4. Aufl. Leipzig: Böhme, 1885. 31 pp. *LF*

2087 Unna, Isak: *Die Stellung Schopenhauers zum Judentum.* Frankfurt a.M.: J. Kauffmann, 1928. 17 pp. *LJ*
Offprint from: *Jüdische Studien, Dr. Josef Wohlgemuth gewidmet.*

2088 Unparteiischer, pseud.: *Richard Wagner und das Judentum; ein Beitrag zur Kulturgeschichte unserer Zeit.* Elberfeld: Lucas, 1869. 16 pp. *LC*

2089 *Der Untergang Israels, von einem Physiologen.* Zürich: J. Schabelitz, 1894. 17 pp. *LJ*

2090 Urbach, R.: Judentum und Christentum. *MGWJ* 50 (1906) 257-288. *LJ*

2091 Valentin, Hugo Maurice (1888-1963): *Antisemitism, Historically and Critically Examined.* Tr. from the Swedish by A.G. Chater. London: V. Gollancz, 1936. 324 pp. *LJ*

2092 Veit, Moritz (1808-1864): *Sendschreiben an meine Wähler.* Berlin: Veit & Co., 1849. 60 pp. *Unseen*

2093 Venetianer, A.: *Zum Zeugnis; offener Brief an den würdigen Herrn J. Lichtenstein, Bezirksrabbiner zu Tápio-Szele in Ungarn als Widerhall zu seinem "Mein Zeugniss."* Wien: Verlag des Autors, 1886. 13 pp. *LJ*

2094 Venetianer, Lajos (1867-1922): *Jüdisches im Christentum.* Frankfurt a.M.: J. Kauffmann, 1913. 82 pp. (Volksschriften über die jüdische Religion, vol. 1, 5) *LJ*

2095 Verband der Deutschen Juden: *Bericht über die Tätigkeit des Verbandes der Deutschen Juden bei der Vorbereitung des Preußischen Volksschulunterhalt-ungsgesetzes von 1906, erstattet von F. Makower.* Berlin: H.S. Hermann, 1907. 95 pp. *LJ*

2096 Verband der Deutschen Juden: *Denkschrift zum Entwurf eines Gesetzes betreffend die Unterhaltung der öffentlichen Volksschulen.* Berlin: H.S. Hermann, 1906. 24 pp. *LJ*

2097   Verband der Deutschen Juden: *Wie wird im Preußischen Heer die Beförderung von Juden zu Reserveoffizieren vereitelt?* Berlin: H.S. Hermann, 1911. 79 pp. *LJ*

2098   Die Verbreitung der Juden in Deutschland. *N.Z.* 11, 1 (1892–1893) 57–59. *LJ*

2099   Verein der Freunde Israel zu Basel: *Seine Entstehung und seine Arbeit während 50 Jahren.* Basel: 1881. 70 pp. *Unseen*

2100   Verein für die Statistik der Juden e. V. in München: *Jahresbericht des Vereins . . . über das Vereinsjahr 1904.* München: B. Heller, 1905. 25 pp. *LJ*

2101   Verein für jüdische Statistik: *Jüdische Statistik.* Hrsg. vom Verein für jüdische Statistik unter der Redaktion von Alfred Nossig. Berlin: Jüdischer Verlag, 1903. 452 pp. *LJ*

2102   Verein für Sozialpolitik, Berlin: *Untersuchungen über die Lage des Hausiergewerbes in Deutschland.* Bd. 77–81. Leipzig: Duncker & Humblot, 1898. 5 vols. *LJ*

2103   Verein zur Abwehr des Antisemitismus, Bibliothek: *Bibliothek des Vereins zur Abwehr des Antisemitismus, Frankfurt a.M. Neu aufgestellt am 27. Dezember 1908.* Frankfurt a.M.: 1908. 45 pp. *Unseen*

2104   Verein zur Abwehr des Antisemitismus, Berlin: *Der Deutschnationale Handlungsgehilfenverband.* Berlin: 1911. 51 pp. *LJ*

        Offprint from: *Mitteilungen aus dem Verein zur Abwehr des Antisemitismus,* 1911.

2105   Verein zur Abwehr des Antisemitismus, Berlin: *Die Juden im Heere.* Berlin: Verein zur Abwehr des Antisemitismus, 1909. 88 pp. *LJ*

2106   Verein zur Abwehr des Antisemitismus, Berlin: *Der Prozeß Rohling kontra Bloch.* Berlin: M. Hoffschläger, 1892. 22 pp. *LJ*

        Offprint from: *Mitteilungen aus dem Verein zur Abwehr des Antisemitismus.*

2107   Verein zur Abwehr des Antisemitismus, Berlin: *Die wirtschaftliche Lage, soziale Gliederung und die Kriminalstatistik der Juden.* Berlin: Verlag des Vereins zur Abwehr des Antisemtismus, 1912. 64 pp. *LJ*

2108   Verein zur Abwehr des Antisemitismus, Wien: *Schädlinge der Gesellschaft.* Wien: Verein zur Abwehr des Antisemitismus, 1910. 23 pp. *LJ*

        Concerns the Leopold Hilsner case on ritual murder in Polna.

2109 Veyrac, S.: Karl Marx et l'antisémitisme. *Revue des Revues* 9 (1894) 117–119. *Unseen*

2110 Victor, Wilhelm: *Die Emanzipation der Juden in Schleswig-Holstein.* Hamburg: M. Philipsen, 1913. 65 pp. *LJ*

Date of publication taken from preface.

2111 Vishnitser, Mark L'vovich: *A History of Jewish Crafts and Guilds.* Foreword by Salo W. Baron. Introduction by Werner J. Cahnman. New York: J. David, 1965. XXVII, 324 pp. *LJ*

2112 Vitting, M. Oskar: Psychologie der jüdischen Rasse. *Pol.Anthrop.Rev.* 5 (1906) 295–297. *LJ*

2113 Vogel, Georg: *Licht für Israel; ein siebenarmiger Leuchter für Israel und Israel's Freunde angezündet.* Leipzig: W. Faber, 1894. 20 pp. (Schriften des Institutum Judaicum in Leipzig, 40) *LJ*

2114 Vogel, Rolf: Die Juden in Armee und Gesellschaft im 19. Jahrhundert. *Ein Stück von uns; deutsche Juden in deutschen Armeen 1813–1976; eine Dokumentation.* Mainz: v. Hase & Köhler Verlag, 1977. pp. 11–48. *LJ*

2115 Vogelstein, Hermann (1870–1942): *Der Zionismus; eine Gefahr für die gedeihliche Entwicklung des Judentums.* Stettin: 1906. 14 pp. *LTA*

Offprint from: *Mitteilungen des Liberalen Vereins für die Angelegenheiten der Jüdischen Gemeinde zu Berlin, 22–23.*

2116 Volkov, Shulamit: Antisemitism as a Cultural Code; Reflections on the History and Historiography of Antisemitism in Imperial Germany. *LBIYB* 23 (1978) 25–46. *LJ*

2117 Volkov, Shulamit: Antisemitismus in Deutschland als Problem jüdisch-nationalen Denkens und jüdischer Geschichtsschreibung. *Geschichte und Gesellschaft* 5 (1979) 519–544. *LJ*

2118 Volkov, Shulamit: The Dynamics of Dissimilation; Ostjuden and German Jews. *The Jewish Response to German Culture; from the Enlightenment to the Second World War.* Eds. Jehuda Reinharz, Walter Schatzberg. Hannover: N.H., 1985. pp. 195–211. *LJ*

2119 Volkov, Shulamit: Jüdische Assimilation und jüdische Eigenart im Deutschen Kaiserreich. *Jüdisches Leben und Antisemitismus im 19. und 20. Jahrhundert.* München: C.H. Beck, 1990. pp. 131–145. *LJ*

2120  Volkov, Shulamit: Kontinuität und Diskontinuität im deutschen Antisemitismus, 1878–1945. *Vierteljahrshefte für Zeitgeschichte* 33 (1985) 221–244. *LJ*

2121  Volkov, Shulamit: Popular Anti-Modernism; Ideology and Sentiment among Master-Artisans during the 1890's. *TAJfDG* 3 (1974) 203–225. *LJ*

2122  Volkov, Shulamit: *The Rise of Popular Antimodernism in Germany; the Urban Master Artisans 1873–1896*. Princeton: Princeton University Press, 1978. IX, 399 pp. *LJ*
       About the campaign of the antiliberal forces in Imperial Germany and the change from liberalism to conservatism by the artisans.

2123  Volkov, Shulamit: The Social and Political Function of Late 19th Century Antisemitism; the Case of the Small Handicraft Masters. *Sozialgeschichte heute. Festschrift für Hans Rosenberg zum 70. Geburtstag*. Göttingen: Vandenhoeck & Ruprecht, 1974. pp. 416–431. *LJ*

2124  Von Judentaufen. *SaH* 46 (1909) 56–58. *LJ*

2125  *Vorurteile gegen Minderheiten; die Anfänge des modernen Antisemitismus am Beispiel Deutschlands*. Für die Sekundarstufe. Hrsg. von Hans Gert Oomen und Hans Dieter Schmid. Stuttgart: Reclam, 1978. 174 pp. (Universalbibliothek, 9543) *LB*

2126  Vorwald, Heinrich: Neues über den Rembrandtdeutschen. *Hochland* 6 (1908) 126–127. *LJ*

2127  Wägner, Richard: *Das Judentum in der Schule; ein pädagogischer Bericht für Eltern, Lehrer und alle, denen die moderne Erziehung nicht gleichgültig ist*. Zürich: Verlags-Magazin, 1873. 24 pp. *Unseen*

2128  Wäntig, Heinrich (1870–1944): Der Antisemitismus. *Gewerbliche Mittelstandspolitik . . . Auf Grund österreichischer Quellen*. Leipzig: Duncker & Humblot, 1898. pp. 136–168. *LV*

2129  Wätjen, Hermann Julius Eduard (1876–): *Das Judentum und die Anfänge der modernen Kolonisation; kritische Bemerkungen zu Werner Sombarts "Die Juden und das Wirtschaftsleben."* Stuttgart: W. Kohlhammer, 1914. 72 pp. *LJ*

2130  Wagener, Friedrich Wilhelm Hermann (1815–1889), ed.: *Das Judentum und der Staat; eine historisch-politische Skizze zur Orientierung über die Judenfrage*. Berlin: F. Heinicke, 1857. 95 pp. *LJ*

2131 Wagener, Friedrich Wilhelm Hermann (1815–1889): *Der Mädchenhandel.* 2. unveränd. Aufl. Berlin: P. Langenscheidt, 1911. 113 pp. (Sammlung Langenscheidt. Beiträge zur Kritik der Gegenwart) *Unseen*

2132 Wagner, Carl: *Was sagt Christus von den Juden; ein Beitrag zur Lösung der Judenfrage. Festpredigt.* 2. Aufl. Berlin: Deutsche Evangelische Buch- und Traktatgesellschaft, 1893. 31 pp. *Unseen*

2133 Wagner, Carl: Welche Mittel sind bei der praktischen Ausübung der Judenmißion sittlich zuläßig. *Nathanael* 23 (1907) 23–28. *LJ*

2134 Wagner, Curt, ed.: *Die in der Verfassung garantierten Rechte der Juden im Preußischen Staate.* Berlin: Jacoby, 1882. 6 pp. *LTA*

2135 Wahrmund, Adolf (1827–1913): *Der Kulturkampf zwischen Asien und Europa; ein Beitrag zur Klarlegung des heutigen Standes der orientalischen Frage.* Berlin: Reuther, 1887. 63 pp. *LJ*

2136 Walch, J. G. A.: *Die Judenfrage — eine von Staats wegen zu behandelnde religiöse Frage.* Dessau: Paul Baumann, 1893. 26 pp. *LTA*

2137 Wald, Alexander: *Der jüdische Mythos; eine Studie.* 2. verm. Aufl. Preßburg: G. Heckenast's Nachf., 1890. 32 pp. *LJ*

The first ed. has been confiscated in Austria.

2138 Waldenburg, Alfred: *Das isocephale blonde Rassenelement unter Halligfriesen und jüdischen Taubstummen.* Berlin: S. Calvary, 1902. 47 pp. *LJ*

2139 Walter, Ingrid: *Moritz Benedikt und die "Neue Freie Presse.* Wien: 1950. 231 l. *Unseen*

Diss. Typescript.

2140 Wander, Paul: Review of Werner Sombarts "Die Juden und das Wirtschaftsleben." *The American Journal of Sociology* 17 (1911/12) 838–841. *LJ*

2141 Wandruszka, Adam: Der Aufstieg der "Neuen Freien Presse"; Weltblatt der Donaumonarchie. *Geschichte einer Zeitung.* Wien: Neue Wiener Presse Druck- und Verlagsanstalt, 1958. pp. 64–122. *LJ*

2142 Wank, Solomon: A Case of Artistocratic Antisemitism in Austria; Count Aehrenthal and the Jews, 1878–1907. *LBIYB* 30 (1985) 435–456. *LJ*

2143 *Warum treten wir nicht in das Christentum ein. Von einem Juden.* Leipzig: Kössling, 1882. 34 pp. *LJ*

2144  *Was lehrt der Talmud.* Leipzig: Th. Fritsch, 1887. 8 pp. (Brennende Fragen, 29) *LJ*

2145  *Was lehrt der Talmud?* Kaiserslautern: Gotthold's Verlag, 1887. 16 pp. *Unseen*

2146  *Was lehrt der Talmud?* Münster: Nasse'sche Verlagshdlg., 1876. 24 pp. (Broschüren-Cyclus für das katholische Deutschland, vol. 11, 3) *Unseen*

2147  *Was lehrt uns der Sturz von Hirschfeld und Wolff, Maass und Genossen.* Potsdam: E. Döring, 1892. 18 pp. *Unseen*

2148  Wasinski, A.: *Die Situation; Extrafahrt der Dampfwalze mit Anhang: "Der Stechapfel." Harmlose und gemütsinnige Betrachtungen, von Carl Wald.* Berlin: O. Lorenz, 1881. 19 pp. (Broschüren-Cyclus, 1) *LJ*

2149  Wassermann, Henry: "Die Fliegenden Blätter." *LBIYB* 28 (1983) 93–138. *LJ*

2150  Wassermann, Henry: Jews and Judaism in the "Gartenlaube." *LBIYB* 23 (1978) 47–60. *LJ*

2151  Wassermann, Henry: Jews in Jugendstil; the "Simplizissimus," 1896–1914. *LBIYB* 31 (1986) 71–104. *LJ*

2152  Wassermann, Henry: "Kauft nicht bei Juden"; der politische Antisemitismus des späten 19. Jahrhunderts in Darmstadt. *Juden als Darmstädter Bürger.* Darmstadt: Eduard Röther Verlag, 1984. pp. 123–136. *LJ*

2153  Wassermann, Rudolf (1884–): *Beruf, Konfession und Verbrechen; eine Studie über die Kriminalität der Juden in Vergangenheit und Gegenwart.* München: Reinhardt, 1907. 106 pp. (Statistische und Nationalökonomische Abhandlungen, 2) *LJ*

2154  Wassermann, Rudolf (1884–): Ist die Kriminalistik der Juden Rassenkriminalistik. *ZfDSJ* 7 (1911) 36–39. *LJ*

2155  Wassermann, Rudolf (1884–): Die Juden und das deutsche Wirtschaftsleben der Gegenwart. *Pr. Jhrb.* 149 (1912) 267–275. *LJ*

2156  Wassermann, Rudolf (1884–): Judenfrage und Ostmarkenpolitik. *Zeitschrift für Politik* 3 (1910) 608–613. *LJ*

2157  Wassermann, Rudolf (1884–): *Kriminalität der Juden in Deutschland 1882–1906.* Heidelberg: C. Winter, 1910. pp. 609–618. *LJ*

Offprint from: *Monatsschrift für Kriminalpsychologie und Strafrechtsreform.*

2158 Wassermann, Rudolf (1884–): Kritische und ergänzende Bemerkungen zur Literatur über die Kriminalität der Juden. *ZfDSJ* 2 (1906) 73–77. *LJ*

2159 Wassermann, Rudolf (1884–): Kritische und ergänzende Bemerkungen zur neuen Literatur über die Kriminalität der Juden. *ZfDSJ* 4 (1908) 172–174. *LJ*

2160 Wassermann, Rudolf (1884–): Wolf'sche Bevölkerungsgesetze und das Bevölkerungsproblem der Juden in Deutschland. *Zeitschrift für Sozialwissenschaft* 12 (1909) 663–671. *LJ*

2161 Wawrzinek, Kurt: *Die Entstehung der deutschen Antisemitenparteien, 1873–1890.* Berlin: E. Ebering, 1927. 97 pp. (Historische Studien, 168) *LJ*

2162 Weber, Adam, ed.: *Das Blutritual der Juden; oder, Der Ritualmord in Polna vor dem Schwurgericht in Nürnberg vom 9. März 1900.* Fürth: 1900. 80 pp. *LJ*
Trial against the Adam Weber, editor of the newspaper *Freie Beobachter* in Fürth.

2163 Weber, Ludwig (1846–1922): Die Judenmission des neunzehnten Jahrhunderts; Portraits. *Werkshagen: Der Protestantismus am Ende des XIX. Jahrhunderts.* Vol. 1. Berlin, 1902. pp. 551–552. *Unseen*

2164 Weber, Max (1864–1920): Die Kulturreligionen und die Welt. *Grundriß der Sozialökonomik. Abt. III, Halbbd. 1. Wirtschaft und Gesellschaft. 2. Aufl.* Tübingen: J.C.B. Mohr, 1925. pp. 349–356. *LJ*

2165 Weder, Johann Baptist: *Bericht und Anträge der Kommissionsminderheit an den Großen Rat betr. das Gesuch um hoheitliche Anerkennung einer israelitischen Kultusgemeinde in St. Gallen vom 29. Oktober 1864.* St. Gallen: 1864. 1 vol. *Unseen*

2166 Wehleid, Hans: Vom Schächten. *Der Hammer* 10 (1911) 102–104. *LJ*

2167 Wehler, Hans Ulrich: Antisemitismus und Minderheitenpolitik. *Das Deutsche Kaiserreich, 1871–1918.* Göttingen: Vandenhoeck & Ruprecht, 1973. pp. 110–118. (Kleine Vandenhoek-Reihe, 13807. Deutsche Geschichte, 9) *LJ*

2168 Weichert, Friedrich: Die Anfänge der Berliner Judenmission. *Jahrbuch für Berlin-Brandenburgische Kirchengeschichte* 38 (1963) 106–141. *Unseen*

2169 Weichmann, Friedrich: *Das Schächten; das rituelle Schlachten bei den Juden.* Mit einem Vorwort von Hermann L. Strack. Leipzig: J.C. Hinrichs' Verlag, 1899. 48 pp. (Schriften des Institutum Judaicum in Berlin, 25) *LJ*

2170  Weicker Georg: *Zur Lösung der Judenfrage; Briefwechsel zwischen einem christlichen Pfarrer und einem jüdischen Lehrer im Großherzogtum Hessen.* Darmstadt: C.F. Winter'sche Buchdruckerei, 1894. 40 pp. *LJ*

2171  Weidenfeld, Josef: *Die gesetzliche Stellung der Juden Galiziens von der Märzrevolution bis zum Verfassungsjahr 1867.* Wien: 1936. 194 l. *LJ*
      Diss. Photocopy of the typescript.

2172  Weil Bruno: *Juden in der deutschen Burschenschaft; ein Beitrag zum Streit um die konfessionelle Studentenverbindung.* Straßburg i.E.: Singer, 1905. 64 pp. *LJ*

2173  Weil, Jakob (1792-1864): *Wagener, Stahl, die Juden und die protestantischen Dissidenten.* Frankfurt a.M.: F.B. Auffarth, 1857. 28 pp. *LJ*
      Offprint from: Steins Israelitischer Volkslehrer.

2174  Weiler, Gershon: Fritz Mauthner: A Study in Jewish Self-Rejection. *LBIYB* 8 (1963) 136-148. *LJ*

2175  Weinberg, Max: Lassalle und seine Stellung zum Judentum. *Israelitische Wochenschrift* 9 (1878) 320-321, 328. *LJ*

2176  Weinberg, Max: Von der Geldmacht der Juden. *Israelitische Wochenschrift* 10 (1879) 17-18. *LJ*

2177  Weinberg, Paul: *Ahlwardt, die Presse und die Parteien; ein objektives Mahnwort eines parteilosen Juden.* Charlottenburg: A. Michow, 1892. 36 pp. *LJ*

2178  Weinberg, Richard: Das Hirngewicht der Juden. *ZfDSJ* 1 (1905) 5-10. *LJ*

2179  Weiner, Paula (Odenheimer): *Die Berufe der Juden in Bayern.* Hrsg. vom Verein für Statistik der Juden in München. Berlin: Max Schildberger, 1918. 131 pp. (Veröffentlichungen der Bureaus für Statistik der Juden, 10) *LJ*

2180  Weiner, Paula (Odenheimer): Die Berufe der Juden in München. *ZfDSJ* 11 (1915) 85-96; 12 (1916) 34-43 *LJ*

2181  Weingarten, Ralph: Gleichberechtigt in die neue Zeit; Die Gründerzeit des Schweizer Judentums, 1866-1920. *Juden in der Schweiz; Glaube, Geschichte, Gegenwart.* Zürich: Edition Kürz, 1982. pp. 54-68. *LJ*

2182 Weinryb, Bernard Dov Sucher (1900–): *Der Kampf um die Berufsumschichtung; ein Ausschnitt aus der Geschichte der Juden in Deutschland.* Berlin: Schocken, 1936. 63 pp. (Jüdische Lesehefte, 13) *LJ*

2183 Weinryb, Bernard Dov Sucher (1900–): Prolegomena to an Economic History of the Jew in Germany in Modern Times. *LBIYB* 1 (1956) 279–306. *LJ*

2184 Weinstein, Marcos: Marx y la cuestion judia. *Judaica* 5 (1938) 1–19. *LJ*

2185 Weinzierl-Fischer, Erika: Antisemitismus als österreichisches Phänomen. *Die Republik* 3 (1970) 28–35. *LV*

2186 Weinzierl-Fischer, Erika: On the Pathogenesis of the Antisemitism of Sebastian Brunner 1814–1893. *Yad Vashem Studies on the European Jewish Catastrophe and Resistance* 10 (1974) 217–239. *LJ*

2187 Weinzierl-Fischer, Erika: Die Stellung der Juden in Oesterreich seit dem Staatsgrundgesetz von 1867. *ZfGJ* 5 (1968) 89–96. *LJ*

2188 Weiss, Matthias: Der politische Antisemitismus im Wiener Kleinbürgertum 1867–1895. *Emuna* 8 (1973) 94–103. *LJ*

2189 Weissberg, Leib: *Die Judenemanzipation und die österreichische Reichsverfassung von 1849; ein Beitrag zur Geschichte der Juden in Oesterreich.* Wien: 1921. III, 110 l. *Unseen*

Diss.

2190 Weissenburg, S.: Die russisch-jüdischen Studenten an den deutschen Universitäten. *ZfDSJ* 10 (1914) 60–62. *LJ*

2191 Weissmann, Arthur Simhah: *Ernste Antworten auf "Ernste Fragen," Franz Delitzsch's neueste Schrift.* 2. Aufl. Wien: Commissionsverlag C.D. Lippe, 1888. 35 pp. *LJ*

On Delitzsch's *Ernste Fragen an die Gebildeten Jüdischer Religion.*

2192 Weisz, Heinrich: *Die Judengesetzgebung der österreichischen Regierung in Bezug auf den Realitätenbesitz, Ehe und Taufe vom Jahre 1848-1867.* Wien: 1927. VI, 267 l. *Unseen*

Diss.

2193 Weldler, Augusta (Steinberg): *Geschichte der Juden in der Schweiz vom 16. Jahrhundert bis nach der Emanzipation. Bearb. und erg. durch Florence Guggenheim-Grünberg.* Bd. 1-2. Hrsg. vom Schweizerischen Israelitschen Gemeindebund. Goldach: 1966–1970. 2 vols. *LJ*

2194  Weller, Bjoern Uwe: *Maximilian Harden und die "Zukunft."* Bremen: Schünemann, 1970. 485 pp. (Studien zur Publizistik, 13) *LJ*

2195  Weltsch, Robert (1891–): Aus dem Jahrhundert der Judenemanzipation. *An der Wende des neuzeitlichen Judentums.* Tübingen: J.C.B. Mohr, 1972. pp. 81–93. *LJ*

2196  Wengraf, Edmund: *St. Georg von Zwettl, i.e. Georg von Schönerer.* Wien: M. Gottlieb, 1887. 47 pp. (Wiener Flugschriften, 1) *LJ*

2197  Wenzel, Stefi: Die Lage von Minderheiten als Indiz für den Stand der Emanzipation einer Gesellschaft. *Sozialgeschichte heute. Festschrift für H. Rosenberg.* Ed. H.U. Wehler. Göttingen: Vandenhoeck & Ruprecht, 1974. pp. 365–387. *LJ*

2198  Werlhof, B. von: Der Jude als Ackerbauer und Handwerker. *Israelitische Monatsschrift Suppl.* 13 (1894) 136–137. *LJ*

2199  Werner, Alfred (1901–): Heinrich Heine; Jewish Nationalist. *Judaism* 5 (1956) 76–84. *LJ*

2200  Werner, Eric: Juden um Richard und Cosima Wagner. *Oesterreichische Akademie der Wissenschaften. Phil. Hist. Klasse. Anzeiger* 12 (1984) 131–169. *LJ*

2201  Werner, Lothar: *Der Alldeutsche Verband, 1890–1918; ein Beitrag zur Geschichte der öffentlichen Meinung in Deutschland in den Jahren vor und während des Weltkrieges.* Berlin: Eberring, 1935. 294 pp. (Historische Studien, 278) *LTA*

      Reprint of 1935 ed. Vaduz, Kraus, 1965.

2202  Werth, E. von: An Wilhelm Marr, 27.11.1889. *Staatsarchiv Hamburg.* StA Hbg. NL Marr, A 282. *Unseen*

2203  Wertheimer, Jack L.: The "Ausländerfrage" at Instututions of Higher Learning — a Controversy over Russian-Jewish Students in Imperial Germany. *LBIYB* 27 (1982) 187–218. *LJ*

2204  Wertheimer, Jack L.: *German Policy and Jewish Politics; the Absorption of East European Jews in Germany 1868–1914.* Ann Arbor, Mich.: University Microfilms International, 1980. 2 vols. VI, 634 l. *LJ*

      Diss. Columbia University, 1978.

2205 Wertheimer, Jack L.: Jewish Lobbyists and the German Citizienship Law of 1914; a Documentary Account. *Studies in Contemporary Jewry* 1 (1984) 140–162. *LJ*

2206 Wertheimer, Josef von (1800–1887): *Jüdische Lehre und Jüdisches Leben mit besonderer Beziehung auf die Juden von Oesterreich und auf die Pflichten gegen Vaterland und Mitmenschen.* Wien: Hölder, 1883. 34 pp. *LJ*

2207 Wertheimer, Josef von (1800–1887): *Die Stellung der Juden in Oesterreich.* Wien: Typ. Keck & Pierer, 1853. 42 pp. *LTA*

2208 Wertheimer, Mildred Salz: *The Pan-German League, 1890–1914.* New York: Columbia University, 1924. 256 pp. (Studies in History, Economics and Public Law, vol. 112, no. 2, whole no. 251) *LJ*

2209 Wesselhöft, E.: *Herschel-Augusti; eine abenteurliche wunderliche und doch durchaus wahre Geschichte.* 2. Aufl., neu bearb. Leipzig: Dörffling & Franke, 1885. 47 pp. *LJ*

2210 West, Caroline: Erlebnisse in der Judenmission. *SaH* 33 (1896) 197–206, 240–251; 34 (1897) 51–61, 105–110, 174–188, 224–243. *LJ*

2211 Westphal, Uwe: *Berliner Konfektion und Mode; die Zerstörung einer Tradition, 1836–1939.* Berlin: Hentrich, 1986. 208 pp. (Stätten der Geschichte Berlins, 14) *LC*

2212 Whiteside, Andrew Gladding: *Austrian National Socialism before 1918.* The Hague: M. Nijhoff, 1962. 143 pp. *LJ*

2213 Whiteside, Andrew Gladding: *Georg Ritter von Schönerer; Alldeutschland und sein Prophet.* Aus dem Amerikanischen von Gerhard Hartmann. Graz: Verlag Styria, 1981. 344 pp. *LJ*

Original title: *The Socialism of Fools.*

2214 Whiteside, Andrew Gladding: *The Socialism of Fools; Georg Ritter von Schönerer and Austrian Pan-Germanism.* Berkeley: University of California Press, 1975. 404 pp. *LJ*

2215 Wickert, Lothar: Theodor Mommsen und Jacob Bernays; ein Beitrag zur Geschichte des deutschen Judentums. *Historische Zeitschrift* 205 (1967) 265–294. *LJ*

2216 Wiegand, A.: Achte internationale Konferenz für Judenmission in Stockholm. *SaH* 48 (1911) 106–123. *LJ*

2217  Wiegand, A.: Dr. Heynemann und die Judenmission. *SaH* 46 (1909) 120–132, 145–157. *LJ*

2218  Wiegand, A.: Die Fortdauer jüdischer Volkszugehörigkeit zu Judenchristen. *SaH* 47 (1910) 113–128. *LJ*

2219  Wiegand, A.: Judenchristliche Gedanken und Hoffnungen. *SaH* 37 (1900) 7–35, 59–71, 140–153. *LJ*

2220  Wiegand, A.: Sendschreiben an die Mitglieder der juden-christlichen Konferenz in Nordamer. *SaH* 41 (1904) 131–142. *Unseen*

2221  Wiegand, A.: Wie kann man unseren modernen Juden das Evangelium nahe bringen. *SaH* 34 (1897) 24–35. *Unseen*

2222  Wielandt, Friedrich: *Die Badischen Gesetze vom 4. Oktober 1862 über Niederlassung und Aufenthalt, Aufhebung einiger Beschränkungen des Rechts zur Verehelichung und bürgerliche Gleichstellung der Israeliten im Zusammenhang mit der bisherigen Gemeindegesetzgebung. Nach amtlichen Quellen bearb.* Karlsruhe: A. Bielefeld, 1863. IV,93 pp. *LJ*

2223  Wiener, Max (1882–1950): *Jüdische Religion im Zeitalter der Emanzipation.* Berlin: Philo-Verlag, 1933. 278 pp. *LJ*

2224  Wiernik, Peter: Switzerland's Discrimination. *History of the Jews in America.* New York: Jewish Press Publ. Co., 1912. pp. 199–205. *LJ*

2225  Der wildgewordene Kleinbürger und Bauer und die Wahlen. *N. Z.* 11, II (1893) 389–392. *LJ*

2226  Wilhelm, Hermann: *Dichter, Denker, Fememörder; Rechtsradikalismus und Antisemitismus in München von der Jahrhundertwende bis 1921.* Berlin: Transit-Buchverlag, 1989. 192 pp. *LJ*

2227  Wilhelm, Kurt (1900–1905): The Jewish Community in the Post-Emancipation Period. *LBIYB* 2 (1957) 47–75. *LJ*

2228  Winkelmann, Walter: *Die rechtliche Stellung der außerhalb der Landeskirche stehenden Religionsgemeinschaften in Hessen; geschichtliche Entwicklung und geltendes Recht. Ein Beitrag zur Geschichte der Bekenntnisfreiheit.* Darmstadt: H.C. Schlapp, 1912. III, 144 pp. *Unseen*

2229  Winter, Georg (1856–1912): *Der Antisemitismus in Deutschland, vom kulturhistorischen und sozialpolitischen Standpunkt beleuchtet.* Magdeburg: Salinger, 1896. VI, 125 pp. *LJ*

2230 *Wirtschaftliche Zustände Galiziens in der Gegenwart; sechs Vorträge.* Mitarbeiter Fr. Bujak u.a. Wien: Braumüller, 1913. 110 pp. *LC*

2231 Wistrich, Robert Solomon (1945–): Anticapitalism or Antisemitism; the Case of Franz Mehring. *LBIYB* 22 (1977) 35–54. *LJ*

2232 Wistrich, Robert Solomon (1945–): Austrian Socialdemocracy and Antisemitism, 1890–1914. *J.S.St.* 37 (1975) 323–333. *LJ*

2233 Wistrich, Robert Solomon (1945–): Eduard Bernstein and the Jewish Problem. *TAJfDG* 8 (1979) 243–256. *LJ*

2234 Wistrich, Robert Solomon (1945–): Eduard Bernstein und das Judentum. *Bernstein und der demokratische Sozialismus.* Eds. Horst Heimann, Thomas Meyer. Berlin, 1978. pp. 149–165. *LJ*

2235 Wistrich, Robert Solomon (1945–): Ferdinand Lasalle; the Gladiator. *European Judaism* 10 (1976) 15–24. *LJ*

2236 Wistrich, Robert Solomon (1945–): Georg von Schönerer and the Genesis of Modern Austrian Antisemitism. *Wien.Lib.Bull.* 29 (1976) 20–29. *LJ*

2237 Wistrich, Robert Solomon (1945–): *The Jews of Vienna in the Age of Franz Joseph.* Oxford: Published for the Littman Library by Oxford University Press, 1989. XIV, 696 pp. *LJ*

2238 Wistrich, Robert Solomon (1945–): Karl Kraus, Jewish Prophet or Renegade? *European Judaism* 9 (1975) 32–38. *LJ*

2239 Wistrich, Robert Solomon (1945–): Karl Lueger and the Ambiguities of Viennese Antisemitism. *J.S.St.* 45 (1983) 251–262. *LJ*

2240 Wistrich, Robert Solomon (1945–): Karl Marx and the Jewish Question. *Soviet Jewish Affairs* 4 (1974) 53–60. *LJ*

2241 Wistrich, Robert Solomon (1945–): Karl Marx, German Socialists and the Jewish Question, 1886–1914. *Soviet Jewish Affairs* 3 (1973) 92–97. *LJ*

2242 Wistrich, Robert Solomon (1945–): Socialism and Antisemitism in Austria before 1914. *J.S.St.* 37 (1975) 323–332. *LJ*

2243 Wistrich, Robert Solomon (1945–): *Socialism and the Jews; the Dilemmas of Assimilation in Germany and Austria-Hungary.* Rutherford, N.J.: Fairleigh Dickinson University Press, 1982. 435 pp. (The Littman Library of Jewish Civilization)

2244  Wistrich, Robert Solomon (1945–): The SPD and Antisemitism in the 1890's. *European Studies Review* 7 (1977) 177–197. *LJ*

2245  Wistrich, Robert Solomon (1945–): Victor Adler; a Viennese Socialist against Philosemitism. *Wien.Lib.Bull.* 27 (1974) 26–33. *LJ*

2246  Witte, Carl: *Mein Konflikt mit dem Herrn Hof- und Domprediger Stoecker; eine Rechtfertigung und ein Appell.* Berlin: F. Fontane, 1899. 57 pp. *LJ*

2247  Witte, Carl: *Schneider Grüneberg und Hofprediger Stoecker; oder, Der gefälschte Brief.* Berlin: F. Fontane, 1896. 51 pp. *LJ*

2248  Witte, Carl: *Wider das Stoecker'sche "Volk."* Berlin: F. Fontane, 1890. 99 pp. *LJ*

2249  Wittels, Fritz: *Der Taufjude.* Leipzig: M. Breitenstein, 1904. 40 pp. *LJ*

2250  Wolf, Arthur: *Die Juden in Basel, 1543–1872.* Basel: 1909. 157 pp. *LJ*

2251  Wolf, Gerson (1823–1892): *Der Abfall vom Christentum und der Uebertritt zum Judentume.* Wien: Herzfeld & Bauer, 1868. 21 pp. *LJ*

2252  Wolf, Gerson (1823–1892): *Geschichte der Juden in Wien 1156–1876.* Wien: Alfred Hölder, 1876. 282 pp. *LJ*

2253  Wolf, Gerson (1823–1892): *Die Juden. Mit einer Schlußbetrachtung von Wilhelm Goldbaum.* Wien: K. Prochaska, 1883. 177 pp. (Die Völker Oesterreich-Ungarns, 7) *LJ*

2254  Wolf, Gerson (1823–1892): *Judentaufen in Oesterreich. Nach Archivalien des K.K. Ministerium des Aeußern, der k.K. Staats-, Finanz- und Justizministerien der k. ungarischen Hofkanzlei, etc.* Wien: Herzfeld, 1863. 209 pp. *LJ*

2255  Wolff, Isidor: *Die Verbreitung des Turnens unter den Juden.* Berlin: L. Lamm, 1907. 12 pp. *LJ*

2256  Wolff, Siegfried: *Das Recht der israelitischen Religionsgemeinschaft des Großherzogtums Baden.* Karlsruhe: G. Braun, 1913. XVII, 250 pp. (Freiburger Abhandlungen aus dem Gebiete des öffentlichen Rechts, 22) *LJ*

2257  Wolff, Theodor (1867–1943): Der Jude Ballin. *Der Marsch durch zwei Jahrzehnte.* Amsterdam: De Lange, 1936. pp. 238–282. *LJ*

2258 Wolffberg, D.: *Mortara; oder, Das Ereignis von Bologna. Nach den authentischen Quellen erzählt und betrachtet: Ein Beitrag zur Kulturgeschichte des 19. Jahrhunderts.* Stettin: Grassmann, 1859. 30 pp. *Unseen*

2259 *Ein Wort an die deutschen Staatsbürger jüdischen Glaubens.* Mainz: J. Wirth'sche Hofbuchdruckerei, 1896. 10 pp. *LJ*

2260 *Ein Wort zur Judenfrage.* Von einem ehemaligen Juden. Berlin: Heinicke, 1880. 19 pp. *Unseen*

2261 *Worte des Dankes an Seine Ehrwürden Herrn Bezirksrabbiner Dr. J. S. Bloch.* Gesammelt und hrsg. von Mitgliedern der Israelitischen Kultusgemeinde Floridsdorf. Wien: M. Waizner, 1883. 21, 15 pp. *LJ*

2262 *Wozu der Lärm! Talmudauszüge in philosemitischer und antisemitischer Beleuchtung.* Leipzig: Verlag der Neuen Deutschen Zeitung, 1892. 47 pp. *Unseen*

2263 Wünsche, August: *Der Talmud; eine Skizze.* Zürich: Verlags-Magazin, 1879. 40 pp. *LJ*

2264 Wüst, Fritz: *Eine Entgegnung auf "Die Grundlagen des 19. Jahrhunderts," von Houston Stewart Chamberlain.* Stuttgart: Strecker & Schröder, 1905. 245 pp. *LTA*

2265 Wussow, Otto Erich von: *Geschichte und Entwicklung der Warenhäuser nach Mitteilungen von Oskar Tietz.* Berlin: Verlag für Sprach- und Handelswissenschaft, 1906. IV, 84 pp. (Handel, Industrie und Verkehr in Einzeldarstellungen, 5) *Unseen*

2266 Wutzdorff (district judge): Fruchtbarkeit der letzten Zeit unserer Kirche für die Judenmission. *SaH* 33 (1896) 39-49. *LJ*

2267 Wutzdorff (district judge): Israel wird in die Wüste geführt werden. *SaH* 33 (1896) 103-110. *LJ*

2268 Wutzdorff (district judge): Judenchrist ohne Sakramentsglauben. *SaH* 33 (1896) 232-240. *LJ*

2269 Wutzdorff (district judge): Zeit der Bekehrung des israelitischen Volkes. *SaH* 34 (1897) 95-104. *Unseen*

2270 Wutzdorff (district judge): Zu den jüdisch-christlichen Gedanken und Hoffnungen. *SaH* 38 (1901) 39-41. *Unseen*

2271  Wyler, Fritz: *Die staatsrechtliche Stellung der israelitischen Religionsgenossenschaften in der Schweiz.* Glarus: Tschudy, 1929. 206 pp. (Glarner Beiträge zur Geschichte, Rechtswissenschaft, Sozialpolitik und Wirtschaftskunde, 10) *LJ*

      Diss. Zürich.

2272  *Der Xantener Knabenmord vor dem Schwurgericht zu Kleve 4-14 Juli 1892.* Vollständiger stenographischer Bericht. Berlin: S. Cronbach, 1893. 8, 507, 2 pp. *LJ*

2273  Yerushalmi, Yosef Hayim: *Assimilation and Racial Antisemitism; the Iberian and the German Models.* New York: Leo-Baeck-Institute, 1982. 38 pp. (LBI memorial lecture, 26) *LJ*

2274  Young, E. J.: *Gobineau und der Rassismus; eine Kritik der anthropologischen Geschichtstheorie.* Meisenheim am Glan: Hain, 1968. XVI,363 pp. (Archiv für vergleichende Kulturwissenschaft, 4) *LV*

2275  Zach, Franz (1876-): *Die Juden — die Herren der Welt.* Klagenfurt: Corinthia, 1912. 64 pp. (Volksaufklärung, 161-162) *Unseen*

2276  Zander, Alfred: *Dokumente zur Judenfrage in der Schweiz. T. 2: Seit 1789; Juden werden Schweizer, von Arnold Ambrunnen, pseud.* Zürich: Verlag Eidgenössische Schriften, 1935. 64 pp. *LB*

2277  Zander, C., ed.: *Handbuch enthaltend die sämtlichen Bestimmungen über die Verhältnisse der Juden.* 2. Aufl. Leipzig: K. Scholtze, 1885. XII, 124, 13 pp. *LJ*

      Despite new legislation granting Jews equality before the law, many restrictions still exist with regard to them.

2278  Zelinsky, Hartmut: Der Kapellmeister Hermann Levi und seine Stellung zu Richard Wagner und Bayreuth; oder, Der Tod als Gralsgebiet. *TAJfDG* Beiheft 6 (1984) 309-351. *LJ*

2279  Zelle, W.: *Wer hat Ernst Winter ermordet? Eine psychologische Studie.* Braunschweig: R. Sattler, 1904. 24 pp. *LJ*

2280  *Zentral-Anzeiger für Jüdische Literatur.* Hrsg. von N. Brüll. Nr. 1-6. Frankfurt a.M.: 1890. 1 vol. *LJ*

      Supersedes *Jahrbücher für Jüdische Geschichte und Literatur.* No more published.

2281 *Zentralverein des Nichtjudenbundes von Ungarn: Statuten-Entwurf . . .*
Ausgearb. von Victor Istóczy. Berlin: O. Hentze, 1880. 11 pp. *LJ*

2282 Zepler, Georg: Demokratie und Antisemitismus; zur Judenfrage. *Neue Demokratie — Richtlinien für bürgerliche Politik.* Berlin: Walther, 1909. Pp. 114–142. *LTA*

2283 *Eine zerstörte Kultur; jüdisches Leben in Wien seit dem 19. Jahrhundert.* Hrsg.: Gerhard Botz, Ivar Oxaal, Michael Pollak. Buchloe: Obermayer, 1990. 427 pp. *LJ*

2284 Zetterbaum, Max: Klassengegensätze bei den Juden. *N.Z.* 11, 2 (1892/93) 4–12, 36–43. *LJ*

2285 *Zeuge Stoecker; ein Zeitbild aus dem Jahre 1885. Die Prozeßverhandlungen wegen Beleidigung des Hofpredigers Stoecker vor der 2. Strafkammer des Landesgerichts Berlin I am 9., 10., 13. und 16. Juni.* Nebst erläuternden und ergänzenden Anmerkungen. Berlin: Fortschritt, 1885. 62 pp. *LB*

2286 Ziegler, Theobald (1846–1918): Th. Ziegler über den Antisemitismus. *Populärwissenschaftliche Monatsblätter zur Belehrung über das Judentum* 19 (1899) 145–148. *LJ*

2287 Ziethe, Wilhelm (1824–1901): *Israels Notstand und Nothelfer; Predigt über Apostelgeschichte 3, 1–10 am Jahresfeste der Gesellschaft zur Beförderung des Christentums unter den Juden , des 5. Juni 1860 in der Louisenstadt-Kirche gehalten.* Berlin: Jahnke, 1860. 16 pp. *Unseen*

2288 Zimmer, Georg, ed.: *Der Mord in Konitz am 11. März 1900. Die öffentlichen Gerichtsverhandlungen in der Winter'schen Mordaffäre.* Bearb. und hrsg. Konitz: Selbstverlag des Verfassers, 1900. 6 pts. *LJ*

2289 Zimmermann, Moshe (1943-): From Radicalism to Antisemitism. *Antisemitism through the Ages; a Collection of Essays.* Ed. Shmuel Almog. Oxford: Pergamon Press, 1988. pp. 241–254. *LJ*

On Wilhelm Marr's development from a radical socialist to a reactionary antisemite and champion of the antisemitic movement.

2290 Zimmermann, Moshe (1943-): Gabriel Riesser und Wilhelm Marr im Meinungsstreit; die Judenfrage als Gegenstand der Auseinandersetzung zwischen Liberalen und Radikalen in Hamburg, 1848–1862. *Zeitschrift des Vereins für Hamburgische Geschichte* 61 (1975) 59–84. *Unseen*

2291 Zimmermann, Moshe (1943-), ed.: *Hamburgischer Patriotismus und deutscher Nationalismus; die Emanzipation der Juden in Hamburg, 1830–1865.* Hamburg:

H. Christians, 1979. 266 pp. (Hamburger Beiträge zur Geschichte der deutschen Juden, 6) *LJ*

2292  Zimmermann, Moshe (1943–): Two Generations in the History of German Antisemitism — the Letters of Theodor Fritsch to Wilhelm Marr. *LBIYB* 23 (1978) 89–100. *LJ*

2293  Zimmermann, Moshe (1943–): *Wilhelm Marr; the Patriarch of Antisemitism.* New York: Oxford University Press, 1986. XII, 178 pp. (Studies in Jewish History) *LJ*

On the development of modern antisemtism in the 19th century, as shown by Wilhelm Marr, one of the first champions of antisemitism. At the end of his life he became one of the strongest critics of the movement.

2294  Zischka, Julius: *Entstehung und Wesen der politischen Parteien.* München: Buchhdlg. des Nationalverein, 1911. 24 pp. (Badische national-liberale Bibliothek, 5) *Unseen*

2295  Zmarzlik, Hans Günther: Antisemitismus im Deutschen Kaiserreich, 1871–1918. *Die Juden als Minderheit in der Geschichte.* Eds. Bernd Martin, Ernst Schulen. München: Deutscher Taschenbuch-Verlag, 1981. pp. 249–270. *LJ*

2296  Zmarzlik, Hans Günther: Der Antisemitismus im Zweiten Reich. *Geschichte in Wissenschaft und Unterricht* 14 (1963) 273–286. *LJ*

On two sources of the antisemitic movement: Anticapitalism, nationalism and the Jewish problem which is actually a non-Jewish one.

2297  Zohn, Harry: Fin de Siècle; the Jewish Contribution. *The Jewish Response to German Culture; from the Enlightenment to the Second World War.* Eds. Jehuda Reinharz, Walter Schatzberg. Hannover: N.H., 1985. pp. 137–149. *LJ*

2298  Zollschan, Ignaz (1877–1948): *Jewish Questions; Three Lectures.* New York: Bloch Publ. Co., 1914. 66 pp. *LJ*

2299  Zollschan, Ignaz (1877–1948): *Das Rassenproblem unter besonderer Berücksichtigung der theoretischen Grundlagen der jüdischen Rassenfrage.* Wien: Braumüller, 1910. VII, 491 pp. *LJ*

2300  Zollschan, Ignaz (1877–1948): Taufe, Rasse, Zukunft; Vortrag gehalten in der "Oesterreichisch-Israelitischen Union" am 26. November 1910. *Monatsschrift der Oesterreichisch-Israelitischen Union* 22, 12 (1910) 1–28. *LJ*

2301  Zoltai, Denes: Wagner, hier et aujourdhui. *Neohelicon* 11 (1984) 43–63. *LJ*

2302  Zschäck, Fritz: War Wilhelm Marr ein Jude? *Weltkampf* 4 (1944) 94–98. *LB*

2303  Zucker, Stanley (1936–): Ludwig Bamberger and the Rise of Antisemitism in Germany, 1848–1893. *Central European History* 3 (1970) 332–352. *LJ*

2304  Zucker, Stanley (1936–): *Ludwig Bamberger; German Liberal Politician and Social Critic, 1823–1899.* Pittsburgh: University of Pittsburgh Press, 1975. XI, 343 pp. *LJ*

2305  Zuckermann, Mendel: *Die Stellung der Hannoverschen Regierung zur Judenemanzipation auf dem Wiener Kongreß und der Bundesversammlung zu Frankfurt a.M.* Hannover: 1901. 14 pp. *LC*

2306  Zuckermann, Mosche: Die Ideologie Richard Wagners als politisches Paradigma Deutschlands. *TAJfDG* 13 (1984) 179–212. *LJ*

2307  *Der zukünftige Musik-Heiland Richard Wagner vor der öffentlichen Meinung; Antwort auf dessen Broschüre "Das Judentum in der Musik." Von einem Christen, den die Natur mit gesunder Vernunft und natürlicher Logik versehen hat.* Leipzig: F. Arndt, 1869. 16 pp. *Unseen*

2308  Die Zukunft der Juden. *I.Dt.R.* 18 (1912) 209–215. *LJ*

2309  Zunz, Leopold (1794–1886): *Die Vorschriften über die Eidesleistung der Juden.* Berlin: J. Springer, 1859. 29 pp. *LJ*

2310  Zur Judenfrage. *Deutsche Worte* 18 (1898) 535–552. *LF*

    Viewpoint on N. Syrkin's article in the July issue of 1898.

2311  Zur Mühlen, Patrik von: *Rassenideologien; Geschichte und Hintergründe.* Berlin: Dietz, 1977. 278 pp. (Internationale Bibliothek, 102) *LJ*

    Summary of the various racial theories in western countries and their influence on antisemitism, the Jews and politics.

# LITERATURE AND THE ARTS

## 2312

שטיין, אריה: דמות היהודי בחיי החברה בגרמניה ביצירת סופרים לא יהודיים
בהבט היסטורי; משנות האיחוד הלאומי עד תקופת ווימאר. ת"א, 1985, 2
כרכים. דיס. אונ. ת"א.

[Stein, Arjeh: *The Image of the Jew in the German Society according to Works of German Non-Jewish Authors during the Period of National Unification until the Weimar Era As Seen from an Historical Aspect.* Tel-Aviv: 1985. 2 vol.] *LJ*

2313 Allenspach, Alfred: *Dreizehn Lieder und Parodien.* Kassel: Selbstverlag, 1897. 8 pp. *LJ*

2314 Ambach, Eduard von: *Der Jude; oder, Neigung und Pflicht. Ein Charakter- und Zeitgemälde aus dem vorigen Jahrhundert. Der reiferen Jugend gewidmet von dem Verfasser "Die Kinder der Witwe."* Regensburg: Manz, 1850. 184 pp. *Unseen*

2315 Angel, Pierre: *Le personnage juif dans le roman allemand (1855–1915). La racine littéraire de l'antisémitisme outre-Rhin.* Paris: Didier, 1973. 223 pp. (Coll. Germanica, 12) *LJ*

2316 *Antisemitische Harfenklänge; ernste und heitere Deklamationen.* 5. bedeutend verm. Aufl. Marburg: Reichs-Herold, 1889. 232 pp. *LJ*

2317 Arnim, Bettina (Brentano) von (1785–1859): Die Klosterbeere. Zum Andenken an die Frankfurter Judengasse. *Gespräche mit Dämonen. Bd. 7.* Berlin: Propyläen-Verlag, 1922. Pp. 18–70. *LJ*

First published in 1852.

2318 Barre, Ernst: *Bekehrt; Lustspiel in einem Akt.* Leipzig: A. Edelmann, 1869. 28 pp. *LF*

2319   Bartels, Adolf (1862–1945): *Ein Berliner Literaturhistoriker Dr. Richard M. Meyer und seine "Deutsche Litteratur."* Leipzig: G.H. Meyer, 1900. 80 pp. (Flugschriften der Heimat, 1) *LF*

2320   Bartels, Adolf (1862–1945): *Deutsches Schrifttum; Betrachtungen und Bemerkungen.* Weimar: A. Duncker, 1911. 192 pp. *LTA*

2321   Bartels, Adolf (1862–1945): *Friedrich Hebbel und die Juden; das literarische Judentum seiner Zeit.* München: Deutscher Volksverlag, 1922. 64 pp. (Deutschlands führende Männer und das Judentum, vol. 5) *LJ*

2322   Bartels, Adolf (1862–1945): *Kritiker und Kritikaster; pro domo et pro arte. Mit einem Anhang: Das Judentum in der deutschen Literatur.* Leipzig: E. Avenarius, 1903. 124 pp. *LC*

2323   Bartsch, Rudolf Hans (1873–1952): *Elisabeth Kött.* Leipzig: L. Staakmann, 1910. 312 pp. *LJ*

2324   Bartsch, Rudolf Hans (1873–1952): *Der letzte Student. Roman.* Berlin: Ullstein, 1913. 318 pp. *LJ*

   Revision of *Als Oesterreich zerfiel*, 1848.

2325   Bartsch, Rudolf Hans (1873–1952): *Zwölf aus der Steiermark.* Leipzig: L. Staakmann, 1909. 383 pp. *LJ*

2326   Bass, Josef: Darstellung der Juden im deutschen Roman des 20. Jahrhunderts. *MGWJ* 57 (1913) 641–665; 58 (1914) 97–112, 359–377; 59 (1915) 13–33; 60 (1916) 140–148, 302–312. *LJ*

2327   Bass, Josef: Die Juden bei Wilhelm Raabe. *MGWJ* 54 (1910) 644–680. *LJ*

2328   Bauer, Edwin: *Der Baron Vampyr; ein Kulturbild aus der Gegenwart.* Berlin: P. Heichen, 1892. 129 pp. *LB*

2329   Becker, August (1828–1891): *Des Rabbi Vermächtnis: Roman.* Abt. 1–3. Berlin: O. Janke, 1866. 3 vols. *LC*

2330   Behr, J.: *Das Opfer des Wucherers; soziale Novelle.* Kaiserslautern: Gotthold's Verlag, 1888. 142 pp. *LTA*

2331   Bierbaum, Otto Julius (1865–1910): *Prinz Kuckuck; Leben, Taten, Meinungen und Höllenfahrt eines Wollüstlings. In einem Zeitroman.* München: Georg Müller, 1907–1908. 3 vols. *LJ*

2332 Blechner, Heinrich: *Schmul-Leeb-Kohn; ein zeitgeschichtliches Kulturbild, von Intimus, pseud.* Wien: Typ. A. Scharf, 1892. 52 pp. *LJ*

2333 Borchardt, Georg Hermann (1871–1943): *Jettchen Geberts Geschichte; Roman.* 2. Aufl. Berlin: E. Fleischel & Co., 1912–1914. 2 vols. *LJ*

2334 Borchardt, Georg Hermann (1871–1943): *Die Nacht des Dr. Herzfeld.* Berlin: E. Fleischel & Co., 1912. 297 pp. *LJ*

2335 Bramsted, Ernest Kohn: Middle Class Superiority, 1850–1870; Towards the Jews. *Aristocracy and the Middle Classes in Germany. Social Types in German Literature, 1830–1900.* Rev. ed. With a foreword by G.P. Gooch. Chicago: University of Chicago Press, 1964. Pp. 132–149. *LJ*

2336 Brod, Max (1884–1968): *Jüdinnen; Roman.* Berlin: A. Juncker, 1911. 270 pp. *LJ*

2337 Brod, Max (1884–1968): *Die Retterin.* Leipzig: K. Wolff, 1914. 101 pp. *LJ*

2338 Bronner, Ferdinand (1867–1948): *Schmelz, der Nibelunge; Komödie, von Franz Adamus, pseud.* Wien: Wiener Verlag, 1905. 243 pp. *LJ*

2339 Brown, G.: *Strousberg; oder, Es ist nicht alles Gold was glänzt; Zeitgemälde in 7 Abteilungen.* Berlin: Typ. R. Bittner, 1875. 37 pp. *Unseen*
    A play.

2340 Bunte, Wolfgang: *Peter Rosegger und das Judentum; Altes und Neues Testament, Antisemitismus, Judentum und Zionismus.* Hildesheim: Olms, 1977. 453 pp. (Judaistische Texte und Studien, 61) *LJ*

2341 Burte, Hermann, pseud. (1879–1960): *Wiltfeber — der ewige Deutsche.* 5. Aufl. Leipzig: G.K. Sarasan, 1912. 353 pp. *LJ*

2342 Capilleri, Wilhelm: *Die Antisemiten; episches Zeitgedicht.* Wien: D. Löwy, 1884. 16 pp. *LV*

2343 Caspari, Karl Heinrich: *Christ und Jude; eine Erzählung aus dem 16. Jahrhundert für das deutsche Volk in Stadt und Land.* Erlangen: Bläsing, 1861. 232 pp. *LJ*

2344 Claussen, A.: *Nach der goldenen Stadt: Erzählung . . .* Mit einem Nachwort von W. Faber. Leipzig: W. Faber, 1893. 102 pp. (Institutum Judaicum in Leipzig, 35–36) *Unseen*

2345 Cohn, Clementine: *Der Herr Hofprediger hat gesagt . . . und anderes. Moderne Zeitbilder, von C. Berg, pseud.* Berlin: S. Cronbach, 1892. 103 pp. *LJ*

2346 Cohnfeld, Adalbert Dorotheus Salomon (1809–1868): *Neue Verfassung! Halt! Dir muß ick mir koofen; ein Lebenszeichen von August Buddelmeier, Dages Schriftsteller mit jroßem Bart.* Berlin: W.Rosahl, 1848. 7 pp. *Unseen*

2347 Cohnfeld, Adalbert Dorotheus Salomon (1809–1868): *Die pollitischen Bandjuden und die kurze Elle, die muß der Deibel holen; eine Jahrnachtsrede.* Berlin: Typ. J. Sittenfeld, 1848–1849. 1l. (Flugblatt, 1848–1849) *Unseen*

2348 Cumberland, Richard (1732–1811): *Der Jude; Schauspiel in 5 Akten.* Stuttgart: Verlag der Expedition Freys, 1868. 52 pp. *LC*

Tr. from the English.

2349 Dahn, Felix (1834–1912): *Ein Kampf um Rom.* Leipzig: Breitkopf & Härtel, 1938. 2 vols. *LJ*

First published in 1876.

2350 David, Jakob Julius (1859–1906): *Die Hanna; Erzählungen aus Mähren.* Berlin: Schuster & Löffler, 1904. 258 pp. *LJ*

2351 Diel, Johannes Baptiste: *Der Steinmetz zu Köln.* Einsiedeln: Eberle und Rickenbach, 1893. 64 pp. (Nimm und lies! Ser. 2, 29) *Unseen*

2352 Dingelstedt, Franz: *Die Amazone; Roman.* Stuttgart: Hallberger, 1868. 2 vols. *Unseen*

2353 Dresch, Joseph Emile (1871–): Doit et avoir. *Le roman social en Allemagne.* Paris: F. Alcan, 1913. Pp. 100–123. *LF*

*Doit et avoir* first published in 1855.

2354 Ebner-Eschenbach, Marie von (1830–1916): Der Kreisphysikus. *Sämtliche Werke. Bd. 2.* Berlin: Pätel, 1920. Pp. 3–81. *LJ*

First published in 1883.

2355 Elisa, Baronin von . . . : *Juden und Christen; oder, Die Zivilehe. Eine Geschichte aus Hamburg.* 2 Bde. Leipzig: Kollmann, 1852. 347 pp. (2 vols.). *LJ*

2356 Elmar, Karl, pseud. (1815–1888): *Ein Jüdischer Dienstbote; Charakterbild mit Gesang in 3 Akten. Musik von J.B. Klerr.* Wien: Wallishaussersche Buchhdlg., 1867. 32 p. (Wiener Theater — Repertoir, 168) *Unseen*

2357  Elösser, Arthur (1870–1938): *Vom Ghetto nach Europa; das Judentum im geistigen Leben des 19. Jahrhunderts.* Berlin: Jüdische Buchvereinigung, 1936. 292 pp. *LJ*

2358  Engel de Janosi, Joseph (1851–): *Der Kabbalist; Trauerspiel in 3 Aufzügen.* Dresden: E. Pierson, 1909. 6, 80 pp. *Unseen*

2359  Ertl, Emil (1860–): *Freiheit, die ich meine; Roman aus der Sturmzeit.* Leipzig: L.Staakmann, 1925. 582 pp. *LF*

      First published 1909.

2360  Fockt, Carl Theodor: *Esther Solymossy, das Mädchen von Tísza-Eszlár; Sensationsroman.* Leipzig: Hugo Kröhl, 1883–84. 416 pp. *Unseen*

2361  Fontane, Theodor (1819–1898): *L'Adultera. Romane und Erzählungen. Bd. 3.* Berlin: Aufbau-Verlag, 1969. Pp. 109–251. *LJ*

      First ed.: 1882.

2362  Franzos, Karl Emil (1848–1904): *Die Juden von Barnow; Geschichten.* 5. stark verm. Aufl. Stuttgart: A. Bonz, 1894. IX, 348 pp. *LJ*

2363  Franzos, Karl Emil (1848–1904): *Judith Trachtenberg; Erzählung.* 2. Aufl. Breslau: E. Trewendt, 1891. 339 pp. *LJ*

2364  Franzos, Karl Emil (1848–1904): *Leib Weihnachtskuchen und sein Kind; Erzählung.* Jena: H. Costenoble, 1896. 351 pp. *LJ*

2365  Franzos, Karl Emil (1848–1904): *Moschko von Parma; Geschichte eines jüdischen Soldaten.* Leipzig: Duncker & Humblot, 1880. 311 pp. *LJ*

2366  Franzos, Karl Emil (1848–1904): *Der Pojaz; eine Geschichte aus dem Osten.* 2 Aufl. Stuttgart: J.G. Cotta, 1905. 486 pp. *LJ*

2367  Frenzel, Elisabeth: *Judengestalten auf der deutschen Bühne; ein notwendiger Querschnitt durch 700 Jahre Rollengeschichte.* München: Deutscher Volksverlag, 1942. Pp. 76–216. *LJ*

2368  Freytag, Gustav (1816–1895): *Die Journalisten; Lustspiel in vier Akten.* 16. Aufl. Leipzig: S. Hirzel, 1902. 152 pp. *LJ*

2369  Freytag, Gustav (1816–1895): *Soll und Haben; Roman.* Leipzig: Hirzel, 1855. 3 vols. *LJ*

2370 Friedländer, Moritz (1844-1919): *Vom Cheder zur Werkstätte; eine Erzählung aus dem Leben der Juden in Galizien, von F. v. St. G., pseud.* Wien: A. Hölder, 1885. 40 pp. *LJ*

2371 Frisch, Efraim (1873-1942): *Das Verlöbnis; Geschichte eines Knaben.* Berlin: S. Fischer, 1902. 199 pp. *LJ*

2372 Geiger, Ludwig (1848-1919): *Die deutsche Literatur und die Juden.* Berlin: G. Reimer, 1910. X, 304 pp. *LJ*

2373 Geiger, Ludwig (1848-1919): Die Juden und die deutsche Literatur. *MGWJ* 50 (1906) 351-369, 444-468. *LJ*

2374 Gelber, Mark H. (1951-): Wandlungen im Bild des "gebildeten Juden" in der deutschen Literatur. *TAJfDG* 13 (1984) 165-178. *LJ*

2375 Gelber, Mark H. (1951-): What is Literary Antisemitism. *J.S.St.* 47 (1985) 1-20. *LJ*

2376 Gödsche, Hermann (1816-1878): *Auf dem Judenkirchhof in Prag.* Eingeleitet und hrsg. von Johann v. Leers. Berlin: P. Stegemann, 1933. 46 pp. (Die Erhebung; Dokumente zur Zeitgeschichte) *LJ*

A chapter from the author's book *Biarritz*, 187-.

2377 Gödsche, Hermann (1816-1878): *Biarritz; historisch-politischer Roman aus der Gegenwart.* Straubing: F. Klüber, 1909. 8 vols. *LC*

2378 Gödsche, Hermann (1816-1878): *Gäeta-Düppel.* Berlin: Verlagsgesellschaft Berlin, 1906. 4 vols. *LC*

2379 Gödsche, Hermann (1816-1878): *Das Geheimnis der jüdischen Weltherrschaft. Aus einem Werke des vorigen Jahrhunderts, das von den Juden aufgekauft ward und aus dem Buchhandel verschwand.* Berlin: Verlag "Deutsches Wochenblatt," 1919. 47 pp. *LJ*

Offprint of a chapter from the author's book *Biarritz*, 187-.

2380 Goldstein, Moritz: Deutsch-jüdischer Parnass. *Der Kunstwart* 25 (1912) 281-294. *LJ*

2381 Goldstein, Moritz: German Jewry's Dilemma before 1914; the Story of a Provocative Essay. *LBIYB* 2 (1957) 236-254. *LJ*

This article deals with Goldstein's essay "Deutsch-Jüdischer Parnass" in the *Kunstwart*, 1912, vol. 25, pp. 281-294.

2382  Gordon, Ph: *Jom Kippur; eine Erzählung aus dem jüdischen Volksleben.*
      Leipzig: Ev.-Luth. Zentralverein für Mission unter Israel, 1902. 16 pp.
      (Kleine Schriften zur Judenmission, 3) *Unseen*

2383  Graetz, Heinrich Hirsch (1817-1891): *Shylock in der Sage, im Drama und in
      der Geschichte.* Krotoschin: V.L. Monasch, 1880. 36 pp. *LJ*

2384  Grillparzer, Franz (1791-1872): Esther. *Dramatische Werke. Bd. 1.* Vaduz:
      Liechtenstein Verlag, 1947. Pp. 99-143. *LJ*
      First performance in 1868.

2385  Grillparzer, Franz (1791-1872): Die Jüdin von Toledo. *Sämtliche Werke. Bd.
      9.* Stuttgart: Cotta, 1892. Pp. 133-219. *LJ*

2386  Grünau, Heinrich: *Exil; Drama aus dem jüdischen Leben.* Dresden: E. Pierson,
      1902. 90 pp. *LJ*

2387  Haffner, Adalbert: *Wiener Geschicht'n; für Antisemiten unterm Christbaum.*
      Wien: Selbstverlag, 1895. 76 pp. *LC*

2388  Hainschink, Wiltrud: *Die witzige Kritik; dargestellt an dem als ihren Begründer
      verschrieenen M. G. Saphir unter Berücksichtigung seiner Beeinflussung durch
      Ludwig Börne.* Wien: 1950. 101 l. *Unseen*
      Diss.

2389  Halm, Friedrich, pseud. (1806-1871): *Eine Königin; dramatisches Gedicht in
      4 Akten und einem Nachspiel.* Wien: C. Gerold's Sohn, 1857. 3 l, 168 pp.
      *Unseen*

2390  Hamerling, Robert (1830-1889): *Homunculus; modernes Epos in 10 Gesängen.*
      5. Aufl. Hamburg: Verlagsanstalt und Druckerei Aktiengesellschaft, 1890.
      319 pp. *LJ*

2391  Hansen, H.: *Gefühls-Antisemiten; ein Wiener Zeitbild.* Zürich: C. Schmidt,
      1898. 80 pp. *LJ*

2392  Hansjakob, Heinrich (1837-1916): *In der Karthause; Tagebuchblätter.* Stuttgart:
      A. Bonz, 1901. 415 pp. *Unseen*

2393  Hansjakob, Heinrich (1837-1916): *Schneeballen; Erzählungen aus dem Kinzig.*
      Freiburg: Rombach, 1964. 2 vols. *LF*
      First published in 1893.

2394 Hartmann, Moritz (1821–1872): Der arme Jude. *Reimchronik des Pfaffen Maurizius.* Stuttgart: Cotta, 1874. Pp. 119–122. *LF*

2395 Hauptmann, Karl (1858–1921): *Ismael Friedmann; Roman.* Leipzig: K. Wolff, 1915. 395 pp. *LJ*

First published in 1913.

2396 Hauschner, Auguste (Sobotka) (1851–1924): *Familie Losowitz, Bd. 1; Rudolf and Camilla, Bd. 2.* Berlin: Fleischel, 1908–1910. 2 vols. *LF*

2397 Hauser, Otto (1876–): *Die Juden und Halbjuden in der deutschen Literatur.* Leipzig: E. Schade, 1933. 103 pp. *LC*

2398 Hauser, Otto (1876–): *Das neue Jerusalem; ein jüdischer Roman.* Stuttgart: A. Bonz, 1905. 410 pp. *LJ*

2399 Helbig, Friedrich: *Die Sage vom "Ewigen Juden"; ihre poetische Wandlung und Fortbildung.* Berlin: C.G. Lüderitz, 1874. 56 pp. *LJ*

2400 Hermann, C.: *Jude und Christ; ein Gemälde aus unserer Zeit.* Freiburg i.Br.: Herdersche Verlagsbuchhdlg., 1864. 272 pp. *LJ*

2401 Herzberg-Fränkel, Leopold (1827–1915): *Abtrünnig; ein Lebensbild aus Galizien.* Berlin: H. Engel, 189–. 31 pp. *LJ*

2402 Herzberg-Fränkel, Leopold (1827–1915): *Geheime Wege; Erzählung.* Prag: J.B. Brandeis, 1897. 134 pp. *LJ*

2403 Herzberg-Fränkel, Leopold (1827–1915): *Polnische Juden; Geschichten und Bilder.* 3. verm. Aufl. Stuttgart: C. Grüninger, 1888. 442 pp. *LJ*

2404 Herzberg, Wilhelm: *Jüdische Familienpapiere; Briefe eines Missionairs.* Hamburg: Meissner, 1868. 384 pp. *LJ*

2405 Herzl, Theodor (1860–1904): Altneuland; Roman. *Gesammelte Zionistische Werke. Bd. 5.* Tel Aviv: Hoza'ah Ivrith, 1935. Pp. 125–420. *LJ*

First published in 1902.

2406 Herzl, Theodor (1860–1904): *Das neue Ghetto; Schauspiel in 4 Akten.* Wien: Verlag der Welt, 1897. 100 pp. *LJ*

2407 Heyse, Paul (1830–1914): Judith Stern: Erzählung. *Novellen und Romane. Bd. 6.* Berlin: Hertz, 1881–82. *Unseen*

2408  Hirsch, T. L., ed.: *Jüdisches Witzbuch; amüsante Witze, Humoresken und Anekdoten.* Berlin: Reform-Verlagshaus, 1913. 80 pp. *LJ*

2409  Holitscher, Arthur (1869–1941): *Der Golem; Ghettolegende in 3 Aufzügen.* Berlin: Fischer, 1908. 135 pp. *LJ*

2410  Horch, Hans Otto: Admonitio Judaica; jüdische Debatten über Kinder- und Jugendliteratur im 19. und beginnenden 20. Jahrhundert. *Das Bild des Juden in der Volks- und Jugendliteratur vom 18. Jahrhundert bis 1945.* Ed. Heinrich Pleticha. Königshausen: Neumann, 1985. Pp. 85–102. *LJ*

2411  Hubrich, Peter: *Gustav Freytags deutsche Ideologie in "Soll und Haben."* Kronberg: Scriptor Verlag, 1974. (Scriptor-Hochschulschriften. Literaturwissenschaft, 3) *LC*

2412  Huldschiner, Richard (1872–1931): *Die stille Stadt.* Berlin: E. Fleischel, 1904. 223 pp. *Unseen*

2413  Jäger, Johann Martin (–1923): *Itzick Veit; Original-Schwank in 4 Akten, von Fritz Claus, pseud.* Paderborn: Kleine, 1890. 31 pp. (Kleines Theater, 175) *Unseen*

2414  Jäger, Johann Martin (–1923): *Der Wucherer; tragikomisches Lustspiel in 5 Aufzügen, von Fritz Claus, pseud.* Paderborn: Kleine, 1890. 54 pp. (Kleines Theater, 57) *Unseen*

2415  Jakobowski, Ludwig (1868–1900): *Werther der Jude; Roman.* 6. Aufl. Berlin: Verlag "Berlin-Wien," 1910. 354 pp. *LJ*

2416  Jekelius, Josef Johann: *Pestbeulen; ein Dutzend Dutzendgeschichten aus dem gleichberechtigten Zusammenleben Israels mit Teut. Nebst einem Anhang: ein Satyrspiel nach den Tragödien.* Kronstadt: Jekelius, 1902. 127 pp. *LB*

2417  Jensen Wilhelm (1837–1911): *Die Juden zu Köln; Novelle aus dem Mittelalter.* 2. durchges. Aufl. Berlin: Cronbach, 1897. XV, 278 pp. *LJ*

2418  Jordan, Wilhelm: *Die Sebalds; Roman aus der Gegenwart.* Stuttgart: Deutsche Verlags-Anstalt, 1886. 2 vols. *LJ*

2419  *Ein Jude des 19. Jahrhunderts; historisch-romantisches Charaktergemälde neuerer Zeit.* 2 Bde. Wien: Gerold Verlag, 1850. XII, 454 pp. *LJ*

2420  Jüdische Dramen der Gegenwart. *MGWJ* 12 (1863) 81–92, 121–130. *LJ*

2421 Kahlenberg, Hans von, pseud. (1870–): *Ahasvera.* Berlin: Vita, 1910. 312 pp. *LJ*

2422 Kaiser, Friedrich (1814–1874): *Ein getaufter Jude. Ein Pfaffenleben; Abraham a Santa Clara. Ein historischer Volksroman.* Wien: von Waldheim, 1871. 2 vols. *Unseen*

2423 Kaiser, Friedrich (1814–1874): *Stadt und Land; oder, Der Viehhändler aus Oberösterreich. Posse mit Gesang in 2 Akten.* 4. Aufl. Wien: Wallishauser Buchhdlg., 1875. 37 pp. (Wiener Theater-Repertoir, 261) *LJ*

2424 Kaiser, Georg (1878–): Die jüdische Witwe: biblische Komödie. *Werke. Bd. 1.* Frankfurt a.M.: Propyläen-Verlag, 1971. Pp. 117–198. *LJ*

First published in 1911.

2425 Kalisch, David (1820–1872): *Hunderttausend Taler; Posse in 3 Akten.* Berlin: Hofmann & Comp., 1849. 108 pp. *Unseen*

2426 Katz, Jakob (1904–): Rezeption jüdischer Autoren durch deutsche Kritik und deutsches Publikum. *LBI Bull.* 75 (1986) 41–53. *LJ*

2427 Kaufmann, David (1852–1899): George Eliot und das Judentum. *MGWJ* 26 (1877) 172–188, 214–231, 255–270. *LJ*

2428 Kayserling, Meier (1829–1905): *Die jüdischen Frauen in der Geschichte der Literatur und Kunst.* Leipzig: Brockhaus, 1879. 375 pp. *LJ*

2429 Königsbrun-Schaup, Franz von: *Der ewige Jude in Monte Carlo; ein Wintermärchen von der Riviera.* Leipzig: E. Pierson, 1892. 111 pp. *Unseen*

Poems about Heine.

2430 Kohn, Hans (1891–): *Karl Kraus, Arthur Schnitzler, Otto Weininger; aus dem jüdischen Wien der Jahrhundertwende.* Tübingen: J.C.B. Mohr, 1962. 72 pp. (Schriftenreihe wissenschaftlicher Abhandlungen des LBI, 6) *LJ*

2431 Kompert, Leopold (1822–1886): *Gesammelte Schriften.* Berlin: L. Gerschel, 1882. 2 vols. *LJ*

2432 Kraus, Konrad: *Clarissa; eine Erzählung aus der Rokokozeit.* Mainz: Kirchheim, 1880. 388 pp. *LF*

2433 Kretzer, Max (1854–1941): *Irrlichter und Gespenster; Volksroman.* Weimar: Schriften-Vertriebsanstalt, 1893. 3 vols. *Unseen*

2434  Kretzer, Max (1854–1941): *Die Verkommenen; Berliner Sittenroman.* Mit einem
      Vorwort des Verfassers. Berlin: F. Luckhardt, 1883. 2 vols in 1. *LC*

2435  Landsberger, Artur (1876–1933): *Millionäre; ein Berliner Roman.* 20. Aufl.
      München: G. Müller, 1918. 389 pp. *LJ*
      First published in 1913.

2436  Lange, Ernst Philipp Karl (1813–1899): *Jane, die Jüdin; Roman.* 4. Aufl.
      Leipzig: A. Schumann, 18––. 2 vols. *LJ*
      First published in 1867.

2437  Laube, Heinrich (1806–1884): Ruben; ein moderner Roman. *Gesammelte
      Werke. Bd. 48.* Leipzig: Max Hesse, 1909. Pp. 1–221. *LJ*

2438  Lea, Charlene Ann: *Emancipation, Assimilation and Stereotype; the Image of
      the Jew in German and Austrian Drama, 1800–1850.* Bonn: Bouvier–Verlag,
      1978. VIII, 171 pp. *LJ*

2439  Levita, Benedictus, pseud.: *Der König von Juda; eine Geschichte die einmal
      wahr werden könnte.* Leipzig: Dietrichsche Verlagshdlg., 1912. V, 376 pp. *LJ*

2440  L'gocki, Josef von: *Der antisemitische Vogel; Humoreske.* Budapest: Posner,
      1884. IV, 63 pp. *LC*

2441  Lichtenstein, Edmund (1864–): *Der Fluch auf Juda! Von Lorenz Stahl, pseud.*
      Berlin: J. van Groningen, 1893. 39 pp. *LJ*

2442  Lindau, Paul (1839–1917): *Gräfin Lea; Schauspiel in 5 Aufzügen.* Berlin:
      Freund & Jeckel, 1880. V, 112 pp. *LV*

2443  Lindauer, Saul: *Die Schöpfungsgeschichte der "Gräfin Lea"; ein deutscher
      Fastnachtsschwank.* Berlin: O. Lorentz, 1881. 35 pp. *LJ*

2444  Liptzin, Solomon (1901–): *Germany's stepchildren.* Philadelphia, PA: Jewish
      Publication Society, 1944. VIII, 298 pp. *LJ*

2445  Löns, Hermann (1866–1914): *Das zweite Gesicht; eine Liebesgeschichte.* Jena:
      Diederichs, 1918. 272 pp. *LJ*
      First ed. 1911.

2446  Löwenberg, Jakob (1856–1929): *Aus zwei Quellen; Roman.* Berlin: E. Fleischel,
      1919. 295 pp. *LJ*
      First ed. 1914.

2447  Lorens, Carl: *Die kleine jüdische Fischerin; Parodie im jüdischen Dialekt nach bekannter Melodie.* Wien: 1885. 1 vol. *Unseen*

2448  Louis-Gabriel, Sister: The Jew in 19th Century Literature. *Jewish Affairs* 19 (1964) 17–20. *LJ*

"Article . . . condensed . . . of a thesis . . . published in 'Common Ground' . . . Council of Christians and Jews in England."

2449  Lucka, Samuel Benedikt: *Die Antisemiten und das Blutmärchen; Novelle, von Dr. S.L. Senex, pseud.* Wien: M. Waizner, 1887. 56 pp. *LJ*

2450  Ludwig, Otto (1813–1865): *Die Makkabäer; Trauerspiel in 5 Akten.* Hrsg. und bearb. von Robert Petsch. Leipzig: B. G. Teubner, 1902. XIV, 95 pp. (Teubners Sammlung, vol. 28) *LJ*

First ed. 1852.

2451  Mann, Heinrich (1871–1950): *Im Schlaraffenland.* München: A. Langen, 1900. 494 pp. *LJ*

2452  Martell, Carl: *Der letzte Jude; antisemitischer Roman.* Berlin: G.A. Dewald, 1893. 210 pp. *Unseen*

2453  Mauthner, Fritz (1849–1923): *Der neue Ahasver; Roman aus Jung-Berlin.* 2. Aufl. Dresden: Minden, 1882. 2 vols. *Unseen*

2454  Meissner, Alfred (1822–1885): *Lemberger und Sohn.* Berlin: O. Janke, 1865. 222 pp. *LJ*

2455  Mendelssohn, Erich von: *Nacht und Tag; Roman.* Leipzig: Verlag der Weißen Bücher, 1914. 283 pp. *LV*

2456  Meyer, Rachel (Weiß): *In Banden frei; Roman von Rahel.* Berlin: O. Janke, 1865. 3, 742 pp. (Schriften hrsg. vom Institut zur Förderung der israelitischen Literatur, vol. 10, 1864/1865) *LJ*

2457  Meyr, Melchior (1810–1871): Gleich und gleich. *Neue Erzählungen aus dem Ries. Gesamtausg.; Bd. 4.* Leipzig: Hesses Klassiker-Ausgaben, [n.d.]. *Unseen*

First published in 1856.

2458  Michaelis, Karin (1872–): *Rachel; ein Ghetto-Roman.* Berlin: Concordia, 1910. 246 pp. *LJ*

2459  Mirani, Johann Heinrich: *Eine Judenfamilie; Orginal-Charakterbild in 4 Abteilungen.* Wien: Typ. L. Sommer, 1859. 59 pp. *LJ*

2460  Möbius, Paul: *Bar-Kochba; Trauerspiel in 5 Aufzügen.* Leipzig: J.J. Weber, 1863. 157 pp. *LJ*

2461  Mosenthal, Salomon Hermann von (1821-1877): *Deborah; Volksschauspiel in 4 Aufzügen.* Mit einer biographischen Einleitung. Leipzig: Ph. Reclam jun., [n.d.]. 75 pp. (Reclams Universal-Bibliothek, 4978) *LJ*

2462  Mosenthal, Salomon Hermann von (1821-1877): *Erzählungen aus dem jüdischen Familienleben.* Stuttgart: E. Hallberger, 1878. 2 vols. *LJ*

2463  Mosse, George Lachman (1918-): The Image of the Jew in German Popular Culture; Felix Dahn and Gustav Freytag. *LBIYB* 2 (1957) 218-227. *LJ*

2464  Münchhausen, Börries von (1874-1945): *Juda; Gesänge.* Goslar: F.A. Lattmann, 1900. 95 pp. *LJ*

2465  Münzer, Kurt (1879-1944): *Der Weg nach Zion; ein Roman.* Berlin: A. Juncker, 1907. 604 pp. *LJ*

2466  Nestroy, Johann Nepomuk (1801-1862): *Judith und Holofernes; Travestie in einem Aufzug.* Durchges. und hrsg. von Carl Friedrich Wittmann. Leipzig: Ph. Reclam jun., [n.d.]. 31 pp. (Universal-Bibliothek, 3347) *LJ*

      First published in 1849.

2467  Nordau, Max Simon (1849-1923): *Doktor Kohn; bürgerliches Trauerspiel aus der Gegenwart in 4 Aufzügen.* Berlin: E. Hofmann, 1902. 200 pp. *LJ*

2468  Oertel, Georg: *Der Rainhof; eine Erzählung für das Volk.* Marburg: Verlag des "Reichsherold," 1888. 52 pp. *Unseen*

2469  Oeser, Rudolf Ludwig (1807-1859): *Das Volk und seine Treiber.* Hrsg. von dem Christlichen Vereine im Nördlichen Deutschland. Eisleben: Christlicher Verein für das Nördliche Deutschland, 1859. 276 pp. *LJ*

      An antisemitic novel.

2470  *Oliver, die schwarzen Juden und der jüdische Mädchenhandel; Sensations-Roman.* Berlin: A. Weichert, 1893. 900 pp. *Unseen*

2471  Oppermann, Heinrich Albert: *Hundert Jahre; 1770-1870; Zeit- und Lebensbilder aus drei Generationen.* Leipzig: Brockhaus, 1870. 9 vols. *Unseen*

2472  Pasqué, Ernst (1821-1892): *Der Goldengel von Köln; eine Erzählung aus französischer Zeit. Mit einem Prolog: Anno 1784.* Berlin: Janke, 1867. 940 pp. *Unseen*

2473 Pastor, Willy (1867–1933): *Stimmen der Wüste*. Berlin: Ribera, 1895. 119 pp. *Unseen*

2474 Pazi, Margarita: Berthold Auerbach and Moritz Hartmann; Two Jewish Writers of the Nineteenth Century. *LBIYB* 18 (1973) 201–218. *LJ*

2475 Pazi, Margarita: Jüdisch-deutsche Schriftsteller in Böhmen im 19. Jahrhundert. *TAJfDG* Beiheft 4 (1982) 203–258. *LJ*

2476 Polenz, Wilhelm von (1861–1903): *Der Büttnerbauer*. Berlin: F. Fontane & Co., 1895. 427 pp. *LV*

2477 Polenz, Wilhelm von (1861–1903): *Der Grabenhäger; Roman*. Berlin: F. Fontane, 1898. 2 vols. *LV*

2478 Praxmarer, Josef (1820–1883): *Die Verbrecher der Hochstraße; Erzählungen aus Tirols Vergangenheit*. Innsbruck: Vereinshandlung, 1902. 136, 84 pp. *Unseen*

2479 Prellwitz, Gertrud (1869–1942): Notizen und Besprechungen über Wilhelm von Scholz' Der Jude von Konstanz; Tragödie. *Pr. Jhrb.* 123 (1906) 574–576. *LJ*

2480 Raabe, Wilhelm (1831–1910): *Höxter und Corvey*. Stuttgart: Philipp Reclam jun., 1981. 213 pp. (Universal-Bibliothek, 7729) *LJ*

First published in Westermann's *Illustrierte Deutsche Monatshefte*, April-Mai 1875.

2481 Raabe, Wilhelm (1831–1910): *Hollunderblüte; eine Erinnerung aus dem Hause des Lebens*. Mit Steinzeichnungen von Hugo Steiner-Prag. Weimar: Gesellschaft der Bibliophilen, 1925. 51 pp. *LJ*

First published 1908.

2482 Raabe, Wilhelm (1831–1910): *Der Hungerpastor*. 25. Aufl. Berlin: Otto Janke, 1906. 397 pp. *LJ*

First published 1864.

2483 Reich, Moritz: *An der Grenze; Dorfgeschichten aus Böhmen*. Leipzig: P. Reclam, 1889. 102 pp. *LJ*

2484 Ring, Max (1817–1901): *Der große Krach; Roman*. Jena: Costenoble, 1881. 4 vols. *Unseen*

2485 Riotte, Hermann: *Lippold, der Hofjude; ein Schauspiel in 5 Aufzügen*. Berlin: M. Schulze, 1884. 64 pp. *Unseen*

2486   Rülf, Gutmann: Ein Nachtrag zu Wilhelm Raabe und die Juden. *MGWJ* 55 (1911) 247–251. *LJ*

2487   Saar, Ferdinand von (1833–1906): Seligman, Hirsch. *Novellen aus Oesterreich.* Vol. *3* Leipzig: Max Hesse, [189?]. Pp. 77–115. *LJ*

2488   Sacher-Masoch, Leopold von (1836–1895): *Der Ilau.* Leipzig: E.L. Morgenstern, 1882. 184 pp. *LJ*

2489   Sacher-Masoch, Leopold von (1836–1895): *Judengeschichten.* Leipzig: J.F. Hartknoch, 1878. 128 pp. *LJ*

2490   Salburg-Falkenstein, Edith von (1868–): *Judas im Herrn.* Dresden: Karl Reisner, 1912. 321 pp. *Unseen*

2491   Salburg-Falkenstein, Edith von (1868–): *Ein Konflikt.* 2. Aufl. Dresden: C. Reisner, 1910. 153 pp. *Unseen*

2492   Samuely, Nathan (1846–1921): *Kulturbilder aus dem jüdischen Leben in Galizien.* Prag: Jakob B. Brandeis, 1885. 226 pp. *LJ*

2493   Scherff, Johann: *Das Erntefest; ein humoristisch-patriotisches Festspiel.* Berlin: Dewald, 1890. 12 pp. *LB*

2494   Scherr, Johannes (1817–1886): Die Jesuitin. *Novellenbuch.* Vol. *6.* Leipzig: Hesse and Becker, 1874. 239 pp. *Unseen*

2495   Scherr, Johannes (1817–1886): *Porkeles und Porkelessa; eine böse Geschichte.* Stuttgart: Spemann, 1882. 292 pp. *LJ*

2496   Schiff, Hermann: *Schief-Levinche mit seiner Kalle; oder, Polnische Wirtschaft. Ein komischer Roman.* Vorrede von Isaak Bernays. Hamburg: Hoffmann and Campe, 1848. XXXVI, 287 pp. *LJ*

2497   Schiff, Hermann: *Die wilde Rabbizin; Novelle. Nebst Anhang: I. Corolaria II: Schabbesschmuck der Familie Absatz. Humoristisch-politische Gespräche aus den Jahren 1850–51.* Hamburg: J. P. F. E. Richter, 1866. 69, 40 pp. (Israelitische Novellen, vol. 4) *LJ*

2498   Schlieben, Erwin: *Das Judenschloß. Roman.* Bd. 1–3. Preßburg: G. Heckenast, 1876. 3 vols. *LJ*

2499   Schnitzler, Arthur (1862–1931): Professor Bernhardi; Komödie. *Gesammelte Werke: Die dramatischen Werke.* Vol. *2* Frankfurt a.M.: S. Fischer Verlag, 1962. Pp. 337–463. *LJ*

Opening night, 1912.

2500  Schnitzler, Arthur (1862–1931): *Der Weg ins Freie*. Berlin: S. Fischer, 1908. 491 pp. *LJ*

2501  Schönaich-Carolath, Emil von (1852–1908): *Tauwasser*. Leipzig: G.J. Göschen, 1907. 144 pp. (Gesammelte Werke, vol. 4) *LJ*

2502  Scholz, Marie (Stonawski) (1861–1944): *Rachel*. Dresden: Karl Reissner, 1909. 317 pp. *Unseen*

2503  Scholz, Wilhelm von (1874–1969): *Der Jude von Konstanz; Tragödie in 4 Aufzügen*. Mit einem Nachspiel. München: G. Müller, 1905. 187 pp. *LJ*

2504  Schüller, Helene: *Die Erzählungen von Wilhelm Fischer in Graz; ein Beitrag zur Erkenntnis artfremder Assimilationsliteratur*. Wien: 1939. *Unseen*

Diss.

2505  Shedletzky, Itta: *Literturdiskussion und Belletristik in den jüdischen Zeitschriften in Deutschland 1837–1918*. Jerusalem: 1986. V, 420, 33 l. *LJ*

Ph.D. Thesis, Hebrew University. Hebrew summary.

2506  Sion, Chr.: *Das moderne Ghetto; Berliner Roman*. Berlin: Hesperus Verlag, 1911. 279 pp. *LJ*

2507  Sittenfeld, Konrad (1862–1918): *Wer ist der Stärkere? Ein sozialer Roman aus dem modernen Berlin*. Leipzig: Friedrich, 1888. 2 vols. *LM*

2508  Spielhagen, Friedrich (1829–1911): *Freigeboren*. Leipzig: L. Staakmann, 1900. IV, 399 pp. *LM*

2509  Spielhagen, Friedrich (1829–1911): *In Reih' und Glied*. Leipzig: L. Staakmann, 1883–1888. 2 vols. (Sämtliche Werke, vols. 5–6) *LJ*

2510  Spielhagen, Friedrich (1829–1911): *Die Sturmflut*. 4. Aufl. Leipzig: L. Staakmann, 1878. 2 vols. *LJ*

About the stock market scandal in 1873, and the period thereafter.

2511  Stein, Leopold (1810–1882): *Der Knabenraub von Carpentras; Drama in 4 Aufzügen*. Berlin: G. Heymann, 1863. VIII, 91 pp. *LJ*

2512  Sternberg, Adalbert von: *Der Christengott und der Judengott; Roman*. Wien: Wiener Verlag, 1907. 142 pp. *LJ*

2513 Stoffers, Wilhelm: *Juden und Ghetto in der deutschen Literatur bis zum Ausgang des Weltkrieges.* Graz: H. Stiasnys and Söhne, 1939. 800 pp. *LJ*

Offprint from vol. 12: *Deutsche Quellen und Studien.* Hrsg. von Wilhelm Kosch.

2514 Sturm, Julius (1816-1896): *Israelitische Lieder; eingeführt von F. Delitzsch.* 2. Aufl. von "Israels Weg zur Herrlichkeit." Halle: G. Emil Barthel, 1867. 116 pp. *LJ*

2515 Sudermann, Hermann (1857-1928): *Der Sturmgeselle Sokrates; Komödie in 4 Akten.* Stuttgart: J.G. Cotta, 1903. 170 pp. *LJ*

2516 Teut, pseud.: *Moiseles; Epos in 5 Gesängen.* Wien: Lesk, 1894. 65 pp. *LB*

Illus. by the author.

2517 Teut, pseud.: *Schmule; lustige Reiseabenteuer in 4 Gesängen.* Wien: Selbstverlag, 1905. 70 pp. *LV*

2518 Türk, Karl: *Die Ritter vom Gelde; sozialer Roman.* Leipzig: Th. Fritsch, 1891. 254 pp. *LB*

2519 Voss, Richard (1851-1918): *Dahiel, der Konvertit.* Stuttgart: Deutsche Verlags-Anstalt, 1889. 3 vols. *LJ*

2520 Wächter, Hermann: *Schmock; auch ein Wiener; Roman.* Berlin: Thiel, 1888. 100 pp. *LJ*

2521 Wassermann, Jakob (1873-1934): *Die Juden von Zirndorf; Roman.* Leipzig: Langen, 1897. 459 pp. *LJ*

2522 Weiser, Karl (1848-1910): *Rabbi David; Schauspiel in 5 Aufzügen, von P.W.N. v.S. pseud.* Leipzig: F. Reclam, 189-. 126 pp. *LJ*

Based on Heine's Rabbi von Bacharach.

2523 Wiesinger, Albert: *Das Kruzifix des Juden; historischer Roman aus der Wiener Geschichte des 17. Jahrhunderts.* Klagenfurt: Verlag der St. Joseph Bücherbruderschaft, 190-. 128 pp. *LC*

2524 Wiesinger, R.: *Das Judentum in der deutschen Literatur.* Großenhain: Baumert, 1906. 26 pp. (Deutsche Fragen) *Unseen*

2525 Wrede, Friedrich von: *Die Goldschilds; die Geschichte einer jüdischen Familie.* 3. Aufl. Berlin: E. Hofmann, 1912. 324 pp. *LJ*

2526  Zentner, Herbert: *Das Eindringen des Judentums in die deutsche Literatur des XIX. Jahrhunderts; dargestellt an Moritz Gottlieb Saphir.* Wien: 1939. 216 l. *Unseen*

Diss.

2527  Zweig, Arnold (1887–1968): *Ritualmord in Ungarn; jüdische Tragödie in 5 Aufzügen.* Berlin: Hyperion-Verlag, 1914. 125 pp. *LJ*

# ANTISEMITIC WORKS

2528   *Ahlwardt vor seinen Wählern; Rede gehalten am 14. Mai 1893 in Waldenberg.*
       Dresden: Glöss, 1893. 23 pp. *Unseen*

2529   *Ahlwardt's Heldentaten.* Dresden: Glöss, 1893. 1 l. (Politischer Bilderbogen,
       7) *Unseen*

2530   *Der Antisemitismus und die ethische Bewegung. Mit einem Anhang: Der
       Antisemitismus im Vorschreiten und Die Natur als Anwalt des Rassen-
       antisemitismus.* Berlin: Struppe & Winckler, 1893. 60 pp. *LJ*
       From: *Westfälische Reform.*

2531   Bartels, Adolf (1862–1945): *Judentum und deutsche Literatur; Vortrag gehalten
       am 29. Juni 1910 im Deutschvölkischen Studentenverband in Berlin.* Berlin:
       Volkstümliche Bücherei, 1912. 24 pp. *LJ*

2532   Bauer, Erwin (1857–1901): *Das literarische Berlin, 1887–1892. Offenherzige
       Briefe an den Bankier Itzig Teiteles in Posen von Dr. Isidor Feilchenfeld,
       pseud.* Leipzig: R. Werther, 1893. II, 261 pp. (Aus der Mischpoke, 1) *LJ*

2533   Böttger, Ernst: Trutzjudentum. *Der Hammer* 11 (1912) 93–94. *LB*

2534   Braumann, A.: *Die Antisemiten und Bismarck, dazu einiges über alten und
       neuen Kurs, Bedientenhaftigkeit usw. Ein offenes Wort von dem Verfasser der
       Schriftsr "Großpreußen oder die Neugestaltung Deutschlands."* Leipzig: C.
       Minde, 1892. 50 pp. *Unseen*

2535   Buchholz, Johannes: *Großgrundbesitzer, Bauer und Landarbeiter.* Berlin:
       Hoffschläger, 1893. 48 pp. *LJ*

2536   Bückmann, Karl: *Jugendbewegung und Judenfrage.* Leipzig: Volkeŗ-Verlag,
       191–. 29 pp. *LJ*

2537 Deckert, Joseph (1843–1901): *Jüdische Stechpalmen; Satyren auf Exrabbi Bloch und Cohnsorten.* Wien: "Sendbote des hl. Joseph," 1895. 139 pp. *LTA*

2538 Deckert, Joseph (1843–1901): *Der neugeplante jüdisch-freimaurerische Weltbund; eine kritische Beleuchtung.* Wien: Warnsdorf, 1896. 31 pp. *Unseen*

2539 Deckert, Joseph (1843–1901): *Rassenantisemitismus; auch ein Situationsbild.* Wien: Verlag des "Sendbote des hl. Joseph," 1895. 43 pp. *LJ*

2540 Deckert, Joseph (1843–1901): *Semitische und antisemitische Schlagworte in Doppelbeleuchtung.* Wien: "Sendbote des hl. Joseph," 1897. 87 pp. *LTA*

2541 Deckert, Joseph (1843–1901): *Türkennot und Judenherrschaft. 3 Konferenzreden gehalten den 8. 9. und 10. September 1893 in der St. Joseph-Votivkirche zu Wien XVIII. Weinhaus.* 5. Aufl. Wien: Verlag des "Sendbote des hl. Joseph," 1894. 24 pp. *LJ*

2542 Deckert, Joseph (1843–1901): *Vier Tiroler Kinder, Opfer des chassidischen Fanatismus.* Urkundlich dargestellt. Wien: C. Lesk, 1893. VII, 130 pp. *LJ*

2543 Deckert, Joseph (1843–1901): *Der wahre Israelit vor den Wiener Geschworenen.* Wien: Verlag des "Sendbote des hl. Joseph," 1896. 119 pp. *LTA*

2544 Deckert, Joseph (1843–1901): *Wunder und Wundertäter. 3 Konferenzreden gehalten am 14., 15. und 16. September 1896 in der St. Joseph-Votivkirche zu Weinhaus-Wien.* Wien: Verlag des "Sendbote des hl. Joseph," 1896. 35 pp. *LTA*

2545 Deckert, Joseph (1843–1901): *Die Zivilehe und ihre Gefahren für das christliche Volk; mit besonderer Berücksichtigung der Verhältnisse in Oesterreich-Ungarn.* Wien: H. Kirsch, 1895. XII, 72 pp. *LTA*

2546 *Deckert-Prozeß.* Wien: Verlag der "Reichspost," 1896. 40 pp. *LTA*

   Offprint from: *Reichspost.*

2547 Deeg, Peter: *Hofjuden.* Hrsg. Julius Streicher. Nürnberg: Der Stürmer, 1938. 547 pp. *LJ*

2548 Dehn, Paul (1848–1938): *Diplomatie und Hochfinanz in der rumänischen Judenfrage.* Berlin: W. Giese, 1901. 33 pp. *LJ*

2549 Delff, Heinrich Karl Hugo: *Judentum und Christentum in Veranlassung der Schrift des Herrn Professors Dr. Paulus Cassel "Wider Heinrich von Treitschke."* Husum: C.F. Delff, 1880. 26 pp. *LJ*

2550  Delitzsch, Franz Julius (1813-1890): *Christentum und Jüdische Presse. Selbsterlebtes.* Erlangen: A. Deichert, 1882. 69 pp. *LJ*

2551  Delitzsch, Friedrich (1850-1922): *Babel und Bibel; ein Vortrag.* Leipzig: J.C. Hinrichs, 1902. 55 pp. *LJ*

2552  Delitzsch, Friedrich (1850-1922): *Zweiter Vortrag über Babel und Bibel.* Stuttgart: Deutsche Verlagsanstalt, 1903. 48 pp. *LJ*

2553  Delitzsch, Friedrich (1850-1922): *Dritter Schlußvortrag.* Stuttgart: Deutsche Verlagsanstalt, 1905. 69 pp. *LJ*
      About "Babel und Bibel."

2554  Deutsch-Sozialer (antisemitischer) Parteitag, Leipzig, 1891: *Bericht . . .* Leipzig: T. Fritsch, 1891. 42 pp. *Unseen*

2555  Deutscher Antisemiten-Bund: *Deutscher Weckruf; von einem deutschen Manne.* Berlin: G.A.Dewald, 1892. 32 pp. *Unseen*

2556  Deutscher Volksverein: *Die Fälschung der öffentlichen Meinung nachgewiesen durch den stenographischen Bericht über die erste öffentliche Sitzung des neugegründeten Volksvereins am 14. März 1881 im großen Konzertsaale der Tivoli Aktien Brauerei.* Hrsg. vom Vorstande des Deutschen Volksvereins. Berlin: Luckhardt, 1881. 46 pp. *LJ*

2557  Deutscher Volksverein in Wien: *Deutsch-national und christlich-sozial; ein Ruf zur Mahnung und Abwehr an die deutsche Bauern- und Bürgerschaft.* Wien: Kubasta and Voigt, 1894. 92 pp. *Unseen*

2558  Deutschnationaler Handlungsgehilfen-Verband: *Die deutschnationale Handlungsgehilfenbewegung und die politischen Parteien. Vortrag gehalten auf dem zwölften Deutschen Handlungsgehilfentage am 18. Juni 1911 in Breslau, von Hans Bechly.* Hamburg: Verlag der Buchhdlg. des Deutschnationalen Handlungsgehilfen-Verbandes, 1911. 63 pp. *LJ*

2559  Deutschsoziale Partei. Verband Nordmark: *Deutschsoziales Liederbuch enthaltend 142 der besten deutschen und antisemitischen Lieder.* Hamburg: Verlag des Verbandes Nordmark der Deutschsozialen Partei, 189-. 112 pp. *LJ*

2560  Diest-Daber, Otto von: *Bismarck und Bleichröder. Deutsches Rechtsbewußtsein und die Gleichheit vor dem Gesetze. Lebenserfahrungen aus Akten, Tagebüchern, Briefen, u.a. Ein ernster Mahnruf an jeden wahrhaften und festen Patrioten.* München: Th. Wenng, 1897. 201 pp. *LJ*

2561 Dobner, W.: *Aufruf zur Wachsamkeit; gegen die Juden-Emanzipation.* Wien: Ludwig, 1848. 1 l. *LC*

2562 Drumont, Edouard Adolphe (1844–1917): *La France juive: essai d'histoire contemporaine.* Paris: C. Marpon et E. Flammarion, 1886. 2 vols. *Unseen*

2563 Drumont, Edouard Adolphe (1844–1917): *Das verjudete Frankreich. Versuch einer Tagesgeschichte.* Deutsche Ausg. von A. Gardon. 6. Aufl. Berlin: A. Deubner, 1889. 2 vols. *LJ*

Original title: *La France juive; essai d'histoire contemporaine.*

2564 Dühring, Eugen Karl (1833–1921): *Der Antisemitismus an den Toren der Sozialdemokratie. Mit einem Verzeichnis einiger Schriften Eugen Dührings.* Berlin: Struppe & Winckler, 1893. 32 pp. *LJ*

Offprint from: *Westfälische Reform.*

2565 Dühring, Eugen Karl (1833–1921): *Der Antisemitismus und die ethische Bewegung. Mit einem Anhang: Der Antisemitismus im Vorschreiten und die Natur als Anwalt des Rassenantisemitismus.* Berlin: Struppe & Winckler, 1893. 60 pp. *LJ*

Offprint from: *Westfälische Reform.*

2566 Dühring, Eugen Karl (1833–1921): *Dühringwahrheiten in Stellen aus den Schriften des Reformators, Forschers und Denkers.* Hrsg. mit einer sachlichen und biographischen Einleitung von Prof. Dr. Döll. Leipzig: Theodor Thomas, 1908. VIII, 159 pp. *LF*

2567 Dühring, Eugen Karl (1833–1921): *Der Ersatz der Religion durch Vollkommeneres und die Ausscheidung alles Judentums durch den modernen Völkergeist.* 3. umgearb. Aufl. Leipzig: Th. Thomas, 1906. VIII, 239 pp. *LJ*

2568 Dühring, Eugen Karl (1833–1921): *Die Judenfrage als Frage der Rassenschädlichkeit für Existenz, Sitte und Kultur der Völker. Mit einer weltgeschichtlichen, religionsbezüglichen, sozial und politisch freiheitlichen Antwort.* 4. Aufl. Berlin: H. Reuther und O. Reichard, 1892. VII, 184 pp. *LJ*

2569 Dühring, Eugen Karl (1833–1921): *Die Judenfrage als Rassen-, Sitten- und Kulturfrage. Mit einer weltgeschichtlichen Antwort.* Karlsruhe: H. Reuther, 1881. VIII, 160 pp. *LJ*

2570 Dühring, Eugen Karl (1833–1921): *Die Parteien in der Judenfrage.* Leipzig: Th. Fritsch, 1882. Pp. 401–421, 473–494. *LJ*

Offprint from: *Schmeitznersche Internationale Monatsschrift.*

2571  Düsing, Dr.: *Die Verjudung der Aerzte und das dadurch veranlasste Eindringen des Zynismus in die Medizin. Ein Beitrag zur Frauenärztinnen-Frage.* Münster i. W.: J. Basch, 1895. 84 pp. *LJ*

2572  Dukmeyer, Friedrich: *Gastgeschenke für Freund und Feind.* Berlin: E. Rentzel, 1893. 97 pp. *LTA*

2573  Eccarius, Karl Theodor: *Die Juden nach ihrer Emanzipation psychologisch dargestellt.* 2. Aufl. Wien: Typ. J. Kock, 1849. 10 pp. *Unseen*

2574  Eichenlaub, Siegfried Wolfgang: *Judenlob! Judenchristliche Erkenntnisse und Bekenntnisse: Bibeljuden, Babeljuden, Berliner Juden.* Berlin: Deutscher Liederverlag, 189–. 16 pp. *LJ*

2575  Ellenbogen, Wilhelm (1863–1951): Der Wiener Antisemitismus. *Sozialistische Monatshefte* (1899) 418–425. *LJ*

About the Austrian antisemtism from the socialist viewpoint.

2576  Endlich, Johann Quirin: *Der Einfluß der Juden auf unsere Zivilisation mit besonderer Rücksicht auf Industrial-Anstalten in Oesterreich.* Wien: Typ. U. Klopf sen. und A. Eurich, 1848. 80 pp. *LJ*

2577  Endner, Wilhelm: *Zur Judenfrage; offene Antwort auf das offene Sendschreiben des Herrn Dr. H. Bresslau an Herrn von Treitschke.* Berlin: S. Hahne, 1880. 29 pp. *LJ*

2578  Engel, H.: *Das Judentum im Staate.* Berlin: Verlag der Redaktion des "Reichsbote," 1884. 46 pp. *LJ*

Offprint from: *Reichsbote.*

2579  Ernst, Christian: *Der Mauschel-Christ nach seinem Leben und Streben dargestellt.* Paderborn: Verlag der Bonifacius Druckerei, 1880. 36 pp. *LJ*

2580  Fiegl, Josef: *Die Rede des Abgeordneten Professor Josef Fiegl, gehalten im Abgeordnetenhause des Reichsrates am 23. Oktober 1886 zur Begründung seines Antrages betreffend die Aufhebung bzw. Einschränkung des Hausierhandels.* Wien: Fiegl, 1886. 16 pp. *LJ*

Offprint from: *Unverfälschte Deutsche Worte*, 1. November 1886.

2581  *Die Flucht vor den Juden aus Oesterreich; oder, Hat der sogenannte "Schandfleck" des 19. Jahrhunderts eine Existenzberechtigung. Von einem katholischen Geistlichen Oesterreichs.* Stolberg: Hoffmeyer, 1898. 56 pp. *LJ*

2582 Förster, Bernhard (1843–): *Richard Wagner in seiner nationalen Bedeutung und seiner Wirkung auf das deutsche Kulturleben.* Leipzig: Fock, 1886. IV, 90 pp. *LJ*
2nd ed. of *Parsifal-Nachklänge.*

2583 Förster, Bernhard (1843–): Text und Begleitbriefe an Wilhelm Marr, 11. und 16.12. 1879 und 17.7. 1880. *Staatsarchiv Hamburg.* Nachlaß Marr. STA Hbg NL Marr, A 63. *Unseen*

2584 *Fragen und Antworten über das Juden-Thema I.* Leipzig: Th. Fritsch, 1888. 8 pp. *LJ*

2585 Frank, Walter (1905–1945): *"Höre Israel": Harden, Rathenau und die moderne Judenfrage.* Hamburg: Hanseatische Verlagsanstalt, 1939. 251 pp. (Schriften des Reichsinstituts für die Geschichte des neuen Deutschlands) *LJ*

2586 Frank, Walter (1905–1945): *"Höre Israel": Studien zur modernen Judenfrage.* 2. erw. Aufl. Hamburg: Hanseatische Verlagsanstalt, 1943. 327 pp. *LJ*

2587 Frankenberg, Fred von Frankenberg and Ludwigsdorf (1835–1897): An Wilhelm Marr, 28.9.1887 and 1.11.1888. *Staatsarchiv Hamburg.* Nachlaß Marr STA Hbg, NL Marr A 65. *Unseen*

2588 *Frankreich unter Judenherrschaft.* Leipzig: Th. Fritsch, 1887. 8 pp. (Brennende Fragen, 23) *LJ*

2589 Frantz, Gustav Adolph Constantin (1817–1891): Die Juden. *Das größere Deutschland.* Ed. Eugen Stamm. Breslau: W. Korn, 1935. Pp. 123–147. *LB*

2590 Frantz, Gustav Adolph Constantin (1817–1891): *Der Nationalliberalismus und die Judenherrschaft.* München: Verlag des Literarischen Instituts, 1874. 64 pp. *LJ*

2591 Frantz, Gustav Adolph Constantin (1817–1891): *Wissenschaftliche Beiträge zur Judenfrage; patriotische Untersuchungen. 1. Die Juden vom Standpunkte der christlichen Sittlichkeit, Geschichte, Staats- und Gesellschaftpolitik. 2. Zwischenbemerkungen zur Judenfrage.* Berlin: Klein, 1881. 192 pp. *Unseen*

2592 Franzen, Theodor: *Die Juden in Köln von den Römerzeiten an bis auf die Gegenwart.* Köln: Verlag der antisemitischen Buchhdlg. E. Hensel, 1901. 38 pp. *LJ*

2593 *Die Fremdlinge in unserm Heime! Ein Mahnwort an das deutsche Volk von einem Berliner Bürger.* Berlin: M.A. Niendorf, 1877. 52 pp. *LJ*

2594  Freund, Josef: *Die Juden werden immer zudringlicher! Hütet und aber und abermals hütet euch vor der Judenherrschaft.* Wien: Typ. M. Lell, 1848. 2 pp. *Unseen*

"Datiert und gezeichnet: Wien, am 31. Juli 1848, Josef Freund."

2595  Freydank, R.: *Triumph Israels.* Rodaun bei Wien: Verlag der Ostara, 1907. 12 pp. (Ostara, 14) *LB*

2596  Friese, G.A.: *Rothschild oder Morgan? Eine unparteiische Studie über ideale und praktische Rassenveranlagung sowie über die modernen wirtschaftlichen Machtverhältnisse.* Leipzig: G. Vogt, 1904. 37 pp. *LJ*

2597  Fritsch, Theodor (1852–1933): An Wilhelm Marr, 1.12.1885 und 12.11.1890. *Staatsarchiv Hamburg.* Nachlaß Marr-StAHbg NL Marr A 67. *Unseen*

2598  Fritsch, Theodor (1852–1933):*Antisemiten-Katechismus: eine Zusammenstellung des wichtigsten Materials der Judenfrage.* 5. Aufl. Leipzig: Th. Fritsch, 1888. 260 pp. *LTA*

2599  Fritsch, Theodor (1852–1933):*Deutsche National-Untugenden.* Leipzig: Verlag des Deutschen Müller, 1884. 8 pp. (Brennende Fragen, 1) *LJ*

2600  Fritsch, Theodor (1852–1933): Ethik des Judentums. *Der Hammer* 3 (1904) 361–366. *LB*

2601  Fritsch, Theodor (1852–1933): *Fragen und Antworten über das Juden-Thema. Aus "Antisemiten-Katechismus."* Leipzig: Beyer, 1892. 29 pp. (Kleine Aufklärungsschriften. Sammlung, 6) *Unseen*

2602  Fritsch, Theodor (1852–1933): *Die geistige Unterjochung Deutschlands. Zugleich eine Antwort an Dr. G. Lomer und Prof. Werner Sombart.* Leipzig: Hammer-Verlag, 1911. 24 pp. (Hammerschriften, 3) *LJ*

2603  Fritsch, Theodor (1852–1933): *Die geistige Unterjochung Deutschlands. Der Hammer* 9 (1910) 57–62. *LB*

2604  Fritsch, Theodor (1852–1933): *Handbuch der Judenfrage. Eine Zusammenstellung des wichtigsten Materials zur Beurteilung des jüdischen Volkes.* 26 Aufl. Hamburg: Hanseatische Druck- und Verlags-Anstalt, 1907. 440 pp. *LJ*

The first ed., 1887, published under the title: *Antisemiten-Katechismus*; the last ed. (49th) printed in 1944.

2605 Fritsch, Theodor (1852–1933): *Die Juden im Handel und das Geheimnis ihres Erfolges. Zugleich eine Antwort und Ergänzung zu Sombarts Buch: Die Juden und das Wirtschaftsleben, von F. Roderich-Stoltheim, pseud.* Berlin: P. Hobbing, 1913. 254 pp. *LJ*

2606 Fritsch, Theodor (1852–1933): *Jüdische Selbstbekenntnisse. Aus "Antisemiten-Katechismus."* Leipzig: Hermann Beyer, 1892. 16 pp. (Kleine Aufklärungsschriften. Sammlung, 9) *Unseen*

2607 Fritsch, Theodor (1852–1933): *Kurze Geschichte des jüdischen Volkes.* Aus "Antisemiten-Katechismus." Leipzig: Hermann Beyer, 1892. 32 pp. (Kleine Aufklärungsschriften. Sammlung, 3) *Unseen*

2608 Fritsch, Theodor (1852–1933): *Leuchtkugeln. Altdeutsch-antisemitische Kernsprüche.* Leipzig: J. Müller, 1882. 24 pp. *LJ*

2609 Fritsch, Theodor (1852–1933): Der Richter und der Talmud. *Der Hammer* 9 (1910) 519–522, 545–548. *Unseen*

2610 Fritsch, Theodor (1852–1933): *Der Sieg der Sozialdemokratie als Frucht des Kartells; nüchterne Wahlbetrachtungen — Judentum und Antisemitismus. Glossen zu einem lehrreichen Aufsatze. Zwei Abhandlungen über brennende Fragen.* 3. Aufl. Leipzig: Th. Fritsch, 1890. 31 pp. *LTA*

2611 Fritsch, Theodor (1852–1933): *Statistik des Judentums. Aus "Antisemiten-Katechismus."* Leipzig: Hermann Beyer, 1892. 75 pp. (Kleine Aufklärungsschriften. Sammlung, 10) *LC*

2612 Fritsch, Theodor (1852–1933): *Talmud und Schulchan Aruch, die Sittenlehre des Judentums. Aus "Antisemiten-Katechismus."* Leipzig: Hermann Beyer, 1892. 40 pp. (Kleine Aufklärungsschriften. Sammlung, 8) *LC*

2613 Fritsch, Theodor (1852–1933): *Tatsachen zur Judenfrage. Das ABC der Antisemiten.* Auszug aus dem Antisemiten-Katechismus. Leipzig: Th. Fritsch, 1889. IV, 130 pp. *LJ*

2614 Fritsch, Theodor (1852–1933): *Urteile berühmter Männer über das Judentum. Aus "Antisemiten-Katechismus."* Leipzig: Hermann Beyer, 1892. 87 pp. (Kleine Aufklärungsschriften. Sammlung, 4–5) *LC*

2615 Fritsch, Theodor (1852–1933): *Verteidigungsschrift gegen die Anklage wegen groben Unfugs, verübt durch Verbreitung antisemitischer Flugblätter.* Leipzig: T. Fritsch, 1891. 52 pp. *LJ*

2616 Fritsch, Theodor (1852–1933): Vom parteipolitischen Antisemitismus. *Der Hammer* 11 (1912) 153–158. *LB*

2617 Fritsch, Theodor (1852–1933): *Die Wahrheit über den Beilis-Prozeß in Kiew.* Nach zuverläßigen russischen Quellen dargestellt. Leipzig: Hammer-Verlag, 1914. 45 pp. (Hammer-Schriften, 6) *LJ*

2618 Fritsch, Theodor (1852–1933): Was ist es um die Religion. *Der Hammer* 10 (1911) 421–425. *LB*

2619 Fritsch, Theodor (1852–1933): *Was kosten uns unsere Juden.* Leipzig: Th. Fritsch, 189–. 1 1. (Flugblatt no. 39) *LTA*

2620 Fritsch, Theodor (1852–1933): Die Weltmission des Judentums. *Der Hammer* 11 (1912) 393–397. *LJ*

2621 Fritsch, Theodor (1852–1933): Wesen des Judentums. *Der Hammer* 7 (1908) 513–519; 9 (1909) 15, 161 *LJ*

2622 Fritsch, Theodor (1852–1933): *Zur Bekämpfung zweitausendjähriger Irrtümer.* Leipzig: Th. Fritsch, 1886. 84 pp. *LJ*

2623 Fritsch, Theodor (1852–1933): *Zwei Grundübel; Boden-Wucher und Börse. Eine gemeinverständliche Darstellung der brennendsten Zeitfragen.* Leipzig: H. Beyer, 1894. 299 pp. *LJ*

2624 Frohme, Karl (1850–1933): *Das Judentum und die Tagespresse; ein Mahnwort in ernster Stunde. Von Junius, pseud.* Leipzig: H. Junge, 1879. 32 pp. *LJ*

2625 Frohme, Karl (1850–1933): *Paul Lindau und das literarische Judentum; eine Kontroverspredigt aus der Gegenwart.* Leipzig: C. Minde, 1879. 32 pp. *LJ*

2626 Fuchs, Josef: *Kirchenvermögen — Judenvermögen: untersucht für Freund und Feind. Fördert die Katholische Kirche den Aberglauben von R.H.* Warnsdorf: A. Opitz, 1898. 31 pp. (Kleine Handbibliothek zur Lehr und Wehr für Freunde der Wahrheit, 6) *Unseen*

2627 Fulda, Friedrich Wilhelm, ed.: *Wandervogel; deutsch oder national. Beiträge des Wandervogels zur Rassenfrage.* Hrsg. von Friedrich Wilhelm Fulda unter Mitwirkung vieler Wandervögel. Leipzig: Matthes, 1914. 27 pp. *LJ*
Articles against the admission of Jews into the Wandervogel.

2628 Gauvain, Hermann von: *Zur Judenfrage. Zwei Sendschreiben.* Berlin: E. Bidder, 1881. V, 72 pp. *LJ*

2629  *Der gefärbte Jude; oder, Was 'm Samuel Liebermann is gebassirt in der Farbenfabrik.* 3. Aufl. Kassel: Bickhardt, [n.d.]. 8 pp. *LJ*

2630  *Geheimnisse; ein Blick hinter die Kulissen.* Berlin: Verlag der Deutschen Hochwacht, 1902. 16 pp. *LJ*

2631  Gehlsen, Heinrich Joachim: *Aus dem Reiche Bismarcks; der Protest eines Patrioten gegen moderne Geschichtsfälschung.* Berlin: G.A. Dewald, 1894. 80 pp. *Unseen*

2632  *Gemeinplätze wie sie von Jüdisch-Freisinnigen und Sozialdemokraten gegen den Antisemitismus gebraucht werden und deren Widerlegung.* Berlin: Geschäftsstelle der Antisemitischen Vereinigung, 1894. 32 pp. *Unseen*

2633  Gerber, Heinrich: *Die "Weisheit Salomonis" und ihr Einfluß auf deutsche Art und Sitte, insbesondere auf die deutsche Rechtspflege.* Sternberg: Selbst-Verlag des Verfassers, 1906. 1 vol. (unpaged) *LJ*

2634  Gibt es eine Judenfrage? *Der Hammer* 6 (1907) 193–200. *LJ*

2635  Giese, Wilhelm: *Die Judenfrage am Ende des XIX. Jahrhunderts. Bericht erstattet dem V. allgemeinen Parteitage der Deutsch-Sozialen Reformpartei zu Hamburg am 11. September 1899.* Berlin: W. Giese, 1899. 16 pp. *LJ*

2636  Giese, Wilhelm: *Die Judenfrage am Ende des XIX. Jahrhunderts. Nach den Verhandlugen des V. allgemeinen Parteitages der Deutsch-Sozialen Reformpartei zu Hamburg am 11.XI. 1899 dargestellt. Anhang: Presse und Judentum von O.H. Böckler.* Berlin: W. Giese, 1899. 96, IV pp. *LJ*

2637  Giese, Wilhelm: *Vorwärts oder rückwärts? Beiträge zur Revision des Börsengesetzes.* Berlin: Luckhardt, 1904. 120 pp. (Der Volkswohlstand und seine Feinde, II, 1) *Unseen*

2638  Giese, Wilhelm, ed.: *Antisemitisches Handbuch.* Berlin: W. Giese, 1896. X, 144 pp. *LJ*

2639  Giese, Wilhelm, ed.: *Antisemitisches Jahrbuch für 1897–1903.* Berlin: W. Giese, 1897–1903. 6 vols. *LC*

2640  Glagau, Otto (1834–1892): *Der Bankerott des Nationalliberalismus und die "Reaktion."* 4. Aufl. Berlin: Friedrich Luckhardt, 1878. 72 pp. *LJ*

2641  Glagau, Otto (1834–1892): *Der Börsen- und Gründungsschwindel in Berlin. Gesammelte und stark verm. Artikel der "Gartenlaube."* Leipzig: P. Frohberg, 1876. XXXVI, 366 pp. *LC*

2642  Glagau, Otto (1834–1892): *Der Börsen- und Gründungsschwindel in Deutschland.* Leipzig: Frohberg, 1877. XXXVIII, 582 pp. *LJ*

2643  Glagau, Otto (1834–1892): *Des Reiches Not und der neue Kulturkampf.* Osnabrück: B. Wehberg, 1879. 272 pp. *LTA*

2644  Glagau, Otto (1834–1892): *Der Kulturkämpfer.* Berlin: F. Luckhardt, 1880. 48 pp. *LJ*

      Forerunner and program of a new periodical under the same title.

2645  Glagau, Otto (1834–1892): *Ludwig Löwe als politischer und moralischer Charakter.* Berlin: Lehmann, 1882. 8 pp. *LJ*

      Offprint from: *Kulturkämpfer*, 44.

2646  Glagau, Otto (1834–1892): Die Petition gegen Israel. *Der Kulturkämpfer* 1 (1880) 13. *LF*

2647  Glasenapp, Gregor von (1855–): *Der Charakter der Israeliten, die Art ihres Wirkens und die Stellung, die die Nichtisraeliten zu ihnen zu nehmen haben.* Riga: Jonek & Poliewsky, 1912. 56 pp. *LJ*

2648  Glasenapp, Gregor von (1855–): *Der Jahwismus als Gottesvorstellung; religionsphilosophische Forschungen auf dem Gebiet des Alten Testaments.* Hrsg. von Philipp Stauff. Weimar: F. Roltsch, 1915. III, 64 pp. (Denkschrift des Deutsch-Völkischen Schriftstellerverbandes, 4) *Unseen*

2649  Grävell van Jostenode, Harald: *Das Ariertum und seine Feinde.* Rodaun bei Wien: Verlag der Ostara, 1908. 16 pp. (Ostara, 25) *LB*

2650  Grau, Rudolf Friedrich (1835–1893): *Die Judenfrage und ihr Geheimnis.* Gütersloh: Bertelsmann, 1881. 56 pp. *LJ*

2651  Graue, Georg: *Ein Votum über das Judentum; Vortrag.* 2. Aufl. mit einer Antwort auf den offenen Brief des Herrn Rabbiner Dr. Mühlfelder. Chemnitz: Kommissionsverlag C. Strauss, 1894. 45 pp. *LJ*

      Epilogue to his "Friedenswort in der Judenfrage" published in 1881.

2652  Griebel, Karl: *Unter jüdischer Diktatur oder Impfung; Reichsseuchengesetz und der "Deutsche Michel." Eine Kulturstudie.* Lichtenthal bei Baden-Baden: Selbstverlag, 1894. 20 pp. *LB*

2653  Grimpen, Albert: *Judentum und Sozialdemokratie. In ihren Beziehungen beleuchtet.* Hamburg: A. Grimpen, 1913. 53 pp. *LJ*

2654 Gröner, Maria: *Schopenhauer und die Juden.* München: Deutscher Volksverlag, 1920. 52 pp. (Deutschlands führende Männer und das Judentum, 1) *LJ*

2655 *Der große Schwindel und der große Krach.* Rostock: W. Werther, 1875. XIII, 96 pp. *Unseen*

The material for this publication was gathered largely from the *Kladderadatsch, Ulk* and *Wespen,* three satirical journals.

2656 *Großpreußen; oder, Die verfehlte Neugestaltung Deutschlands; eine Auseinandersetzung für den Spießbürger von dem Verfasser der Flugschrift "Berlin, eine französische Stadt."* Berlin: A. Reinecke, 1891. 58 pp. *LTA*

2657 Grousilliers, Hector de: *Gegen Virchow und Genossen; oder, Offenbarung und Wissen.* Berlin: H. Polenz, 1880. 38 pp. *LJ*

Based on spiritualism.

2658 Grousilliers, Hector de: *Nathan der Weise und die Antisemitenliga.* Berlin: H. Polenz, 1880. 32 pp. *LJ*

2659 Grunsky, Karl R.: *Wagner und die Juden.* München: Deutscher Volksverlag, 1919. 96 pp. (Deutschlands führende Männer und das Judentum, 2) *LJ*

2660 *Die Güter-Schlächterei in Hessen.* Leipzig: Th. Fritsch, 1887. 8 pp. (Brennende Fragen, 21) *LJ*

2661 H., C. von: *Adel und Judenfrage vom Standpunkte des Adels.* Frankfurt a.M.: A. Föner Nachf., 1893. 138 pp. *Unseen*

2662 H., W.: *Die Juden und wir; Vortrag gehalten am 19. April 1895 in einer Mitglieder-Versammlung des Parochial-Vereins der St. Thomas Gemeinde, von W.H.* Berlin: Dr. von Funke und Nüter, 1895. 22 pp. *Unseen*

2663 Haiser, Franz: *Aufruf an die deutschen Hochschüler Wiens.* Wien: Selbstverlag, 1907. 15 pp. *LJ*

2664 *Hamburger Geschichten und Zustände.* Berlin: M. Schulze, 1886. 16 pp. *LJ*

2665 Hammer, A. Th.: *Juda und die deutsche Gesellschaft; eines freisinnigen Mannes Gedanken über die Judenfrage.* Berlin: H.T. Mrose, 1881. 46 pp. *LJ*

2666 Hammerstein, Wilhelm von (1838–1904): *Zur Judenfrage; Vortrag gehalten auf der evangelisch-lutherischen Konferenz des 25. August 1881.* Berlin: Expedition der Neuen Preußischen (Kreuz) Zeitung, 1892. 20 pp. *LF*

2667 Haug, H.: *Auch ein Kulturbild.* Gotha: Privatdruck, 1894. 35 pp. *LJ*

2668 Hein, Oskar: *Der Experte des Grafen Egbert Belcredi; Portrait eines* "*Vereinigten Christen.*" Wien: Hein, 1889. 36 pp. *LJ*

2669 Hellenbach von Paczolay, Lazar von (1827–1887): *Die antisemitische Bewegung.* Leipzig: W. Besser, 1883. 55 pp. *LJ*

2670 Henningsen, J.: *Professor Sombarts Forschungsergebnisse zur Judenfrage. Eine zeitgemäße Betrachtung.* 3. Aufl. Hamburg: Deutscher Verlag, 1913. 58 pp. *LJ*

2671 Henrici, Ernst (1854–1915): *Der Neustettiner Synagogenbrand vor Gericht. Schilderung des Prozeßes, nebst einem Gedenkwort und einer Schlußbetrachtung.* Berlin: M. Schulze, 1883. 28 pp. *LJ*

2672 Henrici, Ernst (1854–1915): *Reichshallen-Rede am 17. Dezember 1880.* Berlin: M. Schulze, 1880. 4 pp. *Unseen*

2673 Henrici, Ernst (1854–1915): *Toleranz und nationale Ehre; Rede gehalten am 10. Februar 1881 zu Dresden.* Berlin: M. Schulze, 1881. 13 pp. *LJ*

2674 Henrici, Ernst (1854–1915): *Was ist der Kern der Judenfrage; Vortrag gehalten am 13. Januar 1881.* Berlin: Verlag der "Wahrheit," 1881. 14 pp. *LJ*

2675 Henrici, Ernst (1854–1915): *Wie hat sich die Bevölkerung Berlins bei den bevorstehenden Reichstagswahlen zu verhalten; zugleich ein Mahnwort an alle deutschen Wähler. Rede gehalten am 17. Februar 1881 zu Berlin.* Berlin: M. Schulze, 1881. 14 pp. *LF*

2676 Herdach, Karl: *Geldgeber und Diktatoren der Sozialdemokratie.* 2. Aufl. Warnsdorf: Opitz, 1906. 34 pp. (Volksaufklärung, 95) *Unseen*

2677 Herman, Otto, member of the Hungarian parliament: *Judenverfolgung und Psychiatrie.* Budapest: C. Grill, 1881. 26 pp. *LJ*

2678 Hermann, Grandson of the Cherusker, pseud.: *Die krumme Art; Aufruf an das deutsche Volk.* Berlin: Selbstverlag der Antisemiten-Liga, 1879. 4 pp. (Flugblatt der Antisemiten-Liga, 2; Kriegslieder, 1) *LJ*

2679 *Herrn Stoeckers Rede, 22. XI. 1880, im Lichte der Wahrheit.* Berlin: C.Barthel, 1880. 33 pp. *LJ*

2680 Hessen, Robert (1854–): Unsere Aufgaben gegenüber dem Judentum; ein Rückblick auf den Antisemitismus. *Pr. Jhrb.* 64 (1889) 560–579. *LF*

2681 Heyse, M.L.: *Ansichten der Juden*. 3. verm. Aufl. Berlin: M.A. Niendorf, 1877. 37 pp. *LJ*

2682 Hodenberg, Bodo von: *Die Stellung der Deutschen Rechtspartei zum Antisemitismus; Vortrag gehalten . . . 1894*. Leipzig: Verlag der Akademischen Buchhdlg., 1894. 37 pp. *LJ*

2683 Hoffmann-Kutschke, Arthur: *Die Wahrheit über Kyros, Darius und Zarathustra; Beiträge zur Erforschung der älteren arischen Geschichte. Die Perser zur Zeit des Darius I, nach Zarathustra Spitama und ihre Bedeutung für die Weltgeschichte*. Berlin: W. Kohlhammer, 1910. 34 pp. *LJ*

2684 Hoffmann, Paul: *Die Judenfrage in Ungarn*. Aus dem Ungarischen . . . verdeutscht vom Verfasser. Budapest: Typ. Schlesinger, 1881. 64 pp. *LJ*

2685 Hoffmeister, Hermann Wilhelm: *Die jüdische Erziehung der christlichen Jugend; eine Vergewaltigung unseres deutschen Volksgewissens*. Leipzig: A. Friese, 1897. 320, 64 pp. *LJ*

2686 Hoffmeister, Hermann Wilhelm: *Zur Deutschreformation unseres Judenchristentums. Ein Weckruf für denkende Patrioten*. Leipzig: R. Friese, 1896. 98 pp. *LJ*

2687 Hohenlohe-Ingelfingen, Kraft Karl, prince of (1827-1892): An Wilhelm Marr 14.9.1878 und 28.7.1879. *Staatsarchiv Hamburg* Nachlaß Marr StA Hbg NL Marr A 108. *Unseen*

2688 Hollomay, Ludwig: *Mechaniker Ernst Schneider und sein Antisemitismus*. Wien: Selbstverlag, 1886. 15 pp. *LTA*
   "Anti-Schneider."

2689 Horina, Hans: *Lustige Ringellocken; eine Sammlung heiterer Erzählungen*. Wien: Lesk and Schwiedernoch, 1892. 173 pp. *Unseen*

2690 *Humoristisches Bilderbuch aus Neu-Jerusalem*. Berlin: Deutsches Witzblatt, 190-. 1 vol. with 17 plates. *LJ*

2691 Hundt-Radowsky, Hartwig (1759-1835): *Die Naturgeschichte der Juden. Memoiren zur Emanzipationsfrage der Juden*. Wien: A. Dorfmeister, 1848. VIII, 70 pp. *LJ*

2692 Hutter, Theodor: *Der Schatten der Zivilisation; oder, Das Judentum in Böhmen. Von einem Deutsch-Böhmen*. Marburg: Verlag des Reichs-Herold, 1888. 24 pp. *LJ*

2693 Il'ish, Robert Fedorovich: Die antisemitischen Gebrüder Herrnfeld, von
Flaneur, pseud. *Die Standarte* 2, 44 (1908) 1391–1393. *LJ*

2694 Irresperger, Carl C.: *Grand-Unsinn des Dr. Schöpf beleuchtet von einem
Salzburger.* 2. verb. Aufl. Wien: Selbstverlag, 1888. 14 pp. *LTA*

2695 Islebiensis, pseud.: *Dr. M. Luther und das Judentum.* Berlin: Lorentz, 1883.
16 pp. *LJ*

2696 *Ist die Judenfrage eine Kulturfrage? Ein Beitrag zur Charakteristik des
modernen Judentums, von xxx.* Berlin: Sallis'scher Verlag, 1890. 29 pp. *LJ*

2697 Istoczy, Győző (1842–1915): *Emlékiratfélék és egyebek.* Budapest: F.
Buschmann, 1911. 64 pp. *LJ*

2698 Istoczy, Győző (1842–1915): *A magyar antiszemitapárt megsemmisítése s ennek
kővetkezmenyei.* Budapest: Saját Kiadás, 1906. 16 pp. *LJ*

2699 Istoczy, Győző (1842–1915): *Manifest an die Regierungen und Völker der durch
das Judentum gefährdeten christlichen Staaten laut Beschluß des Ersten
Internationalen Antijüdischen Kongresses zu Dresden am 11. und 12.
September, 1882.* Chemnitz: E. Schweitzer, 1883. 16 pp. *LJ*

2700 Istoczy, Győző (1842–1915): *Die Wiederherstellung des jüdischen Staates
in Palästina; aus den Reden Viktor Istoczy's gehalten im ungarischen
Abgeordnetenhaus während der Reichstage von 1872–1896.* Ins Deutsche übers.
und mit Vorwort und Anmerkungen versehen von ihm selbst. Budapest: Typ.
F. Buschmann, 1905. 27 pp. *LJ*

2701 *Jacob und seine Söhne in Deutschland; das deutsche Trauerspiel der
Gegenwart.* Berlin: M. Schulze, 1883. 93 pp. *Unseen*

2702 Jäger, Adolf: *Krach in Sicht? Eine jüdische Kritik der Goldwährung sowie der
Doppelwährung und eine lehrreiche jüdische Finte.* 2. Aufl. Bielefeld: E.
Siedhoff, 1893. 31 pp. *LJ*

2703 Jäger, Otto Heinrich: *Unsere Korpsburschen, Börsenjuden und Semitenturner;
omnia deo juvante juventuti virtus! Im Germanen-Dreibunde des Turnerhort.*
Hannover: Ost, 1892. XII, 190 pp. *Unseen*

2704 Jedzink, P.: *Der Christ; eine Entgegnung auf die von einem Geistlichen der
Erzdiözesen Gnesen und Posen verfasste Broschüre, die den Titel führt "Der
Jude."* Posen: Verlag der Drukarnia Kuryera Poznans Kiego, 1892. 66 pp. *LJ*
Contemporary study about antisemitism.

2705 The Jews in Germany. *Contemporary Review* 39 (1881) 31–43. *LJ*

2706 John, Ludwig: *Gegen die Juden; die Juden wie sie sind* . . . Preßburg: 1848? *Unseen*

2707 *Jude, Sozialdemokratie, Militär; eine sozialpolitische Skizze, von einem Süddeutschen.* Berlin: Germania, 1892. 32 pp. (Katholische Flugschriften zur Wehr und Lehr, 65) *Unseen*

2708 *Juden A-B-C.* Dresden: Glöss, 1893. 1 l. (Politische Bilderbogen, 8) *LJ*

2709 Juden, Antisemiten und wir; ein offener Brief an den Verein zur Abwehr des Antisemitismus. *Der Kunstwart* 26 (1912) 297–303. *LJ*

2710 *Der Juden-Baron: Bleichröder — Rothschild — Rakonitz.* Berlin: Th. Heinrich, 189–. 129 pp. *Unseen*

2711 *Die Juden im deutschen Staats- und Volksleben.* Frankfurt a.M.: Verlag der "Deutschen Reichs-Post," 1878. 49 pp. *LJ*

Offprint from: *Deutsche Reichs-Post.*

2712 *Die Juden im Reichstag.* Dresden: Glöss, 1895. 1 l. (Politischer Bilderbogen, 16) *LJ*

2713 *Die Juden in der Musik.* Berlin: Hentze's Verlag, 1881. 19 pp. *LJ*

Offprint from: *Die Deutsche Wacht.*

2714 *Juden in der Sommerfrische.* Dresden: Glöss, 1895. 1 l. (Politischer Bilderbogen, 18) *LJ*

2715 *Juden in Deutschland.* Dresden: Glöss, 1893. 1 l. (Politischer Bilderbogen, 2) *LJ*

2716 Die Juden in Deutschland. *Der Kulturkämpfer* 2 (1881) 441–454. *LJ*

2717 *Die Juden in Friedrichsruh.* Dresden: Glöss, 1893. 1 l. (Politischer Bilderbogen, 10) *LJ*

2718 Die Juden in Oesterreich. *Historisch-Politische Blätter für das Katholische Deutschland* 142 (1908) 35–45. *LJ*

2719 *Juden-Sünden; die Kunst reich zu werden.* Zur Warnung des Publikums geschrieben. München: Wenger, 1894. 14 pp. *LB*

2720  *Die Juden und Jüdinnen in München (auch anderwärts)*. München: Bauer, 1876. 15 pp. *LTA*

2721  *Judenflinten und Juristenflinten; kritische Beleuchtung des Prozeßes Ahlwardt, von Faust*. Berlin: G.A. Dewald, 1892. 16 pp. *LJ*

2722  *Die Judenfrage in Oesterreich*. Warnsdorf: A. Opitz, 1899. 52 pp. (Volksaufklärug; kleine Handbibliothek zur Lehr und Wehr für Freunde der Wahrheit, 18) *Unseen*

2723  *Die Judenfrage in Oesterreich und Europa. Von einem praktischen Standpunkte allseitig beleuchtet, von Justus Anonymus*. Wien: Mayer and Co., 1860. 31 pp. *Unseen*

2724  *Die Judenfrage in Rostock*. Rostock: Leopold's Universitäts-Buchhdlg., 1861. 16 pp. *Unseen*

2725  *Der Judenspiegel; ein Bilderbuch für Alle, besonders solche aus dem Stamme Ham und Japhet. Mit Fleiß gesammelt und erbaulich gestaltet, von Arius*. Mit vielen Illustrationen erster Künstler. Leipzig: Gautzsch, W. Malende Nachf., 1901. VIII, 152 pp. *Unseen*

2726  *Das Judentum im eigenen Spiegel beleuchtet von einem Juden*. Berlin: Paul Bernhardi, 1885. 54 pp. *LJ*

2727  *Das Judentum in Oesterreich und die Wiener Presse. Von einem Oesterreicher*. Hannover: Westen, 1893. IV, 36 pp. *LJ*

2728  *Judentum und Antisemitismus; Glossen zu einem lehrreichen Aufsatze*. Leipzig: Fritsch, 1890. 17–31 pp. *LTA*

2729  *Judenverfolgungen und Emanzipation von den Juden*. 2. Aufl. Münster: Aschendorff'sche Buchhdlg., 1861. 51 pp. *LJ*

2730  *Jüdische Mysterien*. Leipzig: Th. Fritsch, 1887. 8 pp. (Brennende Fragen, 14) *LJ*

2731  *Jüdische Schweinereien; stenographischer Bericht über den großen Fleischbesudelungs-Prozeß in Würzburg am 28.3.1901*. Würzburg: Memminger, 1901. 60 pp. *LJ*

2732  *Jüdisches Athenäum: Galerie berühmter Männer jüdischer Abstammung und jüdischen Glaubens von der letzten Hälfte des 18. Jahrhunderts bis zum Schluß der ersten Hälfte des 19. Jahrhunderts*. Grimma: Verlag-Comptoir, 1851. VIII, 253 pp. *LJ*

2733 Jurik, Josefine: *Episteln gegen die allgemeine Verjudung.* Aarau: Huber & Comp., 1885. 160 pp. *LJ*

2734 Kämpfer, Ernst: *Jüdische Selbstbekenntnisse.* Berlin: Volkstümliche Bücherei, 1914. 32 pp. (Deutschvölkische Hochschulschriften, 3) *LJ*

2735 *Der Kaiser in der Mitte.* Dresden: Glöss, 1892. 70 pp. *LJ*
   "Motto: Der Deutsche rechts, der Jude links, der Kaiser in der Mitte."

2736 Kannengieser, Alphonse (1855–1914): *Juden und Katholiken in Oesterreich-Ungarn.* Aus dem Französichen. Trier: Paulinus, 1896. 308 pp. *LJ*
   Biography of Sebastian Brunner: Pp. 3–130.

2737 Karbach, Oscar: The Founder of Political Antisemitism: Georg von Schönerer. *J.S.St.* 7 (1945) 3–30. *LJ*

2738 Karl, Alexander: *Die Judenfrage in der Wiener satirisch-humoristischen Presse von 1855 bis zum Auftreten Schönerers.* Wien: 1941. 101 l. *Unseen*
   Diss. 1941.

2739 *Die Katholiken in Baden und die Juden in Wien; eine Berufung an das deutsche Rechtsgefühl.* Freiburg i.Br.: Herder, 1867. 40 pp. *LJ*
   "Aus dem 'Badischen Beobachter' abgedruckt und mit Zusätzen vervollständigt."

2740 Kayser, Franz: *Die Ausbeutung der christlichen Konfessionen und politischen Parteien durch die Juden.* Münster: A. Russell, 1895. 41 pp. *LJ*

2741 Kayser, Franz: *Die Ausbeutung des Arbeiterstandes durch die Juden.* Münster: A. Russell, 1894. 53 pp. *LJ*

2742 Kayser, Franz: *Die Ausbeutung des Bauernstandes durch die Juden.* Münster: A. Russell, 1894. 51 pp. *LJ*

2743 Kayser, Franz: *Die Ausbeutung des Handwerkerstandes durch die Juden.* Münster: A. Russell, 1894. 59 pp. *LJ*

2744 Kayser, Franz: *Die Ausbeutung des Kaufmannsstandes durch die Juden.* Münster: A. Russell, 1894. 56 pp. *LJ*

2745 Keller, R.: *Was ist's mit den Antisemiten? Ein Wort an alle Einsichtvollen in deutschen Landen.* Berlin: A. Winser, 1892. 30 pp. *LJ*

2746 Kikut, Edmund: *Jüdische Börsenjobber.* Berlin: Selbstverlag, 1895. 24 pp. *LJ*

2747  *Kirche und Juden. Von einem Theologen.* Dresden: Verlag der Druckerei Glöss, 1894. 51 pp. *LJ*

2748  Klenz, Wilhelm Heinrich: *Alban Stolz und die Juden; ein zeitgemäßer Beitrag zur Judenfrage für das deutsche Volk.* Münster: A. Russell, 1893. 80 pp. *LJ*

2749  Klenz, Wilhelm Heinrich: *Der Kirchenväter Ansichten und Lehren über die Juden.* Den Christen in Erinnerung gebracht. Münster: A. Russell, 1894. 50 pp. *LJ*

2750  Klenz, Wilhelm Heinrich: *Der Jude im Handel und Wandel; in der Beleuchtung eines vielgenannten katholischen Publizisten, Seb. Brunner vorgeführt, von H.K. Lenz, pseud.* Münster: A. Russell, 1894. 52 pp. (Billige Flugschriften über das Judentum, 2) *LJ*

2751  Klenz, Wilhelm Heinrich: *Judenliteratur und Literaturjuden. Aus Sebastian Brunners Werken dargestellt.* Münster: A. Russell, 1893. 67 pp. *LJ*

2752  Klenz, Wilhelm Heinrich: *Jüdische Eindringlinge im Wörter- und Zitatenschatz der deutschen Sprache; allen Sprachreinigern gewidmet, von H.K. Lenz, pseud.* Münster: A. Russell, 1894. 28 pp. *LJ*

2753  Klopp, Wiard von: *Leben und Wirken des Sozialpolitikers Karl Freiherr von Vogelsang.* Wien: Typographische Anstalt, 1930. XII, 479 pp. *LJ*

2754  Knepler, Hermann: *Der Prozeß Goldmark.* Wien: Herzfeld und Bauer, 1868. 132 pp. *LJ*

2755  Köhler, Paul: *Die Verjudung Deutschlands und der Weg zur Rettung. Noch einmal ein Wort für und wider "W. Marr: Der Sieg des Judentums über das Germanentum."* Stettin: O. Brandner, 1880. 62 pp. *LF*

2756  König, Adolf: *Der Antisemitismus und seine Gegner; Vortrag gehalten am 31. Januar 1892.* Hrsg. nach stenographischer Niederschrift von Max Müller. Weidenau: P. Westphal, 1892. 27 pp. *Unseen*

2757  König, Adolf: *Ein Bubenstück ersonnen, um eines Mannes Ehre zu vernichten; aktenmäßige Darstellung seines Prozeßes gegen Hirsch Hildesheimer.* Hagen: H. Risel, (Preface, 1888). 47 pp. *LJ*

2758  König, Adolf: *Die Verjudung der Justiz; ein Vortrag gehalten am 22. November 1891.* Hrsg. nach stenographischer Niederschrift von Max Müller. Weidenau: P. Westphal, 1891. 20 pp. *Unseen*

2759 Köster, Max: *Die Juden bei Bismarck; Dichtung nach einem Artikel der "Deutsch-Sozialen Blätter."* Nossen: P. Westphal, 1893. 14 pp. *Unseen*

2760 Kolb, George: *Schutz der nationalen Arbeit.* Bayreuth: Giessel, 1883. 16 pp. *Unseen*

2761 Kolk, Franz: *Altes und Neues von der Börse.* Zittau: Pahl, 1893. 39 pp. *LTA*

2762 Kolk, Franz: *Das Geheimnis der Börsen-Kurse und die Volks-Ausraubung durch die internationale Börsenzunft.* Leipzig: H. Beyer, 1893. 63 pp. *LTA*

2763 Kolk, Franz: *Mißstände an der Börse; zeitgemäße Untersuchungen.* Leipzig: B. Franke, 1894. 24 pp. *Unseen*

2764 Kolk, Franz: *Schlachtenbilder von der Börse.* Berlin: Verlag der Geschäftsstelle der Antisemitischen Vereinigung für Norddeutschland, 1894. 54 pp. *LF*

2765 *Die kolossale Ausbeutung des deutschen Nationalvermögens durch die Börse, das Ausland, die Deutsche Reichsbank usw. nebst Vorschlägen zur Besserung und Heilung des Uebelstandes.* Hannover: Klindworth, 1878. 44 pp. *Unseen*

2766 Koniecki, Hermann: *Die antisemitische "Canaille" vor Gericht. Vier neue Dokumente den kaiserlichen Räten empfohlen.* Berlin: G.A. Dewald, 1893. 32 pp. *LJ*

2767 Koniecki, Hermann: *Antisemitische Wüstenpredigt; ein verlorener Weckruf an das deutsche Weib.* Berlin: G.A. Dewald, 1891. 2 pp. *Unseen*

2768 Koniecki, Hermann: *Ave Caesar! Der Wille des Königs und das Notgesetz der Völker. Ein Wort vom jüdischen Reich deutscher Nation.* Berlin: G.A. Dewald, 1892. 15 pp. *LJ*

2769 Koniecki, Hermann: *Damaskus; eine Dichtung.* Berlin: Schneider and Co., 1890. 60 pp. *Unseen*

2770 Koniecki, Hermann: *Feuerfunken; vier antisemitische Gedichte.* Berlin: G.A. Dewald, 1891. 4 pp. *Unseen*

2771 Koniecki, Hermann: *Fredegod oder Godofred ohne Cothum. Auch ein zeitgemäßes Märchen.* Halle a.S.: F. Starke, 1889. 84 pp. *Unseen*

2772 Koniecki, Hermann: *Der Gipfel jüdischer Frechheit; das Gesetz ist tot — es lebe Bleichröder.* Hrsg. von H. Ahlwardt. Berlin: G.A. Dewald, 1891. 13 pp. *LJ*

2773  Koniecki, Hermann: *Die Götterdämmerung unserer Zeit*. Berlin: G.A. Dewald, 1892. V, 112 pp. *Unseen*

2774  Koniecki, Hermann: *Neueste Enthüllungen! Die Verschwörung Ahlwardt! Judenflinten und Antisemiten*. Leipzig: Minde, 1892. 30 pp. *LTA*

2775  Koniecki, Hermann: *Qousque tandem; oder, Das Neujahrsgastmahl. Antisemitisches Schauspiel in einem Akt*. Berlin: G.A. Dewald, 1892. 16 pp. *Unseen*

2776  Koniecki, Hermann: *Volksverräter! Die "oberen" Zehntausend und das Löwe'sche Attentat! Antisemitische Antwort auf "Ahlwardtflinten."* Leipzig: C. Minde, 1892. 32 pp. *LJ*

2777  Koniecki, Hermann: *Wuotan; die Götterdämmerung unserer Zeit*. Berlin: G. A. Dewald, 1891. 64 pp. *LJ*

2778  *Die Konservativen als Partei der verpassten, großen Gelegenheiten*. Betrachtungen anläßlich der letzten Reichstagswahlen. Marburg: Verlag des Reichs-Herold, 1890. 24 pp. *LTA*

2779  *Kooscher: ein neues Lied — net for a Jüd*. Kaiserslautern: Gotthold, 1891. 3 pp. *Unseen*

2780  Krämer, Ed., ed.: *Ein Bubenstück der Börse, ersonnen, einen deutschen Mann und sein deutsches Unternehemen zu verderben. Streiflichter über das Schicksal des freien Wortes in Varzin, an der Börse und bei der Polizei*. Erste Flugschrift als Ersatz für durch Intrigen unterdrückte Deutsche Freie Zeitung; Organ für die Interessen aller Erwerbstätigen. Berlin: Selbstverlag, 1873. 48 pp. *LJ*

2781  Krahn, Adalbert: *Die löblichen Eigenschaften der Juden. Vortrag gehalten in der ersten Versammlung des deutschen Reformvereins zu Leipzig*. Leipzig: E. Kempe, 1884. 13 pp. *LJ*

2782  Krajcsovich, Coloman von: *Der Antisemitismus in Ungarn*. Budapest: Pester Buchdruckerei, 1884. 52 pp. *LJ*

2783  Kreisau, Clemens: *Bauer und Jude. Soziales Lebensbild*. Leipzig: Th. Fritsch, 1891. 68 pp. *LJ*

2784  *Die Kreuzspinne; ein Blick hinter die Kulissen der Zeitgeschichte*. Berlin: Verlag "Deutsche Hochwacht," 1901. 40 pp. *LC*

2785  *Kronzeugen des Antisemitismus*. Wien: Verlag des "Stürmer," 1933. 32 pp. *LB*

2786 Krüger, Eduard: Judentümliches. *Neue Zeitschrift für Musik* 32–33 (1850) 145–147. *LJ*

2787 Kühn, pseud.: *Zu Schutz und Trutz; Zeitgedichte.* 4. Aufl. Berlin: O. Lorentz, 1881. 37 pp. *Unseen*

2788 *Kundgebungen: anläßlich des Tages (20. Dezember 1893) an dem Herr Georg Schönerer wieder in den Vollgenuß seiner bürgerlichen und politischen Rechte getreten ist, 20. Dez. 1888 — 20. Dez. 1893.* Horn: Berger, 1894. 110 pp. *LB*

2789 Lagarde, Paul Anton de (1827–1891): *Deutsche Schriften.* Göttingen: Dieterich's Verlag, 1878–1881. 2 vols. *LJ*

2790 Lagarde, Paul Anton de (1827–1891): *Erinnerungen an Friedrich Rückert, Lipmann Zunz und seine Verehrer.* Göttingen: Dieterich'sche Universitäts-buchhdlg., 1886. 82 pp. *LJ*

"Aus dem 2. Bande der *Mitteilungen* besonders abgedruckt."

2791 Lagarde, Paul Anton de (1827–1891): *Erinnerungen aus seinem Leben, zusammengestellt von Anna de Lagarde.* Göttingen: Dieterich, 1894. 191 pp. *LJ*

About the Jewish Question: Pp. 142–146.

2792 Lagarde, Paul Anton de (1827–1891): *Juden und Indogermanen; eine Studie nach dem Leben.* Göttingen: Dieterich'sche Verlagshdlg., 1887. 95 pp. *LJ*

"Aus dem 2. Bande der *Mitteilungen* besonders abgedruckt."

2793 Lagler, Heinrich: *Das Judentum im Spiegel der Geschichte. Ein Mahnruf an das Volk Israels, von Friedrich Freimund, pseud.* München: C. Hebelen, 1888. 32 pp. *LJ*

2794 Lange, Friedrich (1852–1917): *Deutsche Worte; Blüten und Früchte deutschnationaler Weltanschauung. Weihe- und Hermannsfest-Reden an den Deutschbund und Nachweis über Wesen und Wirken des Bundes seit 1894.* Hrsg. von H. Ehrhard. Berlin: H. Pilger Nachf., 1907. VIII, 128 pp. *LF*

2795 Lange, Friedrich (1852–1917): *Reines Deutschtum; Grundzüge einer nationalen Weltanschauung.* 4. Aufl. Berlin: A. Duncker, 1904. XV, 443 pp. *LJ*

2796 Lehmann, Johannes Georg (1851–1925): *Ihm hat die lange Nase nicht geblutet. Illustrierter Kriegs-Kladderadatsch.* Landberg: Volger & Klein, 1871. 8 pp. *Unseen*

2797  Lehnhardt, Erich: *Die antisemitische Bewegung in Deutschland, besonders in Berlin, nach Voraussetzungen, Wesen, Berechtigung und Folgen dargelegt. Ein Beitrag zur Lösung der Judenfrage.* Zürich: Verlags-Magazin J. Schabelitz, 1884. 104 pp. *LJ*

2798  Lehnhardt, Erich: Judentum und Antisemitismus. *Pr. Jhrb.* 55 (1885) 667–680. *LJ*

2799  Leila, Ada: *Leben und Ende einer israelitischen Jungfrau.* Basel: Verlag der Freunde Israels zu Basel, 1853. 76 pp. *LJ*

2800  Lerique, Josef: *Das Judentum in der deutschen Literatur.* Frankfurt a.M.: A. Fösser, 1882. 34 pp. (Frankfurter zeitgemäße Broschüren, 3, 9) *LJ*

2801  Leroy-Beaulieu, Anatole (1842–1912): *Die Juden und der Antisemitismus. Israel unter den Nationen. Ins Deutsche übertragen von Carl von Vincenti.* Wien: Verlag des "Freien Blattes," 1893. XV, 349 pp. *LJ*

2802  Lesowsky, A.: *Karl von Vogelsang; zeitwichtige Gedanken aus seinen Schriften.* Wien: Typographische Anstalt, 1927. 96 pp. *LJ*

2803  Leuss, Hans (1861–1920): Die antisemitische Bewegung. *Die Zukunft* 7 (1894) 327–332. *LJ*

2804  Leuss, Hans (1861–1920): *"Das richtige Wanzenmittel," ein jüdischer Staat; ein Vorschlag zur Güte.* Leipzig: H. Beyer, 1893. 27 pp. *LF*

2805  Liebermann von Sonnenberg, Max (1848–1911): *Die Bauernwürger; eine Geschichte mit 12 Bildern aus dem Leben.* Leipzig: H. Beyer, 1894. 13 pp. *LF*
Published anonymously under the title.

2806  Liebermann von Sonnenberg, Max (1848–1911), ed.: *Beiträge zur Geschichte der antisemitischen Bewegung vom Jahre 1880–1885, bestehend in Reden, Broschüren, Gedichten.* Berlin: Selbstverlag des Herausgebers, 1885. 331 pp. *LJ*

2807  Liebermann von Sonnenberg, Max (1848–1911): *Bericht über den Deutsch-Sozialen (antisemitischen) Parteitag zu Leipzig am 18. und 19. Mai 1891.* Leipzig: Th. Fritsch, 1891. 1 vol. *Unseen*

2808  Liebermann von Sonnenberg, Max (1848–1911): *Gegen die Börse; Reichstagsrede vom 7. Dezember 1893.* Leipzig: H. Beyer, 1894. 16 pp. *Unseen*

2809 Liebermann von Sonnenberg, Max (1848–1911): *Die Judenfrage und der Synagogenbrand in Neustettin; Rede nach dem Stenogramm gehalten am 25. Oktober 1883 in der großen Volksversammlung auf dem Berliner Bock.* Berlin: Karl Schwarz, 1883. 32 pp. *LJ*

2810 Liebermann von Sonnenberg, Max (1848–1911): *Jüdische Phrasen und deutsche Gedankenlosigkeit; Vortrag im Reformverein zu Leipzig am 1. April 1887.* Kassel: Werner, 1887. 20 pp. *LTA*

2811 Liebermann von Sonnenberg, Max (1848–1911): *Neue Zeiten — neue Parteien. Vortrag gehalten in der 1. öffentlichen Versammlung des Deutschen Reform-Vereins zu Leipzig am 23.1.1885 im großen Saale der Centralhalle.* Stenographische Niederschrift aufgenommen von Herrn Referendar Dr. jur. A. Kaltschmidt und Herrn B. Mühlig. Anhang: "Zur Charakteristik der Leipziger Presse. Leipzig: im Selbstverlag des Deutschen Reform-Vereins, 1885. 31 pp. *LJ*

2812 Liebermann von Sonnenberg, Max (1848–1911): *Die Schädigung des deutschen Nationalgeistes durch die jüdische Nation. Vortrag gehalten am 7. November 1891 auf dem Deutsch-Sozialen Parteitag zu Breslau.* Stenographischer Bericht der Neuen Deutschen Zeitung. Leipzig: H. Beyer, 1891. 37 pp. (Sammlung deutsch-sozialer Flugschriften, 3) *LJ*

2813 Liebermann von Sonnenberg, Max (1848–1911): *Die soziale Frage ist zunächst Judenfrage; Rede.* 3. Aufl. Bochum: Selbstverlag des Patriotischen Vereins, 1884. 16 pp. *LTA*

2814 Liebermann von Sonnenberg, Max (1848–1911): *Verträgt sich die Talmud-Moral mit dem deutschen Staatsbürgerrecht?* Vortrag gehalten am 8. Dezember 1891. Leipzig: Hermann Beyer, 1892. 32 pp. (Kleine Aufklärungsschriften, Sammlung 2, 1) *LV*

2815 Liszt, Franz (1811–1886): Des Zigeuners Gegensatz; der Israelit. *Gesammelte Schriften. Bd. 3: Die Zigeuner und ihre Musik in Ungarn.* Leipzig: Breitkopf & Härtel, 1910. Pp. 9–20. *LJ*

New rev. ed.

2816 Luckhardt, Friedrich: *Juden und Christen; Skizzen aus dem modernen Geschäftsleben.* 2. Aufl. Leipzig: F. Luckhardt, 1895. VIII, 87 pp. *LJ*

No more published. Vol. 1: 1. *Fürst Bismarck und die Berliner-Bewegung.* Vol. 2: *Moderne Ehrenmänner.*

2817  Ludendorff, Mathilde (Spiess) (1877-1966): *Hinter den Kulissen des Bismarckreiches.* München: Ludendorffs Volkswarte Verlag, 1931. 31 pp. *LJ*

Deals with Hermann Ahlwardt's antisemitic activities.

2818  *Ludolf; wie Berolinensis Silesiacus der Dichter des "jüdischen Referendar" ward.* Löbau: Skreczek, 1879. 12 pp. *Unseen*

2819  Lücker, Gerhard: *Das Judentum in der Wiener Journalistik, 1848.* Wien: 1939. III, 119 l. *LJ*

Diss. Reprint of typescript.

2820  Lueger, Karl (1844-1910): *"I Decide Who is a Jew"; the Papers of Dr. Karl Lueger.* Introduced, tr. and ed. by Richard S. Geehr. Washington, D.C.: University Press of America, 1982. VIII, 360 pp. *LJ*

2821  Lützen, Werner: Der Einbruch des Ostjudentums in die Berliner Presse; ein Kapitel Berliner Zeitungsgeschichte des 19. Jahrhunderts. *Zeitungswissenschaft: Mitteilungsblatt des Deutschen Zeitungswissenschaftlichen Verbandes* 18 (1943) 53-60. *Unseen*

2822  Luzsénszky, Alfonz: *Tőrtenetek, 1879-1919. Regény.* Budapest: 1944. 216 pp. *LJ*

2823  M. M.: *Warum sind Sie Antisemit? Ein Mahnruf und Weckruf für das christliche Volk, zugleich ein Mahnruf für die bevorstehenden Weihnachtseinkäufe.* Wien: W. Arming's Wwe., 1896. 72 pp. *LV*

2824  Maier, Hans: *Die Antisemiten.* München: Buchhdlg. Nationalverein, 1910. 24 pp. (Deutsches Parteiwesen dargestellt von Freunden des Nationalvereins, 2) *LJ*

2825  Marr, Wilhelm (1819-1904): Brief an den "Courier an der Weser," no. 161, 13. Juni 1862, Bremen. *Wilhelm Marr; the Patriarch of Antisemitism.* By Moshe Zimmermann. New York: Oxford University Press, 1986. Pp. 116-118. *LJ*

First antisemitic publication by Wilhelm Marr in English translation.

2826  Marr, Wilhelm (1819-1904): *Goldene Ratten und rote Mäuse.* Chemnitz: E. Schmeitzner, 1880. 32 pp. (Antisemitische Hefte, 2) *LJ*

2827  Marr, Wilhelm (1819-1904): *Der Judenkrieg, seine Fehler und wie er zu organisieren ist.* Chemnitz: E. Schmeitzner, 1880. 32 pp. (Antisemitische Hefte, 1) *LJ*

Pt. 2. of *Der Sieg des Judentums über das Germanentum.*

2828 Marr, Wilhelm (1819–1904): *Der Judenspiegel.* 5. mit einem andern Vorwort versehene Aufl. Hamburg: Selbstverlag des Verfassers, 1862. 58 pp. *LJ*

2829 Marr, Wilhelm (1819–1904): *Lessing contra Sem; allen "Rabbinern" der Juden-und Christenheit, allen Toleranz — Duselheimern aller Parteien, allen "Pharisäern und Schriftgelehrten" tolerantest gewidmet.* Berlin: M. Schulze, 1885. 44 pp. *LJ*

2830 Marr, Wilhelm (1819–1904): *Oeffnet die Augen, Ihr deutschen Zeitungsleser. Unentbehrliches Büchlein für jeden deutschen Zeitungsleser.* Leipzig: Fritsch, 1885. 32 pp. (Antisemitische Hefte, 3) *LJ*

2831 Marr, Wilhelm (1819–1904): Philo-Semitism. *Wilhelm Marr; the Patriarch of Antisemitism.* By Moshe Zimmermann. New York: Oxford University Press, 1986. Pp. 118–133. *LJ*

English translation of *Philosemitismus,* first published in 1887.

2832 Marr, Wilhelm (1819–1904): *Religiöse Streifzüge eines philosophischen Touristen.* Berlin: Denicke, 1876. 198 pp. *LJ*

2833 Marr, Wilhelm (1819–1904): *Der Sieg des Judentums über das Germanentum. Vom nicht konfessionellen Standpunkt aus betrachtet.* 2. Aufl. Bern: R. Costenoble, 1879. 50 pp. *LJ*

2834 Marr, Wilhelm (1819–1904): The Testament of an Antisemite. *Wilhelm Marr; the Patriarch of Antisemitism.* By Moshe Zimmermann. New York: Oxford University Press 1986. Pp. 133–155. *LJ*

English translation of: *Das Testament eines Antisemiten,* first published in 1891.

2835 Marr, Wilhelm (1819–1904): *Vom jüdischen Kriegsschauplatz; eine Streitschrift.* 2. Aufl. Bern: R. Costenoble, 1879. 48 pp. *LJ*

2836 Marr, Wilhelm (1819–1904): *Wählet keinen Juden; der Weg zum Siege des Germanentum über das Judentum. Ein Mahnwort an die Wähler nichtjüdischen Stammes aller Konfessionen. Mit einem Schlußwort "An die Juden in Preußen."* Berlin: Hentze, 1879. 48 pp. *LJ*

2837 Marr, Wilhelm (1819–1904): *Der Weg zum Siege des Germanentums über das Judentum.* 4. Aufl. von "Wählet keinen Juden." Berlin: O. Hentze, 1880. 48 pp. *LJ*

2838 Marx, Karl (1818–1883): Die Judenfrage. *Aus dem literarischen Nachlaß.* Bd. 1. Stuttgart: Dietz, 1902. Pp. 352–356. *LJ*

2839  Masaidek, Franz Friedrich: *Herzerfrischungen.* Wien: Lesk & Schwidernoch, 1893. VIII, 157 pp. *LV*

2840  Maurer, August: *Das Börsen-Raubrittertum in Verbindung mit dem Antisemitentum unserer Zeit; die Mittel für ihre Besiegung. Ein wohlgemeinter und rechtzeitiger Mahnruf an das deutsche Judentum.* 3. verm. u. verb. Aufl. Weinheim, Baden: F. Ackermann, 1882. 28 pp. *LJ*

2841  *Der Mauscheljude, von einem deutschen Advokaten.* Ein Volksbüchlein für deutsche Christen aller Bekenntnisse. Paderborn: Bonifacius-Druckerei, 1880. 39 pp. *LJ*

2842  *Das Mauschellied.* Bei jeder fröhlichen Zusammenkunft zu singen. Kaiserslautern: Gotthold, 1887. 3 pp. *Unseen*

2843  Max, Robert: *Nationale Pflichten zur Lösung der Judenfrage.* Kiel: Lipsius & Tischer, 1893. 40 pp. (Deutsche Schriften für nationales Leben, ser. 2, 6) *LJ*

2844  *Mazzes; jüdischer Mutterwitz in Bild und Wort.* Hrsg. von Spaßvogel. Berlin: Frankl, 1889. 65 pp. *Unseen*

2845  *Mazzes for Lachhungerige; jüdische Schwänke. Frisch 'erausgebacken von Isidor Humoreles.* Wien: Neidl, 1879. 39 pp. *Unseen*

2846  Memminger, Thomas, defendant: *Jüdische Schweinereien; stenographischer Bericht über den großen Fleischbesudelungsprozeß in Würzburg, am 28. März 1901.* Würzburg: Memmingers Verlagsanstalt, 1901. 60 pp. *LJ*

2847  *Merk- und Gedenkblätter für selbständige Wähler; Aussprüche antisemitischer Vertreter.* Gesammelt von einem Wiener Bürger. Wien: Vereins-Buchdruckerei, 1895. 1 v. *LV*

2848  Merunowicz, Teofil: *Zydsi.* Lwow: Nakładem Ksiegarni, 1879. 222 pp. *Unseen*
      Published in Vienna the same year in German translation: *Die Juden.*

2849  Messner, Hermann: Blicke ins moderne Judentum. *Neue Evangelische Kirchenzeitung* 28–30 (1877) *Unseen*

2850  Meyer, Paulus (1862–): *Wölfe im Schafsfell — Schafe im Wolfspelz. Enthüllungen über die Judenmission und eine Abrechnung mit Professor Strack.* Mit einem Vorwort von H. Wesendonck. Leipzig: Ernst Rust, 1893. X, 94 pp. *LJ*

2851  Meyer, Rudolf Hermann (1839–1899): *Politische Gründer und die Korruption in Deutschland.* Leipzig: E. Bidder, 1877. 204 pp. *LJ*

2852 Michaelis, Herbert: Bethel Henry Strousberg. *Forschungen zur Judenfrage* 8 (1943) 81-133. (Schriften des Reichsinstituts für Geschichte des neuen Deutschlands) *LJ*

2853 *Moderne Heuchelei; oder, die Interessen des allgemeinen Wohles und der Moral im christlichen Staate gegenüber der Stellung der Wortführer des Zeitgeistes und ihrer Judenpresse zur Frage der notwendigen Zucht der heranwachsenden Jugend und der angemessenen Besserungsmittel für jugendliche Verbrecher, von L. v.E.* Leipzig: Uhlig, 1886. 64 pp. *LJ*

2854 Moderne Juden und die soziale Frage. *Historisch-Politische Blätter für das Katholische Deutschland* 130 (1902) 743-752. *LJ*

2855 *Das moderne Judentum und seine Erlösung.* München: im Selbstverlag des Verfassers, 1878. 122 pp. *LJ*

2856 Mosch, Hans von: *Neue politische Gedichte, 1907-1913.* Berlin: Verlag Deutsche Hochwacht, 1913. 32 pp. *LTA*

2857 Mosch, Hans von: *Das Wiedererwachen des deutschen Geistes; eine dramatische Dichtung.* Berlin: G.A. Dewald, 1894. 15 pp. *Unseen*
Suitable to be performed in antisemitic organizations.

2858 Moses & Cohn als Fabrikanten der öffentlichen Meinung. *Der Kulturkämpfer* 4 (1883) 70-78. *LJ*

2859 Moszkowski, Alexander (1851-1934): *Auserwählte Volkswitze; 399 Juwelen aus dem jüdischen Kronschatz echt gefaßt.* Neue Ausg. Berlin: "Lustige Blätter," 1911. 144 pp. (Der unsterblichen Kiste zweiter Teil) *LJ*

2860 Müller (Author of "Die Nationalheldin der Juden"): *Meister Josephus und das Märchen von Jerusalem; ein wenig Geschichtskritik.* Leipzig: H. Beyer, 1896. 88 pp. *Unseen*

2861 Müller (Author of "Meister Josephus und das Märchen von Jerusalem"): *Die Nationalheldin der Juden und das Purimfest.* Berlin: W. Giese, 1898. 16 pp. *Unseen*

2862 Müller, Dr.: An den Journalisten Wilhelm Marr, 5.12.1879. *Staatsarchiv Hamburg.* Nachlaß Marr STA Hbg NL Marr A 164. *Unseen*

2863 Müller, Josef: *Die Entwicklung des Rassenantisemitismus in den letzten Jahrzehnten des 19. Jahrhunderts.* Dargestellt hauptsächlich auf Grundlage der "Antisemitischen Correspondenz." Vaduz: Kraus Reprint, 1965. 95 pp. (Historische Studien, 372) *LJ*

Reprint of the author's thesis, published in 1940.

2864  Müller, Kurt (1865–): *Juden, ein nationales und soziales Elend. Kulturgeschichtliche und nationalökonomische Studie.* Leipzig: A. Bouman, 1891. 32 pp. *LJ*

2865  Müller, Kurt (1865–): *Das Judentum in der deutschen Studentenschaft.* Leipzig: A. Bouman, 1891. 16 pp. (Cyclus akademischer Broschüren, 10) *LJ*

2866  *Die Münchner Schwindelbanken: ihre Ursachen und ihre Folgen.* München: Verlag der J.J. Leutner'schen Buchhdlg, 1873. 69 pp. *LB*

2867  *Neu-Palästina; oder, Das verjudete Deutschland; ein milder Beitrag zur Kenntnis der Judenherrschaft im sogenannten "Deutschen" Reiche. Von einem Konservativen.* Berlin: Otto Hentze's Verlag, 1879. 52 pp. *LJ*

2868  *Neuere Urteile über die Juden. I-II (Dühring).* Leipzig: Verlag des Deutschen Müller, 1885–1887. 8, 8 pp. (Brennende Fragen, 18) *LJ*

2869  Neumann, Kurt H.: *Die jüdische Verfälschung des Sozialismus in der Revolution von 1848.* Berlin: Junker und Dünnhaupt, 1939. 80 pp. (Veröffentlichungen der Hochschule für Politik. Forschungsabteilung Sachgebiet: Geschichte, 3) *LV*

2870  *Nieder mit den Antisemiten!* 5. Massen-Neudruck. Leipzig: Hammer-Verlag, 1910. 1 l. (Flugblätter zur Volks-Aufweckung, 3) *LM*

2871  Niendorf, Marc Anton: *Die Juden und der deutsche Staat.* 9. Aufl. Berlin: Niendorf, 1879. 90 pp. *LV*

2872  Nietzsche, Friedrich Wilhelm (1844–1900): *Judentum, Christentum, Deutschtum.* Berlin: P. Stegemann, 1934. 84 pp. (Die Erhebung: Dokumente zur Zeitgeschichte) *LJ*

Extracts from Nietzsche's works, selected and arranged by Paul Bergenhagen.

2873  Nordmann, Johannes (1820–1887): *Israel im Heere. Von H. Naudh (pseud.).* Berlin: O. Hentze, 1879. 19 pp. *LJ*

Offprint from: *Deutsche Wacht.*

2874  Nordmann, Johannes (1820–1887): *Die Juden und der deutsche Staat.* Berlin: Nicolai, 1861. 63 pp. *LJ*

2875  Nordmann, Johannes (1820–1887): *Minister Maybach und der "Giftbaum."* 3. Aufl. Berlin: Hentze, 1880. 33 pp. *LJ*

2876 Nordmann, Johannes (1820–1887): *Professoren über Israel; von Treitschke und Bresslau. Von H. Naudh (pseud.).* Berlin: O. Hentze, 1880. 29 pp. *LJ*

2877 *Nützen oder schaden die Zeitungen?* Leipzig: Th. Fritsch, 1887. 8 pp. (Brennende Fragen, 5) *LJ*

2878 Oesterreicher, Leopold: *Der deutsche Michel und die Juden.* Wien: M. Lell, 1848. 1 l. *Unseen*

2879 Ohme, Anton: *Ein offenes Wort an die antisemitischen Gesinnungsgenossen im Deutschen Reiche.* Zwettl: Ohme, 1891. 8 pp. *LV*

2880 Olscher, Bruno: *Die Judenlaus im Christenpelz. Ernste Worte über den Ruin des Mittelstandes durch die Juden und die jüdischen Geschäftskniffe.* Berlin: P. Heichen, 1892. 24 pp. *LJ*

2881 Orel, Anton (1881–1959): *Judaismus, Kapitalismus, Sozialdemokratie; die Väter des modernen Kapitalismus. Im Anschluß an Werner Sombart.* 3. Aufl. Wien: Karl-Vogelsang-Verlag, 1912. 59 pp. *LV*

2882 Orel, Anton (1881–1959): *Das jüdisch-kapitalistische Problem in Shakespeare's Kaufmann von Venedig.* Mit Erläuterungen. 2. Aufl. Wien: H. Kirsch, 1911. 38 pp. *LC*

2883 Osman, bey Vladimir Andrejevich: *Enthüllungen über die Ermordung Alexanders II; veröffentlicht aus Anlaß des 5. Jahrestages des Todes Alexanders II.* Bern: Nydegger & Baumgart, 1886. 223 pp. *LTA*

2884 Osman, bey Vladimir Andrejevich: *Die Eroberung der Welt durch die Juden. Deutsche Uebersetzung. Versuch nach Geschichte und Gegenwart.* Basel: C. Krüsi, 1873. 48 pp. *LJ*

Also published in Russian, Odessa 1874.

2885 Osman, bey Vladimir Andrejevich: *Die Eroberung der Welt durch die Juden.* 2. internationale Aufl. verm. durch Enthüllungen über die Universelle Israelitische Allianz von Major Osman Bey, Kibrizle-Zade. Bern: H. Köber, 1888. 56 pp. *LJ*

2886 Paasch, Karl (1848–1916): *Auf Deutsche! Zum Kampf gegen das Judentum; ein patriotischer Aufruf an sämtliche Deutsche, vom Fürsten bis zum geringsten Arbeiter.* Leipzig: C. Minde, 1892. XLI pp. (Geheimes Judentum, Nebenregierungen und jüdische Weltherrschaft, 1) *LJ*

2887 Paasch, Karl (1848–1916): *Delatoren-Wirtschaft; die Ursache und die Entstehung des Prozeßes Lakert-Lützow, Dr. Schumann, Freiherr von Tausch,*

*Liebermann von Sonnenberg.* "*Ein Spitzel im Deutschen Reichstag.*"
*Zeitgemäße psychologische Skizzen nebst politischen Dokumenten.* Zürich:
Verlags-Magazin, 1897. 99 pp. *LJ*
"Antisemiten unter sich."

2888   Paasch, Karl (1848–1916): *Ein deutscher Pentateuch; Rüstzeug zum Kampfe
       gegen das Judentum. Für Politiker und Abgeordnete aller Parteien.* Leipzig: C.
       Minde, 1892. 72 pp. (Geheimes Judentum, Nebenregierungen und Jüdische
       Weltherrschaft, 3) *LJ*

2889   Paasch, Karl (1848–1916): *Geheimrat Professor Dr. Rudolph Virchow aus
       Schivelbein, unser großer Gelehrter. Eine psychologische Skizze.* Leipzig: C.
       Minde, 1892. 31 pp. (Geheimes Judentum, Nebenregierungen und jüdische
       Weltherrschaft, 2) *LJ*

2890   Paasch, Karl (1848–1916): *Eine Jüdisch-Deutsche Gesandtschaft und ihre
       Helfer. Geheimes Judentum, Nebenregierungen und jüdische Weltherrschaft.*
       Leipzig: der Verfasser, 1891. 4 vols. *LJ*

       Contents: 1: *Mein Freund von Brandt.* 2: *Dokumente.* 3–4: *Der jüdische
       Dämon,* (I–II).

2891   Paasch, Karl (1848–1916): *Der jüdische Dämon.* Leipzig: C. Minde, 1892.
       177 pp. *LJ*

2892   Paasch, Karl (1848–1916): *Die Kaiserlich-Deutsche Gesandschaft in China; eine
       Denkschrift über den Fall Karl Paasch für die deutschen Landesvertretungen
       insbesondere den Reichstag.* [n.p.]: Selbstverlag, 1892. 19 pp. *Unseen*

2893   Paasch, Karl (1848–1916): *Mein gutes Recht.* Zürich: Meyer & Hendeß, 1906.
       XXXII, 173 pp. *LJ*

2894   Paasch, Karl (1848–1916): *Offener Brief an Seine Excellenz den Herrn
       Reichskanzler von Caprivi.* Nebst diversen Anlagen. Leipzig: C. Minde, 1891.
       62 pp. *LJ*

2895   Paasch, Karl (1848–1916): *Plaudereien mit Herrn Heinrich Rickert aus Putzig,
       General der Gardebrigade des freiheitlich menschlichen deutschen Geistes in
       blanken Rüstungen.* Berlin: G.A. Dewald, 1892. 36 pp. *LJ*

2896   Pacher, Paul: *Ein Pröbchen reichsdeutscher Politik.* Berlin: G.A. Dewald,
       1894. 22 pp. *Unseen*

2897 Pape, Justus: *Der Beleidigungsprozeß Conitzer kontra Pape, nebst einigen andern Beiträgen zur Frage der Sittlichkeit im deutschen Buchhandel.* Hamburg: Herold'sche Buchhdlg., 1892. 34 pp. *LJ*

About J. Stettenheim and his book *Welche Frau ist die Beste.*

2898 Pattai, Robert (1846–1921): *Die Judenfrage in Deutschland und Oesterreich; die antisemitische Bewegung in Deutschland und überhaupt. 2 Reden. 3. Aufl.* Wien: Vetter, 1885. 24 pp. *LJ*

Offprint from: *Oesterreichischer Volksfreund.*

2899 Pennell, Joseph: *The Jew at Home; Impressions of a Summer and Autumn Spent with Him in Russia and Austria.* London: W. Heinemann, 1892. 130 pp. *LJ*

2900 Perrot, Franz Fürchtgott (1833–1891): *Die Aera Bleichröder — Delbrück — Camphausen.* Berlin: M.A. Niendorf, 1876. 79 pp. *LJ*

Offprint from: *Kreuzzeitung*, with bibliography, preface and afterword.

2901 Perrot, Franz Fürchtgott (1833–1891): *An die deutschen Handwerker; Aufruf zur Bildung von Vereinen zum Schutze des Handwerks.* Frankfurt a.M.: Typ. Hey, 1881. 26 pp. *LJ*

2902 Perrot, Franz Fürchtgott (1833–1891): *Bismarck und die Juden. "Papierpest" und "Aera-Artikel von 1875."* Erg. durch Karl Perrot. Neu hrsg. mit Einleitung und Nachwort von L. Feldmüller-Perrot. Berlin: Galle, 1931. 288 pp. *LJ*

2903 Perrot, Franz Fürchtgott (1833–1891): *Das Handwerk, seine Reorganisation und seine Befreiung von der Uebermacht des Großkapitals.* Leipzig: Bidder, 1876. 31 pp. *Unseen*

2904 Perrot, Franz Fürchtgott (1833–1891): *Die Juden im deutschen Staats- und Volksleben. 5. Aufl.* Frankfurt a.M.: Verlag der Schriften-Niederlage des Evangelischen Vereins, 1881. 114 pp. *LJ*

2905 Perrot, Franz Fürchtgott (1833–1891): *Die sogennante "Deutsche Reichsbank" — eine privilegierte Aktiengesellschaft von und für Juden. Nebst Betrachtungen über Lasker'hafte und Bamberger'liche Politik.* Berlin: Niendorf, 1876. 92 pp. *LJ*

2906 Petersdorff, Hermann von (1864–1929): *Die Vereine deutscher Studenten; neun Jahre akademischer Kämpfe.* Im Auftrage des Kyffhäuser-Verbandes. Leipzig: Breitkopf & Härtel, 1891. 247 pp. *LTA*

2907  Philippikus, pseud.: *Die jüdische Invasion und das katholische Deutschland. Eine Rede an die deutsche Nation, von einem katholischen Deutschen.* Leipzig: E. Rust, 1893. 46 pp. *LJ*

2908  Pieper, Hans (1913-): *Die Judenschaft in Münster, Westfalen im Ablauf des 19. Jahrhunderts unter besonderer Berücksichtigung freimaurerischer Einflüsse.* Münster i.W.: 1940. 53 pp. *LJ*
Diss. 1940.

2909  Pinkert, Alexander Friedrich: *Die Judenfrage gegenüber dem deutschen Handel und Gewerbe; ein Manifest an die Deutsche Nation, von Egon Waldegg, pseud.* 2.-3. Aufl. Dresden: R. v. Grumbkow, 1879. 49 pp. *LJ*

2910  Pinkert, Alexander Friedrich: *Judenhetze oder Notwehr? Ein Mahnwort.* 2. verm. Aufl. Dresden: R. v. Grumbkow, 1880. 40 pp. *LJ*

2911  Piwonka, Wilhelm von: *Antisemitisches. Eine Weihnachtsgabe für die christlich-arischen Völker.* Wien: Kreisel, 1903. 45 pp. *LV*

2912  Piwonka, Wilhelm von: *Für meine Landsleute; Aufsätze sozial-politischen Inhaltes.* Wien: K. Vetter, 1897. 36 pp. *Unseen*

2913  Piwonka, Wilhelm von: *Die Judenfrage und ihre Lösung. Objektiv dargestellt und einheitlich behandelt.* Wien: C. Vetter, 1894. 104 pp. *LJ*

2914  Piwonka, Wilhelm von: *Der letzte Versuch; ein Ruf zur Ehre, Einigkeit und Vernunft.* Wien: Kommissionsverlag von H. Kirsch, 1898. 28 pp. *LV*

2915  Piwonka, Wilhelm von: *Die Sache liegt so einfach.* Wien: Cornelius Vetter, 1895. 1 vol. *LC*

2916  Piwonka, Wilhelm von: *Schädlinge des Deutschtums; Betrachtungen über die korrumpierte Tätigkeit gewisser verjudeter Kreise.* Wien: H. Kirsch, 1902. 32 pp. *LV*

2917  Piwonka, Wilhelm von: *Unrecht; Worte der Abwehr.* Gewidmet der Deutsch-Oesterreichischen Schriftstellergesellschaft. Wien: H. Kirsch, 1899. 33 pp. *LV*

2918  Piwonka, Wilhelm von: *Unter rot-weißem Banner; Aufsätze verschiedenen Inhaltes.* Wien: H. Kirsch, 1900. 99 pp. *LV*

2919  Plack-Podgorski, Rudolf: *Ahlwardt vor Gericht; eine kritische Beleuchtung des Judenflinten-Prozeßes.* Dresden: Glöss, 1892. 40 pp. *LJ*

2920 Plack-Podgorski, Rudolf: *Mahnwort an den Mittelstand des deutschen Volkes und Aufruf zum Kampf gegen die hohe Finanz und den Börsenschwindel der Welt. Eine Folge des "Prozeß Polke."* Berlin: "Charlottenburger Kritik," 1893. 16 pp. *Unseen*

2921 Plack-Podgorski, Rudolf: *Pharisäer und Heuchler; oder, Die Leuchten des deutschen Parlaments und die Stützen des Staates.* Geschildert nach dem Ahlwardtschen Aktenmaterial und anderen Quellen als eine Ergänzung seiner öffentlichen Anklagen im Deutschen Reichstage. Unter wortgetreuem Abdruck von Akten und Belegen. 3. Aufl. Berlin: G.A. Dewald, 1893. 68 pp. *Unseen*

2922 Plack-Podgorski, Rudolf: *Der Prozeß Polke vom Standpunkte der reinen Vernunft zur Aufklärung der öffentlichen Meinung über Schuld oder Unschuld des Angeklagten im Interesse der Wahrheit und Strafpflege beschrieben und hrsg. Eine Widerlegung des gerichtlich. Urteils vom 3. Juni 1892, Strafkammer 3 des Landgerichts I Berlin unter Nachweis von Falsch- bzw. Meineiden.* Dresden: Glöss, 1892. 134 pp. *LTA*

2923 Plack-Podgorski, Rudolf: *Rechtsanwalt Hertwig, eine Zierde des Anwaltstandes.* Charlottenburg: Fänger & Heimann, 1904. 20 pp. *LTA*

2924 Platon, pseud.: *Die Freimaurerei als Zerstörerin Deutschlands und Europas.* Leipzig: "Wahrheit und Recht," 1882. 100 pp. *LJ*

Offprint from the weekly: *Wahrheit und Recht*; of an article series called "Die letzte Festung."

2925 *Die politische Wochenstube, von einem deutschen Sozialisten.* Nossen i.S.: P. Westphal, 1892. 121 pp. *LJ*

2926 *Der Prozeß Fenner nach den Akten dargestellt und beleuchtet.* Marburg: Verlag des Reichsherold, 1888. 69 pp. *LTA*

2927 Pudor, Heinrich (1865-): *Deutschland für die Deutschen; Vorarbeiten zu Gesetzen gegen die jüdische Ansiedlung in Deutschland.* Bd. 1-2. München: Hans Sachs-Verlag, 1912-1913. 2 vols. *LJ*

2928 Pudor, Heinrich (1865-): *Gedenke, daß Du ein Deutscher bist.* München: Kupferschmied, 1912. 2 vols. (Sammlung Kupferschmied, 3, 8) *LV*

2929 Pudor, Heinrich (1865-): *Hansabund und Judentum.* Hamburg: Deutschnationale Buchhdlg., 1912. 15 pp. *LJ*

2930 Pudor, Heinrich (1865-): *Landwirtschaft und Judentum.* Berlin: Priber & Lammers, 1913. 16 pp. *LJ*

2931 Pudor, Heinrich (1865–): *Wie kriegen wir sie hinaus? Deutsche Nutzanwendungen; eine deutsche Antwort auf die Berliner Tageblatt Pöbelei.* Leipzig: G. Hedeler, 1913. 43 pp. *LTA*

2932 Pudor, Heinrich (1865–): *Zur Sozialpolitik des Mittelstandes.* Gautzsch bei Leipzig, F. Dietrich, 1913. 26 pp. (Kultur und Fortschritt, 477–478) *LJ*

2933 Quidde, Ludwig: *Die Antisemitenagitation und die deutsche Studentenschaft.* Göttingen: Vandenhoeck & Ruprecht, 1881. 18 pp. *LJ*
Published anonymously under the title.

2934 Rabbow, Eduard, ed.: *Die Firma Adolph Ehrlich "Holzhandlung en gros," Universitätsstraße 2 in Verwaltung ihrer 54 Häuser in Berlin. Beiträge zur Beleuchtung des Grundstückswuchers und der "rationellen" Ausnutzung Berliner Warenhäuser.* Berlin: Selbstverlag, 1886. 48 pp. *LJ*

2935 Radenhausen, Christian (1813–): *Esther; die semitische Unmoral im Kampfe wider Staat und Kirche.* Leipzig: E. Thiele, 1887. VIII, 253 pp. *LJ*

2936 Ratzinger, Georg (1844–1899): *Das Judentum in Bayern; Skizzen aus der Vergangenheit und Vorschläge für die Zukunft.* München: R. Abt, 1897. 84 pp. *LJ*

2937 Ratzinger, Georg (1844–1899): *Jüdisches Erwerbsleben, von Robert Waldhausen, pseud.* Passau: R. Abt, 1892. 90 pp. *LJ*

2938 Rauch, Franz: *A.B.C. Büchlein für Arbeiter, Bürger und Christenleute, die der Schule entwachsen sind.* Wien: C. Sartori, 1873. 1 vol. (Weckstimmen für das katholische Volk, 4, 4–5) *LV*

2939 Rausch, Karl (1847–): *Oesterreich; ein Juwel in jüdischer Fassung.* Berlin: O. Hentze, 1880. 46 pp. (Judenherrschaft und Judenwirtschaft in Oesterreich-Ungarn) *Unseen*

2940 Rausch, Karl (1847–): *Wählet keinen Juden! Ein Mahn- und Warnungsruf an die Völker Oesterreich-Ungarns.* Berlin: O. Hentze, 1881. 35 pp. *Unseen*

2941 Rebbert, Joseph: *Blicke ins talmudische Judentum; nach den Forschungen von Dr. Konrad Martin, Bischof von Paderborn, dem christlichen. Volke enthüllt. Nebst einer Beleuchtung der neuesten Judenverteidigung.* Paderborn: Bonifacius-Druckerei, 1876. 96 pp. *LJ*

2942 Rebbert, Joseph: *Christenschutz — nicht Judenhatz; ein Volksbüchlein.* 2. Aufl. Paderborn: Bonifacius-Druckerei, 1876. 32 pp. *LJ*

2943  *Rede Bismarck's über die Judenfrage.* Leipzig: Th. Fritsch, 1887. 8 pp.
(Brennende Fragen, 22) *LJ*

2944  Redlich, J. (ascribed author): *Der Juden-Galgen.* Wien: 1848. 1 l. *Unseen*
Broadside. Signed J.R. From: *Oesterreichisches Jahrbuch,* vol. 7, pp. 72.

2945  *Die Regierung und der Antisemitismus. Von einem Nichtoffiziösen.* Berlin: L.
Friese & A. Pritschow, 1893. 28 pp. *LJ*

2946  Reichenau, Walther von: *Judentum und Deutschtum; über den Einfluß der
jüdischen auf die deutsche materielle und besonders höhere Kultur.* Stuttgart:
Süddeutsche Verlagsbuchhdl. D. Ochs, 1902. 32 pp. *LJ*

2947  Reichenberg, Ch. N.: *Der Wiener Gemeinderat und der Hausierhandel, nebst
dem Bilde eines Hausierers.* Wien: im Selbstverlage des Verfassers, 1887.
14 pp. *LJ*

2948  Retterspitz, Friedrich: *Die Geheimnisse des Judentums gegen alle Nichtjuden;
wissenswerte und sehr interessante Enthüllungen von unschätzbarem Wert und
zur Aufklärung und Bekehrung für alle Kreise und Schichten der ganzen
christlichen Bevölkerung.* Leipzig: H. Beyer, 1892. VIII, 92 pp. *LJ*

2949  Reuss, Kurt: *Der Messias der Juden; ein Appell an das deutsche Volksgewissen.*
Gera: J. Becker, 1896. 61 pp. *LJ*

2950  Reymond, Moritz von (1833–1921): *Jeiteles Teutonicus; Harfenklänge aus dem
vermauschelten Deutschland, von Marr dem Zweiten.* Bern: Rudolf Costenoble,
1879. 62 pp. *LV*

2951  Reymond, Moritz von (1833–1921): *Wo steckt der Mauschel? oder, Jüdischer
Liberalismus und wissenschaftlicher Pessimismus. Ein offener Brief an W.
Marr.* 2. Aufl. Bern: Georg Frobeen, 1880. 62 pp. *LJ*
On Wilhelm Marr's *Der Sieg des Judentums über das Christentum.*

2952  Richter, Emil (1839–1888): *Anfang und Ende der Frankfurter Judengasse, von
Germanicus, pseud.* Leipzig: Germanicus, 1886. 1 vol. *Unseen*

2953  Richter, Emil (1839–1888): *Die Bank- und Bankiersdiebstähle und die
Auflösung von Eigentum und Besitz im Scheinbesitz, von Germanicus, pseud.*
Frankfurt a.M.: Germanicus-Verlag, 1888. 69 pp. *LJ*

2954  Richter, Emil (1839–1888): *Die deutschen Juden in Gegenwart und Zukunft, von
Germanicus, pseud.* Berlin: A. Eckstein Nachf. 1888. 22 pp. (Eckstein'sche
Flugschriften-Sammlung, 10) *LJ*

2955 Richter, Emil (1839–1888): *Die Frankfurter Juden, und die Aufsaugung des Volkswohlstandes; eine Anklage wider die Agiotage und wider den Wucher, von Germanicus, pseud.* Leipzig: Glaser & Garte, 1880. 95 pp. *LJ*

2956 Richter, Emil (1839–1888): *Geschichte der Judenschaft von Frankfurt a.M.; dargestellt von einem Deutschen.* Berlin: W. Giese, 1897. 45 pp. *LC*

2957 Richter, Emil (1839–1888): *Juden und Junker; eine Beleuchtung des Spieler- und Wucherer-Prozeß in Hannover, von Germanicus, pseud.* Leipzig: H. Beyer, 1893. 50 pp. *LJ*

2958 Richter, Emil (1839–1888): *Das Kreditsystem der modernen Mißwirtschaft und die Mobilisierung des Besitzes als Hauptquelle der sozialen Gefahr.* Heilbronn: Gebr. Henninger, 1884. 61 pp. (Zeitfragen des christlichen Volkslebens, 9, 2) *LC*

2959 Richter, Emil (1839–1888): *Memorandum über den Schwindel mit Geheimmitteln in der 2. Hälfte des 19. Jahrhunderts.* Reichenberg: Schopfer, 1884. 1 vol. *LV*

2960 Richter, Emil (1839–1888): *Neuer Börsenschwindel, von Germanicus, pseud.* Leipzig: Glaser & Garte, 1880. 31 pp. *LJ*

2961 Richter, Emil (1839–1888): *Neuer Börsenschwindel, von Germanicus, pseud.* Frankfurt a.M.: Germanicus-Verlag, 1880–1881. 2 vols. *LJ*

2962 Richter, Emil (1839–1888): *Der neueste Raub am deutschen Nationalwohlstand, von Germanicus, pseud.* Frankfurt a.M.: Germanicus-Verlag, 1881. 42 pp. (Neuer Börsenschwindel, 2) *LJ*

2963 Richter, Emil (1839–1888): *Die Rothschild-Gruppe und der "monumentale" Konversions-Schwindel von 1881; eine zweite Anklage wider die Agiotage, von Germanicus, pseud.* Frankfurt a.M.: Germanicus-Verlag "E. Richter," 1881. 58 pp. *LJ*

2964 Richter, Emil (1839–1888): *Wer wird das deutsche Volk vom Untergang retten; eine ernste Frage, von Germanicus, pseud.* Berlin: Eckstein Nachf., 1887. 64 pp. (Ecksteinsche Flugschriften-Sammlung, 4) *Unseen*

2965 Rittner, C.H.: *Der ungarische Reichstags-Abgeordnete Ivan von Simonyi; oder, Die Verjudung des Antisemitismus in Ungarn. Selbsterlebnisse eines deutschen Journalisten.* Hagen i.W.: Risel, 1886. 71 pp. *LJ*

2966 Robolsky, Hermann (1822–1901): *Aus der Wilhelmstraße: Erinnerungen eines Offiziösen.* Berlin: Eckstein Nachf., 1887. III, 319 pp. *Unseen*

2967  Robolsky, Hermann (1822–1901): *Der Deutsche Reichstag, 1867–1892;*
      *Geschichte seines 25 jährigen Bestehens.* Berlin: C. Skopnik, 1893. VIII, 480,
      XLII pp. *Unseen*

2968  Robolsky, Hermann (1822–1901): *Der Deutsche Reichstag; seine Parteien und*
      *Größen, von H. Wiermann, pseud.* Leipzig: Renger, 1884–1885. 2 vols.
      *Unseen*

2969  Rocholl, Heinrich Wilhelm (1845–): *Ueber die Stellung der evangelischen*
      *Christen zur sogenannten Judenfrage der Gegenwart; ein Vortrag.* Köln:
      Römke & Co., 1881. 41 pp. *LJ*

2970  Rödenbeck, Walther: *Die antisemitische Bewegung; ein nationaler*
      *Freiheitskampf.* Spandau: Gustav Schob, 1893. 8 pp. *LTA*

2971  Rohling, August (1839–1931): *Die Ehre Israels; neue Briefe an die Juden.*
      Prag: Cyrillo-Method'sche Buchhdlg., 1889. 88 pp. *LC*
      With Hebrew translation.

2972  Rohling, August (1839–1931): *Franz Delitzsch und die Judenfrage; antwortlich*
      *beleuchtet.* Prag: J.B. Reinitzer, 1881. 155 pp. *LJ*

2973  Rohling, August (1839–1931): *Das Judentum nach neurabbinischer Darstellung*
      *der Hochfinanz Israels.* München: J. Schuch, 1903. 120 pp. *LJ*

2974  Rohling, August (1839–1931): *Le Juif-Talmudiste. Résumé succinct des*
      *croyances et des pratiques dangereuses de la Juiverie . . .* Rev. et corrigé, par
      Maximilian de Lamarque. Paris: Vromant, 1888. 69 pp. *Unseen*

2975  Rohling, August (1839–1931): *Die konfessionelle Schule; vertrauliche Briefe an*
      *einen Drei-Punkte-Bruder.* Dem hohen Wiener Reichsrate gewidmet. Linz
      a.D.: Heindl, 1888. 50 pp. *LV*

2976  Rohling, August (1839–1931): *Louise Lateau, die Stigmatisierte von Bois*
      *d'Haine. Nach authentischen, medizinischen und theologischen Dokumenten für*
      *Juden und Christen aller Bekenntnisse.* Paderborn: Schöningh, 1874. 79 pp. *LV*

2977  Rohling, August (1839–1931): *Talmud-Jude.* Mit einem Vorwort von Edouard
      Drumont aus der auch anderweitig verm. französischen Ausg., von. A.
      Pontigny. In das Deutsche zurückübertragen von Karl Paasch. Leipzig: Th.
      Fritsch, 1891. XV, 144 pp. *LJ*

2978  Rohling, August (1839–1931): *Der Talmudjude; zur Beherzigung für Juden und*
      *Christen aller Stände dargestellt.* Mit einem Vorwort über Gottes- und

Menschensatzung, über neue Rabbiner und ein Geschäftchen. 4. Aufl. Münster: A. Russel's Verlag, 1873. 72 pp. *LJ*

2979  Rohling, August (1839–1931): *Die Wirtschaft der guten Juden und die Weltnot der Gegenwart. Ein Wort für das Volk.* Wien: Lesk & Schwidernoch, 1892. 99 pp. *LJ*

2980  Rohling, August (1839–1931): *Zum Pressprozeß wider den Bezirksrabbiner und Reichsratsabgeordneten J.S. Bloch.* Wien: 1883. 20 pp. *Unseen*

2981  Roi, Johann Friedrich Alexander de la: *Israel, sonst jetzt und einst; Vortrag gehalten auf der Pastoral Konferenz in Berlin, 26. Mai 1880.* Berlin: Verlag der Deutschen Evangelischen Traktat-Gesellschaft, 1880. 34 pp. *LJ*

2982  Rost, Hans (1877–): *Gedanken und Wahrheiten zur Judenfrage; eine soziale und politische Studie.* Trier: Verlag der Paulinus Druckerei, 1907. 101 pp. *LJ*

2983  Rost, Hans (1877–): *Die Juden im Wirtschafts- und Kulturleben.* Klagenfurt: Druck und Buchhdlg. Carinthia des St. Josefs-Vereines, 1911. 64 pp. (Volksaufklärung; kleine Handbibliothek zur Lehr und Wehr für Freunde der Wahrheit, 153/154) *LJ*

2984  Rost, Hans (1877–): Zerfall des deutschen Judentums. *Hochland* 11 (1914) 545–558. *LJ*

2985  Roth, J.: *Antisemiten und Berufsgenossen; ein politisches Zeitbild der Gegenwart.* Wien: 1896. 1 vol. *LV*

2986  *Der Ruin des Mittelstandes, von einem Mann aus dem Volke.* Dresden: Glöss, 1891. 41 pp. *LV*

2987  Rupert, Louis: *Die Kirche und die Synagoge. Aus dem Französischen. Mit Beilagen von Sebastian Brunner.* Schaffhausen: F. Hurter, 1864. VIII, 287 pp. *LJ*

2988  S.R.: *Mißglückte Angriffe auf die mosaischen Berichte.* Warnsdorf: A. Opitz, 1901. 48 pp. (Kleine Handbibliothek zur Lehr und Wehr für Freunde der Wahrheit, 40) *Unseen*

2989  Saldenhofen, Fr. von: *Ausgewähltes über das "Auserwählte Volk." Neuer Beitrag zur Klärung und Lösung der Judenfrage.* Würzburg: Etlinger, 1892. 79 pp. *LJ*

2990 Saulus, pseud.: *Neue Epistel an die Hebräer*. Preßburg: G. Heckenast's Nachf., 1884. 103 pp. *Unseen*

On conditions in Austria.

2991 *Scharfe Patronen für Judenflinten. Von einem höheren Verwaltungsbeamten und deutschen Offizier a.D.* Berlin: P. Heichen, 1892. 39 pp. *LJ*

2992 Scharff-Scharffenstein, Herman von: Ein Blick in das gefährliche Treiben der Judensippschaft. Von einem Deutschen. Augsburg: Anton Herzog, 1851. 23 pp. *LV*

2993 Scharff-Scharffenstein, Herman von: *Das entlarvte Judentum der Neuzeit*. Bd. 1–2. Zürich: Verlags Magazin, 1871. 2 vols. *LJ*

Contents: 1. *Die Juden in Frankfurt a.M.* 2. *Die Juden in Bayern.*

2994 Scheicher, Josef: *Aus dem Jahre 1920; ein Traum vom Landtags- und Reichsratabgeordneten Dr. Joseph Scheicher*. St. Pölten: Gregora, 1907. 89 pp. *LV*

2995 Scheicher, Josef: Reaktion; oder, Die gute alte und die sichtvolle neue Zeit. *Weckstimmen für das Katholische Volk* 2, 11 (1870). *LV*

2996 Schell, Josef Copertin: *Essay mit Gegenüberstellung der Autorität, Solidarität und des Antisemitismus gegen das Reform- und Pluto-Judentum, den Individualismus, den Manchester-Liberalismus, das Anti-Christentum; die Juden- und Zola-Literatur, Zeitungswucherungen und deren wurmstichiges, kernfaules Kind, die Prostitution und Menschenelend.* Wien: Selbstverlag des Verfassers, 1888. 79 pp. *LJ*

2997 Scherb, Friedrich von: *Geschichte des Hauses Rothschild*. Berlin: G.A. Dewald, 1892. 147 pp. *LJ*

2998 Scheuer, Oskar Franz: *Burschenschaft und Judenfrage; der Rassenantisemitismus in der deutschen Studentenschaft*. Berlin: Verlag Berlin-Wien, 1927. 68 pp. *LJ*

2999 Schickert, Klaus: *Die Judenfrage in Ungarn; jüdische Assimilation und antisemitische Bewegung im 19. u. 20. Jahrhundert*. Essen: Essener Verlagsanstalt, 1937. 201 pp. *LJ*

Diss. 1937.

3000 Schmidt, Franz: *Bittschrift der Christensklaven an die Herrn Juden um Christenemanzipation*. Wien: Bader, 1848. 1 l. *LC*

3001  Schmidt, Richard: *O diese Juden; humoristische Satyren aus dem Volke Israel.*
      Berlin: Paul R. Schmidt, 1905. 4 pp. *LJ*
      Publisher's prospectus.

3002  Schmitt, Henryk: *Einige Worte über den neuerlichen Vorschlag der unbedingten*
      *Gleichberechtigung der Juden, zugleich Entgegnung auf die Anklagen womit die*
      *heutigen Verfechter der Juden-Emanzipation gegen die polnische Nation*
      *auftreten. Geschrieben von Heinrich Schmitt. Aus dem polnischen Orginal*
      *übers. von . . . ske.* Lemberg: E. Wincarz, 1860. 74 pp. *LJ*

3003  Schneider, Ernst: *Das Judentum in Oesterreich; Rede des . . . in der Sitzung*
      *des Reichsrates vom 10.11.1899.* Vienna: Vergani, 1899. 1 vol. *LV*

3004  Schneider, Ernst: *Rede über Rothschild . . . Versammlung des Oesterreichischen*
      *Reform-Vereines am 26.2.1885.* Wien: Oesterreichischer Volksfreund, 1885.
      4 pp. *LV*

3005  Schön, Max (1848–): *Die Geschichte der Berliner Bewegung.* Leipzig: M.
      Oberdörffer, 1889. 479 pp. *LJ*

3006  Schönerer, Georg von (1842–1921): *Anfänge und Ziele der deutschnationalen*
      *Antisemiten in Oesterreich. Vortrag von . . . gehalten am 8. März 1902.* Wien:
      A. Amonesta, 1902. 1 vol. *Unseen*

3007  Schönerer, Georg von (1842–1921): *Anträge, welche Reichstagsabgeordneter*
      *Georg Ritter von Schönerer . . . in der Zeit seiner Wirksamkeit im*
      *Abgeordnetenhause zwischen dem 4. November 1873 und dem 11. Juni 1888*
      *dortselbst eingebracht hat . . . Nebst einem Anhange enthaltend das Programm*
      *des Verbandes der Deutschnationalen im Abgeordnetenhause.* Horn: Berger,
      1888. 41 pp. *LJ*
      Proposals nos. 24, 30, 58, 63, 65 serve to foster the antisemitic aims of the
      proponent.

3008  Schönerer, Georg von (1842–1921): *Die Aufgaben und Ziele der*
      *deutschnationalen Antisemiten in Oesterreich; Vortrag gehalten in der am 8.*
      *Mai 1892 vom Heidelberger Deutsch-Sozialen Antisemitischen Verein . . .*
      *abgehaltenen Versammlung.* Heidelberg: Deutsch-Sozialer Antisemitischer
      Verein, 1892. 23 pp. *LM*

3009  Schönerer, Georg von (1842–1921): *Auszug aus der Rede, welche Abgeordneter*
      *von Schönerer in der Wanderversammlung des Vereines der Deutschnationalen*
      *in Steiermark am 5. September 1886 zu Marburg gehalten hat.* Bruck a.d.M.:
      Jilg, 1886. 6 pp. *LJ*

3010 Schönerer, Georg von (1842–1921): *Die Beschlüße des deutschen Bauerntages. Zwei Anträge betreffend die Erlassung von Gesetzen gegen die Juden.* Wien: Kubasta & Voigt, 1891. 131 pp. *LM*

3011 Schönerer, Georg von (1842–1921): *Fünf Reden; nach den stenographischen Aufzeichnungen. Nebst einem Anhang enthaltend: Die Verteidigungsrede des Abgeordneten G. von Schönerer, gehalten in dem wider ihn angestrengten Prozeße am 5. Mai. 1888 und das Urteil vom 5. Mai und vom 27. Juni 1888, wodurch G. v. Schönerer auch des Reichsratsmandates verlustig erklärt wurde. — Das Programm der Deutsch-Nationalen Antisemiten: Linzer Programm. Die Beschlüsse des deutschen Bauerntages. Zwei Anträge des Abgeordneten G. v. Schönerer betreffs die Erlassung von Gesetzen gegen die Juden.* Horn: F. Berger, 1892. 135 pp. *LB*

3012 Schönerer, Georg von (1842–1921): *Georg Schönerer Gesamtwerk.* Hrsg. mit Unterstützung des Reichsinstituts für Geschichte des neuen Deutschlands, von Eduard Pichl. Oldenburg: G. Stalling, 1938. 6 vols. *Unseen*

3013 Schönerer, Georg von (1842–1921): *Judentum und Deutschtum in der Ostmark; 4 Reden.* 2. Aufl. Marburg: Verlag des "Reichsherold," 1887. 72 pp. *LJ*

3014 Schönerer, Georg von (1842–1921): *Rede, gehalten in der Sitzung des Abgeordnetenhauses zu Wien am 28. April 1887 in der Generaldebatte über den Staatsvoranschlag.* Marburg: Verlag des "Reichsherold," 1887. 21 pp. *Unseen*

3015 Schönerer, Georg von (1842–1921): *Rede über die Presse, gehalten vom Reichsrats-Abgeordneten Georg Ritter von Schönerer in der von über 4000 Personen besuchten Versammlung im Stefan-Saale zu Wien, am 13. Febr. 1885.* Wien: 1885. 1 vol. *Unseen*

Offprint from: Schönerers Journal: *Unverfälschte Deutsche Worte*, 1885, vol. 16.

3016 Schönerer, Georg von (1842–1921): *Reden des . . . Nach den stenographischen Aufzeichnungen. Nebst einem Anhang enthaltend: Die Verteidigungsrede des Abgeordneten G. von Schönerer gehalten in der wider ihn angestrengten Prozeße am 5. Mai 1888. und dem Urteil vom 5. Mai 1888 und vom 27. Juni, wodurch G. v. Schönerer auch des Reichsratsmandates verlustig erklärt wurde. Das Programm der deutschnationalen Antisemiten (Linzer Programm). Die Beschlüße des deutschen Bauerntages. Zwei Anträge des Abgeordneten Ritter v. Schönerer betreffs der Erlassung von Gesetzen gegen die Juden.* Horn: F. Berger, 1896. 93 pp. *LJ*

3017 Schönerer, Georg von (1842–1921): *Reden nach den stenograpfischen Aufzeichungen nebst einem Anhange.* Horn: F. Berger, 1898. 80 pp. *LB*

3018 Schönerer, Georg von (1842–1921): *Reden und Anträge des Abgeordneten Georg Ritter von Schönerer, gehalten und gestellt im Abgeordnetenhause des Reichsrates zwischen dem Beginne der X. Session am 22. September bis zum 22. Juni 1886.* Horn: Berger, 1886. 37 pp. *LJ*
Offprint from: *Stenographische Protokolle des Hauses der Abgeordneten.*

3019 Schönerer, Georg von (1842–1921): *Ueber das Vorgehen bei Güter-Ausschlachtungen.* Wien: Kubasta & Voigt, 1899. 80 pp. *Unseen*
Offprint from: *Unverfälschte Deutsche Worte.*

3020 Schönerer, Georg von (1842–1921): *Verteidigungsrede gehalten im Tagblatt-Prozeße zu Wien am 5. Mai 1888.* Horn: Berger, 1888. 3 pp. *LTA*

3021 Schönerer, Georg von (1842–1921): *Zehn Reden . . . aus den Jahren 1882–1888.* Wien: Alldeutscher Verein für die Ostmark, 1914. 203 pp. *LB*

3022 Schönerer, Georg von (1842–1921): *Zur Judenfrage; Rede des . . . gehalten in der Sitzung des Abgeordnetenhauses zu Wien am 28. April 1887 in der Generaldebatte über den Staatsvoranschlag. Nebst einem Anhang mit dem Wortlaut des Antrages betreffend ein Gesetz gegen die Einwanderung ausländischer Juden.* Schloß Rosenau: Verlag von G.R. v. Schönerer, 1887. 23 pp. *LJ*
Offprint from: *Stenographische Protokolle des Oesterreichischen Abgeordneten-haus.*

3023 Schönerer, Georg von (1842–1921): *Zur Sprachenfrage; Rede gehalten in der 16. Sitzung des Abgeordnetenhauses zu Wien am 29.IV.1898.* Horn: F. Berger, 1898. 80 pp. *LB*

3024 Schönerer, Georg von (1842–1921): *Zwölf Reden. Nebst einem Anhang enthaltend: Das Program der Deutschnationalen. Die Beschlüße des deutschen Bauerntages. Die Satzungen a) des Schulvereins für Deutsche b) des Deutsch-Nationalen Vereins.* Wien: Kubasta & Voigt, 1886. 147 pp. *Unseen*

3025 Schorlemer, Hubert von: *Geschütztes Judentum und schutzloses Christentum; eine Zeitbetrachtung.* Traunstein: Typ. C. Werkmeister, 1904. 70 pp. *LJ*

3026 Schorlemer, Hubert von: *Talmi-Antisemitismus, von einem zielbewußten Antisemiten.* Großenhain: H. Starke, 1895. V, 50 pp. *LJ*

3027 Schrenzel, Moses (1838–1912): *Die Lösung der Judenfrage.* Allen Angehörigen des jüdischen Stammes zur Beherzigung empfohlen. Wien: Lippe, 1881. 30 pp. *Unseen*

3028 Schroot, A.: *Die jüdische Moral in alter und neuer Zeit; ein Beitrag zur Lösung der Judenfrage*. Leipzig: K. Krause, 1892. 15 pp. *LJ*

3029 Schulze, P.: *Eine Stimme aus dem Volke über die Judenfrage. Offener Brief an Herrn Egon Waldegg*. Köln: Selbstverlag, 1888. 47 pp. *LJ*

3030 Schwechten, Eduard: *In Sachen kontra Sem*. Köln: Antisemitische Buchhdlg. E. Hensel, 1894. 20 pp. *LJ*

3031 Schwechten, Eduard: *Das Lied vom Levi. Frei nach Schillers "Lied der Glocke."* Köln: Antisemitische Buchhdlg. E. Hensel, 1894. 15 pp. *LJ*

3032 Schwechten, Eduard: *Schlaglichter von Abraham bis auf Dreyfus; gesammelte antihebräische Gedichte*. Berlin: Verlag der "Deutsche Hochwacht," 1902. 160 pp. *LB*

3033 *Schwurgerichtsverhandlung gegen den Schriftsteller Franz Holubek wegen der in den "Drei Engel-Sälen" zu Wien gehaltenen antisemitischen Rede*. Nach stenographischer Aufzeichnung. Wien: Verlag des "Oesterreichischer Volksfreund," 1882. 48 pp. *LV*

3034 Sedinus, Johannes: *Judengift in Einzel-Dosen. Dosis, Nr. 1. Die Verseuchung des deutschen Volkes durch die verjudete Presse*. Berlin: P. Heichen, 1892. 32 pp. *LC*

3035 Sedinus, Johannes: *Press-Israel oder die Berliner Zeitungs-Mischpoke. Fortsetzung zu Sally Simon Tilles' "Mischpoke im Berliner Buchhandel."* Berlin: P. Heichen, 1892. 32 pp. *LJ*

3036 Segel, Binjamin Wolf: *Die Entdeckungsreise des Herrn Dr. Theodor Lessing zu den Ostjuden*. Lemberg: Verlag "Hatikwa," 1910. 74 pp. *LJ*

3037 Seidl, J.: *Der Jude des 19. Jahrhunderts; oder, Warum sind wir antisemitisch*. München: R. Abt, 1900. XV, 184 pp. *LJ*

3038 Seidl, J.: *Der Jude in Oesterreich-Ungarn. Skizzen aus dem sozialen Leben des 19. Jahrhunderts*. München: Abt, 1900. VIII, 184 pp. *LC*

3039 Seifert, Theodor: Ist der Antisemitismus vom kirchlichen Standpunkt aus berechtigt oder nicht? *Allgemeine Konservative Monatsschrift für das Christliche Deutschland* (1899) 1288–1293. *Unseen*

3040 *Die selbstlosen Antisemiten und die ausbeuterischen Sozialdemokraten. Beginnend: Wähler Wiens! Wenn Ihr Euch zu entscheiden habt, etc*. Wien: J. Popp, 1897. 1 vol. *LV*

3041  *Semi-Imperator, 1888–1918: Semi-Alliancen Folge; judaisierte Hohenzollern.*
      *Eine genealogisch-rassengeschichtliche Aufklärung zur Warnung für die*
      *Zukunft; ein packender Kommentar zu den Semi-Alliancen im besonderen und*
      *semigothaischen Erkenntnissen im allgemeinen.* München: F. Eher Nachflg.,
      1919. 206 pp. *LJ*

3042  *Semigothaismen; Allgemeines und Persönliches vom Semigothaismus. Beiträge*
      *zu dessen Sein und Werden, nebst einer Auswahl der wertvollsten Aeußerungen*
      *aus den dies- und jenseitigen Lagern über die semigothaischen Ereignisse, Um-*
      *und Zustände vorzüglich des Jahres 1913.* München: Kyffhäuser Verlag, 1914.
      XVI, 384 pp. *LJ*

3043  Semitha, pseud.: *Semita in Aengsten; authentisches Schreiben eines polnischen*
      *Rabbiners an den Verfasser der Sittenlehre des Talmuds und des zerstörerischen*
      *Einflußes des Judentums im Deutschen Reiche.* Berlin: M. A. Niendorf, 1877.
      22 pp. *LJ*

3044  Seneca, pseud.: *Die Sittlichkeitsverbrechen eines Breslauer Zeitungs-Redakteurs.*
      Mit einer Einleitung von Alex Berg. Berlin: G.A. Dewald, 1894. 16 pp.
      *Unseen*

3045  Sevin, Hermann (1841–): *Semitische und indogermanische Rechtsbegriffe; eine*
      *volkswirtschaftlich ortsgeschichtliche Studie.* Leipzig: H. Beyer, 1889. 16 pp.
      *Unseen*

      Offprint from: *Antisemitische Correspondenz.*

3046  Seyppel, Karl Maria: *Er, Sie, es? IIte ägyptische Humoreske. Nach der Natur*
      *abgemalt und niedergeschrieben 1302 Jahre vor Christi Geburt durch C.M.*
      *Seyppel, Hofmaler und Poet der seligen Majestät König Rhampsinit III.*
      *Memphis, Pyramidenstr. N 36, Ite Etage. Meldung beim Portier.* Düsseldorf:
      F. Bagel, 1883. VI, 42 pp. *LTA*

3047  Seyppel, Karl Maria: *Die Plagen. 3te ägyptische Humoreske. Aufgeschrieben*
      *und abgemalt bei dem Auszuge der Juden aus Aegypten, von C.M. Seyppel,*
      *Hofmaler und Poet der seligen Majestät, König Rhampsinit III. Memphis,*
      *Krokodilenstraße, Villa Seyppel. Sprechstunde: 6–7 vormittags.* Düsseldorf:
      Bagel, 1884. 42 pp. *LJ*

3048  Seyppel, Karl Maria: *Schlau, schläuer, am schläusten; ägyptische Humoreske.*
      *Niedergeschrieben und abgemalt 1315 Jahre vor Christi Geburt von . . .*
      *Hofmaler und Poet Seiner Majestät des Königs Rhampsinit III.* Düsseldorf:
      Bagel, 1882. 40 pp. *LV*

3049 Siecke, Ernst (1846–1935): *Die Judenfrage und der Gymnasiallehrer. Ein Beitrag zur Richtigstellung der öffentlichen Meinung.* Berlin: F. Luckhardt, 1880. 23 pp. *LJ*

3050 *Sigilla Veri; Philipp Stauff's Semi-Kürschner. Lexikon der Juden-Genossen und- Gegner aller Zeiten und Zonen, insbesondere Deutschlands, der Lehren, Gebräuche, Kunstgriffe und Statistiken der Juden, sowie ihrer Gaunersprache, Trugnamen, Geheimbünde usw. 2. um ein Vielfaches verm. Aufl. Unter Mitwirkung gelehrter Männer und Frauen aller in Betracht kommenden Länder im Auftrage der Weltliga gegen die Lüge; in Verbindung mit der Alliance chrétienne arienne.* Hrsg. von E. Ekkehard. Erfurt: U. Bodung, 1929–31. 4 vols. *LJ*

No more published. 1st ed., 1913.

3051 Silberner, Edmund (1910–): Was Marx an Anti-Semite? *Hist. Jud.* 11 (1949) 3–52. *LJ*

3052 Silberstein, Meyer: *Hersch Goldmann's Soll und Haben; ahne Familiengeschichte im 24 Guldenfuss aus' m Cassabuch . . .* Leipzig: Wengler, 1861. 23 pp. *LJ*

3053 Simonyi, Ivan von: *Der Antisemitismus und die Gesetze der menschlichen Gesellschaft; Antisemiten-Kongress zu Dresden.* Preßburg: 1884. 1 vol. *Unseen*

3054 Simonyi, Ivan von: *Der Judaismus und die parlamentarische Komödie; Rede über die Täuschungen und die notwendige Reform unseres modernen Repräsentativsystems, gehalten bei der Gelegenheit der Budgetdebatte im ungarischen Abgeordnetenhaus. Mit einer Einleitung: Die Juden und die Hohlheit unserer modernen Politik und Verfassung.* Preßburg: G. Heckenast, 1883. 94 pp. *LJ*

3055 Simonyi, Ivan von: *Vorträge über die Judenfrage gehalten am 5. Februar 1883 im deutschen Reformverein zu Chemnitz.* Chemnitz: E. Schmeitzner, 1883. 24 pp. *LJ*

3056 Simonyi, Ivan von: *Die Wahrheit über die Judenfrage; zu Nutz und Frommen des jüdischen und nichtjüdischen Publikums geschrieben.* Preßburg: Heckenast's Nachf., 1882. 126 pp. *Unseen*

3057 Simplex, Justus, pseud.: *Der Anti-Verjüdelungs-Verein; ein komisches Epos in 10 Gesängen.* Berlin: E. Staude, 1880. V, 111 pp. *LJ*

3058 Simplex, Justus, pseud.: *Werden und Vergehen des Anti-Verjüdelungs-Vereins; ein harmloser Beitrag zur modernen Judenbewegung in lustigen Reimen. 2.* Aufl. Berlin: E. Staude, 1881. 111 pp. *LJ*

3059   Simplicissimus, Simplicius, pseud.: *Der Fall Kantorowicz als Symptom unserer Zustände; eine Neujahrsbetrachtung auf Grund harmlosen Quellenstudiums.* Berlin: J. Ruppel, 1881. 67 pp. *LTA*

3060   *Sittenlehre des Juden; Auszug aus dem Talmud (Schulchan Aruch). Zusammenstellung rabbinischer Lehren und jüdischer Sittengesetze.* Kommentiert von . . . Prof. Eisenmenger . . . und Prof. Dr. August Rohling in Prag. Veröffentlicht auf Grund des eidlichen Gutachtens des gerichtlichen Sachverständigen Prof. Dr. Jakob Ecker in Trier. Stuttgart: Deutschvölkischer Schutz- und Trutzbund, 189–. 15 pp. *LJ*

3061   Solger, Friedrich (1877–): *Der nationale Geist als Naturerscheinung; Vortrag im Werdandibunde am 25. Februar 1909.* Leipzig: F. Eckardt, 1909. 15 pp. (Wertung; Schriften des Werdandibundes, 4) *Unseen*

3062   Sombart, Werner (1863–1941): Grund zu dem jüdischen Wesen. *Oesterreichische Rundschau* 26 (1911) 127–135. *Unseen*

3063   Sombart, Werner (1863–1941): *Die Zukunft der Juden.* Leipzig: Duncker & Humblot, 1912. 91 pp. *LJ*

3064   Sontag, Leon: *So ist der Herd der sozialen Uebel? Ein Wahlaufruf an die deutschen Männer, den deutschen Frauen ehrfurchtsvoll gewidmet.* Breslau: A. Goscharsky, 1878. 56 pp. *Unseen*

3065   Sorger, H.: *Die 10 Gebote in talmudisch-jüdischer Beleuchtung und das daraus sich ergebende Urteil über das moderne Judentum.* Münster: A. Russell, 1894. 67 pp. *LM*

3066   Sozial-Konservative Vereinigung, Berlin: *Denkschrift nebst den dazu gehörigen Referaten für die erste General-Versammlung der Sozial-Konservativen Vereinigung zu Berlin am 18. und 19. Mai 1881.* Hrsg. von dem Bureau des provisorischen Vorstandes. Berlin: M. Schultze, 1881. 159 pp. *LJ*

3067   Soziale Frage und Antisemitsmus. *Konservatives Wochenblatt* 2, 48 (1891) [n.p.]. *Unseen*

3068   *Sozialpolitische Beiträge zur Judenfrage in Deutschland.* Aus dem praktischen Leben der Provinz und Großstadt. Berlin: A. Klein, 1881. 44 pp. *LJ*

3069   Spigl, Elisabeth: *Das Wiener Judentum der achtziger Jahre in Literatur und Presse.* Wien: Oest. Nationalbibliothek, 1959. 108 pp. *LJ*
       Diss. Wien 1943.

3070 Spitta, Heinrich (1849–1929): *Ein Blick in unsere Zeit*. Freiburg: J.C.B. Mohr, 1888. 44 pp. *Unseen*

3071 Stanojevič, Simon: *Die Judenfrage vom slavischen Standpunkte*. Zombor: Verlag von Sztanojévics, ZS, 1881. 32 pp. *LJ*

3072 Stanojévič, Simon: *Die Wirkung der jüdischen Sittenlehre in der menschlichen Gesellschaft*. 2. Aufl. Zombor: Stanojevics Zs, 1880. 31 pp. *Unseen*

3073 Stauff, Philipp (1876–1923): *Deutsche Judennamen. Zusammengestellt nach den Verzeichnissen jüdischer Religionsbehörden*. Hrsg. im Auftrage des Deutsch-Völkischen Schriftstellerverbandes. Berlin: K.G.Th. Scheffer, 1912. X, 49, III pp. (Denkschrift des Deutsch-Völkischen Schriftstellerverbandes, 1) *LJ*

3074 Stauff, Philipp (1876–1923): *Semi-Kürschner; oder, Literarisches Lexikon der Schriftsteller, Dichter Bankiers, Geldleute, Aerzte . . . jüdischer Rasse und Versippung, die von 1813–1913 in Deutschland tätig oder bekannt waren . . .* Berlin: Selbstverlag, 1913. XXVI, 308 pp. *LJ*

3075 Stauff, Philipp (1876–1923): *Voltaire über die Juden*. Hrsg. im Auftrage des Deutsch-Völkischen Schriftstellerverbandes. Berlin: K.G.Th. Scheffer, 1913. 26 pp. (Denkschrift der Deutsch-Völkischen Schriftstellerverbandes, 2) *LJ*

3076 Stauff, Philipp (1876–1923): Zwei Rassenideale. *Pol. Anthrop.Rev.* 13 (1914) 151–155. *LJ*

3077 Stein, Franz: *Schönerer in der Arbeiterfrage*. Horn: 1893. 53 pp. *LV*

3078 Steiner, Friedrich: *Die neue Jüden-Bürger-Miliz*. Wien: Typ. M. Lell, 1848. 4 pp. *LJ*

3079 Steinmann, Friedrich Arnold: *Das Haus Rothschild, seine Geschichte und seine Geschäfte; Aufschlüße und Enthüllungen zur Geschichte des Jahrhunderts, insbesondere des Staatsfinanz- und Börsenwesens*. Prag: I.L. Kober, 1857. 2 vols. in one. *LJ*

3080 Stettinger ,M.: *Die Sozialdemokratie unter jüdischem Joche*. Klagenfurt: Carinthia, Buchdr. u. Buchhdlg., 1911. 31 pp. (Volksaufklärung, 145) *LV*

3081 Stille, Gustav Wilhelm Bernhard (1845–1920): *Die deutsche Schule in Gefahr*. Berlin: W. Giese, 1899. 63 pp. *LM*

3082 Stille, Gustav Wilhelm Bernhard (1845–1920): *Der Kampf gegen das Judentum*. 8. Aufl. Hamburg: Verlag der Deutschnationalen Buchhdlg., 1912. 219 pp. *LJ*

3083  Stoecker, Adolf (1835–1909): *Die antijüdische Bewegung gerechtfertigt vor dem Preußischen Landtag; Rede des Hofprediger, Stoecker am 25. Februar 1882.* Berlin: Typ. Thormann, 1882. 16 pp. (Flugblatt no. 33 der Christlich-Sozialen Partei) *LJ*

3084  Stoecker, Adolf (1835–1909): *Christlich-soziale Reden und Aufsätze.* 6. Aufl. Berlin: Berliner Stadtmission, 1890. LX, 496 pp. *LJ*

3085  Stoecker, Adolf (1835–1909): *Dreizehn Jahre Hofprediger und Politiker.* 2. Aufl. Berlin: Berliner Stadtmission, 1895. 53 pp. *LJ*

3086  Stoecker, Adolf (1835–1909): *Der Kern der Judenfrage; Rede des Hofprediger Stoecker in der Versammlung der Christlich-Sozialen Arbeiterpartei zu Berlin am 9 April.* Berlin: Typ. Thormann, 1880. 11 pp. (Flugbatt der Christlich-Sozialen Arbeiterpartei, 21) *LJ*

3087  Stoecker, Adolf (1835–1909): *Das moderne Judentum in Deutschland, besonders in Berlin; zwei Reden in der Christlich-Sozialen Arbeiter-partei.* 4. Aufl. Berlin: Wiegandt und Grieben, 1880. 40 pp. *LJ*

3088  Stoecker, Adolf (1835–1909): *Notwehr gegen das moderne Judentum; zweite Rede.* Berlin: Typ. J. Windolff, 1879. 20 pp. (Flugblatt der Christlich-Sozialen Arbeiterpartei, 14) *LJ*

3089  Stoecker, Adolf (1835–1909): *Prozeß Stoecker wider die "Freie Zeitung." Nach stenographischen Aufzeichnungen vervollständigt.* Berlin: Freie Zeitung, 1885. 95 pp. *LJ*

      The defendant, Heinrich Bäcker, was editor of the *Freie Zeitung.*

3090  Stoecker, Adolf (1835–1909): *Rede des Herrn Hofprediger a.D. Stoecker zu Bielefeld, 28. Februar 1893.* Bielefeld: Typ. E. Siedhoff, 1893. 22 pp. *LJ*

3091  Stoecker, Adolf (1835–1909): *Reden im Reichstag. Amtlicher Wortlaut.* Hrsg. von Reinhard Mumm. Schwerin: F. Bahn, 1914. VII, 510 pp. *LB*

3092  Stoecker, Adolf (1835–1909): *Reden und Aufsätze.* Bielefeld: Velhagen und Klasing, 1885. 526 pp. *Unseen*

3093  Stoecker, Adolf (1835–1909): *Reden und Aufsätze.* Mit einer biographischen Einleitung. Hrsg. von Reinhold Seeberg. Leipzig: A. Deichertsche Verlagshdlg. Nachf., 1913. IV, 276 pp. *LV*

3094  Stoecker, Adolf (1835–1909): *Die soziale Lage und Frage; Vortrag gehalten in Billingen.* Gernsbach: Christlicher Kolportage-Verein, 1890. 24 pp. *LTA*

3095 Stoecker, Adolf (1835–1909): *Unsere Forderungen an das moderne Judentum; Rede des Hofpredigers Stoecker, gehalten am 19.* September 1879 in der *Versammlung der Christlich-Sozialen Arbeiterpartei.* Berlin: Typ. Thormann & Götsch, 1879. 12 pp. (Flugblatt, 13. Christlich-Soziale Arbeiterpartei) *LJ*

3096 Stoecker, Adolf (1835–1909): *Vorträge des Herrn Hofpredigers Stoecker aus Berlin und des Herrn Dr. König aus Witten.* Hagen i. W.: Typ. Risel, 1887. 68 pp. *LJ*

3097 Stoecker, Adolf (1835–1909): What We Demand of Modern Jewry. *Rehearsal for Destruction.* By Paul W. Massing. New York: Harper & Brothers, 1949. Pp. 278–287. *LJ*

Translation of: *Unsere Forderungen an das moderne Judentum, 1879.*

3098 Stoecker, Ernst: *Geschichte der Judenschaft von Frankfurt, dargestellt von einem Deutschen.* Berlin: W. Giese, 1897. 45 pp. *LJ*

3099 Stöter, Ferdinand (1811–): *Stoeckers agitatorische Tätigkeit. Aufsatz gelesen im theologischen Verein am 29.6.1885.* Als Manuskript gedruckt. Hamburg: 1885. 16 pp. *LTA*

3100 Stolz, Alban (1808–1883): Licht, Fortschritt, Freiheit; wie dieselben von der schlechten Presse verstanden und gepriesen werden. *Weckstimmen für das Katholische Volk* 1, 1 (1870) *Unseen*

3101 Strösser: *Drei Reden über die Judenfrage, die Handwerkerfrage und die Stellung der konservativen Partei zu verschiedenen politschen und sozialen Fragen.* Breslau: Dülfer, 1881. 66 pp. *Unseen*

3102 *Die studentische Petition als Annex der allgemeinen Petition, betreffend die Einschränkung der jüdischen Machtstellung. Ein Beitrag zur Orientierung über Gründe und Zweck desselben. 2. durchgesehene und bedeutend verm. Doppel-Aufl.* Leipzig: Paul Frohberg, 1881. 32 pp. *LJ*

3103 Stützer, Friedrich G.: *Israel auf dem Scheidewege.* Wien: Selbverlag, 1903. 20 pp. *LJ*

3104 Stusslieb, Ernst: *Der aufgeblasene Talmudlöwe; ergötzliche und lehrreiche Gespräche des Herrn Schochet Isidor Eisenstein mit seinem Sohne Moritz über die unleugbaren Vorzüge und unbestrittenen Vorteile der Jehudim über die Gojim.* Würzburg: Etlingersche Verlagshdlg., 1892. 90 pp. *LJ*

3105  *Talmud-Auszug   (Schulchan-Aruch).   Enthaltend:   die   wichtigsten   bisher übersetzten, noch heute gültigen Gesetze der jüdischen Religion.* Berlin: F.W. Baade, 1892. 4 pp. *LJ*
Antisemitic pamphlet.

3106  *Der Talmud; oder, Die Sittenlehre des Judentums. Nebst einem Anhang: enthaltend Aussprüche deutscher Geistesheroen mit Portraits, Episoden über den zerstörenden Einfluß des Judentums, Statistisches, usw.* Volksausg. Berlin: M. Schulze, 1881. 64 pp. *LJ*

3107  *Der Talmud; oder, Die Sittenlehre des Judentums, nebst Kulturgeschichte des Judentums, Aussprüchen hervorragender Männer aller Zeiten, jüdisch-deutschem Wörterbuch, usw.* 3. Aufl. Wohlfeile Ausg. Berlin: Schulze, 188-. 47 pp. *LJ*

3108  *Th. Mommsen und sein Wort über unser Judentum.* Berlin: O. Hentze, 1881. 8 pp. *LJ*
Offprint from: *Deutsche Wacht.*

3109  Thiele, A.F.: *Juda's Ahnen-Saal; oder, Die jüdischen Gauner in Deutschland, nach den amtlichen Ermittlungen des ehemaligen Kriminal-Aktuars Thiele in Berlin 1841.* Berlin: Julius Ruppel, 1881. 96 pp. *LJ*

3110  Treitschke, Heinrich Gotthard von (1834-1896): Antwort auf eine studentische Huldigung. *Deutsche Kämpfe, N.F.* Leipzig: S. Hirzel, 1896. Pp. 119-122. *LB*

3111  Treitschke, Heinrich Gotthard von (1834-1896): Ein Antwortschreiben des Herrn Professor H. von Treitschke. *Israelitische Wochenschrift* 10 (1879) 145. *LJ*

3112  Treitschke, Heinrich Gotthard von (1834-1896): Eine Erwiderung. *Deutsche Kämpfe, N.F.* Leipzig: S. Hirzel, 1896. Pp. 123-125. *LB*

3113  Treitschke, Heinrich Gotthard von (1834-1896): Erwiderung an Theodor von Mommsen. *Pr. Jhrb.* 46 (1880) 661-663. *LJ*

3114  Treitschke, Heinrich Gotthard von (1834-1896): Herr Graetz und sein Judentum. *Pr. Jhrb.* 44 (1879) 660-670. *LJ*

3115  Treitschke, Heinrich Gotthard von (1834-1896): Die jüdische Einwanderung in Preußen. *Pr. Jhrb.* 52 (1883) 534-538. *LJ*

3116  Treitschke, Heinrich Gotthard von (1834-1896): Noch einige Bemerkungen zur Judenfrage. *Pr. Jhrb.* 45 (1880) 85-95. *LJ*

3117 Treitschke, Heinrich Gotthard von (1834–1896): *Reden im deutschen Reichstage, 1871–1884.* Mit Einleitung und Erläuterungen, hrsg. von O. Mittelstaedt. Leipzig: S. Hirzel, 1896. VIII, 223 pp. *LM*

3118 Treitschke, Heinrich Gotthard von (1834–1896): Unsere Aussichten. *Pr. Jhrb.* 44 (1879) 559–576. *LJ*

3119 Treitschke, Heinrich Gotthard von (1834–1896): *Ein Wort über unser Judentum.* Berlin: Reimer, 1880. 27 pp. *LJ*

  Offprint from: *Pr. Jhrb.*, 1879, vols. 44 and 45; also includes "Unsere Aussichten," published on 15th November 1879 in Pr. Jhrb.

3120 Treitschke, Heinrich Gotthard von (1834–1896): Zuschrift an die Post. *Deutsche Kämpfe, N.F.* Leipzig: S. Hirzel, 1896. Pp. 116. *LB*

3121 Treter, Miecislaus von Lubomir: *E pur si muove! Ein Beitrag zur Lösung der Judenfrage.* Lemberg: Selbstverlag, 1881. 48 pp. *LV*

3122 Treter, Miecislaus von Lubomir: *Frohe Botschaft; wahre Lösung der Judenfrage.* Wien: Ficht, 1882. 110 pp. *Unseen*

  "Concourspreisschrift."

3123 Türk, Karl: *Die Verjudung Oesterreichs; eine Warnung für das Deutsche Reich. Rede.* Berlin: Dewald, 1889. 22 pp. *LJ*

3124 Tulpenthal, Jakob Leibche: *Gott der Gerechte! Berlin geiht pleite! Eine Rede geredt zu seine Frau Hannche von Jakob Leibche Tulpenthal, emanzipierter Isrelit aus dem Großherzogtum Posen.* Berlin: Marquardt & Steinthal, 1848–1849. 1 l., fol. *LJ*

3125 Tulpenthal, Jakob Leibche: *Weih geschrigen; die Welt is meschugge. Dritte Rede geredt zu seine Frau Hannche.* Berlin: Marquardt & Steinthal, 1848. 1 l. *LJ*

3126 Tulpenthal, Jakob Leibche: *Wrangelsche in Berlin will schießen; Branneborghe in Breslau will och schießen. Haste gesehen, wie heißt; zweite Rede geredt zu seine Frau Hannche.* Berlin: Marquardt & Steinthal, 1848. 1 l. *LJ*

3127 *Der Ultramontanismus, der Antisemitismus und die freie Volksschule, von einem christlichen Oberlehrer.* Wien: Jacobi, 1889. 1 vol. *LV*

3128 Ungern-Sternberg, E. von: *Zur Judenfrage.* Stuttgart: Belser, 1892. 44 pp. (Zeitfragen des christlichen Volkslebens, 17, 7) *LJ*

3129   Urteile hervorragender Männer über das Judentum. Leipzig: Th. Fritsch, 1885.
       8 pp. (Brennende Fragen, 16) LJ

3130   Válasz Kossuth Lajos legutóbbi levelére a zsidó kérdésben: 'Szegyen es gyálazat
       hogy Magyarorszagon zsidó kérdés is lehet! Budapest: Typ. S. Kocsi, 1883.
       16 pp. LJ
       Signed by M.M.M.

3131   Valentin, Conrad: Der Kaiser hat gesprochen; wie haben wir Konservativen uns
       jetzt zu verhalten. Berlin: Deubner, 1889. 50 pp. LM

3132   Vampyr; oder, Das Wucherjudentum. 4. Aufl. Riedlingen: Ulrich, 1895. 47 pp.
       Unseen

3133   Varicourt, Br.: Die Juden und die Judenfrage. Pest: Typ. J. Beimel & Bazil
       Kozma, 1861. 32 pp. LJ

3134   Verein für Sozialpolitik, Berlin: Der Wucher auf dem Lande. Berichte und
       Gutachten. Leipzig: Duncker & Humblot, 1887. XII, 354 pp. (Schriften des
       Vereins für Sozialpolitik, 35) LJ

3135   Vergani, Ernst: Die Judenfrage in Oesterreich; zusammengestellt nach den
       Vorträgen gehalten am 21. und 25. November in Potsdam und am 3. Dezember
       1891 in Dresden. Leipzig: Germanicus-Verlag, 1892. 55 pp. LV

3136   Verhandlungen des pfälzischen Schwurgerichts in Zweibrücken; Freisprechung
       des Verlagsbuchhändlers August Gotthold in Kaiserslautern von der Anklage
       der Beschimpfung der jüdischen Religion durch die Presse. Wörtlicher Bericht
       der Sitzung. Kaiserslautern: A. Gotthold, 1888. 31 pp. LJ

3137   Die Verjudung des christlichen Staates. Ein Wort zur Zeit. Leipzig: H. Matthes,
       1865. 31 pp. LJ

3138   Die Verjudung des deutschen Theaters. Die Grenzboten 39 (1880) 28–38,
       71–83. LC

3139   Victor, Klemens: Prof. Dr. Rohling, die Judenfrage und die öffentliche
       Meinung. Eine kurzgefasste Beleuchtung des neulich durch . . . J. Kopp . . .
       veröffentlichten Gutachtens sogenannter "Sachverständiger" in Sachen des
       Prozeßes Rohling-Bloch, usw. Leipzig: Th. Fritsch, 1887. IV, 84 pp. LJ

3140   Vigyázó, Gyula: A magyar zsidóság és a keresztény társadalom. Budapest:
       1908. 71 pp. LJ

3141 Völske, Arnold (1906–): *Die Entwicklung des "rassischen Antisemitismus" zum Mittelpunkt der Weltanschauung Eugen Dührings.* Hamburg: Verlag Hans Christian, 1936. 59 pp. *LJ*

Diss. 1936.

3142 Vogel, Emil Ferdinand: *Offener Brief an alle Innungsgenossen Deutschlands sowie zugleich an alle Bürger und Hausväter, von 22 Innungen zu Leipzig.* Leipzig: Joachim Matthes, 1848. 24 pp. *Unseen*

3143 Vogel, Rudolph: *Herr Minister Buchenberger und der Antisemitismus.* Leipzig: H. Beyer, 1894. 30 pp. *LB*

3144 Vogelsang, Karl von (1818–1890): *Die sozialen Lehren des Freiherrn Karl von Vogelsang: Grundzüge einer christlichen Gesellschafts- und Volkswirtschaftslehre.* Aus dem literarischen Nachlaß desselben zusammengestellt von Wiard von Klopp. St. Pölten: F. Chamra, 1894. 643 pp. *LJ*

One of his social doctrines is that the Jews, after the emancipation, control Austria except for the administration.

3145 Voges, Erich: *Im jüdischen Zeitalter; eine Betrachtung unserer heutigen Zustände in wirtschaftlicher, politischer, sozialer und religiöser Beziehung.* Nordhausen: C. Kirchner, 1895. 22 pp. *LJ*

3146 *Votum eines Unbefangenen; ein Beitrag zur Judenfrage, von einem ehemaligen Liberalen.* Berlin: F. Heinicke, 1881. 36 pp. *LJ*

3147 Vrba, Rudolf (1860–): *Národní sebeochrana; úvahy o hmotném a mravnim úpadku národa Českého.* Praha: Nákl spisovatelovým, 1898. 320 pp. *LJ*

3148 Wälsung, Widar: *War Jesus ein Jude? Eine deutsche Antwort.* Nürnberg: L. Spindler, [n.d.]. 24 pp. *LJ*

3149 Wagner, Cosima (Liszt) (1837–1930): *Cosima Wagner und Houston Stewart Chamberlain im Briefwechsel, 1888–1908.* Hrsg. von Paul Pretzsch. Leipzig: P. Reclam, 1934. 713 pp. *LV*

3150 Wagner, Cosima (Liszt) (1837–1930): *Die Tagebücher.* Ediert und kommentiert von Martin Gregor-Dellin und Dietrich Mack. München: R. Piper, 1976–1977. 2 vols. *LJ*

Vol. 1: 1867–1877; Vol. 2: 1878–1883.

3151 Wagner, Richard (1813–1883): Erkenne dich selbst. *Gesammelte Schriften. Bd. 10, 3. Aufl.* Leipzig: C.F.W. Siegel, 1897. Pp. 263–274. *LJ*

3152  Wagner, Richard (1813–1883): *Judaism in Music.* London: William Reeves, 1910. XV, 95 pp. *LJ*

Original essay together with the later suppl. Tr. from the German and furnished with explanatory notes and introduction by Edwin Evans.

3153  Wagner, Richard (1813–1883): *Das Judentum in der Musik.* Leipzig: J.J. Weber, 1869. 57 pp. *LJ*

First published under the pseudonym K. Freidank, in *Neue Zeitschrift für Musik*, 1850 (no. 19, pp. 101–107; no. 20, pp. 109–112).

3154  Wagner, Richard (1813–1883): *Das Judentum in der Musik, 1869.* 1. Neudruck, hrsg. von Philipp Stauff. Weimar: F. Roltsch, 1914. IX, 51 pp. (Denkschrift des Deutsch-Völkischen Schriftstellerverbandes, 3) *LJ*

3155  Wagner, Richard (1813–1883): Das Judentum in der Musik, von K. Freigedank, pseud. *Neue Zeitschrift für Musik* 33 (1850) 101–107, 109–112. *LJ*

3156  Wagner, Richard (1813–1883): *Die Kunst und die Revolution; das Judentum in der Musik. Was ist Deutsch?* Hrsg. und kommentiert von Tibor Kneif. München: Rogner & Bernhard, 1975. 133 pp. (Reihe Passagen) *LJ*

3157  Wagner, Richard (1813–1883): Modern. *Gesammelte Schriften und Dichtungen. Bd. 10.* Leipzig: E.W. Fritzsch, 1883. Pp. 75–84. *LJ*

3158  Wagner, Richard (1813–1883): Religion und Kunst. *Bayreuther Blätter* 4 (1881) 33–41. *LJ*

3159  Wagner, Richard (1813–1883): Was ist deutsch? *Gesammelte Schriften und Dichtungen. Bd. 10.* Leipzig: E.W. Fritzsch, 1883. Pp. 50–73. *LJ*

3160  *Die Wahrheit über die deutsche Universität Wien und die Lage der deutschen akademischen Jugend. Ein Mahnwort an das deutsche Volk.* Verfasst im Auftrage der deutsch-nationalen Studenten-Versammlung vom 9.12.1892. Horn: F. Berger, 1894. 94 pp. *LJ*

3161  Wahrmund, Adolf (1827–1913): *Babyloniertum, Judentum und Christentum.* Leipzig: F.A. Brockhaus, 1882. XI, 294 pp. *LJ*

3162  Wahrmund, Adolf (1827–1913): *Die christliche Schule und das Judentum.* Wien: Kubasta & Voigt, 1885. IV, 83 pp. *LJ*

3163  Wahrmund, Adolf (1827–1913): *Das Gesetz des Nomadentums und die heutige Judenherrschaft.* Karlsruhe: Reuther, 1887. X, 251 pp. *LJ*

3164  Wahrmund, Adolf (1827–1913): *Juda's Geldmonopol im Aufgang und im Zenith; zwei Zeitgeschichten.* Rodaun — Wien: "Ostara," 1907. 13 pp. (Ostara, 16) *LV*

3165  Wahrmund, Adolf (1827–1913): *Los vom Antisemitismus! Offener Brief an einen Unverfälschten.* Linz: J. Wimmer, 1891. 42 pp. *LTA*

3166  *Wai geschrirn, jetzt fangen die Jüdinnen a schon an.* n.p.: Lell, 1848. 1 l. *LC*

3167  *Warum gibt es in Deutschland eine Judenfrage; eine Antwort in 16 graphischen Tafeln. Von xxx.* Hannover: Verlag der "Heimat," 1898. 17 pp. *LJ*

3168  *Warum ist der Deutsche im Ausland verhaßt?* Leipzig: Th. Fritsch, 1887. 8 pp. (Brennende Fragen, 8) *LJ*

3169  *Warum muß der Antisemitismus siegen. Vom Verfasser des "audiatur et altera pars."* Spandau: G. Schob, 1893. 16 pp. *LJ*

3170  *Was ist Antisemitismus?* Berlin: H. Lüstenöder, 1893. 14 pp. *LJ*

3171  *Was will der Fortschritt?* Leipzig: Th. Fritsch, 1887. 8 pp. (Brennende Fragen, 9) *LJ*

3172  Wawrud-Roscholf: *Der Antisemitismus und die Deutschnationalen in Oesterreich.* Wien: Keiss, 1890. 43 pp. *LV*

3173  Weber, Beda (1798–1858): *Cartons aus dem deutschen Kirchenleben.* Mainz: Kirchheim, 1858. VIII, 789 pp. *LV*

3174  Weber, Hans: *Geschichte des Vereins Deutscher Studenten zu Berlin, 1891–1906, vom 2.–3. Kyffhäuserfest des Kyffhäuserverbandes.* Berlin: V.A.H. Bund des V.D. St., 1912. 304 pp. *LTA*

3175  Wechsler, Bernhard (–1874): *Mallet und die Juden; einige Noten zum Texte einer Predigt.* Hamburg: J. F. Richter, 1858. 16 pp. *LJ*

3176  Wedell, R.A.C. von: *Vorurteil; oder, Berechtigter Haß; eine vorurteilslose Besprechung der Judenfrage.* Berlin: O. Hentze, 1880. 44 pp. *LJ*

3177  Wehleid, Hans: Frank Wedekind über die Aufgabe des Judentums. *Der Hammer* 11 (1912) 215–217. *LB*

3178  *Weimarer historisch-genealoges Taschenbuch des gesamten Adels jehudäischen Ursprungs . . . vom Rassenstandpunkte aus besehen.* Weimar: Kyffhäuser-Verlag, 1912–1913. 2 vols. *LJ*

3179  Weininger, Otto (1880–1903): Das Judentum. *Geschlecht und Charakter. Eine prinzipielle Untersuchung.* Wien: Wilhelm Braumüller, 1903. Pp. 409–452. *LJ*

3180  *Weitere Urteile über das Judentum.* Leipzig: Th. Fritsch, 1885. 8 pp. (Brennende Fragen, 17) *LJ*

3181  *Welchen Anteil hatte Gerson von Bleichröder an dem Sturze des Fürsten Bismarck? Der Schlüssel zur Erkenntnis der gegenwärtigen Lage.* Berlin: K. Sedlatzek, 1890. 24 pp. *LJ*

       Controversy about the book *Das Deutsche Reich zur Zeit Bismarcks*, by Hans Blum.

3182  Welcker, Viktor Hugo: *Die nationalen und sozialen Aufgaben des Antisemitismus; Vortrag.* Ulm: Verlag der Ulmer Schnellpost, 1892. 37 pp. *LV*

       From: *Ulmer Schnellpost*, nos. 45–60.

3183  Wenng, Ludwig, ed.: *Judenfrage vor der bayerischen Kammer der Abgeordneten; Statistisches und anderes über die Judeninvasion in München.* Mit Zugrundelegung der offiziellen stenographischen Kammerberichte. München: Deutsches Volksblatt, 1901. X, 36 pp. *LJ*

3184  *Wer regiert heute? und welcher Partei schließe ich mich an?* Leipzig: Verlag des Deutschen Müller, 1883. 8 pp. *LJ*

3185  Wer schreibt unsere Zeitungen? *Hammer; Blätter für deutschen Sinn* 204 (1912) 8. *LJ*

3186  *Wer trägt die Schuld an der Antisemitenbewegung. Ein Beitrag zur Geschichte unserer Zeit.* Berlin: E. Hübsch, 1886. 23 pp. *LJ*

3187  Werner, Ferdinand (1876–): *Ein öffentliches Heinedenkmal auf deutschem Boden.* Leipzig: G. Hedeler, 1913. 95 pp. *LJ*

3188  Wesendonck, Hermann: *Der jüdisch-christliche Jehova ist kein wahrer, kein würdiger Gott und keine Quelle reiner geläuterter Sittlichkeit.* Leipzig: Spohr, 1892. 184 pp. (Volksaufklärungbibliothek, 1) *LJ*

3189  Wesselsky, Anton: *Oesterreichertum; eine arische Denkschrift.* Wien: Kreisel & Gröger, 1896. 159 pp. *LV*

3190  Westernhagen, Kurt von: *Nietzsche, Juden, Antijuden.* Weimar: A. Duncker, 1936. 78 pp. *LJ*

3191 Westphal, P.: *Illustrierter Führer durch die antisemitische Literatur unter Berücksichtigung beachtenswerter anderweitiger Erscheinungen. Mit einem ausführlichen Verzeichnis der antisemitischen Vereine und einer Tafel empfehlenswerter Lokale.* Nossen i. S.: P. Westphal, 1893. 100 pp. *LJ*

3192 Whitman, Sidney (1848–1925): *Die antisemitische Bewgegung. Aus dem Englischen übers. von O.Th. Alexander.* Berlin: C. Urich, 1893. 32 pp. *LJ*

3193 *Wie macht der Jude das Geschäft?* Leipzig: Th. Fritsch, 1887. 8 pp. (Brennende Fragen, 25) *LJ*

3194 *Wie wird man Millionär?* Leipzig: Verlag des Deutschen Müller, 1883. 8 pp. (Brennende Fragen, 2) *LJ*

3195 Wieringer, Adolf: *Selbsthilfe gegen die fortschreitende Verjudung und Verarmung unseres Volkes.* Wien: Selbstverlag des Verfassers, 1881. 64 pp. *LJ*

3196 Wiesinger, Albert: *Die Kanzel, die Juden und die Judengenossen; zur Abfertigung für jüdische Predigt-Schnüffler und nicht jüdische Predigt-Kritiker.* Wien: Mayer, 1869. 59 pp. *Unseen*

Offprint from: *Vierzehn Fragen aus der Leidensgeschichte*; lent sermons, published in 1869.

3197 Wiesinger, Albert: *Literarische Bildergalerie von antisemitischen Dummköpfen, Narren und Verbrechern; erstes Christenwort zur Judenfrage.* Münster: A. Russell, 1894. 61 pp. *Unseen*

3198 Wilmanns, Carl: *Die "goldene" Internationale und die Notwendigkeit einer sozialen Reformspartei.* Berlin: Niendorf, 1876. 106 pp. *LJ*

3199 Winter, Joseph: *Zur Judenfrage; ein neuer Literatur-Schädling, Herr Isidor Singer.* Wien: Verlag der "Deutschen Worte," 1885. 24 pp. *LJ*

3200 *Wo ist unser Geld geblieben?* Leipzig: Verlag des Deutschen Müller, 1883. 8 pp. (Brennende Fragen, 3) *LJ*

3201 Wohlfarth, Dr.: *Bilder aus der antisemitischen Bewegung I.* Berlin: W. Giese, 1898. 50 pp. *LJ*

3202 Wolf, Athanas: *Der ewige Pressjude; oder, Die Mauschelperiode der deutschen Literatur.* Berlin: Germania, 1891. 64 pp. (Katholische Flugschriften zur Wehr und Lehr', 32) *LJ*

3203  *Woran erkennt man den wahren deutschen Michel.* Leipzig: Th. Fritsch, 1887.
8 pp. (Brennende Fragen, 10) *LJ*

3204  *Ein Wort an die deutsche Frau.* Leipzig: Th. Fritsch, 1888. 8 pp. (Brennende
Fragen, 26) *LJ*

3205  *Ein Wort über unser Verhältnis zu den unter uns lebenden Israeliten.* Halle:
1880. 217–233 pp. *LJ*
Offprint from: *Deutsch-Evangelische Blätter,* vol. 5, no. 4, 1880.

3206  *Die Wucher-Pest; eine zeitgemäße populäre Studie, von A.H.* Brünn: C.
Winkler, 1879. 23 pp. *LV*

3207  *Wucherjude und Vorschußverein; oder, Wo borgt man am Besten. Von einem
Bauernfreund im Eisenacher Oberlande.* 2. Aufl. Berlin: Germania, 1878.
31 pp. *LV*
Offprint from: *Schwarzes Blatt.*

3208  Zach, Franz (1876–): *Das Programm der Reformjuden.* Klagenfurt: Carinthia,
1912. 32 pp. (Volksaufklärung, 160) *Unseen*

3209  Zimmermann, Oswald: *Die nationalen und sozialen Aufgaben des
Antisemitismus; Rede gehalten am 26. Juni 1890 in Magdeburg.* Hrsg. vom
Deutschen Reformverein zu Magdeburg. Berlin: Dewald, 1890. 18 pp. *LB*

3210  Zimmermann, Oswald: *Sind die Juden noch das auserwählte Volk? Ein Beitrag
zur Aufklärung über die Judenfrage zugleich eine Frage und eine Antwort an
Prof. Delitzsch.* Dresden: "Deutsche Wacht," 1889. 55 pp. *LJ*

3211  Zöllner, Johann Karl Friedrich (1839–1882): *Beiträge zur deutschen Judenfrage
mit akademischen Arabesken als Unterlagen zu einer Reform der deutschen
Universitäten.* Hrsg. und mit einer Einleitung versehen von M. Wirth. Leipzig:
O. Mutze, 1894. XXXIII, 760 pp. *LJ*

3212  *A zsidókérdés. Irta egy zsidó.* Budapest: Typ. Wilckens és Waidl, 1882. 24 pp.
*LJ*

3213  *Zum Verständnis des Judencharakters.* Leipzig: T. Fritsch, 1885. 8 pp.
(Brennende Fragen, no. 20) *LJ*

3214  *Zur Klärung.* Wien: 1890–91. 2 vols. *LTA*
Offprint from: *Illustrierte Wiener Volkszeitung.*

3215  Zur Verteidigung der Christen gegen Juden und Judengenossen. *Germania* 13, 178 (1883) *Unseen*

3216  *Zwei Freisprechungen antisemitischer Agitation I. Prozeß gegen Th. Fritsch und Genossen in Leipzig II. Prozeß gegen Buchholtz und Genossen in Dortmund.* Leipzig: T. Fritsch, 1888. 16 pp. *LJ*

3217  *Der zweite Prozeß Ahlwardt wegen Beleidigung des Magistrats und anderer Personen.* Berlin: G.A. Dewald, 1892. 41 pp. *LJ*

# APOLOGETICS

**3218**

לוי, זאב: מיקומה של האפולוגטיקה ב"אגודה המרכזית" של יהודי גרמניה
בשנים הראשונות לקיומה. ילקוט מורשת, 12 (1970), 63–86 ע'.

[Levy, Zeev: The Role of Apologetics in the "Centralverein Deutscher Staatsbürger Jüdischen Glaubens" during the First Years of Its Existence. *Yalkut Moreshet* 12 (1970) 63–86.] *LJ*

English summary.

**3219**

רודקינזון, מיכאל לוי: לבקר משפט: א) היודענשפיעגעל פראצעס במינסטר.
ב) אחוזת קבר לבעל היהודיה בברלין שהובאו לפני כס המשפט. ברלין: דפוס
דוד לאווי ואברהם אלקלעי, תרמ"ד, 4, 52 ע'.

[Rodkinssohn, Michael Levi (1845–1904): *L'baqer mishpat: Critical Review on A) The Trial of the Judenspiegelprozeß in Münster (10 Dec. 1883). B) Debate of the Berlin Representatives of the Jewish Community about the Internment of a Non-Jewish Husband in the Family Vault of his Jewish Wife (23 Dec. 1883).* Berlin: David Lavi and Abraham Alcalay, 1884. 4, 52 pp.] *LJ*

**3220** Abwehr: *Sammelschrift*. Berlin: 1893. *LJ*

Contents: Der echte Talmud-Auszug (4 pp.); Der wahre Wert des jüdischen Eides, von Hirsch Hildesheimer (1 l.); Die Juden als Verbrecher: Flugblatt, no. 16 (2 pp.); Die Güterschlächterei in Hessen: Flugblatt no. 15 (2 pp.); Die Alliance Israélite Universelle (die allgemeine israelitische Allianz) und die Verlogenheit der Antisemiten (1 l.); Ein Urteil des preußischen Minister-präsidenten Graf zu Eulenburg über den Rektor Ahlwardt (1 l.); Moltke als Antisemit: Flugblatt no. 10 (2 pp.); Luthers Urteil über die Juden: Flugblatt no. 13 (2 pp.); Katholische Stimmen über die Juden: Flugblatt no. 15 (2 pp.).

3221 Ackermann, Aron: *Judentum und Christentum*. Leipzig: M.W. Kaufmann, 1903. 32 pp. *LJ*

3222 Adler, Felix (1851–1933): *The Anti-Jewish Agitation in Germany; Larger Tolerance. Two Addresses*. New York: Typ. Lehmaier, 1880. 32 pp. *LJ*

3223 Allgemeine Versammlung der Rabbiner Deutschlands: *Die interkonfessionelle Stellung des Judentums; Kundgebung der. . .* Berlin: Typ. J.S. Preuß, 1884. 15 pp. *LJ*

3224 Almogen, D.: *Worte der Abwehr. Antwort auf die Briefe eines Ariers an einen Semiten.* Leipzig: Oskar Kuß, 1887. 31 pp. *LJ*

3225 Amitti, K.: *Zur Kritik der Antisemiten und Semiten; ein Beitrag zur Bekämpfung der vom Prof. Mommsen erwähnten "antipathischen Gefühle" gegen die letzteren.* Eisenach: Hofbuchdruckerei, 1881. 40 pp. *LV*

3226 *An Herrn Professor Dr. Lazarus, von einem deutschen Juden.* 2. Aufl. Magdeburg: J. Neumann, 1887. 13 pp. *LJ*

Reprint of: Rahmer's *Israelitische Wochenschrift* of March, 10, 1887.

3227 Anti- und Philosemitisches. *N.Z.* 9, 2 (1890–1891) 585–588. *LJ*

3228 *Antisemiten-Hammer; eine Anthologie aus der Weltliteratur.* Mit einem Vorwort von Jacob Moleschott. Hrsg. von Josef Schrattenholz. Düsseldorf: E. Lintz, 1892. 26, 9 pp. *LJ*

3229 *Antisemiten-Hammer; eine Anthologie aus der Weltliteratur.* Mit einem Vorwort von Jacob Moleschott und einer Einleitung von Josef Schrattenholz. Düsseldorf: E. Lintz, 1894. XVIII, 648 pp. *LJ*

3230 *Die Antisemiten in Deutschland.* Danzig: A.W. Kafemann, 1897. 8 pp. *LJ*

3231 Antisemiten-Spiegel: *Die Antisemiten im Lichte des Christentums, des Rechtes und der Moral.* Danzig: A.W. Kafemann, 1892. 388 pp. *LJ*

3232 Antisemiten-Spiegel: *Die Antisemiten im Lichte des Christentums, des Rechtes und der Wissenschaft.* 2. vollständige umgearb. und erw. Aufl. Danzig: A.W. Kafemann, 1900. VIII, 499 pp. *LJ*

3233 Antisemiten-Spiegel: *Die Antisemiten im Lichte des Christentums, des Rechtes und der Moral.* Lfg. 1–3. Danzig: A.W. Kafemann, 1890–1891. 3 vols. *LJ*

The continuation in parts was suspended. The complete publication includes pts. 1–3, entirely rev.

3234  Antisemiten-Spiegel: *Die Antisemiten im Lichte des Christentums, des Rechtes und der Wissenschaft.* Hrsg. im Auftrage des Vereins zur Abwehr des Antisemitismus von seinem Geschäftsführer Curt Bürger. Berlin: Verlag des Vereins zur Abwehr des Antisemitismus, 1911. 457 pp. *LJ*

3235  *Die Antisemiten und das Christentum.* Danzig: A.W. Kafemann, 1900. 28 pp. *LJ*

Offprint from: *Antisemiten-Spiegel*, 1900. Published by Verein zur Abwehr des Antisemitismus.

3236  *Antisemitennot in Wien; Vexierbilder aus dem Antisemitenlager.* (Von einem christlichen Wiener.) Wien: Selbstverlag, 189-. 24 pp. *LJ*

3237  *Apostel des Antisemitismus, deren schädigendes Treiben für Volk und Land und die Mittel zur Abwehr.* Wien: Helios, 1893. 16 pp. *LTA*

3238  Apt, Max (1869-): *Antisemitismus und Strafrechtspflege. Zur Auslegung und Anwendung der Paragraphen 130, 166, 185, 193, 360 des Strafgesetzbuches in höchstrichterlicher und erstinstanzlicher Praxis.* 2. Aufl. Berlin: S. Cronbach, 1894. 138 pp. *LJ*

3239  *Der arme Jude, wie ihn der große Demokrat Herr W. Marr besp. . . (richt). Beleuchtet von keinem Juden.* Hamburg: R. Falcke, 1862. 15 pp. *LJ*

3240  Aub, Joseph (1805-1880): *Toleranz und Humanität; ein Wort der Abwehr und Verständigung.* Mainz: M. Jourdan, 1859. 15 pp. *LJ*

3241  Auerbach, Fritz: *Der Antisemitismus und das freisinnige Judentum; ein offenes Wort an die freidenkenden Juden.* Frankfurt a.M.: Mahlau und Waldschmidt, 1893. 21 pp. *LTA*

3242  Auerbach, Leopold (1847-1925): *Das Judentum und seine Bekenner in Preußen und in den anderen deutschen Bundesstaaten.* Berlin: S. Mehring, 1890. VIII, 488 pp. *LJ*

3243  Auerbach, Leopold (1847-1925): *Wie ist die Judenhetze mit Erfolg zu bekämpfen?* Berlin: R. Lesser, 1893. 20 pp. (An der Tagesordnung, 3) *Unseen*

3244  Aussprachen mit Juden. *Der Kunstwart* 25 (1912) 225-261. *LJ*

3245  Back, Samuel (1841-1899): *An Israels Gemeinden und ihre Rabbinen; eine Stimme der Gegenwart zur Gestaltung der Zukunft.* Prag: Brandeis, 1883. 7 pp. *LF*

3246 Balakan, David: *Die Sozialdemokratie und das jüdische Proletariat.* Czernowitz: H. Pardini, 1905. 63 pp. *LJ*

3247 Baum, Moritz: *Ein wichtiges Kapitel über die Bedeutung und Würde der Völker unserer Zeit, sowie derjenigen der Vorzeit, welche im Talmud gewöhnlich "akkum" genannt werden, nach den Vorschriften der Tora.* Aus Anlaß des jüngst zu Münster i. W. verhandelten Press-Prozeßes. 2. verb. und mit Anmerkungen vers. Ausg. Frankfurt a.M.: Selbstverlag, 1884. 7, 48, 11 pp. *LJ*

3248 Baum, Moritz, ed. and tr.: *Stimmen über Juden und Judentum von hervorragenden christlichen Gelehrten Nord-Amerikas.* Erschienen im "American Hebrew" in New York. Ins Deutsche übertragen und mit Anmerkungen versehen. Frankfurt a.M.: M. Slobotzky, 1890. 72 pp. *LJ*

3249 Beaconsfield, Benjamin Disraeli, 1st earl of (1804–1881): *Die Juden; eine Verteidigungsschrift.* Aus D'Israeli's politischer Biographie über Lord George Bentinck ins Deutsche übers. Leipzig: E.F. Steinacker, 1853. 25 pp. *LJ*

3250 Bebel, August (1840–1913): *Sozialdemokratie und Antisemitismus; Rede des Reichstagsabgeordneten Bebel auf dem 4. Parteitag der Sozialdemokratischen Partei zu Köln am Rhein.* Nebst einem Nachtrag. Berlin: Vorwärts, 1894. 32 pp. *LJ*

3251 Beer Bernhard (1801–1861): *Die freie christliche Kirche und das Judentum; Sendschreiben an Herrn Johannes Ronge, in Bezug auf mehrere Aeusserungen in dessen neuester Schrift: Das Wesen der freichristlichen Kirche.* Leipzig: H. Hunger, 1848. 39 pp. *LJ*

3252 Ben-Hezekia, Moses: *Zur Lösung der Judenfrage durch die Juden; ein jüdischer Osterabend des Jahres 1884 n. Chr.* Berlin: Wilhelm Issleib, 1884. 63 pp. *LTA*

3253 Bender Hermann: *Wahn und Wirklichkeit; eine Streitschrift für und gegen die Juden.* Berlin: E. Rentzel, 1897. 29 pp. *LJ*

3254 Bergman, Shmuel Hugo (1883–1975): Eduard von Hartmann und die Judenfrage in Deutschland. *LBIYB* 5 (1960) 177–197. *LJ*

3255 Berliner, E., ed: *Professor Dr. M. Lazarus und die öffentliche Meinung.* Berlin: Walther & Apolant, 1887. 42 pp. *LJ*

3256 Bernstein, Eduard (1850–1932): Das Schlagwort und der Antisemitismus. *N.Z.* 11, 2 (1892–93) 228–237. *LJ*

Attack on antisemitism from the socialist point of view.

3257  Biach, Adolf: *Friedrich Hebbel und die Juden unter besonderer Berücksichtigung der Briefe und Tagebücher Hebbels.* Brüx: J. Ach & Co., 1897. 26 pp. *LJ*

3258  Binder Carl (1829–1894): *Antisemitische Wühlereien und Raufereien in Pleiss-Athen; ein Beitrag zur Kulturgeschichte unserer Zeit.* Leipzig: Expedition der Zeit- und Kulturbilder, 1881. 46 pp. (Zeit- und Kulturbilder, 2) *LF*

3259  Birnbaum, Nathan (1864–1937): *Ausgewählte Schriften zur jüdischen Frage.* Czernowitz: Verlag der Buchhdlg. Birnbaum und Kohut, 1910. 2 vols. *LJ*

3260  Blau, Julius: *Rückblick und Ausblick.* Berlin: Brodacz, 1900. 7 pp. *LF*

3261  Bloch, Joseph Samuel (1850–1923), ed.: *Akten zur rumänischen Judenfrage; aus Anlaß des Klausenburger Memorandum-Prozeßes.* Wien: Oesterreichische Wochenschrift, 1894. 40 pp. *LF*

3262  Bloch, Joseph Samuel (1850–1923), ed: *Gegen die Antisemiten; eine Streitschrift zusammengestellt.* Wien: D. Löwy, 1882. 39 pp. *LJ*

3263  Bloch, Joseph Samuel (1850–1923): Geistliche Talmudisten im ungarischen Abgeordnetenhause. *Aus der Vergangenheit für die Gegenwart.* Wien: H. Engel, 1886. Pp. 151–166. *LJ*

3264  Bloch, Joseph Samuel (1850–1923): *Die guten Dienste, welche die Antisemiten den Juden leisten; nach einem Vortrage . . .gehalten im Vereine der "Oesterreichischen-Israelitischen Union."* Wien: Oesterreichische Wochenschrift, 1890. 16 pp. *LF*

3265  Bloch, Joseph Samuel (1850–1923): Lessing's Nathan; Vortrag . . . 31. Jänner 1880 . . . *Aus der Vergangenheit für die Gegenwart.* Wien: H. Engel, 1886. Pp. 167–218. *LJ*

3266  Bloch, Joseph Samuel (1850–1923): *Der nationale Zwist und die Juden in Oesterreich.* Wien: M. Gottlieb, 1886. 92 pp. *LJ*

The articles published in this volume were first printed in the *Oesterreichische Wochenschrift.*

3267  Bloch, Joseph Samuel (1850–1923): *Talmud und Judentum in der österreichischen Volksvertretung. Dr. Bloch's Parlamentsreden.* Wien: A. Landau, 1900. XV, 174 pp. (Dokumente zur Aufklärung, 3) *LJ*

3268  Böhlich, Walter, ed: *Der Berliner Antisemitismusstreit.* Frankfurt a.M.: Insel-Verlag, 1965. 265 pp. (Sammlung Insel, 6) *LJ*

3269 Börne, Ludwig (1786–1837): *Das Judentum in Börne's Schriften.* Mit einer Einleitung. Prag: J.B. Brandeis, 189–. X, 106 pp. (Jüdische Universal-Bibliothek, 69) *LJ*

3270 Börne, Ludwig (1786–1837): *Ueber den Antisemitismus. Ein Mahnruf aus vergangenen Tagen.* Wien: O. Frank, 1885. 67 pp. *LJ*

3271 Brandt, Hans: *Der Staat und die Juden.* Königsberg i.Pr.: Hartungsche Zeitung, 1928. 46 pp. *LJ*

3272 Braun, Hermann: *Nach Jerusalem gehen wir nicht, sondern ziehen, wenn es nötig ist, gleich unsern christlichen Brüdern, mit Gott für Kaiser und Vaterland gegen die Feinde Deutschlands.* Ein Schriftchen gewidmet aus Liebe seinen katholischen und protestantischen Mitbrüdern von einem Deutschen mosaischer Religion. Nürnberg: Commissions-Verlag von Heerdegen-Barbeck, 1893. 20 pp. *LJ*

3273 Bresslau, Harry (1848–1926): *Zur Judenfrage. Sendschreiben an . . . Heinrich von Treitschke.* Berlin: F. Dümmler, 1880. 25 pp. *LJ*

3274 Bronsen, David, ed: *Jews and Germans from 1860 to 1933; the Problematic Symbiosis.* Heidelberg: C. Winter, 1979. 383 pp. (Reihe Siegen, vol. 9) *LJ*

3275 Brüll, Adolf (1846–1908): Emile Zola über den Antisemitismus. *Populärwissenschaftliche Monatsblätter zur Belehrung über das Judentum* 16 (1896) 169–173. *LJ*

3276 Brunner, Constantin (1862–1937), pseud.: *Der Judenhaß und die Juden.* Berlin: Oesterheld, 1910. 533 pp. *LJ*

3277 Brunner, Sebastian (1814–1893): *Pressprozeß Sebastian Brunner kontra Ignaz Kuranda; öffentliche Verhandlung vor dem Landgerichte in Wien am 10. Mai.* Nach den stenographischen Aufzeichnungen. Wien: Carl Gerold's Sohn, 1860. 55 pp. *LJ*

3278 Bürger, Kurt: *Deutschtum und Judentum.* Berlin: Verein zur Abwehr des Antisemitismus, 1913. 132 pp. *LJ*

3279 C. Dr.: *Unmusikalische Noten zu Richard Wagner's Judentum in der Musik; von Dr. C.* München: Neuburger & Kalb, 1869. 15 pp. *LJ*

3280 Cahen, Gustav (1840–1918): *Die Judenfrage und die Zukunft.* Hamburg: Philipsen, 1896. 46 pp. *LF*

3281 Caro, Leopold (1864-1939): *Die Judenfrage, eine ethische Frage.* Leipzig: Fr. Wilh. Grunow, 1892. 66 pp. *LJ*

3282 Cassel, David (1818-1893): *Offener Brief eines Juden an Herrn Prof. Dr. Virchow.* Berlin: L. Gerschel, 1869. 38 pp. *LJ*

3283 Cassel, Paulus Stephanus (1821-1892): *Ahasverus; die Sage vom ewigen Juden. Eine wissenschaftliche Abhandlung.* Mit einem kritischen Protest wider Eduard von Hartmann und Adolf Stoecker. Neue Ausg. Berlin: Kühl-Internationale Buchhdlg., 1887. 70 pp. *LJ*

3284 Cassel, Paulus Stephanus (1821-1892): *Die Antisemiten und die evangelische Kirche; Sendschreiben an einen evangelischen Geistlichen.* Berlin: A. Wohlgemuth, 1881. 46 pp. *LJ*

3285 Cassel, Paulus Stephanus (1821-1892): *Christliche Sittenlehre. Eine Auslegung des Briefes Pauli und Titus. Mit einer Schlußbemerkung über Semitismus. Zur Erinnerung an den 28. Mai 1855.* 2. Aufl. Berlin: Stahr, 1880. 112 pp. *LJ*

3286 Cassel, Paulus Stephanus (1821-1892): *Die Juden in der Weltgeschichte.* Berlin: L. Gerschel, 1880. 30 pp. *LJ*

3287 Cassel, Paulus Stephanus (1821-1892): *Wider Heinrich von Treitschke. Für die Juden.* 6. Aufl. Berlin: F. Stahn, 1880. 28 pp. *LJ*

3288 Centralverein Deutscher Staatsbürger Jüdischen Glaubens: *Antisemitische Wahrhaftigkeit.* Frankfurt a.M.: M. Lehrberger, 189-. 4 pp. *Unseen*

3289 Centralverein Deutscher Staatsbürger Jüdischen Glaubens: *Bericht der Rechtsschutz-Kommission über ihre bisherige Tätigkeit erstattet in der ordentlichen Versammlung vom 16. April 1894 durch Eugen Fuchs.* Berlin: Typ. Schmitzer & Bukofzer, 1894. 45 pp. *LJ*

3290 Centralverein Deutscher Staatsbürger Jüdischen Glaubens: *An die deutschen Staatsbürger jüdischen Glaubens; ein Aufruf.* Berlin: Typ. M. Hoffschläger, 1893. 12 pp. *LJ*

3291 *Civis Germanus sum.* Von einem Juden deutscher Nation. T. I. Berlin: R. Wilhelmi, 1891. 24 pp. *LJ*

3292 Cohen, Hermann (1842-1918): *Ein Bekenntnis in der Judenfrage.* Berlin: Dümmler's Verlag, 1880. 25 pp. *LJ*

3293 Cohn, Bernhard: *Jüdisch-politische Zeitfragen.* Berlin: L. Simion, 1899. 79 pp. *LJ*

3294 Cohn, Bernhard: *Vor dem Sturm. Ernste Mahnworte an die deutschen Juden.* Berlin: Wesemann, 1896. 58 pp. *LJ*

3295 Cohn, Elias: *Zwei Erwiderungsvorträge gehalten in den Versammlungen der Christlich-Sozialen Arbeiterpartei am 19. September und 10. Oktober 1879 gegen den Hof- und Domprediger A. Stoecker über das Thema: Unsere Forderungen an das moderne Judentum.* Berlin: Selbstverlag, 1879. 20 pp. *LJ*

3296 Conti, Berthold W.: *Stoecker wider Ahlwardt und Genossen. Offener Brief an den Hofprediger a.d. Stoecker.* Berlin: Selbstverlag, 188-. 14 pp. *LJ*

3297 Cronje, Jan: *Ich werde nie Antisemit. Zur Aufklärung für jedermann.* München: A. Schupp, 1900. 20 pp. *LJ*

3298 Danzig, Moses: *Zur Judenfrage.* Odessa: typ. Ulrich, 1872. 32 pp. *LJ*

3299 Delitzsch, Franz Julius (1813–1890): *Neueste Traumgesichte des antisemitischen Propheten. Sendschreiben an Prof. Zöckler in Greifswald.* Erlangen: A. Deichert, 1883. 32 pp. *LJ*

3300 Delitzsch, Franz Julius (1813–1890): *Rohling's Talmudjude beleuchtet.* 7. durch Beleuchtung der Gegenschrift Rohling's erw. Ausg. Leipzig: Dörffling und Franke, 1881. 120 pp. *LJ*

3301 Delitzsch, Franz Julius (1813–1890): *Schachmatt den Blutlügnern Rohling und Justus entboten.* Erlangen: A. Deichert, 1883. 43 pp. *LJ*

3302 Delitzsch, Franz Julius (1813–1890): *Sind die Juden wirklich das auserwählte Volk? Ein Beitrag zur Lichtung der Judenfrage.* Leipzig: W. Faber, 1889. 64 pp. (Schriften des Institutum Judaicum zu Leipzig, 22) *LJ*

3303 Delitzsch, Franz Julius (1813–1890): *Was Dr. Aug. Rohling beschworen hat und beschwören will. Zweite Streitschrift in Sachen des Antisemitismus.* Leipzig: Dörffling und Franke, 1883. 39 pp. *LJ*

3304 *Die deutsche Flotte und die jüdischen Reichstagswähler.* Berlin: A. Katz, 1897. 14 pp. *LJ*

3305 Döllinger, Johann Josef Ignaz von (1799–1890): *Die Juden in Europa.* Linz: C. v. Kissling, 1891. 34 pp. *LJ*

A lecture.

3306 Döllinger, Johann Josef Ignaz von (1799–1890): *Das Judentum in Europa; Rede vom 25. Juli 1881.* Berlin: Philo-Verlag, 1921. 27 pp. *LF*

3307 Donner, Friedrich: *Das Judentum in den Vereinigten Staaten von Nord-Amerika. Eine Bekehrungsschrift für die H.H. Pastoren Stoecker, Henrici, sowie für alle Judenhetzer.* Wien: Bretzner & Co., 1881. 29 pp. *LJ*

3308 Dreifus, Markus G.: *Zur Würdigung des Judentums unter seinen Nichtbekennern.* Winterthur: G. Lücke, 1860. 63 pp. *LJ*

3309 Durege, Jenny: *Judentum im Christentum; Vortrag.* Magdeburg: Zacharias, 1912. 27 pp. *LJ*

3310 Duschak, Moritz (1815–1890): *Geschichte der Verfassung mit besonderer Beziehung auf die österreichisch-ungarischen Israeliten aus Anlaß des 40-jährigen Regierungsjubiläums Seiner Majestät des Kaisers Franz Josef I.* Wien: Lippe, 1888. 71 pp. *LJ*

3311 Eisler, Moritz (1818–1890): *Die Judenfrage in Deutschland.* New York: Selbstverlag, 1880. 94 pp. *LJ*

3312 Elbogen Friedrich: *Die neue Aera; ein Aufruf.* 2. Aufl. Wien: C. Konegen, 1895. 15 pp. *LTA*

3313 Eliot, George (1819–1880), pseud.: The Modern Hep! Hep! Hep! *The Complete Works: Impressions of Theophrastus Such; Miscellaneous Essays.* Vol. 8. Boston: Colonial Press Co., 189–. Pp. 184–213. *LJ*

3314 Elisamter, pseud.: *Offenes Sendschreiben an den Herrn Baron Albert von Rothschild in Wien.* Berlin: Selbstverlag, 1883. 11 pp. *LJ*

3315 Ellenberger, Heinrich (1806–1883): *Geschichtliches Handbuch. Chronologische Reihenfolge der heiligen jüdischen Tradition von Moses 1540 v. Ch. Geburt bis zum Schluß des Talmuds 500 n. Ch. Geburt, nebst Anhang über die spätere Entwicklung derselben und einem Schlußworte an Prof. Dr. August Rohling.* Budapest: Pester Buckdruckerei, 1883. XV, 61 pp. *LJ*

3316 Ellenberger, Heinrich (1806–1883): *Leiden und Verfolgungen der Juden und ihre Beschützer in chronologischer Reihenfolge; von Pharao 1650 vor Christi Geburt bis zur Gegenwart.* Budapest: Zilahy, 1882. XVI, 141, 10 pp. *LJ*

3317 Enodatus, pseud.: *Juden und Judenhetze.* Löbau: R. Skrzeczek, 1879. 33 pp. *LJ*

3318 Erichson, A.: *Offener Brief an die Antisemiten. Berlin, im November 1880.* Berlin: S. Liebrecht, 1880. 7 pp. *LJ*
In verse.

3319 Ernst, Ludwig: *Die Juden, die verjudeten Christlichsozialen und Deutschnationalen.* Leipzig: Literarische Austalt, 1896. 36 pp. *LJ*

3320 *Ernste Plaudereien über die Judenfrage; Erlebnisse, Geständnisse und Vorschläge eines germanisierten Talmudjuden.* Berlin: R. Wilhelmi, 1893. 80 pp. *LC*

3321 *Erster und zweiter offener Brief an den August Rohling als Antwort auf sein Pamphlet "Der Talmudjude." Von einem Münster Juden im Namen vieler.* Münster: Obertüschen, 1871. 14, 11 pp. *Unseen*

3322 Eschelbacher, Josef (1848–1916): *Aufgaben einer jüdischen Apologetik.* Berlin: 1908. 12 pp. *LJ*

Offprint from: *Korrespondenzblatt des Verbandes der Deutschen Juden*, no. 3, October 1908.

3323 Ettinger, Markus: *Psychologie und Ethik des Antisemitismus im Altertum, Mittelalter und in der Neuzeit.* Wien: Gottlieb, 1891. 29 pp. *LJ*

3324 Farkas, Ödön: *A Zsidó kérdés Magyarországon.* Budapest: L. Aigner, 1884. 56 pp. *LJ*

The Jewish Question in Hungary.

3325 Feuerring, Josef: *Der Antisemitenapostel; ein Wort der Entgegnug an Rektor Hermann Ahlwardt auf seine letzte Broschüre; "Neue Enthüllungen, Judenflinten."* Berlin: Verlag Der Splitter, 1892. 16 pp. *LJ*

3326 Fiebig, Paul Wilhelm Julius (1876–1949): *Juden und Nichtjuden; Erläuterungen zu Th. Fritschs "Handbuch der Judenfrage."* Leipzig: Dörffling & Franke, 1921. 100 pp. *LJ*

3327 Fiedler, Peter Josef: *Die Antisemitenbewegung in Deutschland in ihren Ursachen und Folgen. Vortrag gehalten in der Bezirkslehrerversammlung zu Darmstadt am 17. Januar 1891.* Darmstadt: H. Schmitt, 1891. 24 pp. *LJ*

3328 Fiedler, Peter Josef: *Sind die heutigen Judenverfolgungen gerechtfertigt? Ein Appell an das Gerechtigkeitsgefühl des deutschen Volkes.* Darmstadt: H. Schmitt, 1891. 27 pp. *LJ*

3329 Fischer, Jakob: *Widerlegung der von seiner Hochwürden Herrn Hofprediger Stoecker an uns Juden gestellten Forderungen.* 2. Aufl. Berlin: G. Schultze, 1879. 16 pp. *LJ*

3330   Fischer, Karl (1840–): *Antisemiten und Gymnasiallehrer; ein Protest.* Berlin:
       F. Dümmler, 1881. 40 pp. *LJ*

       Reply to Dr. Siecke's *Judenfrage und der Gymnasiallehrer.* 3rd. ed. Berlin,
       1880 — see entry no. 3049.

3331   Förster, Wilhelm Julius (1832–1921): *Zur Ethik des Nationalismus und der
       Judenfrage; Vortrag gehalten am 23. November 1892.* Berlin: F. Dümmler,
       1893. 20 pp. *LJ*

3332   Fränkel, Jakob Emanuel: *Erwiderung auf die von Prof. Dr. August Rohling
       verfasste Schrift "Der Talmudjude." Dazu als Anhang: Ein Schreiben des Dr.
       Philipp Mansch an den Verfasser.* Lemberg: Typ. S.L. Kugel, 1874. 52 pp. *LJ*

3333   Frank, Friedrich (1832–1904): *Die Kirche und die Juden; eine Studie.* 3.
       neudurchges. Aufl. mit einer Kapiteleinteilung vers. Aufl. Regensburg:
       Verlagsanstalt vormals J.G. Manz, 1893. VII, 88 pp. *LJ*

3334   *Freiheit, Liebe, Menschlichkeit; ein Manifest des Geistes von hervorragenden
       Zeitgenossen.* Berlin: J. van Groningen, 1893. 79 pp. *LJ*

3335   Freystadt, Moritz: *Der Christenspiegel von Anti-Marr. Ein offenes Send-
       schreiben an die modernen Judenfeinde.* 2. Aufl. Königsberg: T. Theile, 1863.
       40 pp. *LJ*

       In answer to Wilhelm Marr's *Judenspiegel.*

3336   Freytag,   Gustav   (1816–1895):   *Ueber   den   Antisemitismus;   eine
       Pfingstbetrachtung.* Hrsg. vom Centralverein Deutscher Staatsbürger jüdischen
       Glaubens. Berlin: Lewit, 1910. 14 pp. *LJ*

       From: *Wiener Neue Freie Presse,* 1893.

3337   Friedeberg, Meyer (1858–): *Praktisches Judentum; ein Wort zur Verständigung,
       insbesondere an seine Glaubensgenossen.* Leipzig: Friese, 1881. 58 pp. *LJ*

3338   Friedemann, Edmund (1847–): *Jüdische Moral und christlicher Staat.* Berlin:
       S. Cronbach, 1893. 45 pp. *LJ*

3339   Fuchs, Eugen (1856–1923): Rückblick auf die zehnjährige Tätigkeit des
       "Central-Vereins Deutscher Staatsbürger Jüdischen Glaubens." Rede gehalten
       am zehnten Stiftungsfest, 2. Februar 1903. *I.Dt.R.* 9 (1903) 197–211. *LJ*

3340   Fuchs, Eugen (1856–1923): *Um Deutschtum und Judentum; gesammelte Reden
       und Aufsätze, 1894–1919. Im Auftrage des Central-Vereins Deutscher
       Staatsbürger Jüdischen Glaubens.* Hrsg. von Leo Hirschfeld. Frankfurt a.M.:
       Kauffmann, 1919. 382 pp. *LJ*

3341 Fuld, Ludwig (1850–): *Das jüdische Verbrechertum; eine Studie über den Zusammenhang zwischen Religion und Kriminalität.* Leipzig: Th. Huth, 1885. VI, 39 pp. *LJ*

Also published under the title: *Christen-, Juden- und Verbrechertum.*

3342 Georg, Wilhelm: *Hinter den Kulissen der Antisemiten. Mein Austritt aus der antisemitischen Partei; Erinnerungen aus dem antisemitischen Hauptquartier.* Hannover: Gebr. Schmidt, 1895. V, 32 pp. *LJ*

3343 Gerecke, Adolf: *Die Verdienste der Juden um die Erhaltung und Ausbreitung der Wissenschaften.* Zürich: Verlags-Magazin, 1893. 47 pp. *LJ*

3344 Gerhardt, Dagobert von (1831–1910): Noch einmal die Juden. *Auf der Bresche; Feuilletons, Skizzen, Erzählungen.* Berlin: F. Luckhardt, 1879. Pp. 109–117. *LJ*

3345 *Der Getreue Ekkehard; Ergebnisse einer Forschungsreise ins Gebiet des heutigen religiösen Lebens. Geordnet und in spezieller Bezugnahme auf die in der Antisemiten-Liga von H. de Grousilliers gehaltene und unter dem Titel "Nathan der Weise und die Antisemiten-Liga" im Druck erschienene Rede als Erwiderung niedergeschrieben.* Berlin: Selbstverlag des Verfassers, 1880. 15 pp. (Ursachen und Wirkungen, 4) *LJ*

3346 Glück, J.: *Ein Wort an den Herrn Professor Heinrich von Treitschke.* Oldenburg: F. Schmidt, 1880. 16 pp. *LJ*

3347 Götz, Marie: *Die Frauen und der Antisemitismus. Allen guten Menschen gewidmet.* Wien: Selbstverlag, 1900. 30 pp. *LJ*

3348 Goldmann, S.: *Ueber den Antisemitismus; ein Wort an meine Mitbürger, insbesondere an meine Glaubensgenossen.* Berlin: H. Lazarus, 1893. 16 pp. *LJ*

3349 Goldschmidt, Alfred: *Auf dem Wege der Freiheit zur Gleichheit und Brüderlichkeit; eine historisch-jüdische Betrachtung.* Breslau: Köbner, 1906. 34 pp. *LJ*

3350 Goldschmidt, Israel: *Ueber die Zukunft und Berechtigung des Judentums.* Leipzig: Heuser, 1883. 41 pp. *LJ*

3351 Grant, Charles: The Jewish Question in Germany. *Contemporary Review* 39 (1881) 366–384. *LJ*

3352 Graue, Georg: *Ein Friedenswort in der Judenfrage; Vortrag im Verein der Liberalen zu Chemnitz gehalten.* Chemnitz: E. Locke, 1881. 20 pp. *LJ*

3353  Gruber, Bernhard: *Christ und Israelit; ein Friedenswort zur Judenfrage.*
      Reichenbach i. Schlesien: Heege & Güntzel, 1880. 23 pp. *LJ*

3354  Gruber, Bernhard: *Der neue Sturm der Judenfrage; noch ein Friedenswort.*
      Reichenbach im Schlesien: Heege & Güntzel, 1880. 23 pp. *LJ*

3355  Grünebaum, Elias: *Die Sittenlehre des Judentums andern Bekenntnissen
      gegenüber; nebst dem geschichtlichen Nachweise über Entstehung und
      Bedeutung des Pharaismus und dessen Verhältnis zum Stifter der christlichen
      Religion.* 2. sehr verm. Aufl. Straßburg: J. Schneider, 1878. XXXVI, 448 pp.
      *LJ*

3356  Grünfeld, Carl Sigmund: *Berühmte (israelitische) Männer und Frauen; ein
      illustrierter Protest gegen den Antisemitismus.* Ser. 1, Bd. 1. Wien: Waizner,
      1886. 1 vol. *LF*

3357  Gugenheimer, Joseph: *Kritische Beleuchtung des in Paderborn 1883 von
      Dr. Justus Brimanns erschienen "Judenspiegel."* Wien: M. Hirschler, 1885.
      33 pp. *LJ*
      Offprint from: *Jeschurun,* Feb.-May 1883.

3358  Haase, Theodor Karl (1834–1909): *Antisemitismus; kleine Studien.* 3. Aufl.
      Wien: Karl Prochaska, 1887. IV, 45 pp. *LJ*

3359  Haffner, Adalbert: *Ist es denn wahr, daß die Juden herzlos sind?* Wien: der
      Verfasser, 1902. 12 pp. *Unseen*

3360  Haffner, Adalbert: *Die Juden im Dienste der Menschheit und des Vaterlandes.*
      Wien: Selbstverlag, 1904. 35 pp. *LC*

3361  Haffner, Adalbert: *Was Frau Weber über den Antisemitismus sagt.* Wien:
      Selbstverlag, 1892. 38 pp. *LJ*

3362  Haffner, Adalbert: *Was mei Bedienerin über den Antisemitismus sagt.* Wien:
      Selbstverlag, 1901. 24 pp. *LJ*

3363  Hallgarten, Charles L. (1838–1908): *Neues über den Antisemitismus. Vortrag
      gehalten am 14.2.1897.* Frankfurt a.M.: Typ. L. Golde, 1897. 18 pp. *LJ*

3364  Hausig, F.: *Christ und Jude: ein Vortrag.* Diesdorf bei Kuhnern: Typ.
      Schreiberhau-Diesdorfer Rettungsanstalten, 188-. 12 pp. *LJ*

3365  Hausmeister, Max: *Die Mittel zur geistigen Hebung des Judentums.* Stuttgart:
      Süddeutsches Verlags-Institut, 1900. 32 pp. *LJ*

3366 Hecht, David: *Der Antisemitismus — eine erbliche Belastung; Nachweis von einem Wiener Kommunallehrer.* Wien: R. Löwit, 1913. 17 pp. *LC*

3367 Hein, Oskar: *Auch ein Abgeordneter: Porträt eines unverfälschten Deutschen, Karl Türk.* Wien: Selbstverlag, 1889. 22 pp. *LTA*

3368 Hein, Oskar: *Aus der Werkstatt der Reaktion; die Prozeßaffaire gegen Mechaniker Schneider in aktenmäßiger Darstellung.* Wien: Typ. A. Alkalay, 1891. 96 pp. *LJ*

3369 Heine, Heinrich (1797-1856): *Jüdisches Manifest; eine Auswahl aus seinen Werken, Briefen und Gesprächen.* Hrsg. von Hugo Bieber. 2. Aufl. der "Confessio Judaica." New York: Mary S. Rosenberg, 1946. VIII, 315 pp. *LJ*

3370 Helmdörffer, F.X.: *Politik und Wucher der Juden. Zu den Schriften W. Marr's.* Freiburg i. Br.: Trömer in Komm., 1879. 34 pp. *LJ*

3371 Henne am Rhyn, Otto (1828-1914): *Die Schmach der modernen Kultur.* Leipzig: H. Lemme, 1885. 143 pp. *LF*

3372 Herrmann, Felix: *Das Ende des Antisemitismus; ein Friedensgruß an die deutsche Nation.* Berlin: J. Zenker, 1887. 36 pp. *LJ*

3373 Hersch, Isaac Moses: *Offener Brief an das Ministerium Auerswald.* Berlin: S. Löwenherz, 1848. 1 l. *LJ*

3374 Hersch, Isaac Moses: *Offener Brief an die Berliner Börsenleute; als da sind Banquiers, Kortiers, Kornhändler und die ganze übrige Maschpoche.* Berlin: S. Löwenherz, 1848. 1 l. *LJ*

3375 Hersch, Isaac Moses: *Offener Brief an die Hohe National-Versammlung.* Berlin: S. Löwenherz, 1848. 1 l. *LJ*

3376 Hersch, Isaac Moses: *Offener Brief an seine Mitberger.* Berlin: S. Löwenherz, 1848. 1 l. *LJ*

3377 Hersch, Isaac Moses: *Offener Brief an unsere liebe Wall-Gäste.* Berlin: S. Löwenherz, 1848. 1 l. *LJ*

3378 Hersch, Isaac Moses: *Sendschreiben an das Ministerium Camphausen über den neuen Verfassungs-Entwurf und andere Sachen.* Berlin: S. Löwenherz, 1848. 1 l. *LJ*

3379 Hertz, Friedrich Otto (1878-): *Antisemitismus und Wissenschaft.* Wien: C.W. Stern, 1904. 32 pp. *LJ*

3380 Hertzka, Adolf (1845-1924): *Drei galgenhumoristische Studien über den Antisemitismus*. Wien: M. Waizner, 1885. 32 pp. *LJ*

3381 Hertzka, Theodor: Freiland und Antisemitismus. *Die Zukunft* 5 (1893) 505-513. *LJ*

3382 Herzfeld, Michael: *Auf nach Palästina! Ein Wort über den "Judenfreund" Victor Istoczy, Reichstagsabgeordneter in Ungarn*. Wien: Selbstverlag, 1878. 16 pp. *LJ*

3383 Hildesheimer, Israel (1820-1899): *Die jüdische Solidarität; Vortrag gehalten im Sefath-Emeth Verein*. Berlin: J. Benzian, 1880. 35 pp. *LJ*

3384 Hillel, Karl: *Die Versöhnung des Judentums mit dem Christentum*. Frankfurt a.M.: Knauer, 1898. 59 pp. *LJ*

3385 Hirsch, Isaak: *Das Programm der nationalliberalen Provinzial-Wahlkomitees und der Antisemitismus*. Hannover: 1893. 8 pp. *Unseen*

3386 Hirsch, Markus (1833-1909): *Kulturdefizit am Ende des 19. Jahrhunderts*. Frankfurt a.M.: J. Kauffmann, 1893. 140 pp. *LJ*

3387 Hirsch, Mendel: *Das reine Menschentum im Lichte des Judentums*. Frankfurt a.M.: J. Kauffmann, 1893. 36 pp. *LJ*

3388 Hirschfeld, Carl: *Offener Brief eines Juden gerichtet an Herrn von Egidy; bestimmt für alle*. Frankfurt a.M.: Selbstverlag des Verfassers, 1891. 67 pp. *LC*

3389 Hofferichter, Theodor: *Für die Semiten; Vortrag gehalten am 28. November 1880 vor der freireligiösen Gemeinde zu Breslau*. Breslau: Preuß & Jünger, 1880. 12 pp. *LJ*

3390 Hoffmann, David (1843-1921): *Der Schulchan-Aruch und die Rabbinen über das Verhältnis der Juden zu Andersgläubigen*. 2. verm. und verb. Aufl. Berlin: "Jüdische Presse," 1894. XII, 234 pp. *LJ*

3391 Hoffmann, Mór: *A sémiták és antisémiták*. Nagy-Kanizsa: Typ. F. Fischel, 1883. 80 pp. *LJ*

3392 Hofmann, Emil: *Eine brennende Frage des gegenwärtigen Israels*. Reichenberg: P. Sollors, 1896. 54 pp. *LJ*

   An appeal for the establishment of societies for the study of Jewish history and literature.

3393 Holländer, Ludwig (1877–): *Die sozialen Voraussetzungen der antisemitischen Bewegung in Deutschland.* Berlin: Levy, 1910. 30 pp. *LJ*

3394 Holzhausen, Paul: *Judenhatz in deutschen Nordseebädern; ein Reiseabenteuer auf Spiekeroog.* Mühlheim, Ruhr: M. Röder, 1893. 8 pp. *LJ*

3395 Horovitz, Markus (1844–1910): *Zur Abwehr; ein Sendschreiben über zwei falschgedeutete Talmudstellen.* Frankfurt a.M.: J. Kauffmann, 1892. 23 pp. *LJ*

3396 Horwitz, Maximilian: *Ehrenpflichten; Vortrag gehalten im Centralverein Deutscher Staatsbürger Jüdischen Glaubens.* Berlin: E. Billig, 1898, 16 pp. *LJ*

3397 Houben, Heinrich Hubert: Karl Gutzkow und das Judentum. *Gutzkow-Funde; Beiträge zur Literatur- und Kulturgeschichte des 19. Jahrhunderts.* Berlin: A.L. Wolff, 1901. Pp. 144–280. *LJ*

3398 Illmer, Charles: *Méditations sur le mouvement anti-sémitique.* Florence: Typ. Successeurs Le Monnier, 1884. 45 pp. *LJ*

3399 Israel, Frederick (1846–): *Die Juden und das Deutsche Reich; offener Brief an eine deutsche Frau von F. Sailer, pseud.* 5. Aufl. Berlin: Stahn, 1879. 43 pp. *LJ*

Against W. Marr's *Der Sieg des Judentums über das Germanentum* and *Vom jüdischen Kriegsschauplatz.*

3400 *Ist der Antisemitismus berechtigt, von einem Staatsbürger.* Frankfurt a.M.: J. Kauffmann, 1893. 18 pp. *LF*

3401 Jacob, Nathan: *Held und das Judentum als eine von der germanischen Rasse abweichende Nation; eingehende Beleuchtung auf die Wahnsinnstheorien des Chef-Redakteurs der Staatsbürgerzeitung praktische Wiederlegung aller Angriffe des sogenannten Reform-Theoretikers gegen das Judentum als konfessionelles und nationales Glied der deutschen Nation, von N.J. Anders, pseud.* Berlin: E. Schlesinger, 1871. 16 pp. *LJ*

3402 Jacoby, Julius: *Die antisemitische Bewegung in Baden.* Karlsruhe: Selbstverlag, 1897. 30 pp. *LJ*

3403 Jakobowski, Ludwig (1868–1900): *Offene Antwort eines Juden auf Herrn Ahlwardt's "Der Eid eines Juden."* Berlin: Küchenmeister, 1891. 32 pp. *LJ*

3404 Jellinek, Adolf (1821–1893): *Die Apologetik des Judentums.* Wien: Oesterreichische Wochenschrift, 1892. 11 pp. *LJ*

Offprint from: *Oesterreichische Wochenschrift.*

3405  Jellinek, Adolf (1821–1893): *Aus der Zeit; Tagesfragen und Tagesbegeben-heiten.* I.–II. Ser. Budapest: Typ. von Sam. Markus, 1884–1886. 2 vols. *LJ*

3406  Jellinek, Adolf (1821–1893): *Franzosen über Juden.* Wien: M. Gottlieb, 1880. XXVI, 36 pp. *LJ*

3407  Jellinek, Adolf (1821–1893): *Organisation gegen Organisation.* Wien: M. Waizner, 1882. 6 pp. *LJ*
Offprint from: *Neuzeit*, no. 47.

3408  Joel, Manuel (1826–1890): *Gegen Gildemeister; Herrn Prof. Gildemeisters Gutachten über den jüdischen Ritualcodex (Schulchan Aruch) und das Verhältnis der Juden zu demselben.* Kritisch beleuchtet. Breslau: W. Jacobsohn & Co., 1884. 34 pp. *LJ*

3409  Joel, Manuel (1826–1890): *Offener Brief an . . . Heinrich von Treitschke.* Breslau: L. Weigert, 1879. 14 pp. *LJ*

3410  Jolenberg, L.: *Ein Briefwechsel zwischen L. Jolenberg und Herrn Hofprediger Stoecker; noch ein Friedensversuch in der leidigen Judenfrage.* Berlin: L. Jolenberg, 1880. 15 pp. *LJ*
Offprint from: *Jüdische Presse.*

3411  Jolenberg, L.: *Ein zeitgemäßes Wort an unsere christlichen Mitbürger, die sogenannte Judenfrage betreffend.* Berlin: Selbstverlag, 1881. 24 pp. *LJ*

3412  Joseph, Max (1868–): *Zur Sittenlehre des Judentums.* Berlin: M. Poppelauer, 1902. 56 pp. *LJ*

3413  Judaeus, pseud.: *Was müssen wir Juden tun?* Zürich: Trüb'sche Buchhdlg., 1881. 57 pp. *LJ*

3414  *Eine Juden-Antwort.* Wien: Typ. L.C. Zamarski & C. Dittmarsch, 1860. 23 pp. *LJ*
Offprint from: *Zeitung des Judentums*, 1860.

3415  *Juden, Studenten, Professoren; Frage- und Antwortspiel, von J.H.M.* Leipzig: C.W. Vollrath, 1881. 52 pp. *LJ*

3416  *Die Judenfrage und der Antisemitismus vor dem Richterstuhl der Menschlichkeit.* Hamburg: Hermann Beyer, 1890–91. 40 pp. *LC*
A reference to "Wehrdich, Michel, pseud." in *Gesamtverzeichnis des deutschen Schrifttums*, 1700–1910.

3417 *Die jüdische Tragödie der Irrungen; ein ernstes Mahnwort zur ernsten Zeit, von einem Juden.* Berlin: Fr. Wesemann, 1897. 103 pp. *LJ*

3418 Kahn, Arthur: *Der Judentag.* Bonn: Trapp, 1900. 24 pp. *LJ*

3419 Kalthoff, Albert (1850–1906): *Judentum und Christentum; Rede, gehalten im oberen Saale der Reichshallen zu Berlin.* Berlin: Hornberg, 1879. 16 pp. (Schriften des protestantischen Reformverein zu Berlin 1880, 3) *LJ*

3420 Kalthoff, Albert (1850–1906): *Die neueste Maßregel zur Bekämpfung des Judentums; Vortrag gehalten im Saale des Handwerker-Vereins zu Berlin.* Berlin: H. Würtzburg, 1880. 20 pp. *LJ*

3421 Kaufmann, David (1852–1899): *Die Lichter am Abend; Predigt . . . in der Synagoge der Landes-Rabbinerschule zu Budapest.* Budapest: S. Zilahy, 1880. 14 pp. *LJ*

3422 Kaufmann, David (1852–1899): *Vom jüdischen Katechismus.* Budapest: S. Zilahy, 1884. 19 pp. *LJ*

3423 Kaufmann, David (1852–1899): *Ein Wort im Vertrauen an Herrn Hofprediger Stoecker, von einem dessen Name nichts zur Sache tut.* Berlin: L. Gerschel, 1880. 20 pp. *LJ*

3424 Kautsky, Karl (1854–1938): Das Judentum, von S., pseud. *N. Z.* 8 (1890) 23–30. *LJ*

3425 Kayserling, Meier (1829–1905): *Die Juden als Patrioten; ein Vortrag gehalten in den Vereinen für jüdische Geschichte und Literatur in Berlin und Leipzig am 18. und 20. Januar 1898.* Berlin: Albert Katz, 1898. 15 pp. *LJ*

3426 Kayserling, Meier (1829–1905): *Vollständige Widerlegung der wider die Juden erhobenen Anklagen und Verleumdungen.* Baden: 1862. 24 pp. *LJ*

3427 Kayserling, Meier (1829–1905): *Der Wucher und das Judentum.* Budapest: Wodianer, 1882. 20 pp. *LJ*

3428 Kelchner, Ernst: *Wozu der Lärm? Ein Beitrag zur Klärung der sogenannten Judenfrage.* Frankfurt a.M.: Selbstverlag, 1881. 24 pp. *LF*

3429 Kissling, Karl von: *Offenes Schreiben an den Hochwürdigen Herrn Johann Hauser, Redakteur des "Linzer Volksblattes."* Linz: Kissling, 1893. 18 pp. *LTA*

3430  Kittel, Rudolf (1853–1929): *Judenfeindschaft; oder, Gotteslästerung? Ein gerichtliches Gutachten. Mit einem Schlußwort: Die Juden und der gegenwärtige Krieg.* Leipzig: Otto Wigand, 1914. III, 92 pp. *LJ*

      About the lawsuit of the Centralverein Deutscher Staatsbürger Jüdischen Glaubens against Theodor Fritsch.

3431  Klausner, Max Albert: *Zu Lehr und Wehr! Jüdische Zeitfragen.* Berlin: S. Calvary, 1903. 125 pp. *LJ*

3432  Klein, Gottlieb (1852–1914): *Zur Judenfrage; unsere Anforderungen an das Christentum des Herrn Stoecker.* Zürich: Verlags-Magazin Schabelitz, 1880. 23 pp. *LJ*

3433  Kleinmann, Adolf: *Anarchismus und Antisemitismus.* Wien: Verlag des Verfassers, 1888. 23 pp. *LC*

3434  Kleist, L.: *Der Apostel Stoecker, seine Jünger und der deutsche Bürgerkrieg; ein Beitrag zur Entwicklungsgeschichte der antisemitischen Bewegung.* Berlin: Stuhr'sche Buchhdlg., 1881. 26 pp. *LJ*

3435  Klötzel, Cheskel Zwi: *Das große Hassen; ein Beitrag zur Judenfrage in Deutschland.* München: Janus-Verlag, 1912–13. 57–60 pp. *LJ*

      Offprint from: *Janus; kritische Halbmonatsschrift für deutsche Kultur und Politik*, no. 2, 1912–13.

3436  Klopfer, Carl Eduard (1865–), ed.: *Zur Judenfrage; zeitgenößische Orginalaussprüche.* Mit einer Vorbemerkung von Ernst Haller. München: J.F. Lehmann, 1891. 63 pp. *LJ*

3437  König, Eduard (1846–1936): *Das antisemitische Hauptdogma.* Bonn: A. Marcus und E. Weber, 1914. 64 pp. *LJ*

3438  Kohler, Kaufmann (1843–1926): *Deutschland und die Juden. Der jüdische Kosmopolitismus.* New York: E. Steiger, 1881. 15 pp. *LJ*

      Offprint from: *Zeitgeist.*

3439  Kohn, Samuel (1841–1920): *Mit tegyünk az ellenünk intézett támadásokkal szemben?* Budapest: 1880. 10 pp. *LJ*

3440  Kohut, Adolph (1848–1917): *Gekrönte und ungekrönte Judenfreunde.* Berlin: Basch, 1913. 199 pp. *LJ*

3441  Kolkmann, Joseph: *Die gesellschaftliche Stellung der Juden.* Löbau i. Westpr.: R. Skrzeczek, 1876. 34 pp. *LJ*

3442 Kolkmann, Joseph: *Die gesellschaftliche Stellung der Juden, Löbau, 1876. Mit einer Vorbewerkung von Chajim Bloch. Anhang: Beim Nestor des Antisemitismus Dr. August Rohling.* Berlin: Philo-Verlag, 1933. VIII, III, 47, 12 pp. *LJ*

3443 Kramer, Franz: *Wie ich die Juden sah; aus den Erinnerungen eines 78-jährigen Katholiken.* Berlin: Selbstverlag, 191–. 11 pp. *LJ*

3444 Krause, Gerhard: *Zur Naturgeschichte der antisemitischen Bewegung.* Berlin: Verlag des "Vorwärts," 1890. 32 pp. (Berliner Arbeiterbibliothek, ser. 2, no 2) *LJ*

3445 Kroner, Philipp: *Der vierfüßige Speisvogel und die zweifüßigen Spaßvögel; ornithologische Glossen zur Kritikasterei.* Löbau: R. Skrzeczek, 1882. 44 pp. *LJ*

A review of Hermann Schell's book *Grundzüge einer vernunftmäßigen Auffassung des Christentums.*

3446 Kroner, Theodor (1845-1923): *Entstelltes, Unwahres und Erfundenes in dem "Talmudjuden" Professor Dr. August Rohlings. Nachgewiesen von Rabbiner Dr. Kroner.* T. 1-2. Münster: E. Obertüschen, 1871. 2 vol. *LJ*

3447 Kroner, Theodor (1845-1923): *Judenhaß oder Nächstenliebe; eine Erklärung des großherzoglichenLandesrabbinerDr. Kroner.* Eisenach:Hofbuchdruckerei, 1878. 15 S. *LJ*

3448 Krzesinski, Bogumil: *Der Jude; zeitgemäße Betrachtung von einem katholischen Geistlichen der Erzdiözese Gnesen-Posen.* Posen: Selbstverlag des Verfassers, 1892. 20 pp. *LJ*

3449 Küchenmeister, Karl: *Antwort des Herrn Karl Küchenmeister in der Volksversammlung vom 18. Dezember 1891 auf die öffentliche Herausforderung des Deutschen Antisemitenbundes in der Versammlung vom 11. Dezember 1891.* Hrsg. von der Vereinigung zur Bekämpfung der Rassenhetze. Berlin: Typ. C. Küchenmeister, 1891. 15 pp. (Zur Bekämpfung der Rassenhetze, Flugschrift 1) *LJ*

3450 Küchenmeister, Karl: *Kritische Proteste eines germanischen Christen gegen die neueste Bleichröder- und Judenhetze, von Kaberlin, pseud.* Berlin: Verlag der Illustrierten Berliner Gerichtshalle, Carl Küchenmeister, 1891. 30 pp. *LJ*

3451 Kümmel, Werner: Rudolf Virchow und der Antisemitismus. *Medizinhistorisches Journal* 3 (1968) 165-179. *LC*

3452 Kurrein, Adolf (1846–1919): Arbeit und Arbeiter im jüdischen Volke. *Populärwissenschaftliche Monatsblätter zur Belehrung über das Judentum* (1890) 73–76, 201–205, 228–231, 253–258, 278–283. *LJ*

3453 Kurrein, Adolf (1846–1919): Die soziale Frage im Judentum. *Populärwissenschaftliche Monatsblätter zur Belehrung über das Judentum* (1888) 185–188, 228–232; (1889) 36–39, 157–160, 230–233, 251–254, 274–277. *LJ*

3454 Lamberti, Marjorie (1937–): *Jewish Activism in Imperial Germany; the Struggle for Civil Equality.* New Haven: Yale University Press, 1978. 235 pp. (Yale Historical Publications; miscellany, 119) *LJ*

3455 Lamberti, Marjorie (1937–): The Prussian Government and the Jews; Offical Behavior and Policy-Making in the Wilhelminian Era. *LBIYB* 17 (1972) 5–17. *LJ*

3456 Landau, Leopold (1848–1920): *Lüge und Wahrheit; Dichtung.* 2. Aufl. Pforzheim: Selbstverlag, 188–. 11 pp. *LJ*

"Den deutsch-sozialen und verwandten Blättern ins Album."

3457 Landau, Saul Raphael (1870–): *Fort mit den Hausjuden! . . . Grundlinien jüdischer Volkspolitik. (Anhang: Tabellarische Uebersicht der jüdischen Reichsratsabgeordneten seit dem Jahr 1867. Umschlag: Der Polenklub und seine Hausjuden.* Wien: C.W. Stern, 1907. V, 42 pp. *LJ*

3458 Landsberger, Julius (1819–1890): *Wahrheit, Recht und Friede; eine Kanzelrede für Freunde und Feinde des Judentums.* Berlin: Peiser, 1881. 16 pp. *Unseen*

3459 Landsberger, Julius (1819–1890): *Zur Abwehr; Widerlegung der im Starkenburger Boten Nr. 92, resp. Augsburger Postzeitung Nr. 96 gegen das Judentum erhobenen Beschuldigungen.* Darmstadt: Typ. Gebr. Edelmann, 1871. 16 pp. *LJ*

Offprint from: Supplement in the *Main-Zeitung*, no. 294 and in the *Hessische Volksblätter*, no. 295.

3460 Lang, Julius (Vienna): *Der Antisemitismus vom katholischen Standpunkte als Sünde verurteilt. Studien über die Fragen: Kann der gläubige Katholik Antisemit sein? . . .von einem katholischen Privatgelehrten.* Volksausg. 3. Aufl. Wien: Verein zur Abwehr des Antisemitismus, 1891. 58 pp. *LJ*

3461 Lankes-Uhlemann, Fernanda: *Ein Streiflicht auf den Antisemitismus.* Berlin: E. Apolant, 1899. 26 pp. *LV*

3462 Lazar, Julius: *Das Judentum in seiner Vergangenheit und Gegenwart. Mit besonderem Hinblick nach Ungarn.* 2. Aufl. Berlin: Otto Hentze, 1880. 127 pp. *LJ*

3463 Lazare, Bernard (1865–1903): *Antisemitism, its History and Causes.* Tr. from the French. New York: International Library Publications, 1903. 384 pp. *LJ*

3464 Lazarus, Moritz (1824–1903): *An die deutschen Juden.* Berlin: Walther und Apolant, 1887. 30 pp. *LJ*

3465 Lazarus, Moritz (1824–1903): *Einiges aus den Motiven welche in der Koblenzer Konferenz vom 11. und 12. August 1883 zu dem Beschluß geführt haben, ein grundlegendes Werk über jüdische Ethik ins Leben zu rufen.* Berlin: Typ. J.S. Preuß, 1884. 8 pp. *LJ*

3466 Lazarus, Moritz (1824–1903): *Die Erneuerung des Judentums; ein Aufruf.* Berlin: G. Reimer, 1909. XVI, 120 pp. *LJ*

3467 Lazarus, Moritz (1824–1903): *Treu und frei; gesammelte Reden und Vorträge über Juden und Judentum.* Leipzig: C.F. Winter, 1887. VI, 355 pp. *LJ*

3468 Lazarus, Moritz (1824–1903): *Unser Standpunkt; zwei Reden an seine Religionsgenossen am 1. und 16. Dezember 1880.* Berlin: Stuhr, 1881. 40 pp. *LJ*

3469 Lazarus, Moritz (1824–1903): *Was heißt national? Ein Vortrag.* Berlin: F. Dümmler Verlagshdlg., 1880. 61 pp. *LJ*

3470 Lefson, E.: *Anti-Stoecker; offener Brief und Nachwort.* Berlin: M. Schildberger, 1879. 16 pp. *LJ*

3471 Lehmann, Emil (1829–1898): *Die Juden jetzt und einst; ein Beitrag zur Lösung der "Judenfrage."* Dresden: Pierson's Verlag, 1886. 37 pp. *LJ*

3472 Lehmann, Emil (1829–1898): *Offener Brief an Herrn Professor Friedrich Paulsen.* Berlin: E. Billig Nachf., 1898. 16 pp. *LJ*

Offprint from the monthly: *Im deutschen Reich,* no. 12, 1898.

3473 Lehmann, Emil (1829–1898): *Ueber die judenfeindliche Bewegung in Deutschland.* Leipzig: Offenhauer & Co., 1880. 15 pp. *LJ*

3474 Lehmann, Emil (1829–1898): Zur Geschichte des Judenhaßes. *Gesammelte Schriften.* Berlin: H.S. Hermann, 1899. Pp. 100–116. *LJ*

3475  Lehr, Elias: *Reflexionen eines Verurteilten*. Wien: Selbstverlag, 1902. 114 pp.
      *LJ*

      Lehr was sentenced to one month in prison because he published pamphlets in
      favor of the defendant Hilsner in the Polna blood libel process.

3476  Lengsfelder, Salomon: *Beleuchtung der Herzens- und Verstandesergiessung
      eines anonymen Judenfeindes in der "Agramer-Zeitung" Nr. 87 und 89,
      bezüglich der Juden-Emanzipation*. G. Kanizsa: Typ. J. Markbreiter, 1861.
      55 pp. *LJ*

3477  Lengsfelder, Salomon: *Erwiderung auf Dr. Rohlings Pamphlet "Der
      Talmudjude."* Preßburg: Typ. Löwy & Alkalay, 1883. 48 pp. *LJ*

3478  Leroy-Beaulieu, Anatole (1842-1912): *Der Antisemitismus. Autorisierte
      Uebersetzung von Wilhelm Thal*. Berlin: J. Edelheim, 1901. 37 pp. *LJ*

3479  Leschmann, Georg Friedrich: *Hofprediger Stoecker; oder, Meine persönlichen
      Erlebnisse unter den Christlich-Sozialen in Berlin. Ein Beitrag zur Beleuchtung
      und Abwehr der antisemitischen Bewegung der Gegenwart*. Offenbach am
      Main: J.P. Strauß, 1881. 16 pp. *LJ*

3480  Levi, Leo N.: *Was soll aus den Juden werden? Eine Abhandlung über die
      Judenfrage*. Aus dem Englischen übers. von H. Berliner. Zürich: C. Schmidt,
      1895. 29 pp. *LJ*

      Original title: *What shall become of the Jew?*

3481  Levinstein, Gustav (1842-1910): *Professor Paulsen und die Judenfrage*. Berlin:
      M. Poppelauer, 1897. 24 pp. *LJ*

3482  Levinstein, Gustav (1842-1910): *Wissenschaftlicher Antisemitismus; Vortrag*.
      Berlin: E. Billig, 1896. 20 pp. *LJ*

3483  Levinstein, Gustav (1842-1910): *Zur Ehre des Judentums; gesammelte
      Schriften*. Berlin: Verlag des Central-Vereins Deutscher Staatsbürger Jüdischen
      Glaubens, 1911. XV, 193 pp. *LJ*

3484  Levy, Alphonse (1838-1917): Antisemitismus in der Schweiz. *I.Dt.R.* 8 (1902)
      65-73. *LJ*

3485  Levy, Alphonse (1838-1917): *Sanitätsrat Stilles "Kampf gegen das Judentum."*
      Berlin: Centralverein Deutscher Staatsbürger Jüdischen Glaubens, 1913. 16 pp.
      *LJ*

      Offprint from: *Im Deutschen Reich*.

3486 Levy, Heymann: *Eppes Rores über der Berger Katzenjammer bei der Berger Katzenmusik.* Berlin: C.A.Schienentz, 1848. 1 l. *LJ*

3487 Lewald, Fanny (1811–1889): *Meine Lebensgeschichte.* Hrsg. und eingeleitet von Gisela Brinker-Gabler. Frankfurt a.M.: Fischer Taschenbuch Verlag, 1980. 303 pp. (Die Frau in der Gesellschaft; Lebensgeschichten) *LJ*
First published in 1861–62 in Berlin.

3488 Lewin, Adolf (1843–1910): *Der ewige Jude; eine Ansprache an viele wenn nicht an alle, von Alwin Dolfe, pseud.* Trier: Gebr. Maas, 1891. 32 pp. *LJ*

3489 Lewin, Adolf (1843–1910): *Naturwissenschaft oder Judenhaß? Eine Beleuchtung des Artikels: "Der Judenstamm in naturhistorischer Bedeutung."* Breslau: Leuckert'sche Buchhdlg., 1880. 29 pp. *LJ*
Offprint from: *Jüdisches Literaturblatt, Ausland*, no. 22–27, 1880.

3490 Lewy, Joseph: Antisemitismus und Medizin. *I.Dt.R.* 5 (1899) 1–19. *LJ*

3491 Lichtenstein, Edmund (1864–): *Ahlwardt im Kampf mit dem Gesetz; Ahlwardt's Zusammenbruch.* Vortrag gehalten in einer Versammlung der "Vereinigung zur Bekämpfung der Rassenhetze" am 5. August 1892, von Ed. Mund, pseud. Berlin: J. van Groningen, 1892. 32 pp. (Berliner Fanfaren, 4) *LJ*

3492 Lichtenstein, Edmund (1864–): *Ahlwardt's Ende! Authentische Enthüllungen Eingeweihter. Gesammelt von Ed. Mund, pseud.* 3. Aufl. Berlin: J. van Groningen, 1892. 38 pp. (Berliner Fanfaren, 3) *LJ*

3493 Lichtenstein, Edmund (1864–): *Das antisemitische "Deutsche Tageblatt" im Lichte der Wahrheit. Zur Abwehr.* Schönebeck a. E.: Georg Wolff, 1882. 16 pp. *LJ*

3494 Lichtenstein, Edmund (1864–): *Papa Ahlwardt's Heldentaten in 5 Gesängen, von Ed. Mund, pseud.* Berlin: J. van Groningen, 1892. 15 pp. (Berliner Fanfaren, 5) *Unseen*

3495 Lichtenstein, Edmund (1864–): *Sibirien in Preußen, von Ed. Mund, pseud.* Berlin: J. van Groningen, 1892. 36 pp. (Berliner Fanfaren, 2) *Unseen*

3496 Liebermann, Arthur: *Religionsvorschriften des Judentums über Tierschutz und Tierfürsorge.* Königsberg i. Pr.: D. Kahan, 1906. XIII pp. *LJ*

3497 Liebermann von Sonnenberg, Max (1848–1911): *Die Herabwürdigung des christlichen Eides durch den Rabbiner Dr. Münz in Gleiwitz; Wortlaut des Rabbinerbriefes an den Reichstags-Abgeordneten Liebermann von Sonnenberg und Wortlaut von dessen Antwort und Widerlegung.* Berlin: Deutschnationale Buchhdlg. und Verlags-Anstalt, 1902. 13 pp. *LJ*

3498  Liebknecht, Wilhelm (1826–1900): *Rede über den Kölner Parteitag mit besonderer Berücksichtigung der Gewerkschaftsbewegung, gehalten zu Bielefeld am 29.10.1893.* Bielefeld: Schumann & Co., 1893. 40 pp. *LJ*

3499  *Lieder eines Semiten.* Hamburg: A. Goldschmidt, 1892. 32 pp. *LJ*

3500  Liéser, E.: *Die modernen Judenhasser und der Versuch von Julius Lang, das Judentum mit Richard Wagner zu versöhnen.* Nakel: Kallmann, 1869. 16 pp. *LJ*

3501  Linden, Gustav von: *Der Sieg des Judentums über das Germanentum; eine Widerlegung der Marr'schen Polemik in historischer und allgemeiner Beziehung, zugleich eine Mahnung an das deutsche Volk und an die deutschen Fürsten.* 2. Aufl. Leipzig: G. Körner, 1879. VI, 41 pp. *LJ*

3502  Lippe, Karpel (1830–1915): *Die Gesetzsammlung des Judenspiegels, zusammengestellt und gefälscht von Aron Briman, Pseudodoktor Justus.* Beleuchtet und berichtigt. Jassy: Typ. H. Goldner, 1885. XIV, 288 pp. *LJ*

3503  Lippe, Karpel (1830–1915): *Die Menschenliebe, die Zivilisation und die Gerechtigkeit, vom Standpunkte der jüngsten Vorgänge in Tiszá-Eszlár aus betrachtet.* Preßburg: Typ. Löwy & Alkalay, 1883. 24 pp. *LJ*

3504  Lippe, Karpel (1830–1915): *Symptome der antisemitischen Geisteskrankheit.* Jassy: Typ. H. Goldner, 1887. 92 pp. *LJ*

3505  Lippe, Karpel (1830–1915): *Der Talmudjude vor dem katholisch-protestantisch-orthodoxen Dreirichter-Kollegium Rohling-Stoecker-Pobedonoscew.* Wien: D. Löwy, 1884. 41 pp. *LJ*

3506  Lippert, Julius (1839–1909): *Der Antisemitismus.* Prag: Deutscher Verein zur Verbreitung gemeinnütziger Kenntnisse, 1883. 18 pp. (Sammlung gemeinnütziger Vorträge, 88) *LJ*

3507  Löb, Moritz: *Ein Ausnahmegesetz gegen die jüdischen Handlungsgehilfen; eine Erwiderung.* Berlin: Typ. J. Sittenfeld, 1913. 5 pp. *LJ*

Against an article, published by Dr. Schweitzer. Offprint from: *Soziale Praxis und Archiv für Volkswohlfahrt,* vol. 23, no. 30.

3508  Löhneysen, Heinrich von: *Antisemitismus und Nächstenliebe. Von einem positiv-christlichen Standpunkt aus betrachtet.* Berlin: H. Walther, 1893. 35 pp. *LJ*

3509 Löw, Albert: *Unsere Freunde und unsere Feinde; Vortrag gehalten . . . in seiner geliebten Vaterstadt Holleschau nach den im Monat Oktober 1899 daselbst erfolgten antisemitischen Umtrieben.* Budapest: Typ. F. Buschmann, 1903. 18 pp. *LJ*

3510 Löwe, Ludwig (1837–1886): *Kontra Stoecker; 3 Reden der Abgeordneten Ludwig Löwe Adolf Stoecker und Hänel gehalten in der Sitzung des Preußischen Abgeordnetenhauses vom 11.2.1880.* Berlin: Barthel, 1889. 16 pp. *LJ*

3511 Löwenfeld, Raphael (1854–1910): *Schutzjuden oder Staatsbürger?* Berlin: Schweitzer & Mohr, 1893. 19 pp. *LJ*

3512 Löwenfeld, Raphael (1854–1910): *Schutzjuden oder Staatsbürger?* 3. Aufl. verm. um Stimmen der Presse und Zuschriften aus dem Publikum. Berlin: Schweitzer & Mohr, 1893. 27 pp. *LJ*

3513 Löwy, David: *Der Talmudjude von Rohling in der Schwurgerichtsverhandlung vom 28. Oktober 1882; zur Abwehr und Verständigung. Mit einem Vorwort von A. Wünsche.* Wien: D. Löwy, 1882. 40 pp. *LJ*

3514 Löwy, David: *Unverfälschte Worte, von einem Theologen.* 2. Aufl. Wien: D. Löwy, 1889. 36 pp. *LJ*

3515 Looshorn, Johann: *Des Juden Mayer Prozeß gegen Bamberger Fürstbischöfe, von J. L.* München: G. Schub, 1899. 8 pp. *Unseen*

3516 Lowenfeld, David: A Futile Defense; Jewish Responses to German Antisemitism, 1879–1914. *Olam (World Union of Jewish Students), London* no. 1 (1976) 38–47. *LJ*

3517 Lublinski, Samuel (1868–1910): Der Antisemitismus; Heinrich von Treitschke als Politiker. *Nachgelassene Schriften.* München: G. Müller, 1914. Pp. 92–119, 156–168. *LJ*

3518 Lucko, Hermann: *Ein Jahr im Zentrum der Deutsch-Sozialen Partei; ein offenes Wort.* Leipzig: Selbstverlag des Verfassers, 1892. 28 pp. *LJ*

3519 Lübeck, Karl: *Eine Rechtfertigung der Juden und wahre Lösung der Judenfrage, von C.L. Beck, pseud.* Leipzig: Morgenstern, 1881. V, 105 pp. *LJ*

3520 *Luther und die Juden.* Den deutschen Studenten gewidmet, von einem Kommilitonen. Leipzig: Frohberg, 1881. 32 pp. *LJ*

3521 Lux, Heinrich (1863-): *Die Juden als Verbrecher; eine Beleuchtung antisemitischer Beweisführung.* München: M. Ernst, 1893. 32 pp. (Sammlung gesellschaftswissenschaftlicher Aufsätze, 3) *LJ*

3522 *Luxemburg: Anklagrede der königlichen Großherzoglichen Staatsanwaltschaft in Luxemburg wegen Beleidigung der jüdischen Religion und ihrer Bekenner.* Mit einem Vorwort von Förder. Berlin: Philo-Verlag, 1925. 28 pp. *LJ*

This speech was first published in 1889. The defendant was the editor of the newspaper *Luxemburger Wort.*

3523 Macaulay, Thomas Babington, 1st baron (1800-1859): *Civil disabilities of the Jews. Eine . . . Abhandlung.* Hrsg. und mit Anmerkungen versehen von Dr. F. Fischer. Berlin: L. Simion, 1882. 29 pp. *LJ*

3524 Macaulay, Thomas Babington, 1st baron (1800-1859): *Macaulay über die Judenfrage.* Aus dem Englischen von Philipp Siegfried Bauer. Frankfurt a.M.: F.B. Auffarth, 1852. 16 pp. *LJ*

3525 Maier, Gustav (1844-1923): *Mehr Licht; ein Wort zur "Judenfrage" an unsere christlichen Mitbürger.* Ulm: H. Kerler, 1881. 23 pp. *LJ*

3526 Mandl, Leopold: *Psychologie zum Verständnis des Antisemitismus; treue Worte an Freund und Feind.* Wien: Selbstverlag, 1882. 1 vol. *Unseen*

3527 Mandl, Leopold: *Zur Abrechnung; eine Zurückweisung der babylonisch-germanischen Angriffe auf den Prophetismus Israels.* Wien: M. Waizner, 1903. 16 pp. *LJ*

3528 Marbach, Oswald (1810-1890): *Ueber die sittlichen Ausartungen und Bedrohungen des Kulturlebens in der Gegenwart.* Leipzig: Zechel, 1880. 8 pp. *LJ*

Reprinted from the masonic monthly: *Am Reisbrette.*

3529 Margulies, Samuel Hirsch (1858-1922): *Haman an die Antisemiten.* Lübeck: Typ. Werner & Höring, 1893. 15 pp. *LTA*

3530 Matók, Béla: *A zsidó kérdés, Nro. 2: történelmi társadalmi és törvényes szempontból tárgyalva.* Budapest: 1881. 135 pp. *LJ*

3531 Mayer, Ernst (1862-1932): *Der Antisemitismus und das deutsche Bürgertum; ein Vortrag.* 2. Aufl. Würzburg: L. Kressner, 1893. 16 pp. *LC*

3532 Mayer, Israel: *Antisemtismus in der Pfalz? Ein offener Brief an die "Pfälzische Presse."* Zweibrücken: Typ. A. Kranzbühler, 1888. 27 pp. *LJ*

3533 Mayer, Michael A.: Jewish Reactions to New Hostility in Germany, 1879-1881. *LBIYB* 11 (1966) 137-170. *LJ*

3534 Mendelsohn, Martin (1860-1930): *Die Pflicht der Selbstverteidigung; eine Rede.* Jahresbericht des Vorsitzenden in der ersten ordentlichen Generalversammlung des Centralvereins Deutscher Staatsbürger Jüdischen Glaubens. Berlin: Imberg & Lefson, 1894. 37 pp. *LJ*

3535 Merx, Ernst Otto Adalbert (1838-1909): *Wissenschaftliches Gutachten über den wahren Sinn der Stellen aus dem Sohar und aus Vital's liqqutim, auf die Herr Prof. Rohling seine Blutbeschuldingung gründen will.* Wien: J.C. Fischer, 1885. 21 pp. *LJ*

3536 Meyer, Seligmann (1853-1925): *Ein Wort an Herrn Hermann Messner.* Berlin: Edition Götz, 1877. 50 pp. *LJ*

Review on Messner's article "Blicke ins moderne Judentum" published in *Neue Evangelische Kirchenzeitung*, 1877, 28-30.

3537 Meyer, Seligmann (1853-1925): *Zurückweisung des dritten judenfeindlichen Artikels des Herrn Professors Dr. H.v. Treitschke.* Berlin: Stuhr, 1880. 20 pp. *LJ*

3538 Mintz, Meir: *Lelewel, Kämpfer für Recht und Wahrheit und die Judenfeinde; Betrachtungen.* Lemberg: Poremba, 1860. 48 pp. *LF*

3539 Mommsen, Theodor (1817-1903): *Auch ein Wort über unser Judentum.* Berlin: Weidmannsche Buchhdlg., 1880. 18 pp. *LJ*

3540 Mühlfelder, Jakob: *Offener Brief an den Oberpfarrer Herrn Dr. Graue zu Chemnitz.* Chemnitz: M.Lohse, 1894. 61 pp. *LJ*

3541 Müller, Johannes (1864-): Judenfrage und Antisemitismus, christlich beurteilt. *SaH* 28 (1891) 249-264. *LC*

3542 Müller, Johannes (1864-): *Der Weg zur Verständigung zwischen Judentum und Christentum.* Leipzig: W. Faber, 1892. 84 pp. (Schriften des Institutum Judaicum in Leipzig, 39) *LJ*

3543 Münz, Lazar (1837-1921): *Die modernen Anklagen gegen das Judentum als falsch nachgewiesen; ein Rede.* Frankfurt a.M.: J. Kauffmann, 1882. 29 pp. *LJ*

3544  Muscat, Perez Paul: *Die Rasse der Israeliten; oder, Ehrenname und Erziehung Israels. Vierter Abschnitt des Werkes: Das Leben und die Krone Israels . . . nebst einem Anhange: 3 Arten in der Christenheit und der Antisemit . . .* Mainz: O. Lehmann, 188-. 65 pp. *LJ*

3545  Muscat, Perez Paul: *Der Reichtum der Israeliten; oder, Der aufrichtige Israelit ist kein Materialist.* Nice: 1886. 13 pp. *LJ*

3546  Neumann, Wilhelm: *Der Friede unter den Kindern der Bibel. Judentum und Christentum.* Prag: J.B. Brandeis, 1883. 31 pp. *LJ*
       Ecumenical.

3547  Neustadt, Pinkus: *Zur jüdischen Feindesliebe.* Breslau: Schatzky, 1879. 16 pp. *LJ*
       Offprint from: *12. Bericht der Hebräischen Unterrichtsanstalt.*

3548  Nikel, Johannes: *Alte und neue Angriffe auf das Alte Testament; ein Rückblick und Ausblick.* Münster: W. Aschendorff, 1908. 46 pp. (Biblische Zeitfragen, Ser. 1, 1) *LJ*

3549  Norton, Richard: *Die Epoche der Begriffsverwirrung.* 2. Aufl. Berlin: Steinitz, 1881. 84 pp. *LJ*

3550  Oettinger, Eduard Maria (1808-1872): *Offenes Billet-doux an den berühmten Hepp-hepp Schreier und Judenfresser Herrn Wilhelm Richard Wagner.* Dresden: L. Wolf, 1869. 22 pp. *LJ*

3551  *Offener Brief eines geborenen alten Salzburgers an Herrn Schöpf; Kritik der hierorts erschienen antisemitischen Schriften.* Salzburg: Kerber, 1888. 16 pp. *Unseen*

3552  *Offener Brief eines jüdischen Predigers an den Hofprediger Herrn Adolf Stoecker in Berlin.* 3. verm. Aufl. Magdeburg: Friese, 1879. 18 pp. *LJ*

3553  Oppenheimer, Ludwig J.: Juden in Oesterreich. *Austriaca; Betrachtungen und Streiflichter.* Leipzig: Dunker & Humblot, 1882. Pp. 187-224. *LJ*

3554  Oppenheimer, Moses: *Offener Brief an Herrn Adolph Stoecker, Hofprediger und Mitglied des Oberkirchenrates in Berlin.* 2. Aufl. Mannheim: Selbstverlag, 1879. 14 pp. *LJ*

3555  Oppenheimer, Moses: *Semiten und Arier. 2. Brief an Herrn Adolph Stoecker, Hofprediger und Mitglied des Oberkirchenrates in Berlin, zugleich Landtags-*

*Abgeordneter für Bielefeld.* Mannheim: Selbstverlag des Verfassers, 1880. 15 pp. *LJ*

3556 Pariser, Kurt (1863–): *Antisemitismus-Anarchismus; Vortrag gehalten in der allgemeinen Versammlung der Centralvereins Deutscher Staatsbürger Jüdischen Glaubens am 3. Dezember 1895.* Berlin: E. Billig, 1896. 26 pp. *LJ*

3557 Pawel-Rammingen, Alexander, von (1855–): *Gedanken eines deutschen Edelmannes über die Judenfrage.* Berlin: H. Walther, 1904. 47 pp. *LJ*

3558 Pawel-Rammingen, Alexander, von (1855–): *Gedanken eines Kavaliers über Antisemitismus.* Berlin: Walther & Apolant, 1887. 29 pp. *LJ*

3559 Perinhart, J.: *Die deutschen Juden und Herr W. Marr.* 2. Aufl. Löbau Wstpr.: R. Skrzeczek, 1879. 42 pp. *LJ*

3560 Pestalozzi, Johannes: *Antichristentum in alter und neuer Zeit; Versuch einer Darstellung als ein Hülfsmittel zur Orientierung für alle Stände deutscher Christenheit.* Leipzig: Grunow, 1887. III, 436 pp. *Unseen*

3561 Pestalozzi, Johannes: *Der Antisemitismus; ein Krebsschaden, der am Marke unseres Volkslebens frißt.* Leipzig: W. Faber, 1891. 103 pp. *LJ*

3562 Pestalozzi, Johannes: *Antisemitismus und Judentum; ein Beitrag zur Beleuchtung der Stoeckerschen Agitation.* Halle: E. Strien, 1886. VIII, 69 pp. *LJ*

3563 Philagathos, pseud.: *Die Judenfrage und ihre Lösung.* Neustadt, O.S.: H. Raupach, 1890. 25 pp. *LJ*

3564 Phillips, A.: *Gegen Stoecker und Wagner: Rede des Reichstagsabgeordneten Dr. Phillips gehalten am 23. September 1884 in Berlin.* Berlin: Fortschrittlicher Verein der Potsdamer Vorstadt, 1884. 4 pp. *LJ*

3565 Piton, Heinrich: *Die "Judenfrage." Predigt über Matth. VII, 12.* 3. Aufl. Annweiler: Meissner und Philippson, 1881. 16 pp. *LJ*

3566 Plessner, Elias: *Die Stellung der Juden im Staate; ein Wort zu seiner Zeit.* Nebst einem Anhange: Das gedankenharmonische Doppelfest. Vortrag gehalten zum 25-jährigen Jubiläum der Alliance Israélite Universelle. Berlin: Driesner, 1885. 20 pp. *LJ*

3567 Pohl, Karl: *Semitismus.* 2. Kapitel für Wahrheit und Recht, von K.P. Wien: T. Dorfmeister, 1900. 40 pp. *LJ*

3568  Pohlmann, Walter: *Christen und Juden.* Neuwied: Heuser's Verlag, 1894.
      47 pp. *LJ*

3569  Pohlmann, Walter: *Die Juden und die körperliche Arbeit; ein Vortrag gehalten
      am 27. März 1894 zu Berlin im Centralverein Deutscher Staatsbürger Jüdischen
      Glaubens.* Berlin: M. Harrwitz, 1894. 21 pp. *LJ*

3570  Pohlmann, Walter: *Das Judentum und sein Recht.* 12. Aufl. Neuwied: Heuser's
      Verlag, 1893. 47 pp. *LJ*

3571  Pohlmann, Walter: *Das Judentum und seine Feinde.* Berlin: M. Harrwitz, 1893.
      46 pp. *LJ*

3572  Pohlmann, Walter: *Jüdische Leiden.* Neuwied: Heuser's Verlag, 1893. 48 pp.
      *LJ*

3573  *Die Preußische Staatsverwaltung und die Juden; Protestversammlung vom 10.
      Februar in Berlin.* Stenographischer Bericht. Berlin: H.S. Hermann, 1901. 50
      pp. *LJ*

3574  Preußisches Abgeordnetenhaus: *Die Judendebatte im Preußischen Abgeordneten-
      hause. Reden Seiner Excellenzen, der Herrn von Gossler und der Herrn
      Stoecker und Rickert, anläßlich der zweiten Beratung des Kulturetats am 20.
      u. 21. März 1890.* Berlin: Aktiengesellschaft für Druckerei und Verlag, 1890.
      42 pp. *LJ*

3575  Priluker, Jakob: *Zwischen Judentum und Christentum und allen andern
      Religionen; Drama in einem Aufzuge und 2 Bildern.* 2. Aufl. Hamburg:
      Priluker, 1882. 32 pp. *LJ*

3576  Prof. Dr. Strack über den Antisemitismus. *I.Dt.R.* 14 (1908) 686–690; 15
      (1909) 15–21 *LJ*

3577  Rádin, Adolph Moses (1845–1909): *Offener Brief eines polnischen Juden an den
      Redakteur Herrn Heinrich von Treitschke von Moses Aron Nadyr, pseud.*
      Löbau: R. Skrzeczek, 1879. 28 pp. *LJ*

      About Treitschke's article in Pr. Jhrb. 1879: *Unsere Aussichten.*

3578  Rathenau, Walther (1867–1922): Staat und Judentum. *Zur Kritik der Zeit.*
      Berlin: S. Fischer, 1912. Pp. 219–243. *LJ*

3579  *Reden gegen den Antisemitismus gehalten in den Sitzungen des
      Oesterreichischen Abgeordnetenhauses bei Gelegenheit der Beratung des
      Gesetzes zur Regelung der äußeren Rechtsverhältnisse der Israelitischen*

*Religionsgesellschaft. Nach den stenographischen Protokollen des Reichsrates.* Wien: Oesterreichische Wochenschrift, 1890. 28 pp. *LJ*

3580 Reich, Heinrich Leo: *Zur Wehr und Lehr; ein Wort zur Zeit an die denkenden ungarischen semitischen und nicht semitischen Bürger.* Ung. Altenburg: 1882. 20 pp. *LJ*

3581 Reichenbach, A.: *Die moderne Judenhetze; nach einem öffentlichen Vortrage.* Breslau: Selbstverlag, 1879. 14 pp. *LJ*

3582 Reichenbach, A.: *Nach der Hatz; kritische Betrachtung der letzten Judenhetze in Deutschland als der neuesten Krankheitserscheinung des deutschen Volkes.* Zürich: Verlags-Magazin, 1881. 67 pp. *LJ*

3583 *Der reine Mosaismus; interkonfessionelle Religionslehre II. Vom Verfasser der "Religion des kommenden Jahrhunderts."* Budapest: Aigner, 1882. 56 pp. *Unseen*

3584 Reinharz, Jehuda: *Deutschtum and Judentum; Jewish Liberalism and Zionism in Germany, 1893-1914.* Waltham, Mass.: Brandeis University, 1972. V, 442 pp. *LJ*

Diss. 1972.

3585 Revel, Wilhelm: *Der Wahrheit die Ehre; ein Beitrag zur Judenfrage in Deutschland.* Nürnberg: Wörlein & Co., 1881. 30 pp. *LJ*

3586 Rieger, Paul (1870-1939): Antisemitismus und Wissenschaft. *I.Dt.R.* 8 (1902) 473-480, 537-542. *LJ*

3587 Rieger, Paul (1870-1939): *Ein Vierteljahrhundert im Kampf um das Recht und die Zukunft der deutschen Juden; ein Rückblick auf die Geschichte des C.V. in den Jahren 1893-1918.* Berlin: Philo-Verlag, 1918. 88 pp. *LJ*

3588 Ritter, Immanuel Heinrich: *Beleuchtung der Wagner'schen Schrift; das Judentum und der Staat.* Berlin: in Komm. bei Kasselberg, 1857. 23 pp. *LJ*

3589 Ritter, Immanuel Heinrich: *Ein Wort an Juden und Christen; Rede am Neujahrstage.* Berlin: Stuhr'sche Buchhdlg., 1883. 13 pp. *LJ*

3590 Rodkinssohn, Michael Levi (1845-1904): *Der Schulchan Aruch und seine Beziehungen zu den Juden und Nichtjuden.* Ins Deutsche übertragen von D. Löwy. Wien: D. Löwy, 1884. 68, X pp. *LJ*

3591 Röhrich, Wilhelm: *Wucher und Intoleranz; zugleich eine Antwort auf die Schrift von W. Marr "Der Sieg des Judentums über das Germanentum."* *Von einem Unparteiischen.* Zürich: Verlags-Magazin, 1879. 36 pp. *LJ*

3592 Rosenberg, Aron: *Antisemiten sind Rschoim; zweckdienliche Broschüre aus dem "Wiener Blatt zur Belehrung und Bekehrung der christlichen und auch der jüdischen Rschoim-Antisemiten.* Wien: Wiener Blatt, 1896. 24 pp. *LJ*

3593 Rosenberg, Aron: *"Judenblut-Christenblut."* Wien: Wiener Blatt, 1897. 29 pp. *LJ*

3594 Rosenberg, Aron: *Der papierne Weltkrieg im XX. Jahrhundert n. Chr.* Wien: im eigenen Verlage, 1903. 64 pp. *LJ*

3595 Rosenmann, Moses: *Jüdische Realpolitik in Oesterreich; ein Vademecum für ernst Denkende.* Wien: R. Löwit, 1900. 30 pp. *LJ*

3596 Rosenow, Emil (1871–1904): *Kapital und Judenfrage.* 2. Aufl. Chemnitz: A. Langer, 1890. 16 pp. *LJ*

3597 Rosenthal, Ludwig A. (1855–1928): Deutsche und Juden. *Jüdisches Literatur-Blatt* 30 (1907) 38–40, 62–65. *LJ*

3598 Rosenthal, Ludwig A. (1855–1928): *Ein jüdischer Egidy; offener Brief an den Verfasser der Flugschrift "Die Zukunft des deutschen Judentums."* *Von einem Juden.* Dresden: H. Oskar Damm, 1892. 16 pp. *Unseen*

3599 Rost L.: *Zur Berufstätigkeit der Juden; gegen den Vorwurf ihrer Arbeitsscheu.* Alzey: A. Meschett, 1880. 56 pp. *LJ*

3600 Rothe, Emil: *Die Judenfrage; Vortrag . . . gehalten zu Cincinnati, den 22. Jan. 1881.* Cincinnati: 1881. 16 pp. *LJ*

3601 Rothenbücher, Adolf: *Sohar, Talmud und die Antisemiten.* Berlin: Neufeld & Henius, 1895. 91 pp. *LJ*

3602 Rothschild, Albert von: *Offenes Sendschreiben von A. Freiherr v. Rothschild in Wien an Hofprediger Stoecker in Berlin.* Uebers. ins Hebräische von A. Rudall. Preßburg: Typ. Löwy & Alkalay, 1880. 15 pp. *LJ*

German and Hebrew on opposite pages.

3603 Rothschild, Clementine von: *Briefe an eine christliche Freundin über die Grundwahrheiten des Judentums.* Mit einem biographischen Vorwort von Leopold Stein. Leipzig: E.L. Morgenstern, 1883. XIII, 88 pp. *LJ*

These letters are signed with the author's pseud.: Esther Izates. First edition published in 1867.

3604 Rülf, Isaak (1831–1902): *Entstehung und Bedeutung des Antisemitismus in Hessen.* Mainz: J. Wirth, 1890. 30 pp. *LJ*

3605 Rülf, Isaak (1831–1902): *Zur Verteidigung der Juden hier und überall. Mit besonderer Rücksicht auf ihre Stellung und Beaufsichtigung in Kurhessen.* Marburg: Selbstverlag des Verfassers, 1858. 25 pp. *LJ*

3606 *Das Rüstzeug der Antisemiten; im Interesse des sozialen Friedens.* Hrsg. von einer Anzahl deutscher Juden. Leipzig: Täschner, 1892. 62 pp. *LJ*

3607 Salinger, Eugen: *Hep! Hep! Ein Blick in den Judenspiegel des Herrn W. Marr.* Hannover: Meyer, 1862. 41 pp. *Unseen*

3608 Sanders, Daniel (1819–1897): *Die beiden Apostel; ein Schwank von Hans Sachs dem Jüngern.* Zürich: J. Schabelitz, Verlags-Magazin, 1881. 8 pp. *LJ*

3609 Schach, Fabius (1868–1930): *Volks- oder Salonjudentum? Von xxx.* Berlin: Schildberger, 1893. 22 pp. *LJ*

3610 Schacht, F.: *Der Antisemitismus der Gegenwart und seine Abwehr; ein Weckruf an die deutschen Juden, von F.S.* Mühlheim am Rhein: K. Glitscher, 1895. 27 pp. *LJ*

3611 Schanz, Uli: *Es werde Licht! Ein Friedenswort in Versen zur Glaubens- und Nationalitätenfrage in Deutschland und Oesterreich, zugleich als Gruß an das kommende Jahr. Hierzu: Die Judenhetze "La caccia ai Giudei" in italienischer Beleuchtung durch Ruggiero Bonghi. Deutsch von Uli Cavaliere Schanz.* Auma, Thur. A. Jügelt, 1895. 51 pp. *LJ*

3612 Schatt, L.G.: *Herr Liebermann von Sonnenberg und der Antisemitismus; eine ungehaltene Rede.* Mannheim: K. Schatt, 1891. 15 pp. *LJ*

3613 Schirmer, Wilhelm: *Ahasver; ein Mahnruf in der Judenfrage.* Danzig: A.W. Kafemmann, 1891. 15 pp. *LJ*

3614 Schleinitz, Alexander von (1807–1885): *An die Judenverfolger; zur Entgegnung auf das Buch "Israel und die Gojim."* Berlin: Stuhr, 1881. 51 pp. *LJ*

3615 Schlesinger, Markus: *Neki Kapayim; reine Hände. Widerlegt die wider die Juden erhobenen Beschuldigungen.* Deutsch von Adolf Hirtenstein. Budapest: Selbstverlag, 1882. 30 pp. *LJ*

3616 Schmidt, Karl: *Die Judenhetze*. 2. Aufl. Wiesbaden: C. Limbarth, 1889. 32 pp.
LJ

3617 Schneidt, Karl: *Der Prozeß Ahlwardt und anderes*. Berlin: Moderner-Verlag, 1892. 32 pp. (Sammlung volkstümlicher Streitschriften, 1) *LJ*

3618 Schöler, Hermann (1869–): *Die antisemitische Bewegung, ihre Entstehung und Ueberwindung; vom Standpunkte liberaler Weltanschauung, staatsphilosophisch beleuchtet. Vortrag*. Berlin: R. Schnürpel, 1911. 31 pp. *LJ*

3619 Schöpf, Joseph Anton: *Antisemitische, zu deutsch judenhetzerische Bestrebungen in der Saison-Stadt Salzburg!!! Grandverwunderung des Dr. Schöpf*. Salzburg: Selbstverlag, 1888. 16 pp. *LJ*

Suppl. to *Grandverwunderung*. Salzburg: Selbstverlag, 1888. 16 pp.

3620 Schöpf, Joseph Anton: *Nachtrag zu Grandverwunderung*. Salzburg: Selbstverlag, 1888. 16 pp. *LJ*

3621 Scholem, Theobald: Die "Deutsche Turnerschaft" und der Antisemitismus. *Israelitische Wochenschrift* 11 (1902) 37–38. *LJ*

3622 Scholl, Karl (1820–1907): *Der Antisemitismus, betrachtet vom sittlichen Standpunkt. Mit besonderem Hinweis auf den Meineids-Prozeß des Rabbiners und Reichstags-Abgeordneten Bloch gegen Rohling, Verfasser des "Talmudjuden." Zugleich mein erstes und letztes Wort gegen niedere Verdächtigung*. Bamberg: Handelsdruckerei und Verlagshdlg, 1894. 36 pp. *LJ*

Date taken from preface.

3623 Scholl, Karl (1820–1907): *Hundert Jahre nach Lessings Nathan; den Judenhassern zur Beschämung, ernsten Juden zur Selbstprüfung*. Bamberg: Verlag der Handelsdruckerei, 1893. VIII, 196 pp. *LJ*

3624 Scholl, Karl (1820–1907): *Jesus von Nazareth, auch ein Semite*. 3. Aufl. Leipzig: R. Friese, 1881. 23 pp. *LJ*

3625 Scholl, Karl (1820–1907): *Das Judentum und seine Weltmission*. Leipzig: Robert Friese, 1880. 26 pp. *LJ*

Offprint from: *Es werde Licht; Monatsblätter zur Förderung der Humanität*, 1880, vol. XI, February.

3626 Scholl, Karl (1820–1907): *Die Rockfahrt nach Trier und die Judenverfolgungen in Russland*. Mannheim: Löffler, 1891. 16 pp. *LJ*

Offprint from: *Es werde Licht*.

3627 Scholl, Karl (1820-1907): *Zwei Antisemiten; ein Freidenker und ein Hofprediger. Nebst einem Anhang: Die wirkliche semitische Unmoral; oder, Grundsätze der jüdischen Sittenlehre.* Leipzig: R. Friese, 1890. 52 pp. *LJ* Offprint from: *Es werde Licht.*

3628 Schoppe, Wilhelm: *Der Jude wird verbrannt; zeitgemäße Abhandlung.* Dresden: Schoppe, 1892. 32 pp. *LJ*

3629 Schorsch, Ismar (1935-): *Jewish Reactions to German Antisemitism, 1870-1914.* New York: Columbia University Press, 1972. 291 pp. (Columbia University Studies in Jewish History, Culture and History, 3) *LJ*

3630 Schrattenholz, Josef (1847-): *Großpapa Stoecker; ein Beitrag zur Deszendenz-Theorie des modernen Antisemitismus.* Leipzig: Breitkopf und Härtel, 1893. 35 pp. *LJ*

3631 Schrattenholz, Josef (1847-): *Vor dem Scheiterhaufen; ein Wort für die Juden und ein Vorwort für den Zaren.* Breslau: Leopold Freund, 1891. 80 pp. *LJ*

3632 Schreiber, Emanuel (1852-1932): *Die Prinzipien des Judentums; verglichen mit denen des Christentums zur Abwehr der neuesten judenfeindlichen Angriffe.* Leipzig: Baumgärtner in Komm, 1877. VI, X, 252 pp. *LJ*

3633 Schreiber, Emanuel (1852-1932): *Die Selbstkritik der Juden.* Berlin: C. Duncker, 1880. XVI, 167 pp. *LJ*

3634 Schreiber, Emanuel (1852-1932): *Die soziale Stellung der Juden; offenes Sendschreiben an Herrn Dr. Maass-Breslau.* Königsberg: Typ. Prange, 1877. 30 pp. *LJ*

3635 Schreiber, Ignatz L.: *Replik auf die von Freiherrn von Königswarter am 23. März 1888 in der Sitzung des Hohen Oesterreichischen Herrenhauses gehaltene Rede.* Wien: Verlag des Verfassers, 1888. 1 vol. *LV*

3636 Schreiner, Martin (1863-1926): *Die jüngsten Urteile über das Judentum kritisch untersucht.* Berlin: S. Cronbach, 1902. X, 184 pp. *LJ*

3637 Schütz, Max: *Franz Liszt über die Juden, von Sagittarius, pseud.* Budapest: Grill, 1881. 38 pp. *LJ*

3638 *Schuldig oder nichtschuldig; die Judenfrage vom objektiven Standpunkte betrachtet, von einem Deutschen.* Berlin: E. Schlesinger, 1880. 24 pp. *LJ*

3639 *Schutz und Förderung jeder redlichen Arbeit.* Dresden: H. Grünberg, 188-. 6 pp. *LC*

The Jewish Question 1848–1914

3640 Schwalb, Moritz (1833–1916): *Zur Beleuchtung des Stoecker Mythus*. Berlin: Walther & Apolant, 1885. 47 pp. *LJ*

3641 Seligmann, Caesar (1860–1950): *Judentum und moderne Weltanschauung; 5 Vorträge*. Frankfurt a.M.: Kauffmann, 1905. 117 pp. *LJ*

3642 Seligmann, S.: *Förderung der Landwirtschaft unter den Israeliten. Rechenschaftsbericht. . .* Freiburg i.Br.: Lorenz & Wätzel, 1906. 93 pp. *LJ*

3643 Siegfried, Heinrich, ed.: *Zwei Betrachtungen über die Antisemitenbewegung in Deutschland. 1. Eine französische Abfertigung der Marr und Genossen. 2. Ein Wort zur Judenfrage von A. Bernstein*. Berlin: Freund und Jeckel, 1881. 36 pp. *LJ*

3644 Silberhein, F.: *Semiten und Antisemiten; ein Wort der Gerechtigkeit nach allen Seiten*. Frankfurt a.M.: Gebr. Fey, 1881. 8 pp. *LJ*

3645 Silberner, Edmund (1910–): Friedrich Engels and the Jews. *J.S.St.* 11 (1949) 323–342. *LJ*

3646 Simon, F.: *Wehrt Euch! Ein Mahnwort an die Juden. Mit einem offenen Briefe der Frau Baronin Bertha von Suttner an den Verfasser*. Berlin: Centralbuchhdlg., 1893. 24 pp. *LJ*

3647 Singer, Isidore (1859–1939): *Berlin, Wien und der Antisemitismus*. Wien: D. Löwy, 1882. 34 pp. *LJ*

3648 Singer, Isidore (1859–1939): *Briefe berühmter christlicher Zeitgenossen über die Judenfrage . . . zum ersten Male,.* hrsg. mit biographischen Skizzen der Autoren und einem Vorworte versehen. Wien: O. Frank, 1885. XLV, 200 pp. *LJ*

3649 Singer, Isidore (1859–1939): *Der Juden Kampf ums Recht; Vortrag gehalten 1902*. New York: E. Zunser, 1902. 15 pp. *LJ*

3650 Singer, S.: Jews in Their Relation to Other Races. *National Life and Thought of the Various Nations throughout the World. A Series of Addresses*. London: T.E. Unwin, 1891. Pp. 363–378. *LTA*

3651 Sonnenfeld, Hugo: Der Centralverein und die politischen Wahlen vom 15. Oktober 1903. *I.Dt.R.* 9 (1903) 619–650. *LJ*

3652 Sonsheim, Konrad von: *Zur Judenfrage; Inquisition und Scheiterhaufen, oder Stöcker contra Lessing. Ein Appell an die Vernunft des deutschen Volkes*. Stettin: B. Behrendt, 1880. 15 pp. *LJ*

3653 Spangenberg, Max: *Der Standpunkt der "Freien Wissenschaftlichen Vereinigung an der Universität Berlin." Zur Judenfrage und zur Wissenschaft. Zwei Reden gehalten am 4. Juli 1881 und 30. Oktober 1882.* Berlin: Lehmann, 1882. 35 pp. *LJ*

3654 Sprechsaal unter eigener Verantwortung der Einsender; Deutschtum und Judentum. *Der Kunstwart* 25 (1912) 6-15. *LJ*

3655 Steckelmacher, Moritz (1851-): *Randbemerkungen zu Werner Sombart's "Die Juden und das Wirtschaftsleben."* Berlin: L. Simion, 1912. 63 pp. *LJ*

3656 Stein, A.: *Der große Prophet, Rektor Ahlwardt. Ein Mahn- und Abschiedswort an meine antisemitischen Freunde.* Berlin: J. van Groningen, 1892. 47 pp. (Berliner Fanfaren, 1) *LJ*

3657 Stein, Julius, ed.: *Börne und Treitschke; offenes Sendschreiben über die Juden von Löb Baruch (Dr. Ludwig Börne) an . . . Heinrich Gotthard von Treitschke.* Berlin: Stein, 1880. 20 pp. *LJ*

3658 Stein, Leopold (1810-1882): *Bileam; eine semitische Stimme.* Frankfurt a.M.: Mahlau and Waldschmidt, 1881. 16 pp. *LJ*

3659 Stein, Leopold (1810-1882): *"Contra Rüppell"! Ein Akt der Intoleranz von einem Mann der Wissenschaft; zur Abwehr.* Frankfurt a.M.: F.B. Auffarth, 1858. 15 pp. *LJ*

3660 Stein, Leopold (1810-1882): *Der geklärte Judenspiegel; zur getreuen Darstellung des jüdischen Wesens und Lebens.* Leipzig: E. L. Morgenstern, 1882. 31 pp. *LJ*

3661 Steinthal, Heymann (1823-1899): *Ueber Juden und Judentum; Vorträge und Aufsätze.* Hrsg. von Gustav Karpeles. Berlin: M. Poppelauer, 1925. XIII, 305 pp. *LJ*

3662 Steinthal, Heymann (1823-1899): Ueber religiöse und nationale Vorurteile. *Deutsche Revue* (1879) 189-206. *Unseen*

3663 *Die Stellung der Arbeiter zur Judenfrage.* Berlin: W. & S. Löwenthal, 1881. 14 pp. *LJ*

3664 Sterling, Eleonore: Jewish Reaction to Jew Hatred in the First Half of the 19th Century. *LBIYB* 3 (1958) 103-121. *LJ*

3665 Stern, Jakob (1843-1911): *Tierquälerei und Tierleben in der jüdischen Literatur.* Zürich: J. Schabelitz, 1880. 48 pp. *LJ*

3666  Stern, Ludwig Lämmlein (1824–1890): *Die Lehrsätze des neugermanischen Judenhaßes mit besonderer Rücksicht auf W. Marr's Schriften.* Historisch und sachlich beleuchtet. Würzburg: Verlag Stahel, 1879. IV, 63 pp. *LJ*

3667  Stettenheim, Julius (1831–1916): *Der Judenfresser. Ein "Wohl bekomm's."* 4. Aufl. Hamburg: M. Rosenberg, 1862. 2 l. fold. *Unseen*

3668  Stöpel, Franz: *Apologie der Juden, von einem Germanen.* Berlin: Expedition, 1880. 37 pp. *LJ*

       From: *Merkur; deutsche und internationale Revue*, vol. 1, no. 1.

3669  Strack, Hermann Leberecht (1848–1922): Aus der Rüstkammer des Antisemitismus. *Nathanael* 29 (1913) 54–58. *LJ*

3670  Strack, Hermann Leberecht (1848–1922): *Das Blut im Glauben und Aberglauben der Menschheit. Mit besonderer Berücksichtigung der "Volksmedizin" und des jüdischen Blutritus.* 8. Aufl. Neubearb. der Schrift "Der Blutaberglaube." München: C.H. Beck, 1900. XVI, 206 pp. (Schriften des Institutum Judaicum in Berlin, 14) *LJ*

3671  Strack, Hermann Leberecht (1848–1922): *Der Blutaberglaube bei Christen und Juden.* München: C.H. Beck, 1891. VI, 59 pp. (Schriften des Institutum Judaicum in Berlin, 14) *LJ*

3672  Strack, Hermann Leberecht (1848–1922): *Der Blutaberglaube in der Menschheit; Blutmorde und Blutritus. Zugleich eine Antwort auf die Herausforderung des "Osservatore Cattolico."* 4. neubearb. Aufl. München: C.H. Beck, 1892. XII, 155 pp. (Schriften des Institutum Judaicum in Berlin, 14) *LJ*

3673  Strack, Hermann Leberecht (1848–1922): *Herr Adolf Stoecker, christliche Liebe und Wahrhaftigkeit.* Karlsruhe: H. Reuther, 1885. IV, 98 pp. *LJ*

3674  Strack, Hermann Leberecht (1848–1922): *Die Juden, dürfen sie "Verbrecher von Religions wegen," genannt werden? Aktenstücke, zugleich als eine Beitrag zur Kennzeichnung der Gerechtigkeitspflege in Preußen.* Berlin: H. Walther, 1893. 30 pp. (Schriften des Institutum Judaicum in Berlin, 15) *LJ*

3675  Strack, Hermann Leberecht (1848–1922): *Sind die Juden Verbrecher von Religions wegen? 1. Der Fleischbesudlungs-Ritus. 2. Jüdische Geheimschriften und jüdische Sekten. 3. Die Sittenlehre des Judentums der Gegenwart.* Leipzig: J.C. Hinrichs' Verlag, 1900. 138 pp. (Schriften des Institutum Judaicum in Berlin, 28) *LJ*

       Offprint from: *Nathanael.*

3676 Sulpicius, pseud.: *Der Judenhaß und die Mittel zu seiner Beseitigung. Ein ernstes Mahnwort an unsere Zeit.* Wesentlich erw. Separat-Abdruck aus der "Allgemeinen Monatspresse." 2. Aufl. Stuttgart: Verlag der Allgemeinen Monatspresse, 1882. 16 pp. *LJ*

3677 Sulzbach, Abraham (1838–1925): *Rischuss oder Judenidiosynkrasie.* Löbau Westpr.: Skrzeczek, 1879. IV, 39 pp. *LJ*

3678 Szántó, Simon (1819–1882): *Zwei Briefe an den Heiligen Geist im Konzil.* Wien: Herzfeld & Bauer, 1870. 15 pp. *Unseen*

3679 Das Talmud-Flugblatt des Centralvereins; eine Beleuchtung antisemitischer Wahrhaftigkeit. *I.Dt.R.* 18 (1912) 305–317. *LJ*

3680 Te-Kio, pseud.: *Judenmord und Christenliebe; ein Kraftwörtchen.* Berlin: E. Wertheim, 1906. 14 pp. *Unseen*

3681 Toury, Jakob: Organizational Problems of German Jewry. *LBIYB* 13 (1968) 57–90. *LJ*

3682 Toussaint, Friedrich Wilhelm: *Der moderne Staat und das Judentum.* Minden i. Westf.: J.C.C. Brun, 1886. 52 pp. (Soziale Zeitfragen, 12) *LJ*

3683 Tschernichoff, M.: *Die Aufgabe der jüdischen Wohltätigkeit.* Berlin: H. Schildberger, 1894. 28 pp. *LJ*

3684 Tschernichoff, M.: *Das Stiefkind der Menschheit.* Leipzig: M. Kaufmann, 1900. 29 pp. *LC*

3685 Ukrainy, Lew Z.: *Was wollen die Antisemiten?* Rostock i. M.: C.J.E. Volckmann, 1905. 128 pp. *LJ*

3686 *Unsere Judenfrage, von einem Juden deutscher Kultur.* Berlin: L. Lamm, 1906. 35 pp. *LJ*

3687 Unterweger, Rose (Krausse) Stolle (1849–): *Der Antisemitismus im Lichte des gläubigen Christentums.* Berlin: H. Maueroth, 1892. 16 pp. *LJ*

3688 Valentiner, Christian August: *An die Juden und für die Juden; ein Wort aus der Sprache des Herzens.* Hamburg: 1862. 20 pp. *Unseen*

Reply to Marr's pamphlet *Der Judenspiegel*; first published anonymously under the title.

3689 Velter, Camill: *Anklagrede gehalten . . . in der Sitzung des Zuchtpolizeigerichtes am 12. März 1889 in Sachen des öffentlichen*

*Ministeriums gegen die Redaktion des "Luxemburger Wort" wegen Beleidigung der jüdischen Religion und ihrer Bekenner. Autorisierte Uebersetzung des französichen Orginaltextes.* Luxemburg: Typ. T. Schröll, 1889. 30 pp. *LJ*

3690  Verband der Deutschen Juden: *Soziale Ethik im Judentum; zur fünften Hauptversammlung in Hamburg 1913.* Frankfurt a.M.: Kauffmann, 1913. 134 pp. *LJ*

3691  Verband der Deutschen Juden: *Stenographischer Bericht über die . . . Hauptversammlung des Verbandes,.* Bd. 1-5 Oktober 1905-1907, 1909, 1911, 1913. Berlin: 1905-1914. 5 vols. *LJ*

3692  Verein zur Abwehr des Antisemitismus, Berlin: *Abwehr-Flugblätter.* Berlin: Verein zur Abwehr des Antisemitismus, 1895. 1 vol. *LJ*

      Collection of 9 articles.

3693  Verein zur Abwehr des Antisemitismus, Berlin: *Die Antisemiten und das Christentum.* Danzig: A.W. Kafemann, 1900. 28 pp. *LJ*

      Offprint from: *Antisemitenspiegel 1900.*

3694  Verein zur Abwehr des Antisemitismus, Berlin: *Der Juden Anteil am Fortschritt der Kultur.* Berlin: 1911. 68 pp. *LJ*

      Offprint from: *Mitteilungen aus dem Verein zur Abwehr des Antisemitismus.*

3695  Verein zur Abwehr des Antisemitismus, Berlin: *Ergänzung zum Antisemiten-spiegel. (2. Aufl., 1900) Die Antisemiten im Lichte des Christentums, des Rechtes und der Wissenschaft.* Berlin: M. Hoffschläger, 1903. 34 pp. *LJ*

3696  Verein zur Abwehr des Antisemitismus, Berlin: *Der politische Antisemitismus von 1903-1907.* Berlin: F. Sommer, 1907. 68 pp. *LJ*

3697  Verein zur Abwehr des Antisemitismus, Berlin: *Die Verhandlungen des Reichstags über den Wucher und des preußischen Abgeordneten-Hauses über die Juden als Geschworene und Richter.* Berlin: J. Buchholz, 1891. 4 pp. (Flugblatt, 5) *LJ*

3698  Verein zur Abwehr des Antisemitismus, Wien: *Berichte der General-versammlung des Vereins zur Abwehr des Antisemitismus, 1892-98.* Wien: 1892-1898. *LJ*

3699  Verein zur Abwehr des Antisemitismus, Wien: *Pro memoria.* Wien: Verein zur Abwehr des Antisemitismus, 1896. 8 pp. *LJ*

      Signed by: Arthur Gundaccer, Freiherr von Suttner.

3700 Verein zur Abwehr des Antisemitismus, Wien: *Stenographisches Protokoll der am 13. Oktober . . . veranstalteten Protest-Versammlung*. Wien: Verlag des Vereines, 1892. 29 pp. *LJ*

3701 Verein zur Abwehr des Antisemitismus, Wien: *Steonographische Aufnahme der am geselligen Abend des Vereins zur Abwehr des Antisemitismus am 5. April 1894 gehaltenen Reden*. Wien: Verlag des Vereins zur Abwehr des Antisemitismus, 1894. 23 pp. *LJ*

3702 Verein zur Abwehr des Antisemitismus, Wien: *Wiener Kalender für Stadt und Land*. Hrsg. von A.G. von Suttner. Wien: 1895. 1 vol. *Unseen*

3703 Der verstorbene Kanzler Caprivi über den Antisemitismus. *Populärwissenschaftliche Monatsblätter zur Belehrung über das Judentum* 19 (1899) 82–83. *LJ*

3704 *Die Verurteilung der antisemitischen Bewegung durch die Wahlmänner von Berlin. Bericht über die allgemeine Versammlung der Wahlmänner aus den vier Berliner Landtagswahlkreisen am 12. Januar 1881*. Berlin: C. Bartel, 1881. 16 pp. *LJ*

3705 Vindex, Carl: *Antisemitische Wühlereien und Raufereien in Pleiss-Athen; ein Beitrag zur Kulturgeschichte unserer Zeit*. Leipzig: Expedition der Zeit- und Kulturbilder, 1881. 46 pp. (Zeit- und Kulturbilder, 2) *LJ*

3706 Vogelstein, Hermann (1870–1942): Bemerkungen zu B. Levitas Aufsatz "Erlösung des Judentums." *Pr. Jhrb.* 102 (1900) 510–515. *LJ*

3707 Wachtel, Friedrich: *Offener Brief an Herrn Dr. Fritz Reuter*. Leipzig: Komm. Verlag Oskar Leiner, 1870. 13 pp. *LTA*

3708 Wagener, Karl: *Die Judenfrage im Lichte der Heiligen Schrift*. Berlin: Selbstverlag, 1886. 16 pp. *LJ*

3709 Walcker, Karl (1839–1909): *Die Judenfrage vom staatswissenschaftlichen Standpunkte aus betrachtet*. Sonderhausen: F.A. Eupel, 1894. IX, 24 pp. *LTA*

3710 Waltemath, Georg: *Rede . . . gegen die Antisemiten gehalten am 1. September 1891 in der Versammlung des Hamburger Vereins der Deutschen Freisinnigen Partei*. Hrsg. vom Vorstand des Vereins. Hamburg: Typ. A. Scheibenhuber, 1891. 14 pp. *LJ*

3711 Walter, Emil (1860–): *Stoecker kontra Walter; Verteidigungsrede gehalten vor dem Königl. Schöffengericht zu Magdeburg am 11. April 1881 von Emil Walter, Redakteur des "Kobold."* Stenografischer Bericht. Magdeburg: H. Leuschener, 1881. 13 pp. *LJ*

3712  Walther, G.: *Herr Schreier, der Antisemit wie er leibte und lebte und was er getrieben, in kunstvolle Reimlein gebracht und beschrieben; wahrheitsgetreue Dichtung in sechs Kapiteln.* Leipzig: Literarische Anstalt A. Schulze, 1896. 30 pp. *LJ*

3713  Wartensleben-Schwirsen, Alexander von: *Gegen die Antisemiten. Ueber Religionsfreiheit und Religionsfrieden und Verhältnis der Christen zu den Juden; Vortrag.* Cammin an der Ostsee: H.L. Behrendt, 1881. 15 pp. *LJ*

3714  Wassermann, Jakob (1873–1934): Das Los der Juden. *Die Neue Rundschau* (1904) 940–948. *LJ*

3715  Wechsler, Elchanan Pinchas Moshe Haim: *Ein Wort der Mahnung an Israel um Beherzigung der Judenhetze und merkwürdige darauf bezügliche Träume von Jaschern milo Debor [pseud.] in Würzburg.* Würzburg: Typ. M. Richter, 1881. 60 pp. *LJ*

3716  Weinreich, H.: *Ob der Jude oder Christ, saget mir, wer besser ist? Historisch-sozialpolitische Betrachtungen über die Unbilligkeit und Unklugheit der antisemitischen Bestrebungen von einem Ultramontanen [pseud.].* 2. Aufl. München: Weinreich, 1882. 30 pp. *LJ*

3717  Wertheimer, Josef von (1800–1887): *Gesinnungstüchtigkeit des jüdischen Stammes in humaner und staatlicher Beziehung und dessen Leistungsfähigkeit auf allen Gebieten des menschlichen Wissens und Könnens. Zur Wahrung der menschen- und staatsbürgerlichen Rechte der Juden durch Tatsachen erhärtet.* Wien: A. Hölder, 1886. 57 pp. *LJ*

3718  Wertheimer, Josef von (1800–1887): *Zur Emanzipation unserer Glaubensgenossen.* Wien: A. Hölder, 1882. 29 pp. *LJ*

3719  Wessely, Moritz: *Der Antisemitismus; ein Schandfleck des 19. Jahrhunderts. Kultur-historische Studie.* Nürnberg: Rosenfeld, [n.d.]. 11 pp. *LC*

3720  Wichert, Ernst (1831–1902): Kammergerichtsrat Ernst Wichert in "Ritter und Dichter" über den Antisemitismus. *Populärwissenschaftliche Monatsblätter zur Belehrung über das Judentum* 20 (1900) 32–33. *LJ*

3721  *Wie ich ein Agitator ward. Eine kulturhistorische Plauderei.* Gotha: F.W. Runze, 1892. V, 41 pp. *LJ*

3722  Wiener, J.: *Judentum und Christentum; ein Beitrag zur Klärung einer religiösen-sozialen Streitfrage.* Zürich: Verlags-Magazin, 1877. 29 pp. *LJ*

3723 Willheimer, Jonas: *Der Judenhaß, von J. W-m-r.* Wien: Typ. L. Hahn, 1873. 20 pp. *LJ*

3724 Willheimer, Jonas: *Die Schmach des Jahrhunderts; nebst der Denkschrift welche der Vorstand der Wiener Kultusgemeinde dem gewesenen Minister-präsidenten Grafen Taaffee überreichte.* Wien: Selbstverlag, 1900. 56 pp. *LJ*

3725 Witt, A.: *Die Juden in ihrer sozialen und bürgerlichen Stellung.* Augsburg: Selbstverlag, 1879. 22 pp. *LJ*

3726 Wolff, Georg: *An das Gewissen des deutschen Volkes.* Kassell: Centralverein Deutscher Staatsbürger Jüdischen Glaubens, 1901. 46 pp. *LJ*

3727 Wolff, Georg: *Ist die antisemitische Bewegung ein nationaler Freiheitskampf?* 9. Aufl. Velten bei Berlin: Veltener Zeitung, 1894. 24 pp. *LJ*

3728 Wolff, Lion: *Handel, Schacher und Wucher der Juden im Kalender von Alban Stolz. Ein Wort der Verwahrung und zur Abwehr.* Karlsruhe: Macklot, 1874. 44 pp. *LJ*

3729 Zehn Thesen gegen den Antisemitismus. *AZJ* 66 (1902) 85–86. *LJ*

3730 Zenker, Ernst Viktor (1865–): *Mystizismus, Pietismus, Antisemitismus am Ende des neunzehnten Jahrhunderts. Kultur-philosophische Studie* . . . Wien: Verlag des "Freien Blattes," 1894. 88 pp. (Kollektion des "Freien Blattes," vol. 2) *LJ*

Solution of the Jewish Question and antisemitism by scientific understanding and not through existing or new religions and social movements.

3731 Ziemlich, Bernhard (–1907): *Einer der nicht Liturgiker sein will; Antwort an Herrn Professor de Lagarde i.e., auf sein Pamphlet "Lipmann Zunz und seine Verehrer."* Leipzig: R. Friese, 1887. 24 pp. *LJ*

3732 *Die Zukunft des deutschen Judentums, von einem Juden.* Dresden: O. Damm, 1891. 13 pp. *LJ*

3733 Zuns, Julius: *Denkschrift über die antisemitische Bewegung in Oesterreich.* Frankfurt a.M.: Mahlen & Waldschmidt, 1891. 46 pp. *LTA*

3734 Zuns, Julius: *Der "Wucher auf dem Lande"; eine Kritik des Fragebogens, der vom Verein für Sozialpolitik veröffentlichten Wucherenquête.* Frankfurt a.M.: Mahlau & Waldschmidt, 1888. 49 pp. *LJ*

# APPENDIX

# NEWSPAPERS AND PERIODICALS

## General

*Die Gartenlaube; illustriertes Familienblatt.* Leipzig, 1853–1937. *LB*

A great number of antisemitic articles were published during the years 1874–1875.

*Die Grenzboten; Zeitschrift für Politik und Literatur.* Leipzig: F.L. Herbig, 1843–1914. *LJ*

Antisemitic material published particularly in the years 1879–81. Last published in 1944.

*Neue Freie Presse.* Wien, 1864–1939. Eds: Eduard Bacher and Moritz Benedikt. *LJ*

*Neue Preußische (Kreuz) Zeitung.* Berlin, 1848–1929. *LF*

Published daily since 1848 till February 1929.

*Die Neue Zeit; Wochenschrift der deutschen Sozialdemokratie.* Stuttgart: Dietz, 1883–1923. 41 Vols. *LJ*

*Politisch-Anthropologische Revue; Monatsschrift für das soziale und geistige Leben der Völker.* Ed. Ludwig Woltmann und Hans K.E. Buhlmann. Eisenach: Thüringische Verlagsanstalt, 1902–1918. 17 vols. *LJ*

*Das Zwanzigste Jahrhundert; Deutschnationale Monatshefte für Soziales Leben, Politik, Wissenschaft und Literatur.* Berlin, H. Lüstenröder, 1890–95. *LV*

Numerous antisemitic articles were published in 1891.

## Antisemitic

*Alldeutsche Blätter, 1. Januar 1894/5–Mai 1939.* Berlin: Thormann und Götsch, 1894–1939. *Unseen*

Formerly: *Mitteilungen des Allgemeinen Deutschen Verbandes*, 1891–1893.

*Alldeutscher Verband: Flugschriften des Alldeutschen Verbandes.* Nr. 1–34. Mainz, 1896–1912. *LV*

*Allgemeine Konservative Monatsschrift für das Christliche Deutschland.* Leipzig: Böhme, 1879–1909. *Unseen*

Numerous antisemitic articles in: 1879–80, 1883, 1888–1889.

*Die Antikorruption; völlig unabhängiges Wochenblatt zur Bekämpfung der Mißstände, Schäden und Auswüchse des öffentlichen und privaten Lebens.* Ed. Hermann Wesendonck, Bd. 1–2. Leipzig: F.E. Fischer, 1892–94. *Unseen*

Continuation under the title: *Der Zeitspiegel*, vols. 3–4, 1894–95.

*Der Antikrat; Gegen Parteigewalt und Hebräer-Einfluß, für selbständige Geistesführung und soziale Gerechtigkeit.* Ed. A. Enss. Berlin: A. Enss, 1887–1896. *Unseen*

*Antisemitische Blätter aus dem nationalen Lager.* Bd. 1, Nr. 1–6. Wien: Kreisel & Gröger, 1889. *LV*

*Antisemitische Correspondenz; Zentralorgan der deutschen Antisemiten.* Bd. 1–18. Leipzig: H. Beyer, 1886–1903. *LB*

Also published under the title: *Deutsch-Soziale Blätter*, and continued under this title.

*Antisemitische Flugblätter.* Berlin, 1879–1880. *LJ*

Contents: Israel an allen Orten [*Deutsche Wacht*]; Herr Prof. Lazarus und die jüdischen Deutschen; Die Mäßigkeitsjuden; Israelitisches Mosaik [*Deutsche Wacht*]; Wie sich einmal . . . ein Prediger über die Juden ausließ [*Deutsche Reform*].

*Auf Vorposten; Monatsschrift des Verbandes gegen Ueberhebung des Judentums, Oktober 1913–September 1914.* Berlin: Verlag "Auf Vorposten," 1913–1914. *LTA*

Ceased publication in 1926, vol. 14, nos. 1–2.

*Bayreuther Blätter; Deutsche Zeitschrift im Geiste Richard Wagners.* Leipzig: Breitkopf and Härtel, 1878–1932. 61 vols. *LJ*

Subtitle varies.

*Deutsch-Soziale Blätter.* Hrsg. Theodor Fritsch. Leipzig: Berger, 1886–1893. *Unseen*

Since 1894 published as supplement to *Antisemitische Correspondenz.* See also *Reichssturmfahne.*

*Deutsch-Sozialer Reformverein, Berlin: Antisemiten-Kalender, 1898.* Leipzig: H. Beyer, 1898. 48, 16 pp. *Unseen*

No more published.

*Deutsche Reform.* Dresden, 1879–1887. *Unseen*

Journal of the Deutsche Reformpartei.

*Deutsche Tageszeitung; das Organ des "Bundes der Landwirte" gegründet für deutsche Interessen.* Berlin, 1894–1934. *Unseen*

*Deutsche Wacht; Wochenschrift für nationales Deutschtum und soziale Reform. Organ der Deutschen Reformpartei.* Dresden, 1887–1906. *Unseen*

*Die Deutsche Wacht; Monatsschrift für nationale Kulturinteressen. Organ der Antisemitischen Vereinigung.* Hrsg. Wilhelm Marr. Berlin: Hentze, 1879–1881. 3 vols. *Unseen*

*Deutsche Weckschriften.* Hrsg. von einer Vereinigung Deutscher Männer, no. 1–2. Berlin: G. A. Dewald, 1892. 2 vols. *Unseen*

*Deutschlands Entjüdelung.* Hrsg. A. Enss. Berlin, 1883?–1887. *LJ*

No more published. Superseded by *Der Antikrat.*

*Die Geißel: Tageblatt aller Tageblätter.* Nr. 1–113, hrsg. von J. Ertl. Wien: Ertl, 1848. 468 pp. *LJ*

*Hammer; Blätter für deutschen Sinn.* Leipzig: T. Fritsch, 1902–1914. *LJ*

*Hammer Jahrbuch.* Wien: F. Schalk, 1908–1914. *Unseen*

Ed.: Franz Stein.

*Der Hammer; Zeitschrift der deutschnationalen Arbeiterschaft.* Hrsg. von Franz Stein. Wien: Der Hammer, 1895–1902. 7 vols. *LB*

In 1896 the name of the journal was changed to *Der Hammer; Zeitschrift für soziale Reform auf nationaler Grundlage*.

*Die Judenfrage; antisemitische Monatschrift*. Jhrg. 1, Nr. 1. Hrsg. unter Mitwirkung hervorragender Gelehrter und Politiker. Wien, 1909. 40 pp. *LJ*

*Der Judenspiegel; eine Monatsschrift*. Berlin: Verlag der "Deutschen Hochwacht," 1901–1902. 2 vols. *Unseen*

Ed.: Friedrich Poppe. Published from November 1901 to October 1902.

*Kehraus; antisemitischer Volkskalender, 1889–1894*. Marburg: Verlag des Reichsherold, 1889–1894. 6 vols. *LJ*

*Kehraus-Bibliothek; illustrierte Monatsschrift für Unterhaltung und deutschen Humor*. Berlin: M. Schulze, 1884–1885. *Unseen*

*Kehraus! Humoristisch-satirischer Volkskalender der Wahrheit für die Jahre 1883–1887*. Berlin: M. Schulze, 1883–1887. 5 vols. *LJ*

*Der Kulturkämpfer; Zeitschrift für öffentliche Angelegenheiten*. Hrsg. von Otto Glagau. Berlin: F. Luckhardt, Expedition, 1880–1886. 7 vols. *LJ*

*Der Kulturkämpfer; Zeitschrift für öffentliches Leben, Politik, Wissenschaft, Kunst und Literatur*. 1. Jhrg., Febr.–Juli 1901, Nr. 1–6 Red. Oskar Webel. Leipzig: C. Minde — Alldeutscher Verlag, 1901. 1 vol. *Unseen*

No more published.

Marr, Wilhelm (1819–1904): *Antisemitische Hefte*. Chemnitz: E. Schmeitzer, 1880. 2 v. *Unseen*

*Mitteilungen des Allgemeinen Deutschen Verbandes*. Berlin: Thormann und Götsch, 1891–1893. 3 vols. *Unseen*

From 1894, superseded by *Alldeutsche Blätter*

*Odin; ein Kampfblatt für die alldeutsche Bewegung*. Bd. 1–3. München: J. Kutschera & Co., 1899–1901. 3 vols. *Unseen*

*Oesterreichischer Volksfreund*. Wien: Mayer & Co., 1851–55. *LV*

Semi-monthly.

*"Ostara"; österreichisches Flugschriften-Magazin*. Bd. 1–84. Graz: Deutsche Vereinsdruckerei, 1905–1915. *LV*

Ed.: Jörg Lanz-Liebenfels.

*Personalist und Emanzipator; Organ Dührings. Halbmonatschrift für aktionsfähige Geisteshaltung und gegen korrupte Wissenschaft.* Ed. Ulrich Dühring. Berlin: Expedition, 1899–1914. *LJ*

This periodical was the mouthpiece for Dühring's ideas and theories about racial antisemitism, social democracy, university professors and cosmopolitans.

*Politische Bilderbogen.* Nr. 1–33. Dresden: Glöss, 1892–1901. *LJ*

Antisemitic subjects in cartoons with corresponding text on verso.

*Der Reichsbote; antisemitisches Volksblatt. Organ für das christliche Volk Oesterreichs.* Wien: Kreisel, 1903. nos. 1–5 in 1 vol. *LV*

No more published.

*Reichsbote; deutscher Kalender für Stadt und Land auf die Jahre 1878–1881.* Bielefeld: Velhagen & Klasing, 1878–81. 3 vols. *Unseen*

*Reichsgeldmonopol; Organ für sozial-politische Reform.* Kassel, 1882–1895. 12 vols. *LJ*

Weekly. The years 1893, 1894/95 were published under the title: *Antisemitisches Volksblatt.*

*Die Reichsglocke; Organ für Volkswirtschaft, Politik und soziales Leben.* Hrsg. H.J. Gehlsen. Berlin: A. Michow, 1883–1907. *Unseen*

Also published under the title: *Die (Deutsche) Reichsglocke.*

*Der Reichsherold; einziges freisinniges nationaldeutsches (antisemitisches) Organ.* Hrsg. Otto Böckel. Marburg, 1887–1894. 9 vols. *Unseen*

Weekly.

*Reichssturmfahne.* Leipzig, 1885–1890. *Unseen*

Continued as *Deutsch-Soziale Blätter* from 1890–October 14, 1914, and as *Deutsch-Völkische Blätter* from October 17, 1914–1923.

*Schild und Schwert; neue österreichische Zeitung, politisch-konservatives Journal.* Wien: Bader, 1848. 180 pp. *LV*

*Schmeitzners Internationale Monatsschrift; Zeitschrift für allgemeine und nationale Kultur und deren Literatur.* Chemnitz: Schmeitzner, 1882–1883. 2 vols. *LJ*

*Staatsbürgerzeitung ("Alte Held'sche").* Berlin: Selbstverlag, 1865–1914. *LM*

Founded in 1865, from 1875 antisemitic; continued from 1917 until 1926.

*Unverfälschte deutsche Worte.* Bd. 1–33. Hrsg. Georg Ritter von Schönerer. Wien: Keiss, 1883–1914. *LV*

*Die Wahrheit, humoristich-satirisches Wochenblatt; Skizzenbuch der "Wahrheit."* Berlin: A. Werkenthin, 1881. 32 pp. *LJ*

*Die Wahrheit; humoristisch-satyrisches Wochenblatt.* Bd. 1–6. Berlin: M. Schulze, 1880–1885. 6 vols. *Unseen*

*Westfälische Reform; Wochenblatt zur Pflege des Deutschtums und des ehrlichen Geschäftsverkehrs. Organ der antisemitischen Vereine Westfalens und Rheinlands.* Jhrg. 1–14. Dortmund: R. Grenz & Co., 1883–1895. *Unseen*

*Der Zeitspiegel; Wochenschrift zur Bekämpfung der Mißstände.* Hrsg. Hermann Wesendonck und A. Schmidt, Jhrg. 4–5 der "Antikorruption." Leipzig: Grübel und Sommerlatte, 1894–5. *Unseen*

Continuation of *Antikorruption.* No more published.

## Confessional

*Germania; Zentralorgan der deutschen Katholiken.* Berlin: Germania Aktiengesellschaft für Druck und Verlag, 1871–1938. *Unseen*

Antisemitic articles in 1875, in nos. 174, 185, 189, 190, 201, 203, and 228.

*Historisch-Politische Blätter für das Katholische Deutschland.* Jhrg. 1–154. München, 1838–1914. *LJ*

The years 1873–1879 contain numerous articles on antisemitism. Ceased publication in 1923 with vol. 171.

*Der Sendbote des Heiligen Joseph; eine Monatschrift zur Verbreitung der Verehrung des Heiligen Joseph, des Schutzpatrons der Katholischen Kirche.* Bd. 1–14. Hrsg. und redigiert von Joseph Deckert. Wien, 1876–1914. *Unseen*

## Jewish

*Allgemeine Zeitung des Judentums [AZJ]. Ein unparteiisches Organ für alles jüdische Interesse.* Berlin: Mosse, 1837–1922. *LJ*

*Ben-Chananja; Zeitschrift für jüdische Theologie und für jüdisches Leben in Gemeinde, Synagoge und Schule.* Bd. 1–10. Szegedin: Typ. S. Burger, 1858–1867. 10 vols. *LJ*

Deutsch-Israelitischer Gemeindebund, Leipzig: *Mitteilungen.* Leipzig, 1873–1914. *LJ*

*Dr. Bloch's Wochenschrift; Zentralorgan für die gesamten Interessen des Judentums.* Wien, 1884–1914. *LJ*

Continued till 1936. Also called *Oesterreichische Wochenschrift.*

*Freies Blatt; Organ zur Abwehr des Antisemitismus, Nr. 1–221.* Wien: Freies Blatt, 1892–1896. 5 vols. *LJ*

*Die Freistatt; alljüdische Revue.* Eschweiler, 1913–14. 2 vols. *LJ*

*Hebräische Bibliographie; Blätter für neuere und ältere Literatur des Judentums.* Bd. 1–21. Redigiert von M. Steinschneider zugleich eine Ergänzung zu allen Organen des Buchhandels. Berlin: J. Benzian, 1858–1882. *LJ*

*Historia Judaica; Journal of Studies in Jewish History Especially in the Legal and Social History of the Jews.* New York, 1938–1961. 23 vol. *LJ*

*Illustrierte Monatshefte für die gesamten Interessen des Judentums.* Wien: A. Hilberg, 1865–1866. 2 vols. *LJ*

*Im Deutschen Reich; Zeitschrift des Centralvereins Deutscher Staatsbürger Jüdischen Glaubens.* Berlin, 1895–1922. 28 vols. *LJ*

*Der Israelit; ein Zentralorgan für das orthodoxe Judentum.* Begründet von Dr. Lehmann in Mainz. Frankfurt a.M., 1860–1938. 43 vols. *LJ*

Ceased publication with vol. 79, no. 43 in 1938.

*Israelitische Wochenschrift für die religiösen und sozialen Interessen des Judentums.* Magdeburg, 1870–1894. *LJ*

*Israelitische Wochenschrift.* Berlin: Cronbach, 1892–1906. 15 vols. *LJ*

Ceased publication with vol. 15, no. 13 in 1906.

*Israelitisches Familienblatt.* Bd. 1, 1898 — Bd. 17, 1914. Hamburg: Israelitisches Familienblatt, 1898–1914. *LJ*

The last volume (40) was published in 1938.

*Israelitisches Wochenblatt für die Schweiz.* Bd. 1, 1900–1914. Zürich, 1900. *LJ*

The paper is published weekly to this day.

*Israelitisches Wochenblatt; Generalanzeiger für die gesamten Interessen des Judentums.* Jhrg. 1 (1902)–15 (1916). Berlin: Wolf, 1902–1916. 15 vols. *LJ*

Ceased publication. Vol. 1–9 was published under the title: *Generalanzeiger für die gesamten Interessen des Judentums, 1902–1910.*

*Jahrbuch für jüdische Geschichte und Literatur.* Hrsg. vom Verband der Vereine für Jüdische Geschichte und Literatur. Bd. 1–17. Berlin: M. Poppelauer, 1898–1914. 17 vols. *LJ*

The last volume was published in 1938.

*Jahrbücher für jüdische Geschichte und Literatur.* Hrsg. von Nehemia Brüll. Frankfurt a.M.: W. Erras, 1874–1890. 10 vols. *LJ*

Continued as *Zentral-Anzeiger für Jüdische Literatur.*

*Die Jüdische Presse; konservative Wochenschrift.* Berlin: H. Itzkowski, 1870–1914. 45 vols. *LJ*

Ceased publication with vol. 54, no. 35 in 1923.

*Die Jüdische Rundschau.* Jhrg. 1–20. Berlin: Jüdische Rundschau, 1895–1914. 20 vols. *LJ*

No. 89 of vol. 43, 1938, was the last to be published.

*Der jüdische Student.* Berlin: 1903–1914. 11 vols. *LJ*

The last volume, no. 30, was published in 1933.

*Jüdische Turnzeitung; Monatsschrift für die körperliche Hebung der Juden.* Jhrg. 1–15. Hrsg. von der Jüdischen Turnerschaft. Berlin: Meysel, 1900–1914. *LF*

Vols. 14–15, 1913–1914, were published under the title: *Jüdische Monatshefte für Turnen und Sport.*

*Jüdische Zeitschrift für die Wissenschaft des Judentums.* Jhrg. 1–11. Hrsg. von A. Geiger. Breslau: Schletter'sche Buchhdlg., 1862–1875. *LJ*

*Jüdische Zeitung (Jüdische Volkszeitung).* Jhrg. 1–20. Breslau, 1896–1914. *LJ*

On April 30, 1937, the last no. (17) was published.

*Jüdisches Litteraturblatt.* Begründet von M. Rahmer. Hrsg. von L. A. Rosenthal. Berlin, 1872–1913. 35 vols. *LJ*

Ceased publication with vol. 35, no. 3, in 1913.

*Jüdisches Volksblatt.* Wien: Administration, 1899–[?]. *LJ* Weekly.

*Jüdisches Volksblatt; zur Belehrung und Unterhaltung auf jüdischem Gebiete.* Leipzig: Baumgärtner, 1853–1866. *Unseen*

This paper merged with the *AZJ* in 1866.

*K.C. Blätter (Kartell-Convent Blätter).* Berlin: Philoverlag, 1910–1914. 4 vols. *LJ*

Ceased publication with vol. 23 in 1933.

*Liberales Judentum; Monatschrift für die religiösen Interessen des Judentums.* Hrsg. von der Vereinigung für das Liberale Judentum in Deutschland. Frankfurt a.M.: Vereinigung für das Liberale Judentum, 1908–1923. 15 vols. *LJ*

*Monatsschrift der Oesterreichisch-Israelitischen Union.* Bd. 1–31. Wien, 1889–1919. 31 vols. *LJ*

Vols. 1–12 were published as *Mitteilungen der Oesterreichisch-Israelitischen Union.*

*Monatsschrift für Geschichte und Wissenschaft des Judentums.* Bd. 1–83. Dresden: R. Kuntze, 1852–1939. *LJ*

Index for the years 1851–1939, published in 1966; VIII, 250 pp.

*Die Neuzeit; Wochenschrift für politische und religöse Kulturinteressen.* Wien, 1861–1903. 43 vols. *LJ*

*Oesterreichisches Central-Organ für Glaubensfreiheit, Kultur, Geschichte und Literatur der Juden.* Bd. 1, Nr. 1–49. Redakteur: Isidor Busch und M. Letteris. Wien: Somnier, 1848. 426, 8 pp. *LJ*

No more published.

*Ost und West; Monatschrift für modernes Judentum.* Berlin, 1901–1923. *LJ*

Ceased publication in 1923.

*Populärwissenschaftliche Monatsblätter zur Belehrung über das Judentum; für Gebildete aller Konfessionen. Organ für freisinnige Bestrebungen im Gemeindeleben.* Frankfurt a.M., 1881–1908. *LJ*

*Reichsbote; Zeitschrift für soziale, wissenschaftliche und Kultus-Interessen des Judentums.* Wien: Knöpfelmacher, 1894. 1 vol. *LV*

"Beilage; Vollständige Uebersetzung des Talmud, von Wilhelm Reich."

*Schlemiel; jüdische Blätter für Humor und Kunst.* Jhrg. 1–3, Mai 1903 — June 1905; Februar 1907, Nr. 1–24. Berlin: L. Lamm, Welt-Verlag, 1903–1907. 2 vols. *LJ*

*Die Schmach des Jahrhunderts; Halbmonatschrift zur Bekämpfung des Antisemitismus.* Ed. Karl Schneidt. Berlin: Moderner Verlag, 1892–1893. *LJ*

*Studia Judaica Austriaca.* Bd. 1–10. Wien, Verlag Herold, 1974–1984. 10 vols. *LJ*

Ed: "Oesterreichisches Jüdisches Museum in Eisenstadt."

Verband der Deutschen Juden: *Korrespondenzblatt.* Berlin, 1907–1914. 14 vols. *LJ*

Verein zur Abwehr des Antisemitismus, Berlin: *Mitteilungen aus dem Verein . . .* Bd. 1–24. Berlin, 1891–1914. 24 vols. *LJ*

One of the best sources about antisemitism in Germany during the years 1891–1914; published weekly. Each volume has an index.

*Die Welt; Zentralorgan der zionistischen Bewegung.* Bd. 1–18, Nr. 31, 1897–Juli 31, 1914. Wien, 1897–1914. 18 vols. *LJ*

No more published.

*Wiener Mitteilungen; Zeitschrift für israelitische Kulturzustände.* Hrsg. von Meir Max Letteris. Wien: M. Letteris, 1854–1870. *LJ*

*Zeitschrift für Demographie und Statistik der Juden.* Hrsg. vom Bureau für Statistik der Juden. Jhrg. 1–12. Berlin, 1905–1916. *LJ*

*Zeitschrift für die Geschichte der Juden in Deutschland.* Hrsg. von Ludwig Geiger. Bd. 1–5. Braunschweig: C.A. Schwetschke, 1887–1892. 5 vols. *LJ*

*Zeitschrift für Hebräische Bibliographie.* Unter Mitwirkung namhafter Gelehrter, hrsg. von H. Brody u.a. Bd. 1–23. Berlin: S. Calvary, 1896–1920. *LJ*

*Zion; Monatsschrift für die nationalen Interessen des Jüdischen Volkes.* Berlin, 1895–1900. 6 vols. *LJ*

Continuation of *Jüdische Volkszeitung*; formerly *Selbstemanzipation*."

# Missionary

*Dibre Emeth oder Stimmen der Wahrheit an Israeliten und Freunde Israels.* Frankfurt an der Oder: Trowitzsch und Sohn in Comm., 1845-1912. *LJ*

*Der Freund Israels; Nachrichten von der Ausbreitung des Reiches Gottes unter Israel.* Basel: Schneider, 1835-1914. *LJ*

Continued till today.

*Der Friedensbote für Israel; Im Auftrag der Berliner Gesellschaft zur Beförderung des Christentums unter den Juden.* Jhrg. 1-4. Berlin: Wiegandt und Grieben, 1863-1866. 4 vols. *LJ*

Ed.: Wilhelm Ziethe.

*Friedensbote; Missionsblatt der Gesellschaft zur Beförderung des Christentums unter den Juden in Berlin.* N.F. Jhrg. 1-14. Hrsg. von F.W.S. Schwarz. Berlin: Wiegandt & Grieben, 1869-1883. *LJ*

Superseded by *Nathanael*.

*Der Messiasbote; ein Nachrichtenblatt der Berliner Judenmission.* Jhrg. 1, Nr. 1-Jhrg. 11, Nr. 3. Hrsg. von R. Bieling. Berlin: Verlag des Christlichen Zeitschriftenvereins, 1906-1916. *LJ*

Suppl. to *Nathanael; Zeitschrift für die Arbeit der evangelischen Kirche an Israel.*

*Missionsblatt des Rheinisch-Westfälischen Vereins für Israel.* Bd. 1-49. Hrsg. F. Stolle. Köln, 1845-1910. *Unseen*

New series published under the title: *Missionsblatt des Westdeutschen Vereins für Israel*, vols. 51-66. Köln, 1895-1910.

*Nathanael; Zeitschrift der Berliner Gesellschaft zur Beförderung des Christentums unter den Juden.* Bd. 1-34. Hrsg. Hermann L. Strack. Berlin: Wiegandt und Grieben, 1885-1918. *LJ*

Continuation of *Friedensbote*.

*Saat auf Hoffnung; Zeitschrift für die Mission der Kirche an Israel.* Hrsg. von Franz Delitzsch u.a. Leipzig, 1863-1914. *LJ*

*Zions Freund.* Hrsg. Pastor Arnold Frank. Jhrg. 1-15. Elmshorn bei Hamburg: Typ. Braunstedt, 1899-1914. *LJ*

Discontinued in 1936, with vol. 38.

# AUTHOR INDEX

Antisemitisches Volksblatt 94
Apostata, pseud. see Harden,
  Maximilian
Appelbaum (lawyer) 106
Apt, Max (1869–) 3238
Arendt, Hannah (1906–1975) 107, 108
Arianus, Friedrich 109
Arius 2725
Ark, B. 111
Arkel, Dirk van 112
Arndt, Hans 113
Arnim, Bettina (Brentano) von
  (1785–1859) 2317
Aryan, pseud. 114
Asch, Adolf 115
Aschaffenburg, Gustav (1861–1944)
  116
Ascher, Arnold 117, 118
Aschheim, Steven Edward 119, 120
Aschkewitz, Max (1901–) 121
Astfalck, Caesar 122–124
Aub, Joseph (1805–1880) 3240
Auerbach, Berthold (1812–1882)
  125
Auerbach, Elias (1882–1971) 126
Auerbach, Fritz 3241
Auerbach, Leopold (1847–1925) 3242,
  3243
Austerlitz, Friedrich 129
Austria. Polizei Direktion, Wien.
  Zentral Evidenz Bureau see
  Oesterreichische Polizei-Direktion,
  Wien. Zentral-Evidenz Bureau
Austriacus, pseud. see Rausch, Karl
Avé-Lallemant, Friedrich Christian
  Benedict 130–132
Avineri, Shlomo (1933–) 1, 133
Axenfeld, Karl 134
Ayerst, William 135

B.J.C. see Kartell Jüdischer
  Verbindungen
Bach, Albert 136
Bacharach, Zvi see Bachrach, Walter
  Zwi

Bachem, Julius (1845–1921) 137, 138
Bacher, Albert 139
Bachrach, Walter Zwi 6, 7, 140–142
Back, Samuel (1841–1899) 3245
Back, Wilhelm 143
Backhaus, Simon 144
Bäntsch, Bruno 145
Bagge, Adam 1154
Bahr, Hermann (1863–1934) 146
Balakan, David 3246
Balder, Benno, pseud. 147
Bamberger, Ludwig (1823–1899) 148
Bamberger, Seligmann Beer
  (1807–1878) 149
Bankberger, Dr. Hilarius see Perrot,
  Franz Fuerchtgott
Barasch, Iuliu 150
Barden, Brünhild, pseud. see Hahn,
  Adele
Barkai, Abraham 151–153, 1658
Barkenings, Hans-Joachim 154
Baron, Salo Wittmayer (1895–1989)
  155–157
Barre, Ernst 2318
Bartels, Adolf (1862–1945) 158–164,
  2319–2322, 2531
Barth, Theodor 165
Bartsch, Rudolf Hans (1873–1952)
  2323–2325
Bartys, Julian 166
Baruch, Löb see Börne, Ludwig
Bary, Jozsef 167
Bass, Josef 2326, 2327
Baudisch, Ursula 168
Bauer, Bruno (1809–1882) 169
Bauer, Edwin 2328
Bauer, Erwin (1857–1901) 170–177,
  2532
Bauer, Otto (1881–1938) 178, 179
Baum, Moritz 3248, 3247
Baumgarten, Emanuel Mendel
  (1828–1908) 180, 181
Baumgarten, Michael (1812–1889) 182,
  183
Bauwerker, Carl 184

Dithmar, minister 547
Dittmar, Peter 548
Dix, Arthur (1875–) 549
Dobner, W. 2561
Dodel, Arnold (1843–1908) 1310
Döll, Emil 2566
Döllinger, Johann Josef Ignaz von
  (1799–1890) 3305, 3306
Dönges, Emil 550
Dolfe, Alwin, pseud. see Lewin, Adolf
Donath, Endre 551
Donner, Friedrich 3307
Dorée, Nadage 552
Doron, Joachim 553
Doron, Yehoyakim 9
Dreifus, Markus G. 556, 3308
Dreifuss, Emil 557
Dresch, Joseph Emile (1871–) 2353
Dreydorff, Johann Georg 558
Dreyfus, Robert (1873–1939) 559
Drumont, Edouard Adolphe
  (1844–1917) 2562, 2563
Dubnow, Semen Markovich
  (1860–1941) 560–562
Düding, Dieter 563
Dühring, Eugen Karl (1833–1921) 564,
  565, 2564–2570
Düsing, Dr. 2571
Duggan, Paul R. 566
Dukmeyer, Friedrich 567, 2572
Durege, Jenny 3309
Duschak, Moritz (1815–1890) 568,
  569, 3310

E., H. see Ellenberger, Heinrich
Eberle, Josef 570
Eberstein, Alfred von 571, 572
Eberswalde. Synagogengemeinde 573
Ebner-Eschenbach, Marie von
  (1830–1916) 2354
Eccarius, Karl Theodor 2573
Ecker, Jakob (1851–1912) 575, 594,
  3060
Eckert, Willehard Paul 576
Eckstein, Adolf (1857–1935) 577–579

Eckstein, Gustav 580
Edinger, Dora 581
Eduard, Daniel 582
Effertz, Otto 584
Eger, Heinrich 585
Eheberg, Karl Theodor von (1855–)
  586
Ehrke, Thomas 587
Ehrlich, Ernst Ludwig 588
Ehrmann, Herz 589
Eichenlaub, Siegfried Wolfgang 2574
Ein Deutsch-Böhme see Hutter,
  Theodor
Einhart, pseud. see Class, Heinrich
Einhorn, Ignaz, pseud. see Horn, Ede
Einig, Peter 590
Eisen, Arnold M 592
Eisenmenger, Johann Andreas
  (1654–1704) 593, 594, 3060
Eisler, Moritz (1818–1890) 3311
Elbogen Friedrich 595, 3312
Elbogen, Ismar (1874–1973) 596, 597
Eliav, Mordechai 3, 598, 599
Eliot, George (1819–1880) 3313
Elisa, Baronin von . . . 2355
Elisamter 3314
Ellenberger, Heinrich (1806–1883)
  3315, 3316
Ellenbogen, Wilhelm (1863–1951) 600,
  2575
Elmar, Karl 2356
Elmayer-Vestenbrugg, Rudolf von
  (1881–) 601
Elösser, Arthur (1870–1938) 2357
Eloni, Yehuda 2
Emanuel, B. 602
Emmerich, Wolfgang 604
Endlich, Johann Quirin 605, 2576
Endlich, Quirin see Endlich, Johann
  Quirin
Endner, Wilhelm 2577
Engel de Janosi, Joseph (1851–) 607,
  2358
Engel, H. 2578
Engel, Joseph 608

Harmelin, Wilhelm 912
Harpf, Adolf 913, 914
Harrassowitz, Otto 915
Harris, James F. 916
Hartleben, A. 917
Hartmann, Eduard von (1842–1906)
918
Hartmann, Moritz (1821–1872) 919,
2394
Hartwig, Edgar 920
Hartwig, Otto (1830–1903) 921
Hasse, Ernst (1846–1908) 922
Haug, H. 2667
Haumann, Heiko (1945–) 923
Hauptmann, Karl (1858–1921) 2395
Hauschner, Auguste (Sobotka)
(1851–1924) 2396
Hauser, Otto (1876–) 2397, 2398
Hausig, F. 3364
Hausmeister, Jakob August 924, 925
Hausmeister, Max 3365
Hawlik, Johannes 926
Hayn, Hugo (1843–1923) 927
Hecht, Alexander 928
Hecht, David 3366
Hecht, Georg 929
Heckel, Johannes (1889–1963) 930
Heckscher, M 931
Heger, Adolf 932
Heilbrunn, Rudolf M. 933
Heimberger, Joseph 934
Hein, Oskar 935, 2668, 3367, 3368
Heine, Heinrich (1797–1856) 3369
Heinen, Ernst 936
Helbig, Friedrich 2399
Hellenbach, Lazar von see Hellenbach
von Paczolay, Lazar von
Hellenbach von Paczolay, Lazar von
(1827–1887) 2669
Hellwig, Albert Ernst Karl Max
(1880–) 937–939
Hellwing, Isak A. 940
Helmdörffer, F.X. 3370
Heman, Karl Friedrich (1839–1919)
941–943

Henle, von 1066
Henne am Rhyn, Otto (1828–1914)
3371
Henningsen, J. 2670
Henrici, Ernst (1854–1915) 944, 2671,
2672, 2673, 2674, 2675
Hentsch, Gerhard 945
Hentschel, Willibald 946
Heppner, Ernst 947
Herdach, Karl 2676
Herman, Otto, member of the
Hungarian parliament 2677
Hermann, C. 948, 2400
Hermann, Georg, pseud. see Borchardt,
Georg Hermann
Hermann, Grandson of the Cherusker
2678
Hermann, Heinrich (1852–) see Balder,
Benno, pseud.
Herrmann, Felix 3372
Hersch, Isaac Moses 950, 3373–3378
Hersch, Jekef Mosche 951
Hertl, Paul 952
Hertz, Friedrich Otto (1878–) 953,
3379
Hertzka, Adolf (1845–1924) 3380
Hertzka, Theodor 3381
Herwig, pseud. see Pichl, Eduard
Herz, Hugo 954
Herz, Sophony (1905–) 955
Herzberg-Fränkel, Leopold
(1827–1915) 2401–2403
Herzberg, Wilhelm 2404
Herzfeld, Michael 956, 3382
Herzig, Arno 957
Herzl, Theodor (1860–1904) 959–961,
2405, 2406
Herzstein, Robert Edwin 962
Hess, Moses (1812–1875) 963
Hessen, Robert (1854–) 2680
Heuch, F.C. 964
Heynemann, Sigismund Sussmann 965
Heyse, M.L. 2681
Heyse, Paul (1830–1914) 2407
Hieber, Otto 966

Sandvoss, Franz 1822
Saner, Marcel 1823
Saphir, Adolph (1831–1891) 1824–1827
Sauer, August 2385
Saulus, pseud. 2990
Schach, Fabius (1868–1930) 1828, 1829, 3609
Schacht, F. 3610
Schacht, Hjalmar Horace Greeley (1877–1970) 1830
Schadäus, Elias (fl.1591) 1831
Schächter, Hersch 1832
Schäffer, Ernst 1834
Schaffer, Schepsel 1835
Schanz, Uli 3611
Scharf von Scharffenstein, Hermann Martin see Scharff-Scharffenstein, Hermann von
Scharff-Scharffenstein, Herman von 1836, 2992, 2993
Scharlowski, Werner (1933–) 1837
Schatt, L.G. 3612
Schatzberg, Walter 1136
Schechter, Solomon (1850–1915) 1838
Schedukat, Klaus 1839
Scheftelowitz, Isidor (1876–1934) 1840
Scheicher, Josef 1841, 2994, 2995
Scheidemann, Philipp (1865–1939) 1842
Schell, Josef Copertin 2996
Schemann, Ludwig (1852–1938) 1843, 1844
Scherb, Friedrich von 2997
Scherff, Johann 2493
Scherr, Johannes (1817–1886) 2494, 2495
Scheuer, Oskar Franz 2998
Schickert, Klaus 2999
Schiefer, Franz Xaver 593
Schiff, Hermann 2496, 2497
Schiff, Maximilian Paul see Paul-Schiff, Maximilian
Schilling, Konrad 1845
Schimmer, Gustav Adolf 1846, 1847
Schippel, Max (1859–1928) 1848

Schirmer, Wilhelm 3613
Schläpfer, Rudolf 1849
Schleier, Hans 1850
Schleinitz, Alexander von (1807–1885) 3614
Schlesinger, Markus 3615
Schlieben, Erwin 2498
Schlotzhauer, Inge 1851
Schmeisser, E. 1852
Schmidl, Erwin A. 1853
Schmidt-Clausing, Fritz (1902–) 1854
Schmidt, Ferdinand Jakob (1860–) 1855
Schmidt, Franz 3000
Schmidt, Gerhard Karl (1908–) 1856
Schmidt, K. 1857
Schmidt, Karl 3616
Schmidt, Richard 3001
Schmidtbauer, Peter 1858
Schmitt, Heinrich see Schmitt, Henryk
Schmitt, Henryk 3002
Schnee, Heinrich (1871–1949) 1859
Schnee, Heinrich (1895–) 1860–1862
Schneider, Ernst 1863, 3003, 3004
Schneider, J. 1864
Schneidewin, Max Paul Ernst (1843–) 1865
Schneidt, Karl 3617
Schnitzler, Arthur (1862–1931) 2499, 2500
Schochow, Werner 1866
Schöler, Hermann (1869–) 3618
Schön, Max (1848–) 3005
Schön, Theodor 1867
Schönaich-Carolath, Emil von (1852–1908) 2501
Schönerer, Georg von (1842–1921) 1868, 3006–3024
Schönwald, Alfred (1835–1894) 1869
Schöpf, Joseph Anton 3619, 3620
Schöps, Hans Joachim (1909–) 1870
Schöps, Julius 835
Scholem, Theobald 3621
Scholl, Karl (1820–1907) 1871, 1872, 3622–3627

# SUBJECT INDEX